Criminology

Third edition

The third edition of *Criminology: A Sociological Introduction* offers a comprehensive overview of the study of criminology, from early theoretical perspectives to pressing contemporary issues such as the globalization of crime, crimes against the environment and state crime.

New to the third edition is a refreshed focus on the social, political and economic context of crime in the post-financial-crisis world as well as two separate chapters on terrorism and counter-terrorism and state crime and human rights. New developments in the field, including psychosocial criminology are also reflected upon and considered.

This popular international textbook offers a challenging and critical approach to the study of criminology and is essential reading for students looking to expand their understanding of crime and the world in which they live.

The book is supported by a free companion website featuring a wealth of additional resources including, for instructors, a testbank of questions, assignable critical thinking questions with outline answers, assignable exercises, and downloadable illustrations, and for students, links to useful websites and an interactive flashcard glossary. These resources can be accessed at www.routledge.com/cw/carrabine.

Eamonn Carrabine, Pam Cox, Pete Fussey, Dick Hobbs, Nigel South, Darren Thiel and **Jackie Turton** are all based in the Department of Sociology at the University of Essex, Colchester, UK.

 A range of further resources for this book are available on the Companion Website: www.routledge.com/cw/carrabine.

'This new edition of *Criminology: A Sociological Introduction* not only offers an essential grounding in how to think *sociologically* about crime, from the histories of crime to the futures of crime and crime control, but provides new and exciting insights in relation to the ever-changing contours of criminological debate. The contemporary nature of the material and issues covered, combined with critical questions posed by the authors, make this a rich, authoritative and stimulating resource!'
Loraine Gelsthorpe, University of Cambridge, UK

'There are now several introductory criminology texts but in a crowded marketplace *Criminology: A Sociological Introduction* stands out. Written by the internationally renowned team at Essex University, this third incarnation builds on the success of previous editions and includes chapters on some of the most pressing concerns in the field, including terrorism and counter-terrorism, state crime and human rights. Accessible, stimulating and sometimes provocative, this book takes students through the most important socio-criminological issues of our time and is a resource that they will return to again and again.'
Yvonne Jewkes, University of Leicester, UK

'This book provides a vibrant, exciting guide to the relationship between crime and society. With important insights into the history, theory and practice of crime and crime control from a sociological perspective, the book lays down conceptual and methodological foundations that allow us to better understand and appreciate the key criminological issues of the contemporary era. Highly recommended.'
Rob White, University of Tasmania, Australia

'A very fine critical introduction to criminology has gotten better in this most recent edition. The text provides a good balance of breadth with depth. It unpacks and makes digestible often complex perspectives on crime and justice and, for this reason, it is one of the better texts on the market today for first year students. The sweep of ideas and topics is impressive, giving ample scope to the "new" without trying to be fashionable.'
John Scott, University of New England, Australia

'I have been using *Criminology: A Sociological Introduction* in my Crime and Punishment courses for several semesters now. I chose this particular text out of several that I have examined because it has a global perspective, a critical lens, and it provides a comprehensive overview of criminological issues that I have been unable to find in other texts. This book is very accessible to my students without sacrificing sophistication and nuance.'
Miriam J. Konrad, Georgia State University, USA

'This third edition retains all the strengths of earlier editions while adding important new work on contemporary issues. It gives students a thorough grounding not just in the traditional aspects of the discipline to do with crime, policing and punishment but in more current issues facing society like the "war on terror" and the impact of globalization. The critical thinking questions listed in each chapter encourage students to think and read more deeply than many textbooks while the "Further Study" suggestions are invaluable resources for directing their reading and research.'
Mary Bosworth, University of Oxford, UK

'This is an essential resource for anyone interested in the study of crime and social control. This resource is distinct with its frame of the "criminological imagination," and provides a systematic and critical examination of the historical and contemporary context of crime, thinking about crime and its control, and globalization and crime. Already a terrific reference, this third edition offers additional and very timely insights into some of the key global issues in criminology, including terrorism, state crime and human rights.'
Karen Laidler, University of Hong Kong

'The latest edition of this textbook provides students new to the field with a comprehensive introduction to the sociology of crime. The book is accessible without being overly simplistic and it encourages students to think sociologically about crime and popular responses to it. This new edition combines important coverage of key aspects of theory and analysis with new work and new fields of study that are at the very heart of sociological criminology today. I'm sure it will prove to be an excellent resource for students.'
Simon Winlow, Teesside University, UK

Criminology

A sociological introduction

Third edition

Eamonn Carrabine, Pam Cox,
Pete Fussey, Dick Hobbs,
Nigel South, Darren Thiel
and Jackie Turton

 Routledge
Taylor & Francis Group

LONDON AND NEW YORK

First published 2004
Third edition 2014
by Routledge
2 Park Square, Milton Park, Abingdon, Oxon, OX14 4RN

and by Routledge
711 Third Avenue, New York, NY 10017

Routledge is an imprint of the Taylor & Francis Group, an informa business

© 2014 Eamonn Carrabine, Pam Cox, Pete Fussey, Dick Hobbs, Nigel South,
Darren Thiel and Jackie Turton

British Library Cataloguing in Publication Data
A catalogue record for this book is available from the British Library

Library of Congress Cataloging in Publication Data
Carrabine, Eamonn.
   Criminology: a sociological introduction / Eamonn Carrabine, Pam Cox, Pete Fussey,
   Dick Hobbs, Nigel South, Darren Thiel and Jackie Turton . – Third edition.
      pages cm
   1. Criminology. 2. Crime–Sociological aspects. I. Title.
   HV6025.C7456 2014
   364–dc23   2013045629

ISBN: 978-0-415-64078-7 (hbk)
ISBN: 978-0-415-64080-0 (pbk)
ISBN: 978-1-136-17955-6 (ebk)

Typeset in Frutiger
by Keystroke, Station Road, Codsall, Wolverhampton

We dedicate the book to Stan Cohen, Barbara Hudson, Mary Macintosh, Terrence Morris, Geoffrey Pearson and Jock Young, who died in 2013.

Contents

List of illustrations

Plates

Figures

Tables

Boxes

Notes on the authors

All the authors work in the Department of Sociology at the University of Essex, Colchester, UK.

Eamonn Carrabine is Professor of Sociology, and his teaching and research interests lie in the fields of criminology, cultural studies and sociology more generally. He has published prolifically in leading journals including the British Journal of Criminology, The Howard Journal of Criminal Justice, Punishment and Society, Sociological Review, Theoretical Criminology, and Crime, Media, Culture. His books include Crime in Modern Britain (co-authored, 2002), Power, Discourse and Society: A Genealogy of the Strangeways Prison Riot (2004) and Crime, Culture and the Media (2008). He is currently writing a book on Crime and Social Theory, and then plans to write a book on the Iconography of Punishment, focusing on how punishment has been represented in the literary and visual arts.

Pamela Cox is a Senior Lecturer specializing in criminal justice history, social history, comparative criminology and gender. She has worked as a youth justice and family justice consultant for UK local authorities and international NGOs. Her books include: Bad Girls in Britain: Gender, Justice and Welfare, 1900–1950 (2012/2003), Becoming Delinquent: British and European Youth, 1650–1950 (co-edited with H. Shore, 2002) and Crime in Modern Britain (co-authored, 2002). In 2012, she co-wrote and presented a BBC TWO series, Servants: The True Story of Life Below Stairs, drawing on Bad Girls' analysis of domestic service training homes for girls.

Pete Fussey is Professor of Sociology, and his main research interests focus on security, social control and the city. He has worked on multiple large-scale projects and published widely in these areas. Recent books include Terrorism and the Olympics (co-edited, 2010), Securing and Sustaining the Olympic City (co-authored, 2011) and Researching Crime (co-authored, 2013). He is currently completing a monograph on human trafficking in the EU, due to be published in 2014.

Dick Hobbs is Professor of Sociology at the University of Essex, and fractional Professor at the University of Western Sydney. He previously held Chairs at the University of Durham, and the London School of Economics. His most recent book is Lush Life: Constructing Organized Crime in the UK (2013).

Nigel South is Professor of Sociology, and his research interests include environmental crime, green criminology and human rights; illegal and legal drug use; crime, inequalities and citizenship; theoretical and comparative criminology; and public health and community services. He has held teaching and research posts in London and New York, and is an Adjunct Professor in the School of Justice at Queensland University of Technology. He serves on several editorial boards and is the European Editor of *Critical Criminology* (the journal of the Critical Criminology Division of the American Society of Criminology). Recent books include: *Green Cultural Criminology: Constructions of Environmental Harm, Consumerism and Resistance to Ecocide* (co-authored with A. Brisman, 2014) and *The Routledge International Handbook of Green Criminology* (co-edited with A. Brisman, 2013).

Darren Thiel is a Senior Lecturer with research interests in public policy, criminal justice, policing and economic sociology. He has worked as a researcher at the Home Office and the Police Foundation. His publications include: *Policing Terrorism: A Review of the Evidence* (2009) and *Builders: Class, Gender and Ethnicity in the Construction Industry* (2012).

Jackie Turton is a Senior Lecturer. She is a very experienced researcher particularly in qualitative methodology using in-depth interviews to gather sensitive data. She has completed a number of projects for various national and local government agencies including the Home Office, Department of Health and the Royal College of Paediatrics and Child Health. Her research activities have included child protection, studies of marginalized groups and women as offenders. Recently Jackie's work has focused on children as victims of abuse including child trafficking. Publications include: *Child Abuse, Gender and Society* (2008); articles on 'Maternal Abusers: Underlying Concerns for Children' (2010), 'Female Sexual Abusers: Assessing the Risk' (2011); and book chapters, 'Maternal Abuse: The Emerging Phenomenon of Child Sexual Abuse' (2012) and 'Betrayal of Trust: Victims of Maternal Incest' (2013).

Acknowledgements

For this third edition we welcome Pete Fussey, Dick Hobbs, Darren Thiel and Jackie Turton to the writing team and thank Maggy Lee (who has since moved to the University of Hong Kong) and Ken Plummer for their excellent contributions to the second edition.

The Department of Sociology at the University of Essex continues to provide a supportive and engaging home for our collaborative criminological work. We are now very pleased to be one of the largest groups of academics teaching criminology in the UK and have learnt a great deal from our own students. We hope that the Department's interdisciplinary spirit runs through and enlivens this book. On a personal note we thank Mo Doshi, Jai and Mia Fussey, Bill, Tess and Patrick Hayton, Alison Inman, Linsey McGoey, Chrissie Rogers, Daniel South, Sherrie Tuckwell, Mike Turton, Sue, Pat, Nik, Lisa and the Bruise.

Thanks are also due to Holly Davis, Carrie Bell and Thomas Sutton at Routledge who have given expert advice and helped guide the manuscript though to publication. We also thank our anonymous reviewers who have provided very constructive feedback on all three editions.

EC, PC, PF, DH, NS, DT, JT
Colchester, October 2013

Permissions

Data and tables obtained from the Home Office are reproduced by permission.

Every effort has been made to contact copyright holders for their permission to reprint material in this book. The publishers would be grateful to hear from any copyright holder who is not here acknowledged and will undertake to rectify any errors or omissions in future editions of this book.

part 1

The Criminological Imagination

Timeline

1750s and 1760s	The Classical School and Beccaria
	Fielding's London policing experiments
1780s	Bentham's panopticon
1820s	Collection of criminal statistics
1870s	The Italian or Positivist School and Lombroso
1870s–1900s	Heredity and criminal families
1910s	Intelligence theories
	Twin research, somatotypes and endocrinology
	Durkheim and functionalist criminology
	Early African American socio-criminology
1920s	Psychoanalytic theories
1920s/1930s	Early Chicago School
	Zonal theory, life story research
1930s	Anomie theory
1930s/1940s	Differential association
1960s	Neo-Chicago School
1960s/1970s	Subcultural theory, labelling theory
	Control theory, Marxist/conflict criminologies
1970s onwards	Moral panic theory
	New criminology
	Critical criminology
	Birmingham Centre for Contemporary Cultural Studies
	The political economy of crime
	The justice model
	Administrative/actuarial criminology
	Feminist criminology
	Black and anti-racist criminology
	Foucauldian genealogies and governance
1980s	Left realism
	Resurgence of radical right
1990s	Reintegrative shaming theory
	Cultural criminology
	Postmodern criminology
	Green criminology
2000s	Globalization of crime
	Risk and actuarialism
	Criminologies of war and terrorism
	Human rights
	Public criminology

chapter 1

Introduction

Key issues

- What is criminology?
- What is sociology?
- Why a sociological introduction to criminology?
- Why are 'social divisions' important?
- How does this book work?

An introduction: the many meanings of criminology

Criminology has many meanings but at its widest and most commonly accepted it is taken to be the study of crime, criminals and criminal justice. There are many different approaches to criminology and the subject itself has been shaped by many different academic disciplines. This book focuses on sociology and criminology. It outlines the distinctiveness of a sociological approach to crime and suggests how this differs from other approaches.

What does criminology mean to you? Why have you chosen to study it? Whatever your reasons, you are not alone. Criminology is a fast-growing subject attracting thousands of students across the world. The criminal justice 'industry' is, for better or worse, expanding at a similar rate as ideas continually change about how crime should be defined, how it should be dealt with and how all this should be measured and financed. Daily life in many parts of the world is closely influenced by crime. Many newspapers, TV schedules, websites, films, books and computer games are built around crime stories of various kinds. This book offers a sociological view of these and other developments.

What counts as a criminological topic?

Criminology is relatively new as a degree subject but it began at least 250 years ago. Since then, it has been shaped by philosophers, psychologists, anthropologists, psychiatrists, medics and lawyers as well as by sociologists, social theorists, cultural analysts and historians. As Zedner (2007a) observes, one of criminology's greatest strengths is its disciplinary hybridity.

Any study of crime must involve the study of law. Criminology explores the bases and implications of criminal laws – how they emerge, how they work, how they get violated and what happens to violators. But we know that laws vary from time to time and from place to place. Laws are relative, and always historically shaped. Even something as seemingly universally condemned as killing others has its moments when it is acceptable (for example, in war). Many criminologists believe therefore that they should not be confined by the bounds of law – this would make criminology a very traditional, orthodox and even conservative discipline. Rather, criminologists should also be able and willing to take on wider matters. The most common form of crime around the world is **property crime** or different kinds of theft. Clearly, however, there is much more to criminology than the study of theft. As you will see, although we focus on current laws in this book, we also include an array of areas that are not quite so clearly defined by them such as crimes against **human rights**, damage to the environment, hate crimes and some state crimes. To include these kinds of areas is to maintain a broad vision of forms of order and disorder and the power relations that uphold these.

It is arguably this broad vision that characterizes a more sociological approach to crime. By contrast, psychosocial and bio-medical approaches have tended to focus more closely on individual dispositions and personal motivations in relation to crime and much greater attention on physical, **emotional** and cognitive issues. In terms of criminal justice interventions, they have tended to be linked to evidence gathering and to the design or evaluation of strategies aiming to change criminal or chaotic behaviour. In this sense, they have viewed criminology as a more expert-based **forensic science**. This leads some to conclude that they are more grounded in the realities of crime than sociologists who work with a more 'general' approach to crime and 'less specific' notions of disorder. This books sets out what a sociologist, while respecting this view, might say in defence.

Criminological methods

It follows from this that, in the same way that different disciplines focus on different criminological topics, they also favour different kinds of research methods. Depending on their orientation and training, a criminologist might use anything from psychological testing to global crime statistics, or from life-stories to media analysis. Chapter 2 outlines the main research methods used within sociological criminology although we aim to illustrate how these methods have been used in different studies discussed across the book. Chapter 2's website allows you to explore some of these methods for yourself and see how others have used them.

Different research methods often result directly from different approaches to knowledge. The ways in which we choose to find out about the world – which can be called our **epistemology** – are linked to our views of what we think might be relevant, what it might be linked to and why it matters. Some criminologists make very orthodox claims to be scientists: observing, testing, measuring and trying to produce law-like statements around crime. We will meet some of this work in chapters 2 and 3 where we introduce **positivism** and **experimental criminology**. However, other criminologists do not claim to be scientific in this way. For instance, in 1958, G. B. Vold published a text called *Theoretical Criminology*. Here, he was simply concerned with laying out major ways of theorizing crime rather than with testing these. Likewise, when Ian Taylor, Paul Walton and Jock Young published *The New Criminology* in 1973, their aim was not to make a scientific study but rather to make space for a new critical stance. More recently, Jack Katz (1988) and Jeff Ferrell (1998) have used **cultural criminological methods** to analyse the 'seductions' or attractions of crime, risk-taking and thrill-seeking. So, as we shall see, the study of crime takes researchers in a number of different and often conflicting directions.

Sociology and the 'sociological imagination'

Sociology can be defined as the *systematic study of human society*. But it is much more than a series of facts and theories about society. Instead it becomes a form of consciousness, a way of thinking, a critical way of seeing. As Peter Berger (1963: 34) says: 'The first wisdom of sociology is this: things are not what they seem.' By this he means that nothing is self-evident, fixed or 'obvious'.

Thus, in criminology, a sociological approach does not take for granted 'common-sense' discussions of crime – as found for example in the media or even the news. Instead, it always challenges the taken for granted and asks questions about what we believe to be true about crime, why we might believe this and how crime is shaped by wider social factors.

Over fifty years ago, Charles Wright Mills claimed that developing what he called the 'sociological imagination' would help people to become more active citizens. C. Wright Mills (1916–62) was a US sociologist who held up sociology as an escape from the 'traps' of our lives. It can show us that society – not our own foibles or failings – is responsible for many of our problems. In this way, Mills maintained, sociology transforms personal problems (like criminal behaviour) into public and political issues (like 'the crime problem'). For Mills 'The sociological imagination enables us to grasp history and biography and the relations between the two within society. That is its task and its promise' (Mills, 1959: 4).

Sociology and the 'criminological imagination'

In this book we aim to provide a sociological introduction to criminology. From its origins in the nineteenth century, sociology has been concerned with a fundamental question: What is society? This leads us to some other basic but vital questions. What brings people into relationships with others? What holds them there? What can cause these relationships to break down? How can such breaches be repaired? If they are not repaired, what are the consequences? Sociology's focus on society as a social order means that it has always had, from its earliest days, a corresponding focus on social disorder.

As outlined in the previous sections, sociology is also about seeing the human world with a critical eye – realizing that there are general patterns of social life that shape people's life experiences, their attitudes, beliefs, behaviour and their identity. The human world that sociologists are interested in is broad and diverse in scope, ranging from day-to-day interactions between people to historical and global social phenomena. Taking a sociological perspective on that world involves trying to step outside society, becoming a stranger, so that the familiar becomes a field of adventure, not a refuge of common sense. It involves trying to look at society as a newcomer.

This way of looking at the social world involves nurturing and applying the 'sociological imagination'. In particular, it involves developing our minds to see that many personal troubles experienced by individuals – unemployment, poverty, crime victimization, to name just a few – are also public issues and that, in turn, these are interrelated with wider social forces.

In this book we aim to apply, and hopefully nurture, a 'criminological imagination'. This involves appreciating that:

- ■ Crime is a truly sociological concept. It does not exist as some autonomous entity but is a **social construct**. While there is much agreement, what is regarded as crime varies across time, place and people.
- ■ The criminal is also socially constructed, defined as such by the same social processes that define certain acts as crimes and others not.
- ■ Crime control and punishment are also shaped by social influences that determine the seriousness of acts defined as criminal, and the priority with which they are to be addressed.

Sociology, social divisions and crime

The analysis of social divisions is central to the sociological enterprise. For a long time though, sociologists focused primarily upon one major system of social division: inequalities associated with social and economic positions. Such a focus looks at how people are ranked in terms of their economic situation, their power and their prestige. It focuses especially on social class (and on caste and slavery in some kinds of societies). More recently, sociologists have recognized that other divisions are very relevant in framing all kinds of social relations, including those linked to crime and control:

- ■ social and economic divisions: here a person's labour, wealth and income play a key role in crime;
- ■ gender and sexuality divisions: here a person's position as a man or as a woman plays a key role in crime;
- ■ ethnic and racialized divisions: here a person's 'race' and ethnicity plays a key role in crime;
- ■ age divisions: here a person's age plays a key role in crime.

Each of these areas of inequality and social division is addressed in this book. In particular, Chapter 5 discusses the work of criminologists who have argued that understanding of the causes and the experience of crime needs to be looked for in entrenched structural – social and economic – inequalities. Conflict analyses of crime, for instance, have drawn attention to how the crimes that poor people commit are subject to disproportionate attention by criminal justice systems.

However, it is an odd irony that conflict analyses – concerned about class and power differences – for so long neglected the importance of gender despite their focus on social inequality. If, as conflict theory suggests, economic disadvantage is a primary cause of crime, why do women (whose economic position is, on average, much worse than that of men) commit far fewer crimes than men?

Up until the 1970s, the study of crime and deviance was very much a male province. British sociologists Frances Heidensohn (1968, 1996) and Carol Smart (1976) documented the neglect of women in such study. They also showed that when women had been included, the approach had usually been highly sexist or outrightly misogynist.

The contributions of feminist scholars to the study of crime raised some fundamental questions. One relates to what Kathleen Daly and Meda Chesney-Lind (1988) have called 'the generalisability problem'. This refers to whether theories generated to explain male offending can be used to explain female offending. Can women simply be inserted into theories that explain male offending, or are new theoretical developments necessary to explain female crime?

In redressing the omissions of criminology, feminist scholars saw an additional – but also an obvious – neglect of a focus upon men as men. Although crime is indeed largely – although not exclusively – committed by men, this dimension of analysis had been largely ignored: it was a key missing link. Hence, feminist criminologists began to raise the issue of masculinity and crime. They have suggested that since more men are involved in crimes, there may be a link between forms of masculinity and forms of crime. It is only relatively recently, then, that the obvious fact that crime is in some way bound up with masculinity has been taken up as in any way problematic.

We address gender, sexuality and masculinity centrally in chapters 6 and 9, but relevant issues are also raised elsewhere throughout the book. A further social division addressed in the book concerns 'race' and ethnicity. Across Western countries some minority ethnic groups, and especially black communities, are over-represented in the criminal justice process – in police stops, in appearances in court and in the prison population. Many commentators give the impression – especially in elements of the popular press – that some minority ethnic communities are somehow more criminally inclined than others. Such an impression both reflects and reinforces racist ideologies. Various factors are at work that account for crime. Crime is not evenly distributed across the social spectrum, and age, location, gender and socio-economic position are important variables in accounting for offending and victimization.

Analysing the relationship between 'race' and crime seriously also means taking account of discrimination in the criminal justice system – a point first raised by black criminologists in the United States in the early twentieth century. In Britain, the racist murder of black teenager Stephen Lawrence by a gang of white youths at a bus stop in London in 1993 – and the inquiry into the police investigation that followed – thrust the tragedy of violent racism into the public consciousness with a potency never present before. The flawed police investigation into the murder became, for many, symbolic of the character of relations between the police and minority ethnic communities in Britain. Fundamentally, using the language of 1960s Black Power activists in the United States, the 'Macpherson Inquiry' (1999) observed that the police investigation was characterized by institutional racism. Prior to the investigation, researchers had been producing evidence of racial prejudice and discrimination among some police officers for over two decades. We focus further on issues of 'race' and criminal justice in Part 4 of this book, 'Controlling Crime'.

However, the salience of focusing on 'race' and ethnicity in criminological inquiry is observed in a number of other places in the book.

To this point, we have discussed social divisions around class, gender, sexuality and 'race' as if they are discrete categories in which people live their lives. Yet in practice they are experienced 'as a totality' by individuals (Allen, 1987: 169–70). Any one person's experience at any one moment in time is a product of interacting divisions. One response to this reality, which has been put forward by Kathleen Daly (1997), is the 'multiple inequalities' approach around the class–race–gender axis of investigation. She suggests that everyone is located in a matrix of multiple social relations. This means that race and gender are just as relevant to the analysis of white men as they are to that of black women.

Structure of the book

The book is organized into five parts. Following this introduction and the next two chapters on 'Histories of Crime' and 'Researching Crime', Part 2 – 'Thinking about Crime' – introduces the major movements in thought and theory, organized – to help you make sense of it all – as a chronological narrative of the key theoretical developments in historical and criminological debates. The timeline at the start of this chapter shows the major movements in criminological thinking covered by the book as a whole. The third part – 'Doing Crime' – focuses on developing an understanding of experiences and patterns of criminal activity and victimization and also considers where crime takes place. Part 4 – 'Controlling Crime' – focuses on processes, theories and problems about crime control and punishment. The fifth and final part – 'Globalizing Crime' – introduces perspectives on how global forces impact upon crime and crime control. We also look to the dynamic boundaries and likely future directions of the criminological imagination.

How to use the book

We would like you to use the book in the same way that we encourage students to use our university lectures – as a path to learning. Our lectures provide a guide to key issues – a road map of ideas, if you like – and a route through the maze of reading material. The chapters in this book serve in the same way. We try to guide you through the key topics, debates and research relevant to taking a sociological approach to criminology. However, in no way do we claim to provide the final word! Learning comes through a process of exploration, and especially through the struggle to comprehend. We will not serve you well by removing the need for that struggle. Therefore, we aim to point you in the right direction but you must take the next steps yourself. Hence, reading this book alone will not suffice. We try to guide you to the reading that we have found to be the most informative and influential for the criminological issues we deal with. But we provide only an outline. We hope that you will use our guide to select your further study and engage with it yourself. After all, in thinking critically, we are providing only our perspectives. You may develop your own. Consequently, as with all journeys, there is more than one way of reaching your destination. Some paths are obviously the best way; for others, you must make your own informed judgement.

Special features

Chapter summaries

At the end of each chapter you will find a summary listing the key points. They are intended not to provide a full summary of the chapter, but to serve as a reminder about the key issues raised. They probably won't make much sense until you have read the whole chapter first!

Critical thinking questions

You will also find a number of 'critical thinking questions' at the end of each chapter. These are not examination questions. They are intended to get you thinking about what we see as some of the most important issues raised in the chapters. You will see that they are not questions to which you can give a 'yes' or 'no' answer. Instead, you will need to think carefully about them, revisit some of the points made in the chapter in question and in some cases consult the further reading recommended for that chapter. The book's website suggests ways of tackling these questions and also offers longer case studies and example boxes.

Suggestions for further study

At the end of each chapter you will also see a section labelled 'Further study'. This section has a number of purposes. In general, it is hoped that it will serve as a resource for you for future use – something that you can return to as a guide for your reading. Under this section we list key books – and articles in some cases – that we think make the most valuable contribution to understanding the issues covered by the chapter. The reading listed ranges from books that are suitable for the new student to criminology in general, for those new to the topic of the chapter in particular, and to the student (or tutor!) wishing to develop a more in-depth understanding of the subject. Again, the book's website offers links to some full-length versions of the recommended texts.

Suggestions about useful websites

Finally, at the end of each chapter, under the heading 'Useful websites', we list websites that provide useful information. These, and more, are also listed on the book's own website which we hope will be a valuable resource for you and your studies.

Glossary

A glossary of key concepts used – highlighted in **bold** – is provided at the end of the book. Concepts – abstract representations, or mental images of things observed and experienced in the real world – provide the foundations of sociological thinking. They are therefore fundamental to a sociological approach to the study of crime, deviance and social control. 'Crime' itself is a concept. We don't witness, hear or read about 'crime' when it happens. What we do see or learn are things that we have come to think of – or conceptualize – as crime.

In the glossary we provide a short definition of the key concepts used. While the glossary is intended to help you, do think about the definitions provided. Concepts don't just exist 'out there' somewhere; they are made up as abstract representations of things. In thinking about the meaning of concepts you may find it useful to consult a good encyclopedia of sociology and a good criminological dictionary where you should find the particular concept you are interested in discussed in much more detail than provided in our glossary.

chapter 2

Histories of Crime

Key issues

- What can history add to criminology?
- What have crime historians focused on and why?
- Do societies today experience more crime than in the past?
- How have understandings of different groups of offenders changed over time?
- Are digital research methods transforming crime history?

Introduction

This chapter takes a step back and looks at histories of crime. It outlines key changes in the ways historians have researched crime and criminals. Many of the other chapters include historical material on, for example, criminological theories (chapters 4 and 5), policing (Chapter 17), prisons (Chapter 18) and particular crimes (e.g. Chapter 10 on **property crime**, Chapter 11 on sexual crime and Chapter 14 on drug-related crime). These show how ways of dealing with and thinking about criminals have changed over time.

Many people believe that crime has got 'worse' in modern societies. By this they often mean that society has become 'more violent' and that communities have become 'less safe'. But what is this view based on? Is it accurate? What do historians and historical criminologists say on the matter? This chapter starts with an overview of recorded crime patterns, with a particular focus on violence, and then moves on to track key changes in historical studies of crime. It focuses on British examples but also uses some comparative material.

Historical patterns: declining violence

Many historians argue that past societies have been far more violent than contemporary ones. Julius Ruff's important text, *Violence in Early Modern Europe, 1500–1800* (2001), details the violence of everyday life in past societies. This took many forms, from military and political to community and interpersonal. Some of this violence was sanctioned by law (e.g. judicial torture) though much was not. Ruff argues that this violence reached a peak in sixteenth-century Europe but then declined over the next two centuries as European elites started to turn to other means of handling disputes and became less 'accepting' of violence.

This kind of study has been strongly influenced by German-English sociologist Norbert Elias's classic text, *The Civilising Process* (1939/1978). Elias argues that from the Middle Ages on, Europeans began to exercise new kinds of self-control over their bodies and behaviour. The emerging civilized society was marked by greater self-discipline as well as new forms of state sanctions for unruliness. Knafla (2003: xi) argues that this 'civilising process' is 'still with us today' and that it is 'bringing to an end traditional forms of social violence . . . through expanded institutions of government and police, positive law and professional courts, more rational forms of proof and a pluralistic society'.

Other comparative historical research seems to bear this out. Eisner shows that there was a 'long-term decline in homicide rates' from the sixteenth to the early twentieth century (Eisner, 2003: 1). Spierenburg (1998a) argues that codes of honour became less violent. Godfrey *et al.* (2003b: 9) suggest that there was a widespread decline in recorded violence per capita between the 1870s and the 1910s in Europe, Australia and New Zealand. Knafla finds the same for North America (Knafla, 2003). Notably, Braithwaite's comparison of 'Australian convict society' and 'American slave society' links the marked decline of Australian crime rates in the nineteenth century to the latter's long-standing use of reintegrative punishment strategies (Braithwaite, 2001).

This historical decline in violent crime arguably ended in the mid- to late twentieth century. For example, British homicide rates have increased significantly since the 1980s due mainly to a doubling in the number of murders of men aged 20 to 24 (Dorling, 2005: 29). This raises complex questions for criminologists as to the broader social shifts behind this 'return' to violence. It also raises new challenges for historians of crime who have yet to take on comparative analysis of this later period.

There have been fewer large-scale or comparative historical studies of non-violent crime. One reason for this is the difficulty of comparing the ways that different states categorize different offences and how these categorizations change over time. However, national studies show that theft and property offences were very common in the past, just as they are today. Emsley (2005) estimates that theft accounted for between a half and three-quarters of all recorded crime in England between 1750 and 1900. Petty street-based offences were also prominent, with many prosecutions for drunkenness, gambling, illegal selling and vagrancy in the same period (Gatrell, 1990). The next section suggests how and why patterns of recorded crime changed in the British case.

British prosecution patterns

British prosecutions followed the same broad pattern found in Europe and the wider English-speaking world. Recorded crime rose sharply in the early nineteenth century, then stabilized until the early twentieth century, then rose again very sharply after the Second World War and particularly after the 1970s (see Figure 2.1).

Historians have explained the British pattern in different ways (see Emsley, 2005). The first sharp rise (1790s–1840s) is often linked to the modernization of society: **urbanization**, **industrialization**, migration and economic depression after the Napoleonic wars. These changes probably resulted in more people, especially younger men, committing more crime. However, historians also argue that changes in control caused an increase in prosecutions. New criminal offences were created, the courts were reorganized (which made it easier for ordinary people to initiate a case) and the new police force was set up. In addition, national criminal statistics were collected from 1805 which turned crime into a national and more easily measured phenomenon.

The long 'plateau' period where this rise flattened out (1850s–1910s) is more difficult to explain. Social changes may have meant that fewer crimes were actually committed, rather than fewer prosecutions brought. Rising living standards, lower food prices, political stability, declining interpersonal violence and adjustment to new urban industrial lifestyles, combined with the workings of a strong centralized regulatory state, seem to have created – temporarily at least – more law-abiding subjects and a new public order consensus (Gatrell, 1990).

The twentieth-century rise in prosecutions is commonly explained in terms of increased opportunities to commit new kinds of crime, trends in the economic cycle, and a breakdown in the fragile public order consensus of the late Victorian period, especially in the wake of the social upheavals of the two world wars. Recorded crimes rose steeply from about half a million in 1950 to 1.6 million in 1970 and then to 5.5 million in 1991 (Home Office, 1999). Post-Second World War consumer booms generated both more goods for those with disposable income as well as the desire for more goods which very likely resulted in increased property crime. In line with this, car-related offences – relatively rare in the 1950s – grew rapidly (Corbett, 2003). As discussed above, violent offences have also been increasing.

So, crime patterns have clearly changed over time. Recorded crime rates have increased dramatically relative to population in the last thirty years. However, the value of historical studies here is to show that there was no 'golden age' where crime did not occur.

Trends in historical writing

Historians' views on crime have altered a lot since the 1970s, especially with the challenges of, first, 'history from below' or social history, and later, gender history and cultural history (see Godfrey et al., 2003a; Emsley and Knafla, 1996; King, 1999). As this chapter shows, social historians' initial and ground-breaking concern with white male working-class criminals has given way to a broader range of studies of women, juveniles, 'race', the 'underclass' and **colonialism**. There is also a comprehensive body of work on the history of policing, prisons and punishment which is discussed in chapters 15, 17 and 18.

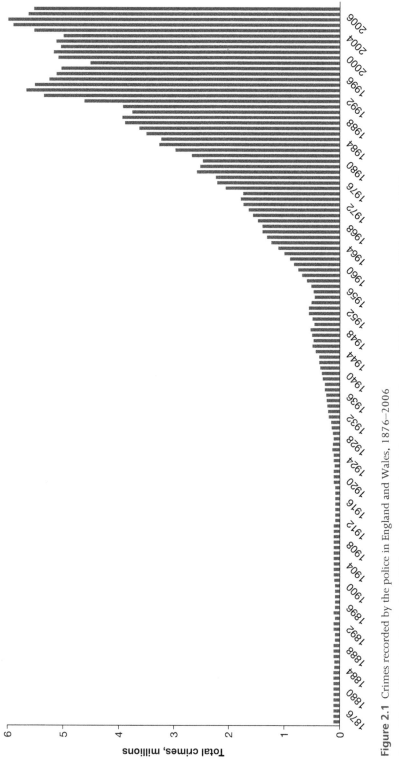

Figure 2.1 Crimes recorded by the police in England and Wales, 1876–2006

Source: Criminal Statistics, England and Wales (various years) and Crime in England and Wales 2005/06 (Walker *et al.* 2006).

Men and crime

In the 1960s and 1970s, radical historians began to turn away from traditional areas of research (high politics, diplomacy, war, state formation and so on) to investigate what came to be widely called 'history from below', or 'social history'. This focused on working-class lives, everyday survival and political struggles. These historians, many working within a leftwing and Marxist perspective, were interested in understanding the impact of **capitalism**, urbanization, industrialization and class formation upon people's lives.

Male workers were viewed as particular casualties of capitalism and its new levels of poverty and exploitation but also as being radicalized by these. Historians like E. P. Thompson, Eric Hobsbawm, Douglas Hay and Peter Linebaugh wrote powerful studies of the many (male) agricultural labourers, (male) industrial workers and (male) unemployed who were prosecuted in their thousands for '**social crimes**' in the eighteenth and early nineteenth centuries. Many of these prosecutions resulted from the criminalization of old customs – customs that had traditionally helped ordinary people put more food on their tables. For example, with changing definitions of private property, small-scale hunting and trapping were criminalized as 'trespass' and 'poaching', and collecting (or 'gleaning') crops left over from a harvest became a form of theft. Others were prosecuted for political crimes linked to protests to protect these customary **rights** and also to the harsh repression of new illegal organizations (like trade unions and working men's associations) and new political activities like mass rallies calling for working men to be given the vote (Thompson, 1963, 1975, 1991; Hobsbawm and Rudé, 1969; Archer, 1990). British social historians' work in this field influenced similar studies of 'social crime' in continental Europe (Godfrey et al., 2003a: 21). Again, the aim was to examine how far the broad social and economic changes linked to modernity led to the criminalization of the poor.

According to these historians, a defining feature of 'social crime' was that most ordinary people believed these actions were justifiable. Crime was therefore interpreted as a political act, criminals as conscious or unconscious class rebels, policemen as class traitors (being of working-class origins themselves), and the courts as instruments of class oppression (Hobsbawm, 1972; Hay et al., 1975; Linebaugh, 1976, 1991). Although this broad approach attracted criticism from other historians (Blok, 1972; Langbein, 1983; Innes and Styles, 1993; Lea, 1999), it remained dominant into the late 1980s (for an overview of these debates, see Philips, 1983; Weiss, 1999: xiii–xxiv).

From the late 1980s, this view of history, class and crime began to change. Social history was critiqued from three different directions. First, studies of pre-capitalist or early modern societies (1500–1800) showed that crime and disorder were not just by-products of 'modern' struggles (Beattie, 1986; Sharpe, 1999). Second, cultural historians argued that crime and its control held many and varied social meanings, and that these were as much bound up with issues of nation, race, sensation and science as they were with economic inequalities (Pick, 1989; Walkowitz, 1992; Kohn, 1992). Third, historians of gender and family relations highlighted many kinds of less than heroic male crimes, including domestic violence and child abuse (Behlmer, 1982; Clark, 1987; Doggett, 1992). This opened the way for new historical studies that focused on the construction of criminal masculinities.

A major claim in this work is that Western societies became increasingly intolerant of male violence. Evidence for this included harsher penalties for 'everyday' crimes such as assault. Acts of interpersonal violence which may not even have been prosecuted in the early eighteenth century were punished by large fines, imprisonment and sometimes the death penalty by the early nineteenth (Wiener, 1998). Intolerance of male violence was also expressed through the criminalization of much 'traditionally acceptable' male behaviour, from duelling to bare-knuckle boxing to wife-beating. This shift was linked to growing divisions between rough and respectable cultures, the physical withdrawal of elites from ordinary communities, the separation of public and private spaces and the introduction of the new police force in the 1830s to control unruly working-class communities (Barrie and Broomhall, 2011). Eisner similarly argues that the 'long-term decline in homicide rates' from the sixteenth to the early twentieth centuries 'seems to go along with a disproportionate decline in elite homicide and a drop in male-to-male conflicts in public space' (Eisner, 2003: 83). Feminist and gender historians have examined women and children's (predominantly girls') experiences of rape, sexual assault, incest and domestic violence (Clark, 1987; D'Cruze, 1998; Jackson, 2000) and analysed how men's intimate violence could be challenged.

Male violence may have been less tolerated but it remained embedded in everyday life as shown by apprentice riots (Griffiths, 1996), late nineteenth-century public holiday skirmishes involving 'hooligans', 'scuttlers' and other gangs (Pearson, 1983; Davies, 2000) and mid-twentieth-century clashes between different kinds of young (mostly male) **subcultures** (S. Cohen, 1972/2002; Hall and Jefferson, 1976). Spectacular outbreaks like these, however, seem to be rooted in more general cultures of 'ordinary' violence among young men in playgrounds, schools, pubs, clubs, homes and workplaces. This is not to imply that violence and crime is an unchanging or natural part of modern masculinities (see Messerschmidt, 1993; Newburn and Stanko, 1994; Collier, 1998). Definitions of 'acceptable' male violence have been contested between men themselves since at least the 1500s. The key point is that, historically, the negotiation of everyday violence has played a major role in the construction of everyday masculinities and has quite frequently resulted in informal policing directed at, or court appearances by, young men.

Women and crime

Concern about rising crime rates among women has grown in recent years. Yet historical studies show that women have a long history of offending. There is a significant pattern to this: high female prosecution rates from 1500 to 1800, falling rates from the 1800s to 1945 and higher rates from 1945 onwards. In other words, the gap between male and female prosecution rates was narrow in the first and last periods but much wider in the second.

Women in early modern Britain and Europe often appeared before courts. They were most commonly charged with property crime, slander, assault and infanticide (Walker, 2003; Arnot and Usborne, 1999a; Beattie, 1975). Slander or defamation of character was considered a much more serious offence at this time than it is today. In early modern society, to lose one's 'good name' was to lose trade, customers, trust and face. Local reputations were at the heart of local village and small town life, not least because it was difficult to make a fresh start by moving away to another community. This was to change with nineteenth-century migration and urbanization and, as a result, slander became a less important crime among ordinary people although it remained very important for elites where personal reputation still mattered. In the early modern period, however, slander was a significant offence, frequently prosecuted and frequently committed by women. In continental Europe slander, gossip and rumour-spreading were often among the charges levelled at the many women accused of witchcraft (Wiesner, 2007; Roper, 2004). The same was true in Britain although there were far fewer cases (Sharpe, 2001).

Female prosecution rates were high in the early modern period for two key reasons. First, women arguably committed more offences because they were more fully engaged in public, street

FREE FIGHT IN A COTTON MILL.
ANNISTON, ALA., FACTORY GIRLS JOIN SIDES IN A RIOT IN WHICH MISS BROWN IS FATALLY INJURED.

Plate 2.1 Women millworkers in a free fight in a cotton mill.

Source: Unattributed nineteenth-century engraving in *Police Gazette*. Mary Evans Picture Library.

and neighbourhood life (Eales, 1998). Long before capitalism and industrialization they were almost all economically active (apart from a small group of elite families). Women worked in many areas, including agriculture, baking, textiles, fishing and brewing and, crucially, combined this with domestic work and childcare. Very often, children worked alongside their parents and work itself was done in or near the home. This meant that there was no clear separation of home and work as there was in the nineteenth century when capitalism transformed work. Tasks became more specialized, workplaces were separated from homes, child labour was first intensified then banned. Women continued to work but their lives became more closely associated with the home, childcare and domesticity (the private sphere) rather than with places outside the home (the public sphere). Some historians (Feeley, 1994) argue that early modern women's greater public presence had a clear impact on their offending behaviour in that they arguably had more opportunities to commit crime than their nineteenth-century counterparts. Others (see Arnot and Usborne, 1999a, for overview) disagree, mainly because they argue that later generations of women were not rigidly confined to the private sphere after capitalism.

The second reason why women's prosecution rates were higher in the early modern period was because of the particular nature of early modern modes of law enforcement. These were more informal and community-based than they were to become in the nineteenth century and were applied more equally to the whole community, including to women and children. As law enforcement became more professionalized, specialized and nationalized it became more masculinized. From the 1830s it could be argued that the criminal justice system revolved around entirely male police officers arresting mostly male offenders and those offenders being sent by male-dominated courts to mostly male prisons. As a result, some historians argue that women were less likely to face prosecution for serious offences in the nineteenth century than they were before because prosecution itself had become a much more serious matter (Feeley, 1994). This argument certainly works in relation to the higher courts. However, women continued to appear frequently in the lower courts (summary courts) which dealt with offences seen as less serious such as habitual drunkenness, soliciting, petty theft or child neglect. As Arnot and Usborne argue in their discussion of European trends, '[t]he lower the historian moves down the jurisdictional ladder, the larger the proportion of women' (1999b: 8).

Many thousands were also dealt with *outside* the criminal justice system for minor and moral offences such as vagrancy, alcoholism, destitution, sexual promiscuity or illegitimate pregnancy. This is an important point because it means that their experiences were not recorded in criminal statistics. Inebriates' reformatories (homes for alcoholics), religious rescue homes, hostels and, up to a point, asylums, workhouses and mental hospitals all housed large numbers of women and girls across the Western and wider English-speaking world (on the United States, see Pascoe, 1990; on Australia and Canada, see Langfield, 2004; on Britain, see Zedner, 1991b, Mahood, 1995 and Cox, 2012). Time spent in these institutions was very often much longer than an average female prison sentence. Some women and girls approached these institutions for help or shelter themselves, though the 'freedom' of such a choice was often very constrained. Many of these institutions survived well into the twentieth century but have not featured in many criminological studies (see Barton, 2005) apart from some work on the **pathologization** (or medicalization) of female crime (Dobash *et al.*, 1986).

Twentieth-century women's experiences of crime and control have so far been studied rather less by historians, though this is beginning to change. Boritch and Hagan's (1990) study of male and female arrest rates in Toronto from the 1850s to the 1950s found that these both declined overall and showed marked similarities in relation to different kinds of offences. Most of those arrested, especially for very common public order offences, were from lower-class backgrounds. The study therefore stresses the importance of class in any study of gender and crime – a view shared by a **survey** of gender and violence in Britain over the same historical period (D'Cruze, 2000).

Histories of women's involvement in policing from the early twentieth century onwards (Brown and Heidensohn, 2000; Jackson, 2006; Schulz, 1995) also open a window on women's crime, much of which remained property- and public order-based. A high-profile minority of women were involved in more serious crimes such as murder, as detailed in two studies (Ballinger, 2000; D'Cruze et al., 2006). Prostitution prosecutions declined in early twentieth-century Europe (Bartley, 2000) but remained prominent at a more global level, as shown by Ringdal's (2003) ambitious 'world history' of this subject (see also Hershatter, 1997, on Shanghai).

Early feminist criminologists writing from the 1970s analysed rising female crime rates – much of what we know about late twentieth-century women's crime comes from them. Freda Adler's *Sisters in Crime* (1975), a study of US women, sparked a controversial debate still invoked today. Adler argued that a 'new female criminal' had been created by women's social liberation from the 1960s onwards. Late modern women had, first, a greater public role and therefore more opportunities to commit crime, and, second, were more likely to face prosecution as they were more likely (in contrast to their nineteenth-century counterparts) to be treated in similar ways to men.

Others rejected Adler's claims. Box and Hale (1984) argued that women might have become more socially liberated in the late twentieth century but that they also remained economically marginal (see also Smart, 1979). Structural inequalities meant that as a group they had, historically, always been poorer than men (occupying more low-paid jobs, combining periods of paid employment with periods of unpaid childcare, earning less during their working lives therefore having fewer savings and reduced pensions, and so on). If women were committing more crime it was because of their continuing social marginality, not their greater legal equality.

Other feminist criminologists focused on the treatment of women by the police, courts and prisons. In this they have also increasingly focused on the differences *between* women rather than the differences between women and men, and asked which kinds of women are more likely to be arrested, found guilty, imprisoned or referred for psychiatric treatment. Important as gender difference is in shaping crime patterns, it is by no means the only difference that counts. Some research has found that, on the whole, women who present themselves as more traditionally feminine, and above all as respectful and remorseful, tend to get treated more 'leniently' than other women (Carlen and Worrall, 1987; Worrall, 1990; Heidensohn, 1996). Others have shown how this construction of women can mean that some of their crimes, such as maternal child abuse, continue to remain invisible (Turton, 2007).

Youth and crime

Most prosecuted crime is committed by younger people. There are two reasons for this. This group (and young men in particular) commit more crime of a kind that people feel should be reported and younger offenders are more likely to be pursued by the criminal justice system.

Youth crime has a long and complex history. Research here focuses on two broad issues: disorderly youth cultures and youth justice procedures. From at least 1500, boys, but also girls, have been involved in riotous street cultures, gangs, property crime and violent crime, from theft, assault and vandalism to manslaughter and murder (for an overview see Cox and Shore, 2002; on girls see Davies, 1999 and Cox, 2012). From the 1800s, ways of dealing with youth crime changed significantly as this section will show.

The idea that juvenile delinquency is far from 'new' was set out most comprehensively by sociologist Geoff Pearson (1983) in his now classic text, Hooligan. The book charts a century of British panics around disorderly youth starting with the Conservative government's 'short, sharp, shock' programme of the 1980s and going back to the 'hooligan' rioters of the 1890s. Pearson argued that all these were linked by a recurring and familiar set of 'respectable fears' – unruly behaviour in public space, lack of respect for traditional values, unwillingness to 'settle down'. Each adult generation experienced these as 'new' and each believed that young people's behaviour was 'worse' than it had been when they were young themselves. He explained this in terms of ongoing inter-generational tensions and the life course. The ageing process means that adults always experience the social worlds of the young as unfamiliar and as posing a threat to 'established' ways of doing things, whatever these might be. This process has been exaggerated in modern times because of the faster pace of socio-economic and technological change.

Historians support this view but take it even further by showing that youth crime and disorder has been a subject of British and European public debate since at least the 1500s. The key point here is that these debates took place long before large-scale urbanization and industrialization. Griffiths (1996, 2002) details the wide range of measures taken against unruly youths in early modern England by the Church, employers, poor law authorities and the courts. European studies offer a similar picture. Parents, especially elite ones, went to great lengths to punish their young sons' immoral behaviour. Drinking, gambling, fighting and promiscuity could ruin a family's good name, with dire economic consequences. Dutch parents sent their sons away to work in the Dutch East Indies while some Spanish parents sent their sons to correctional orphanages, sometimes for several years (Roberts, 2002; Tikoff, 2002). These extreme measures show how seriously early modern youthful disorder was taken. They also highlight the overlooked fact that the sexual and moral behaviour of young men as well as young women was subject to regulation.

Industrialization and urbanization created more opportunities for youth crime and new responses to youth crime. Recorded prosecutions of children and adolescents, particularly in urban areas, rose dramatically from the late eighteenth century onwards and the new term 'juvenile delinquency' emerged soon after (see Box 2.1). This youth crime wave was linked to massive population growth and a simple increase in numbers of people under the age of 30. It was seen by authorities at the time, however, as evidence of the collapse of traditional social controls. Changes to the apprenticeship system were widely blamed. Young people had traditionally left home to learn a trade as apprentices or domestic servants. Apprentices had to work for a set period (often seven years) for low wages. In return, they gained a training, sometimes housing, and, crucially, longer-term job security. Young people thus swapped parental discipline for employer discipline. Further, it was expected that they would eventually marry and be 'disciplined' by their own family responsibilities. The breakdown of apprenticeship – due to demands for more flexible and mobile labour – gave young workers a new freedom (though also a new economic vulnerability) that few of their parents and grandparents had known. In

the criminological imagination

BOX 2.1 Extract from 'The Report of the Committee for Investigating the Causes of the Alarming Increase of Juvenile Delinquency in the Metropolis', 1816

It was found that Juvenile Delinquency existed in the metropolis to a very alarming extent; that a system was in action, by which . . . unfortunate Lads were organised into gangs; that they resorted regularly to houses, where they planned their enterprises, and afterwards divided the produce of their plunder.

Source: 'Report of the Committee for Investigating the Causes of the Alarming Increase of Juvenile Delinquency in the Metropolis', London, 1816: 5; cited in Shore (1999: 6).

some developing regions such as Southeast Asia and Africa it is possible to see similar inter-generational tensions today and comparable concerns about new levels of juvenile crime (see United Nations Asia and Far East Institute for the Prevention of Crime and the Treatment of Offenders for more on this: http://www.unafei.or.jp/english/index.htm).

Youth migration was not new but large-scale urban migration was. This shaped juvenile delinquency in two key ways: by providing more opportunities for 'dissolute' leisure activities (Springhall, 1998) and by providing more possibilities of surveillance and regulation. Towns and cities had coffee houses, gaming rooms, pubs and brothels but they also had moral vigilante groups (such as the Society for the Promotion of Christian Knowledge, or societies for the 'reformation of manners'), Christian crusaders (such as Anglican evangelists and Methodists), thief-takers, prosecution associations and later public health reformers and the police themselves. This historical period is most often read by sociologists in terms of dislocation and alienation but overlooks the many steps taken to prevent and contain these processes. The development of new ways to deal with something now named as 'juvenile delinquency' in the early nineteenth century was part of a wider development of a new kind of state, community and control.

New ways of dealing with delinquency across the West included, from the early nineteenth century onwards, setting up juvenile reformatories, moving child cases to lower courts, abolishing child imprisonment in adult jails and creating juvenile courts. Increasing numbers of non-offending children were brought into these new juvenile justice systems through new child protection legislation (1880s onwards). Young victims of crimes such as neglect and abuse and those thought to be at risk of offending could be 'put into care' in juvenile reformatories. This kind of 'welfare policing' has been most commonly studied through the experiences of girls (Mahood, 1995; Cox, 2012) but also involved large numbers of boys.

Studies of twentieth-century juvenile delinquency are less concerned with when and why it was 'invented' and focus more on when and why formal responses to it shifted from justice (punishing deeds) to welfare (meeting needs). Historians stress that these two elements have been part of the juvenile justice system ever since it was set up (Wills, 2007). For example, in the 1940s hardliners felt that abolishing birching (corporal punishment ordered by a court) was 'too soft' on young offenders whereas 'liberals' in the same period called for careful casework by new kinds of welfare professionals such as social workers and psychologists.

That said, in Britain, the 1969 Children and Young Persons Act and its (partial) implementation by the 1970 Conservative government marked a new turn towards welfarism. Care proceedings and community-based treatment or residential care were favoured over criminal proceedings and custodial responses. The discretionary powers of social workers were enhanced and those of magistrates reduced (Pitts, 2003; Muncie, 1999). This drive to 'liberalize' had earlier historical roots but was also linked to a new post-war political consensus across social policy issues in general.

Well-known studies of twentieth-century youth subcultures such as Stan Cohen's classic *Folk Devils and Moral Panics* (1972/2002) or Hall and Jefferson's *Resistance Through Rituals* (1976) describe a very different scene to that documented by juvenile justice studies. With their focus on the more spectacular world and public presence of older teenage subcultures they have more in common with early modern studies of disorderly, but not necessarily law-breaking, youths. These studies (discussed in more detail in Chapter 6) have an important place in the development of academic criminology because they analysed the media's role in constructing 'deviant' subcultures and exaggerating (or amplifying) the destructive effects of these. Yet these more spectacular behaviours have historically only ever accounted for a small number of youth prosecutions. More mundane cases of shop-lifting, fare-dodging, theft, vandalism and car crime accounted for the vast majority in the 1970s and 1980s when these classic studies were written. The introduction of ASBOs (anti-social behaviour orders) by the 1998 Crime and Disorder Act arguably blurred the boundary between spectacular youth cultures and actual youth crime, for example by allowing the banning of certain kinds of clothes (such as hoodies) in certain kinds of places (such as some shopping malls).

The 'dangerous class', 'underclass', race and crime

Many sociologists and criminologists argue that today's society is much more unequal than it was in the past and that social inclusion has given way to extreme social exclusion (Young, 1999a). While such inequalities are certainly deep-rooted, historical studies show that they are not new. Concerns about the 'dangerous classes' and their links to crime can be traced back in Western societies to the early nineteenth century (Morris, 1994; Crowther, 2000). They have much in common with debates around the 'underclass' in the 1990s and 'social exclusion' more recently. Broadly speaking, all these terms refer to social groups who are economically marginalized, socially stigmatized and who appear to others to live by a 'different' set of moral standards.

Definitions of 'dangerousness' were, and remain, closely linked to perceptions of class and race. In colonial contexts, native and aboriginal peoples were thought to require closer policing by white settler authorities. Special measures, such as missions and forced adoptions, were set up in the United States, Canada, Australia and New Zealand to reform these groups (Langfield, 2004; Byrne, 1993; Choo, 2001; Pascoe, 1990, see also Stoler, 2002). In societies with a history of slavery, like the USA, black people faced huge discrimination in the criminal justice system (see Chapter 5 for discussion of early black criminologists' work on this).

In Europe, the 'dangerous classes' tended to be poor, urban and white but were commonly framed as a 'race apart', as a distinctive 'breed' of person (Davis, 1989; Cox, 2002). These discourses became more pronounced with the mass migrations of people out of Ireland and southern and eastern Europe to North America, Britain and Australia. **Social Darwinist** models of the 'survival of the fittest' and racial degeneration suggested that the 'unfit' were threatening to outbreed the 'fit'. This thinking influenced criminal justice. In Britain, the 1869 Habitual Criminal Act and the 1879 Habitual Drunkards Act were designed to detect and detain 'habitual' criminals of various kinds. It also influenced criminology. American criminologist Richard Dugdale analysed 'criminal families'. His infamous 1875 study of the Jukes family – showing how murderers had married prostitutes, how mentally defective women had mothered many delinquent children and so on – inspired similar studies in Britain and Europe (Hahn Rafter, 1997; Pick, 1989). Lombroso's efforts to define 'criminal types' (through their faces, bodies, expressions and inherited characteristics, as discussed in Chapter 4) were clearly part of a much broader cultural turn towards the pathological or scientific explanations for crime (Lombroso, 1876). After 1945, the term 'problem family' was used by many social workers dealing with juvenile delinquency. Today, the term 'troubled families' is preferred by government. At one level the use of these new terms has been a positive development as they analyse delinquency alongside wider family relations. At another it replicates earlier characterizations of 'degenerate' families. In the 1980s and 1990s, American Charles Murray's controversial work on the 'underclass' and ethnicity continued this line of enquiry (Murray *et al.*, 1990; see also Lister *et al.*, 1996 for critique).

Given this context it is easy to see how racialized discourses of crime were applied to non-white immigrants. In Britain, beliefs about 'deviant foreigners' have been attached to many groups over time from Irish, East European Jewish, Malay and Chinese migrants in the nineteenth century to West Indian migrants of the mid-twentieth to certain 'asylum seekers' of the present. Concerns about 'foreigners' of all kinds have often been accompanied by concerns about white 'under-class' behaviour. The cafés, clubs, drugs and music that grew up around historic migrant cultures in many Western cities were new cosmopolitan urban spaces which were often subject to heightened police surveillance as sites of potential 'trouble'.

Of all these groups the experiences of West Indians (mainly young men) within the criminal justice system have attracted most criminological attention in Britain. Classic studies of race and crime were closely connected to studies of class and crime. For Hall *et al.* (1978), historical moral panics around white underclass criminality took on new politicized forms when they settled on a new target: post-war West Indian, particularly Jamaican, migrants and their children; and the 'new' kinds of criminal behaviours they apparently brought to the deprived inner-city areas. 'Mugging' (simply a new name for the old crime of 'aggravated robbery'), 'hustling' (petty criminality involving gambling, prostitution and unlicensed gatherings) and marijuana-linked crimes (which represented a new phase of a much longer history of British drug use) were all heavily associated by the press and the public with black immigrants.

Other writers extended Hall *et al.*'s work, critiquing the 'over-policing' of young West Indians (notably through the use of notorious 'sus' laws – being stopped 'on suspicion' of being involved in criminal activities) and the part these played in the urban riots of the early 1980s in London, Birmingham, Manchester, Liverpool and Bristol (Whitfield, 2004; Holdaway, 1996; Keith, 1993).

For much of the 1980s, perceived links between class and crime were highly racialized, with urban black people viewed by liberals and hardliners alike as among the most seriously socially excluded and, by extension, among the most likely to commit crime. Of course, liberal and left-leaning commentators, including most criminologists writing on this subject, also argued that high rates of crime and imprisonment among young blacks were also the product of the systematic racial discrimination against this group operating at all levels of the criminal justice system. As this section has suggested, this discriminatory thinking has a long history.

BOX 2.2 Crime history and the digital revolution

In the last decade, new digital research techniques have revolutionized crime history. Historians have long used criminal statistics, institutional records, census records and newspapers alongside other cultural and more personal individual and family records. However, the digitization of many of these records has transformed their work. Digitization makes it possible to conduct new large-scale searches of traditional modern sources.

Tim Hitchcock and Robert Shoemaker have been at the forefront of this work in the UK. Their 'Old Bailey Proceedings Online' (2006) is a ground-breaking project which has created searchable texts of 198,000 criminal trials held at London's central criminal court between 1674 and 1913. Their second project, 'London Lives, 1690–1800' (2012) has opened access to 240,000 searchable biographical records around crime, poverty and social policy relating to over 3 million individuals. Both initiatives have created remarkable new ways of researching 'history from below' and have helped to re-connect crime history with broader social history. They have also made key computing techniques, such as **data mining,** accessible to historians.

Digitization has also allowed historians to 'follow' offenders across their life course. In *Serious Criminals* (2011) and *Criminal Lives* (2007), Godfrey, Cox and Farrell combine digitized census returns, criminal registers, newspaper reports and other personal geo-data (such as an offender's places of residence, school or work and shifting proximity to family members) to evaluate the long-term effect of sentencing policy on large cohorts of repeat offenders from the north-west of England in the nineteenth century. They conclude that sentencing strategies were often much less relevant than other life-changing factors such as employment and marriage in reducing recidivism.

Similarly, Hamish Maxwell Stewart (2010) uses this kind of **record linkage** to track transported convicts from their court cases in England and Ireland to their cemetery plots in Tasmania and to correlate their death rates with trends in crime rates, food prices, labour regimes and other socio-economic data. His research draws on the 'Founders and Survivors' (2012) initiative, another large-scale digital data project piecing together the lives of the 73,000 men, women and children who survived the convict experience to become Tasmania's settler population.

Digital crime history has its limits. Only a fraction of historical sources have been digitized and most of these relate to the period 1700–1930. Transcription and coding errors compromise the accuracy of digitized search mechanisms. Some fear that this new 'quantitative turn' could undermine the more discursive insights of cultural histories of crime. Nevertheless, digitization allows us to make exciting new connections between macro and micro history, between the structural and the personal, between the bio-medical and the biographical.

Summary

1   Recorded crime rose sharply in the early nineteenth century, then stabilized until the early twentieth century, then rose again very sharply after the Second World War and particularly after the 1970s. Property crime was the most common offence throughout this period.

2   Historical studies of crime have changed in focus and nature. From the 1970s, social historians interpreted crime in class terms whereas from the late 1980s onwards, this class-based view has broadened to encompass other issues like gender and age.

3   The history of crime from the nineteenth century on can be read as the history of men policing men.

4   Women and young people have long histories as offenders. Ways of dealing with both groups changed in the nineteenth century with the result that both groups were dealt with in specific parts of, as well as outside, the criminal justice system.

5   Perceived links between social exclusion, 'race' and criminality are very long-standing. Terms for excluded groups have changed over time and have included 'the dangerous classes' and 'the underclass'. These groups have often been presented as if they were a distinct social type.

6   Digital research techniques have transformed crime history by generating large searchable resources and allowing historians to search for macro-patterns within these.

Critical thinking questions

1   What does a historical perspective add to the study of criminology?
2   How would you summarize crime patterns, 1500–2000?
3   What factors need to be considered when trying to assess and interpret historical crime patterns?

Further study

Emsley, Clive (2005) *Crime and Society in England, 1750–1900*, 3rd edn, London: Longman. A very comprehensive and accessible overview of the history of crime and control.

Ruff, J. R. (2001) *Violence in Early Modern Europe 1500–1800*, Cambridge: Cambridge University Press. Important study of long decline in violence.

Walker, Garthine (2003) *Crime, Gender and Social Order in Early Modern England*, Cambridge: Cambridge University Press. Very good overview of early modern crime, often overlooked by criminologists and sociologists!

Eisner, Manuel (2003) 'Long-term Historical Trends in Violent Crime', *Crime and Justice: A Review of Research*, 30: 83–142. An unusual and valuable long-term and comparative look at patterns of violent crime.

D'Cruze, Shani, Walklate, Sandra and Pegg, Samantha (2006) *Murder: Social and Historical Approaches to Understanding Murder and Murderers*, Cullompton: Willan. Puts modern murder in historical perspective.

Pearson, Geoff (1983) *Hooligan: A History of Respectable Fears*, London: Macmillan. Classic analysis of modern historical youth cultures

Cox, Pamela (2012) *Bad Girls in Britain: Gender, Justice and Welfare, 1900–1950*, Basingstoke: Palgrave (paperback edition of 2003 text). Looks at the other side of Geoff Pearson's story by charting a history of delinquent girls.

Useful websites

National Archives
http://www.nationalarchives.gov.uk/
The UK government's official archive which includes historical records relating to crime, policing and prisons.

Old Bailey Proceedings Online
http://www.oldbaileyonline.org/
A fully searchable resource containing over 197,000 full records of criminal trials held at London's central criminal court from the seventeenth to the twentieth centuries.

London Lives, 1690–1800: Crime, Poverty and Social Policy in the Metropolis
http://www.londonlives.org/
Original historical sources on criminal justice, poor relief, charities and hospitals.

British Newspaper Archive
http://www.britishnewspaperarchive.co.uk/
Can be searched for national and local media coverage of specific criminal cases, national crime trends and popular and political debate about these.

chapter 3

Researching Crime

Key issues

■ What counts as criminological data?

■ Why is it necessary to think critically about criminal statistics?

■ What kinds of research methods do criminologists and sociologists use?

■ Must criminological researchers 'take sides'?

Introduction

Specialist texts on research methodology and methods have proliferated in the social sciences. In both criminology and sociology, the study of 'methodology' – the theoretical principles and framework behind different ways of carrying out research – and research 'methods' – the tools or instruments used by researchers to gather their evidence – have become distinct areas within the subject.

Criminological researchers come from a variety of disciplines and draw from a range of research techniques. In recent years, criminologists along with other social scientists have become more reflective about research techniques and outcomes. This chapter explores these issues in relation to the nature of criminological data and commonly used research methods, the use of criminal statistics and **ethics**. It closes by considering a long-standing question within the discipline: Whose 'side' are criminological researchers on?

Criminological research methods

Criminologists generate their own data through their own research projects. They select their research methods according to their expertise and area of interest. Psychological profiling, genetics, urban ethnography, cultural history and social theory – and many more besides – are all currently used. As this brief list indicates, the criminological research field is very diverse (Westmarland, 2011; King and Wincup, 2007; Champion, 2005; Maxfield and Babbie, 2007; Coleman and Moynihan, 1996). Opinions are often sharply divided as to the 'best' methods to use and many researchers are unaware of work outside their own discipline. Whilst preference for particular research methods may relate to deeply held epistemological and ontological beliefs – such as whether the social world can be objectively 'captured' and measured or not – practical considerations – such as applying the appropriate method depending on the type of research question – also play a significant part.

Sociological approaches to crime research are themselves very diverse but until recently two have dominated: **qualitative** – involving methods such as interviews, **participant observation** and **ethnography** (Noaks and Wincup, 2004); and **quantitative** using tools like surveys, statistical analysis and **prediction studies** (Bushway and Weisburd, 2005). In recent years 'mixed methods' approaches have become more prominent across the social sciences which aim to combine these two approaches in creative ways (Creswell, 2003). New kinds of criminological work are beginning to emerge along these lines (e.g. Schulenberg, 2007). Mixed methods are increasingly favoured among those involved in **evaluation research** and **evidence-based policy making**. Here, criminologists and other social scientists evaluate policy initiatives or generate evidence about a particular social problem with a view to designing an intervention to help ease that problem (see website for exercises to allow you to practise your own criminological research skills).

Experimental criminology takes this further. Its defining feature is that it seeks to test out its theories in the criminal justice field and to make policy recommendations based on 'hard' evidence of what works. Sherman (2005) traces this tradition from Henry Fielding's eighteenth-century policing experiments in London (see Chapter 4) through von Liszt's offender reform programme in late nineteenth-century Marburg through to the current randomized controlled fieldwork of the Pennsylvania-based Academy of Experimental Criminology. He argues that, this tradition notwithstanding, 'the vast majority of published criminology remains analytic and nonexperimental' (2005: 129). Sherman and his colleagues believe that criminology's future lies in a closer collaboration between analytical and the experimental approaches which will help to make the subject 'more useful'. They would like to see experimental techniques used to link criminality to the life course as well as to provide evidence to counter the United States' 'three-decade increase in prisoners'. Nevertheless, experimental criminology is problematic for many sociologists because it is based on the idea that it is possible to provide 'unbiased empirical guidance' (Sherman, 2005: 129) to shape policy debates. It favours medical-style randomized controlled experiments and tends to separate crime, criminality and control out from the wider social relations that construct them.

In the UK such approaches to crime and justice research were brought into the heart of government policy during the 'what works' agenda of the Blair years (1997–2007). This in turn impacted on academia and encouraged the development of 'crime science', 'the application of science to the control of crime' (Laycock, 2008: 149) often for policy ends, an approach that styles itself as radically new and one of great significance. Regarding the latter, proponents of crime science have immodestly related their approach to other areas of criminology as akin to that between medicine and the sociology of medicine (Smith and Tilley, 2005). Here, presumably, crime scientists bestow their healing powers to address the problems of society whilst other criminologists, diminished in their importance, are seen to do little more than engage in abstract theorizing and critique. Despite its stated novelty, there is much here that is not new. For example, the theoretical assumptions of routine activity and rational choice theories of crime prevention – or 'criminologies of everyday life' (Garland, 1996) – that guide much crime science research have existed within criminology for decades. More established still is the application of scientific method to understand society, as practised by Durkheim ([1897] 2002) in the nineteenth century.

Crime science is not without its detractors, however. These include criticisms that such approaches often assume particular and partial versions of criminal action that lack internal coherency, erroneously claim value-free objectivity, may uncritically finesse socially repressive policies, ignore the visceral pleasures and 'seductions' of crime, and conduct analysis abstracted from the social and emotional contexts in which crime is enacted (Hayward, 2007). On this latter point, Jock Young (2004) has pilloried such approaches and their claims of scientific rigour, labelling them 'voodoo criminology'.

Social psychologists studying crime also use experimental and mixed method approaches. **Social psychology** analyses the relationships between individuals and society. It examines how individuals relate to each other as well as to groups and institutions. Compared to other forms of mainstream psychology, it is less concerned with bio-medical and neurological matters and more concerned with questions of social action and perception. It generally seeks to explore the connections between individual perceptions, beliefs and behaviours and social structures and processes. Classic social psychological approaches to crime and deviance – such as symbolic interactionism – are discussed in Chapter 5. Social psychologists involved in crime research today are likely to use mixed methods and to focus on questions such as motivation, stigma, emotions, individual and community perceptions of crime and the receptiveness, or otherwise, of particular kinds of offenders to particular kinds of sanction (see Chapter 12).

Criminological research is funded in different ways and its **outputs** can take various forms. University-based criminological research is mostly funded by academic research agencies such as the UK's Economic and Social Research Council or the Australian Research Council. These agencies allocate funds mostly derived from governments. Alternatives include research commissioned and paid for by other state bodies or by the voluntary or private sectors. Funding inevitably raises issues of ownership, the tailoring of aims to meet funders' (and the government's) ambitions and the question of 'whose side' criminologists are on – an issue to be explored later in the chapter. Research findings are typically presented at academic conferences or policy consultations and published as academic journal articles or policy reports. Box 3.1 shows something of the range of outlets available and the accompanying website offers links to some of these.

BOX 3.1 Some academic criminological associations and journals

American Society of Criminology
http://www.asc41.com/
Publishes two journals, *Criminology* and *Criminology & Public Policy*.

Australia and New Zealand Society of Criminology
http://www.anzsoc.org/

British Society for Criminology
http://www.britsoccrim.org/

European Society of Criminology
http://www.esc-eurocrim.org
Publishes the *European Journal of Criminology*: http://www.esc-eurocrim.org/journal.shtml

Socio-Legal Studies Association
http://www.slsa.ac.uk/

British Journal of Criminology
http://bjc.oxfordjournals.org/

Criminological data

What counts as criminological data? Many people – other than criminologists – produce information about criminals, victims, law enforcers, sanctions and rights. Criminal justice agencies themselves such as the police, courts and prisons are very important here as the main source of criminal statistics (discussed below). However, criminologists also use information that comes from outside the criminal justice system. These include:

- *Mass media* contain vast amounts of crime coverage and comment. Television, film, news media and the Internet represent crime and justice in many different ways. Many students are initially attracted to criminology as a subject through these sorts of channels which are covered in detail in Chapter 20.
- *Charities and voluntary organizations* have a long global history of intervening in crime and deviance and this involvement continues today. Organizations like the Howard League for Penal Reform, Women's Aid or the National Association for the Care and Resettlement of Offenders (NACRO) in the UK or Equal Justice USA in the United States play a significant role in criminal justice by providing services but also by creating criminological data and research reports. Others, like Amnesty International or Human Rights Watch, publicize state crime around the world.

- *Private companies* like banks, credit suppliers and insurance agencies store and exchange huge amounts of information about their customers. A person with a criminal record or unreliable financial record can be refused some financial services. High crime rates in particular residential areas (as calculated by risk assessors and loss adjusters) can raise domestic and commercial insurance premiums quite dramatically.
- *International bodies* are a further important source of global and comparative criminological data. Specialist agencies here include the United Nations Interregional Crime and Justice Research Institute (UNICRI), the United Nations Office on Drugs and Crime (UNODC), the European Commission's (EC) Europa – Justice and Home Affairs Unit, and the Association of Southeast Asian Nations (ASEAN) which also deals with transnational crime.

Thinking critically about statistics

Joel Best (2001) argues that people respond to statistics in three distinct ways. The 'awestruck' treat them with reverence and as if they represent the clear truth about a particular issue. The 'naïve' are more critical but also tend to accept statistics as 'hard facts'. The 'cynical' are very suspicious about statistics, believing that they are often flawed, that they can be manipulated to prove anything and, even worse, that they are deliberately used to mislead and deceive.

Best advises us, however, against being awestruck, naive or cynical. Instead, we need to be critical and to develop a questioning perspective which allows us to evaluate the merits and limitations of statistics. The critical appreciate that in summarizing complex information, statistics do not capture every intricacy. Simplifications and omissions result: choices are made about how to define the problem being measured, and how to go about measuring it. In evaluating these choices, the critical make informed judgements about how to use and value statistics. The aim of this section is to encourage a critical approach to crime statistics.

Recorded crime

Criminologists generate their own statistical data in the course of their research projects. Alongside this, however, they are very likely to draw on official criminal statistics. In most countries, the main sources of formally recorded crime statistics are government departments responsible for criminal justice. In Britain, the Home Office publishes annual Criminal Statistics, with separate volumes for England and Wales, Scotland and Northern Ireland, on the Internet as well as in printed reports. These statistics are readily available to students, the general public, journalists and anybody else with an interest. In Canada, criminal and other social statistics are collated by federal agency Statistics Canada. It is important to note here that some governments do not routinely publish this kind of information and that some authoritarian regimes – such as China, Burma and Vietnam – actively withhold it (see UNICRI and Human Rights Watch websites for information on this kind of material).

The crimes recorded by no means reflect the full extent of unlawful activity, however. To take the case of England and Wales, the Criminal Statistics do not include data from police forces for which the Home Office is not responsible – for instance, the British Transport Police (Department for Transport), Ministry of Defence Police (MoD) and the Civil Nuclear Constabulary (Department for Energy and Climate Change) publish their own statistics. They also exclude cases of tax and benefit fraud known to agencies such as HM Revenue and Customs and the Department for Work and Pensions (respectively) which have their own investigative functions. Even where a category of crime is included in the Criminal Statistics, many crimes committed do not appear in police records for a variety of reasons (see Muncie, 2001: 25–39 on these omissions).

Recorded crime statistics are not the product of a neutral fact-collecting process. The recording process itself is governed by guidelines. The appendix to the *Criminal Statistics England and Wales* states that 'the . . . process starts when someone reports to the police that an offence has been committed or when the police observe or discover an offence'. The National Crime Reporting Standard (NCRS) (introduced in the UK in 2002) requires any reported incident – whether or not it is classified as a crime – to be recorded. The police make an initial examination of the facts to determine if there is prima facie evidence that an offence has been committed; a crime report may then be made out. However, for a crime to be registered in official data, a number of things need to happen:

- recognition by a victim or possibly a witness that a potentially criminal incident has taken place
- reporting of that incident to the police
- acknowledgement by the police that a potentially criminal incident has occurred
- recording by police of the incident as an alleged crime.

There are many factors along the way that can prevent a crime being recorded. Only a proportion of possible crimes make it through what has been called 'the crime funnel' (see also Chapter 15).

BOX 3.2 Some sources of official statistics on the Internet

Statistics Canada:
www.statcan.ca
(Key words: justice and crime)

The UK Office of National Statistics:
www.ons.gov.uk
(Key words: crime and justice)

For neighbourhood statistics:
http://www.neighbourhood.statistics.gov.uk/
For police-only statistics: http://www.police.uk/

Federal Bureau of Investigation:
www.fbi.gov
(Key words: Uniform Crime Reports)

Scottish Executive:
www.scotland.gov.uk
(Key words: recorded crime, crime statistics)

Australian Bureau of Statistics:
www.abs.gov.au
(Key words: recorded crime)

Sources: the individual government departments.

It is well known, consequently, that only a small proportion of incidents that would be classified as crime are recorded by official statistics. The statistics represent only the tip of the iceberg. Early local crime surveys – to be discussed in a later section – revealed that many victims do not report crimes to the police. These survey findings are supported by anecdotal accounts from victims. For instance, a victim's perception about how seriously their allegation will be taken by the police will affect the reporting of crime. Once it has been reported, the police are able to exercise a certain amount of discretion in deciding what to record. Victims' complaints may be disbelieved or dismissed as too trivial. They may even be excluded to avoid work and improve the clear-up rate. Other factors affect crime records: reporting requirements for insurance claims, for instance, result in a high level of reporting of property crimes; and changing patterns of policing and targeting of crimes affect the numbers of particular crimes that come to the attention of the police (Maguire, 1997). In short, the recording of crime involves complex processes of interpretation and interaction. It is certainly not a straightforward process, hence the need to be 'critical'.

Racist incidents: an example of thinking critically about recorded crime

Racist crime – where victims are targeted because of their 'race' or ethnicity – provides a very useful example here. Data on racist incidents for England and Wales can be found in *Statistics on Race and the Criminal Justice System*, published by the Ministry of Justice. Britain has a long history of racist crime (Bowling, 1998; Witte, 1996), but in statistical terms it simply did not exist before 1979, as it was not recorded in official statistics until then.

There has since been a huge increase in the number of recorded incidents, especially from the late 1990s (see Figure 3.1). The data seem to suggest that racist crime has escalated: certainly the awestruck and the naive – to use Joel Best's categories – might think so. But is this really the case?

To think critically about the statistics, we would need to bear in mind the observation made above that not all crimes appear in police records. In the case of racist incidents it is clear that in the past there has been significant under-reporting by victims due – to some extent – to dissatisfaction with the police handling of reported incidents. A number of common allegations have been made by victims. Often, they have complained about considerable delays before police attend incidents (Gordon, 1990: 13). It has also been alleged that the police have frequently refused to acknowledge the racial motives behind incidents, often explaining them away as minor disputes between neighbours (Dunhill, 1989: 70). Victims of racist incidents have also complained that the police are reluctant to prosecute the perpetrators, and on occasion the victims themselves have been subject to hostile treatment from the police (Gordon, 1990: 20–1; see also Chapter 9 of this book); fear of such hostility has served as a deterrent to reporting incidents.

In taking a critical view of the number of recorded racial incidents, the apparent increase over time could quite conceivably reflect changes in police recording practices and also perhaps a greater motivation by victims to report crimes (for discussion of similar upward trends in reported sex crime, see Chapter 11). The sharp rise in the number of recorded incidents in the late 1990s following the publication of the inquiry into the racially motivated murder of teenager Stephen Lawrence (Macpherson, 1999) supports such an observation. The report not only drew

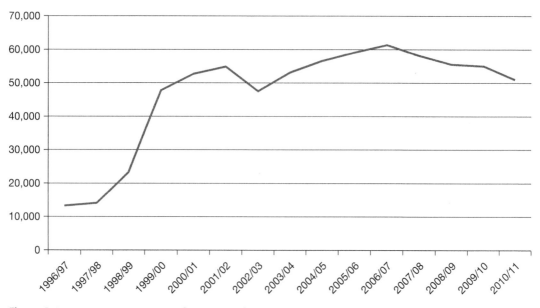

Figure 3.1 Recorded racist incidents for all police force areas in England and Wales, 1996–2011.

Sources: Home Office (2004); Ministry of Justice (2008); Ministry of Justice (2011).

widespread public attention to the problem of racist crime, but in labelling the Metropolitan Police Service as 'institutionally racist' it led to a major examination by police forces concerning how they respond to racist incidents. The definition of an incident was also broadened to include any incident that is perceived to be racist by the victim or any other person – previously, it was limited to the perception of the victim and the police. It is also likely that the establishment of racially aggravated offences for the first time in Britain under the 1998 Crime and Disorder Act made police forces more alert to such offences. The 2006 Racial and Religious Hatred Act took further action against activities that stirred up hatred against persons on racial or religious grounds. In addition to these shifts in reporting and recording habits, the way in which such data are presented by state agencies also requires scrutiny. For example, in their report on statistics on race and the criminal justice system for 2010/11 the Ministry of Justice (2011: 12) declare a decrease of 'almost 18 per cent in the number of racist incidents reported across England and Wales over the five-year period (2006/07 to 2010/11)'. Whilst this may be true, the authors have selected the highest point in the statistical trend (the highest recorded number of racist incidents was during 2006/07) against which to compare the 2010/11 statistics and thus present their efforts in the best possible light. Their statistics also state a 389 per cent increase in racist incidents between 1996/97 and 2010/11.

As this example shows, a comparison of recorded crime data over time is important if hazardous. Comparison of data between countries is also problematic but raises important methodological questions for criminologists. In the USA, for example, rates of recorded race crime (e.g. those recorded by the Federal Bureau of Investigation (FBI) Uniform Crime Reports) are proportionally much lower than they are in England and Wales. One reason for this is that the criteria used for defining these crimes are far more stringent.

the criminological imagination

In 2007, disputes around the definition and policing of race crime in the USA grew into a major public issue, with many calling for a new civil rights movement as a result. Protests focused around the Jena Six – six black youths charged with the 'attempted murder' of a white co-student in Jena, Louisiana. The six and their many supporters claim that the white student had, with others, committed race crimes against black students in the school, including the hanging of a noose in the school grounds. The key point of their claim is that the white students' actions had gone unpunished whereas the actions of the six black students (which might have been charged as 'assault', for example) had been treated disproportionately. In Florida during 2012 the Sanford Police Department's decision not to charge George Zimmerman for fatally shooting black teenager Trayvon Martin further ignited such debates. Such high-profile cases may yet precipitate a new approach to race crime in the USA.

National crime victimization surveys

Since the 1970s, many countries have established official crime victimization surveys. These provide an important alternative way of generating data about crime (and especially unrecorded crime) by asking samples of people directly about their experiences of crime victimization. As Coleman and Moynihan argue, they are a key way of addressing the '**dark figure**' of unreported crime and can also be usefully compared with **self-report** studies in which different groups of people are asked, for example, to complete an 'anonymous delinquency checklist' (1996: xi–xii, 49).

The first large-scale government deployment of such research was the US National Crime Victimization Survey established in 1972, and now conducted annually. The first such national crime victimization survey in Britain was the British Crime Survey (BCS), carried out in 1982, with further surveys in 1984, 1988, 1992, 1996 and 1998. In the 2000 British Crime Survey, close to 23,000 people aged 16 and over were interviewed. From 2001 the BCS moved to an annual cycle, with 40,000 respondents to be interviewed per year (46,000 were interviewed in 2010/11). More changes followed in 2011/12 with the renaming of the BCS as the Crime Survey for England and Wales (CSEW) and the inclusion of younger people (4,000 people aged 10–15) in the survey sample. The BCS/CSEW measures the amount of crime in England and Wales by asking people about crimes they have experienced in the past year. It asks people about their attitude to crime, whether or not they fear crime and what measures they take to avoid it. It also asks them about their attitudes to the criminal justice system, including the police and the courts. The survey findings are published in a variety of specialist reports available online on the Home Office website, and complete datasets of primary data are available for secondary analysis and can be obtained from the University of Essex Data Archive. The questions used in the BCS/CSEW are also published online by the Question Bank at the University of Surrey (see the website accompanying this book for direct links and exercises on this).

National crime victimization surveys, with their focus on victims' experiences, can present a very different picture of crime than that offered by national criminal statistics, with their focus on recorded crime. For example, a comparison of BCS data for 2002–3 with recorded crime statistics for 2002 suggests some major differences (Simmons and Dodd, 2003). According to the BCS, there were:

- three times as many offences of vandalism
- three times as many thefts from the person
- over twice as many woundings
- twice as many bicycle thefts.

In other important respects, there is less discrepancy between these two kinds of data. Broad trends for vehicle theft, for example, are relatively similar across the BCS/CSEW and recorded crime figures because victims more readily report such thefts to the police and to insurance companies (see Maguire, 2012).

As discussed in Chapter 9, crime victimization surveys have been very useful in providing insights into under-reported and under-recorded crime and to sensitize policymakers to the range and diversity of victim experiences. However, as with all research methods, these surveys have their limitations. In almost all cases, victim surveys focus on crimes experienced by individuals or households. They do not focus on, for example, collective victims of corporate or state crime. They arguably define 'crime', 'victim' and 'criminal' in very limited terms and highlight 'conventional' crimes over others.

International, local and commercial crime victimization surveys

Large-scale international victim surveys have also been carried out so some international comparisons can be made here. For example, the European Union International Crime Survey (EU ICS) surveys residents above the age of 16 in eighteen (of 27) European Union countries. Despite its apparent reach, significant differences in relative sample sizes generate questions over the ability to generalize findings across national boundaries. For example, the EU ICS samples similar numbers of participants in France and Northern Ireland despite their dramatically different sizes of population (65 million and 1.8 million respectively). The International Crime Victim Survey (ICVS) series has further reach. Initiated in 1988 it has since been deployed in some 55 different countries. The project was set up to bridge the gap in adequate recording of offences by the police for purposes of comparing crime rates in different nations and to provide a crime index independent of police statistics as an alternative standardized measure. The ICVS is the most far-reaching programme of standardized sample surveys to look at householders' experience of crime, policing, crime prevention and feelings of insecurity in a large number of nations.

Again, as discussed in Chapter 9, there are also specific problems, though, with using international victimization reports to measure crime. The cultural perception of crime in different countries may affect the respondents (Newman, 1999: 25). It is clear that findings from victimization surveys need to be interpreted very carefully, with the knowledge that apparent differences may reflect variations in definition as much as variations in the incidence of crime.

Local victim surveys with a narrower geographical focus have also made a significant contribution to knowledge about crime. They have highlighted the uneven distribution of risks of victimization, showing that certain age or social groups are more frequently subjected to crime than others. For example, by focusing on particular localities, local victim surveys in Britain (notably in Islington, Merseyside, Edinburgh and Rochdale) have shown the higher levels of crime prevailing in socially deprived areas and the disproportionate victimization of women, of minority ethnic groups and of the poor (Crawford et al., 1990; Kinsey, 1984; Mooney, 1993; Forrester et al., 1988). In particular, local victim surveys have revealed levels of violence and sexual crime against women higher than those revealed by mass victimization surveys, and certainly far higher than those indicated by police records (Hanmer and Saunders, 1984; Radford, 1987; Painter and Farrington, 1998). Indeed, the highest estimates of domestic violence have come from local victimization surveys, which probably reflects the problems of using narrow legal definitions in understanding sexual victimization and interviewers' insensitivity to women's personal and often painful experiences in earlier national crime surveys. For example, the first two British Crime Surveys revealed only one (unreported) case of attempted rape and 17 and 18 cases of sexual assault respectively in the 1983 and 1985 reports. By contrast, the first Islington Crime Survey (Jones et al., 1986) showed that one-third of the households in that area contained people who had been sexually assaulted during the previous year, and that younger women were very much more likely to be assault victims than women aged over 45.

Not all victim surveys are directed at individual victims. Commercial victimization surveys ask owners of retail and manufacturing premises about the crime they have experienced in a particular period of time. Such surveys can provide an alternative measure of crime and the extent to which particular premises are subject to repeat victimization. The Home Office carried out the first of these in Britain in 1993 and the second in 2002. The 2002 survey found that 75 per cent of retailers and 50 per cent of manufacturers experienced at least one crime in the previous year with the largest businesses (those with 50 or more employees) at greater risk (Home Office, 2005b). Overall, this kind of crime was lower in 2002 compared with 1993 which found that eight out of ten retailers and two-thirds of manufacturing premises experienced one or more of the crimes covered by the survey (Mirrlees-Black and Ross, 1995). It should be noted that some offences such as theft by staff and fraud are more difficult to detect and more likely to be under-represented.

Thinking positively about crime statistics

The critical perspective applied to crime statistics to this point perhaps suggests that the statistics provide more of an insight into official definitions of crime, crime recording and policing practice than into actual levels of unlawful activity. Thinking critically about crime statistics, though, also involves thinking about the potential they offer. For example, a major aim of the National Crime Recording Standard (NCRS) introduced in 2002 has been to ensure that all incidents reported to the police are recorded – even if some are not subsequently classified as a crime and published as criminal statistics – in order to provide more accurate intelligence for local policing and for intervention by other agencies. Although instituted to address a number of the problems outlined above, this more standardized approach is not without its critics. For example, by setting consistent minimum standards of data collection, the NCRS requires police constabularies to record information about those alleged to have been involved in crime, rather than solely recoding data on those charged. Other criticisms have focused on the increased statistical visibility of seemingly minor disputes such as playground fights (Mortimore, 2011). Overall, while the statistics may not provide the reliable measures of crime that policymakers and journalists, for instance, would wish for, they play a central part in criminological research.

Criminologists and criminals

Generations of criminologists have tried to look beyond formal criminal statistics and to do their own research on criminal activity. In a much-quoted phrase, Robert E. Park, chair of the Department of Sociology at the University of Chicago in the 1920s, encouraged research students to 'go get the seat of your pants dirty in real research' – in short, to go and get acquainted first-hand with the social world around them.

While Western anthropologists at the time were still studying 'exotic' cultures in remote places, Park believed that anthropological methods could be used in Western urban research and that social scientists should study people in their everyday environments. He saw the city as a 'social laboratory' in which social processes and human interactions could be studied *in situ*. Park and his colleagues developed a distinctive approach to social research, social life and the study of deviance – 'the Chicago School'. Researchers in this tradition – which was extremely influential in shaping sociological criminology (as outlined in Chapter 5) – used a particular mix of ethnographic and other qualitative research methods. They aimed to capture the complexity of social life through interviews, the study of personal documents and, famously, observational methods. For real understanding, imaginative participation in the lives of others was required; empathy, as well as an acute eye, was the key (Bulmer, 1984).

An ethnographer participates in a given social setting, 'amid the action' for an extended period of time; makes regular observations of people and events in that setting; listens to people and engages in conversations; interviews informants about issues that cannot be observed directly by the researcher; collects documents about the group under study; and writes up a faithful representation of what they have discovered in a detailed account of their study. Major studies of crime and deviance carried out within the early Chicago School were Nels Anderson's *The Hobo: The Sociology of the Homeless Man* (1923), Frederic Thrasher's *The Gang* (1927), John Landesco's *Organized Crime in Chicago* (1929), Clifford Shaw's *The Jack Roller* (1930) and Paul G. Cressey's *The Taxi-Dance Hall* (1932). Paul Cressey stated that his first objective 'was to give an unbiased and intimate picture of the social world of the typical taxi-dance hall' (a hall where customers paid to dance with young women). According to Cressey, and characteristic of an ethnographic approach:

> Observers were sent into the taxi-dance halls. They were instructed to mingle with the others and to become as much a part of this social world as ethically possible. . . . The investigators functioned as anonymous strangers and casual acquaintances . . . without encountering the inhibitions and resistance usually met in formal interviews.
>
> (Cressey, 1932: xxxiv)

In Britain, the organization Mass Observation conducted similar work and individual writers and journalists published accounts of their 'undercover' encounters. Ada Chesterton's *Women of the Underworld* (1928) and George Orwell's *Down and Out in Paris and London* (1933) are just two of many. Notably, this kind of work was not undertaken in earnest by academic sociologists or criminologists in Britain until the 1970s.

Ethnographic research in the United States lost its momentum from the 1930s with the development of more formalized sociological methodologies which tended to privilege more quantitative methods. After the Second World War, however, members of the 'Second Chicago

School' such as Howard Becker and Erving Goffman (discussed below) gave it a new radical political edge which was taken further by Californian universities in the 1960s with their focus on countercultural, deviant and alternative groups. Some noted studies here include John Lofland's *Doomsday Cult* (1966), Marvin Scott's *The Racing Game* (1968), Jacqueline P. Wiseman's *Stations of the Lost* (1970), and Jack Douglas and Paul Rasmussen's *The Nude Beach* (1977). Adler and Adler (1998: xiii) summarize ethnographic research aims in this period:

> Free to go out and study those groups in close proximity, these ethnographers realized that the only sensible way to get information about hidden populations was to study them naturalistically. Disdaining the research endeavors that analyzed criminals as captured populations, these sociologists and criminologists went into bars, inside gangs, and into the inner sanctums of deviant populations to find out what constituted their realities.

Adler and Adler go on to argue that the late 1970s to the early 1990s were the 'Dark Ages' of ethnographic research. During this period, university ethics committees, cautious of the moral, ethical and legal implications of fieldwork on crime and deviance, inhibited ethnographic research.

Notably, this was much less the case in Britain where the 1970s saw a significant development of this kind of work with studies such as James Patrick's study of gang life in Glasgow (1973), Howard Parker's study of 'joy-riding' in the inner city (1974), Jason Ditton's study of fiddling and pilfering in a bakery (1977), Anne Campbell's study of violence among female gangs (1981, 1984) and Dick Hobbs's study of crime and policing in east London (1988), to name just a few.

Moral, ethical and legal issues

Ethnographic methods can sometimes (though by no means always) raise particular moral, ethical and legal difficulties. Researchers who are closely observing people involved in criminal behaviour have to decide where or whether to draw a line. Taken to its extreme, the logic of the criminological ethnography suggests that researchers should be prepared to engage in or witness criminal acts themselves. This view has been most strongly proposed by US sociological criminologists from the 1960s onwards. Ned Polsky wrote in his study of 'hustlers' that if a researcher were to

> study adult criminals in their natural settings, he must make the moral decision that in some ways he will break the law himself. He need not be a 'participant' observer and commit the criminal acts under study, yet he has to witness such acts or be taken into confidence about them and not blow the whistle.
>
> (Polsky, 1967: 133)

Soloway and Walters (1977) relate a situation in their study of heroin users in which the researcher was unwittingly involved in an armed robbery involving a car in which he was a passenger. James Inciardi inadvertently participated in a convenience store hold-up (1977).

More recently, cultural criminologist Jeff Ferrell, known for his work on US urban youth crime, has argued that 'For the dedicated field researcher who seeks to explore criminal subcultures and criminal dynamics, obeying the law may present as much of a problem as breaking it' (1998: 26). Drawing from Max Weber's notion of *verstehen*, Ferrell argues that to achieve criminological *verstehen* – that is, a deep appreciation of the lived experience of criminals and the situated meanings, emotions and logic of crime – researchers must be prepared to participate in the 'immediacy of crime' themselves.

If they are prepared to do so, however, they will need to make some ethical decisions about how far they are prepared to go, what kind of knowledge it is ethical to possess and what criminal acts are inappropriate for study. They will also need to evaluate what responsibilities they might have to victims, to criminals, to those involved in crime control, to themselves and to their profession.

This kind of approach to criminological research has been critiqued from a number of quarters. Sociological researchers themselves have been divided on this issue. Lewis Yablonsky advised the 'applied sociologist' to 'proceed with caution' and to avoid 'becoming a tool' in illegal activity or 'reinforcing' criminal activity by observing rather than challenging it (1965: 71, 72). In the early 1970s, Kai Erikson attacked the covert research methods favoured by some of his colleagues as deceptive and unethical (Galliher, 1995: 175). Ferrell himself and his co-writer, Mark Hamm, warn researchers against 'thrill-seeking' for its own sake (1998: 7–8). Criminologists working on gender issues – around masculinities and femininities – have criticized this kind of work on the grounds that it can glamorize certain kinds of (male) crime and in doing so marginalize the study of other kinds of crime (see e.g. Scraton, 1990).

Codes of ethics

Most academic associations and research funding bodies have developed codes of professional ethics to promote 'good practice' in research. These, of course, apply to all kinds of research methods – not just ethnographic methods. The codes cover issues such as consent, confidentiality, access, transparency, risk assessment and data protection. Criminological associations such as the British Society of Criminology (BSC) and the International Society for Criminology (ISC) and sociological associations such as the American Sociological Association (ASA) publish these codes on their websites. Researchers at all levels – from undergraduates to professors to consultants – must now show that they have considered them in their research design.

These codes are certainly important as a way of protecting the interests of those taking part in research – those interviewed, surveyed, observed and counted – and in promoting professionalism amongst researchers. However, the problems with restrictive ethical codes highlighted by Ferrell and others in relation to ethnography are arguably relevant to many other areas of criminological and sociological research. Is a criminologist working within tight ethical codes still able to conduct effective research into 'closed' worlds of different kinds, such as the 'closed' worlds of child sexual abuse, people trafficking or corporate crime? Is it always possible or desirable for research aims to be 'transparent' and equally open to all parties? Could excessive risk assessment mean that researchers no longer take risks and, if so, what might be the effects of that? These kinds of questions are in part connected to the question of taking sides in criminological research.

Taking sides in criminological research

Becker and 'underdog sociology'

Many criminologists and sociologists have liberal leanings and a concern for inequality and injustice. Many want their research to be more than an academic exercise; they want it to contribute to social change. Debate about the sympathies of sociologists who study crime and deviance was fuelled by those working in the Chicago School of Sociology in the 1950s and 1960s – what is sometimes called the 'Second Chicago School' (discussed in Chapter 5). The School was characterized by a diverse range of perspectives, but a dominant one emerged – one that was critiqued as 'underdog sociology' (Gouldner, 1973). Prominent characters and studies here included: Howard Becker's work on drug use; Erving Goffman's on asylums and Harold Finestone's on delinquency.

Howard Becker's 1966 presidential address to the Society for the Study of Social Problems, published in his famous essay 'Whose Side Are We On?' (1967), outlines their approach. Although it was published over four decades ago it is still debated in universities. As Martin Hammersley has argued, 'it continues to have relevance for us today, not least in posing fundamental questions that still need answering' (2001: 107).

Becker's point was that sociologists must take sides in their work since they cannot, by definition, be on all sides. Given this, sociologists should take the side of the subordinate party. Since it was not possible 'to do research uncontaminated by personal and political sympathies', researchers should make these sympathies more explicit. For Becker, 'the question is not whether we should take sides, since we inevitably will, but rather whose side are we on?' (1967: 239). By this he did not mean that researchers should reject impartiality, arguing that 'whatever side we are on, we must use our techniques impartially enough that a belief to which we are especially sympathetic could be proved untrue'.

Becker's position was closely connected to his wider and very influential concept of 'labelling'. Researchers should focus on the experiences of groups labelled as deviant by those in authority (who he also called 'moral entrepreneurs'). The experiences of 'deviant' groups were overshadowed because their 'right to be heard' and their 'credibility' was much weaker than that of those with the power to label, control and punish (1967: 241). It was the researcher's job to redress the balance and, in so doing, to challenge authority where necessary.

This view of criminological research has had its opponents both at the time and since. In a famous essay 'The Sociologist as Partisan' attacking Becker, Alvin Gouldner argued that:

> the pull to the underdog's exotic difference takes the form of 'essays on quaintness'. The danger is, then, that such an identification with the underdog becomes the urban sociologist's equivalent of the anthropologist's (one-time) romantic appreciation of the noble savage.
>
> (Gouldner, 1973: 37)

For Gouldner, Becker's approach 'expresses the satisfaction of the Great White Hunter who has barely risked the perils of the urban jungle to bring back an exotic specimen. It expresses the romanticism of the zoo curator who preeningly displays his rare specimens' (1973: 38). Gouldner argues that, in fact, the agenda of truly 'radical sociologists' should be to study the 'overdog', the 'power elites' who shape the legal systems, law enforcement and penal practice, rather than the underdog oppressed by them.

Ohlin and policy-forming sociology

A very different point of view emerged through the work of another scholar connected to the Chicago School, Lloyd Ohlin. Ohlin was a practitioner as well as an academic (Galliher, 1995). His work was shaped by his experiences working on parole boards and as a research sociologist in the correctional system. His methods were quite distinct from Becker's, with more of a focus on surveys than on ethnography. His analysis of deviance was also distinct (as discussed in Chapter 5). The well-known study he completed with Richard A. Cloward in 1960, *Delinquency and Opportunity*, argued that delinquency was the product of blocked opportunities connected to poverty, education and employment (and, by extension, less connected to labelling). According to this view, it was still a researcher's job to challenge authorities and policymakers but to do so by playing an active part in the policy-making process. Researchers should use the kinds of research methods that would generate the kind of data to provide the kind of evidence that policymakers could not ignore.

Many criminologists have adopted this stance, working with campaigners and reformers as well as policymakers. They have been active in penal reform movements, in setting up rape crisis centres and hostels for victims of domestic violence and sexual abuse, and in challenging racism within the criminal justice system (see Knepper, 2007; Ryan and Ward, 1992; Holdaway and Rock, 1998). The emergence of **public criminology** in recent years (see Chapter 22) has given a new emphasis to this kind of public-oriented work.

These two broad concerns – to critique authorities and to work with authorities – have shaped sociological criminology from the 1960s onwards. They have helped to create particular kinds of research methods – some that produce data more easily incorporated into public policy and some less so. They have also informed theoretical debates around conflict criminology, radical criminology, left idealism and cultural criminology – discussed across several chapters here. Of course, it could certainly be argued that these two broad concerns are not mutually exclusive. Nevertheless, the question 'whose side are we on?' remains highly relevant.

BOX 3.3 Research design

As a student, you will probably be asked to conduct your own criminological research project of some kind at some point. Here are some factors you will need to consider in your **research design**:

Research questions

- What do you want to find out and why is it relevant?
- What are your basic theoretical questions?

- What are your corresponding empirical questions?
- How will you turn your theoretical questions into specific researchable questions?

Research methods and data analysis

- What kinds of research methods and data analysis strategies have you chosen to use and why?
- What kind of data will your methods yield and will this help to answer your research questions?
- Can you use the project to develop new practical skills?
- If you're using more than one method or mixed methods how will you draw these together?

Existing research and literature review

- How has your project been shaped by your wider reading?
- How has existing research dealt with the topic you want to study?

Sampling

- How will you select your research materials or respondents?
- What will shape your decisions here?

Access

- How will you contact and negotiate access to the people or materials you want to research?
- Who are the **gatekeepers** in your project?
- Do you have a back-up plan if things don't work out?

Ethics

- What ethical considerations and potential risks do you need to consider?

Time frame

- How much time have you allowed for each research task?
- How can you ensure that you will complete the project by your deadline?

See the website for practical exercises related to this box.

Summary

1   There is no distinctive methodology or set of methods used in criminological research. Criminologists' views on the purpose of crime research differ radically – both between disciplines and within disciplines (like Sociology). This is linked to the fact that the needs of offenders, victims and policymakers are arguably different.
2   Official criminal statistics should always be treated carefully.
3   There are many sources of criminological data – students should try to look beyond their own national criminal justice system where possible.
4   Criminological researchers, like all researchers, need to have a workable research design and give careful consideration to moral, legal and ethical issues.

Critical thinking questions

1   **What does it mean to 'think critically' about crime statistics?**
2   **Whose interests should be served by criminological research?**
3   **When criminological researchers 'take sides', are they 'biased' in their work?**

Further study

King, R. D. and Wincup, E. (eds) (2007) *Doing Research on Crime and Justice*, 2nd edn, Oxford: Oxford University Press. A comprehensive collection of essays on the practicalities and problems of doing criminological research.

Cromwell, P. F. (ed.) (2003) *In Their Own Words: Criminals on Crime*, 3rd edn, Los Angeles, CA: Roxbury. Fieldwork accounts of crime uniquely from the prospects of offenders.

Ferrell, J. and Hamm, M. (eds) (1998) *Ethnography at the Edge: Crime, Deviance, and Field Research*, Boston, MA: Northeastern University Press. A valuable collection of essays that provides methodological, political and theoretical reflections of fieldwork on crime and deviance.

Bushway, S. and Weisburd, D. (2005) *Quantitative Methods in Criminology*, Aldershot: Ashgate. A useful and accessible overview of quantitative approaches.

Maguire, M. (2012) 'Criminal Statistics and the Construction of Crime', in M. Maguire, R. Morgan, and R. Reiner (eds) *The Oxford Handbook of Criminology*, Oxford: Oxford University Press. A good overview of the key issues affecting the recording and measurement of crime.

Westmarland, L. (2011) *Researching Crime and Justice: Tales from the Field*, London: Routledge, chapter 1. This provides a good introduction to the purpose and types of criminological research.

Useful websites

Statistics Canada
http://www.statcan.ca/start.html
Produces national statistics on the population, resources, economy, society and culture of Canada.

Federal Bureau of Investigation
http://www.fbi.gov/homepage.htm
The FBI is the principal investigative arm of the United States Department of Justice. Information about law enforcement and crime statistics can be sourced here.

Australian Bureau of Statistics
http://www.abs.gov.au/
The Australian Bureau of Statistics is Australia's official statistical organization.

The Home Office
http://www.homeoffice.gov.uk/
The Home Office is the government department responsible for internal affairs in England and Wales.

The Office for National Statistics
http://www.ons.gov.uk/
Collects and makes available statistics on a range of social, economic and demographic issues in the UK.

The Scottish Executive
http://www.scotland.gov.uk
The Scottish Executive is the devolved government for Scotland. It is responsible for most of the issues of day-to-day concern to the people of Scotland, including health, education, justice, rural affairs and transport.

United Nations Interregional Crime and Justice Research Institute
http://www.unicri.it/

EC Europa – Justice and Home Affairs
http://ec.europa.eu/justice_home/fsj/crime/fsj_crime_intro_en.htm

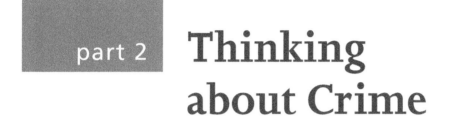

part 2 **Thinking about Crime**

chapter 4

The Enlightenment and Early Traditions

Key issues

- What traditions emerged from the Enlightenment?

- What is the classical inheritance?

- What is the positivist inheritance?

- What are their key differences?

Introduction

The received history of criminology as a discipline of study often starts with influential figures and their links with landmark theoretical perspectives such as **classicism** in the eighteenth century and **positivism** in the nineteenth. This chapter provides an introductory account of criminology's development, starting with the writings of criminal law reformers in the eighteenth century, particularly Cesare Beccaria and Jeremy Bentham. These writers drew upon **Enlightenment** ideals and characterized the offender as a rational, free-willed actor who engaged in crime in a calculated way and was responsive to the deterrent penalties that these reformers advocated. This classical school of criminology was then challenged in the late nineteenth century by writers of the positivist school, including Cesare Lombroso, Enrico Ferri and Francis Galton, who adopted a more empirical, scientific approach to the subject and investigated the criminal using the techniques of anthropology, anthropometry and other new human sciences. The positivist school claimed to have discovered the existence of 'criminal types' whose behaviour was determined rather than chosen, and for whom treatment rather than punishment was appropriate. Subsequent work has refuted many early positivist claims but the project of 'scientific criminology' continues today.

A caution

One of the immediate problems with this characterization of criminology's history is that it implies that people only began to think about crime in an analytical way from the middle of the eighteenth century. This is seriously misleading. As Chapter 2 showed, historians of crime have traced changing of views of crime going back much further than this. Further, many sociologists view the breaking of social rules as an intrinsic element of social organization itself. In other words, crime – and thinking around crime – have been features of many past societies, a point made by Durkheim in the late nineteenth century (see Chapter 5). Discourses on crime and criminals are as old as human civilization. For instance, there are various propositions about crime put forward in the writings of ancient and medieval philosophers, in early theological and other religious texts, and in early modern legal thought. We need to recognize that there are, in fact, a variety of ways of 'thinking about crime', and that criminology is only one version among others.

This is not to say that criminology is simply our modern response to a timeless and unchanging set of questions, not least because in earlier times the cultural sensibilities that governed thinking about crime were very different from our own. For example, early Christianity was a system of thought that did not view the lawbreaker as different or abnormal, but rather understood his or her behaviour as a manifestation of universal human depravity and the sinful state of all humankind. This is clearly a very different way of thinking about crime from that espoused within later criminology.

Nevertheless, traditional accounts of crime, whether these be Christian or otherwise, are not entirely remote from present thinking about the subject. For instance, if we look at the diverse literature of the early modern period, which includes criminal biographies and broadsheets, accounts of the Renaissance underworld, Tudor rogue pamphlets, Elizabethan dramas and Jacobean city comedies, we can see rudimentary versions of our present understandings of how individuals become deviant. Perhaps the most famous example is Daniel Defoe's novel *Moll Flanders*, published in 1722. On one level, it is a tale of sin and repentance, but it is also rich in the elements that feature in some modern criminological theories. The story tells us how Moll fell in with bad company, was sorely tried by temptation, became too fond of drink, lost her reputation and was driven to crime by lust – but if we use more neutral language to tell the tale, then we are not that far removed from some contemporary criminology.

So when we think of the seventeenth- and eighteenth-century understandings of crime, what becomes clear is that crime was often regarded as omnipresent temptation to which all humankind was vulnerable, but when it became a question of why some succumbed and others resisted, the explanations often trailed off into the unknowable, resorting to fate, or the will of God.

There are two points that need to be emphasized in these opening remarks. The first is that we need to be cautious of histories of criminology that begin with classicism and suggest that no one had seriously thought about crime before, even though we are going to do just that! The second is that older ways of thinking about crime did not disappear with the coming of the modern, scientific age. In fact, it is more accurate to say that criminology operates in cultures that continue to combine many modes of thought and action. Traditional understandings are often as pervasive, for example in popular culture, as criminological research.

Enlightenment thinking about crime

A useful way to track major changes in ways of thinking about crime is by comparing an account of a mid-eighteenth century public execution and an early nineteenth-century prison timetable. This is how Michel Foucault opens his classic study, *Discipline and Punish: The Birth of the Prison* (1977): he starts with a description of an execution of a French man accused of a high-profile murder, written in 1757:

> on a scaffold that will be erected [at the Place de Grève], the flesh will be torn from his breasts, arms, thighs and calves with red hot pincer, his right hand . . . burnt with sulphur, and, on those places where the flesh will be torn away, poured molten lead, boiling oil, burning resin, wax and sulphur melted together and then his body drawn and quartered by four horses and his limbs and body consumed by fire, reduced to ashes and thrown to the winds.
>
> (Foucault, 1977: 3)

He moves on to consider a second description of a prison timetable, written just eighty years later:

> Art. 17. The prisoners' day will begin at six in the morning in winter and at five in the summer . . . they will work for nine hours a day . . . Art. 18. Rising. At the first drum-roll, the prisoners must rise and dress in silence . . . at the second drum-roll, they must be dressed and make their beds. At the third, they must line up and proceed to the chapel for morning prayer . . . Art. 19. The prayers are conducted by the chaplain and followed by a moral or religious reading. This exercise must not last more than half an hour.
>
> (Foucault, 1977: 6)

The differences in systems of control are clearly illustrated. In the striking opening pages, Foucault compares the earlier forms of *brutal punishment of the body* with later forms of *surveillance and imprisonment*, which act upon the mind and soul in an effort to reform the offender. What we are seeing here is a shift to an understanding of crime based upon the principles of Enlightenment thinking.

The French *philosophes* – an elite group of eighteenth-century radical thinkers – were one of the cornerstones of such thinking. A 'solid, respectable clan of revolutionaries' (Gay, 1973: 9), they included Montesquieu, Rousseau and Voltaire. In matters of crime, their work contributed to a distinctive move away from systems that were capricious and 'barbaric' to systems that were to become more rational, predictable and disciplining (as we see in many chapters throughout this book). Such thinking signalled the emergence of 'modernity'. Sociologist Peter Hamilton (1996) has suggested that the 'Enlightenment mind' valued ten features:

■ *Reason* – became a key way of gaining and organizing knowledge.
■ *Empiricism* – factual knowledge is gained empirically through the senses and observation.
■ *Science* – in particular, experimental scientific observation and revolution.

- *Universalism* – the search for general laws and principles.
- *Progress* – the idea that 'the human condition' could be improved.
- *Individualism* – individual experience and observation as the starting point for all knowledge.
- *Toleration* – the view that minority religious beliefs were not inherently inferior to majority beliefs.
- *Freedom* – the idea that humans should be free from tyranny.
- *Human nature* – the idea that human nature was universal.
- *Secularism* – a challenge to the cultural dominance of Christianity.

The classical tradition in criminology

Enlightenment thinking underpinned what became known as the classical approach to crime. It introduced a much more rational and fair system for organizing punishment. It had much less of a focus on the criminal per se and it had little concern with establishing the causes of crime. In general, its concern was to establish a more just social order and to try to ensure a greater legal equality of citizens, regardless of social rank.

Cesare Beccaria – 'the Rousseau of the Italians' (Beirne, 1993: 14) – is generally seen, at least symbolically, as the founder of this movement. He was born in Milan, Italy, in 1738. A humanist, he argued for the reform of an 'irrational' judicial system that had existed for centuries (including the abolition of torture and capital punishment). His work was also informed by:

- *Social contract theory* – the theory of how imaginary individuals come together to make a society work (exemplified in the work of Jean-Jacques Rousseau).
- *The view that human beings have '**free will**'* – human actions are not simply determined by inside or outside 'forces' but result from freely made personal decisions.
- *The idea of punishment as **deterrent*** – rational beings will choose not to commit crimes if the punishment 'fits the crime' and they know that they will be punished.
- *Utilitarianism* – laws should be designed to be most useful to the majority of people (a concept developed further by Jeremy Bentham).
- *Secularism* – Beccaria wanted to build a more humanist theory of punishment that focused on living, sentient human beings who were responsive to pain and pleasure, rather than based on traditional ideas of divine law.

At the heart of classic thought were ideas on the nature of punishment (see the more recent development of these ideas in Chapter 15). Punishments could deter only if they were 'proportional' to the crime. Proportionality means (1) that the severity of punishments corresponds to the severity of the harm done by the crime, so that more serious crimes receive more serious punishments; and (2) that the type of punishment resembles the crime, so that others in society can learn to associate the punishment with the crime. In essence, the classical view of punishment is that it should be public, prompt, necessary, the least possible in the given circumstances, proportionate to the crimes and dictated by the laws.

Beccaria started to develop these ideas in *Dei delitti e delle pene* (An Essay on Crimes and Punishments) of July 1764. This is one of the classic texts of Enlightenment thinking and early modern penology. Box 4.1 shows the range of themes he raised in this short but very influential book.

BOX 4.1 Cesare Beccaria's *Essay on Crimes and Punishments*

This key text of classical thinking is a very short book devoting brief chapters to such topics as

- Of the origins of punishments
- Of the right to punish
- Of the proportion between crimes and punishments
- Of estimating the degree of crimes
- Of the divisions of crime
- Of crimes which disturb the public tranquillity
- Of torture
- Of pecuniary punishments
- Of the advantage of immediate punishments
- Of the punishment of nobles
- Of robbery
- Of banishment
- Of the punishment of death
- Of suicide
- Of smuggling
- Of bankrupts
- Of the sciences
- Of education

Plate 4.1 Cesare Beccaria (1738–94), Italian legal theorist and political economist.

Source: Mary Evans Picture Library.

Here are some of his views for discussion:

> By justice I understand nothing more than that bond which is necessary to keep the interests of individuals united; without which, men would return to their original state of barbarity. All punishments, which exceed the necessity of preserving this bond, are in their nature unjust.
>
> (chapter 2)

> A scale of crimes may be formed of which the first degree should consist of those which immediately tend to the dissolution of society and the last of the smallest possible injustice done to a private member of that society.
>
> (chapter 6)

> A punishment may not be an act of violence, of one, or of many against a private member of society; it should be public; immediate and necessary; the least possible in the case given; proportioned to the crime; and determined by the laws.
>
> (chapter 47)

Classical ideas are also found in the work of the English utilitarian philosopher and penal reformer, Jeremy Bentham (1748–1832). Building a moral calculus and arguing for the greatest happiness of the greatest number, he felt that punishments should be calculated to inflict pain in direct proportion to the damage done to the public interest. One of his ideas was the concept of prison design. He argued for a panopticon model, with a tower at the centre and a periphery building composed of cells from which every inmate could be observed (Plate 4.2). The cells would all have windows that would enable surveillance by prison guards. Whereas the old dungeons hurled an indiscriminate group of people together in large, dark and unmonitored cells, Bentham's principles were based on visibility and inspection. Although Bentham's ideal prison was never built, his views did encourage a new approach to penality through which prisons took on a new purpose (Bozovic, 1995).

A key point here is that Enlightenment thinking was also based on efforts to design new, practical measures to control and prevent crime and not just on legal essays like those written by Beccaria. One leading experimental criminologist, Lawrence Sherman, argues that '[c]riminology did not begin in a Milanese salon among the group of aristocrats who helped Beccaria formulate and publish his epigrams . . . but more than a decade earlier in a London magistrate's courtroom full of gin-soaked robbery defendants' (2005: 120). He was referring to Henry Fielding, magistrate at the Bow Street Court in the 1750s, who believed that crime could be drastically reduced through preventive measures including raising the price of gin (see Box 4.2).

Back to justice: some recent classical developments

It is important to realize that just as ideas never appear 'out of the blue' but emerge from historical change, so too do ideas rarely simply 'vanish'. They can be modified, re-branded or re-worked

Plate 4.2 The Panoptican of Jeremy Bentham.

Source: After Barton and Barton (1993: 139).

thinking about crime

BOX 4.2 Henry Fielding: Enlightenment as experiment?

Henry Fielding used his experiences as a magistrate at the Bow Street Court as the basis of his 1751 treatise, 'An enquiry into the causes of the late increase of robbers, etc, with some proposals for remedying this growing evil'. The treatise identified the 1750s gin craze as the cause of the crime wave and looked for alternatives to hanging as a response to this. Fielding's alternatives – a series of measures to prevent crime being committed in the first place – were arguably as dramatic as Bentham's panopticon proposal or Beccaria's proposal to calibrate punishments. These preventive measures included increasing the price of gin (through higher taxation), regulating gambling and providing low-cost housing and food for the very poor. He also began to call for a system of 'socialized' justice where a new state-funded police force, rather than crime victims, would be responsible for apprehending criminals. In 1753, Fielding was asked by the government to test out some of these measures: the result was the Bow Street Runners, forerunners of the modern police. Sherman claims this was 'a turning point in the English **paradigm** of justice' as it had demonstrated the 'failure of relying solely on the severity of punishment' to contain crime. This, we might say, was Enlightenment in practice. Fielding's **'experimental criminology'** plays as important a part in the history of the discipline as Beccaria's more well-known analytic criminology.

Plate 4.3 Henry Fielding.

Source: Mary Evans Picture Library.

HENRY FIELDING.
Aetatis XLVII.

into new concepts. This is very much true of classicism, which remains part of the justice system today. As we see in more detail in Chapter 15, in the latter years of the twentieth century there was a considerable revival of interest in classical thought.

In the early 1970s, an old debate around the definition of 'good' sentencing policy was reopened. What is a just sentence? The 'Back to Justice' model suggested by Von Hirsch and his colleagues claimed that 'The severity of punishment should be commensurate with the seriousness of the wrong' (Von Hirsch, 1976: 66), arguing that:

1 The degree of likelihood that the offender might return to crime should be irrelevant to the choice of sentence. He should be sentenced on what he has done.
2 Indeterminate sentences should be abolished. Particular crimes merit particular punishments, and offenders should know what they will get.
3 Sentencing discretion should be sharply reduced. A system of standardized penalties should be introduced.
4 Imprisonment should be limited to serious offences – usually crimes leading to serious harm.
5 Milder penalties should not claim to rehabilitate, but simply be less severe punishments (Von Hirsch, 1976).

Some problems with the classical model

- The classical model presents an overly rational vision of human nature, arguing that people only behave in a purely self-interested and 'free' fashion. If they can see they will be punished, they will be deterred; if they think they can get away with crime, they will. For many, this is just too simple and ignores the complexities of human behaviour.
- Classicism regards crime as resulting from free choice; but we may be left wondering whether we are all equally 'free' to make these choices, and whether we all face the same choices.
- Classicism assumes that individuals live in societies that are organized in fair and just ways. But can we have 'justice' in an 'unjust society'?

The positivist movement

The criminal type and Lombroso

Writing in the nineteenth century, Lombroso is usually seen as another founder of modern criminology and certainly achieved much fame, or notoriety, in the closing years of the twentieth century. Lombroso viewed many criminals as atavistic throwbacks to an earlier species on the evolutionary scale and as having bodily anomalies. He believed that many criminals had a distinctive physique: low foreheads, prominent jaws and cheekbones, protruding ears, excessive hairiness and unusually long arms. He is often seen as having invented the idea of the 'criminal body', an idea he explored in 1876 in his book *L'uomo delinquente* (The Criminal Man), which went through five editions (Lombroso-Ferrero, 1911). In this study, he observed the physical characteristics of Italian prisoners and compared them to Italian soldiers – focusing on their heads, body, arms and skin. One was a 'brigand', Vilella, whom he studied through a post-mortem examination. In a famous passage, he remarked:

> This was not merely an idea, but a revelation. At the sight of that skull, I seemed to see all of a sudden, lighted up as a vast plain under a flaming sky, the problem of the nature of the criminal – an atavistic being who reproduces in his person the ferocious instincts of primitive humanity and the inferior animals. Thus were explained anatomically the enormous jaws, high cheek-bones, prominent superciliary arches, solitary lines in the palms, extreme size of orbits, handle-shaped or sessile ears found in criminals, savages and apes, insensibility to pain, extremely acute sight, tattooing, excessive idleness, love of orgies, and the irresistible craving for evil for its own sake, the desire not only to extinguish life in the victim, but to mutilate the corpse, tear its flesh, and drink its blood.
>
> (quoted in Wolfgang, 1960: 248)

But Lombroso's experimental work was flawed. Had he looked beyond prison walls, he would have realized that the physical features he attributed exclusively to prisoners were actually found throughout the entire population. His claim that criminals could be distinguished from non-criminals on a physical basis was soon challenged (see Goring, 1913/1972). Yet although his work had many failings, he is usually credited with re-focusing criminological thinking from the workings of the *criminal law* to an understanding of the *criminal type*.

Lombroso worked with others, notably Raffaele Garofalo (1852–1934) and Enrico Ferri (1856–1928). Together they came to be identified as the Italian School. Ferri offered a three-way view of the causes of crime: the anthropological, telluric (physical) and social. He was against the view that any one single factor could cause crime, and saw instead the need to consider factors in combination. For Ferri,

> [E]very crime from the smallest to the most atrocious, is the result of the interaction of these three causes, the anthropological condition of the criminal, the telluric [literally, 'pertaining to the earth'] environment in which he is living, and the social environment in which he is born, living and operating.
>
> (quoted in Muncie *et al.*, 2003: 36)

The anthropological component highlighted heredity and constitution; the physical factors highlighted issues such as climate and season; and the social element stressed population, religion, education and the like. Ferri divided criminals into five basic types: criminal lunatics, the born incorrigibles, habitual criminals, occasional criminals and emotional criminals.

Researchers working on crime began to use this kind of work to examine links between crime, mental incapacity, heredity, 'criminal family' networks and physical attributes. Chapter 2 discusses elements of this work in relation to histories of the criminal 'underclass'. Many of them began to use a new range of scientific tools to measure the incidence and impact of these factors – from IQ tests to criminal photography. Chapter 5 discusses how positivist approaches emphasizing the physical causes of crime influenced early twentieth-century studies of female criminality.

BOX 4.3 Cesare Lombroso (1836–1909) and his photos of criminal types

The man

Born on 6 November 1835 in Verona, perhaps more than anyone else Cesare Lombroso is 'the founder of modern criminology'. An Italian physician who worked in prisons, he was director of a mental asylum in Pesaro, Italy, and professor of psychiatry and criminal anthropology at the University of Turin. Writing at a time where there was a widespread interest in social Darwinism and eugenics, he drew his ideas in part from phrenology, and they were also linked to craniology and physiognomy – which look at the structures of the brain and the mind. He was an early criminal anthropologist, founder of the positivist school of penal jurisprudence. Lombroso was a socialist, and much of his work advocated more humane treatment of criminals. He was an early advocate of the indeterminate sentence, as well as the reduction of the death penalty.

« 1836   CÉSAR LOMBROSO   † 1909
Prof. de Clinique Psychiatrique et d'Anthropologie
à l'Université Royale de Turin,
Fondateur du Musée d'Anthropologie criminelle,
Directeur des Archives de Psychiatrie.

Plate 4.4 Cesare Lombroso (1836–1909), Italian physician and criminologist. Lombroso is considered the founder of modern criminology, though many dispute this.

Source: Elliot and Fry in *Nos Maîtres*, Mary Evans Picture Library.

Reading Lombroso: some extracts from his writing capture his concerns

Spot the criminal through differences

> . . . deviation in head size and shape from the type common to the race and religion from which the criminal came; asymmetry of the face; excessive dimensions of the jaw and cheek bones; eye defects and peculiarities; ears of unusual size, or occasionally very small, or standing out from the head as do those of the chimpanzee; nose twisted, upturned, or flattened in thieves, or swollen nostrils; lips fleshy, swollen, and protruding; pouches in the cheek like those of some animals; peculiarities of the palate, such as a large central ridge, a series of cavities and protuberances such as are found in some reptiles, and a cleft palate; abnormal dentition; chin receding, or excessively long or short and flat, as in apes; abundance, variety, and precocity of wrinkles, anomalies of the hair, marked by characteristics in the pelvic organs; excessive length of arms; supernumerary fingers and toes; imbalance of the hemispheres of the brain (asymmetry of cranium).

> (Wolfgang, 1960: 250)

TYPES DE CRIMINELS MEURTRIERS (Voir *Explication des planches*).

Plate 4.5 Criminal types – an example from Lombroso's study that claimed to relate physiognomy to criminal nature. This plate shows young and female murderers. Lombroso's research involved the measurement and frequently the photographing of body and facial types.

Source: Reproduced in Lombroso, 'L'Homme criminel', plate lxiv, Mary Evans Picture Library.

Types of criminal by physical characteristics

. . . as a rule, the *thieves* have mobile hands and face; small, mobile, restless, frequently oblique eyes; thick and closely set eyebrows; flat or twisted nose; thin beard; hair frequently thin; almost receding brow. Both they and those committing *rape* frequently have ears *ad ansa*. The latter often have brilliant eyes, delicate faces, tumid lips and eyelids; as a rule they are of delicate structure and sometimes hunchbacked. . . . The *habitual homicides* have cold, glassy eyes, immobile and sometimes sanguine and inflamed; the nose, always large, is frequently aquiline or, rather, hooked; the jaws are strong, the cheekbones large, the hair curly, dark and abundant; the beard is frequently thin, the canine teeth well developed and the lips delicate; frequent nystagmus and unilateral facial contractions, with a baring of the teeth and a contraction of the jaws. . . . In general *all criminals* have ears *ad ansa*, abundant hair, thin beard, prominent fronat sinuses, protruding chin, large cheekbones, etc.

(Wolfgang, 1960: 251)

Statistical regularity and positivism

Another early 'scientist of crime' was Adolphe Quetelet (1796–1874), a leading nineteenth-century statistician. Developing a theory of social mechanics, he believed that statistical research could outline the average features of a population, and that it would hence be possible to discover the underlying regularities for both normal and abnormal behaviour. In 1835 he published *Treatise on Man, and the Development of His Faculties*, in which he depicted 'average man', against which abnormal man could be measured. He used bell-shaped curves identify average qualities which could then be studied systematically.

The publication of early criminal statistics in France from the 1820s on meant that regularities could be studied across variables such as sex, age, climate and economic conditions. Likewise, the French sociologist Émile Durkheim (1858–1917) could study suicide rates (at that time when suicide was a crime in most countries) to show that suicides also had a very definite demographic pattern. By examining records in and around his native France, he could show that some categories of people were more likely than others to choose to take their own lives. He found, for instance, that men, Protestants, wealthy people and the unmarried each had significantly higher suicide rates than women, Roman Catholics and Jews, the poor, and married people. Durkheim deduced that these differences corresponded to people's degree of *social integration*. Low suicide rates characterized categories of people with strong social ties; high suicide rates were found among those who were more socially isolated and individualistic. In more male-dominated societies, men certainly had more autonomy than women; individualistic Protestants were more prone to suicide than Catholics and Jews; single people, with weaker social ties than married people, had higher suicide rates; and while the wealthy clearly had much more freedom of action than the poor this appeared to be at the cost of higher rates of personal unhappiness.

The positivist inheritance

A major account of positivistic criminology was offered by the American sociologist David Matza. In an opening chapter of his classic book, *Delinquency and Drift* (1964), he summarized the positivist view (of which he was very critical) as follows:

1   'The criminal is a specific type of person.' Thus, positivistic criminology started to draw up long classification systems of different kinds of offenders. Lombroso and Ferri, for example, identified not just the 'born criminal', but also the 'emotional criminal', the 'morally insane criminal' and the 'masked epileptic criminal'.
2   'The criminal differs from others.' The focus in positivistic criminology is upon finding criminogenic characteristics – which may range from body parts (e.g. the size and weight of skulls), body types (as in Sheldon's work) to personality types (as with the work of Walter Reckless). The emphasis is on developing techniques to show how offenders differ from non-offenders. These techniques have often used new technologies such as photography and fingerprinting in the nineteenth century through to chromosome typing (which links the XYY chromosome to violent offences) and DNA testing in the twentieth century and biometric profiling today.
3   'The criminal is "driven" into crime through factors outside his or her control.' Positivism views criminality as caused by factors, internal or external, that are beyond the control of the individual offender. Thus, crime is 'caused', in this model, by 'feeble-mindedness', 'atavistic regression', 'unsuccessful socialisation' or 'XYY chromosomes'. In this sense, positivism is a deterministic theory.

These arguments can still be found in a great deal of criminological research. One major strand of such work, developed by Sheldon and Eleanor Glueck, uses a 'multi-factor approach'. This entails sampling a large number of delinquents or criminals to see whether they present characteristics in common that are found less frequently in a general population. Often these are prospective longitudinal surveys.

Similarly, the 'criminal career approach' analyses a number of these key factors and shows how they develop over time. It asks why people start offending (onset), why they continue (persistence), whether their behaviour becomes more serious or not (escalation) and why people stop (desistance). The major risk factors ('factors that increase the risk of occurrence of events such as the onset, frequency, persistence, duration of offending'; Farrington, 1997) include impulsivity (now often called HIA – hyperactivity impulsivity attention deficit), low intelligence, poor parental supervision, broken homes, convicted parents, socio-economic deprivation, poor schooling and 'situational factors' (Farrington, 1997). These kinds of studies argue that these factors are highly correlated with crime.

BOX 4.4 Summary of some biologically based theories of crime

William Sheldon's Theory of Somatotypes (based on early work of Kretschmer) links crime to body types:

- endomorph – chubby, round, not criminal;
- ectomorph – skinny, frail, not criminal;
- mesomorph – heavy, muscular, criminal.

Kallikak and Juke families. The descendants of Martin Kallikak's illegitimate son exhibited a remarkably high degree of criminality across several generations, and the descendants of Ada Juke included seven murderers, 60 thieves, 50 prostitutes, etc. These two cases contributed to an early view that crime and deviance were inheritable.

Twin studies compare criminality of identical twins with criminality of fraternal twins. Generally, twin studies have shown a higher rate of similar criminality (concordance) (60–70 per cent) for identical twins than for fraternal twins (15–30 per cent), although some say that these percentages are exaggerated. This provides some support for the idea that genetics may play a role in criminal behaviour. Perhaps the most famous case of twin studies is to be found in the work of Karl Christiansen, who examined 3,586 sets of twins born between 1881 and 1910. In 35 per cent of the cases, both identical twins would have criminal convictions. In only 12 per cent of fraternal twins would both have criminal convictions, which provides some support for a genetic link.

XYY chromosome research. This became a particular controversy in the 1960s. 'Normal' males have an XY sex-chromosome configuration, but some males (1 in 1,000) have an extra Y chromosome, giving them an XYY configuration. Research in the 1960s found a slight suggestion of an association between XYY configuration and criminality. This led to the idea of the 'super-male criminal', full of aggression. More recent studies have refuted the idea that having the XYY configuration 'causes' men to commit crimes.

Biochemical factors. Serotonin deficiency may be related to impulsiveness, crime and violence. An imbalance involving dopamine, noradrenaline and serotonin may be conducive to deviant/criminal behaviour.

Brain dysfunction. There is some evidence that neurological defects are more common among excessively violent people than among the general population. EEG readings on some adult criminals are similar to those of normal people at younger ages (brain immaturity).

Also, old concerns like learning disabilities and new problems like attention deficit hyperactivity disorder (ADHD) may be linked to crime.

Potential criticisms

- Crime is probably the result of a combination of factors, including social, psychological, political, economic and geographic ones – rarely, if ever, biology on its own.
- Unrepresentative samples are very common in such research. Generally, such research raises severe methodological problems (how do you separate out biological from social factors?).
- Causation is often muddled with correlation: an association between bodily features and criminal behaviour does not mean that biology caused the behaviour.
- Sometimes there may be a labelling effect: society reacts to certain types, and this may generate responses that are criminal.
- In general, the evidence for such research is at best limited.

For more on biological perspectives in criminology, see Fishbein (2000).

Problems with the positivist model

- In contrast with the classical model, the positivist model often assumes that people are driven into crime by forces largely out of their control. It implies that people are not free and not wholly responsible for their own actions. It arguably denies the meanings of crime in people's lives or the appeal of offending. A way forward could be to consider crime as resulting from a combination of choice and **determinism**.
- It exaggerates the differences between criminal and non-criminals. By focusing upon what makes a criminal different from the population, it tends to suggest an image of the normal and the abnormal, of them and us.
- It has a tendency to neglect the workings of the penal system: how laws are made, how certain actions come to be defined as crimes and others do not. Crimes are assumed as givens, as unproblematic categories.

Tensions between positivism and classical thinking

Both the classical tradition and positivism come in many different varieties, and although they have their roots in the past, they are both still alive and well in criminological thinking today. As you read this book, you may like to identify aspects of the reappearance of each. They have been extremely influential and can be seen as master moulds that organize many ways of thinking about crime. Table 4.1 contrasts the two positions.

Table 4.1 Comparison of classical and positivist schools

Issue	Classical school	Positivist school
Roots	Enlightenment	Modern science
Focus	Criminal administration	Criminal person
Approach	Philosophical – social contract theory, utilitarianism	Scientific, positivism Laws Measurements
View of human nature	Free will Hedonism Morally responsible for own behaviour	Determined by biological, psychological, and social environment Moral responsibility obscured
View of justice system	Social contract; exists to protect society; due process and concern with civil rights; restrictions on system Definite sentence	Scientific treatment system to cure pathologies and rehabilitate offenders; no concern with civil rights Indefinite sentence
Form of law	Statutory law; exact specification of illegal acts and sanctions	Social law; illegal acts defined by analogy; scientific experts determine social harm and proper form of treatment
Purpose of sentencing	Punishment for deterrence; sentences are determinate (fixed length)	Treatment and reform; sentences are indeterminate (variable length until cured)
Criminological experts	Philosophers; social reformers	Scientists; treatment experts

Summary

1   There is no straightforward 'history of criminology'. Although it is a convention in textbooks to suggest the importance of classical theory and positivism as the founding ideas, these were preceded by earlier ways of thinking about crime.
2   The classical school, commonly associated with Beccaria, is linked to Enlightenment ideas of rationality, free will, choice and progress.
3   The positivist school, commonly associated with Lombroso and Ferri, focuses on the criminal as a particular type, stresses determinism, and looks at the characteristics (social as well as biological) that mark out the criminal from the 'normal' population.
4   Classical and positivist theories have been re-worked and continue to influence criminological thinking and criminal justice systems.

Critical thinking questions

1   What was the Enlightenment? Consider some of the key intellectual contributions it made and then consider the different ways in which people may have thought about crime before the Enlightenment.

2   Consider the idea of 'a criminal type' of person. What are the most recent ways of identifying and defining such a person?

3   Clarify what you understand by a just deserts model (tip: read Von Hirsch, 1976, chs 27 and 28) and try to develop your own penal tariff. What are the limits and difficulties of such an approach?

4   Consider the tensions between classical and positivist thought. How do you see them at work in the modern criminal justice system?

Further study

Beccaria, C. *Beccaria: On Crimes and Punishments and Other Writings*, edited by Richard Bellamy (1995), Cambridge: Cambridge University Press. A short selection of Beccaria's original writings.

Beirne, P. (1993) *Inventing Criminology: Essays on the Rise of 'Homo Criminalis'*, Albany: State University of New York Press. Looks at the intellectual history of criminology from Beccaria to Goring.

Sherman, L. W. (2005) 'The Use and Usefulness of Criminology, 1751–2005: Enlightened Justice and its Failures', *Annals of the American Academy of Political and Social Science*, 600: 115–135. An article offering a critical history of theoretical criminology and arguing for wider use of experimental criminology.

Garland, D. (2003) 'Of Crime and Criminals: The Development of Criminology in Britain', in M. Maguire, R. Morgan and R. Reiner (eds) *The Oxford Handbook of Criminology*, 3rd edn, Oxford: Oxford University Press. An article that critically looks at the growth of criminology (mainly in the UK).

Gould, S. J. (1981) *The Mismeasure of Man*, New York: W.W. Norton. A classic statement of the misuse of biological theories and measurements.

Rafter, N. H. (1997) *Creating Born Criminals*, Chicago: University of Illinois Press. A social history of biologically founded theories of crime in the United States, the study shows their influence on theories today.

Von Hirsch, A. (1976) *Doing Justice: The Choice of Punishments*, New York: Hill and Wang. A clear and useful account of justifications for punishment, heavily derived from classical thinking.

Useful information

For more general guides to theory, see:

Burke, R. H. (2001) *An Introduction to Criminological Theory*, Cullompton: Willan. A comprehensive yet short introduction to the main criminological theories.

Downes, D. and Rock, P. (1998) *Understanding Deviance: A Guide to the Sociology of Crime and Rule Breaking*, 3rd edn (2003, 4th edn), Oxford: Oxford University Press. For a long while this has been the most sophisticated general treatment of the full range of theories of crime discussed in this and other chapters. Regularly updated, it also provides a bibliography that signposts all the major books in the field.

Muncie, J., McLaughlin, E. and Langan, M. (eds) (2003) *Criminological Perspectives: A Reader*, 2nd edn, London: Sage/Open University. An exceptionally valuable collection of around 50 readings extracted from all the major positions and perspectives on crime ranging from Beccaria and Lombroso to Braithwaite and Smart.

Cullen, F. T. and Agnew, R. (2003) *Criminological Theory: Past to Present (Essential Readings)*, 2nd edn, Los Angeles, CA: Roxbury Park. There are many readers in criminology but this one stands out as an excellent collection of classic statements. Useful for the whole of Part 2 of this book.

chapter 5

Early Sociologies of Crime

Key issues

- How did the early sociologists study crime?
- What is the functionalist approach to crime?
- What role did the Chicago School play in developing early sociological criminology?
- What are the strengths and weaknesses of each theoretical approach?

Introduction

In this chapter we turn to some of the major ways of thinking about crime introduced by sociologists, largely – but not exclusively – during the twentieth century, and with prominent focus on delinquency, youthful gangs, the city and crime. Although much of their work has been criticized and subsequently modified, much remains relevant today and underpins a great deal of contemporary thinking about crime.

Six major images capture the basics of these theories, and they are not mutually exclusive – indeed, they benefit from consideration of how they relate to each other, as they each have somewhat different emphases. (And indeed today, criminologists would rarely be happy with just one theory.) These images are as follows:

1   Crime is 'normal' in all societies – it serves certain functions and may even help keep a society orderly. It cannot, therefore, be easily eliminated. Crime may be usefully understood in mapping these functions.

2   Crime is bound up with conflict, often of a class-based nature in which crimes of the powerful are much less noticed than the crimes of the weak. Crime may be usefully understood in terms of social divisions and interests, especially economic interests.

3   Crime is bound up with tension, stresses and strains within societies. Most commonly there is a breakdown of the smooth workings of society – often called anomie (or normlessness) and sometimes referred to as social pathology or social disorganization (especially in earlier studies). Crime may usefully be understood by looking at the tensions and strains that exist within a society.

4   Crime is strongly (but far from exclusively) linked to city life. Modern cities bring with them cultural enclaves that seem more prone to generating criminal/delinquent styles of life with their own values, languages, norms, dress codes, etc. Crime may usefully be understood through mapping these 'criminal areas' and examining the dynamics of such places.

5   Crime is learned in ordinary everyday situations. There is a process of cultural transmission, and crime may be usefully understood through looking at life histories and how people learn their everyday meanings and values.

6   Crime comes about through a lack of attachment to groups valuing law-abiding behaviour. Controls and regulations break down. Crime here may be usefully understood through the breakdown of social controls.

There are many other ways of thinking about the social foundations of crime, and there have been accounts that create bridges between the positions (especially in the work of 'differential opportunity' theory – which attempts to synthesize positions 2, 3 and 4). In what follows, each of these ways of thinking will be briefly introduced.

The normality of crime

In his pioneering study of deviance, Émile Durkheim made the curious claim that there is nothing abnormal about deviance; in fact, it is to be found in all societies and must therefore be seen as a normal part of society. He adopted a **functionalist perspective**: the theory that looks at the ways in which societies become integrated as their various parts perform various vital functions. At base, Durkheim suggests that crime and deviance perform four functions essential to society:

1   Culture involves moral choices over the good and bad life. Unless our lives and societies are to dissolve into chaos, there will usually be a preference for some values and some behaviours over others. Yet the very conception of 'the good' rests upon an opposing notion of 'the bad'; you cannot have one without the other. And just as there can be no good without evil, so there can be no justice without crime. Deviance, in short, is indispensable to the process of generating and sustaining morality.

2   This also means that 'deviance' tends to clarify and stake out moral boundaries. By defining some individuals as deviant, people draw a social boundary between right and wrong. For example, a university marks the line between academic honesty and cheating by disciplining those who commit plagiarism. In all spheres of life – sexuality, religion, family life, work –

people draw up codes of conduct and police 'the good'. Drawing attention to the bad may serve to highlight the good.

3   In fact, Durkheim argues that responding to deviance actually promotes social unity. People typically react to serious deviance with collective outrage. In doing so, Durkheim explained, they reaffirm the moral ties that bind them. Deviance brings people together, creating a moral unity – often built from outrage. In the past, or in less complex societies, this phenomenon was more pronounced. Durkheim claimed that there was more likely to be a shared sense of right and wrong (what he called the 'conscience collective') in these societies and crimes were more likely to be defined as activities that offended the sensibilities of large groups of people. Yet collective outrage persists in more complex and individualized societies too, as evinced in the response to 9/11 for example, and is often expressed through the newspapers and the media generally.

4   On top of this, deviance may also encourage social change. Deviant people, Durkheim claimed, push a society's moral boundaries, suggesting alternatives to the status quo and encouraging change. Moreover, he declared, today's deviance sometimes becomes tomorrow's morality (1895/1988: 71). Since the 1950s, many music-oriented youth cultures – including rock-and-roll, mod, punk and acid house – have been denounced as a threat to the morals of youth and an affront to traditional musical tastes. Since then, however, such movements have been repeatedly swept up in the musical mainstream, becoming multibillion-dollar industries. Similarly, protest movements of one generation may be seen as deviant, but they often bring about change that becomes the norm for subsequent generations.

Functionalist theory, then, teaches us a great paradox about crime and deviance: that far from always being disruptive, it may contribute to a social system and underlie the operation of society. We will always have to live with deviance, suggests Durkheim, because it is bound up with the very conditions of social order. As the anthropologist Mary Douglas (1966: 161), herself strongly influenced by Durkheim, noted, 'where there is no differentiation there is no defilement'. The very act of ordering generates disorder. For as long as we want notions of the good and for as long as we want social change, deviance will be necessary.

Problems with functionalism

It is indeed likely that most societies do have crime, but we know that they differ enormously in their rates of crime. Thus, for example, the United States has extremely high crime rates – whereas some other societies, such as Japan or Iran, seem to have very low crime rates. This account does not really help us see just why these rates are so different, nor expose the deeper dynamics of social control. That said, functionalists such as Durkheim might argue that crime rates soar when societies are under stress (as we will see in the next section), and the responses of others to crime – from media reporting to public concern – serve to strengthen the society by bringing together citizens in common opposition. There is a strong connection here to contemporary moral panic theory which is discussed in Chapter 6.

The egoism of crime in capitalist society

Quite an opposite story is told from Marxist theory and conflict theory. As Box 5.1 shows, although Karl Marx (1818–83) and his collaborator Friedrich Engels (1820–95) were a long way from being criminologists, their observations about the workings of capitalism often highlighted how it was a system that generated relatively high levels of crime.

BOX 5.1 Marx and Engels on crime

Engels

Immorality is fostered in every possible way by the conditions of working-class life. The worker is poor; life has nothing to offer him; he is deprived of virtually all pleasures. Consequently, he does not fear the penalties of the law. Why should he restrain his wicked impulses? Why should he leave the rich man in undisturbed possession of his property? Why should he not take at least a part of this property for himself? What reason has the worker for *not* stealing?

Distress due to poverty gives the worker only the choice of starving slowly, killing himself quickly or taking what he needs where he finds it – in plain English – stealing. And it is not surprising that the majority prefers to steal rather than starve to death or commit suicide.

The clearest indication of the unbounded contempt of the workers for the existing social order is the wholesale manner in which they break its laws. If the demoralization of the worker passes beyond a certain point then it is just as natural that he will turn into a criminal – as inevitably as water turns into steam at boiling point. Owing to the brutal and demoralising way in which he is treated by the bourgeoisie, the worker loses all will of his own and, like water, he is forced to follow blindly the laws of nature. There comes a point when the worker loses all power [to withstand temptation]. Consequently, the incidence of crime has increased with the growth of the working-class population and there is more crime in Britain than in any other country in the world. The annual statistics of crime issued by the Home Office show that there has been an extraordinarily rapid growth of crime. The number of those committed for trial on criminal charges in England and Wales alone has increased sevenfold in thirty-seven years.

There can be no doubt that in England the social war is already being waged. Everyone looks after his own interests and fights only for himself against all comers. Whether in doing so he injures those who are his declared enemies is simply a matter of selfish calculation as to whether such action be to his advantage or not. It no longer occurs to anybody to come to a friendly understanding with his neighbours. All differences of opinion are settled by threats, by invoking the courts, or even by taking the law into one's own hands. In short, everyone sees in his neighbour a rival to be elbowed aside, or at best a victim to be exploited for his own ends.

(Engels, 1845/1958: 130, 145–6, 149, 242, 243)

Marx

Present-day society, which breeds hostility between the individual man and everyone else, thus produces a social war of all against all which inevitably in individual cases, notably among uneducated people, assumes a brutal, barbarously violent form – that of crime. In order to protect itself against crime, against direct acts of violence, society requires an extensive, complicated system of administrative and judicial bodies which requires an immense labour force. In communist society this would likewise be vastly simplified and precisely because – strange though it may sound – the administrative body in this society would have to manage not merely individual aspects of social life, but the whole of social life, in all its various activities, in all its aspects. We eliminate the contradiction between the individual man and all others, we counter-pose social peace to social war, we put the axe to the *root* of crime – and thereby render the greatest, by far the greatest part of the present activity of the administrative and judicial bodies superfluous. Even now crimes of passion are becoming fewer and fewer in comparison with calculated crimes, crimes of interest – crimes against *persons* are declining, crimes against *property* are on the increase. Advancing civilisation moderates violent out-breaks of passion even in our present-day society, which is on a war footing; how much more will this be the case in communist, peaceful society! Crimes against property cease of their own accord where everyone receives what he needs to satisfy his natural and his spiritual urges, where social gradations and distinctions cease to exist.

(Marx and Engels, 1845/1975: 248–9)

Willem Adrian Bonger (1876–1940) was a Marxist Dutch sociologist/criminologist who committed suicide rather than submit to the Nazis, and whose PhD thesis was published in 1916 as 'Criminality and Economic Conditions'. He suggested that major shifts in crime come with the emergence of capitalism, and after an exposition of the working of capitalism, Bonger concluded that the present economic system 'weaken[s] the social feelings . . . breaks social bonds and makes social life much more egoistic'. For him, it was capitalism that generated an egoistic culture – with capitalists being greedy and workers becoming demoralized. It brutalizes many, and helps create an 'insensibility to the ills of others'. As he writes,

Long working hours and monotonous labor brutalize those who are forced into them: bad housing conditions contribute also to debase the moral sense, as does [sic] the uncertainty of existence, and finally absolute poverty, the frequent consequence of sickness and unemployment, ignorance and lack of any training of any kind contribute their quota . . . the demoralizing of all is the status of the lower proletariat.

(quoted in Muncie *et al.*, 1996: 43)

From this he goes on to discuss four different types of crime all linked to economic conditions. These were (a) vagrancy and mendacity; (b) theft; (c) robbery and homicide for economic reasons (mainly by poor people); and (d) fraudulent bankruptcy, adulteration of food, etc. This theory can also be seen in strands of many aspects of Marxist theory that are still alive today.

Problems with Marxism

As is well known, many of Marx's major predictions have simply not come true, and in the eyes of many, the whole theory has been discredited. All the same, Marxist criminologists do see a number of key ideas in Marx's ideas that can help in the study of crime. Those ideas have led to the broader arguments of conflict theory and new left realism, both of which will be discussed later. Moreover, Marx's emphasis on the linkages between social processes and the political economy continues to hold relevance for many scholars in the aftermath of the 2008 global financial crisis.

Again, the structuralist and deterministic assumptions are too strong in this theoretical approach. It is as if being poor would necessarily drive you into crime – whereas we know that the vast majority of poor people never commit serious crimes. There is also a lurking pejorative sense that working-class life is miserable, wretched and immoral; a lot of value claims are imported into the theory, and most contemporary theories of class would find this suspect.

Cultural transmission, city life and the Chicago School

As is shown in Chapter 2, a major tradition for approaching crime and delinquency started to emerge at the University of Chicago in the first four decades of the twentieth century. Chicago was itself a leading centre for the study of sociology. It was the first major department of sociology; it produced the first major textbook; it trained a large number of graduate students; and it produced many monographs on the nature of city life at that time – including tramps, dance halls, prostitution, organized crime, mental illness and slums. Indeed, it has been said that Chicago in the 1920s is the most studied city of all time. Although inspired by European theorists such as Tonnies, Durkheim and Simmel, the unique contribution of the Chicago sociologists was in making the city itself a social laboratory for actual research. And the study of cities and crime has remained important for criminology (see Chapter 8).

Chicago itself was an extraordinary city: a new metropolis exploding with new populations, mass migration from all over Europe and the southern states of America, growing from a few hundred people in the mid-1880s to over 3 million in the 1930s. Its growth brought with it all the signs of modernity – from dance crazes, movies and cars to bootlegging, crime and unemployment. This was the Jazz Age.

Former journalist Robert Ezra Park (1864–1944) was chair of the Department of Sociology and had a passion for walking the streets of the world's great cities, observing the full range of human turbulence and triumph. Throughout his 30-year career at the University of Chicago, he led a group of dedicated sociologists in direct, systematic observation of urban life. In a classic line, he claimed that 'I suspect that I have actually covered more ground, tramping about in cities in different parts of the world, than any other living man' (quoted in Bulmer, 1984). At Park's urging, generations of sociologists at the University of Chicago rummaged through practically every part of their city.

From this research, Park came to understand the city as a highly ordered mosaic of distinctive regions, including industrial districts, ethnic communities and criminal/delinquent/'vice' areas. These so-called natural areas all evolved in relation to one another, forming an urban ecology. To Park, the city operated like a living social organism. Urban variety was central: even though many people saw the city as disorganized and even dangerous, social life in the city was intoxicating. Walking the city streets, he became convinced that urban places offer a better way of life – the promise of greater human freedom and opportunity – than we can find elsewhere. But the downside may well be a growth in crime and dangerousness. These are all themes we recognize in current criminological debates, but they are far from new.

The Chicago School and crime

The Chicago sociologists borrowed from some earlier social work traditions. From the United States they were influenced by the work of Jane Addams (who ran a community project, Hull House, and also worked to map out the different parts of the city and its problems); and from the United Kingdom they drew from the famous poverty studies of Charles Booth, Henry Mayhew and others. From these opening ideas that parts of the city were perhaps more likely to harbour crime than others, the Chicago sociologists pioneered a range of approaches to the study of crime that may be briefly summarized as follows:

1   Crime may be more common in the city, not just because of greater numbers of people, but because the city generates a distinctive way of life. Indeed, and reflecting on the work of Georg Simmel, the blasé attitude of city-dwellers and metropolitan styles – an urban way of living – bring greater tolerance for diversity and, in making the streets less communal and more anonymous, generate the possibility for a less controlling environment, but a more criminogenic one.
2   Crime can be found in 'natural habitats' or ecological zones. The city generates certain ways of life to be found in its various areas – and many of these could be linked to crime and deviance. In 1925 Ernest W. Burgess, a student and colleague of Robert Park, described land use in Chicago in terms of **concentric zones** that look rather like a bull's-eye. City centres, Burgess observed, are business districts bordered by a ring of factories, followed by residential rings with housing that becomes more expensive the further it stands from the noise and pollution of the city's centre.
3   Crime is basically learned in the same ways as everything else; it is normal learning. This idea of **differential association** was linked to the writings of Edwin Sutherland.

thinking about crime

4   Crime is best studied through a range of different methodologies which when put together bring about a much richer understanding of crime than when only one single method is adopted. Thus, in his study of delinquency, Clifford Shaw gathered detailed life histories of delinquent boys and, with Henry McKay, Shaw examined the statistical records of delinquency for different parts of the city and spot-mapped them on to the 'ecological zones' that Robert Park had helped map out. Meanwhile, Frederic Thrasher was studying 1,313 gangs in their everyday life environments – an early and important instance of participant observation. And the backgrounds to delinquency in the city comes alive through studies of tramps (Anderson's *The Hobo*), dance halls (Cressey's *The Taxi-Dance Hall*), the slums (Zorbauigh) and organized crime.

5   Crime may be best dealt with through coordinated agencies: Chicago saw the start of Hull House through to the programmes of the Chicago Area Project.

The zonal theory of crime

At the heart of the Chicago theory was the idea of Park *et al.* (1925) that the urban industrial community of Chicago may be described as consisting of five successive zones (Figure 5.1).

I   In American cities the central business district tends to accommodate the retail, financial, recreational, civic and political centres. The skyscrapers and canyon-like streets of this downtown district are thronged with shoppers, clerks and office workers. Few people live there.

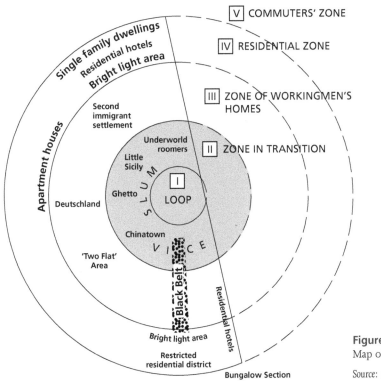

Figure 5.1
Map of the zonal theory of the city.

Source: Adapted from Park *et al.* (1925).

II   The zone in transition. This is an interstitial area characterized by high-density and low-cost housing and where change is rapidly taking place. Here are to be found the slum or semi-slum districts.

III The zone of the workingmen's homes. This lies beyond the factory belt surrounding the central business district. It remains accessible, and is often within walking distance for the workers.

IV   The better residential zone is inhabited chiefly by the families engaged in professional and clerical pursuits. They are likely to have high school if not college education. This is the home of the middle class.

V   The commuters' zone comprises the suburban districts.

Each of these zones could be studied in terms of the kinds of lifestyles that appeared there. This could be done partly through ethnographic research but also through looking at detailed statistical records (see Chapter 3). Thus, parts of the city could be analysed in terms of their crime rates, or measuring rates of mental illness. Of course, as we have seen, there are serious issues in measuring crime and deviance, and figures may only be approximations. Nevertheless, what the Chicago sociologists found was that there were distinctive areas where crime rates were much higher (the zone of transition). Here ethnic cultures conflicted, housing was rundown, poverty was more widespread. *Certain parts of the city are more prone to crime.*

The work of Chicago sociologists has transformed in recent years although it retains a strong emphasis on urban culture and crime (Chapter 8 discusses its broader impact on environmental and spatial criminology). Sudhir Venkatesh (2008), in particular, has renewed Chicago's gang study tradition in his book, *Gang Leader for a Day: A Rogue Sociologist Takes to the Streets.*

Crime as learned: differential association theory

Edwin Sutherland is also identified with Chicago, and among his many significant contributions to criminology, his theory of differential association – developed in various editions of his textbook *Principles of Criminology* (it first appeared in the 1939 edition) – is probably his most prominent. For Sutherland, crime was a normal learning process; we learn crime in much the same way as we learn everything else. Far from being genetic or biological, it was also not a matter of pathology or abnormal learning. Moreover, learning any social patterns – whether conventional or deviant – is seen as a process that takes place in groups. According to Sutherland (1956), any person's tendency towards conformity or deviance depends on the relative frequency of association with others who encourage conventional behaviour or, as the case may be, violation of norms. Sutherland set out nine propositions that formed components of this theory:

1   Criminal behaviour is learned.
2   Criminal behaviour is learned in interaction with other persons in a process of communication.
3   The principal part of learning criminal behaviour occurs within intimate personal groups.
4   When criminal behaviour is learned, the learning includes (a) techniques of committing the crime, which are sometimes very complicated, sometimes very simple; and (b) the specific direction of motives, drives, rationalizations and attitudes.

BOX 5.2 Some classic Chicago studies

Edwin Sutherland (1883–1950): differential association theory

Edwin Sutherland has been called 'the Dean of American Criminology'. He was at Chicago only for a relatively brief time, but he wrote his study *24,000 Homeless Men* (Sutherland with Locke, 1936) and *The Professional Thief* (1937) there – the latter being a classic life story research of a thief, Chic Conwell. He moved on to Indiana University in 1936. *White Collar Crime* (1949) was published just before his death in 1950.

Frederic M. Thrasher (1892–1962): *The Gang: A Study of 1,313 Gangs in Chicago*

Thrasher's classic study took many years to complete, and concluded that there were roughly 25,000 or so members of gangs in Chicago. The gang underwent a kind of evolution from a loose grouping into a more structured form with a strong and binding identity. It tended to emerge from play groups in the poorer part of the city. All the gangs were of boys; there was a general hostility towards girls in general because they were seen to weaken loyalty. Thrasher identified several types of gang:

- the diffuse gang – never gets a proper organization;
- the solidified gang – with a high degree of morale and solidarity, and usually with a clear name;
- the conventionalized gang – the athletic club (these made up about a quarter of all the gangs he observed);
- the criminal gang – can drift into habitual crime.

Later Thrasher moved to New York University and studied the Boys' Club of New York City.

Edward Franklin Frazier (1894–1962)

A leading black sociologist who pioneered the study of black youth as well as the study of the black bourgeoisie, the black church and black families in the United States. He did his PhD at Chicago but later went on to become a leading professor in social work at Howard University.

Clifford Shaw (1895–1957) and Henry D. McKay (1899–1980)

Both were graduate students at Chicago during the 1920s and later worked as a team for the Institute for Juvenile Research near the Chicago loop for 30 years. McKay was the statistician, Shaw was the fieldworker and activist (Snodgrass, 1982). They established the Chicago Area Project in 1932 which worked with the local community in an attempt to resolve the 'delinquency problem'.

5   The specific direction of motives and drives is learned from definitions of legal codes as favourable and unfavourable.
6   A person becomes delinquent because of an excess of definitions favourable to violation of law over definitions unfavourable to violation of law.
7   Differential associations may vary in frequency, duration, priority and intensity.
8   The process of learning criminal behaviour by association with criminal and anti-criminal patterns involves all the mechanisms that are involved in any other learning.
9   Though criminal behaviour is an expression of general needs and values, it is not explained by those general needs and values since non-criminal behaviour is an expression of the same needs and values.

Problems with the Chicago School

Although the Chicago School provided many of the foundational ideas of the sociology of crime, many of them are now not far short of a century old – and have been open to much refinement. Thus, although the city is still known to harbour 'natural areas' of crime, the concentric zones model is usually seen to be only one special case.

There is also a problem with what is called 'the ecological fallacy'. We cannot assume that because certain areas accommodate more criminality, that people in those areas are necessarily criminals; this is simply not true. So the theory is not strong at explaining why some people become criminal and others do not.

Anomie and the stresses and strains of crime

Early social models of crime often assumed a certain harmony or fit between the parts of a society and its overall working. Societies functioned; and the institutions in them (from work and school to family and religion) worked to perform certain functions to keep a society balanced or in a particular state. How then can crime and deviance happen?

Drawing from the traditions established both by Marx and Durkheim, the US sociologist Robert K. Merton (1910–2003) saw crime and deviance emerging as an individual adaptation to pressures flowing from the social structure. In one of the most cited discussions of twentieth-century criminology, Merton's 'Social Structure and Anomie' (1938), modern capitalist society was seen as being under pressure, and the strains and tensions within it, Merton thought, led to crime and deviance. Distinguishing between a social structure (which provided economic roots to success) and a culture (which provided norms, values and goals), Merton argued that deviance occurred where there was an imbalance between social structure (approved social means) and culture (approved goals). Drawing from Durkheim, Merton called this tension or norm breakdown **anomie**. His model was effectively what has been called a materialist one. He looked at how important the cultural goal of the 'American Dream' (of being able to succeed and gain wealth solely through hard work and earning money) was, and found that some people were so placed within society that they were unable to achieve this dream. He argued that this inability opened up a series of responses or adaptations (Table 5.1).

Writing originally about North American society in the 1930s, Merton argued that the path to conformity was to be found in pursuing conventional goals by approved means. The true 'success story', in other words, is someone who gains wealth and prestige through talent and hard work. But not everyone who desires conventional success has the opportunity to attain it. Children raised in poverty, for example, may see little hope of becoming successful if they 'play by the rules'. As a result, they may seek wealth through one or another kind of crime – say, by dealing in cocaine. Merton called this type of deviance innovation – the attempt to achieve a culturally approved goal (wealth) by unconventional means (drug sales). Table 5.1 characterizes innovation as accepting the goal of success while rejecting the conventional means of becoming rich.

Table 5.1 Merton's modes of individual adaptation to anomie

	Culture goals	Institutionalized means
Conformity	+	+
Innovation	+	−
Ritualism	−	+
Retreatism	−	−
Rebellion	+/−	+/−

Key:
+	=	acceptance
−	=	rejection
+/−	=	reject old and substitute new

The inability to become successful by normative means may also prompt another type of deviance that Merton calls *ritualism*. Ritualists resolve the strain of limited success by eschewing cultural goals in favour of almost compulsive efforts to live 'respectably'. In essence, they embrace the rules to the point where they lose sight of their larger goals. Lower-level bureaucrats, Merton suggests, often succumb to ritualism as a way of maintaining respectability.

Merton noted other adaptations. *Retreatism* was the rejection of both cultural goals and means so that one, in effect, 'drops out': some alcoholics, drug addicts and street people are examples. *Rebellion* involves the rejection of both the cultural definition of success and the normative means of achieving it. Those who adopt this response advocate radical alternatives to the existing social order, typically calling for a political transformation of society.

What is important in this kind of explanation is that it looks at society as a whole and finds stresses and strains within the system that seem to generate 'weak spots' – crime is induced through a system that has potentials for contradiction and conflict. Merton's theory has been extremely influential in the development of 'delinquent gang theory' and, also, in attempts to understand the criminogenic effects of rapid social change.

Problems with anomie theory

The problem with Merton's ideas is the presumption of goals and values. It is just possible that life was like this in 1930s America (though we doubt it), but it is certainly not like this in the early twenty-first century – which, as we see throughout this book, is often characterized as a postmodern, risk society. Societies are just too complex, have too many competing values systems and generate too much conflict for this simple unitary idea to be valid.

Nor can we assume that people are simply socialized to a common set of values: quite the contrary, much evidence points to different socialization patterns among different groups.

And more: the theory also largely seems to assume that people are driven into crime through tensions and through grim necessity. As Jack Katz and others have pointed out (see Chapter 15), we do not necessarily need to see crime as motivated by painful sources or solely through 'background' structural factors. Many are drawn to crime for excitement and other emotive reasons.

We do not wish to make Merton's theory sound too facile and simply wrong. Its influence lies in that it pointed sharply to the role of economic factors in shaping crime, and to producing a genuinely social account that found the roots of crime to lie not in individual people, but in the organization, workings and cultural goals found in wider society. It has had many ardent followers, and it still has many adherents today.

Gangs, youth and deviant subcultures

One of these followers is Albert Cohen (1918–), who has been influenced by Merton and Sutherland, who both taught him. His *Delinquent Boys* (1955) became a classic in the field. In this study, Cohen notes that delinquent boys stole for the hell of it. They engaged in short-run hedonism and in what he called a 'reaction formation' to the frustration experienced as part of a class system, especially in school. They did not steal to gain goods or property. Instead, they gained status among their peers through adopting malicious, negative values which were the antithesis of the middle-class values taught in middle-class educational worlds.

Cohen's study of delinquent boys pioneered the idea that boys become delinquent because of what he termed 'status frustration', the process by which people feel thwarted when they aspire to a certain status. In schools especially, Cohen noted that boys from more deprived backgrounds often found school life an alienating and frustrating experience. They were being judged by what Cohen called the 'middleclass measuring rod'. They initially wanted to be successes, but found that they had not developed the skills to do this in their family and community life. For example, reading books was alien, and being polite and well-spoken hard. Their cultural differences had poorly equipped them for school life. Cohen suggests that in their frustration they inverted the values of the school – achievement, hard work, planning for the future and deferring gratification – and developed instead a contra culture in which values of non-achievement, playing around, not thinking of the future and instant gratification deliberately become their goals. Activities become non-utilitarian (they steal 'for the hell of it'), negativistic (opposing the values of adult society), malicious, versatile and characterized by short-run hedonism and group autonomy.

Cohen asserted that delinquency was most pronounced among lower-class youths because it is they who contend with the least opportunity to achieve success in conventional ways. Sometimes those whom society neglects seek self-respect by building a deviant subculture that 'defines as meritorious the characteristics they do possess, the kinds of conduct of which they are capable' (1955: 66). Having a notorious street reputation, for example, may win no points with society as a whole, but it may satisfy a youth's gnawing desire to 'be somebody'. Unlike most of the Chicago sociologists, he did discuss girls, although in very stereotypical terms.

Synthesizing the theories?

The prominent work of Richard A. Cloward (1926–2001) and Lloyd E. Ohlin (1918–2008), *Delinquency and Opportunity* (1960), can be seen as an attempt to form a bridge between the Chicago tradition (especially Sutherland's learning theory) and the strain tradition (especially Merton's anomie theory). They suggest that delinquent subcultures have their own opportunity structures. That is, young people have access to different kinds of youthful cultures. While they may aspire to the goals set by conventional society, working-class youth – as in Merton's and Cohen's model – can easily be thwarted and cannot get ahead. But they also find that they have differential access to youth cultures too. In their own work, Cloward and Ohlin suggest that there were three major kinds of such cultures:

1 *Criminal*. The criminal youth culture is at the top of the hierarchy. Here, alternative routes to financial success are available. In such circumstances, there are 'close bonds between different age levels of offender and between criminal and conventional elements' (Cloward and Ohlin, 1960: 171), so there is rapid integration of new (young) individuals into lives of crime.
2 *Violent/conflict*. Here there is not only little access to the legitimate opportunity structure, but also restricted access to the illegitimate/criminal one. Such youth may live in very unstable

areas, and violence becomes the means therefore by which they seek to resolve their frustrations and problems. Proficiency in violence becomes a source of status.

3   *Retreatist/drug.* Those who have neither access to the criminal culture nor the means to seek violent responses become 'double failures', and they are the most likely simply to 'drop out'. They become retreatists and turn to drink, drugs and other forms of withdrawal from the wider social order.

Thus, Cloward and Ohlin maintain that criminal deviance results not simply from limited legitimate opportunity but also from the availability of illegitimate opportunity. In short, deviance or conformity grows out of the relative opportunity structure that frames young people's lives. It was the nature of these opportunity structures and how they provide opportunities to learn deviant ways that fascinated the Chicago School. In its day – nearly 50 years ago – this was seen as a very elegant way of thinking about crime, bridging as it did the anomie tradition of Merton and the Chicago tradition of Shaw and Sutherland. To modern eyes, however, the theory looks somewhat contrived – and does not take into account a much wider range of forms of youthful culture.

There are more problems with the various Chicago theories:

■   They fall short by assuming that everyone shares the same cultural standards for judging right and wrong.

■   There is an acceptance of more established conceptions of criminality that potentially define deviance in ways that unfairly focus attention on poor people. If crime is defined to include stock fraud as well as street theft, offenders are more likely to include affluent individuals.

■   All structural-functional theories imply that everyone who violates conventional cultural standards will be branded as deviant. Becoming deviant, however, is actually a highly complex process.

Control theories

The term 'social control', initially linked to the work of Edward Ross, who first used the term in the *American Journal of Sociology* in 1896, and linked to the classical school of Durkheim and Mead, started to develop as a broad theory of self-control in the 1950s. Like the other broad ideas already considered, it comes in many guises.

Neutralization theory

One of social control's earliest formulations is to be found in the work of Sykes and Matza. They argue that boys can commit delinquent acts when their commitment to the moral order is weakened, and that they can do this through what Sykes and Matza term **techniques of neutralization**. These techniques are stories people tell themselves which break bonds through such devices as blaming others, denying responsibility or refuting the harm of their actions.

Sykes and Matza suggest five major techniques that enable delinquents to break 'the moral bind to law' (Matza, 1964: 181):

1   *The denial of personal responsibility.* Here the delinquent uses a kind of social word play. 'Of course I'm delinquent. Who wouldn't be, coming from my background?' He then can neutralize personal responsibility by detailing the background of a broken home, lack of love, and a host of other factors.

2   *The denial of harm to anyone.* In this pattern of neutralization, stealing a car is only borrowing it; truancy harms no one; and drug use 'doesn't hurt anyone but me'.

3   *The delinquent denies that the person injured or wronged is really a victim.* 'The [assaulted] teacher was unfair'; the victim of a mugging was 'only queer'; and the gang youth assaulted was 'out to get me'.

4   *The delinquent condemns the condemners.* 'Society is much more corrupt than I am.'

5   *Delinquent group or gang loyalties supersede loyalty to the norms of an impersonal society.* 'When I stabbed him, I was only defending my turf.' The youth places his gang or delinquent group above the law, the school and society.

Developing in close connection with this, *social bond theory* is effectively a theory of self-control. Walter Cade Reckless (1899–1988) and Simon Dinitz (1926–2007) presented it as 'containment theory'. They looked at groups of boys to see what insulated some from crime of all kinds but not others – the techniques that neutralize 'good boys' from crime and foster 'bad boys' in it.

Social control theory

All this anticipated the general question later posed by Travis Hirschi. Most contemporary control theories effectively ask not 'Why do people become criminal and commit crime?' but the reverse and intriguing question: 'Why do people refrain from committing crime?'

In his early work, Hirschi argued that 'delinquent acts result when an individual's bond to society is weak or broken' (1969: 16). Hirschi asserts that conformity arises from four types of social controls that create a social bond (Table 5.2). The weaker any of these controls are, the more likely it is that criminal acts will happen.

Later, Gottfredson and Hirschi used this question of why people are restrained from offending as the basis for their more general theory of crime (1990). Here, however, Hirschi shifted the

Table 5.2 Hirschi's elements of the bond

Element	Examples
Attachment	Identification with peers or parents, emotional bond between child and parent, concern and respect for parents' or peers' opinions, engaging in activities with peers, supervision by parents, intimate communications with parents, attitudes towards school, concern for teachers' opinions, general sensitivity to the opinions of others.
Involvement	Time-consuming activity (work, sports, recreation, hobbies), time spent on homework, lack of boredom, amount of non-active leisure time, time spent talking with friends.
Commitment	Investment in society (education, career, family), academic competence, educational aspirations and expectations, achievement orientation, expected occupation, importance of reputation.
Belief	Respect for authorities, importance of and respect for law, absence of neutralizations.

focus and replaced the emphasis on social control with that of self-control. Individuals with high self-control 'will be substantially less likely at all periods of life to engage in criminal acts' (ibid.: 89). This changes the theory a great deal, as all the other elements now go missing. Gottfredson and Hirschi further highlight the role of opportunity. Here, individuals with such low levels of self-control are argued to be particularly likely to commit crimes once confronted with the opportunities to do so. Over the years, the theory has been much tested, and some criminologists now think it has been the most influential theory of delinquency over the past 30 years.

Problems with control theory

Control theory is an odd theory of crime as it works from the assumption that most of us would commit crimes if we had the chance. It is only the social ties, bonds and attachments that prevent us from doing this. It is at least worth considering whether this is true.

This also means that it neglects offenders' motivations: the cause is apparent – a lack of control. Again, we do not need special reasons to account for crime, except to note that the bonds have broken.

More specifically, there are difficulties in ascertaining just how tight these bonds have to be. Some argue that bonds may have to be too repressive and too overwhelming in modern societies. Other criticisms include the way in which the responsibility for preventing criminality is almost exclusively weighted towards the individual and their families rather than considering broader criminogenic social processes such as inequality. In other respects, there are questions over the quality of Hirschi's research. Hirschi claimed that the strength of his theory lay on robust and transparent empirical foundations, involving the survey of more than 3,000 participants. Yet a close reading of Hirschi's (1969) work reveals some poor research design including ambiguous and leading survey questions and a failure to control for high levels of non-response bias (i.e. that large numbers of specific groups failed to complete Hirschi's excessively long survey and this skewed his results).

Reintegrative shaming?

A theory that has developed more recently than Hirschi's and in many ways is connected is John Braithwaite's 'reintegrative shaming'. In his influential book *Crime, Shame and Reintegration* (1989), Braithwaite highlights the importance of informal, rather than formal, sanctions in checking crime. As he says, 'It would seem that sanctions imposed by relatives, friends or a personally relevant collectivity have more effect on criminal behaviour than sanctions imposed by legal authority' (quoted in Muncie, 1999: 433). Closely allied to the work on shame by Thomas Scheff (which suggests that one of the central features of life is our search for honour and the ways in which shaming plays a role in that search), the emphasis on shaming can be seen to keep us in check. **Shame** is linked to taking the role of 'the other' (cf. Mead, 1934), and links to pangs of conscience when confronted with the possibility of wrongdoing. We want and need the social approval of others.

thinking about crime

Shaming involves all social processes expressing disapproval that have the aim of inducing remorse in the offender. The **shame** that matters most is not that coming from officials such as the police or judges or courts but that from the people we care about most. It is not stigmatizing in so far as it is aimed not at the offender per se but at the act the offender commits; the ultimate aim must be reintegration. The shaming itself creates outcasts, meaning that bonds of respect with the offender are not sustained. In contrast, reintegrative shaming is disapproval dispensed in a relationship with the offender that is based on respect, with the focus on the offence and where 'degradation ceremonies are followed by ceremonies to decertify deviance, where forgiveness, apology and repentance are culturally important' (Muncie et al., 1996).

Braithwaite contends that reintegrative shaming is effective in complex urban societies as well as simpler ones. It is likely that those nations with low crime rates are those in which shaming has the greatest social power (see Chapter 15).

Written out of criminological history?

The studies featured in this chapter laid the foundations of sociological criminology but they did so in ways that prioritized the view of (mostly white) male academics who approached crime as a male phenomenon (with a focus on young white men). This closing discussion looks at the work of early black sociologists and at the few early sociological attempts to address female crime.

Early black sociologists

The study of crime in early twentieth-century America was undertaken at the same time by African American and by white scholars. However, most works by the former remain unknown. As Young and Greene (2002: xi) write, 'the perspectives of African Americans remain on the periphery of the discipline' and 'their contributions continue to be excluded from textbooks and course material'.

Writings by African American scholars link crime to a range of causes although their work is characterized by a focus on race and racism. 'Like other early American sociologists and criminologists, African American scholars were influenced greatly by Durkheim and the "Chicago School" and emphasise social disorganization, anomie and the ecology of crime' (Young and Greene, 2002: 5–6). W.E.B. Du Bois (1868–1963) and Monroe Work (1866–1945) used a form of social disorganization analysis to ask why blacks were so over-represented in the justice system from the nineteenth century onwards. They suggested that the ending of slavery (and the removal of a powerful form of social control) meant that freed African Americans had to adjust to new ways of living and to create new kinds of moral values, as well as having to cope with the new kinds of economic stresses of operating in a 'free market' within a society where racial prejudice continued to run high. In addition, many young southern blacks migrated to find work in northern cities – swapping the social controls of rural home for urban 'disorganization' in ways that mirrored the experiences of much more well-documented European migrants to the United States during that time.

Du Bois and Work also argued that racialized justice was quick to criminalize and then exploit black groups which meant that those groups themselves lost confidence in 'white' justice. For

Table 5.3 Selected African American scholarship on crime and justice, 1900–49

Scholar	Date	Research topic
Work, M.	1900	Crime among Negroes of Chicago
Du Bois, W. E. B.	1901	Convict-Lease system in the South
Miller, K.	1914	Negro crime
Johnson, C. S.	1922	Chicago race riot
Reid, I. de A.	1925/32	Negro prisoners
Washington, F. B.	1932–3	Care of the Negro delinquent
Moses, E. R.	1933	Delinquency in the Negro community
Diggs, M.	1940	Negro juvenile delinquency
Cox, O.	1945	Lynching
Moses, E. R.	1947	Differential crime rates between Negroes and whites
Blue, J. T.	1948	Juvenile delinquency, race and economic status
Frazier, E. F.	1949	Sociological theory, race relations and crime

Source: Adapted from Greene and Gabbidon (2000: 5, table 1).

example, in the southern US states, a 'convict-lease system' operated in which (mostly black) prisoners were 'sold' or leased as workers to local employers – even though slavery had formally been abolished. 'The lessee then took charge of the convicts – worked them as he wished under the nominal control of the state. Thus a new slavery and slave-trade was established' (Du Bois, 1901/2002) – one in which the criminal justice system was closely implicated.

In the 1940s, other black sociologists built on this earlier tradition. E. Franklin Frazier (1947) compiled detailed surveys of work on race and crime, although he is known for his own work on black juvenile delinquency which he linked, like other Chicago scholars, to increasing social disorganization. Earl R. Moses (1949) attributed higher rates of black crime in Baltimore to racial differences in buying power arguing that whites found it easier to get jobs and therefore easier to buy or rent property. Given the centrality of questions of race to questions of criminology, it is very important that these early studies are more fully integrated into criminological history and teaching.

Early sociological studies of women and girls

> An excursion through the twentieth century's developments in criminology is a journey through communities inhabited only by men, passing street corners and sea-fronts occupied exclusively by male youth and into soccer stadia, youth clubs and rock venues where women and their experiences fail to register even a passing comment from the researchers.
>
> (Scraton, 1990: 17)

If much early criminology was written by college boys fascinated by street corner boys (Heidensohn, 1996) where did this leave studies of girls? Most nineteenth- and early twentieth-century studies of female criminality were influenced by medical and psychopathological models

thinking about crime

(see discussion of positivism in Chapter 4). Women and girls' bodies, hormones and sexuality were believed to shape their behaviour as much as, if not more than, socio-economic questions about class, aspiration and anomie (Cox, 2003: 135–61; Campbell, 1981). Puberty could unsettle girls by creating adult desires in adolescent bodies. The resulting sexual tension could cause them to break moral codes or commit crime. Cyril Burt, one of the UK's first educational psychologists, calculated that 'over-potency of the sexual instinct' was linked to a significant proportion of girls' delinquency (Burt, 1925: 432). US criminologists Sheldon and Eleanor Glueck's study of 'five hundred delinquent women' in the 1930s identified a wide range of predisposing factors but still emphasized the physical. These kinds of views were long-lasting: one 1968 study of delinquent girls in London concluded that it was 'quite likely that physical defects and lack of physical attractiveness have played a part in causing delinquency' (Cowie *et al.*, 1968: 64).

Girls and women did feature in a few early sociological studies of crime. William I. Thomas, another Chicago School scholar, edged towards a more gendered account of social disorganization. In *The Unadjusted Girl* (1923) he argued that young women, especially young European migrants to the USA, were caught between old moral values and new social practices. They were more likely to be 'affected by the feeling that much, too much [was] being missed in life' because they had been 'heretofore . . . most excluded from general participation in life'. This might result in 'despair or depression' or cause a young woman to 'break all bounds' (Thomas, 1923: 72).

For many Chicago sociologists, delinquency was a solution to young people's experience of social dislocation. Alfred K. Cohen (1955) argued that girls were less likely to seek a delinquent solution because they could gain social status by forming relationships with men and, later, by becoming mothers. Boys, on the other hand, defined their success in terms of their access to money, influence and power rather than through family life. Furthermore, girls' friendship groups were thought to be very different to those of boys which meant that they rarely joined the street gangs that so fascinated these scholars.

These kinds of views help to explain why these foundational studies paid such fleeting attention to female crime – it just did not fit their moulds. It also explains why feminist sociologists and criminologists later felt compelled to challenge these and find new ways to conceptualize gender and crime (see Chapter 6).

Summary

1   The functionalist perspective on crime suggests that it is 'normal' in all societies – it serves certain functions and may even help keep a society orderly. Crime may be usefully understood in mapping these functions.

2   The Marxist theory of crime suggests that crime is bound up with conflict of a class-based nature in which crimes of the powerful are much less noticed than the crimes of the weak.

3   Anomie theory suggests crime is bound up with tension, stresses and strains within societies. Most commonly there is a breakdown of the smooth workings of society.

4   The Chicago School of sociology saw crime as being strongly linked to city life. Modern cities bring with them cultural enclaves that seem more prone to generating criminal/delinquent styles of life with their own values, languages, norms, dress codes, etc.

5 Differential association theory suggests that crime is learned in ordinary everyday situations through a process of cultural transmission.
6 Social control theory suggests that crime comes about through a lack of attachment to groups valuing law-abiding behaviour.
7 Reintegrative shaming involves all social processes expressing disapproval that have the aim of inducing remorse in the offender. The shame that matters most is not that coming from officials such as the police or judges or courts but that relating to the people we care about most.

Critical thinking questions

1 Compare the following two views – one suggests that crime is normal, the other that capitalism generates crime.

> There must be something rotten in the very core of a social system which increases its wealth without diminishing its misery, and increases in crimes even more rapidly than in numbers.
>
> (Karl Marx, 'Population, Crime and Pauperism',
> *New York Daily Tribune*, 16 September 1859)

> Crime is normal . . . It is a factor in public health, an integral part of all healthy societies.
>
> (Émile Durkheim, *Rules of Sociological Method*: 76)

2 Examine the different kinds of study of crime emanating from the Chicago School. Consider how they complement each other. Do they ultimately add up to a full understanding of delinquency and crime? If not, what is missing?
3 Look at your own home city or town. Can you map out the areas of greatest crime? How would you explain this concentration?
4 Critically discuss the factors that may weaken a person's bond to society. Is such weakening likely to lead to crime and deviance?

Further study

Cloward, R. and Ohlin, L. E. (1960) *Delinquency and Opportunity: A Theory of Delinquent Gangs*, New York: Free Press. A classic study of subculture situated at the intersection of the Chicago School and strain theories.

Gabbidon, S., Greene, H. T. and Young, V. D. (2001) *African American Classics in Criminology and Criminal Justice*, Thousand Oaks, CA: Sage. Important volume examining the 'black' tradition of criminology in the United States.

thinking about crime

Hirschi, T. (1969) *Causes of Delinquency*, Berkeley, CA: University of California Press. This is the classic statement of Hirschi's 'control theory'.

Matza, D. (1969) *Becoming Deviant*, Englewood Cliffs, NJ: Prentice Hall. Although old, this is one of the most sophisticated accounts of crime and deviance available. At its core it reviews the major traditions of anomie, cultural learning and labelling in the study of deviance; but it is highly original in its synthesis.

Merton, R. K. (1938) 'Social Structure and Anomie', *American Sociological Review*, 3 (October): 672–82. One of the most cited papers in the sociology of crime.

Useful websites

University of Chicago: Department of Sociology
http://sociology.uchicago.edu/department/history.shtml
Gives a brief history of the original Chicago School theorists.

Society for Human Ecology (SHE)
http://www.societyforhumanecology.org/
This is an international interdisciplinary professional society that promotes the use of an ecological perspective in both research and application.

Chicago Area Project
http://www.chicagoareaproject.org
Continues to operate today.

chapter 6

Radicalizing Traditions

Key issues

- What is labelling theory?
- How did conflict theory arise and what are the questions posed by a 'new criminology'?
- How did the Birmingham Centre for Contemporary Cultural Studies provide an advance over earlier subcultural theories?
- What is the impact of feminism on criminology?
- What has been the influence of Foucault?

Introduction

The social ways of thinking about crime discussed in Chapter 5 were very influential in shaping contemporary criminology and appeared predominantly in the first six decades of the twentieth century. In this chapter we will look at accounts of crime that came into prominence during the latter part of the twentieth century. Many of these can be seen in some way as a response to earlier theories – challenging them, debating them, extending them. Indeed, during this time there was a constant tendency to find new ways of thinking about crime – but often these new ways turned out to be little more than old ways updated, and often their newness was attacked very rapidly and they fell into decline as quickly as they appeared. But some of the theories had a more enduring impact. This chapter will briefly review these late twentieth-century theories before turning in Chapter 7 to some of the most recent trends.

The 1960s was a watershed decade. Looking back now it seemed like an era when all kinds of established authority came to be challenged. From popular culture to civil rights, revolutionary upheaval was in the air – and academic disciplines also experienced some profound upheavals. In criminology, the very idea of 'crime' and 'deviance' was challenged. Claims from the past that it is self-evident and obvious what constitute 'crimes', that we know what 'deviance' is, that these are 'objective categories' – all these assumptions came under critical scrutiny. The thinking of the 1960s came to see such 'objective' definitions of crime and deviance as problematic. There was now a need to study the categories themselves – what they were, how they came about, and what they did to people. And much of this was political; suddenly, politics became an integral part of criminology.

At the time, this was seen as quite a radical shift in emphasis and it gave rise to what have been called the 'New Deviancy theorists', the 'Societal Reaction Perspective' or **Labelling Theory**. In the United Kingdom it generated an informal organization – the National Deviancy Conference (NDC) – that held regular conferences and discussions at York University between 1968 and 1973 (and resulted in several books: notably *Images of Deviance* (1971) and *Politics and Deviance* (1973)) (see Box 6.1). This grouping lasted a few years until the late 1970s although it had effectively come to an end much earlier. Even so, the NDC was, as Mooney (2012:14) describes, an enormously productive and influential body: 'it attacked positivist and classicist discourses and was concerned with how the criminal justice system was selective and fundamentally flawed, particularly with respect to its focus on the crimes of the working class while ignoring those of the more powerful groups in society.' While this critical momentum did not disappear, new divisions and schisms did subsequently open up.

BOX 6.1 From the National Deviancy Conference to the rise of the new criminologies

Background

The National Deviancy Conference (NDC) was established in 1967 as a reaction against mainstream criminology. It held conferences at the University of York between 1968 and 1973 and thereafter turned for a while into a broader European organization. Among its key founder members in the United Kingdom were Stanley Cohen, Laurie Taylor, Jock Young, Ian Taylor and Mary McIntosh.

What was the NDC responding against?

Its central position was a critique of mainstream criminology – as exemplified in work conducted at the Home Office or at the Institute for Criminology in Cambridge, which used traditional methods, lacked a firm sociological focus and was often rather conservative in outlook. Broadly, this was a time of student rebellion, growth in sociology and also a time for wider activism in various new penal reform and social change movements. These positions were brought together in a desire to radically rethink the problem of crime and deviance.

What theories did it draw from?

The NDC marked a strong concern with sociology and deviance – all its founders were sociologists, though it soon came to include radical practitioners too and members of radical change movements. It initially drew from the theories of symbolic interactionism, ethnomethodology, Marxism, appreciative ethnography, conflict theories, social movement activism, neo-functionalism, labelling theory and anarchistic criminology. Its members were writing before the arrival of a **feminist criminology**, though many of them were part of the newly emerging second-wave women's movement.

Examples of key texts

- Jock Young, *The Drugtakers* (1971)
- Stanley Cohen, *Folk Devils and Moral Panics* (1972/2002)
- Laurie Taylor, *Deviance and Society* (1973)
- Stanley Cohen (ed.) *Images of Deviance* (1971)
- Ian Taylor and Laurie Taylor (eds) *Politics and Deviance* (1973)

Demise and diffusion

The New Criminology (see Box 6.2) eventually critiqued much of this new radicalism and itself unfolded into a number of other positions. Some of those involved left criminology altogether and developed other fields such as cultural studies or sexuality studies. Some remained with a particular theoretical orientation and developed it further – such as those who had initially applied ethnomethodology to the study of criminal statistics (they now went on to apply ethnomethodological reasoning to other areas of social life). And others went on to develop further criminologies – left realism, discourse theory and feminist criminology – which will be discussed later in this, and the next chapter.

See Cohen (1971) and Taylor and Taylor (1973).

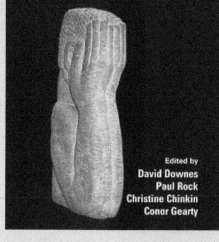

Plate 6.1 Cover of Crime, Social Control and Human Rights: From Moral Panics to States of Denial, Essays in Honour of Stanley Cohen.

Source: © Routledge.

Briefly, these new and critical theories proposed:

- A turning away from conventional theories of crime which assumed the nature of criminal categories and control processes and asked questions about the causes of crime. Instead, it was argued that crime was a socially constructed category, that it differed throughout history and different cultures, and that there could not therefore be any 'criminal type' – since criminal types depended on who defined the laws at particular times.
- A rejection of the view that crime is caused by pathologies, disorganization, strains, stresses and leakage within a consensual society which more or less agreed on values. Instead, its focus moved to pick up on the theme of conflict: to see crime (as some earlier criminologists such as Bonger had indeed done) as a special form of conflict.
- Ways of seeing crime and deviance as ideologically driven categories that stretched the concerns of criminology away from offenders toward the role of social control.
- A re-examination of youth subcultural theories of crime, placing a much greater emphasis upon culture and cultural forms.
- A fresh concern with gender. It is striking how few theories of crime of the nineteenth and twentieth centuries recognized one of the most apparent facts about crime: that it is overwhelmingly committed by men. With the rise of modern (second-wave) feminism, the issue of gender was brought into criminology as a key element for thinking about crime.
- A move to see criminology as part of the very problem it tries to solve. Many interventions directed at criminal actions simply do not work in the way they are supposed to work. Instead, they tend to extend the webs of surveillance and control.

'Deviance' and labelling

For a short while during much of the late 1960s and the 1970s, labelling theory became the dominant sociological theory of crime. In one sense this was very odd, since it made few claims to try to understand what made people criminal. Quite the contrary: it tended to assume we would all be criminal if we could (in this, it had quite a lot in common with control theory, discussed in Chapter 5). Instead, it turned its focus on societal reactions to crime. Societal reactions could range from the informal responses of public opinion, families or the mass media to the more formal responses of police, courts and prisons.

Labelling theory highlights social reaction. In doing so it reworked some old ideas and put them into new contexts and shocked establishment criminology by emphasizing the contingent, constructed, fluid and symbolic dimensions of social life. The elementary understanding of the way in which criminal responses may shape crime goes back a long way: it is captured in popular phrases such as 'give a dog a bad name'. In the twentieth century the origins of the theory are usually seen to lie with Frank Tannenbaum in his classic study *Crime and the Community* (1938). Here he argued that

> The process of making the criminal, therefore, is a process of tagging, defining, identifying, segregating, describing, emphasizing, evoking the very traits that are complained of. . . .

The person becomes the thing he is described as being. . . . The way out is a refusal to dramatize the evil.

(Tannenbaum, 1938: 19–20)

The theory has a number of roots in earlier sociological traditions, but draws heavily on the idea of W. I. Thomas that 'when people define situations as real they become real in their consequences'. This is sometimes also known as the 'self-fulfilling prophecy' (see Janowitz, 1996).

Becker, Lemert and Cohen

The key labelling theorists are usually seen to be the North American sociologists Edwin Lemert and Howard S. Becker and the South African-born but UK-based criminologist Stanley Cohen.

Edwin Lemert (1951, 1967) argued that many episodes of norm violation – from truancy to under-age drinking – often provoke little reaction from others and have little effect on a person's self-concept. Lemert calls such passing episodes **primary deviance**. He asked what happens if other people take notice of someone's deviance and make something of it. If, for example, people begin to describe a young man as a 'boozer' or a 'drunk' or even an 'alcoholic' and then push him out of their group, he may become embittered, drink even more and seek the company of others who condone his behaviour. So the response to initial deviance can set in motion **secondary deviance**, meaning an individual engages in repeated norm violations and begins to take on a deviant identity. The development of secondary deviance is one application of the Thomas theorem, which states that 'Situations defined as real become real in their consequences.'

The terms 'primary' and 'secondary deviance' capture the distinction between original and effective causes of deviance: primary deviation arises from many sources but 'has only marginal implications for the status and psychic structure of the person concerned', whereas secondary deviation refers to the ways in which stigma and punishment can actually make the crimes or deviance 'become central facts of existence for those experiencing them, altering psychic structure, producing specialised organisation of social roles and self regarding attitudes' (Lemert, 1967: 40–1). Deviant ascription became a pivotal or master status. It was Lemert who argued that rather than seeing crime as leading to control, it may be more fruitful to see the process as one in which control agencies structured and even generated crime.

Howard S. Becker was a second-generation Chicago sociologist (identified with the 1950s and 1960s) whose own work focused on marijuana use and its control. Studying the ways in which cultures and careers were transformed by negative sanctions against drug use, he outlined the broad problem of labelling when he asked:

We [should] direct our attention in research and theory building to the questions: who applied the label of deviant to whom? What consequences does the application of a label have for the person so labelled? Under what circumstances is the label of a deviant successfully applied?

(Becker, 1963: 3)

thinking about crime

In what became the canonical statement of labelling theory, he announced that

> Social groups create deviance by making the rules whose infraction constitutes deviance, and by applying those rules to particular people and labelling them as outsiders. . . . Deviance is *not* a quality of the act the person commits, but rather a consequence of the application by others of rules and sanctions to an 'offender'. The deviant is one to whom that label has successfully been applied: deviant behavior is behavior that people so label.
>
> (Becker, 1963: 9)

Becker challenged standard definitions of deviant behaviour. In his research on drug users he could show how sanctions against drug use led to distinctive subcultures and careers as drug users which, he claimed, would not exist without the sanctions. Sanctions shaped the nature of drug use.

Stanley Cohen in his seminal work *Folk Devils and Moral Panics* (1972/2002) looked at one of the first major youth phenomena in the United Kingdom. This was a study of the big English youth phenomenon of the 1960s: the rise of the so-called mods and rockers (see Plate 6.2). Apart from the teddy boys of the 1950s, these were the first major youth phenomenon of the post-war era, and sparked off a great deal of controversy. They seemed to turn the local beaches of Clacton into a battleground. Cohen had an unusual take on all this: for him, the mods and rockers came into being, at least in part, because of the very responses of the media, the police and the courts – which helped define and shape them. The term **moral panic** is introduced to capture the heightened awareness of certain problems at key moments. In his classic formulation:

Plate 6.2 A youth lying on the sand at Margate, Kent, when mods and rockers clashed on the beach on 18 May 1964. The first major study of moral panics was that of this youth phenomenon of the 1960s.

Source: © PA.

a condition, episode, person or group of persons emerges to become defined as a threat to societal values and interests: its nature is presented in a stylised and stereotypical fashion by the mass media; the moral barricades are manned by editors, bishops, politicians and other right thinking people.

(Cohen, 1972: 9)

Moral panics in this sense of applying to 'certain problems' at key moments originally seemed to be short-lived and with a distinct focus: a riot, a drug overdose, a violent crime, a paedophile murder. Yet, perhaps reflecting a greater sense of social anxiety and awareness of risk, it seems that such isolated panics have become almost pervasive and commonplace (McRobbie and Thornton, 1995: 560).

Some of these ideas are discussed further in chapters 7, 12, 20 and 22; for more on the Dramatization of crime and deviance and on Classic Moral Panic theory see Chapter 20.

Wider contributions

Overall, labelling theory has covered a surprisingly wide range of issues and produced many classic studies. Thus, Edwin Schur's *Crimes without Victims* (1965) looked at 'victimless' crimes and showed how the legal response of the times such as prohibition and criminalization of certain behaviours – e.g. homosexuality, abortion, drug use – generated more problems than were solved. Erving Goffman's *Asylums* (1961) and Thomas J. Scheff's *Being Mentally Ill* (1966) developed a controversial theory of mental illness based upon labelling dynamics, suggesting that there was no such simple thing as 'mental illness'; rather, the role of the person defined as mentally ill depended upon a major process of identification. And the criminologist Lesley Wilkins's *Social Policy, Action and Research* (1967) used systems theory to show how a process of deviancy amplification works: how small deviations can, through a process of feedback by control agencies, become major patterns of deviance.

This latter idea was subsequently used to great effect by Jock Young (1971) in his study of drug use in bohemian London, which described how the mass media transformed marijuana use into a social problem through sensationalist and lurid accounts of hippie lifestyles. As the much cited quote from the *News of the World* (21 September 1969) on a squat in a Georgian mansion in Piccadilly makes abundantly clear:

HIPPIE DRUGS – THE SORDID TRUTH
Drug-taking, couples making love while others look on, a heavy mob armed with iron-bars, filth and stench, foul language, that is the scene inside the hippies' fortress in London's Piccadilly. These are not rumours but facts, sordid facts which will shock ordinary decent living people.

(cited in Young, 2007b: 59)

The passage nicely captures the mix of fascination and repulsion, dread and desire that moral guardians exhibit toward the objects of their anxiety. There is a delicious irony here for the report goes on to describe how the hippies sit 'lit only by the light of their drugged cigarettes' led by the enigmatic Dr John, the pseudonym of Phil Cohen, who would subsequently become one of the leading exponents of a radicalized subcultural theory!

All in all, this was a very productive period of research and theory about crime and deviance. The labelling perspective brought political analysis into deviancy study. It recognized that labelling was a political act and that 'what rules are to be enforced, what behaviour regarded as deviant and which people labelled as outsiders must . . . be regarded as political questions' (Becker, 1963: 7). From this it went on to produce a series of empirical studies concerning the origins of the dominant definitions of deviance through political actions (in such areas as drug and alcohol temperance legislation, juvenile delinquency, homosexuality, prostitution and pornography) as well as the political bias in the apprehension and adjudication of deviants.

Labelling theory – with its rejection of so-called positivistic criminology and its deterministic understanding of human action – was a key component in the development of the sociology of deviance. This sociology not only changed the theoretical base for the study of criminals but also brought in its wake a dramatic restructuring of empirical concerns. Sociologists turned their interests to the world of expressive deviance: to the twilight, marginal worlds of tramps, alcoholics, strippers, dwarfs, prostitutes, drug addicts, nudists; to taxi-cab drivers, the blind, the dying, the physically ill and handicapped, and even to a motley array of problems in everyday life. It opened up the field of inquiry so that it was possible to discuss a range of areas hitherto neglected – blindness, obesity, smoking and interpersonal relationships – thereby enabling both the foundations for a formal theory of deviance as a social property and a method for understanding the routine and the regular through the eyes of the ruptured and the irregular. Whatever these studies had in common, it was very clear by this stage that it was not conventional criminology.

Problems with labelling theory

Popular as the theory became, it was soon under attack. Among the most central criticisms made were the following:

- It is seen as a liberal theory that gives too little attention to the state, power and the economy.
- From the political right, it is seen as overly sympathetic to the criminal and deviant – a proposal for going soft on crime.
- For rigorous positivist-minded social scientists, either it is un-testable or, if it is tested, is found to be severely lacking in supportive evidence.
- Criminologists were usually unhappy about its neglect of the origins of deviance. Labelling theory failed to provide any account of the initial motivations steering individuals towards deviance.
- Closely linked to the above is the argument that labelling theorists had rescued the deviants from the deterministic constraints of biological, psychological and social forces only to enchain them again in a new determinism of societal reactions (Plummer, 1979).

Developments

Although labelling theory is always cited as one of the major sociological theories of crime and deviance, the original research and controversies that surrounded it during the 1970s have largely abated. The theory has become a quiet orthodoxy for some sociologists. Yet several of its key themes have entered criminological research under different guises. Three can be highlighted here. The first is the theory of moral panics. An idea discussed by Howard Becker over the initial concern with drugs in the United States, it was developed further in the work of Stanley Cohen in his research on the panics concerning teenage mods and rockers in beach resorts on English bank holidays in the 1960s. The focus here becomes the exaggerated responses of control agencies (largely the media) in stirring up concern and anxiety. The study of moral panics has been applied to many areas and has become a staple feature of sociological research (Thompson, 1998; Critcher, 2003; Jewkes, 2004; in 2011 a special issue of the journal *Crime, Media, Culture* was devoted to the topic; and see Chapter 20).

The second is the theory of social constructionism. Much recent labelling theory has moved under this different name. This is an approach in sociology which argues that 'conditions must be brought to people's notice in order to become social problems' (Best, 1990: 11). Once again closely allied to Becker's notion of moral enterprise, it looks at the ways individuals, groups and societies come to label certain phenomena as problems and how others then respond to such claims. Joel Best, for instance, has traced the 'rhetoric and concern about child victims', while Joseph Gusfield (1981) has analysed the drink–driving problem. Broadly, there is seen to be a 'social problems marketplace' in which people struggle to 'own' social problems. This theory continues to examine the rhetoric, the claims and the power struggles behind such definitional processes.

A third area is the enhanced understanding of social control. Traditionally, many labelling theorists were concerned with the excessive encroachment of technology, bureaucracy and the state upon personal life – often in its grossest forms such as the increasing medicalization of deviance, the bureaucratization of the control agencies and the concomitant dehumanization of the lives of their 'victims', as well as the direct application of technology in the service of control. When there was a political shift to the right in many Western democracies in the 1980s, such concerns were co-opted as part of a market-based laissez-faire liberalism that aimed to roll back the state and introduce privatization into social control. Despite this, labelling theorists have long been concerned with policies of decriminalization, deinstitutionalization, demedicalization, deprofessionalization and the creation of social movements concerned with such activities (Cohen, 1985).

In sum: labelling theory highlights societal reactions to crime and deviance. It has a long history but became particularly prominent in the 1960s and 1970s. Since that time, and after a number of critiques, the theory has become something of an orthodoxy. Currently, the theory of moral panics, social constructionist theories and theories of social control have become its modern-day reincarnations.

thinking about crime

Crime as conflict

A young Karl Marx (1843/1971: 137) once wrote that 'to be radical is to grasp things at root' and at the root of his political vision is the idea of class conflict, which in turn informed the radical criminology emerging in the late 1960s. A key influence here is Alvin Gouldner who launched a scathing critique of the by now dominant liberal sociology of deviance in a well-known feud with Howard Becker.

He begins by denouncing Becker's **partisan** sociology as 'glib' for while it might be at ease in the 'cool worlds' of drug addicts, jazz musicians and mental health patients (amongst other 'outsiders') as well as when taking sides with the 'underdog' against small-minded, middle-class morality, it otherwise amounted to little more than well-meaning 'zookeeping' – observing the often hidden or the exotic aspects of the social world. His complaint is that the

> pull to the underdog is sometimes part of a titillated attraction to the underdog's exotic difference . . . Becker's school of deviance is redolent of romanticism. It expresses the satisfaction of the Great White Hunter who has bravely risked the perils of the urban jungle to bring back an exotic specimen. It expresses the romanticism of the zoo curator who preeningly displays his rare specimens. And like the zookeeper, he wishes to protect his collection; he does not want spectators to throw rocks at the animals behind the bars. But neither is he eager to tear down the bars and let the animals go. The attitude of these zookeepers of deviance is to create a comfortable and humane Indian Reservation, a protected social space, within which these colourful specimens may be exhibited, unmolested and unchanged.
>
> (Gouldner, 1968/1973: 37–8)

Anticipating later developments he criticized the picture painted of the deviant as a passive victim of an intolerant society, rather than a defiant rebel against it.

As he memorably put it, the deviant was understood as 'not as man-fighting-back . . . but rather, man-on-his-back' (Gouldner, 1968/1973: 39) and the focus was on the bureaucratic, caretaking institutions of society rather than the master institutions producing the suffering in the world. Others were quick to take up the challenge and take criminology in a more resolutely Marxist direction (Quinney, 1970; Liazos, 1972; Chambliss, 1976). This had been implicit in Gouldner's intervention and we will just consider one brief example here before turning to important British developments.

Jeffrey Reiman and economic conflicts

One of the most accessible statements of the conflict theory of crime is Jeffrey Reiman's (1942–) *The Rich Get Richer and the Poor Get Prison* (1979; 10th edition, 2013). Reiman shows how the poor are arrested and charged out of all proportion to their numbers for the kinds of crimes poor people generally commit: burglary, robbery, assault, and so forth. Yet when we look at the kinds of crimes poor people almost never have the opportunity to commit, such as serious corporate crimes, antitrust violations, industrial safety violations, embezzlement and serious tax evasion, the criminal justice system is frequently tolerant and merciful. The more likely it is for a particular form of crime to be committed by middle- and upper-class people, the less likely it is that it will be treated as a criminal offence (Reiman, 1979).

Ironically, for Reiman the criminal justice system is designed to fail – any success it achieves is a pyrrhic victory: it succeeds in its failures. As he says, 'On the whole, most of the system's practices make more sense if we look at them as ingredients to maintain rather than reduce crime' (Reiman, 2001: 4). It is a carnival mirror of crime: it reflects real dangers in our society, but it is a truly distorted image. We keep seeing and hearing about the wrong things in crime analysis, and the really serious crimes go missing. There are many other crimes that are far more costly and even dangerous but which never appear in the mirror. Much of his book is full of documentary evidence of the high cost of these crimes we neglect.

So for Reiman, the goals of a policy to eliminate crime are somewhat different. Most of his criteria are linked in various ways to establishing 'a more just distribution of wealth and income and mak[ing] equal opportunities a reality' (1979: 183). His work is often not discussed seriously by either criminologists or textbooks, but his book has now been through ten editions, has a major website (listed at the end of this chapter) and seems to provide an argument and resource that interests students more than it does the criminological profession, providing an accessible introduction to issues that others have developed with varying degrees of theoretical sophistication and nuance.

The new criminology

Although there is a long history of conflict theories of crime (from at least Marx onwards), since the 1970s there has been a significant revitalization of interest.

A key book here was by the British sociologists of crime Ian Taylor, Paul Walton and Jock Young, called The New Criminology (1973; see Box 6.2). This was a substantial critique of all the theories we have so far outlined, and more besides (each chapter takes a particular theory and dissects it).

Broadly, they argued that most existing theories of crimes:

- ■ had not looked at a wide enough range of questions (to take in the wider structural explanations of control as well as of crime, for instance);
- ■ had often ignored wider material conflicts at the root of much of the criminal process;
- ■ too frequently were deterministic in their assumptions and gave little role to the creative human actor willing to commit crimes;
- ■ had inadequate epistemologies (theories of how we know the truth).

They argued that limitations were not just to be found in the early theories (positivism and classicism), but equally to be found in the so-called radical or sceptical theories of the 1970s (labelling, new deviance, etc.). These failed to do many things – and the whole field had become 'exhausted, except as a form of moral gesture' (Taylor et al., 1973: 14). At the time of writing, all the authors were Marxists and they placed an emphasis on both the structural origins of acts seen as deviant or criminal and on the reaction to these acts (Mooney, 2012: 18).

From their work, a new position started to appear that was based on the 'materiality' of crime, and was variously called critical criminology, working-class criminology or neo-Marxist

BOX 6.2 *The New Criminology: For a Social Theory of Deviance*

In this book, published in 1973, the authors, Ian Taylor, Paul Walton and Jock Young, review each of the major theories of criminology and find them lacking. They then argue that a series of key questions need to be addressed in any 'fully social theory of crime'. Their work is interesting both for its critique and for its framing of questions, and for over a decade it was one of the most influential books in British criminology. The questions it posed were:

1 The wider origins of the deviant act.
2 The immediate origins of the deviant act.
3 The actual act.
4 The immediate origins of social reaction.
5 The wider origins of deviant reaction.
6 The outcome of the social reaction on deviant's further action.
7 The nature of the deviant process as a whole.
8 The new criminology.

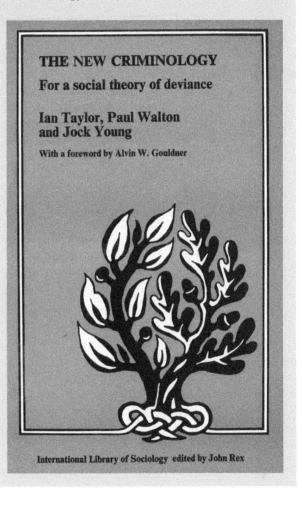

THE NEW CRIMINOLOGY

For a social theory of deviance

Ian Taylor, Paul Walton and Jock Young

With a foreword by Alvin W. Gouldner

International Library of Sociology edited by John Rex

Plate 6.3 Cover of *The New Criminology*, published in 1973. It became a highly important watershed, taking stock of the old field of criminology and designating the requirements for a fully social theory of crime.

Source: © Routledge.

criminology. Much of it borrowed from conflict theory and Marxism. For some of these writers, the problems of the poor and the working class were not the truly serious problems of crime. On the contrary, it was the crimes of the powerful (Pearce, 1976) that deserved focus; the wrong crimes and the wrong criminals were being focused upon. This was the basis of much of the first wave of radical criminology. As Mooney (2012: 19) summarizes:

For the new criminologists the causes of crime are to be found outside the individual, in the social structure, that is, in the 'inequalities of wealth and power, and in particular of inequalities in property and life chances' (Taylor *et al.*, 1975: 281) created by contemporary capitalist society, and, given this, the solution must involve the restructuring of society.

Critics from all sides though were quick to highlight some of the flaws in the radical argument. Socialist critics worried that the 'romanticism of crime, the recognition in the criminal of a rebel "alienated" from society, is, for Marxism a dangerous political ideology' (Hirst, 1975: 218). Stan Cohen (1979a: 44) suggested that socialist legality might in practice mean a 'model of social control in which offenders wear sandwich-boards listing their crimes before a crowd which shouts "Down with the counter-revolutionaries!" and are then led away to be publicly shot'. As we will shortly see a wave of feminist scholarship powerfully challenged many of the assumptions on which Marxist criminology rested, while mainstream voices retorted that the radicals have ignored 'the large measure of consensus, even among the oppressed, in condemning the theft and violence that makes up the bulk of traditional crime' (Radzinowicz and King, 1979: 87). In the context of criticisms both from within 'critical' criminology as well as 'traditional' criminology, a bitter divide would come to split the Left during the 1980s and much of the 1990s.

Left realism

The revisionism of left realism sought to counter the resurgent right-wing criminology (see Box 6.3) through a renewed commitment to social democratic principles and a return to Merton's understanding of anomie to confront crime – where Merton's dire warning that the ceaseless striving for wealth in American society produces a fatal disjuncture between cultural goals and the legitimate ways of achieving them. Seeing crime as a serious problem, especially in inner-city areas, and one that had been growing in recent years, left realism focused on what was conceived of as 'the square' of crime: the state, society and the public at large, offenders and victims (Figure 6.1). All four factors need to be looked at for all types of crime. Victims of crime are overwhelmingly poor, working-class people and, often, those who are marginalized and deprived because of their ethnicity. For example, unskilled workers are twice as likely to be burgled as other workers. *Much crime, then, is committed by the working class against the working class.* Young *et al.* argue that the causes of crime need to be looked for in deep structural inequalities. Crime is produced by **relative deprivation** – a perceived disadvantage arising from a specific comparison – and **marginalization**, where people live on the edge of society and outside of the mainstream with little stake in society overall.

Figure 6.1 The square of crime.

Source: After Young (1997).

thinking about crime

All this calls for the pursuit of justice at a wide level. The left realists argue for policies involving fundamental shifts in economic situations, enlightened prison policies, environmental design and accountable police. They stress that crime needs to be taken seriously and confronted by politicians, policymakers and academics – and the public's concerns listened to.

The stated aims of new left realists are to avoid over-general accounts of crime and to see crime in context. The specific shapes of crime, its causes and the way they are controlled change across the world as the society changes. New causes of crime and new patterns of crime appear worldwide. Ian Taylor (1999), for example, argued that the strong shift to a 'market society' since the time of Margaret Thatcher and Ronald Reagan not only tended to promote more 'ugly' crime but also brought more 'brutish' penal responses. In their more recent contributions to a revitalization of left realism, DeKeseredy and Schwartz (2010) have updated this analysis and also placed gender issues in a central position, so they argue that in the current period 'criminogenic subcultural development in North America and elsewhere is heavily shaped by the destructive consequences of right-wing . . . economic policies and marginalized men's attempts to live up to the principles of hegemonic masculinity' (DeKeseredy and Schwartz, 2012: 107).

Left idealism?

The arrival of a left realism did not pass without criticism from others on the left. Jock Young (1975, 1979) and others summarized the result as an 'idealist–realist' polarity. According to Mooney (2012: 27), realists attached the label of 'left idealism' to some critical approaches not because of any 'perceived utopianism but philosophically because of a stress on ideas rather than material reality' and hence a so-called 'left idealist' position could be seen as covering a range of perspectives on crime and the law such as interactionism's micro-sociological approach (Downes and Rock, 1979), Marxism's macro-sociological approach (Sumner, 1976), abolitionism (Mathiesen, 1974) and analyses of discipline and state power (Boyle et al., 1975; Fitzgerald and Sim, 1979). Arguably, what unites these is an idealization of the working-class criminal, a coercive conception of order, and an unwillingness to deal with aetiology, statistics and reform.

However, those identified as 'idealists' rejected the label and associated criticisms, and argued that their version of a 'criminology from below' against the authoritarian state and alliances with the radical lobbying and pressure groups (e.g. concerned with prisons or the police) was a response to the realities of life under governments, led by Margaret Thatcher at the time but with patterns continuing subsequently, that was keen to implement right-wing and authoritarian policies and measures. From their perspective there is a direct relationship between economic crises and political responses of the state and judiciary, leading to marginalization and criminalization of some groups and not others:

> [W]e are not saying that crime is not a problem for working-class people or that, contrary to the innuendo in some new realist writing, the terrible brutality suffered by many women is not a problem for them. Neither are we saying that the state cannot be reformed. . . . What we are saying is that the new realist position on law and order is theoretically flawed and, from a socialist perspective, it remains politically conservative in its conclusions about what can be done about the state.
>
> (Sim et al., 1987: 59)

Divisions remain between the different strands of critical criminology, with left realism exploring the socio-cultural context of law and order in a more reflexive fashion (DeKeseredy and Schwartz, 2012) while others have oriented themselves towards a human rights discourse (Cohen, 2001; Scraton, 1999).

BOX 6.3 Criminologies from the Right

In much of this chapter we have been describing intellectual developments from the Left, but it is also important to emphasize that over this period the Right were also energetically redefining the crime problem. Indeed, they crucially influenced the 'law and order' politics of the Conservatives under Margaret Thatcher and Ronald Reagan's Republicans in the United States. The New Right combines at least four distinct approaches. One revives nineteenth-century libertarianism and natural law philosophy to chastise the state for criminalizing 'victimless crimes' that do not 'violate anyone's rights; drunkenness, possession of drugs, prostitution, homosexuality . . . in order to police the morals of America' (Wollstein, 1967). Another vigorously emphasizes the virtues of free market economics in a fundamental critique of welfare state solutions to social problems, while the third position associated with traditionalist conservatives argues for the continuing importance of deterrence, free will and individual responsibility (van den Haag, 1975, 1985). A fourth approach is that identified with the criminology of James Q. Wilson who is variously described as a 'neo-conservative' or 'New Realist' (Tame, 1991: 140), but does differ from the libertarians, economists and traditional conservatives in important respects (as demonstrated by his numerous advisory roles during the Reagan and Bush administrations).

Wilson (1975) influentially argued that poverty does not cause crime. Despite the huge investment in welfare programmes in the 1960s and rising affluence over that decade, the crime rate soared. He took this quite startling fact as proof that sociological thinking on the causes of and solutions to crime were seriously mistaken. Instead, he claimed crime was dramatically rising on account of the collapse of the civic socialization of young people, community failure and family breakdown. With his colleague George Kelling he published one of the most influential articles in American criminology, where their 'broken windows' image is used to explain how neighbourhoods descend into crime and disorder (Wilson and Kelling, 1982). They argued that if minor incivilities – like vandalism, graffiti, begging, drunkenness – go unchecked they set in motion a cycle of decline and this argument has achieved a certain orthodoxy amongst policymakers in ways that have not always received the approval of Wilson and Kelling. For example, it was used to justify the tough 'zero tolerance' policing of New York in the 1990s and has informed measures introduced in the UK targeted at anti-social behaviour such as the agenda pursued by the Home Office through the development of new powers. The Anti-Social Behaviour Orders (ASBOs) and dispersal orders have been familiar for a few years and in 2012 the UK government introduced proposals to replace these with new Criminal Behaviour Orders (CBOs) and Crime Prevention Injunctions (CPIs). There remains though considerable disagreement over how successful aggressive policing tactics are in securing order and safety (Harcourt, 2001).

thinking about crime

The Birmingham Centre and the new subcultural theory

Another important development that was taking place during the 1970s and early 1980s was the work based at the Birmingham Centre for Contemporary Cultural Studies (BCCCS), established in 1964 by Richard Hoggart (then a Professor of English). It was Hoggart's deputy, Stuart Hall, who led the Centre through its most influential period in the 1970s. Hall became director in 1968, before leaving in 1979 to take up the chair of Sociology at the Open University (Rojek, 2003). During his time there he encouraged many students to draw upon Marxist and critical thinking while still conducting empirical studies of crime, delinquency and subcultures.

A good example of this was Phil Cohen's (1972) study of the emergence of 'mods' and 'skinheads' in the East End of London during the 1960s. Cohen, who as we have seen was involved in the radical squatter movement in London, published the seminal article 'Subcultural Conflict and Working Class Community' as one of the earliest contributions to the *Working Papers in Cultural Studies* through the Birmingham Centre. In some respects Cohen's analysis shared the Chicago School's emphasis on biography, place and change, but it also offered a distinctive class analysis of the destruction of working-class community and the erosion of its traditional culture. For Cohen (1972: 23), delinquent subcultures 'express and resolve, albeit "magically", the contradictions which remain hidden or unresolved in the parent culture'. In other words, the conflicts in adult culture are felt most acutely by the young and appear at various levels: at the ideological level, between 'traditional working class puritanism' and 'the new hedonism of consumption'; at the economic level, between a 'future as part of the socially mobile elite' or as 'part of the new lumpenproletariat' (Cohen, 1972: 23).

Youth style and delinquency do not solve the real crises in class relations. They are symbolic, or imaginary, attempts at resolving hidden problems, and examples of this, for Cohen, include the ways in which the original mod style was an attempt to realize the lifestyle of the socially mobile white-collar worker, as mods' dress and music reflected the hedonistic image of the affluent consumer. The later phenomenon of the skinhead he reads as a systematic inversion of the mods' pursuit of the upwardly mobile option. Instead, the skinheads followed the downwardly lumpen solution. Music and style were again the central focus of the action as they signified a reaction against the contamination of the parent culture by middle-class values, and the aggressive caricature of working-class values was regressively expressed through boots, braces and racism.

The Birmingham Centre refined this approach by explicitly drawing on Gramsci's (1971) work to locate subcultures not just in relation to parent cultures, but in a fully theorized understanding of class conflict. The conceptual framework is detailed in the chapter 'Subcultures, Cultures and Class' (Clarke et al., 1976) from the collection *Resistance through Rituals* (Hall and Jefferson, 1976). Their argument is that 'cultural configurations will not only be subordinate to [the] dominant order: they will enter into struggle with it, seek to modify, resist or even overthrow its reign – its *hegemony*' (ibid.: 12; emphasis in original). The various post-war working-class youth subcultures discussed in the book are seen as movements that win back space, through issuing challenges to the status quo. However, these are not political solutions. Resistance is played out in the fields of leisure and consumption, rather than in the workplace. For Clarke et al. (1976), a key consequence of resistance through rituals and symbols is that it fails to challenge the broader structures of power.

One of the best examples of this approach is Paul Willis's *Learning to Labor* (1977), an ethnographic study of how school prepares young people for different positions in the labour market, as signalled very clearly in the title and the subtitle: *How Working Class Kids Get Working Class Jobs*. In his analysis of a Midlands secondary school he followed a group of working-class boys – the 'lads' – who oppose school authority and develop a subculture of nonconformity. Yet what he demonstrates is that the oppositional school culture of the lads offers only a limited resistance, and in fact prepares them for the shop-floor culture of general labouring. In other words, having a laugh, skiving, being tough, sexism and racism are all forms of preparation for coping with work and will eventually trap them in dead-end jobs. The overall point is that symbolic resistance expresses the frustrations of working-class youth but will never develop into real power. In fact, as Willis's (1977) work tragically attests, the resistance reinforces inequality.

The Centre's most substantial work is *Policing the Crisis* (Hall *et al.*, 1978), in which Stuart Hall collaborated with Chas Critcher, Tony Jefferson, John Clarke and Brian Roberts to produce the most sophisticated statement of a 'fully social theory of deviance' (Taylor *et al.*, 1973) yet achieved. The book analyses the hegemonic crisis in the United Kingdom that began in the late 1960s and anticipates the victory of Margaret Thatcher's authoritarian 'law and order' programme in the 1979 general election. The first half of the book explores the moral panic that developed in Britain in the early 1970s over the phenomenon of mugging, and the authors demonstrate how the police, media and judiciary interact to produce ideological closure around the issue. Black youth are cast as the folk devil in police and media portrayals of the archetypal mugger – a scapegoat for all social anxieties produced by the changes to an affluent, but destabilized, society.

In the second half of the book they chart how the rapid deterioration of Britain's economic condition from the late 1960s meant that hegemony became increasingly difficult to sustain and the state turned from governance through consent to the adoption of coercion to control the crisis. The state's primary concern is to deflect the crisis away from class relations on to authority relations concerned with youth, crime and race – so that the white working class blame immigrants for the present conditions, rather than the faults contained in the capitalist system. In 2013 a 35th anniversary edition of *Policing the Crisis* was published with reflections from the authors on the continuing relevance of such an analysis.

In a discussion of the 'politics of "mugging"', Hall and his colleagues (1978) attempt to explain the rise in black criminality, which they see largely as the result of police labelling. But they do concede, within a broader consideration of black culture, consciousness and resistance, that some are forced into crime as a result of unemployment and a subcultural refusal to accept the lumpen role assigned to them under capitalism.

Some problems

Stanley Cohen (1980) (see Plate 6.1) developed a forceful critique of the Birmingham Centre's work in the introduction to the second edition of his *Folk Devils and Moral Panics*, which has become highly influential as it suggests the gap that had now developed between criminology and cultural studies. He begins by explaining how the new subcultural theory of the 1970s sought to radically distance itself, in both time and place, from the American functionalism of the 1950s via the 'the latest vocabulary imported from the Left Bank' (1980: xxviii). Yet for all the obscure

Continental language, 'the new theory shares a great deal more with the old than it cared to admit' (1980: iv). The points of similarity are a focus on the same 'problematic':

- growing up in a class society;
- male urban working-class adolescents;
- delinquency as a collective solution to a structurally imposed problem.

Where the recent work does differ is through an 'over-facile drift to historicism' (Cohen, 1980: viii). What he means by this is that too much attention is given to contextualization and historical development within Birmingham work, which often involves a particular emphasis on 'a single and one-directional historical trend' (1980: viii).

Cohen also raises a number of objections against reading resistance through rituals and symbols, which can be summarized as follows.

1   It is oversimplistic to understand resistance only in terms of opposition. Some actions will be conservative, irrational, inconsistent and 'simply wrong' (Cohen, 1980: xi).
2   There is a tendency to read the development of youth style as internal to the group, with commercialization coming only later. This seriously underestimates the ways in which 'changes in youth culture are manufactured changes, dictated by consumer culture' (Cohen, 1980: xii).
3   Too often, subcultural activities are understood to be inherited from long traditions of working-class resistance which lead 'to the vexing issue of consciousness and intent' (Cohen, 1980: xiii) and the playing down of the meaning of style and subcultures to the members themselves.
4   He poses the question of why we should believe the interpretations offered of these subcultures and to what extent there is any sociological rigour in the conclusions drawn.

This is a formidable critique, and it is important to recognize that the Marxist emphasis on class was contested by feminists at the Centre in *Women Take Issue* (Centre for Contemporary Cultural Studies, 1980), and the relative neglect of 'race' was highlighted in *The Empire Strikes Back* (Centre for Contemporary Cultural Studies, 1983). Subsequent developments in cultural studies are too diverse to document here; but as we see in Chapter 7, there have been recent moves to take a cultural criminology further.

Hall and Jefferson (2006) later addressed the criticisms of the *Resistance through Rituals* project in a fascinating encounter with the many developments in subcultural theory that have occurred since the 1970s. One useful illustration of the continuing salience of the approach pioneered at Birmingham was the account provided to *The Guardian* newspaper by Angela McRobbie (one of the Centre's key members) concerning the 'hoodie' phenomenon that was receiving much media attention at the time:

> The point of origin is obviously Black American hip-hop culture, now thoroughly mainstream and a key part of the global economy of music through Eminem and others. Leisure- and sportswear adopted from everyday wear suggests a distance from the world of office [suit] or school [uniform]. Rap culture celebrates defiance, as it narrates the

experience of social exclusion. Musically and stylistically, it projects menace and danger as well as anger and rage. [The hooded top] is one in a long line of garments chosen by young people, usually boys, and inscribed with meaning suggesting that they are 'up to no good'. In the past, such appropriation was usually restricted to membership of specific youth cultures – leather jackets, bondage trousers – but nowadays it is the norm among young people to flag up their music and cultural preferences in this way, hence the adoption of the hoodie by boys across the boundaries of age, ethnicity and class.

(McRobbie, 2005, cited in Hall and Jefferson, 2006: xi)

Her analysis clearly echoes the earlier tradition by situating the origins of the style in a larger context and analyses the distinctive elements in terms of their symbolic significance (distance from the office, projecting menace, celebrating defiance, etc.). But it also moves beyond the classic position by suggesting how the hoodie crosses boundaries and the culture itself must be grasped through understanding the global economy of music. This way of 'acknowledging the new without losing what may still be serviceable in the old' is seen by them as a 'valuable motif to hang on to' as it is 'something our critics have not always managed to do' (Hall and Jefferson, 2006: xii).

Feminist criminology

Another important development within radical traditions was the arrival of feminist criminology in the mid-1970s. It is an odd irony that the conflict analyses of crime we have discussed long neglected the importance of gender – despite their focus on social inequality. If, as conflict theory suggests, economic disadvantage is a primary cause of crime, why do women (whose economic position is, in general, much worse than that of men) commit far fewer crimes than men do?

Until the 1970s, the study of crime and deviance was very much a male province. But the influential work of British sociologist Carol Smart and others changed all that. In Smart's book *Women, Crime and Criminology* (Plate 6.4), originally published in 1976, she both documented the ways in which women had been neglected in the study of crime and deviance and showed that when they had been included the approach had usually been highly sexist or outright misogynist. Much later, Frances Heidensohn (1987, 1996) suggested that feminist scholarship over the past thirty years in criminology can be divided into two phases. First, pioneering work that defined the agenda for the study of gender. Second, consolidation, with a range of studies produced in response to that agenda and debate over whether a feminist criminology is possible, or even desirable. Today there seems little doubt that feminist work in criminology has expanded but is not characterized by any single, unitary feminist or theoretical perspective (Renzetti, 2012: 132).

Broadly, we can suggest three major contributions of the feminist approach:

■ as a critique of existing malestream criminology – showing how women have been neglected, how they have been misrepresented and how they may be brought back into existing theories;

■ as a perspective to suggest new areas of study;

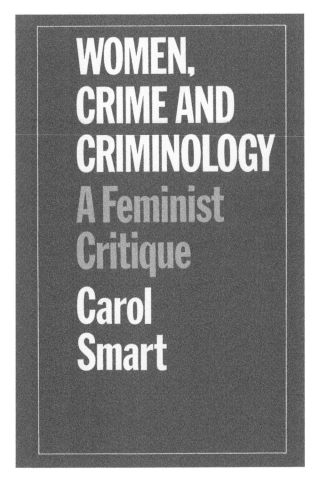

Plate 6.4 Cover of Carol Smart's *Women, Crime and Criminology*, published in 1976. Smart's path-breaking book brought women firmly into the sphere of criminological thinking.

Source: © Routledge.

■ as a way of bringing gender to the forefront and especially the role of men and masculinity in crime.

Many of these issues will feature prominently throughout the book; here though we introduce some of the initial challenges posed by feminism.

Critique of malestream criminology

In the 1970s, feminist criminology made its first contribution by making a major critique of the male bias inherent in the theories and writings of criminologists. Not only were nearly all leading theorists men, they also wrote almost exclusively about men – and when they did look at women offenders, it was usually with a set of assumptions that are at best called sexist. For instance, in one notorious case, a criminologist called Otto Pollak proposed that women are in fact *more* criminal than men: it is just they are also more devious and cunning and hence can 'cover up their crimes' better!

How does gender figure in some of the theories we have already examined? Robert Merton's anomie theory (see Chapter 5) defines cultural goals in terms of financial success, and this has traditionally had more to do with the lives of men, while women have been socialized to view success in terms of relationships, particularly marriage and motherhood (Leonard, 1982). A more woman-focused theory might point up the 'strain' caused by the cultural ideals of equality clashing with the reality of gender-based inequality. It could help us see that different forms of deviance may emerge for women: those that are linked to marriage and motherhood. Indeed, women who do not marry ('spinsters') and who do not have children ('childless') have often been seen as 'problems' in the past. Today different 'problem' labels may be common, for example teenage or unmarried mothers.

But feminist criminologists have gone much further than reappraising past theories and assumptions. They have opened up a whole field of new questions and issues. Among the issues have been the importance of the fear of crime in women's, and especially older women's, lives; the gendering of sexual violence, and especially the growth of awareness of domestic violence, rape and incest; and the gendering of social control.

One aspect of this has been the study of women in crime. Partly this meant the study of criminal women: girls in gangs, women prostitutes, shoplifters and other crimes with which women are more closely identified. But here we will just give two brief examples: the growing interest in the ways in which women are handled differently by the police, the courts and prisons (often through what is called a code of chivalry), and the centrality of sexual violence to much debate.

A code of chivalry?

Much work has focused around the exposure of 'double standards', sometimes related to notions of a 'code of chivalry'. Studies have been unable to come to cut-and-dried conclusions over the issue of whether men and women are treated in different ways by the courts. While some have suggested that women are treated more leniently by courts and the police, others have shown that women who disappoint or violate traditional role expectations can be dealt with harshly. For example, one study indicated that violent women offenders received more sympathetic and individualized justice for serious crimes, while men got no comparable understanding. But the majority of the research does tend to picture courts as places that have conventional and stereotyped views of gender roles, which they then reinforce in sentencing. Carlen's (1983) classic study of Scottish courts found that distinctions were made between 'good' and 'bad' mothers, and the kind of sentence they received depended on the category into which they were perceived to fall.

What unites most authors on this topic of chivalry or special treatment is that women coming before the courts experience what is known as the double bind of 'double deviance' and 'double jeopardy'. 'Double deviance', it is argued, arises primarily as a result of the fact that women's crime rates are so low. This has significant effects, because those women who do offend are seen to have transgressed not only social norms but also gender norms. Or, to put it another way, since courts are so unused to dealing with women offenders, those who do come before them are seen as both rule-breakers and role defiant – and they may be treated accordingly. For example, in Edwards's (1984) study of female defendants before the Manchester City Magistrates' Court, she found that women were much more likely to be subject to an oppressive and paternalistic

thinking about crime

form of individualized justice. She argues that 'Female defendants are processed in accordance with the crimes which they have committed and the extent to which the commission of the act and its nature deviate from appropriate female behaviour' (1984: 213).

The argument is that double deviance leads to paternalism and protectiveness towards women and excessive punishment for women who offend. As a result, many women offenders feel that they are placed in 'double jeopardy'. That is, they are actually punished twice. First, they face the usual sanctions of the criminal justice system, but in addition they may be more harshly treated because they are seen as deviant as women. Therefore, it is not entirely surprising to find that in most of the studies, women characterize their experience in the criminal justice system as one that is particularly unjust. It seems clear too that women also face informal systems of social control and justice. For example, the stigma involved in the loss of reputation is particularly profound and damaging. Carlen (1983) found that a number of women offenders received beatings from their husbands, as well as the punishment meted out by the court sentence. Similarly, Heidensohn (1987) argues that much of the sense of injustice felt by women who come before the courts stems from their perceptions of such agencies as male-dominated and unsympathetic to them.

Violence against women

Another major area of debate opened by feminist criminologists has been the nature of sexual violence. Domestic violence, sexual harassment, child abuse and incest, and of course rape, have all been placed formally on the agenda (they are discussed in more detail in chapters 9, 11, 15, 18 and 20). According to the United Nations, 'At least one in five of the world's female population has been physically or sexually abused by a man or men at some time in their life.' Figures vary across countries and for differing kinds of abuse; but that such abuse is both widespread and frequently condoned makes it a crucial area for understanding patriarchy.

Men, masculinity and crime

Having done this groundwork, feminists saw the obvious failings in criminology as it focused on men as men. Statistics repeatedly show that many more men than women commit crimes. Indeed, as Richard Collier notes, 'most crimes would remain unimaginable without the presence of men' (Collier, 1998; see also Jefferson, 2002b). This dimension had been ignored – it was a key missing link. One further contribution of feminist criminology has been to raise the issue of men and masculinity.

If there is such a skew towards men, could this mean that the whole process of crime is connected to gender? It must be a strong probability. We are not of course saying that all men are criminal and all women are not; but we are suggesting that there is something about 'masculinity' – or at least certain forms of it – that makes it more probable that men will commit crimes. We need, for instance, to explain why it is that men commit more crimes and women fewer. And, indeed, once we start to raise these issues, a whole new field of questions and problems is revealed.

One issue becomes the ways in which girls and women seem to be more regulated. For instance, in virtually every society in the world there would seem to be more stringent controls on women than men. Historically, our society has restricted the role of women to the home. The family is their domain. In many public spaces and bars, women remain decidedly unwelcome: these places are men's domains. And more, women on their own in public places may be looked upon with some suspicion. In some countries the normative constraints placed on women are really very great: in Saudi Arabia, although there have been announcements that change will occur in a few years time, at present women cannot vote or legally operate motor vehicles; in Iran, women who dare to expose their hair or wear make-up in public can be whipped. They are severely restricted in their access to public spaces. In this sense, in many countries women simply have less access to the possibilities of committing crimes.

But another issue is surely the expectation in many cultures of what it means to be a man. There is now a very considerable amount of sociological and criminological research and writing on boys and men – on 'maculinities'. This term is used to denote that there are many ways of being masculine and of 'doing masculinity', and these change with different kinds of social order and society. At the same time, many researchers argue that patriarchy is a key feature of society and underpins the ways in which men come to dominate women (in most if not all societies). These conditions are however bound up with particular times and places and hence are far from always being the same.

Researchers such as Messerschmidt (1993, 2000), Collier (1998), Jefferson (2002b) and Mac an Ghaill (1994) have looked at boys and men in their variety to identify the processes involved in developing different kinds of masculinity. They tend to suggest that there is a dominant mode of masculinity to be found in many societies (what is sometimes called hegemonic masculinity) that highlights such issues as power, dominance, aggressiveness, achievement, competition, status attainment, and the like. Masculinities are always worked at and always contested: they are never fixed and stable once and for all. And researchers also sense a variety of alternative masculinities that develop – sometimes linked to ethnicity, or being gay, or resisting common or dominant patterns (as in some versions of the men's movement). Their concerns suggest that men can be seen often as 'doing their gender' (i.e. performing as men) through various criminal activities such as football hooliganism, violence, road rage, rape and corporate crime. These crimes all have very different styles and meanings, but they can come to display men as certain kinds of men – congruent with what is expected in order 'to be a man'. This is an exciting new area of criminological thinking, and one in which more and more research is being conducted.

Foucault and discourse theory

One final influence on current thinking about crime and control must be mentioned here. One hugely influential inspiration behind many contemporary debates within criminology was the French philosopher Michel Foucault (1926–84). Having said this, it is very important to be aware that Foucault was not a criminologist and indeed had little regard for the subject. He was a philosopher of the history of ideas, and his work looks broadly at a number of institutions each with their accompanying knowledge. So the history and workings of prison and how criminology and penology grew to study and to shape these would be one example. However he also looked across the range of the human sciences and institutions that represent power and knowledge so, for example, he wrote on 'the birth of the clinic' as a distinctly modern way of handling health, on the development of the psychiatric discourse and modern approaches to madness, and the development of our modern languages around sexuality. His intellectual agenda was very wide-ranging and he even asks questions about the very idea of what it means to be an 'individual' human being in Western societies.

Foucault questions the roots and patterns of ideas found in social life and how they help to construct what is going on in social worlds. He holds no simple view of 'cause and effect' or of knowledge being linear and straightforward – the way we sometimes explain problems or present the history of ideas in textbooks! Instead, he sees ideas as circulating in local complexes. They are disordered, contradictory, fragmentary. We can see the influence of his work in discussions elsewhere in this book when we examine his comparison of the transition from forms of punishment in the *ancien régime* classical societies (which focus on the body, especially physical torture) to the micro-politics of modern, capitalist societies (which focus on surveillance, classification and **normalization** – especially through the medium of prisons). His concern – and criticism – about criminology is that he sees it emerging as a discipline at the same time as a whole new apparatus of crime control is brought into being. The whole profession of criminology, he suggests, is there not really to solve the problem of crime but to extend and organize power and surveillance.

Always a radical and critical thinker, he identified and emphasized dramatic ruptures with the past and suggested that these modern developments are not signs of simple 'enlightened' progress, but rather evidence of the extension of power and increasing surveillance. It is easy to see how the work of Stan Cohen (1985) on social control systems was influenced by Foucault. For Foucault, power is everywhere and works its way through **discourses** – bodies of ideas and language, often backed up by institutions. Thus, criminology is a discourse that invents or

Plate 6.5 Michel Foucault (1926–84). Foucault was a leading critical thinker who debunked the notion of criminology as a science. His *Discipline and Punish* (1977) had a striking impact on criminological study, but in many ways, as a philosopher of the history of ideas, he was an anti-criminologist.

Source: Magnum Photos; *photo:* Martine Franck.

produces its own set of ideas and languages about the criminal as an object to be studied, backed up by many institutions such as the prison and the courts. Power works its way distinctly through this discourse to help shape the whole society's view of crime. 'Knowledge' in this view may act as a way of keeping people under control.

Many of Foucault's ideas challenge common sense. Whereas some would present criminology as a *science* that studies and helps us to understand crime, Foucault sees it as a *discourse* that extends surveillance and power relations. Whereas prisons are conventionally understood to combat crime, he sees them as mechanisms for extending crime. He is very clear what he thinks of criminology:

> Have you read any criminological texts? They are staggering. And I say this out of astonishment, not aggressiveness, because I fail to comprehend how the discourse of criminology has been able to go on at this level. One has the impression that it is of such utility, is needed so urgently and rendered so vital for the working of the system, that it does not even need to seek a theoretical justification for itself, or even simply a coherent framework. It is entirely utilitarian. I think one needs to investigate why such a 'learned' discourse became so indispensable to the functioning of the nineteenth century penal system.
>
> (Foucault, 1975/1980: 47)

As you can see, his ideas are controversial, very influential and much discussed. Some say he was one of the most brilliant figures of twentieth-century thought. Others feel that his difficult writing and complexity have detracted from engagement with what is happening in the real world (see also chapters 11, 15 and 18 for further discussion of Foucault's ideas). For some writers, the work of Foucault, and a wave of other French poststructuralist and postmodernist intellectuals, stimulated a critical challenge to modernism and the framework that shaped a modernist criminology (South, 1997). As Milovanovic (2012: 156) argues, this in turn gave rise to an 'affirmative postmodern criminology' that suggests that 'causes of harm' can only be 'understood in a holistic framework that recognizes both agency and structure as co-producers of the harm that it polices'.

Summary

1   Labelling theory focuses upon the societal reactions to crimes – the role of law, social control agencies, the media, etc. in playing their part in shaping the nature of crime. Far from crime control solving the problem of crime, control may actually serve to shape and structure it. Key theorists are Lemert, Becker and Cohen.
2   In the mid-1970s, the publication of *The New Criminology* generated a concern with a wider range of questions about crime and brought neo-Marxism and conflict theory to the fore.
3   The research of the BCCCS re-examined youth subcultural theories of crime, placing a much greater emphasis upon culture and cultural forms. It had clear links to Marxist theorizing.
4   The issue of gender was brought into criminology by feminists as a key element for thinking about crime.
5   Foucault sowed the seeds of a major 'anti-criminology' movement, arguing that criminology was a discourse through which power–knowledge relations were enacted.

Critical thinking questions

1   Discuss the ways in which criminology has become 'radicalized' in recent years. Has this radicalization helped to provide a more satisfactory account of crime?

2   What are moral panics? Identify a recent one you have seen discussed in the media. Does such a panic differ very much from the ones studied by Stan Cohen and Jock Young over 30 years ago?

3   Identify a contemporary youth culture. Which of the theories outlined in this chapter seem best at helping you understand it?

4   Trace the emergence of feminist criminology and assess its impact on redefining what criminology is.

5   How would you account for the fact that men seem much more likely to be criminal than women?

6   Given so much writing and talking about crime, why has there been so little success in its reduction?

Further study

Becker, H. S. (1963) *Outsiders: Studies in the Sociology of Deviance*, New York: Free Press.

Lemert, E. (1967) *Human Deviance, Social Problems and Social Control*, Englewood Cliffs, NJ: Prentice Hall. Two classic studies of labelling.

Maguire, M., Morgan, R. and Reiner, R. (2012) *The Oxford Handbook of Criminology*, 5th edn, Oxford: Clarendon Press. This has become a key text: very comprehensive coverage of the whole field of crime and control by specialist writers. It is, however, expensive.

Useful websites

Howard S. Becker Homepage
http://home.earthlink.net/~hsbecker/
A comprehensive site with a selection of published papers and links.

The Rich Get Richer and the Poor Get Prison
http://paulsjusticepage.com/reiman.htm
A companion website for Jeffrey Reiman's book: *The Rich Get Richer and the Poor Get Prison: Ideology, Class, and Criminal Justice*, 10th edition (2012).

chapter 7

Crime, Social Theory and Social Change

Key issues

- What is a late modern world and how is crime changing within it?
- What is the link between postmodernism and crime?
- What is the globalization of crime?
- What is the impact of the 'risk society' on crime?

Introduction

The past few chapters have suggested a number of ways of thinking about crime that have been developed by criminologists over the past century and a half. Some of the ideas are now seen as outdated, but in general they have all provoked thought and can often be seen to persist – in new forms – to this day. We are still interested in ideas of the criminal person and of justice (Chapter 4). We still look at social explanations of crime and delinquency – such as the ideas established by the Chicago School (Chapter 5). And labelling, conflict theory and feminist theory are very much alive and well (Chapter 6). In this chapter, we will consider a few of the newer social trends as a background to the rest of the book. Once again, some of the ideas will be taken up in more detail later.

   At the heart of this chapter is the idea that the world we live in is undergoing significant and continual social change and that this is having an impact on both the ways we think about crime and on the nature of crime itself. This chapter will suggest four general trends, each of which has specific implications for criminological thinking. These are:

- the movement to a late modern society;
- the drift towards postmodernism;
- the speeding up of globalization;
- the emergence of a risk society.

While these new times call for new ways of approaching questions of crime, punishment and security, it is important to recognize that criminology is always confronted by complex social processes and it is this dynamic of continuity and change that shapes the world around us.

Crime and the movement to late modernity

Over the last couple of decades many sociologists have suggested that a somewhat different kind of society is in the making. In the past, a key distinction that drove sociological work was that between traditional and modern society (Kivisto, 1998). For Marx, this was a move towards capitalism with growing conflict and exploitation; for Durkheim, it was a shift from mechanical society to organic solidarity (from a society based on similarity to one based on differences). And for Max Weber, this was a move towards increased bureaucratization – a process which the contemporary sociologist George Ritzer (2002) has called **McDonaldization**, whereby the principles of the fast food industry – efficiency, calculability, predictability and control – become increasingly applied to all of social life.

However, the modern world is now seen to be giving way to a late modern world, or to what the sociologist Ulrich Beck calls a 'second modernity '(see also Giddens, 1990, 1999; and Box 7.1). As Beck powerfully states:

> We live in an age in which the social order of the national state, class, ethnicity and the traditional family is in decline. The ethics of individual self-fulfilment and achievement is the most powerful current in modern society. The choosing, deciding, shaping human being who aspires to be the author of his or her own life, the creator of an individual identity, is the central character of our time. It is the fundamental cause behind changes in the family and the global gender revolution in relation to work and politics. Any attempt to create a new sense of social cohesion has to start from the recognition that individualism, diversity and scepticism are written into Western culture.
>
> (Beck, 2000: 165)

The criminologists David Garland and Richard Sparks (2000) have succinctly described the 'coming of late modernity' in Box 7.1. Overall these factors imply, with some force, that new ways of thinking about crime and control are now necessary.

It is against the backdrop of such major changes that contemporary crime debates emerge and we can summarize these changes briefly:

- As we enter a period of mass consumerism, so desires for commodities are increased. The need to have commodities grows, and there is an escalation in credit card use, with a potential increase in fraud.

BOX 7.1 The coming of late modernity

By 'the coming of **late modernity**' we mean to refer to the social, economic and cultural configurations brought into being by the confluence of a number of interlinked developments. These include:

a the transformative dynamic of capitalist production and exchange (the emergence of mass consumerism, globalization, the restructuring of the labour market, the new insecurity of employment);
b the secular changes in the structure of families and households (the movement of women into the paid labour force, the increased rate of divorce and family breakdown, the decreasing size of the family household, the coming of the teenager as a separate and often unsupervised age grade);
c changes in social ecology and demography (the stretching of time and space brought about by cars, suburbs, commuting, information technology);
d the social impact of the electronic mass media (the generalization of expectations and fears; the reduced importance of localized, corporatist cultures, changes in the conditions of political speech); and
e the democratization of social and cultural life (the 'desubordination' of lower class and minority groups, shifts in power ratios between men and women, the questioning of authority, the rise of moral individualism).

The second great transformative force was the reorganization of class (and, in the USA, race) relations that occurred in the wake of late modernity's massive disruptions. This was made possible by the shifting economic interests of the skilled working class, the welfare state's self-destructive tendencies and the economic recessions of the 1970s and 1980s. In the end though, it was the political 'achievement' of leaders like Thatcher and Reagan, with their reactionary mix of free-market economics, anti-welfare social policy and cultural conservatism. Together these dynamics changed the collective experience of crime and welfare and the political meaning of both. **Late modernity** brought with it new freedoms, new levels of consumption and new possibilities for individual choice. But it also brought in its wake new disorders and dislocations – above all, new levels of crime and insecurity.

Source: Garland and Sparks (2000: 199).

■ The restructuring of the labour market can lead to much more casual employment and work patterns, with more people entering the informal or underground economy. The new insecurity of employment can mean looking for alternative ways of survival, and crime may be one of these, especially in the informal economy.
■ Changes in families and households have meant the growth of different kinds of household (from living alone to lone-parent households, from more and more people cohabiting to lesbian and gay partnerships) as well as growing numbers of women at work. These changes have led some critics to suggest that as the old traditional family declines, so the older controls

on behaviour become weakened (Dennis, 1993; Morgan, 1978; Phillips, 2001). Others predict that as the population becomes older, so there will be a growth of both crimes among the elderly and the elderly as victims of crime (at present they figure relatively low on both counts) (Rothman et al., 2000).

- As we experience changes in social ecology, so all manner of new crimes connected to the environment come into being. Some writers have called these green crimes (they are discussed in Chapter 19).
- Shifts in demography and city life brought about by cars, suburbs, commuting – we now see the development of a 'night-time economy', and all manner of crimes that are facilitated by movement (some of these issues are addressed in Chapter 8).
- The spread of new forms of information technology brings with it new patterns of crime – from cybercrimes to mobile phone theft.
- The social impact of the mass media such as film and television produce multiple images of crime which frame how people view criminality and how they adjust their behaviour in response (see Chapter 20).
- Since 9/11 the pursuit of security against international terrorism has posed significant threats to the very freedoms liberal principles were designed to protect (see chapters 21 on terrorism and 22 on state crime).

The exclusive society and the vertigo of late modernity

An example of how crime is changing under conditions of late modernity can be found in the work of Jock Young. In his book *The Exclusive Society* (1999a) Young explores three kinds of division: economic (where people are excluded from the labour market), social (where people are excluded from civil society) and the expansion of a criminal justice system (which excludes more and more people from daily life). Young suggests that whereas there used to be a more consensual world of conformity – work and family were core values and the world was 'at one with itself' (Young, 1999a: 4) – from the 1960s onwards we see a world becoming torn more and more by crisis: 'from a society whose accent was on assimilation and incorporation to one that separates and excludes' (1999a: 7). Yet pluralism also grows – what he sees as a diversification of lifestyles, the immigration of people from other societies, and the proliferating glimpses of other societies through global media. In this sense, everyone may now become a potential deviant. We have also seen the arrival of no-go zones, curfews and gated communities, while vast numbers of people experience penal exclusion (1999a: 18). In the new century the numbers of people imprisoned in the United States had risen to 2.2 million, and 1 in 34 of the US population are either in prison, on probation, or on parole on any given day (Young, 2007a: 12). As we will see in Chapter 18 the United States leads the way in confining its citizens through the phenomenon of 'mass incarceration'. What is more there is a clear racial dimension to this social policy, to the extent that 1 in 9 African American males aged 20–29 is in prison and a staggering 1 in 3 is either in prison, on probation or parole (Mauer, 1997).

Young sees crime as the defining feature of modern societies – it is everywhere. Despite attempts to 'sanitize' and order sections of late modern life (for example through the establishment of secure 'gated communities') crime remains ubiquitous, crime has moved from the rare, the abnormal, the offence of the marginal and the stranger, to a commonplace part of the texture of everyday life: it occupies the family, heartland of liberal democratic society as well as extending its anxiety into all areas of the city. It is revealed in the highest echelons of our economy and politics as well as in the urban impasses of the underclass.

(Young 1999a: 30)

In his *Vertigo of Late Modernity*, which Young regards as a sequel to the arguments developed in the *Exclusive Society*, he (2007a: 12–13) insists that vertigo is the 'malaise of late modernity' and it derives from two sources: 'insecurities of status and economic position'. On this reckoning 'turbo-charged capitalism' not only induces anxieties and insecurities in large swathes of the middle class, but also generates an underclass of the economically redundant that are associated with high crime rates in no-go areas of major cities. These are familiar arguments from his work, yet what is new in the book is the return to cultural criminology (through demonstrating the seductions of **transgression** as well as acknowledging the intense experiences of **humiliation** produced by social exclusion) and the place of terrorism in justifying state violence.

Postmodernism and crime

Closely allied to the above is the arrival of ideas and practices that have been called postmodern. **Postmodernism** is a much-contested term, but in general it suggests that a much less certain and more provisional view of the world is in the making. The grand or absolute truths that were being pursued in the modern world are now challenged and in their place we find partial and

Plate 7.1 Robocop – future image of crime control?

Source: © Rank Film Distributors, courtesy of the British Film Institute.

limited truths. Applied to criminology, postmodernism sees the whole modern criminological project as misguided. This is because criminology is seen to ask the same questions and comes up with the same answers despite its failure to ever solve the problem of crime. Postmodernism thus suggests that the entire criminological project, particularly its preoccupation with aetiological and deterministic explanations of criminality, has been misconceived, and that it is time to recognize that.

Postmodernism tends to focus on contexts and meanings that differ from place to place rather than on grander abstractions. It sees a world made up of many shifting differences. And this brings with it a whole series of challenges to criminology – many of which were already there in some earlier versions of labelling theory (see e.g. Cohen, 1997; Young, 1999a: 33). It is perhaps too early to see whether these challenges to criminology are going to become prominent, for in effect they would lead to the abandonment of criminology as a discipline as we know it now. The basic arguments of postmodernism emphasize that the search for a cause of the criminal, the search for general theories of crime, the look for generalities are indeed searches for grand meta-narratives that have now had their day. *There is no one story to be told of crime.* Stories of crime now become fragmented, patchworked, pot-pourried. Indeed, postmodern criminology would probably not have problems with any of the ways of thinking of crime we have outlined above until they make grand claims for themselves – as being the 'truth' regarding crime.

Our view is that postmodernism suggests *a more provisional world – one that is altogether less sure of itself.* Modernity brought many changes, and the criminological challenge of the twentieth century was to sift through these changes to 'solve' the crime problem. As was hinted at in Chapter 6 through the work of Foucault, criminology did not really work very well. Indeed, the more that people studied crime, the more crime seemed to grow! Although there has been much theorizing about crime, many criminology books written and many courses taught, we seem to be no nearer to solving the problem of crime. Criminology as we once knew it may well have failed.

In the twenty-first century, this late or postmodern world is an accelerating one in which there is an increased sensitivity to diversities and differences. In this view, the world becomes less dominated by generalities and 'master narratives', and there is a turn towards 'local cultures' and their 'multiplicity of stories'. As Rob Stones suggests,

> Postmodernists argue . . . for respecting the existence of a plurality of perspectives, as against a notion that there is one single truth from a privileged perspective; local, contextual studies in place of grand narratives; an emphasis on disorder, flux and openness, as opposed to order, continuity and restraint.
>
> (Stones, 1996: 22)

One study that claims to be a postmodern criminology is Stuart Henry and Dragan Milovanovic's *Constitutive Criminology: Beyond Postmodernism* (1996). It calls for 'an abandoning of the futile search for "the causes of crime"' and looks instead for 'the genealogies, drift, seductions, chaos, discourse, social constructions, structuration and structural coupling' (1996: 53) as ways of thinking about crime. **Constitutive criminology** is based on the key assumption that human beings are responsible for actively constructing their social world primarily through language and symbolic representation, but at the same time are also shaped by the world they create.

Constitutive criminologists argue that the basis of crime is the socially constructed and discursively constituted exercise of unequal power relations. For Henry and Milovanovic (1996: 116), crime is defined as 'the power to deny others their ability to make a difference'. For example, crime as 'harm' occurs when people have their property stolen from them or their dignity stripped from them, or when they are prevented from achieving a desired goal because of sexism, racism or ageism. Crime then becomes domination, whether by single individuals (e.g. robbers), collectives (e.g. organized criminals or corporations) or by state governments (as in genocide, for example). Furthermore, crime is the 'co-produced' outcome not only of humans and their environments, but also of human agents and the wider society through its excessive investment in crime – through crime prevention, criminal justice agencies, criminal lawyers, criminologists, crime news, crime shows, crime books, and so on. Indeed, similar to the abolitionists before them (see Chapter 6), constitutive criminologists see criminal justice as part of the problem, not the solution.

In policy terms, constitutive criminologists emphasize the need to transform the prevailing social structures and institutional systems of oppression and to change the ways we think and talk about crime (e.g. through an activist engagement with the mass media – see Barak, 1994, on 'newsmaking criminology'). Although some commentators have described constitutive criminology as one of the 'new criminologies' that warrants attention (Arrigo, 1997), others are more sceptical of constitutive theory's relatively unresearched state, the complexity of its arguments, its limited impact on revolutionizing mainstream criminology, and its questionable ability to offer practical strategies to reduce harm (Croall, 1996). Others worry that, despite its postmodern emphasis, it still manages to assert the primacy of criminology.

Postmodern philosophy has also affected criminology in another way. A number of criminologists have, for example, more or less left the field of criminology for other priorities – priorities that no longer capture and keep them within the field of criminology. Colin Sumner (1994) famously wrote a book-length obituary for the discipline. Carol Smart, in a now classic article, sees no room for feminism within criminology – even though this was indeed her earliest claim (see Chapter 6). She now worries:

> It is a feature of post-modernism that questions posed within a modernist frame are turned about. So, for a long time, we have been asking 'what does feminism have to contribute to criminology?' Feminism has been knocking at the door of established disciplines hoping to be let in on equal terms. These established disciplines have largely looked down their nose (metaphorically speaking) and found feminism wanting. Feminism has been required to become more objective, more substantive, more scientific, more anything before a grudging entry could be granted. But now the established disciplines are themselves looking rather insecure and, as the door is opening, we must ask whether feminism really does want to enter?
>
> (Smart, 1990: 83)

It is an irony of the times that some criminologists have decided to leave the field altogether for other (usually political) concerns at the very time when criminology has never been more popular among students. Indeed, one of the most important developments over the last few years has been the emergence of a new cultural turn in criminology that attends to the disembedded, pluralistic, contested, mediated and hedonistic lifestyles encouraged by postmodernity.

Cultural criminology

The origins of cultural criminology can be traced back to the work of the Birmingham Centre and the New Criminology of the 1960s and 1970s, outlined in the previous chapter, but the 1990s also saw a resurgence of interest in the cultural (Ferrell and Sanders, 1995). In North American criminology Jeff Ferrell (1999, 2004, 2006) has done much to emphasize the role of image, style and meaning in illicit subcultures and the mediated processes through which crime and punishment are constructed. In the British context Mike Presdee (2000, 2004), Keith Hayward (2002, 2004) and Jock Young (2004, 2007a) provide some of the most influential accounts of the commodification of crime and the intense pleasures provoked when doing wrong. Each is influenced by Jack Katz's (1988) path-breaking book on the *Seductions of Crime* (see also Chapter 12 and Ferrell's (1992) review essay on the text). Although much cultural criminology has attracted criticism for being merely decorative or a ghetto of '70s retro chic' (Mason, 2006: 2) that makes many of the same theoretical mistakes as some 1970s radical criminology, it does offer fresh insight into how crime and deviance are constructed, as the following examples demonstrate.

One important article charts how the decline of 'underclass' discourse in the United Kingdom and the rise of the 'chav' phenomenon are intimately related, with the 'chav' representing a popular reworking of underclass ideas (Hayward and Yar, 2006). For example, the website www.chavscum.co.uk describes itself as 'a user's guide to Britain's peasant underclass'. However, a crucial difference pointed out by Keith Hayward and Majid Yar (2006: 10) is that the earlier commentary on the underclass relied on characterizing certain groups in the working class as suffering from a pathological relationship to *production* (i.e. work and socially useful labour), whereas the 'chav' is in contrast defined through a pathological relationship with *consumption* – manifest in the 'flawed consumption' of the lower classes. As they go on to explain:

> The perceived 'problem' with this 'new underclass' is that they consume in ways deemed 'vulgar' and hence lacking in 'distinction' by superordinate classes . . . 'chavs' and 'chavishness' are identified on the grounds of the taste and style that inform their consumer choices. Recent popular discussions correspondingly focus upon: clothing (branded or designer 'casual wear' and 'sportswear'), jewellery ('chunky' gold rings and chains), cosmetics ('excessive' make-up, sunbed tans), accessories (mobile phones), drinks ('binge' drinking, especially 'premium lagers' such as Stella Artois), and music (R&B, hip-hop).
>
> (Hayward and Yar, 2006: 14)

Using concepts derived from the French sociologist Pierre Bourdieu they describe how this is a way of thinking that not only pathologizes but also marginalizes people. Here, new forms of social exclusion may be seen as constructed through consumer aesthetics that discriminate on the grounds of taste.

Bourdieu would describe this antagonistic process as a form of 'symbolic violence' through which class inequalities are socially reproduced. Bourdieu's (1984) understanding of the sharp and often cruel class distinctions that lie behind judgements of taste has also been imaginatively taken up by Angela McRobbie (2005) in an examination of the forms of female symbolic violence found in mid-evening 'make-over' television programmes. Here women of recognized taste (the experts and presenters) publicly denigrate women with little or no taste. The most famous was the BBC's *What Not To Wear* presented by the very middle-class Trinny and Susannah, but there are also many newer hybrid genres that all rely on the transformation of unfortunate victims (with the help of experts) through the acquisition of status-enhancing forms of cultural capital (see also Skeggs, 2009). McRobbie (2005: 150) reveals how comments like 'she looks like a mousy librarian', 'ughh she has yellow stained teeth' and 'she looks like a German lesbian' involve a level of cruelty and viciousness that is 'reminiscent of 1950s boarding school stories where the nasty snobbish girls ridicule the poor scholarship girl for her appearance, manners, upbringing, accent and shabbily dressed parents'.

Globalization and crime

A third trend in which contemporary criminology must be located has been the way the world has become increasingly connected. This growing interrelationship has been seen to influence many criminogenic processes. These include the eased movement of illegal goods, people and money around the planet and, also, significant shifts in the way wealth and inequality have become distributed globally.

BOX 7.2 What does globalization mean?

Globalization is a very controversial topic and it has now entered criminology. What might it mean?

- 'Globalisation has something to do with the thesis that we all now live in one world' (Giddens, 1999).

- 'The process of increasing interconnectedness between societies such that events in one part of the world more and more have effects on peoples and societies far away' (Baylis and Smith, 1997: 7).

- 'Globalisation . . . refers both to the compression of the world and the intensification of consciousness of the world as a whole. . . . [It] does not simply refer to the objectiveness of increasing interconnectedness. It also refers to cultural and subjective matter, namely the scope and depth of consciousness of the world as a single place' (Robertson, 1992: 8).

Globalization

Globalization has become a popular term over the past decade, and is used to cover a wide array of concerns but its meaning is far from clear. To start with, and simply, we can define it as *the increasing interconnectedness of societies*. **Globalization of crime** may then be seen as *the increasing interconnectedness of crime across societies*.

Globalization refers to the various processes by which the peoples of the world are incorporated into a single world or global society (Albrow, 1990). It suggests that 'we all now live in one world' (Giddens, 1999). More formally, David Held and his colleagues have argued that 'Globalization is the widening, deepening and speeding up of worldwide interconnectedness in all aspects of contemporary life, from the cultural to the criminal, the financial to the spiritual' (Held *et al.*, 1999).

We can get some quick idea of what is meant by globalization when we think of the imagery of worldwide multicultural companies such as Coca-Cola, McDonald's, Nike and Disneyland. These companies exist across the globe – and in a number of ways. They *produce* goods across many countries; they *market* goods across many countries; and they *present* their logos and images, which travel the globe ahead of them. Think of how almost identical McDonald's outlets can be found in many countries – even though the company had its origins in the United States. McDonald's are simultaneously loved by millions and hated by millions – as signs of convenience and the modern world, and as signs of corporation takeover and mass culture. Crime can be seen like this. It produces criminal goods, markets them and sends commodities – from arms and drugs and people – all over the globe.

But a linked concept is that of *glocalization* (Robertson, 1995), meaning that each community adapts and responds to the global flow. McDonald's is never quite the same in each country; there are modifications made. And this is true of global crime patterns too: although drug trafficking may involve globalization – flows across the world – each culture has its distinct values and communities, which make its specific responses different.

The sociologist Manuel Castells (1998: ch. 3) has written about the 'global criminal economy' and, following the United Nations Conference on Transnational Crime in 1994, identified at least six main forms it is taking across the world:

- *Arms and weapons trafficking*. This is a multibillion-dollar industry whereby states or guerrilla groups are provided with weapons they should not have.
- *Trafficking in nuclear materials*. This entails the smuggling of nuclear weapon materials.
- *Smuggling of migrants*. There is now a widespread trade in people desperate to leave their home country to find security, work and a new way of life. Some have estimated this to have involved around 27 million people (Bales, 1999). One account estimates that Chinese criminal gangs (Triads) alone make some $2.5 billion a year in trafficking migrants – often with disastrous consequences (Cohen and Kennedy, 2000: 154). For instance, in 2000 some 58 Chinese people being smuggled into the United Kingdom were found dead on arrival; they had been packed into a lorry in unbearable conditions, with air vents closed. The driver was sent to prison for 14 years.
- *Trafficking in women and children*, often linked to prostitution. Significant numbers of women and children may be moved from one country (usually the poor of Eastern Europe or the poor of Asia and Latin America) to richer countries where new sex markets are appearing (Lee, 2011).

- *Trafficking in body parts*, often called 'the new cannibalism'. Nancy Scheper-Hughes and Lois Wacquant say, 'we are now eyeing each other's bodies greedily as a potential source of detachable spare parts with which to extend our lives' (2002: 14). There is now a worldwide and thriving market in body organs from both live and dead donors. Sometimes these organs are taken from condemned or even executed prisoners (especially in China, where it is estimated that perhaps 2,000 organs are removed and sold each year (*New Internationalist*, April 1998: 15–17)). The flow is typically only one way: from the desperate poor to the needy rich (Scheper-Hughes and Wacquant, 2002).

- *Money laundering*. The increasing globalization of markets has generated multiple opportunities for criminal enterprise. The growth of **money laundering**, particularly from drug-related crime, has become a major route for the incursion of criminal activity into the legitimate economic sector. Indeed, the acceleration of free-market policies, the internationalization of major speculative financial activity, the deregulation of stock exchanges since the 1980s combined with the growing bureaucratic complexity of corporate enterprises have expanded the range, scale and opportunities for all kinds of financial crime (Carrabine *et al.*, 2002: 60).

BOX 7.3 International trafficking

The illegal drug trade is found all over the world: cocaine in Colombia and the Andes, opium/heroin from the Southeast Asian Golden Triangle, all along the Mexican border, Turkey and the Balkans, or Afghanistan and Central Asia (Castells, 1998: 169). In part, the proliferation of illegal drugs in the United States and Europe stems from 'demand': there is a very profitable market for cocaine and other drugs, as well as many young people willing to risk arrest or even violent death by engaging in the lucrative drug trade. But the 'supply' side of the issue also propels drug trafficking. In the South American nation of Colombia, at least 20 per cent of the people depend on cocaine production for their livelihood. Furthermore, not only is cocaine Colombia's most profitable export, but it outsells all other exports combined (including coffee). Clearly, then, understanding crimes such as drug dealing requires the analysing of social conditions both in the country of consumption and around the world. More and more, the comprehension of crime and deviance requires moving beyond the borders of one country to look at a host of international connections (see also Chapter 14).

For Manuel Castells, the global criminal economy of trafficking (of drugs, arms, people) has expanded its realm to 'an extraordinary diversity of operations, making it an increasingly diversified, and interconnected, global industry'. Human trafficking is commonly understood to involve a variety of crimes and abuses associated with the recruitment, movement and sale of people (including body parts) into a range of exploitative conditions around the world. There is a substantial amount of literature that points to the structural and ideological conditions in a globally stratified order which are conducive to the trafficking and forced migratory movements of men and women, including economic crises, lack of sustainable livelihoods, political conflict, civil war, ethnic persecution, social inequalities, gender-blind macroeconomic policies and wider processes of global social transformation.

BOX 7.4 The globalization of social control

In addition to crime taking on increasingly international dimensions, social control has also become linked to more and more international agencies. A good example of this is the Centre for International Crime Prevention, a United Nations organization based in Vienna. Indeed, the UN has acknowledged the importance of crime prevention since 1948. At present it has three central programmes:

- The Global Programme against Corruption, which provides technical cooperation to a selection of developing and transitional countries, providing analyses of current problems and policies.
- The Global Programme against the Trafficking in Human Beings, which, as its name suggests, addresses trafficking in human beings, especially women and children. In a selection of countries, new structures are emerging for collaboration between police, immigration authorities, victim support groups and the judiciary, both within countries and internationally (linking countries of origin to destination countries).
- The programme for Assessing Transnational Organized Crime Groups: Dangerousness and Trends looks at organized crime groups across the world, focusing on forecasting future developments and strategies of such groups in order to facilitate the formulation of pre-emptive responses.

Rebirth of human rights theories

One of the consequences of global theories has been a major worldwide resurgence of interest in ideas concerning human rights (see Box 7.5), much of which is linked not just to rights but also to governmental mechanisms and crime. David Held and his colleagues refer to the 'human rights regime' that is spreading around the world, and cite an Argentinian human rights campaigner, Emilio Mignone, as saying 'The defense of human dignity knows no boundaries' (Held *et al.*, 1999: 65–70). There are over 200 human rights non-governmental organizations in the United States, a similar number in the United Kingdom and the rest of Europe, and the number is growing all the time. Criminology's global concerns have aroused more and more interest in such rights issues (see Chapter 21), while Lydia Morris's (2006) edited collection shows how the different traditions in sociology can contribute to the theory and practice of rights.

The risk society: actuarial justice and contradictory criminologies

A fourth major theme in social theories of the late modern world is that of 'risk'. 'Risk' is now a dominant theme in contemporary life, to the extent that virtually everything we do has some danger associated with it. There are two dominant explanations of our contemporary pre-occupation with risk (Johnston, 2000: 23).

One originates in the sociology of modernity and is primarily concerned with the emergence of an entirely new set of 'risky' social circumstances. Anthony Giddens in his book *The Consequences of Modernity* (1990) argues that one of the defining features of late modernity is the development of a 'calculative attitude' in individuals and institutions to deal with the issues of risk, trust and security in what are seen as troubling times. He sees risk as being globalized (something that exists on a global scale rather than at a local level) yet also personalized, as it is built into people's subjective concerns about their identity.

Giddens's argument has much in common with Ulrich Beck's (1992) discussion of what he calls the 'risk society'. For Beck, the 'risk society' is a distinct stage of modernity that has replaced the 'class society' of the industrial era. He argues that politics in class society was concerned not with risk but with the 'attainment and retention of social wealth' (Taylor, 1999: 207). In contrast, in the *world risk society*, new technologies are generating risks that are of a quite different order from those found throughout earlier human history. Of course, past societies were risky and dangerous places too – whole populations could be wiped out by major earthquakes, floods or plagues, for example. But Beck argues that new kinds of risks appear with the industrial world which are not 'in nature' but 'anthropogenic', that is, 'manufactured' by highly developed human societies.

These are associated with the many new technologies that generate new dangers to lives and the planet itself. They are humanly produced, may have massive unforeseen consequences, and may take many, many thousands of years to reverse. These 'manufactured risks' are taking us to the edge of catastrophe. The list of examples of new risks could be quite long: the changes in work and family patterns, fallout from the atomic bomb, the spread of networks of cars and planes throughout the planet, the arrival of AIDS as a major world pandemic, the development of genetically modified crops, the cloning of animals (and people), the deforestation of the planet, 'designer children' and 'surrogate mothering', the intensity of computer games, and so on and on. All have consequences that may be far-reaching and are at present unpredictable. Risk society, then, is a stage of development in which the pace of technological innovation generates global risks, such as nuclear war and environmental pollution.

The risk society is a society of 'fate' as it is maintained by some theorists that class divisions have been overridden by the similarity of destinies that we all share. For Beck, those of us who live in risk societies are no longer concerned with such matters as justice and equality. Instead, we try to prevent bad things happening, and consequently a 'risk society is one obsessed with security' (Johnston, 2000: 24). It is important to recognize that Giddens and Beck are concerned with the sociological preconditions of risk in late modernity, and neither explicitly addresses crime or punishment – although recent discussions of moral panics have found the thesis attractive (see Chapter 20 for further commentary on the reformulation of moral panic theory in light of these developments).

The genealogy of risk

The second major perspective on risk has a rather different orientation, and has had more of an impact in criminology. This can be defined as a genealogy of risk. Broadly speaking, there are a set of authors who have developed Michel Foucault's later work on governmentality (O'Malley, 1992; Garland, 1997; Rose, 1996; Smandych, 1999). In this work, risk is seen as a particular way of thinking born in the nineteenth century and is especially concerned with the historical development of the statistical and human sciences and their use of techniques to manage populations through health, welfare and social security reforms. According to this view, government during the twentieth century has become increasingly preoccupied with the management of risks through applying what are known as 'actuarial' techniques, which were developed in the insurance industries. What is important is that actuarial understandings of risk in insurance are associated with chance, probability and randomness as opposed to notions of danger and peril. It is important to keep this distinction in mind, for Beck and Giddens argue in contrast that in the risk society there has been an increase in the dangers arising from this latest phase in capitalism.

An especially influential statement of this second position is Malcolm Feeley and Jonathan Simon's (1992, 1994) discussion of what they term 'the new penology' in relation to a then largely unremarked set of transformations in criminal justice occurring in the United States. As they put it,

> the new penology is markedly less concerned with responsibility, fault, moral sensibility, diagnosis, or intervention and treatment of the individual offender. Rather it is concerned

with techniques to identify, classify and manage groupings sorted by dangerousness. *The task is managerial, not transformative.*

(Feeley and Simon, 1992: 452; emphasis added)

The new penology is based on **actualarism** – probability calculations and statistical distributions to measure risk – which have come to underpin correctional policies. Feeley and Simon (1992) give the example of how at one extreme the prison provides maximum security at a high cost for those who pose the greatest risk, and at the other, probation provides low-cost surveillance for low-risk offenders. They coin the phrase 'actuarial justice' to express some of the internal tensions posed by the new penology. Jock Young (1999a: 67) develops these arguments further and explains that actualarism is not as morally neutral as it may seem; rather it involves the stripping of human relationships of their moral worth, 'rendering them "morally irrelevant"' (Bauman, 1995: 133, cited in Young, 1999a: 67).

The importance of Feeley and Simon's argument lies not simply in their view that the use of imprisonment, probation, parole and community punishments has in each case accelerated in recent times, but in that 'the new penology is in part the product of a societal accommodation to routinely high volumes of crime, as well as of the refinement of professional practices for monitoring, surveillance and aggregate management' (Sparks, 2000: 131). In other words, the causes of crime are no longer seen as important; instead, probabilities are central, for actuarial justice 'does not see a world free of crime but rather one where the best practices of damage limitation have been put in place' (Young, 1999b: 391).

It is clear that these authors have identified a new trend in crime control. However, one of the defining features of contemporary penal policy and practice is that they are actually governed by contradictory criminologies. In a series of influential publications, David Garland (1996, 2000, 2001b) signposts a set of developments associated with 'the culture of high crime societies' that are heralded in two types of contradictory criminology. One he describes as a *criminology of the self*, which characterizes offenders as rational consumers – just like us. The second is a *criminology of the other*, which defines the offender as a threatening stranger who is not at all like 'us' (Garland, 1996: 446). The criminology of the self gets its support from a wide range of recent theories, which include rational choice theory, routine activity theory and situational crime prevention theory, that combine to form a 'criminology of everyday life' (see Felson, 1998). The defining feature of these theories is that they all start from the understanding that crime is a normal, common aspect of modern living. Consequently, crime has become seen as a risk to be calculated by both offenders and potential victims rather than a deviation from civilized conduct caused by individual pathology or faulty socialization – the hallmark of traditional criminology. Instead, the new criminologies of everyday life see crime as a normal outcome of everyday social interaction.

What is also surprising about these new theories about the everyday nature of crime is the way in which policymakers have enthusiastically taken them up. The key significance of these theories is that their programmes for action are not addressed 'to state agencies such as the police, the courts and the prisons, but *beyond* the state' (Garland, 1996: 451; emphasis in original) to the organizations, institutions and individuals of civil society. The implication, then, is that the state has a limited capacity to effect change, and instead these theories look to the world of everyday life to reduce crime. So instead of relying on prisons to deter offenders, or the ability of the police to catch criminals, the sorts of programmes advocated include things like 'replacing cash with credit cards, building locks into the steering columns of cars', using CCTV in city centres, closing discos at different times, laying on extra late-night buses and using special routes to and from football matches. The central 'message of this approach is that the state alone is not, and cannot effectively be, responsible for preventing and controlling crime' (ibid.: 453).

A central theme of neo-liberalism is being played out here, for what all these programmes are emphasizing is that citizens themselves must take some of the responsibility for controlling crime – a strategy that merges with privatization and welfare cuts that were characteristic of neo-liberal governments in the 1980s and 1990s. These are developments that have recently been analysed by Jonathan Simon (2007), where he argues that the USA is increasingly 'governing through crime' and Richard Ericson's (2007: 1) diagnosis of how neo-liberal politics encourages 'treating every imaginable source of harm as a crime' to be managed by the intensification of surveillance networks and the elimination of procedural safeguards in criminal law. Similarly Lucia Zedner (2005, 2007b) has emphasized how since 9/11 the pursuit of security against international terrorism has seen various provisions in the law become downgraded and even regarded as an obstacle to the fight against terror (see also Chapter 21). Thus, for example, criminal prosecution is increasingly viewed as an impediment to dealing effectively with such matters as anti-social behaviour and terrorism, so that the need for new measures (like anti-social behaviour orders and control orders) that bypass the protections offered by criminal law ominously proliferate. As McRobbie (2006: 82) suggests, the shoot-to-kill policy (Operation Kratos) that was suddenly introduced in the aftermath of the London bombings of 7 July 2005 without 'due discussion across the departments of government, only to be seemingly re-invoked following the killing of an innocent young Brazilian man on his way to work, reflects this cavalier relation to existing law'.

However, it is also important to recognize that accompanying this administrative, and largely technical, actuarial response to crime there has been an upsurge in the increasingly hysterical rhetoric and punitive language articulated by the political arm of the state. As Garland (1996: 460) argues, 'the punitive pronouncements of government ministers are barely considered attempts to express popular feelings of rage and frustration in the wake of particularly disturbing crimes', such as those surrounding the murders of young children that have been a deeply troubling aspect of recent times. These punitive responses are informed by a rather different criminology, which is of 'the other' and essentializes difference. As Garland (1996: 461) explains, it 'is a criminology of the alien other which represents criminals as dangerous members of distinct racial and social groups which bear little resemblance to "us"'. Consequently, offenders are defined as a different species of threatening, monstrous individuals for whom we should have no sympathy and for whom there is no effective help. The only practical and rational response is to have them taken out of circulation and incapacitated for the protection of the public, whether in long-term imprisonment or, as is the case in the United States, by judicial killing.

Indeed, Garland's (2005, 2007) more recent work has been drawn to the dynamics of capital punishment in American culture. He explains that for the most part:

> American capital punishment is not about executions (which are now relatively rare – more Americans are killed each year by lightning). It is about mounting campaigns,

taking polls, passing laws, bringing charges, bargaining pleas, imposing sentences, and rehearsing cases. It is about threats rather than deeds, anticipated deaths rather than actual executions. What gets performed, for the most part, is discourse and debate.

(Garland, 2007: 137)

As can be seen from Figure 7.1, the number of executions in the USA peaked in the 1990s, but since then the number of death sentences has declined – reversing the longer term trend which seemed to suggest a greater cultural acceptance of capital punishment. The reasons for this shift are open to debate, but would include the growing importance of legal clinics and innocence projects (Baumgartner *et al.*, 2008). While the number of executions has decreased in recent years it must be remembered that more than 3,400 prisoners sit on death row with more than 12,000 death-penalty-liable homicides occurring every year (Garland, 2007: 139). Research has consistently shown that ethnicity, class and the quality of legal counsel are the main factors structuring the death penalty. The result is that poorly legally represented blacks, convicted of appalling crimes against white victims, are the groups disproportionately executed (Ogletree and Sarat, 2006).

So, to conclude, contemporary crime control is increasingly dualistic, polarized and ambivalent. As we have seen there is a *criminology of the self* that characterizes offenders as rational

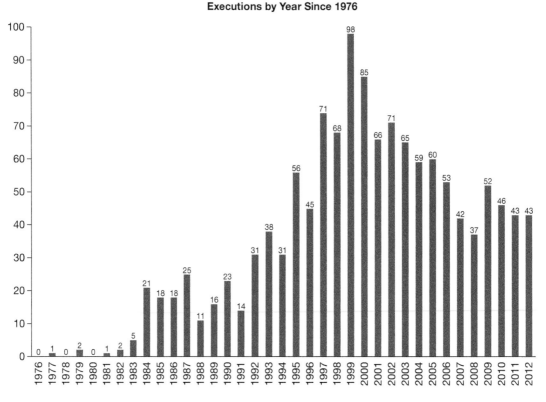

Figure 7.1 Death penalty executions in the United States, 1976–2012.

Source: Death Penalty Information Center.

thinking about crime

consumers, just like us; and there is a *criminology of the other*, which invokes images of dangerous and outcast strangers that are very different to us. In the former, crime is seen as a matter of routine, and the intention is to promote preventive action, whereas the latter is concerned with demonizing the criminal, while exciting popular fears and hostilities, and promoting support for state punishment. For Garland there is

> an emerging distinction between the *punishment* of crime, which remains the business of the state (and . . . becomes once again, a significant symbol of state power) and the *control* of crime, which is increasingly deemed to be 'beyond the state' in significant respects.
>
> (Garland, 1996: 459; emphasis in original)

One sympathetic critic has argued that while Garland has grasped some of the ambivalence generated by the state in confronting its limits, his account 'achieves its effect by ignoring an array of other responses to crime which indicate quite diverse agendas and assessments of the fate of state-based crime control' (O'Malley, 1999: 181). John Braithwaite (2003: 13), moreover, argues that 'Garland makes a number of statements that are wrong at worst, misleading at best'. This is because Garland overlooks social responses to crimes of the powerful, which would reveal a rather different and more nuanced understanding of cultures of control. Jock Young (2002), in an extensive review of Garland's work, applauds the many achievements to be found in the *Culture of Control*, but finds the book guilty of a number of serious elisions (between crime and criminology, the normal and pathological and the very comparison between the USA and the UK). Further critical assessments of the work can be found in Matt Matravers's (2005) edited collection of essays that picks up on the diverse ways that crime and social order have come to structure everyday life.

Summary

1   The contemporary world may be seen through the four key ideas of late modernity, post-modernism, globalization and a risk society.
2   Late modernity brought with it new freedoms, new consumption patterns and new possibilities for individual choice, alongside new levels and forms of crime and insecurity.
3   Postmodernism suggests that there is no longer any chance of developing one general theory of crime or one dominant narrative. Instead, the world is seen to be too eclectic and provisional to be understood by any single grand theory.
4   As globalization speeds up and makes the world more and more 'one place', so there is also a globalization of crime – with criminal activities ranging from money laundering to the trafficking of people – spreading across national borders.
5   'Risk' is now a dominant theme in contemporary life. It flags the ways in which the pace of technological innovation generates global risks, such as nuclear war and environmental pollution.
6   There is a criminology of the self in which offenders are seen as rational consumers and crime is seen as a matter of routine; and there is a criminology of 'the other', in which offenders are seen as dangerous and outcast strangers, exciting popular fears and hostilities, and promoting support for state punishment.

Critical thinking questions

1 Does postmodernism mean the end of modern criminology as we know it? In what ways is criminology changing?

2 Is it fair to say that late modernity brings with it both an increasing crime rate and different patterns of crime?

3 Select any two areas of crime and consider how far they have become increasingly globalized.

4 What is the risk society? How far does this impact on crime?

5 Outline some of the major social changes that sociologists have suggested are taking place in the contemporary world. What implications do these have for (a) our understanding of crime; and (b) the nature and patterns of contemporary crime?

Further study

Aas, K. (2007) *Globalisation and Crime*, London: Sage. A clear, perceptive and concise introduction to global crime and criminology.

Bauman, Z. (1998) *Globalization*, Cambridge: Polity. A useful general guide to globalization which does also suggest how the processes of globalization may well be generating more social disorder and crime.

Cohen, R. and Kennedy, P. (2000) *Global Sociology*, Basingstoke: Macmillan. Excellent student text on globalization, with a key chapter on crime (chapter 9).

Ericson, R. (2007) *Crime in an Insecure World*, Cambridge: Polity. Provides a rich account of how crime has become the central dynamic organizing social relations in Western societies.

Ferrell, J., Hayward, K. and Young, J. (2008) *Cultural Criminology: An Invitation*, London: Sage. A useful introduction to the field by leading exponents of this perspective.

Findlay, M. (1999) *The Globalisation of Crime*, Cambridge: Cambridge University Press. The first major study of crime and its global features.

Henry, S. and Milovanovic, D. (1996) *Constitutive Criminology: Beyond Postmodernism*, London: Sage. This is not an easy book, but it brings together a lot of ideas already discussed. Its claim is to build a new kind of constitutive or postmodern criminology that builds upon an array of different theories and that shuns any grand theory of crime.

Lee, M. (2011) *Trafficking and Global Crime Control*, London: Sage. A comprehensive and up-to-date analysis of this much discussed yet seldom researched form of transnational crime.

Useful websites

New Internationalist
This monthly magazine contains a wealth of global information
http://newint.org

United Nations Crime and Justice Information Network
http://www.uncjin.org
Provides links and information on the United Nations organizations combating crime on an international level.

United Nations Office on Drugs and Crime
http://www.odccp.org/crime_cicp_sitemap.html
The UNODC is a global leader in the fight against illicit drugs and international crime.

United Nations Interregional Crime and Justice Research Institute: LMS bibliographic Database
http://www.unicri.it/bibliographic_database.htm
The Library Collection includes some 6,000 authors, as well as more than 300 series and 600 publishers. Documents are classified according to the LMS bibliographic field structure and subjects are described according to the UNCRI Thesaurus: http://www.unicri.it/unicri_thesaurus.htm

United Nations Interregional Crime and Justice Research Institute: World Directory of Criminal Resources
www.unicri.it/html/world_directory_of_criminology.htm
This site contains more than 470 institutes covering some 70 countries. A number of countries, in particular developing ones, which do not have criminological institutes, have nevertheless requested that some of their bodies' services be included in the Directory.

http://www.culturalcriminology.org
A website produced by criminologists based at the University of Kent, UK, which provides a resource for students interested in this growing area of criminology.

http://www.governingthroughcrime.blogspot.com

Jonathan Simon's blog that interprets current events through his own distinctive criminological analysis.
http://www.deathpenaltyinfo.org
A useful website for data on the death penalty in America.

chapter 8

Crime, Place and Space

Key issues

■ Why are some places more 'crime-prone' than others?

■ What are the connections between crime, control and place?

■ What does it mean to think spatially about crime?

Introduction

Where does most recorded crime occur? Where do offenders and victims live and spend time? Are particular places perceived as more threatening than others and, if so, when and to whom? Is it possible to prevent crime by changing people's surroundings? How can we theorize the surroundings, environments and spaces in which we live? What does it mean to think 'spatially'? The aim of this chapter is to show how questions of **space** can enliven criminology.

Social life is conducted in social space. Consider the range of different spaces you might spend time in or pass through on a typical day: home, street, college, workplace, shop, library, bar, sports centre, cinema, friends' home. Consider by what means and at what times of day you journey between these spaces: bike, on foot, car, bus, train. Each space has its own internal rules of conduct – breaching these rules can create potential for deviance. Geographers argue that these spaces are not simply the inert 'backdrop' for our social interactions but that, by contrast, they help to shape the very nature of our social interactions (Gregory and Urry, 1985; Wolch and Dear, 1989). In other words, space has the power to shape social life.

What does it mean to think spatially about crime? A first stage is to ask *where* recorded crime *takes place* in addition to asking who commits crime and why. This helps to build up a profile of the places or environments where most crime and control encounters occur alongside profiles of offenders and victims. Criminologists began to focus on these issues in earnest in the 1970s, building on the earlier work of the Chicago School. Criminal justice practitioners now make routine use of crime mapping to allow them to observe spatial patterns.

A second stage is to consider *how places can be altered* in ways that might reduce crime. This can involve a number of factors, from definitions of what make a particular location 'crime-prone' or 'safe' to the arrangement and purpose of buildings to local beliefs or memories about a place. It can also involve a number of agents, from planners, developers and politicians who have the power to change spaces to ordinary people who have the everyday task of negotiating existing spaces.

A third stage is to consider *how we come to know about space and crime* in the first place and what we do with that knowledge. **Mapping** statistics has been the central methodological tool in this kind of criminological research. This necessarily raises questions about the source of the statistics and the nature of mapping technology. More recently, the importance of the Internet in both areas has raised the issue of global public access to this kind of **geo-data**. This chapter looks at each of these three stages.

Offenders, offences and place

Social scientists interested in place and crime have identified themselves with different fields since the early twentieth century. Chicago School sociologists used terms such as 'urban sociology', 'human ecology' and '**ecology of crime**'. In the 1970s and 1980s, 'environmental criminology' was used until similar terms began to be more frequently used in relation to green issues (see Chapter 19). Around the same time, many criminological debates moved away from a traditional focus on the causes of crime to a 'post-welfare' focus on crime prevention and management. One of the results of this was new work on 'situational crime prevention' (SCP) and 'crime prevention through environmental design' (CPED). At present there is no single term to denote the study of crime and place. Mike Davis explores crime and control in Los Angeles as an extreme example of the 'ecology of fear' (1999). Others refer to 'socio-spatial criminology' (Bottoms, 2012) or 'crime and community' (Hughes, 2007). On the more quantitative cartographic side, 'geo-criminology' and 'crime mapping' (Vann and Garson, 2001) are more frequently used.

Park and Burgess's work in Chicago in the early twentieth century foregrounded the relationship between urban environment, actions and values. They saw social science as a form of 'human ecology' (1925). Burgess's 'zonal theory of urban development' suggested that Chicago – and other large cities – was structured around five concentric circles (see Figure 5.1). The non-residential 'central business district' was surrounded by the 'zone in transition', an area of cheap rented housing attracting different generations of migrants. Next came three residential areas of increasing affluence. Other Chicago scholars built on this model. Shaw and McKay's (1942) studies of juvenile delinquency showed that a very high proportion of young offenders had grown up in the 'zone in transition'. They explained this as an effect of the 'social dis-organization' that characterized this area. A churning migrant population with shifting moral values, high levels of poverty and low levels of community cohesion produced teenagers prone to commit crime. More recent criminological research (discussed below) linking a community's crime levels to its capacity for '**collective efficacy**' have some clear links to these early Chicago studies.

If early work on crime and place focused on offenders and where they lived and socialized, later work from the 1970s onwards focused on offences and victims (Bottoms, 2012). One influential study argued that offenders tended to commit crimes in areas that were culturally familiar to them in some way but not generally their own neighbourhoods (Brantingham and Brantingham, 1991). Victim surveys (see Chapter 9) allowed '**area victimization rates**' (the level of offences against a particular group in a particular area) to be compared with '**area offence rates**' (all recorded offences in a particular area). Other studies, such as Baldwin and Bottoms's (1976) on Sheffield, questioned the link between offenders and 'zones in transition' in the UK context, stressing instead the importance of the housing market in shaping community relations.

The connections between poverty, place and crime are still much debated by criminologists (see Bottoms, 2012). Weatherburn and Lind (2001) find that 'economic stress' contributes to criminality because of the strains it places on parenting. Oberwittler (2005) argues that the effect of deprivation on crime is greater in the USA than in Europe because the USA, with its weak welfare system, experiences greater levels of extreme deprivation. He also stresses the importance of looking at economic disadvantage in relation to parents, friends, schools and other networks which make up a 'neighbourhood'. This emphasis on networks is echoed in the findings of Wikström and Sampson (2003). They identify two kinds of 'behaviour settings' in relation to crime: those that promote self-control and those that do not. They argue that it is not the setting (or space) alone which does this but the community connected to it. Communities with high levels of 'collective efficacy' – or high levels of cohesion and mutual trust – will be willing to intervene to challenge behaviour in a given setting and stop it from escalating. Communities with low levels of 'collective efficacy' – rather like those Burgess defined as living in the 'zone in transition' – will be less willing or able to intervene. A recent UK team-study of young people in Peterborough, led by Wikström (2012), extends this work (see Box 8.1).

BOX 8.1 Case study: Peterborough Adolescent and Young Adult Development Study: situational resistance and situational vulnerability

The PADS team, led by Wikström, interviewed the same 700 Peterborough teenagers at intervals over five years between the ages of 12 and 16. They asked them about their perceptions of right and wrong and to self-report their own wrongdoing. This information was anonymized and cross checked with local police records.

PADS' key finding is that low level crime peaks in mid-adolescence after which very few young people continue to offend. Most are 'crime-averse'. PADS analysts therefore focused on identifying factors that seem to deter the majority from further offending. They argue that those with a 'strong personal morality' (defined as understanding right and wrong *and* as caring about the consequences of wrongdoing) are more likely to be 'situationally resistant' to crime. This means that they are unlikely to see crime as an 'option' even when they spend time in settings that encourage crime.

By contrast, the minority of young people who continue to offend into their late teens are 'situationally vulnerable' to crime. They are an important group because they account for a high proportion of offending: just 4 per cent of the PADS' sample were responsible for 47 per cent of all self-reported crime in the study period. There are two aspects to their vulnerability. First, they are more likely to have a 'weak personal morality' (in that they may be aware of the difference between right and wrong but, crucially, do not care strongly about the consequences of wrongdoing). Second, they are more likely to spend more time in places where deviance tends to go unchecked by the local community. These are places that have a low sense of public ownership, such as a city centre, or a housing area with low collective efficacy. In short, PADS suggests that heightened youth crime occurs when certain kinds of young people (those with 'weak personal morality') spend time in certain kinds of places (where deviance goes unchecked).

PADS' findings offer an important challenge to routine activity models of crime. According to these models, most of us will commit crime if we have the opportunity to do so. Reducing our opportunities to commit crime, for example, by changing our physical situation (space) or increasing security, therefore becomes the most important means of preventing crime. For PADS researchers, changing space is only one piece of the puzzle. Building personal morality and community efficacy are just as vital.

Sources: www.pads.ac.uk; Treiber (2012); Wikström *et al*. (2012).

Spatial distribution of crime

So, what geographic patterns do we see in current recorded crime? Statistics for England and Wales show a very uneven distribution (Home Office, 2007a). Some local authorities have high levels of recorded crimes across a range of crime types. These tend to be large urban areas with a mix of richer and poorer residents: London, parts of the south-east, south Wales, the north-west and parts of the north-east.

However, patterns and concentrations of crime also vary by crime type. Figures for three types of more serious recorded crime – serious wounding, domestic burglary and robbery – across 376 local authorities in England and Wales demonstrate this. Robbery and serious wounding are both concentrated in a relatively small number of areas. Eighteen local authorities have robbery rates of more than three times the average for England and Wales (average = 1.9 offences per 1,000 population). Four local authorities have serious wounding rates of more than three times the average (average = 0.3 offences per 1,000 population). There is some overlap between these two but also some significant variations: for example, urban south Wales has high rates of serious wounding but relatively low levels of robbery. Domestic burglary rates are more evenly spread across England and Wales with just one local authority with a rate of more than three times the average (average = 13.1 offences per 1,000 population). As these figures and the maps in Figures 8.1, 8.2 and 8.3 show, crime can be highly localized.

Criminologists and policymakers increasingly use geo-demographic information systems to provide a more detailed analysis of the broad spatial patterns displayed in these types of maps. Data from the Crime Survey of England and Wales, for example, can be used in conjunction with the ACORN information system (A Classification of Residential Neighbourhoods) which

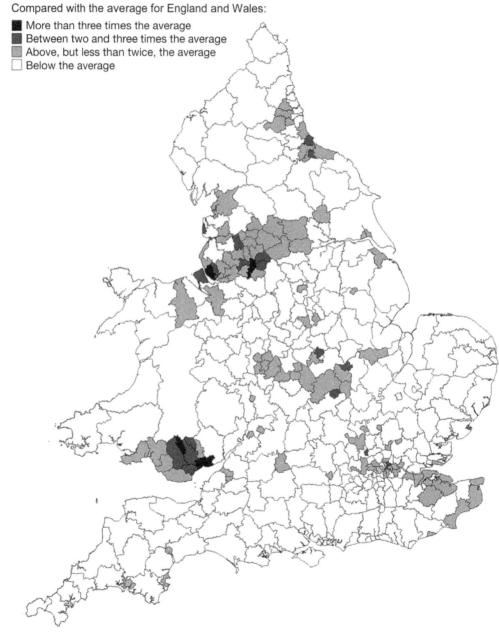

Figure 8.1 Serious wounding in England and Wales. Rates by population at local authority level, 2006–7.
Source: Home Office (2007a: 115).

thinking about crime

categorizes UK postcodes into types based on census data, consumption profiles and lifestyle surveys. Households can then be grouped according to the demographic, employment and housing characteristics of the surrounding area. Developed by a private company, ACORN has been bought by many government agencies and local authorities as a planning tool not least

Figure 8.2 Domestic burglary in England and Wales. Rates by population at local authority level, 2006–7.
Source: Home Office (2007a: 116).

because it presents household data in a more complex way than conventional classifications of class. Richer households are divided into three groups: 'wealthy achievers' (e.g. wealthy executives, affluent older people and well-off families), 'urban prosperous' (prosperous professionals, young urban professionals and students) and 'comfortably off' (e.g. young couples, secure

Figure 8.3 Robbery in England and Wales. Rates by population at local authority level, 2006–7.
Source: Home Office (2007a: 117).

families, older couples living in suburbs). Middling households are described as having 'moderate means' (e.g. post-industrial families, skilled manual workers, Asian communities). Poorer households are described as being 'hard-pressed' (struggling families, burdened singles, high-rise hardship) (http://www.caci.co.uk/acorn/default.asp).

The Home Office have analysed crime risk by ACORN areas. The two types of household at most risk of being a victim of crime (vehicle theft, burglary and violence) were those in 'urban prosperous' and 'hard-pressed' areas. The data also showed there was some correspondence between these figures and levels of concern about crime. Compared with the average in England and Wales, levels of worry about crime and anti-social behaviour were higher in 'hard-pressed' and 'moderate means' areas and lower in 'wealthy achiever' and 'comfortably off' areas. (Home Office, 2007a: 119–20). Urban prosperous groups' attitudes to crime are more complex. They may be less aware of, or less concerned about, the risks they might face. In the case of students they may have much less choice about where they can afford to live than others within this group. Other researchers who have used a similar approach include Pantazis (2000) in relation to crime and social harm, Chandola (2001) on fear of crime and area differences in health and Howe (2001) on deprivation indices and violence in the community.

BOX 8.2 Case study: the night-time economy and violent disorder

In many of Britain's towns and cities the expansion of the **night-time economy** has been an important way of sustaining urban prosperity. Profit derived from alcohol is arguably the driving force behind these developments, rather than the broader cultural renaissance imagined by more utopian planners who envisaged a flourishing of more inclusive European café-culture through this urban restructuring.

Many concerns have been raised about the serious health- and crime-related consequences of the lifestyles linked to the night-time economy revolving around weekend 'binge drinking', drug taking, risky sexual encounters, a diet of high-fat fast food, and the threat of fights and violent assault (see Chapter 14). The task of policing the night has become heavily privatized through bouncers and other forms of private security (Hobbs *et al.*, 2003) but continues to have a signficant impact on public services.

What kinds of social, political and economic forces have shaped this situation? Winlow and Hall (2006) argue that the resulting 'violent nights' are not just the product of drinking, flirting and fighting but result from wider post-industrial restructuring, urban regeneration and broader cultural change. They document young people's feelings about work, relationships, education, consumption and leisure in considerable detail before analysing victims' and perpetrators' accounts of interpersonal violence.

The 'orderly disorder' and 'seductive hedonism' of a big night out leads many into apparently unavoidable violence. The violence gives an edge to the night and often results from the escalation of trivial altercations. It tends to be heavily ritualized, is scarcely reported and flares up in predictable 'hot spots' like taxi queues and fast food outlets. Some perpetrators are self-anointed urban knights on quests to punish the 'arseholes', 'cunts' and 'piss-takers' who cross their path. Others take themselves less seriously and their main motivation is a general 'liking' of violence combined with the 'ability to show fortitude, conquer fear and avoid humiliation' (Winlow and Hall, 2006: 158). What unites both victims and perpetrators is a 'stoical, fatalistic and reactionary attitude to violence', which 'is a deeply entrenched and highly reproductive form of "survivalism" that infuses the localized culture and *habitus* of its male members' (Winlow and Hall, 2006: 161).

Crime prevention, space and communities

So far, we have considered the connection between crime, community and area dynamics. This raises a further question – Is it possible to *change* these dynamics and the places in which they are played out in order to reduce crime? Can crime be cut by reshaping a space or altering community relations in a space or both? Criminological work on this first focused on changing spaces but has since moved on to focus on changing community relations.

Changing spaces: urban design and crime

US architect Oscar Newman (1972) used the concept of **'defensible space'** in the 1970s to argue that it was possible to modify the built environment to reduce the opportunity for crime and to promote community responsibility. Newman's ideas – which centred on public housing design – helped to shape new approaches within what was then still referred to as environmental criminology. 'Situational crime prevention' (SCP) and 'crime prevention through environmental design' (CPED) advocated changes in physical environments and physical objects within them. These strategies have gradually become part of everyday life in public, residential, commercial and financial urban sectors. Street fixtures – such as benches, bus shelters, playgrounds and lighting – were all increasingly designed to screen out undesirable activity. So-called 'tramp-free benches', for example, are designed to allow people to sit only for short periods and to discourage any longer term use or 'loitering'. Surveillance equipment and CCTV is used to monitor but also to deter wrongdoing.

In addition, new rules governing behaviour in many kinds of spaces have been introduced. Most UK football grounds banned standing on the terraces in the wake of the 1989 Hillsborough disaster and introduced all-seater stadia as part of a generally successful effort to combat hooliganism. In 2005, two of the UK's largest shopping malls, Bluewater in Kent and the Trafford Centre in Manchester, banned customers wearing hoodies and baseball caps as part of a general clampdown on intimidating behaviour, swearing and shoplifting (http://news.bbc.co.uk/1/hi/england/kent/4561399.stm). In 2008, there was a controversy surrounding the use of 'mosquitos' – devices that emit a high-frequency buzzing sound – to disperse groups of young people gathering in public spaces (http://www.liberty-human-rights.org.uk).

Urban design and surveillance were taken up by academics and planners at a time when the old focus on the causes of crime was beginning to give way to a new focus on the need to manage crime. SCP and CPED, for example, are clearly linked to Felson's (1998) 'routine activity theory'. All arguably see crime as an inevitable phenomenon that can best be managed by reducing the opportunity to commit an offence rather than by seeking to reduce individuals' desire to commit a crime in the first place.

Criminology remains divided on the implications of this shift. Some argue that it addresses the needs of and empowers those communities – often among the most deprived – that live with the realities of high crime rates. **Community safety** is identified as an important element in any kind of neighbourhood regeneration. Others argue that it fails to address the root causes of the poverty, deprivation and spatial exclusion which, in their view, lies behind so much recorded crime (McLaughlin and Muncie, 1999). Mike Davis (1999) offers an extreme but very interesting view here (see Box 8.3). His account of Los Angeles as an 'ecology of fear' reworks original Chicago School zonal theory and argues that the linking of urban design and policing has led to a destructive militarization of urban landscapes which protects privilege and punishes poverty.

BOX 8.3 *Ecology of Fear: Los Angeles and the Imagination of Disaster*

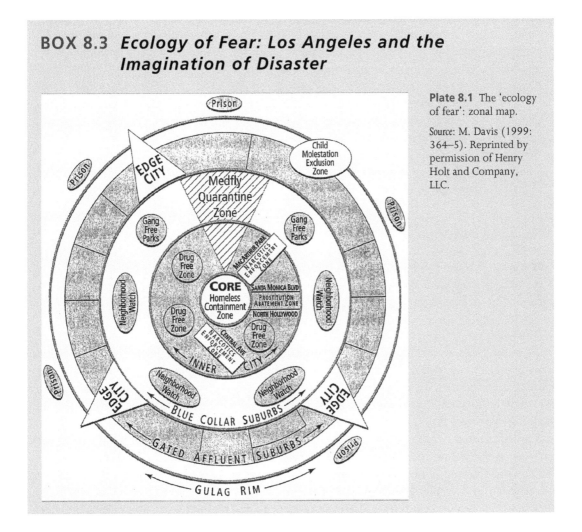

Plate 8.1 The 'ecology of fear': zonal map.

Source: M. Davis (1999: 364–5). Reprinted by permission of Henry Holt and Company, LLC.

Mike Davis charts the remodelling of Los Angeles' central downtown area in the years following the 1965 Watts Riots. Davis argues that, fearing a 'black inundation' of the old business district, leading landowners and financiers worked with the city police department, the LAPD, to design a new riot-proof financial area, Bunker Hill. The new area was put to the test in 1992 in further riots sparked by the televised beating of Rodney King, a black man, by white police officers. As Davis puts it, while other parts of the city were attacked and looted, 'Bunker Hill became a Fortress . . . Bullet-proof steel doors rolled down over street-level entrances, escalators froze and electric locks sealed off pedestrian passage ways.' The 'riot-tested success' of these defences 'stimulated demand for new and higher levels of physical security' causing a further 'erosion of the boundary between architecture and law enforcement' (Davis, 1999: 364–6).

According to Davis's zonal map, more affluent residential areas of LA and its surrounding urban areas developed 'social control districts' as a means of keeping out crime. Certain zones were designated drug-free, gun-free, graffiti-free and even child-molestation-free. This new 'disciplinary order' was created through the merging of criminal and civil codes with landuse planning into a 'new militarized landscape'. CCTV surveillance played a key role here – establishing what Davis calls 'virtual scanscapes', areas of 'protective invisibility that increasingly define where white collar workers and middle class tourists feel safe' (Davis, 1999: 366, 383). Outside these protected areas, life looked very different. Areas like MacArthur Park became 'free fire zones' where 'crack dealers and street gangs settle their scores with shotguns and uzis' and slum landlords conduct 'their own private reign of terror against dealers, petty criminals and deadbeat tenants' and schools became 'more like prisons' (Davis, 1999: 378). At the outer edge of Davis's zonal map – something which he says has 'no equivalent' in Burgess – lies the 'gulag rim' made up of the many kinds of prisons and correction units within the vast Californian penal system (Davis, 1999: 416).

Issues to consider:

- Davis's account is compelling but is it generalizable beyond Los Angeles?
- What are the social costs and benefits of neighbourhood regeneration?

Newman's own reworking of defensible space theory (1996) stresses the need to move beyond urban design to address community relations. People should feel that they 'own' public space and share a responsibility for it – not simply that they are being monitored. This kind of thinking is evident in the more communitarian approaches to governance that emerged in the 1990s and which are also very much linked to post-welfarism. New Labour's 1998 Crime and Disorder Act had a major impact on British approaches to crime and community. Crime was to be tackled not just by the police and the courts but by new Crime and Disorder Reduction Partnerships (CDRPs) which were set up in over 300 local authorities and maintained by the 2010 Coalition government. The partnerships require a multi-agency approach, typically involving the police, local councils, health authorities and voluntary agencies. The emphasis is on identifying both local crime problems and 'what works' to reduce these. There are two key strategies here. First, the community is 'responsibilized' as part of a wider dispersal of power (Hughes, 2002; Crawford, 2002) and, second, these new styles of local policing encourage a new kind of attention to local trouble spots.

Increasing interest in the localized nature of crime has led to highly localized policing strategies and even localized criminal justice legislation. Dispersal orders, ASBOs, curfews and other measures are all 'tailored' to particular environments – they aim to stop certain people behaving in certain ways in certain spaces at certain times. Civil rights campaigners such as Liberty have warned that these spatial techniques represent a dangerous trend because, among other things, they sanction a move away from the principle of a common, universal criminal justice system operating more equally across a state. They have launched a number of legal challenges to the government on these issues (http://www.liberty-human-rights.org.uk).

Some criminologists believe that this kind of work is valuable because it can show precisely *where* crime problems are and *where* police should target their resources. Echoing the earlier discussion of the night-time economy, Bromley and Nelson's study of alcohol consumption and crime in a British city concludes that 'a detailed knowledge of the variety of spaces and times of alcohol-related crime and disorder is key to the development of appropriate urban design, planning and licensing policies and can be used to inform a more closely targeted policing strategy' (2002: abstract). Others are less sure. Herbert and Brown (2006) argue, similarly, that relationships between identities, values and spatial environments are complex and should not be oversimplified. Finally, this kind of analysis may work for public order offences but it must be stressed that it does less to help police to tackle those kinds of crime which take place in private as opposed to public space – white-collar crime, domestic violence, fraud and state crime, for example (for a wider discussion on policing and place, see Braga and Weisburd, 2010, and Fyfe, 2004, 2010).

Living in spaces: everyday negotiations of disorder

Community safety has become part of the UK criminal justice policy framework. But, outside the policy framework, how do communities themselves negotiate crime, risk and fear in their own neighbourhoods? Many UK households may not be aware of the policies of their particular CDRP, for example, but have nevertheless developed their own ways of dealing with crime as it affects, or seems to affect, their everyday lives.

Feminist geographers and criminologists have investigated the many ways in which women routinely adapt their use of urban space in order to guard against possible physical or sexually motivated attack – taking certain routes, avoiding certain places at night, telling others where they are going and so on (Pain, 1991). This kind of work has since been extended to encompass other groups – such as children, teenagers and elderly people (Pain and Smith, 2008). One of the key points about such studies is that they highlight the importance of beliefs and emotions in establishing shared meanings around particular places or routes between places. A given place may have been designed as 'safe' but different groups of people may continue to experience it as risky or dangerous and act accordingly. Cultural geographers such as David Sibley (1995) have explored myth making, meaning and social exclusion in relation to 'marginal' spaces in ways which are very useful to criminology. Drawing on this, Millington's work on local reactions to asylum-seekers in the south-east of England bears this out (2005). Hostile locals tended to attribute much local crime to newcomers living in 'Little Bosnia' – an area which quickly acquired strong negative associations.

Modifying movements around space is one way in which people try to minimize their exposure to crime. Securing their home, workplace or neighbourhood is another. A further option is to relocate altogether. Beliefs about crime and safety play a significant part in determining whether a neighbourhood gains a reputation as 'rough' or 'desirable' and therefore in shaping the workings of housing markets.

The concept of **urban flight** or 'white flight' is relevant here. Derived from the Chicago School work on patterns of ethnic segregation, it has been used in the UK to explain the movement out of the inner city by both the middle and the working classes – a movement partly driven by beliefs about crime. In the 'home counties' of south-east England urban flight is shaped by particular perceptions of ethnicity with the inner city constructed as a hub of disorder associated with a large black and ethnic minority presence (Clapson, 2003; Watt, 1998; Dench et al., 2006). Watt argues, for example, that white East End Londoners have moved into neighbouring Essex because of their perception that 'their' neighbourhoods have been 'taken over' by non-white newcomers. Others suggest that this effect is only strong amongst the older generation (Scharf et al., 2003) and may be less pronounced amongst younger people who have grown up with multiculturalism.

Mapping and the uses of geo-data

As this discussion has shown, mapping (or cartography) is a vital research tool in studies of crime and place. From Quetelet and Mayhew in the nineteenth century to the first environmental criminological studies in the mid-twentieth century, maps provided visual representations of crime and a means of explaining its spatial relationships.

Satellite and Internet technology have transformed cartography, however. Geographical information systems (GIS) combine spatial analysis software, database technology and high-resolution satellite photography to create new interactive spatial visualizations of social science data. These developments are having a major impact on criminal justice practices. One of the first to be developed, Chicago Crime Map, offered an interactive crime map combining the Chicago police department's publicly available crime reports, Google Earth software and Google Maps website. Reported crimes were browsable by location, time and type in what became a classic example of a 'mashup' – a new kind of map combining 'two or more separate data streams to create original content' (Goodman and Moed, 2007). Mashups have rapidly expanded in the commercial sector and now have many civic and criminal justice applications.

In 2011, the Home Office developed the Police.uk website, a free public service offering postcode-based overviews of recorded crime. A recent enhancement to this site means that 'members of the public can now check the safety of their estate, village, or route to work by making their own personalized crime maps' (Home Office, 2013).

Sites like this raise issues about the status of what has been termed 'personal geo-data'. Sharing such data 'outside the context of its creation' has implications for privacy, transparency and ownership (Goodman and Moed, 2007). The site vastly expands the traditional relationship between the police and the public. The police, a public body, have always produced information about private citizens in the public interest. In the past, this data has been circulated by the media and other channels but in a very selective way. The combination of Internet, browser and GIS technologies now allow crime data to be delivered in completely new ways – in a comprehensive, spatial and visual format, which can be used by individuals much more on their own, 'hyperlocal' terms. It remains to be seen what impact access to such information will have on 'democratizing' public experiences and perceptions of crime as well as on authorities' abilities and desire to present crime figures in particular ways. These democratizing tendencies will have to be balanced alongside serious questions of civil liberties. Does the resident whose home is identified as having been the site of crime have a right to privacy? Do his or her neighbours (or local estate agents, schools or doctors' surgeries) have a right to know what kind of crime has been reported? If they do, should they pay for that information? Significantly, the pioneer in this field, Chicago Crime Map later became a commercial 'hyperlocal' crime news site, but was closed down by owners NBC in 2013 due to low profits. The public may be keen on 'hyperlocal' crime news but not so keen that they want to pay to view it online.

Critical cartography

Maps always need to be interpreted. They are never neutral despite the fact that we often treat them as if they are. Many geographers are very critical of mapping. Even the most technologically sophisticated maps offer a representation of a given area rather than a value-free 'real' view of it (Pinder, 2003). These critics argue that whenever we look at a map we see it from the point of view or perspective of the person or object with the power to 'gaze' out over the whole territory from a position of authority. Mapping has always been a powerful tactic of governance and surveillance. Colonizers, urban reformers and police authorities have always drawn maps of 'unruly' or 'ungoverned' areas in ways which justify their efforts to 'restore' order to those areas. For example, Blomley and Sommers (1999) chart the efforts of a group of marginal Vancouver residents to contest the way in which their existing neighbourhood was literally erased from maps drawn up by local planners seeking to 'regenerate' it. In another example, Kurgan and Cadora's mapping of 'million dollar blocks' (see Box 8.4) uses cartography to demonstrate the extremely high cost of incarcerating large numbers of residents from 'crime-prone' zones in US cities. Here, maps are used to raise questions about crime and power not simply presented as a tool in a crime prevention kit. This is a powerful example of what has been termed 'carceral geography' (Moran, 2013).

BOX 8.4 Radical crime mapping

The Justice Mapping Center (JMC) in New York takes a radical approach to crime mapping. It brings together architects, spatial information design experts and criminologists. It has provided powerful visual data to show that a disproportionate number of US prisoners come from a small number of neighbourhoods in big cities.

In an early eye-catching project, the JMC mapped so-called 'million dollar blocks' by mapping the home addresses of state prisoners in order to calculate the total cost of incarcerating large numbers of residents from single neighbourhoods. They used the example of Brownsville's District 16 which accounted for 3.5 per cent of Brooklyn's population but 8.5 per cent of its prisoner population. They estimated that, in one year – 2003 – it cost $11 million to incarcerate people from just 11 local blocks in the District.

In 2010, the JMC launched the National Justice Atlas of Sentencing and Corrections, that offers 'an online, interactive, mapping utility that gives policy makers, the media, researchers and the public a neighborhood-level view of where prison inmates and offenders on probation and parole are from and where corrections spending is highest'.

According to the Atlas:

- In New York City, neighbourhoods that are home to 18 per cent of the city's adult population account for more than 50 per cent of prison admissions each year.
- In Wichita, Kansas, where probation and parole revocations account for more than two-thirds of the city's admissions to prison each year, one-quarter of all people on probation or parole live in only 8 per cent of the city's neighbourhoods.
- In Pennsylvania, taxpayers will spend over $40 million to imprison residents of neighbourhoods in a single zip code in Philadelphia, where 38 per cent of households have incomes under $25,000.
- In Shreveport, Louisiana, nearly 7 per cent of all working-age men living in the neighbourhoods of a single zip code were sent to prison in 2008.
- In Austin, Texas, while neighbourhoods in three of the city's 41 zip codes are home to only 3.5 per cent of the city's adult population, they grapple with over 17 per cent of people returning from prison each year.

For more on this see:

http://www.justicemapping.org/
www.justiceatlas.org

Summary

1   Social life is lived out in social space. A spatially aware criminology considers the relationship between crime, control and place. Various terms are currently in play to describe this kind of work: socio-spatial criminology, geo-criminology, crime and community are all used.

2   Early work (from the 1920s) on place and crime focused on offenders. Later work (from the 1970s onwards) focused on offences, victims and urban design. Current work could be said to fall into two groups: (i) community dynamics in a given place, and (ii) high-tech monitoring of space and crime mapping.

3 Recently, criminologists have tended to focus on analysing formal policies aiming to change places and improve community dynamics. They have mixed views on the success of such policies. Cultural geographers interested in questions of crime and disorder continue to look at ordinary people's everyday understandings and negotiations of space and perceived risk.

4 Mapping is a vital if contested part of many investigations of crime and place. The transformation of the gathering, display, distribution and use of personal geo-data (which combines mapping, Internet and survey technologies) is likely to have profound implications for criminology.

Critical thinking questions

1 What do criminologists gain from looking at crime in terms of where it occurs?

2 Do crime maps change your view of crime rates? If you live in England or Wales, you can use the Home Office's Police.uk website or its Interactive Crime Map to compare police recorded crime at the local authority level: http://webarchive.nationalarchives.gov.uk/20110218135832/http://rds.homeoffice.gov.uk/rds/ia/atlas.html

3 Is it possible to prevent crime just by changing spaces?

4 What is 'collective efficacy' and how is it linked to a local community's sense of informal control over their local space?

Further study

Bottoms, A. E. (2012) 'Developing Socio-spatial Criminology' in M. Maguire, R. Morgan and R. Reiner (eds) *Oxford Handbook of Criminology*, 5th edn, Oxford: Oxford University Press. A broad overview of classic and contemporary studies of this field.

Braga, A. and Weisburd, D. (2010) *Policing Problem Places: Crime Hot Spots and Effective Prevention*, Oxford: Oxford University Press. Explores impact of concentrating policing within certain trouble spots.

Hughes, G. (2007) *The Politics of Crime and Community*, Basingstoke: Palgrave. Connects issues of space with community.

Smandych, R. (ed.) (1999) *Governable Places: Readings on Governmentality and Crime Control*, Aldershot: Ashgate. Suggests how and why control works through the control of particular places.

Pain, R. and Smith, S. J. (2008) *Fear: Critical Geopolitics and Everyday Life*, Aldershot: Ashgate. Asks why certain places and spaces generate fear for particular social groups.

Vann, I. B. and Garson, G. D. (2001) 'Crime Mapping and its Extension to Social Science Analysis', *Social Science Computer Review*, 19 (4): 471–9. An early article on the relationship between crime mapping and broader social science.

Useful websites

Peterborough Adolescent and Young Adult Development Study
www.pads.ac.uk
An ongoing 10-year study investigating situational influences on young people, in particular the impact of their families, schools and communities on their social development.

ACORN
http://acorn.caci.co.uk/
Segments the UK population by combining demographic data, social factors, population and consumer behaviour.

Police.uk
www.police.uk
Uses UK postcode searches to generate street-level maps and data about crime and policing.

Justice Mapping Center
http://www.justicemapping.org/
Provides visual data to argue that large numbers of US prisoners come from a small number of neighbourhoods in big cities.

Carceral Geography
http://carceralgeography.com/
A resource and networking site for those working on prisons, detention and space.

part 3 **Doing Crime**

chapter 9

Victims and Victimization

Key issues

- What are the different forms of victimization? How do they relate to power differentials in society?

- How does crime impact on individuals and the wider communities?

- What kinds of offences and their victims have been subject to most political and public attention, and which overlooked?

- What is the role of victims in the criminal justice process? What is their actual experience of the justice system?

Introduction

Crime is generally understood to be behaviour that is prohibited by criminal law. In other words, no act can be considered a crime, irrespective of how immoral or damaging it may be, unless it has been made criminal by state legislation. This conceptualization appears straightforward enough. However, it tells us very little about the processes whereby certain harmful acts and victims routinely come to be identified and recognized as part of the crime problem while others remain hidden. A critical approach to the study of crime and its impact on individuals and society therefore requires us to reflect on questions such as: What is 'criminal'? How do legal conceptions of 'crime' and its victims come to be constructed?

Clearly, victims play a central role in initiating the criminal justice process. Without them, much of the work of the criminal justice system would come to a halt.

The numbers and types of cases entering the system and thereby eventually providing the workload for the courts, prison service and other conventional agencies, appear largely to be determined by the reporting behaviour of victims and witnesses, not action initiated by the police.

(Shapland, 1986: 210)

While this quote is over 25 years old it remains the case that victim reporting plays a vital part in solving crime (Goodey, 2005). Even so, only a fraction of crime is reported to and recorded by the police and this combined with low clear-up rates means that only a small proportion of offences ever reach the court (see chapters 16 and 17). In all these cases, victim experiences can be prolonged and complex. An incident that occurred in perhaps a few minutes can become the subject of a series of inquiries that may last months or years after the event. Victims who come to court expecting that a trial will be an assertion of their wrongs can find that their probity is on trial as well.

So what do victims think of their experiences of the criminal justice system? Does the system fulfil their expectations of justice, or does the system further distress and disillusion them?

The role of victims within the criminal justice system

In contemporary Britain, the role of victims within the criminal justice process is largely confined to reporting the crime and/or providing evidence. The significance of the victim's role in these areas is compounded by the fact that the vast majority of offences come to police attention through a victim's report rather than through patrolling activities. Furthermore, most crimes are solved through information obtained from the victim or another witness rather than through leads developed independently by detectives (see Reiner, 2000; see also Greenwood et al., 1977, on the United States).

Historically, however, the role of the victim was very different and much more extensive. Until the establishment of the New Police in 1829, local governance was based upon the fundamental principles of deterring and solving crime through individual and community self-regulation. Most crimes were considered to be a private matter between the offender and the victim except, for example, in cases of treason or sedition. Private thief-takers established themselves to investigate offences for victims; many thief-takers also cashed in on the rewards offered by the government for the apprehension of offenders leading to conviction. The victim, or the victim's relatives or friends, would also make the decision whether or not to prosecute an offender, pay for a variety of legal documents and other expenses of prosecution and, more importantly, take on the role of prosecutor in court. This meant in effect some victims had greater access to justice, for instance men of property, than others, for example women, especially in cases of sexual offences (Emsley, 2005; Kearon and Godfrey, 2007). Examples of these early discrepancies in justice for the victims of crime can be found in the proceedings of the Old Bailey online (see: http://www.oldbaileyonline.org/static/history.jsp). Some criminologists (e.g. Scraton, 2009) would argue that access to justice for victims has been slow to improve and part of the reason for this is linked to the ways in which we understand victimization.

Defining crime and victimization

Not all harmful activities are seen as criminal. As Steven Box (1983) has argued, power may itself determine that the crimes of the powerful have generally been excluded from public perceptions of the crime problem and, conversely, the victimization of the powerless may be understated. Criminal negligence leading to workplace injuries and deaths, environmental offences, the manufacture and sale of unsafe products, misconduct of corporations, abuse of power by the state, and so on are rarely perceived as 'real' crime (see chapters 10, 13, 19 and 21). These are often offences that do not have a direct, immediate and tangible victim. They go largely unreported because of the problem of lack of victim awareness despite the considerable risk of long-term impact on the most disadvantaged as suggested by Walklate: 'it is the poorer members of society who are likely to be the least well-equipped to deal with loss of pension funds or long-term loss of work as a result of some accident or disaster' (2007a: 72).

There has been some attempt to broaden the definition of victims to include both direct and indirect victims, and also to include a range of abuses and harms relating to criminal abuse of power, such as the impairment of victims' fundamental rights, notably through the 1985 United Nations Declaration of Basic Principles of Justice for Victims of Crime and Abuse of Power (see http://www2.ohchr.org/english/law/victims.htm). Nevertheless, even when victims are prepared to take action, they and/or their families may have to embark on a long struggle to gain recognition of their victim status often through the formation of a voluntary issue-based pressure group.

BOX 9.1 The Hillsborough disaster

The Hillsborough Family Support Group (HFSG) was founded in May 1989 by a majority of the families who lost loved ones in the football disaster at Hillsborough Stadium Sheffield, England, on 15 April 1989. A few families met whilst travelling to and from the Lord Justice Taylor Inquiry, and decided that they should contact every next of kin and form a group. They held their first meeting at the Vernon Sangster Sports Centre, Liverpool. By July of the same year, they had democratically elected a committee and held the first committee meeting.

Plate 9.1 Memorial to the dead and injured.

Source: Getty Images.

. . . the bereaved families came together to help and support each other throughout the aftermath. It became very clear at an early stage that a strong group was needed if a campaign to bring out the truth and ensure justice was to succeed. This link will help you realize the amount of work the HFSG has done in their search for justice and how hard they had to fight against insurmountable odds: http://hfsg.co.uk/

Ninety-six men, women and children died as a result of the Hillsborough disaster on 15 April 1989. Finally after 23 years of campaigning the report by the Hillsborough Independent Panel has offered the families justice.

Source: http://hillsborough.independent.gov.uk/

That there are no clear and unequivocal criteria to determine that acts defined as 'criminal' always cause harm to society adds a further complication in understanding the relationship between the crime and victimization. 'Victimless crimes' such as certain sexual acts between consenting adults, prostitution, and buying and selling of some illegal drugs, have often been cited in this context (Schur, 1965; Croall, 2001). These are forms of behaviour that may be illegal but are consensual in nature. Because no criminal victimization is occurring, the participants have no reason to complain to the police. The notion of 'victimless crime' has been used by some critics to condemn unjust laws and to further campaigns for legal reform, especially in offences against sexual morality (Jeffery-Poulter, 1991; Higgins, 1996; and see Chapter 11).

Whether or not the notion of 'victimless crime' is a valid one remains open to debate. For example, feminists are split along ideological lines on their views of prostitution as work, women's agency in relation to prostitution, and the distinction between voluntary sex work and sexual exploitation (Murray, 1998; McLeod, 1982; Miller, 1986; also see Sanders *et al.*, 2010). Some have argued that women run the risk of physical and sexual violence at the hands of clients or being harassed by the police on the streets. Others have pointed out that society is affected because prostitution objectifies and reinforces stereotypical notions of women. From a law and order perspective, politicians and local residents who are in favour of clampdowns have also

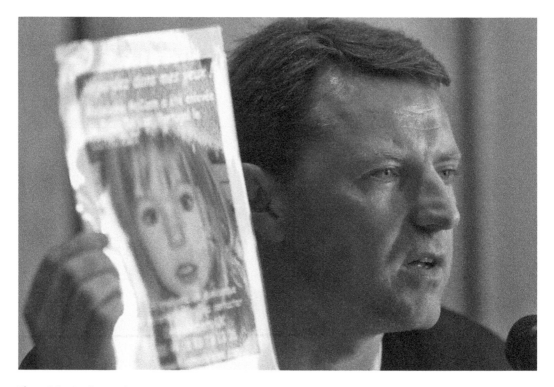

Plate 9.2 The father of Madeleine McCann, the 4-year-old British girl who vanished in Portugal in May 2007, giving a press conference to show a missing persons poster in Arabic and French, in Rabat, in June 2007. The parents launched a campaign to raise public awareness of the case in the hope that people would come forward with information that could help police find their daughter.

Source: AFP/Getty Images.

doing crime

argued that street prostitution is not victimless as it may damage the reputation and quality of life in the neighbourhood. Similar arguments and counter-arguments have been raised in relation to illegal drug use in the context of the decriminalization debate (see Chapter 10). In short, there are no clear, unequivocal definitions of 'consensus', 'harm', 'offender' and 'victim'. Such judgements are always informed by contestable, epistemological, moral and political assumptions (de Haan, 1990: 154).

The hierarchy of victimization

Clearly, some victims enjoy a higher status in the crime discourse, and their experiences of victimization are taken more seriously than others'. Many criminologists have highlighted the dangers of stigmatizing the victims and of creating victim stereotypes. Nils Christie (1986: 18) defines the status of 'ideal victim' in the following way: 'By "ideal victim" I have . . . in mind a person or a category of individuals who – when hit by crime – most readily are given the complete and legitimate status of being a victim.' Put simply, the 'ideal' victim is typified by an elderly woman or child. Such people are considered weak, vulnerable, innocent and deserving of help, care and compassion. On the other hand, young men, homeless people, car owners who do not lock their cars, or a drunken victim of an assault are generally considered to be 'non-ideal victims' and less deserving of sympathy because of their characteristics (e.g. physical strength), action (e.g. their risk-taking behaviour) or inaction (they should have protected themselves).

The **hierarchy of victimization** (Box 9.2) and its impact on certain social groups may be best illustrated by the ambivalent position of women as victims of sexual and domestic violence. Historians have used a variety of sources, including court records, institutional records, newspapers and diaries, to show that in the past, only certain women and girls who presented themselves in certain ways were likely to succeed in bringing their case to public attention, or rarer still, to secure a conviction (Cox, 2003; Zedner, 1991a, 1991b). In the contemporary context, feminist criminologists have argued that focusing on the characteristics or behaviour of individual victims as precipitating factors in crime events has a tendency to reinforce gender stereotypes in explaining cases of rape and violence against women and in distinguishing between 'innocent' and 'blameworthy' victims. Indeed, the notion of victim precipitation can easily become shorthand for 'victim blaming', as the following excerpts illustrate:

> The chronically abused wife is one who permits her husband to beat her, refuses to take punitive action afterward, and remains in the same situation so that she may be beaten again. . . . A wife who has been beaten for the first time may be a victim. A wife who is beaten again is a co-conspirator.
>
> (clinical psychologist and marriage counsellor, quoted in Edwards, 1989: 165)

> Women who say no do not always mean no. It is not just a question of saying no, it is a question of how she says it, how she shows and makes it clear. If she doesn't want it she only has to keep her legs shut.
>
> (Judge Wild, 1982, quoted in Smart, 1989: 35)

It is the height of imprudence for any girl to hitchhike at night. This is plain, it isn't really worth stating. She is in the true sense asking for it.

(Judge Bertrand Richards, 1982, quoted in Smart, 1989: 35)

As we see in what follows, such stereotyping has a serious impact on victims and the ways in which some social groups are dealt with by the criminal justice system. This in turn has led to unwillingness among some victims and witnesses to cooperate with the police and courts.

BOX 9.2 Hierarchy of victimization

The 'low-status, powerless groups' (Reiner, 2000: 93) whom the dominant majority in society see as troublesome or distasteful generally occupy the lower end of the hierarchy of victimization. Examples would be the homeless, the unemployed, those with alcohol and drug problems, prostitutes, refugees, asylum seekers, youth adopting a deviant cultural style, football fans and radical political organizations. The prime function of the police has always been to control and segregate such groups. And when members of such groups do report a crime to the police, they have to engage in a struggle to have their experiences taken seriously. This has often led to complaints from these social groups that they are being 'over-policed' as problem populations but 'under-policed' as victims. For example, the Lesbian and Gay Census 2001 in Britain found that although 1 in 4 respondents had been a victim of serious homophobic crime in the previous five years (including assault, blackmail, arson, rape, hate mail), 65 per cent of the victims did not report the crime to the police, mostly because they feared police harassment or had no confidence that the police would be sympathetic.

The hierarchy of victimization is also shaped by international politics and conditions of war. Ordinary civilians dragged into armed conflicts often suffer heightened victimization from conventional crime (e.g. theft, assault), forced displacement as well as human rights abuses including mass rape, mass killings, trafficking and torture (e.g. in the former Yugoslavia, Rwanda, Israel/Palestine). According to Human Rights Watch, some 50 million people are forcibly displaced as a result of persecution, conflict and human rights violation. Yet not all those who suffer are perceived as innocent victims worthy of our sympathy and support. For example, many refugees, asylum seekers and illegal migrants have been subject to racist attacks and exploitation at the hands of far-right groups, human traffickers, gang masters and unscrupulous employers in the European Union. Yet society's attitudes to the victimization of 'non-citizens' are shaped by stereotypes of the 'undesirable' immigrant as an 'economic scrounger', 'bogus' or 'criminal' (Goodey, 2000).

Different types of victimology

While victimologists are highly critical of the traditional offender-oriented nature of criminology and share a common interest in developing victim-centred research, they differ in their assumptions and the focus of study. Various attempts have been made to classify the different strands of

doing crime

victimological thought. Karmen (1990) identifies three strands within **victimology**: the conservative, the liberal and the radical-critical. Each of these strands defines the scope of the discipline differently, reflects a particular understanding of the problem of crime, and connects with different positions within the victims' movement.

The *conservative* strand within victimology defines the discipline in four ways. First, it views crime as a distinct problem with particular focus on the highly visible forms of crime victimization; second, it is concerned to render people accountable; third, it encourages self-reliance; and, finally, it focuses on notions of retributive justice. This type of victimology generally aims to identify particular patterns of victimization and to examine the actions or patterns of lifestyle of individual victims that may have contributed to the process of crime victimization. Indeed, many of the early victim studies within this tradition shared the assumption that victims are somehow different from non-victims and that they are identifiable because they have particular, distinctive characteristics. For example, some writers set out to develop typologies of victims on the basis of psychological and social variables (von Hentig, 1948). Others, such as Mendelsohn (1956), have used the notion of culpability, ranging from the 'completely innocent' to the 'most guilty victim', to understand the victimizing event (for some of the highly controversial studies, see Wolfgang's (1958) study of homicide and Amir's (1971) study of rape). These so-called 'proto-victimologists' typically referred to victims' conscious and unconscious role in their own victimization, and focused on individual responsibility in the escalation of a situation into a criminal incident. As Jo Goodey (2005: 11) points out, '[m]uch of this early work is now discredited for its limited and damaging interpretation of victimization minus the social context in which crime is committed'.

Although research on victimization proneness is controversial, more recent studies from this tradition have raised some important insights into the nature of relationships between offenders and victims for policymakers and victims' movements and organizations. In particular, the development of victim surveys has helped to place the issues of crime victimization and victimization prevention on the policy agenda (see the next section).

The *liberal* strand within victimology extends the conservative focus by including more hidden types of criminal victimization and abuses by white-collar elites, multinational corporations and businesses in their analyses. Most victims of fraud are, by definition, unaware that they have been victimized at all, or unwilling to recognize that they have been conned (Box, 1983: 17). The intense media attention paid to high-profile business fraud cases and deceptions such as those involving Barings Bank, Bank of Credit and Commercial International (BCCI) and the Maxwell pension fund has highlighted the plight of those who are their victims, including 800,000 depositors in 1.2 million bank accounts in over 70 countries in the case of the collapse of BCCI, and the devastating impact upon them (Levi and Pithouse, 1992; and see Chapter 13). The consequences of corporate crime may also extend to employees, tenants and consumers (Slapper and Tombs, 1999). This type of victimology is often concerned with making 'the victim whole again' – for example, by considering the value of restitution, mediation and reconciliation as appropriate penal strategies (Braithwaite, 2002).

The *radical-critical* strand within victimology sets out to extend the focus of the discipline even further. Its analysis extends to all forms of human suffering and is based on the recognition that poverty, malnutrition, inadequate health care and unemployment are all just as socially harmful as, if not more harmful than, most of the behaviours and incidents that currently make up the official crime problem. Furthermore, it considers the criminal justice system also contributes to the problem of victimization. Thus, 'institutional wrong-doing that violates human rights' (Karmen, 1990: 12), police rule-breaking, wrongful arrest and false imprisonment, political corruption, and deviant or injurious actions of the state that may or may not be defined as 'crimes', are treated as legitimate areas for study. By using broader social conceptions of victimization, this type of victimology promises to challenge dominant understandings of what constitutes the 'crime problem' and its impact on individuals and whole communities. In recent years, victimologists writing from this tradition have also turned to more structural explanations as a way of understanding the nature and process of victimization. For example, they have engaged in analysis of the wider economic and social context of victimization and structural powerlessness, and in political analysis of the rights of victims (see Walklate 2007a; Mawby and Walklate, 1994).

Crime victimization surveys

A key aspect of victim-oriented research has been the development of crime victimization surveys. As Chapter 2 shows, the Crime Survey for England and Wales (CSEW) – previously the British Crime Survey – and other national victim surveys in the United States, Canada, Australia, the Netherlands and Switzerland have provided us with an alternative measure of crime and a more informed understanding of the impact of crime on victims, the social, economic and demographic characteristics of the victim population, and public attitudes to crime and the criminal justice system. Large-scale cross-national victim surveys such as the UN-sponsored International Crime Victimization Survey (ICVS) have also been carried out so that some international comparisons of victimization can be made (see Box 9.3). One of the key findings of the ICVS is that the experience of being criminally victimized has become a statistically normal feature of life around the world, though the type and extent of victimization vary. For all crimes the highest reporting levels are in the industrialized world. In countries of transition and developing countries, crimes were reported less frequently. The survey has also highlighted the experiences of respondents and their anxieties about crime and policing during periods of political, economic and social upheaval. For example, corruption has been identified as a main concern for survey respondents in developing countries and countries in transition. Local victim surveys in Britain with a narrower geographical focus such as the Islington Crime Survey have also made a significant contribution to our knowledge of crime. They have highlighted the uneven distribution of risks of victimization, showing that certain age or social groups are more frequently subjected to crime than others.

   Although crime victimization surveys have helped to redress an imbalance in early criminological works, provide insights into the hidden figures of crime and sensitize policymakers to the range and diversity of victim experiences with crime, they too have serious limitations. For one thing, they suffer from a general inability to tap certain forms of crime where there is no direct or clearly identifiable victim. Many crimes committed in the corporate boardroom, in the financial marketplace, on the Internet, or directed against the environment thus remain characterized by 'no knowledge, no statistics, no theory, no research, no control, no politics, and no panic' (Jupp *et al.*, 1999). Crime victimization surveys therefore carry with them limited notions about what is crime and who are the victims. They have a tendency to focus the notion of criminality on the conventional crimes while other equally harmful acts, and victims, remain hidden. In particular, early surveys that examine people's lifestyle (cf. Hindelang *et al.*, 1978; Gottfredson, 1984) in order to assess how patterns of leisure activities and everyday behaviour affect the risks of victimization have been criticized for ignoring the reality that lifestyles are often shaped by social forces and structural constraints.

There are also specific problems with using international victimization reports as a measure of crime. International victimization surveys that rely on standardized concepts of 'crime' tend to ignore different cultural perceptions that may affect the respondents. Indeed, respondents in different countries may have different notions of thresholds concerning what they perceive as unacceptable and harmful behaviour. All this suggests that findings from victimization surveys must be interpreted very carefully, in the knowledge that any differences may reflect definitional variations as much as variations in prevalence or incidence.

BOX 9.3 The International Crime Victimization Survey

The International Crime Victimization Survey (ICVS) conducted in 1989, 1992, 1996, 2000, 2005 and 2009 is a cross-national comparative measure of victims' experience with crime, policing, and feelings of unsafety in a large number of countries. The 2000 ICVS shows that the most common reason for not reporting in all countries was that the incident was considered 'not serious enough' or there was 'no loss'. Reporting is also influenced by other factors: previous personal experiences of reporting; experience with or attitudes to the police; expectations; factors related to the particular victimization experience in hand; existence of alternative ways of dealing with this; relationship with the offender; and the 'privacy' of the issue. For all countries combined, just over 1 per cent of women reported offensive sexual behaviour. Women know the offender(s) in about half of all the sexual incidents. Victims were also asked why they did report. In general, victims of sexual incidents, assaults and threats were most concerned to stop what happened being repeated. For burglaries and thefts from cars, more than a third reported because they wanted help in getting property back, and a third did so for insurance reasons. Other victims referred to the civic obligation to notify the police. Risks for different social groups were also examined. Households with higher incomes were more at risk than those poorer ones. In poorer neighbourhoods, households in general might have higher risk, but more affluent households emerge as the most vulnerable. Younger respondents were more at risk than older ones. Men were about 20 per cent more at risk than women for robbery and assaults.

Source: Kesteren *et al.* (2000).

Social variables in crime victimization

Individuals are differentially placed in respect of crime – differentially vulnerable to crime, and differentially affected by crime. Indeed, there is evidence to suggest that the risk of crime victimization is unevenly distributed within and between different localities and various sections of the population. Existing victim surveys in Britain and elsewhere have highlighted social class, age, gender and ethnicity as key and intertwining variables in the patterns and rates of crime victimization.

Social class

Crime victimization surveys have consistently shown that the risk from property crime is unequally distributed among the population, with the 'most marginalized social groups living in the poorest areas' generally bearing the greater burden of crime (Davies *et al.*, 2003: 13; Nicholas *et al.*, 2007; Office for National Statistics (ONS), 2013). Similarly, Foster and Hope (1993) found in their analysis of early BCS data that pockets of high unemployment in public housing estates experienced very high rates of victimization. Indeed, many of the most deprived housing estates with drugs and/or high crime problems are found in areas evacuated by business and industry. Closure of local shops and other amenities reinforces a bad reputation for the area that has adverse consequences for the availability of credit and insurance for residents (Pearson, 1987). This has produced what the Rowntree Inquiry described as 'vicious cycles of decline in particular areas and on particular estates' (Rowntree Foundation, 1995).

The significance of class in crime victimization has been a key issue for one particularly influential perspective in British criminology since the mid-1980s. As Young (1986: 21) puts it, the central tenets of 'left realism' are to recognize that crime is 'a very real source of suffering for the poor and the vulnerable' and to 'take crime seriously'. John Lea and Jock Young in their pivotal work *What Is To Be Done about Law and Order?* (1984) drew attention to the fact that most crime is intra-class and intra-racial, committed by relatively disadvantaged perpetrators on similarly relatively disadvantaged victims. Thus, working-class crime, such as street crime, burglary, personal violence, is seen as a problem of the first order. The task of the left, so they argue, is to accept this reality, try to understand it and do something about it, rather than deny or overdramatize it (for a critique of left realism, see Chapter 6).

Age

Contrary to popular imagination, children under the age of 1 are more at risk of being murdered than any other age group (ONS, 2013); many of the victims are killed by their parents or carers in Britain (Home Office, 2005a; NSPCC, 2013). In general, the more socially vulnerable the victim and the more private or intimate the setting of the crime's commission, the less visible the crime. In recent years there have been a growing number of revelations about the extensive abuse of children who have been in the care of local authorities.

By the late 1990s, allegations of sexual abuse and systematic violence by community and children's homes staff in Britain had surfaced in Leicestershire, Islington (London), Dumfries, Buckinghamshire, Northumbria, North Wales, Cheshire and more recently Haut de la Garenne in Jersey. Another example is child sexual abuse by women. Social stereotypes of femininity and motherhood mean that the criminal justice and child protection systems generally fail to identify women as perpetrators of sexual abuse, and accounts of male and female child victims tend to be disbelieved or minimized (Turton, 2007). Even when cases of abuse are reported and recorded, they are often considered to be atypical, one-off scandals, and something distinct from the more familiar crises of law and order.

Victim surveys have shown that young people are at least as much at risk of victimization as adults, and for some types of crime, more at risk than adults irrespective of class, gender or place. According to the 2011/12 Crime Survey for England and Wales just over a quarter of young people aged from 10 to 24 had been a victim of either personal theft, such as mobile phones or of assault in the previous 12 months. Significantly, young males who have committed an offence themselves are more likely to be victims (Wilson et al., 2006). Studies in Edinburgh (Anderson et al., 1994), Glasgow (Hartless et al., 1995) and Teesside (Brown, 1994) have produced startlingly similar results indicating routine experience by children and teenagers of different forms of abuse in the home and on the street, harassment by adults and other young people, bullying as well as other forms of serious crime, including physical assault. Few of these experiences are reported to the police, however, and youth victimization, as opposed to youth offending, remains low on the priority lists of the police and politicians. This, combined with the experience for many young people of being 'moved on', or stopped and searched, contributed to the argument that young people are over-controlled as delinquents but under-protected as victims (Loader, 1996; Anderson et al., 1994; Muncie 2009; see also Brown, 2005: ch.5). Clearly then, children and young people are affected not only by conventional crimes such as theft but also by crimes behind closed doors and crimes specific to the very young including child abuse and school bullying.

Although the elderly have lower rates of victimization from violent street crime than younger age groups, they can be subject to abuse hidden behind closed doors of private households or care homes. There are other problems with assessing the extent of elder victimization: elder abuse is not conceptualized in legal terms, is not a clearly defined offence, and has no satisfactory working definition. According to the Action on Elder Abuse survey 2007, the prevalence rate of abuse at home for those over 66 years is 4 per cent in the UK. More concerning is that 2.6 per cent (that is 227,000 individuals) reported abuse by trusted others including family members, friends and careworkers. This is almost certainly an underestimate. Non-reporting often results from concerns over domestic privacy, and few cases end up in official statistics, let alone in court (Brogden and Nijhar, 2000: 48–9).

Gender

Chapter 2 suggests that victim surveys and official statistics have consistently shown that men are more likely to be victims of violent attacks, particularly by strangers and by other men in public spaces, whereas women are more likely to be victimized in the home. According to the 2011/12 CSEW, young men aged 16 to 24 had the highest risk of being a victim of violent crime (ONS, 2013). Although homicide rates have dropped to the lowest since 1989 (ONS, 2013) young men in Britain are exposed to 'more fights, more brawls, more scuffles, more bottles and more knives . . . These are the same groups of young men for whom suicide rates are rising, the same groups of which almost a million left the country in the 1990s unknown to the authorities, presumably to find somewhere better to live' (Dorling, 2005: 190). Many work-based injuries also take place, where assault and intimidation commonly occur between men – from either managers or colleagues, as a result of unsafe working practices (Stanko et al., 1998), or in the course of providing services to the public, especially in occupations such as the police and health service workers, security guards, publicans and bar staff (Budd, 1999).

Women on the other hand are more likely to be victimized in the home. They are the main victims of reported and unreported sexual violence (Finney, 2006; Nicholas et al., 2007). This gendered pattern of violence is notable around the world, especially in Latin America and Africa (Newman, 1999). Women are more likely to have experienced persistent, unwanted attention, for example stalking and repeat victimization, especially in domestic violence, than men (Nicholas et al., 2007; Budd and Mattinson, 2000; Finney, 2006). Such experiences of victimization are sometimes made invisible in conventional victim studies, however. Indeed, critics have argued that victim surveys that are based on measuring discrete events cannot fully comprehend the pervasive, underlying threat to security or the **'continuum of sexual violence'** (Kelly, 1988) that characterizes the experiences of many women. Women routinely learn to manage their lives structured and informed by their relationships with men they know. In these relationships, many women during their lifetime learn to deal with habitual violence, bullying or prolonged abuse, in what can be described as 'climates of unsafety' (Stanko, 1990). Men can also find themselves in very controlled partnerships as the victims of domestic abuse and they often find their victimization silenced by the social expectations of masculinity (Grady, 2002).

Feminists have highlighted the particularly gendered nature of violence that occurs in both war (mass rape, human trafficking) and peace ('femicide') (Jamieson, 1998; Kelly, 2005). State agents may be the violators rather than protectors of women's rights in some cases. For example, critics have pointed to evidence of international peacekeepers being involved in sex trafficking and other forms of sexual exploitation in conflict and post-conflict regions such as in the Balkans and the existence of a culture of denial and impunity amongst the state and transnational bodies including the UN and NATO (Human Rights Watch, 2000; Mendelson, 2005).

The treatment of women within some groups further highlights the hidden gendered pattern of violence used against young women who do not conform to strict cultural norms. So-called honour killings offer an extreme example of this violent behaviour.

BOX 9.4 'Honour killings'

One in ten young British Asians believes so-called honour killings can be justified, according to a poll for the BBC's Asian Network. Of 500 Hindus, Sikhs, Christians and Muslims questioned, a tenth said they would condone the murder of someone who disrespected their family's honour. Figures show 13 people die every year in honour killings, but police and support groups believe it is many more. Honour killing is a brutal reaction within a family – predominantly Asian and Middle Eastern – to someone perceived to have brought 'shame' upon relatives. What constitutes dishonour can range from wearing clothes thought to be unsuitable or choosing a career which the family disapprove of, to marrying outside of the wider community.

Not tolerated

Dr Aisha Gill, a lecturer in criminology at Roehampton University, told BBC Five Live that convincing the Asian community that honour killings were not acceptable was the right approach:

> I think it's absolutely essential that there is a collective responsibility, and this is not just for agencies but for communities that are affected by it. [The government should] send out a clear message, an unambiguous message that such violence against women will not be tolerated.

Source: BBC News September 2006.
http://newsbbc.co.uk/go/pr/fr/-/1/hi/uk/5311244.stm)

The report below offers a recent case study in which Shafilea Ahmed's parents were found guilty of her murder.

3 August 2012: The parents of Shafilea Ahmed have been jailed after being convicted of her murder

The 17-year-old went missing from her home in Warrington, Cheshire, in 2003 and her body was found in the River Kent in Cumbria six months later. Iftikhar, 52, and Farzana Ahmed, 49, had denied her murder but the jury returned guilty verdicts. The judge said they would both serve 25 years and told them: 'Your concern about being shamed in your community was greater than your love for your child.' The couple suffocated Shafilea with a plastic bag after years of abuse. After the trial the police described the killing as a 'vile and disgraceful act against someone they should have been proud of . . . this is not an honour killing, this is a clear case of murder'. The prosecution claimed her parents murdered her because they believed she had brought shame on the family.

Source: www.bbc.co.uk/news/uk-england-19068490

Ethnicity

Studies have found that in Britain and the rest of Europe, people belonging to ethnic minority groups are generally at greater risk of crime victimization than the indigenous populations (Percy, 1998; Clancy et al., 2001; Albrecht, 2000). But there are some important variations. Smaller-scale, local area studies in Britain have revealed even more complex patterns of risk of victimization and variations within and between different groups, socio-economic factors, localities and offences (Gill, 2006; Jones et al., 1986; Crawford et al., 1990; Jefferson and Walker, 1993; Webster, 1994; Bowling and Phillips, 2002). Ethnic minority groups are also routinely subject to racial violence and harassment. Indeed, some violent offences are best seen as a 'process', as the cumulative impact of threats, domestic assaults, name calling, racial insults, abuse, graffiti and punching cannot be captured by the mere counting of each individual incident (Bowling, 1998).

Perhaps more damagingly, minority ethnic groups have pointed to persistent police failure in protecting them from racist victimization. Such criticisms have gathered momentum in the wake of the Stephen Lawrence scandal in Britain of the late 1990s in which the Macpherson Report (1999) found 'institutional racism' to be pervasive within the Metropolitan Police, and by extension elsewhere, and that, as a result, ethnic minority groups are unjustly treated. The poor response to crime victimization of particular sections of society has serious implications, especially against a background of conflicts between the police and black communities, serious problems long associated with police use of stop and search powers and a number of successful claims against the police for civil damages (see Chapter 17). Confidence in the police and cooperation with investigations have no doubt been harmed by tensions and negative encounters between the police and those belonging to ethnic minority communities. Indeed, victimization and attitudinal surveys have provided evidence to support this. Africans and Caribbeans have generally lower levels of satisfaction with the police than do white respondents, while results are more mixed among Asian respondents (see Bowling and Phillips, 2002: 135–8).

The impact of crime

Not only are social groups and individuals differentially vulnerable to crime victimization, they are also differentially fearful about crime. Fear of crime has come to be regarded as 'a problem in its own right' (Hale, 1992), quite distinct from actual crime and victimization, and distinctive policies have been developed that aim to reduce levels of fear. The Crime Survey for England and Wales regularly investigates the levels and character of this fear, categorizing and measuring the emotional reactions prompted by crime. The BCS shows that those who are most concerned about crime tend to be women, the poor, those in unskilled occupations and those living in the inner cities, council estate areas, or areas with high levels of disorder. The young are most concerned about car-related theft. Women, especially older women, are far more likely to feel unsafe at home or out alone after dark than men. People in partly skilled or unskilled occupations are found to be more fearful than those in skilled occupations, while those who consider themselves to be in poor health or with disability also have heightened levels of concern about crime (Simmons and Dodd, 2003; Nicholas et al., 2007). In another national survey of ethnic minorities, nearly one in four black and Asian respondents reported being worried about being racially harassed (Virdee, 1997). The meaning of such fears and anxieties is discussed in Chapter 12.

Victims of specific crimes may be affected by the crime itself (**primary victimization**) or the way in which others respond to them and the crimes (**secondary victimization**). A particular crime may have an effect on victims directly in a number of ways. They may be physically injured, incur financial loss or damage to property or lose time, as a result of the crime itself or of involvement in the criminal justice process. Most existing studies have concentrated on the impact of more serious personal or property crimes, as opposed to the majority of everyday crimes or other high-profile cases of business crime or criminal negligence. These studies have highlighted the acute stress, shock, sense of intrusion of privacy, and adverse physical, practical or financial effects suffered by many victims (Maguire and Corbett, 1987; Brogden and Nijhar, 2000; Lurigio *et al.*, 1990). In cases of violence, there is evidence from the British Crime Surveys to suggest that the most common emotional reaction is anger, followed by shock, fear, difficulty in sleeping, and crying. Victims of rape, sexual assault and abuse have been found to suffer persisting effects related to their physical and mental health – for example, emotional disturbance, sleeping or eating disorders, feelings of insecurity, or troubled relationships over a period of time (Maguire and Corbett, 1987; Kelly, 1988; Ruback and Thompson, 2001).

"George, this new home security system you bought... how much did it cost?"

Plate 9.3 Cartoon on home security system.

Source: © Cartoon Stock, London, www.CartoonStock.com

The reaction of criminal justice agencies and other experts, such as the medical services, may exacerbate such negative impact for the victim. On the basis of a series of interviews with victims of interpersonal crimes, Shapland *et al.* (1985) found that many victims in Britain were poorly informed about the criminal justice process, including the possibility of state compensation. Perhaps more significantly, the study found that victims began with very positive views of the system's response to their problems, but became increasingly critical as their cases progressed. In the initial stages, much of the sense of secondary victimization felt by victims stems from their perceptions of the police as unsympathetic. Findings that the police are insensitive to victims are common to studies across a wide range of countries in which policing structures are very different (Newman, 1999). Furthermore, in the later stages, victims often perceive court appearances as at best bewildering and at worst intimidating as recent cases have suggested (see Box 9.5).

The failings of the British criminal justice system in the treatment of female victims have been well documented (Stanko, 1994; Dobash *et al.*, 1995; Smart, 1995). In particular, there has been public concern about the police's insensitive or even hostile treatment of female victims of sexual

BOX 9.5 Lawyers' treatment of gang grooming victims prompts call for reform

Campaigners demand urgent shake-up of court procedure after seven barristers cross-examined a girl every day for three weeks in child grooming case.

'I want to ask you once more why you are telling me lies?' demands the defence barrister Tayyab Khan. He is cross-examining a witness on her evidence relating to the multiple violent rapes she suffered at the instigation of a child grooming gang operating in the West Midlands.

'No,' she says. 'I am not telling lies.' She breaks down, but the court transcript shows the barrister pressing the point. 'You're a compulsive liar,' he states. She's shouting and crying now. 'Was you there? Was you there?' she asks. 'You're telling lies,' Khan insists again. 'No, I'm not, shut up, shut up!' she shouts. She's clearly distressed, but this seems not to bother him as he continues with his line of questioning regardless.

Khan's client, Ahdel Ali, was convicted of crimes including the rape of a 13-year-old and multiple sexual offences with children as part of a three-year investigation called Operation Chalice – but not before the main victim in the trial, a girl called Abby, was aggressively cross-examined by seven barristers every day for three weeks. Each represented a different man charged with sexually exploiting her over two years, and all in turn had their go at testing not only her evidence relating to their client, but also calling into question her integrity, lifestyle and issues of consent. Seven men were eventually convicted as a result of Operation Chalice, one of the first cases dealing with grooming of . . . vulnerable girls.

The notion that young victims who have been repeatedly gang-raped should be required to endure multiple aggressive interrogations in order to get justice is now being challenged by child sexual abuse campaigners.

Source: Copyright Guardian News & Media Ltd 2013.

doing crime

offences – for example, in acquaintance attacks or in cases where the woman's demeanour or dress code is seen to be 'provocative' (Edwards, 1989; Hanmer et al., 1989; Gregory and Lees, 1999; see also Chapter 11). The problem of secondary victimization of some victims was dramatically highlighted in 1982 by an episode of Roger Graef's ground-breaking television documentary on the Thames Valley Police that showed a very disturbing interrogation of a rape victim by two male officers. Indeed, the police response to men's violence against women is important not only for the safety of individual women but also because of its social significance. The police define which types of attacks are to be taken seriously and proceeded with, and which types of attacks are to be condoned or dropped (i.e. 'no-crimed'). By making a distinction between 'innocent' and 'blameworthy' victims, the police are also making a distinction between attacks they deem to be justifiable in society and those that are not. This decision-making process demonstrates that the police do not offer unconditional protection to all victims against all forms of violence. Instead, moral judgements are constantly being made based on a variety of socio-cultural factors including gendered assumptions or stereotypical assumptions about race, age and sexuality, biases within the police **occupational culture**, and the associated definition of what counts as 'proper policing'. For example, calls to domestic disturbances have always been a significant part of the police workload but as Robert Reiner argues, '"Domestics" were seen as messy, unproductive and not "real" police work in traditional cop culture' (2000: 135). However, others have pointed to a 'cultural shift' in police policy and practices towards 'service provision' and some of the improvements in police responses to the problem of domestic violence in recent years (Goodey, 2005: 158). It would seem that the experiences of victims have changed little judging by recent cases – such as the West Midland sex trafficking trial (see Box 9.5) and the court case concerning the Manchester music school, which resulted in the key victim committing suicide during the trial – and this is despite attempts to protect victims from the adversarial system.

Finally, there has been an increased recognition of the pains of indirect victimization. For example, the families of murder victims may suffer the profound trauma of bereavement, compounded by the viciousness of the attack or the senselessness of the murder (Rock, 1998). Paul Iganski (2001: 628–31) has also drawn attention to the range of harms generated by certain crimes that extend well beyond the initially targeted victim. The 'waves of harm' (see Figure 9.1) generated by hate crimes spread beyond the individual to the victim's 'group' or community in the wider neighbourhood. As one respondent in his study explains, 'it tends to get people really anxious and excited and . . . we like to call them domestic terrorism' (Iganski, 2001: 630). Other persons who share the victim's characteristics – and come to hear of the victim's plight – may potentially be affected by a hate crime. They may respond as if they have been victimized themselves. In this sense, hate crimes constitute 'message crimes'. The wave of harm can also spread to other targeted or socially vulnerable groups within and beyond the victim's neighbourhood. Furthermore, hate crimes arguably strike at the core of societal values, offending the collective moral code.

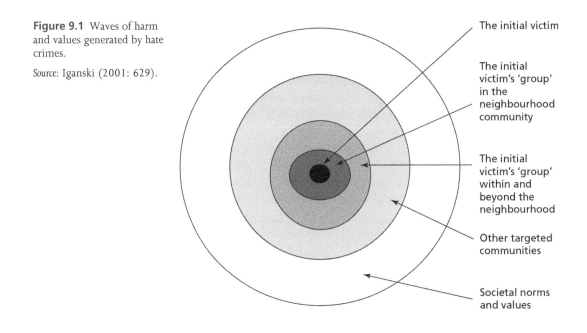

Figure 9.1 Waves of harm and values generated by hate crimes.

Source: Iganski (2001: 629).

The initial victim

The initial victim's 'group' in the neighbourhood community

The initial victim's 'group' within and beyond the neighbourhood

Other targeted communities

Societal norms and values

Towards a victim-oriented criminal justice process?

It has been increasingly recognized that the victim has a key role in the criminal justice process. After all, most crime would remain hidden and unpunished without the cooperation of the victim in reporting the offence, providing evidence and acting as witness in court. The marginalization and 'silencing' of many victims in the court process has been well documented (see Chapter 16), though more recent attempts to develop a more 'victim-oriented' criminal justice system in Britain and elsewhere may have gone some way to address that (Goodey, 2005). There have been calls for increased victim participation in the criminal justice process, often in decisions as to bail, diversion from prosecution, levels of sentence and parole. A formal way of providing for victims' views to be taken into account is through what is known as a 'victim impact statement' (VIS) or 'victim statement' (VS). Such provisions are more developed in the United States than in Britain, and have received rather mixed receptions. In Britain there is evidence to suggest that victim statements are supported by many decision-makers at the level of rhetoric – in other words it is commonplace to endorse the idea of giving victims an opportunity to be 'heard' – but when it comes to the level of action victim statements are sought and used only in a small minority of cases (Morgan and Sanders, 1999). Critics have also argued that sentences should be a matter of public policy rather than dependent on the lottery of the forgiveness or anger of the victim, that the victim might feel even more frustrated and angry if the court appeared to ignore the VS/VIS, and that a more appropriate way forward might be to educate those working in the criminal justice agencies about the physical and psychological impact of victimization on individuals and families (Ashworth, 1993; for a review, see Goodey, 2005 and Walklate, 2007b).

So what are the limits and possibilities of developing a victim-oriented criminal justice system? In recent years, victim groups and voluntary or professional organizations have fought hard to raise the profile of hidden victims (for instance victims of trafficking) and to press for improved

doing crime

BOX 9.6 Victim movements – some examples around the world

Victims, their families, voluntary or professional agencies and communities affected by crimes have mobilized themselves in different ways to force governments to take the problem of crime victimization seriously.

In the People's Republic of China, the 'Tiananmen Mothers' is a group made up of the relatives of 125 victims killed during the Tiananmen Square student movement on 4 June 1989. On that day, the Chinese army, backed by tanks, stormed the square killing demonstrators. Officially, the 1989 student movement remains a 'counterrevolutionary uprising'. The government has never released any official tally of casualties, but outside groups have estimated that the number of those killed or injured runs in the thousands. The 'Tiananmen Mothers' wanted the authorities to set up an inquiry into the killings, impose punishment on the culprits, provide compensation and assistance to those who continue to suffer psychologically or financially from the crackdown, and remove the political and social stigma on victims and their families.

In the United States a more conservative rights-based victim movement has been at the forefront of campaigns for extension of their role in judicial discretion (e.g. the right to make 'victim impact statements' to inform sentencing decisions) and often for a more punitive response to offenders. For example, the national community and victim's rights organization 'Parents for Megan's Law' was set up after a 7-year-old New Jersey girl was raped and murdered in 1994 by a paroled sex offender who had moved into her neighbourhood. The resulting legislative changes provide for stringent community notification requirements for convicted sex offenders if and when they get out of prison and, in some cases, for harsher sentences. Other victim groups have also campaigned for indefinite confinement of sex offenders or for the retention or reintroduction of the death penalty for other offenders. Civil libertarians and other critics, however, have called the **Megan's Law** provisions a 'badge of infamy' that is attached to certain offenders for life. A similar scheme, known as 'Sarah's Law', was rolled out across all police forces in England and Wales from 4 April 2011. It allows anyone to ask the police to check whether people who have contact with children pose a risk.

In Britain the central organ of the victim movement, 'Victim Support', has concentrated on lobbying for and providing services to individual victims (e.g. through the work of local volunteers), compensation, and provision for the victim in court. It has also been highly influential in shaping the government's 'Victim's Charter', which sets out the rights of victims, specifying how they are to be treated and the standards they can expect – for example, information about the progress of their case, about trial dates, and about bail and sentencing decisions. In addition, victim groups and concerned citizens have also been highly vocal in their demands for legislative changes or tougher sentencing in the aftermath of particular crimes (e.g. the murder of children, the Dunblane killings).

victim services and more sensitive treatment of victims by criminal justice agencies. In practice, expressions of victims' needs and interests and their recognition by the state are often mediated by power differentials and political considerations. Vocal, determined victim groups or those with most resources are generally better placed than the most vulnerable and least vocal victim groups to express their needs, lobby for change, or seek practical help or information. Furthermore, many critics have argued that the call for addressing victim needs and for orienting the criminal justice system away from the offender and towards the victim can easily become conflated with a populist 'law and order' approach to punishment.

As Fattah (1986: 2–3) argues,

> Most victim advocates do not restrict their demands to a charter of victim rights or to a better lot for those who are victimized. These demands are usually coupled with, and in fact overshadowed by, calls for harsher penalties, stricter measures and more oppressive treatment of offenders. Getting-tough with offenders is often advanced as the central or, at least, as an essential component, of society's obligation to the victims of crime. . . . In this way, the noble cause of the victims of crime is used as a pretext to unleash suppressed vindictive impulses or as an excuse to act out the inhibited aggression against the offender.

While calls for 'justice' by victim groups can become overshadowed by or equated with a 'get tough' approach to crime and disorder, a victim-oriented criminal justice system also has the potential of paving the way for a more progressive approach to punishment. In recent years, there are signs of a growing interest around the world in communitarian ideas of reintegration and restorative justice whereby justice is primarily a process of reconciling conflicts and repairing harms or ruptures to social bonds resulting from crime (Dignan 2005; McLaughlin et al., 2003; Braithwaite, 1989; Zehr, 1990). As Chapter 15 explains, the restorative justice model, the use of reintegrative shaming techniques, mediation and reparation aim to provide an alternative and more appropriate way of resolving disputes, confronting offenders with their wrongdoing and empowering the victims. However, one can argue that public demands for retribution as the organizing principle of justice remain as strong as ever and while the government appears to support a victim approach, recent budget cuts suggest this might be rhetoric rather than action. For criminologists, the relationships between crime victims, offenders and the community will continue to be an important and highly contentious area of study.

Summary

1   Victims play a central role in initiating the criminal justice process. In addition, there have been moves to increase victim participation at subsequent stages of the criminal justice process and to develop alternative means of resolving disputes, confronting offenders with their wrongdoing and empowering the victims.
2   Victimologists are highly critical of the traditional offender-oriented nature of criminology and share a common interest in developing victim-centred research. At the same time, they differ in their assumptions and the focus of study. There are at least three strands within victimology: the conservative, the liberal and the radical-critical.

3   Some victims enjoy a higher status in the crime discourse, and their experiences of victimization are taken more seriously than others. In this sense, 'victim' is a social construct that reflects broader power differentials and stereotypes in society.
4   The risk of crime victimization is unevenly distributed within and between different localities and various sections of the population. Victim surveys and official statistics have consistently shown that men are more likely than women to be victims of violent attacks, particularly by strangers and by other men in public spaces. Women on the other hand are more likely to be victimized in the home.
5   Victims may be affected by the crime itself or the way in which others respond to them and the crimes. There is also increasing recognition of the impact of indirect victimization on victims' families and communities.

Critical thinking questions

1   Compile a list of five local/national and five international stories about victims of different types of crime from any chosen newspaper. What do these stories tell you about the differential status of victims in media representations of crime? Is there a pattern to the types of victims who are portrayed as innocent and deserving of our help, and those who are seen as blameworthy?

2   Consider the advantages and disadvantages of increasing victim participation at different stages of the criminal justice process. What are the implications for procedural, substantive and negotiated justice?

Further study

Goodey, J. (2005) *Victims and Victimology: Research, Policy and Practice*, Harlow: Longman. A useful text examining the key theoretical, political and policy debates in the field of victims and victimology.

Walklate, S. (ed.) (2007b) *Handbook of Victims and Victimology*, Cullompton: Willan. An authoritative handbook on the nature, extent and impact of criminal victimization and the developments in victimology.

Mawby, R. and Walklate, S. (1994) *Critical Victimology*, London: Sage. A critical and comparative analysis of victim services and other key issues facing crime victims within the criminal justice system.

Walklate, S. (2007a) *Imagining the Victim of Crime*, Maidenhead, UK: Open University Press. An introduction into theoretical, methodological and substantive areas of victiminology.

Schur, E. M. (1965) *Crimes without Victims: Deviant Behavior and Public Policy*, Englewood Cliffs, NJ: Prentice Hall. A classic sociological text examining a range of 'victimless' crimes from the labelling perspective.

Useful websites

Victim Support
http://www.victimsupport.org.uk/
Charity giving free confidential advice and support to victims and their families.

Criminal Justice System Online: 'Victims Virtual Walkthrough'
http://webarchive.nationalarchives.gov.uk/20080107211250/http://www.cjsonline.gov.uk/witness/help_and_support/index.html
An interactive virtual tour that provides information about the British criminal justice process as it relates to victims of crime.

United Nations Declaration of Basic Principles of Justice for Victims of Crime and Abuse of Power
http://www2.ohchr.org/english/law/victims.htm

United Nations Interregional Crime and Justice Research Institute
http://www.unicri.it/documentation_centre/publications/icvs/
Provides information on various international crime victimization surveys.

Human Rights Watch
www.hrw.org
An international watchdog concerned with gathering information about breaches of human rights. The website provides details on their activities.

chapter 10

Crime and Property

Key issues

■ What can be identified as property crimes?

■ How does the pattern of property crime vary across time and place?

■ What are the characteristics of property crime offenders?

■ How is the risk of victimization socially distributed?

Introduction

Official statistics around the world suggest that by far the most frequently reported crime is property crime (Nicholas *et al.*, 2007). So what is property crime?

Broadly speaking, property crime involves stealing and dishonestly obtaining or damaging another's property, whether tangible goods or intangible property. All this may seem very straightforward. However, the distinction between what is unambiguously criminal and what is culturally tolerated behaviour is not always so clear-cut. For example, the dishonest acquisition of another's property is not always perceived as 'theft' by the offender or by the victim. Pickpocketing is seen as unacceptable and criminal, whereas hotel employees stealing food, wine or cash and hotel guests stealing linen, art or silverware from their rooms may be tolerated by the victim or justified as 'perks' or 'souvenirs' by the perpetrator. Similarly, we tend to associate 'fraud' with crime for gain or major financial scandals (see Chapter 13). Yet it is not always easy to draw a line between 'enterprise' and 'dishonesty', or between dishonest behaviour that is clearly 'illegal' and the hustles, scams and confidence tricks of 'con merchants', false advertising of salespersons or pyramid schemes, and the behaviour of many others involved in everyday commercial exchanges.

In this chapter we look at the different forms and patterns of property crime, our attitudes towards its perpetrators, the characteristics of different types of property crime offenders, issues surrounding the risk of victimization and its distribution, and the impact of property crime on individual victims and communities. The aim is to challenge some of the popular assumptions about property crime and property crime offenders and to broaden our understanding of the crime problem and what is to be done about it.

Patterns of property crime

What we place into the category of 'property crime' makes a big difference to the range of behaviour we have to explain. Chapter 2 shows the problems of using crime and judicial statistics as a measure of actual levels of criminal activities in society. Nevertheless, crime statistics provide a useful starting point for understanding patterns of crime and the decisions of those responsible for controlling crime. From the 1830s onwards, crime has been classified into six main types:

- offences against the person;
- offences against property (with violence);
- offences against property (without violence);
- malicious offences against property;
- offences against the currency;
- and miscellaneous offences (Emsley, 2002).

The pattern that can be drawn from the statistics shows a steady increase in crime, especially property crime, in the late eighteenth century, becoming much sharper from the first decade of the nineteenth century to the close of the 1840s, and then a general decline in crime until the end of the nineteenth century, except, most noticeably, for burglary (Emsley, 2005).

Many historians have explained the changing level of property crime by referring to the combined effects of key changes in British social and economic life during this period: population growth; urbanization and the capitalization of industry; and changing levels of unemployment and economic hardship. Historians who adopted a class conflict perception of society saw property crime as an element of the developing struggle between capital and labour. They argued that new work practices brought about by industrialization, and changes in payment for labour and in notions of property ownership, meant that traditional rural popular culture and customs (e.g. gathering fallen wood for fuel, taking wild game, collecting scrap metal) were increasingly criminalized (Thompson, 1975). Seen in this light, the thefts of poor men might be understood as resistance to capitalism and new work discipline. Other historians, however, turn to social and court data that reveal a relationship between capital and labour far more complex than a simple class conflict model might suggest. They stressed the significance of changes in the administration of criminal justice (such as the establishment of the new police forces), the 'civilization' of the population, a diminishing fear about the 'dangerous classes', and a corresponding decline in the reporting and prosecuting of small-scale theft, especially in the second half of the mid-nineteenth century (see Emsley, 2005). Court records show that most thefts involved everyday objects of relatively little value and that very many of the victims were relatively poor people. In the long run, the changes in the economy meant that people had more disposable income and more movable property, and shops had more goods for consumers, which in turn prompted changes in the opportunities for and style of theft.

The dominance of property offences continued into the twentieth century. Conventional and new forms of property crime were rampant during the Second World War even though it was commonly regarded as a golden age of community spirit and national pride. The war created massive opportunities for crime for everyone – from organized gangs and professional criminals to 'ordinary' and 'respectable' people. Blackouts and bombed buildings made looting especially easy; because of rationing, many people took to fiddling and forging their food, petrol and clothes coupons; and profiteering and the black market boomed (Calder, 1991; Fraser, 1994). The steady increase of crime during the inter-war and post-war periods might arguably reflect the economic difficulties generated by the Depression as well as the temptations created by the first signs of the consumer society. For certain social classes and in certain areas of Britain, consumer booms (notably of the 1930s and 1950s) generated both more goods for those with disposable income and the desire for more goods, which very likely resulted in increased property crime. The consumer booms and technological revolution of the post-war decades put into circulation a mass of portable, high-value goods such as televisions, radios and stereos that presented attractive new targets and new opportunities for crime. For example, car crime rose sharply because there were many more valuable cars available on every city street at all times and often unattended than there were before the Second World War.

The range of property crime activities has also broadened significantly and, in some cases, developed into sophisticated transnational businesses generating high profits. For example, car theft is no longer simply a domestic problem or the province of teenagers engaged in random acts of theft. 'Thefts to order' (especially of luxury cars) are now well organized and sophisticated operations – from the theft itself, the forging of plates and documentation, through to the smuggling of the cars across the USA–Mexican border or to 'far-flung destinations' such as Russia and China (see Box 10.1). Developments in computing and telecommunications technology have generated greater opportunities for theft and enabled new or existing forms of deviance to be carried out more extensively, more quickly, more efficiently and with greater ease of concealment (Thomas and Loader, 2000; Jewkes, 2003a).

This argument can be extended to the emergence of 'new' everyday property crimes such as bank or credit card fraud. The expansion of automated banking and the increased use of 'plastic money' have posed a new set of risks to the banking industry and customers. The fraudulent use of stolen credit and bank cards was described as one of the fastest-growing, and most favoured, of financial crimes at local and street level in many societies in the late 1980s (Tremblay, 1986). The availability of cheap technology such as swipe machines, and simple techniques such as 'skimming', which involves reading and copying secret coded details on cards, has pushed up the costs of credit card fraud even further.

BOX 10.1 The globalization of car theft

In the past, stolen vehicles generally stayed inside the country within which they were stolen or, in the case of the USA, either stayed within the country or were taken across the border to Mexico, Central America and South America. Today, however, the exporting of stolen vehicles has become a global phenomenon. Cars, motorcycles, commercial trucks and vans may be stolen in the USA and Western Europe and exported to far-flung destinations such as Eastern Europe, the Middle East, parts of Africa, and China. In Eastern Europe, for example, there has been a move towards capitalist economies and an increased demand for luxury cars such as BMWs and Mercedes since the fall of the Soviet Union in 1991. Given that the local supply of these vehicles is too small to meet demand, a market has been created for stolen vehicles imported from other countries.

Ron Clarke and Rick Brown (2003) suggest there are several other factors that contribute to the growing global problem of car theft. First, so many vehicles are driven across national borders each day that it becomes relatively easy to transport a stolen car across borders. Second, many used cars are routinely and legally shipped from one country to another, and some stolen car rings are able to set up their activities as legitimate enterprises of this type. Third, customs officials rarely examine every container routinely carried on cargo ships given the volume of global trade. Officials in the countries receiving stolen vehicles may also be corrupt, with customs officials and local police taking bribes to look the other way. Fourth, vehicle theft is not a high priority for law enforcement officials in developing countries that receive stolen vehicles because they face much more serious crime problems.

Ron Clarke and Rick Brown also point out that several groups benefit from the exporting of stolen vehicles. For example, car insurance companies often raise their rates to cover the loss of the vehicles and may increase their profits as a result. The companies that ship the stolen vehicles across oceans also make a profit. Finally, car manufacturers benefit by selling new cars to the victims whose vehicles were stolen.

Comparative experiences

With the notable exceptions of Japan and Switzerland, all the available evidence from industrialized countries points to a rapid and sustained increase in crime, especially property crime, in the post-war period. Such increases in crime have occurred not only in periods of economic downturn and depression but also during times of full employment and exceptional living standards. The 1960s were years of affluence, yet against all conventional wisdom, crime continued to rise in cities in the United States as well as in major centres of European countries.

Criminologists are divided as to the reasons behind such increase and, by implication, what should be done about it. For example, neo-conservatives such as James Q. Wilson have singled out the immediate post-war idea of a caring welfare state, the supposed permissiveness of the 1960s and the increases in crime as proof that social democratic theorizing on the causes and solutions to crime was flawed (Wilson, 1975). The focus on the falling moral standards and weakening sources of social authority (especially in family standards) as major causes of crime had a significant influence on the law-and-order agendas on both sides of the Atlantic during the Bush, Reagan and Thatcher administrations. In contrast, writing from a left realist perspective, Jock Young has argued that even an absolute increase of prosperity at a national level tells us little about material inequality in society. According to the relative deprivation thesis, people have different expectations depending on what they feel they deserve. They may compare their economic situation with that of a reference group and feel relatively deprived when these expectations are not met. The argument is that faced with signs of evident wealth and possessions in neighbouring communities, unemployed youth could be motivated to commit street and property crimes because of emotional frustration, latent animosities and lack of opportunities (Young, 1986; Lea and Young, 1984).

However, following almost universal increases in property crime during the 1970s and 1980s, recorded property crimes in the USA, Britain and other European countries have since experienced a general decline. According to the National Crime Victimization Survey in the USA, whilst property crime (comprising mainly burglary, theft and car theft) makes up slightly more than three-quarters of all crime in the United States, property crime rates have continued to decline (www.ojp.usdoj.gov/bjs). In England and Wales, property crime accounted for the majority of both British Crime Survey (BCS) and police recorded crime, but generally fell during the latter part of the twentieth century (Barclay and Tavares, 2002). This trend has continued – according to a more recent BCS, overall household acquisitive crime in England and Wales has fallen by more than half between 1995 and 2004/5 (Nicholas et al., 2005). Criminologists are divided as to the reasons behind such reductions in crime. While some American commentators have drawn attention to the tougher criminal justice policies and substantial increase in imprisonment rates as possible explanations, the experience of

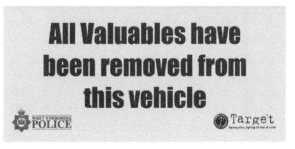

Plate 10.1 Crime prevention posters.

Source: West Yorkshire Police:
http://www.westyorkshire.police.uk/

other countries provides a counter to this. Canada's record on crime, for example, mirrors that of the United States, but without an equivalent increase in prison numbers. Variations in sentencing and imprisonment across Europe also challenge the idea that harsher punishment necessarily underlies the reduction in property crime (Barclay and Tavares, 2002).

The hidden figure of property crime

In 2005/6, property offences accounted for around 80 per cent of all recorded crimes in England and Wales. They include burglary, theft and criminal damage (robbery offences are officially categorized as crimes of violence). As a result, most of the activities of the police and other criminal justice agencies are geared towards preventing and controlling property crime (see chapters 16 and 17). Of course, interpreting official statistics is fraught with difficulties. Official crime statistics do not provide an objective and incontrovertible measure of criminal behaviour. Instead, they often fluctuate according to the organizational constraints and priorities of the criminal justice system. For example, changes in police practices and priorities will have a significant effect on the official crime data. High-profile planned operations against a particular type of offence (such as burglary, drugs or street robberies) will inevitably bring about an increase in arrests and the discovery and recording of many new offences in the targeted areas. Conversely, numbers may fall owing to a withdrawal of police interest in a particular type of crime.

Globally, around two in three victims of burglaries report their victimization to the police. According to the International Crime Victimization Survey (ICVS), the level of reporting is highest in New World nations (the United States, Canada, Australia, New Zealand) and Western Europe but much lower in Latin America, Asia and Africa, mainly because the incident seems too 'trivial' or the victim feels nothing can be done about it (Mayhew and Van Dijk, 1997). In some countries, notably in Latin America, fear or dislike of the police is also a factor. The extent of insurance cover is another important factor. In most African and many Asian and Latin American countries, only between 10 and 20 per cent of the victim survey respondents (as opposed to at least 70 per cent in most industrialized countries) are insured against household burglary. All this suggests that a hidden figure of property crime exists around the world.

The dominance of property crime in the official crime data reflects not only the prevalence of certain types of property crime but also their high reporting rates especially in industrialized countries. For instance, the British Crime Surveys (BCSs) have consistently shown that thefts of cars and burglaries in which something is stolen are almost always reported to the police, partly because of the seriousness of the offence, partly because victims who are insured need to report the crime in order to make an insurance claim. On the other hand, robbery, theft from the person, and attempted burglaries where nothing is stolen have traditionally resulted in much lower reporting and recording rates (Nicholas et al., 2005).

Cross-national comparisons of victim survey data also suggest there are significant variations in the types of goods taken in burglaries, motives behind the theft, and perceptions of the victims. In developing nations, stolen goods often include money, food and simple household objects such as cutlery or linen, most probably for personal use. One study in Central and Eastern Europe found that in many cases the burglars systematically stripped the home, even taking used clothes. 'In such cases the overall value of burglary might have been less, but the relative loss to the victim and the consequential impact of the crime might have been more pronounced' (quoted in Mawby, 2001: 41). Similarly, 42 per cent of the respondents in the ICVS in Africa considered the theft of a bicycle to be 'very serious'. This must be viewed within the social and economic context of the African society where less serious criminal events still pose very serious consequences in the lives of victims (Naudé et al., 2006). In the more affluent countries, where most people keep their money and jewellery in the bank or in safes, burglars generally give preference to objects that are easily resold such as electrical appliances, computers, hi-fi equipment, furniture and art objects.

Profile of property crime offenders

Throughout the eighteenth and nineteenth centuries, only a small number of property crimes involved large sums of money or very valuable objects, and very few cases involved violence. Perhaps unsurprisingly, most of the offenders brought before the courts in England and Wales for petty theft tended to be young, male, poorly educated (if educated at all) and poorly employed (if employed at all) in low-skilled, low-paid jobs such as labouring, domestic service and casual work. This pattern then continued into the early twenty-first century, regardless of changes in the nature of low-skilled employment. All these factors informed the overall perception of criminality and reinforced conventional understandings of 'problem populations' in society.

It is undeniable that some people commit more serious property crimes than do others, and some people are more committed to a criminal lifestyle than others. Edwin Sutherland's (1937) classic formulation of professional thieves demonstrates their characteristics as a specialist occupational group defined by a level of commitment to illegal economic activities as a means of making a living. This insight paved the way for much subsequent criminological thinking and empirical work on the 'all-purpose criminal' who makes crime a career choice and a way of life: from the 'full-time miscreants' in British towns in the early 1960s (Mack, 1964), and short-term groups drawn together for specific 'project crimes' such as the Great Train Robbery (McIntosh, 1975), to the contemporary serious crime groups (Hobbs, 1995; see also Chapter 13).

A very broad distinction can be made between professional property crime and amateur property crime. These categories reflect the different motivations, levels of temptation, degree of skill, experience and planning, and illegitimate opportunity structures. For example, Maguire (1982) has identified three types of burglar: *low level*, *middle range* and *high level*. Low-level burglars are primarily juveniles and young adults. They lack a commitment to crime and do not usually think of themselves as 'thieves'. They tend to be opportunists whose involvement in crime is usually short-lived. Middle-range burglars usually begin their criminal careers at a young age and move into and out of crime. Generally, they are older, more skilful and experienced than low-level burglars and search out targets across a wider geographic area. They also tend to have access to external sources to assist them in the sale of their stolen property. High-level burglars are well connected with sources of information about goods to steal and with 'fences' who can dispose of large quantities of stolen goods. They carefully plan their crimes and possess skills and technical expertise to overcome complex security measures.

Of course, a wide variety of offences and characteristics of offenders can be found across a spectrum of property crime. To date, research on criminal careers has tended to concentrate on (young) offenders involved in 'common' property crimes such as theft and vandalism (Farrington, 2002; Piquero et al., 2007). Little research has been done on careers in other forms of property or financial crime such as consumer fraud, tax evasion, insider trading, embezzlement or money laundering. Some of these offences can be carried out only by those who hold office in a legitimate organization or occupy an advanced position in the occupational hierarchy. Offenders may also move from one form of property crime (e.g. theft) to another (e.g. robbery), or from opportunistic offences (e.g. shoplifting) to more highly planned ones (e.g. stealing of museum pieces).

Everybody does it?

We should note that in between those deeply committed to a criminal lifestyle and those who occasionally steal or defraud lie a vast range of property criminals who are 'ordinary' or socially acceptable people. Almost two-thirds of adults interviewed in a study in England and Wales (including those in the middle classes) admitted to committing minor fraud (e.g. having paid cash in hand to evade taxes, having lied about an insurance claim, having claimed for refunds to which they are not entitled), but rarely think their behaviour is criminal (The Times, 12 September 2003: 16). Similarly, studies in Canada suggest that shoplifting costs the retail trade over $1 million each day, and that between 1 in 12 and 1 in 20 customers admit to having stolen from shops (cited in Gabor, 1994: 73–4). Skyes and Matza's (1957) concept of neutralization is useful to identify the techniques that many shoplifters use to deny or deflect blame for wrongdoing away from the perpetrator (see Chapter 5). For example, shoplifters may claim that shoplifting does not really hurt the store very much (denial of the injury caused) or that a particular store deserves to be ripped off because they exploit customers (denial of the victim). Such neutralizations allow individuals to redefine shoplifting as a more acceptable form of behaviour.

Theft by employees is also extremely widespread. In Britain the British Retail Consortium calculated that staff theft during 1997 cost shops a total of £374 million – that is, more than double the losses caused by burglaries and eight times greater than the cost of robberies (Park, 2001). The workplace has always been a key site of property crime. Indeed, Gerald Mars (1982: 1) wrote about the 'normal crimes of normal people in the normal circumstance of their work'. They include traders dealing in cash to evade VAT (value added tax), taxi drivers who fiddle their takings, warehouse employees who overload and undercharge their friends, and shop assistants and cashiers in the retail trade 'voiding' a transaction or overcharging customers and pocketing the cash.

Occupational structure is a key variable in workplace crime. Mars contends that 'fiddles' are part of the elasticity of some occupations which emphasize individual entrepreneurship, flair, adaptability and professional autonomy, and in which group control of the workforce is low. For travelling sales representatives, journalists, lawyers, health professionals, academics and other relatively independent professionals, the conditions of work may create a criminogenic environment that opens opportunities and rationalizations for rule-bending and rule-breaking. For example, store managers can 'customize' their own 'shoplifting' by recategorizing goods as old or damaged or altering stock records; journalists can fiddle their travelling expenses and slush money and rationalize these as 'perks' that come with the job. In contrast, in occupations that are highly structured and characterized by controlling rules, minimal autonomy and tight work-groups (e.g. in cargo-handling areas at airports, distribution centres and docks), fiddles often take place in the context of teamwork. Such practices are nothing new. Fiddling was common in the eighteenth century, when dockers often stole liquor, sugar or tea from cargoes as they unloaded them. Stolen items were then resold to grocers, publicans or ordinary people in the market (Emsley, 2005).

Social distribution of crime risks

Writing about the first BCS, Hough and Mayhew (1983: 15) cited the average household that could expect to be burgled 'once every 40 years'. The BCS and police recorded crime have both shown considerable falls in burglary levels since peaks in the mid-1990s. The number of domestic burglaries estimated by the BCS fell by 59 per cent from 1,770,000 in 1995 to 726,000 in 2006/7 (Nicholas *et al.*, 2007). What these statistics fail to show is that burglary is unevenly distributed across time and space. For example, researchers from the routine activity perspective have found that the patterns of burglars are often determined by the time patterns and routine activities of their victims. Residential burglary occurs disproportionately during daytime when most households are unoccupied. Studies in the USA also show that residents of large cities, renters and households headed by African Americans, Hispanics or young people are more likely than others to be burgled (Shover, 1991).

In general, the risk of property crime victimization is unevenly distributed within and between different localities and various sections of the population.

Social class

Contrary to popular belief and anxieties about crime in rural and middle-class areas, researchers in Britain have consistently found that people living in run-down inner-city areas and areas of council accommodation are particularly vulnerable to crime problems. Successive BCSs and police statistics have shown that, in general, poorer households with few home security measures in high-crime areas and areas of deprivation are most likely to experience residential burglary (Nicholas *et al.*, 2007). Foster and Hope (1993) found in their analysis of BCS data that households in council estates with the highest levels of council tenure and poverty face a risk of burglary around five times greater than tenants who live in areas with less concentrated levels of council tenure and where tenants are better off. These households are also more likely to suffer a repeat burglary and are most affected by the crime(s).

Repeat victimization occurs when the same location, person, household, business or vehicle suffers more than one crime event over a specified period of time (Pease, 1998; Simmons and Dodd, 2003: 17–18; for repeat victimization amongst retailers, see Taylor, 2004). According to the National Board for Crime Prevention (1994), 4 per cent of victims experience 44 per cent of all crimes in Britain. For those who are subject to repeat victimization, it may become virtually impossible to differentiate the impact of discrete crimes from the generally poor quality of life.

Those living in the inner city, council estates and areas of high physical disorder are also more likely than average to experience a second burglary within the year. In response, there is evidence to suggest that uninsured small businesses and young men living in deprived, high-crime areas are more likely to have purchased stolen goods as a means of minimizing their losses (Sutton, 1998).

A similar pattern has emerged from local studies in Britain, indicating not only the problem of repeat victimization but also the 'lived reality' of people at risk. By focusing on particular localities these surveys (notably in Islington (London), Merseyside, Edinburgh and Rochdale) highlighted the higher levels of crime prevailing in socially deprived areas and the disproportionate victimization of women, of ethnic minority groups and of the poor (Crawford et al., 1990; Kinsey, 1984; Mooney, 1993; Forrester et al., 1988). Significantly, such high levels of social deprivation and crime victimization are also coterminous with higher levels of poor health.

Ethnicity

According to the BCSs, ethnic minority groups (especially Pakistanis and Bangladeshis) are generally more at risk than whites of household crimes. It is, however, extremely difficult to isolate ethnicity as a discrete variable in explaining patterns of victimization. Socio-economic factors and wider processes of racialization may be at work here, if we take into account the fact that ethnic minority households are more likely than white households to experience poverty (that is, with incomes below half the national average) and to live in socially disadvantaged areas (Modood and Berthoud, 1997). Ethnic minority groups are also routinely subject to racial violence and harassment that range from murder, damage to property (including racist graffiti), to verbal and other forms of abuse of an isolated or persistent nature (see also Chapter 9).

Age

Official statistics and self-report studies indicate the prevalence of property crime in young people's everyday life. Crime statistics have consistently found the 'typical offender' to be male (over 80 per cent of offenders known to the authorities) and young. Similarly, according to a recent survey (Wilson et al., 2006), almost 1 in 4 young people in England and Wales admitted to committing at least one offence in the previous 12 months. The most commonly reported offence categories were assault and other thefts. One-fifth of 12–25-year-olds had handled (bought or sold) stolen goods. However, any focus on young people as the perpetrators of crime should not be allowed to obscure or divert our attention away from the worryingly high levels of victimization that young people suffer from their peers and adults. The BCSs have repeatedly shown that young people experience relatively more serious problems as victims of crime irrespective of class, gender or place (see Chapter 9). Few of these experiences are reported to the police, however, and youth victimization (as opposed to youth offending) remains low on the priority lists of the police and politicians.

Geography

Survey data has consistently highlighted the spatial concentration of the incidence of crime victimization – for example, in urban areas (as opposed to rural areas) and in the poorest 'striving areas' (as opposed to the wealthiest 'thriving areas').

It is not just the cities that have become synonymous with the 'crime problem'. Geographical research on crime and the use of computer-generated analyses of patterns of reported crime in different local police force areas (e.g. Crime Pattern Analysis) have pointed to particular concentrations of so-called 'hotspots' of crime. Research evidence in the United States and Britain suggests that even high-crime areas have their relatively safe micro-locations as well as their specific 'trouble-spot' areas (Sherman, 1995; Hope, 1985; Hirschfield *et al.*, 1995).

BOX 10.2 Key developments in the law and punishment of property crime in Britain

1808	Repeal of capital punishment for pickpockets.
1820	Repeal of capital punishment for stealing in shops.
1861 and 1916	Larceny Acts cover many types of stealing and provide for greater or lesser penalties depending on the nature of the property stolen, the place, the relationship between the thief and owner.
1968 and 1978	Theft Acts codify all offences against property and create a simplified definition of theft covering all types of stealing, embezzlement and fraud. The maximum sentence for theft is 10 years' imprisonment, 14 years for burglary and life imprisonment for robbery.
1971	Criminal Damage Act – maximum punishment for damage to property is 10 years' imprisonment, life imprisonment for arson.
1981	Forgery and Counterfeiting Act.
1991	Criminal Justice Act reduces the maximum sentence for theft from 10 to 7 years' imprisonment.
1997	Crime (Sentences) Act increases prison sentences for certain categories of offenders, including a minimum of three years for a third offence of domestic burglary.
2003	Criminal Justice Act provides a wider and more varied range of short custodial sentences (e.g. 'Custody Plus', 'Intermittent Custody') for offenders (including non-violent but persistent offenders).

Writing from a different perspective, Ian Taylor (1997, 1999) highlights the shifting 'urban fortunes' behind the massive increase in crime in specific localities and regions in Britain from the late 1980s to early 1990s. For Taylor, the levels of crime in different localities are related to their varied capacities for responding to global economic competition, deindustrialization and post-industrial restructuring. For example, industrial areas in northern England (such as South Yorkshire) which suffered the most recent loss of what was locally assumed to have been a secure labour market experienced the highest rates of increase in crime. On the other hand, Greater Manchester, 'the "youth capital" of the North of England with one of the largest post-Fordist labour markets in the North', had the smallest increases in property crime and crime in general (I. Taylor, 1999: 134). Yet such 'new leisure zones' and their thriving alcohol-oriented night-time economy have other well-documented problems of violence and disorder (Hobbs *et al.*, 2000; see also chapters 8 and 14).

Controlling property crime

Our ideas about property crime (what form does it take?) and property crime offenders (who are they?) have also shaped our responses to the problem. 'Common' property offences such as petty theft, burglary and forgery were among the 200 or so offences punishable by death under the 'Bloody Code' in the eighteenth century. For example, the shoplifting of goods worth five shillings was a capital offence, as was stealing sheep or cattle. Transportation to penal colonies and prison were also used to punish a range of offenders. Indeed, prisons of different varieties have since emerged to occupy a central role in the criminal justice system even though their precise function and effectiveness are still subject to intense political and academic debate (see Chapter 18). Then as now, it was the 'quantity' rather than 'quality' of the offences that most concerned the public, legislators, the police and commentators on crime alike. The main exception was the periodic panic about violent street robberies (also known as 'garotting', or 'mugging' in the contemporary context) that prompted the revival of whipping for adults in the 1860s (Rawlings, 1999: 100, n. 1). Legislation and its enforcement were slow in keeping pace with the opportunities for large-scale theft, fraud and embezzlement provided by the expansion and development of the business and financial world during the nineteenth and early twentieth centuries (as they still are) (Robb, 1992; and see Chapter 13).

As Steven Box (1983) and others have indicated, there is considerable inconsistency in the way in which the criminal justice system perceives and treats 'the crimes of the powerless' as opposed to 'the crimes of the powerful' – business offenders. For example, if one measures the significance of property offences in terms of the value stolen, rather than the quantity of incidents, fraud has far greater importance than other categories. As Mike Levi (1993) points out, in April 1992 the Frauds Divisions of the Crown Prosecution Service were supervising cases involving nearly £4 billion. By contrast, the combined costs of the vast number of vehicle offences and burglaries for 1990 were estimated by the Association of British Insurers at under £1.3 billion.

Critics argue that the concentration of criminal justice responses against low-level property crime offenders has impacted most on those who are already economically and socially marginalized. For example, studies have shown that the rise in women's prosecutions in Britain from the 1980s onwards has gone hand in hand with the continuing and worsening levels of female poverty (Carlen, 1988, 1998; Pantazis, 1999; Heidensohn, 2006). Similarly, the steep increases in the numbers of women received into prisons from the 1990s in Britain have been linked to a more punitive sentencing culture, the increased numbers of women in the categories of economic and social deprivation who have been traditionally more vulnerable to imprisonment, and the increased use of custody for women convicted of theft, handling stolen goods and fraud (Carlen, 1998: 56; Player, 2005).

BOX 10.3 Looting and state negligence

When property crime takes on a more spectacular form, it forces us to reconsider our conventional assumptions about criminals, victims and the role of the state.

One of the aftermaths of Hurricane Katrina in flood-stricken New Orleans in the USA in August 2005 is looting and lawlessness. More than a million people were evacuated from New Orleans and the surrounding areas before the hurricane struck, but Mayor Ray Nagin has estimated that up to 100,000 people decided to stay in the city. There is a feeling of foreboding as those marooned become more desperate. There is no electricity, and people who have lost everything are struggling to find food and clean water. There are reports of shootings, carjackings and thefts across the city. President Bush condemned the acts and called for 'zero tolerance' against law-breakers. People have faced shoot-outs and some reports say martial law has been imposed in some areas. Armed gangs have moved into some hotels. Some have been breaking into shops, houses, hospitals and office buildings. Thieves used a forklift truck to break into a pharmacy while dozens of carjackings have been reported.

In Mississippi, curfews are in place as the authorities try to prevent the scale of looting seen in New Orleans. In Houston, where thousands of refugees have been taken, the *Houston Chronicle* puts the blame for the disintegration of civilization in New Orleans on inadequate protection by the government. 'Looting and violence are unconscionable but were invited by the failure of federal, state and local authorities to reassert order or even provide basic sustenance for storm survivors,' it says.

Source: BBC News August 2005: http://news.bbc.co.uk

Other forms of property crime

So far we have concentrated on the more conventional forms of crime against property in everyday life. There are of course other forms of property crime with equally, if not more, harmful impact on individuals and communities alike.

Theft and illegal export of cultural property

The theft of **cultural property** is flourishing and now constitutes a major form of transnational crime. **Cultural property** can be defined as movable or immovable property of great importance to the cultural heritage of every people. It can include monuments such as architectural works, sculptures, paintings, manuscripts, structures of an archaeological nature, cave dwellings, and sites that are significant from the historical, aesthetic, ethnological or anthropological points of view. In Iraq, for example, priceless statues, ancient manuscripts (including one of the oldest surviving copies of the Koran) and other treasures were destroyed or stolen from the museums and libraries in a wave of looting and lawlessness following the collapse of the government of Saddam Hussein in Baghdad. Although looting of art treasures has long been a feature of warfare, illegal excavation and trade in stolen art and antiquities have been spurred by increasing pressure from the international art market. Crimes against **cultural property** have the potential for robbing entire cultures and nations of their cultural heritage (United Nations Educational, Scientific and Cultural Organization, 1997). In African countries such as Mali, the purchase for illegal export of cultural objects and looting of archaeological sites has increased rapidly since the 1970s. Objects tend to acquire higher prices the further they travel from 'home'. Art treasures, human remains, religious relics and sacred objects, furniture, and cultural objects in Nigeria, South Africa, Asia, Latin America, former Soviet-bloc countries and, to some extent, Western European countries such as Italy and Britain have been targeted in recent years (Box 10.4). Archaeological sites in the USA have also been looted and vandalized in the hunt for the best 'marketable' Native American artefacts.

The international trade in stolen, smuggled and looted art is estimated to be worth US$4.5–6 billion dollars per year (*New York Times*, 20 November 1995). Elaborate methods of distributing stolen art are often used to conceal the origin of the objects; as a result, it can take years to resolve disputes over the ownership of such art. For example, the Lydian Hoard, a collection of

BOX 10.4 Crime against cultural property

The British Parliamentary Report on Cultural Property: Return and Illicit Trade (2000) highlights the massive scale and impact of illicit excavations around the world. For example, the looting of the Early Bronze Age cemeteries of the Cycladic Islands in the Aegean may have resulted in the loss of 85 per cent of the relevant archaeological contents, and over 1,000 pieces of pottery worth about US$10 million are smuggled out of the Mayan region of Central America every month. Looting of sites in Italy is also a serious problem. A 1998 raid on a villa in Sicily seized some 30,000 Phoenician, Greek and Roman antiquities that were valued at US$20 million. The illegal trade, export and smuggling of Egyptian antiquities for sale abroad are known to cause substantial and irrevocable damage to Egypt's cultural heritage. The report suggests that England is one of the largest markets for illicitly traded property. Studies of antiquities from celebrated private collections in public exhibitions in Britain and North America during the 1990s, and the sale of antiquities in the London antiquities market suggest that an alarmingly high percentage of these objects had no provenance and history.

ancient treasures looted in Turkey, was purchased by New York's Metropolitan Museum of Art in the 1960s. It took the Turkish government almost 20 years to trace the whereabouts of the objects and another six years of legal action before the museum finally agreed to repatriate the objects. The illicit art market is populated by a mix of criminal organizations, individual thieves, 'fences' who act as the middle person, and unscrupulous collectors as well as legitimate traders such as antique dealers and institutions, including reputable auction houses (Conklin, 1994). This is yet another example of the symbiosis between legitimate and criminal activity, just like the cross-over activities in the entertainment and gambling industries, the arms trade and many other areas (see Chapter 13).

Theft of intellectual property

Theft of intangible property, such as copyright infringement, counterfeiting of trademarks and making patented products, exists at different levels, from the individual computer owners who illegally copy video games or music at home (see Chapter 20) to the organized groups that engage in large-scale counterfeiting and smuggling.

Counterfeiting is a major activity for professional criminals in Britain, and has links globally, involving production of goods or currency and then distribution. Generally low risks and high profit margins make counterfeiting a very lucrative activity. Fake designer label clothing and other luxury items, counterfeit computer software and large-scale illegal reproduction of popular CDs and DVDs are well-known examples. Some counterfeit luxury items may be produced in the same factories as legitimate goods in developing countries, which in turn raises broader questions about consumer products, value and neo-liberal capitalism. More everyday items such as soap powder, toys, shampoos, cleaning products and even tea bags have also been subject to counterfeit and have resulted in injury (Croall, 1997). Currency counterfeiting faces the problem that daily use of money makes fake versions harder to pass, but this does not mean that such counterfeit circulation is uncommon.

BOX 10.5 Jail for forgery clan who flooded Britain with counterfeit £20 notes

Nine members of a gang of money forgers, including three generations of the same family, were jailed for up to seven years yesterday for what the prosecution claimed was Britain's biggest ever counterfeiting operation.

Two-thirds of all the fake £20 notes circulating in 2005 were produced by the gang and the Bank of England recovered more than £14m . . . All the defendants admitted conspiracy to counterfeit notes. Passing sentence, Judge William Kennedy said: 'Each of you who participated in these conspiracies were part of the biggest and most effective counterfeiting operation ever encountered by the Bank of England.

'At first sight, someone who had given little thought to the true nature of this enterprise might ask why this sort of offence is regarded with such seriousness. With an economy measured in trillions of pounds, does counterfeiting, even of tens of millions of pounds, really matter? The answer to that is a resounding yes – it matters enormously. This is not some quaint cottage industry organised by otherwise law-abiding citizens to eke out in an unusual way a few extra pounds to spend. This is a prime example of organised crime.' It would also have helped to fund organised crime, he said.

The judge added: 'It is for all those reasons that counterfeiting has for hundreds of years been regarded as an offence of great seriousness.' In medieval times offenders were charged with treason.

Tim Cray, prosecuting, told the court: 'This is believed to be the largest counterfeiting case ever to come before the courts in this jurisdiction. This conspiracy was regarded by the fiscal authorities as a threat of the highest order to the banking system. It also involved the production of counterfeit notes on an industrial scale and was organised by dedicated and resourceful criminals.'

He added: 'The impossibility of estimating the number of notes that might remain in circulation is in itself an indication of the effectiveness of the counterfeiting.'

Source: *The Guardian*, Friday 24 November 2006.

So who suffers and who benefits from the global trade in counterfeit goods? The answer is not always so clear-cut. Manufacturers and consumers (especially the poorer consumers who buy substandard or even dangerous counterfeit goods) are generally considered to be the 'legitimate' victims (see Chapter 9). But what about those working in factories with substandard conditions and pay? According to the World Health Organization, there is widespread availability of counterfeited medicines in developing countries for the treatment of life-threatening conditions such as malaria, tuberculosis and HIV/AIDS. In Nigeria, for example, shortages of drugs and other technologies in the medical care system have led to the sale of 'counterfeit, substandard and otherwise dangerous substances', accounting for as much as 60–70 per cent of all drugs, and causing many instances of drug poisoning and death (Alubo, 1994: 97–8; and see Chapter 14). On the other hand, the counterfeiting industry arguably enables those who cannot afford the full prices to obtain similar consumer products and provides income for the unemployed, especially workers in developing nations.

Biopiracy

Finally, the question of 'who is the offender?' becomes even more contentious when applied to other non-conventional forms of property. 'Biopiracy' is a term that has been given to the practices of some companies that have asserted the right of ownership over genetic materials taken from living organisms (Manning, 2000). For instance, patent law has been extended in recent years in such a way as to allow the ownership of DNA, cell lines and other biological materials. It has become possible for transnational corporations to 'own' DNA sequences and modified genes of animals and plants and to make significant profits through royalty charges for their use. Supporters of patent law point out that weak intellectual property regimes could foreclose opportunities for biotechnology research and product development. High research costs can drive up the price of the end products, many of which are important for public health needs.

Critics, however, argue that the patenting of medicines, seeds, plants and – potentially – higher life forms by multinational corporations amounts to biopiracy and can have particularly serious consequences for the developing countries. For example, the Africa Group in the World Trade Organization has highlighted the serious implications that patents on seeds of staple food crops would have on the rights of indigenous communities to food security. It proposed that the mandated review of the Agreement on Trade-Related Aspects of Intellectual Property Rights should make clear that plants, animals and micro-organisms and their parts, and all living processes, cannot be patented. To some extent, these issues are related to the over-exploitation of the earth and its resources especially by those in a position of power; they have prompted some criminologists to reappraise more traditional notions of crimes and injurious behaviours and to examine the role that transnational corporations and governments play in creating 'green crimes' (see Chapter 19).

New horizons in understanding property crime

There is no doubt property crime makes up an inordinate amount of reported and unreported crime. As Part 2 of this book shows, criminological explanations of why individuals commit property crime span a variety of perspectives from the dispositions of the individual offender to the social conditions associated with crime. For some offenders, survival, subsistence and drug habits may well be the primary motivations for committing property crime. Other criminologists have argued that crimes such as shoplifting have to be understood in the broader context of the creation of needs, the structuring of consumption and the commodification of desire under late capitalism. Yet these societal processes alone cannot explain the meaning or the attractions of criminality.

Cultural criminologists (see Chapter 12) argue that criminology has traditionally under-estimated the attractions in doing wrong or living 'on the edge'. The concept of 'edgework' was first put forward by the sociologist Stephen Lyng (1990; Lyng and Snow, 1986) in his analysis of voluntary risk-taking. He argues that 'edgework' can be understood as 'a type of experiential anarchy in which the individual moves beyond the realm of established social patterns to the very fringes of ordered reality' (Lyng, 1990: 882). Edgework activities that involve an observable threat to one's physical or mental well-being can be best illustrated by dangerous sports (such as skydiving, hang-gliding and rock-climbing) or by dangerous occupations (such as fire-fighting, combat soldiering, movie stunt work). More generally, edgework can also take the form of excessive drug use (which involves negotiating the boundary between sanity and insanity) or marathon running (which tests the limits of body). Lyng (1990: 863) argues that voluntary risk-taking provides 'a heightened sense of self and a feeling of omnipotence' for those who succeed in getting as close as possible to the edge without 'going over it'.

These ideas have been further developed by cultural criminologists such as Jeff Ferrell and Jack Katz. Katz (1988: 54) suggests that shoplifting can be understood as a version of a 'thrilling and sensually gratifying game'. It can be rewarding beyond the monetary gains – for example, providing the feelings of accomplishment when a theft is successful. Katz found that expressive motivations were highly prevalent in his interview data obtained from well-off college student shoplifters. Studies also found that burglars frequently cited excitement as part of their motivation, while others targeted occupied homes because such burglaries provide an 'illicit adventure' (cited in Mawby, 2001: 69).

Similarly, if we turn to the world of business, bank fraud, price-fixing or manipulating the stock market, all contain elements of the thrills and spills of risk-taking common to other aspects of social life. As Stan Cohen (1973b: 622) reminds us, 'some of our most cherished social values – individualism, masculinity, competitiveness – are the same ones that generate crime'. Indeed, it is the excitement and a sense of machismo in beating the competition in our 'enterprise' culture that arguably induces some managers and young city professionals to perform 'dirty deeds' in covert business activities – for example, to act as spies, phone-tappers, computer hackers, safe-breakers, forgers and saboteurs (Punch, 2000).

Property crime also has to be understood within the context of the expansion of the hidden economy and increased blurring of boundaries between employment and unemployment and between legal and illegal work. Hutton's (1995) influential '40:30:30' thesis argued that in an increasingly polarized society (only 40 per cent of the population have secure employment, while the others are split between those in insecure employment and a marginalized underclass of the unemployed), the gap between benefit entitlements and realistic standards of living in a consumer-oriented society is widening. Subsequent critics have quarrelled over the exact figures (Young, 2007a: 60), but the underlying social processes continue to divide the world. In particular, commentators have argued that those young people who are without the protection of employment, family and welfare, or are trapped in the 'magic roundabout' of different training and enterprise schemes, are most likely to adopt one of the transient lifestyles or alternative 'careers' thrown up by local hidden economies, including 'fencing' stolen goods, 'hustling', unlicensed street trading, or acting as 'lookouts' or 'touts' (Carlen, 1996; Craine, 1997). Perhaps more significantly, many of these illegal activities are not considered as crime, just 'ordinary work' (Foster, 1990: 165; Taylor and Jamieson, 1997). All this points to the need to understand crime as a 'normal' rather than an 'exceptional' social phenomenon (Hall, 2012).

Although property crime has been a constant focus of public and political attention, this chapter suggests that there is no singular 'crime problem' as such. Instead, there is a wide spectrum of illicit behaviour, misconduct, troubling and alarming events that are widespread and constantly occurring, and a variety of ways of conceiving of and thinking about everyday property crime.

Summary

1   Official statistics and victimization surveys have consistently indicated the prevalence of various types of property crime over time, among different social groups and across societies.
2   This is evident in the vast range of illegal activities committed by the general public, the hidden and petty-criminal economies of everyday survival, the crimes committed by respectable people in the normal circumstances of their everyday jobs and by those who simply get a buzz out of leading life 'on the edge'.
3   While the risks of victimization and the impact of property crime remain highly differentiated and unevenly distributed, research studies have generally pointed to the higher levels of property crime prevailing in socially deprived areas and the disproportionate victimization of the poor, of young people and of minority ethnic groups.
4   Against a background of social change and technological advances, the range of property crime activities has broadened significantly or even developed into transnational businesses. New or existing forms of property crime can also be carried out more extensively, more quickly, more efficiently and with greater ease of concealment.
5   In addition to crimes that take place in the street or are directed at households, property crime also includes theft and illegal export of cultural property and theft of intellectual property. A critical study of these forms of crime requires reappraisal of more traditional notions of offending, harmful behaviour and property.

Critical thinking questions

1   **What evidence is there to suggest that many crimes against property are committed by socially acceptable people in their everyday life?**
2   **What are the limitations of the official picture of property crime?**
3   **How might criminological research advance our understanding of previously hidden forms of property crime around the world?**
4   **Discuss how techniques of neutralization could be applied to the following acts: (a) theft by employees, (b) selling of DVDs that infringe copyright.**

Further study

Emsley, C. (2005) *Crime and Society in England 1750–1900*, 3rd edn, London: Longman. An accessible introduction to the history of the crime problem, perceptions of criminality and changes in the courts, the police and the system of punishment.
Mawby, R. (2001) *Burglary*, Cullompton: Willan. A useful overview of the key aspects of the problem of burglary and some of the developments and research studies in policy responses.

Newman, G. (ed.) (1999) *Global Report on Crime and Justice*, New York: Oxford University Press. A comprehensive text from the United Nations on crime, criminal justice and international crime victimization surveys.

Shover, N. (1996) *Great Pretenders: Pursuits and Games of Persistent Thieves*, Boulder, CO: Westview Press. A fascinating book on the criminal pathways and decision-making of offenders based on original studies and autobiographies of persistent thieves in the USA.

Useful websites

The Home Office: Research Development Statistics – Publications
http://www.homeoffice.gov.uk/rds/bcs.html
The National British Crime Survey provides up-to-date annual information on different types of crime, including property crime, which may or may not be reported to and recorded by the police. Full reports and summaries of BCS findings and many other research studies funded by the Home Office can be found here.

International Crime Victims Survey
http://www.unicri.it/icvs/
Information, publications and statistics on international crime victimization surveys are available at this site.

chapter 11

Crime, Sexuality and Gender

Key issues

- What are the major patterns of crimes linked to sex?
- How do they link to gender?
- Why do they provoke such hysteria?
- How are sex crimes changing?
- What can be done about them?

Introduction

In the grand sweep of crime, sex offences are officially not as common as many other offences. The UK Home Office recorded 54,982 sex offences for 2010–11 – this amounts to around just 5 per cent of all violent crime. However, these crimes continue to provoke a great deal of anxiety and concern. For reasons discussed in Chapter 3, being precise about criminal statistics is very difficult but figures for serious sexual offences including both female and male rape have been increasing over the last decade despite the fact that these cases remain severely under-reported. There is always a large hidden figure of crime, but in the case of sex offences such problems may be magnified because many victims do not wish to report the crimes at all – finding the glare of public recognition and scrutiny too traumatic. In some cases – often involving under-age offences – victims may not be aware that a crime has been committed. Even when a crime is reported, getting a conviction may be difficult; according to the Fawcett Society, a UK women's rights organization, only 1 in 20 rapes reported to the police leads to a conviction. In their recent study Lovett and Kelly (2009) also found that attrition rates in England and Wales were very low and that there was: '[A] virtually continuous year-on-year rise in reporting and only a nominal increase in prosecutions and convictions, with the effect of an ever-decreasing conviction rate' (2009: 45; also see Figure 11.1).

Sometimes the accusations made by women in rape cases are not taken seriously. As the late Sue Lees (1996a: x–xi) argued, from her extensive analysis of the police, courts and victims in London:

> [I]t is simply inconceivable that the vast majority of women who report rape to the police are lying. Moreover, there is evidence that those women who do report are merely the tip of the iceberg, and yet this tip is further decimated as the criminal justice system runs its course.

The evidence therefore, suggests that sexual offences, especially rape, are under-reported and when they are recorded the attrition rate is high. Many feminists and criminologists have considered ways to understand these anomalies.

Understanding sex offences: sex crimes, gender and violence

There are two major sets of explanations that have been used to understand an array of sex offenders. The first sets out psychological and psychiatric problems (for overview see Holmes and Holmes, 2008). With extreme cases of psychopathological sex killers, these probably have some major validity. But many sex crimes are much more common and 'everyday' than this. The most conspicuous feature of these crimes is that they are overwhelmingly committed by men. James Messerschmidt suggests that many sex offences originate with the 'ordinary' violence of boys. He suggests that:

> approximately 25 percent of adult male sex offenders report that their first sexual offence occurred during adolescence. Moreover a significant proportion of all male sexual offences are committed by persons under the age of eighteen.
>
> (Messerschmidt, 2000: 3–4)

In many ways, sociologists see sex crimes as a way of 'doing gender'. Messerschmidt has powerfully merged ideas of 'structured action' and 'doing gender' to show the ways in which men can draw upon social resources in the wider culture to give different meanings to their masculinities and to make sense of various criminal actions. Certain boys use sexual and assaultive violence as what might be called a 'masculine practice'. For example recent news reports have indicated some girls and young women who join gangs may experience high levels of sexual abuse as initiation into gang membership or as a more permanent form of social control within the gang culture.

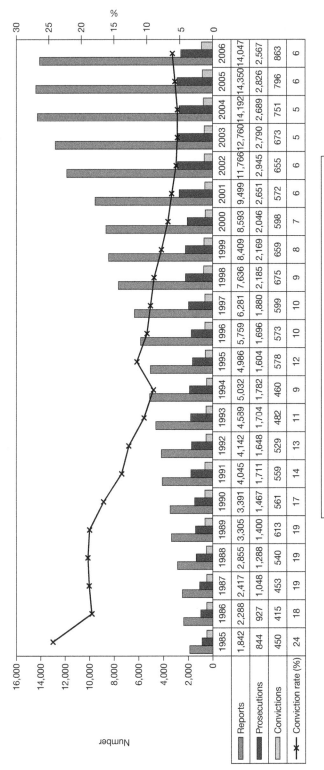

	1985	1986	1987	1988	1989	1990	1991	1992	1993	1994	1995	1996	1997	1998	1999	2000	2001	2002	2003	2004	2005	2006
Reports	1,842	2,288	2,417	2,855	3,305	3,391	4,045	4,142	4,589	5,032	4,986	5,759	6,281	7,636	8,409	8,593	9,499	11,766	12,760	14,192	14,350	14,047
Prosecutions	844	927	1,048	1,288	1,400	1,467	1,711	1,648	1,704	1,782	1,604	1,696	1,880	2,185	2,169	2,046	2,651	2,945	2,790	2,689	2,826	2,567
Convictions	450	415	453	540	613	561	559	529	482	460	578	573	599	675	659	598	572	655	673	751	796	863
Conviction rate (%)	24	18	19	19	19	17	14	13	11	9	12	10	10	9	8	7	6	6	5	5	6	6

Figure 11.1 Reports, prosecutions and convictions for rape in England and Wales, 1985–2006.

Source: Lovett and Kelly (2009: 45, fig. 5.6); Kelly et al. (2005) supplemented by latest figures supplied by RDS – Office for Criminal Justice Reform.

Notes: Cases include minors. Data are collated on the principal offence rule, so only the most serious offence with which an offender is charged is included. Excludes convictions on lower offences.

BOX 11.1 Two social theories of sexuality

Gagnon and Simon's *Sexual Conduct* (1973/2005) is one of the landmark texts in the sociology of sexuality and is seen as the foundational text of what is now commonly known as the 'social constructionist' approach to sexuality. Gagnon and Simon claim that there is no one, unified pattern of sexuality; instead, there are 'many ways to become, to be, to act, to feel sexual. There is no one human sexuality, but rather a wide variety of sexualities' (Gagnon, 1973/2005, preface).

Three of their main themes will help us think about sexuality and crime:

- *Beware of the biological: it claims too much*. Sex crimes are rarely a matter of sex being a simple biological release. In contrast to classic ways of thinking about sexuality as biological, bodily and 'natural' – as *essentially* given – Gagnon and Simon aimed to show the ways in which human sexualities are always organized through economic, religious, political, familial and social conditions; any analysis that does not recognize this must be seriously flawed. Sexuality, for humans, is never just a free-floating desire. It is always grounded in wider material and cultural forces.
- *Look for the symbols and meanings*. Human sexualities are always symbolic. With sex crimes we should always be looking out for motivations that are not simply or straightforwardly sexual. Sex may be performed out of rage, as aggression, as a hunt, as a hobby, because of a scarring experience, as a mode of transgression, as a form of violence.
- *Examine sexual scripts*. Human sexualities – including sex crimes – are probably best seen as evolving through scripts that suggest the Who? What? Where? When? and Why? of sexual conduct as they guide our sexualities at personal, interactional and cultural-historical levels.

A second major contribution comes from the French historian of ideas Michel Foucault (introduced in Chapter 6). He argued that sexuality 'is the name given to a historical construct . . . a great surface network in which the stimulation of bodies, the intensification of pleasures, the incitement to discourse, the formation of knowledge, the strengthening of controls and resistances, are linked to one another, in accordance with a few major strategies of power' (Foucault, 1978: 106). Startlingly challenging conventional wisdom, he attacked the notion that sex had been repressed in the Victorian world, and claimed instead that sexuality in this period was a discursive fiction which had actually organized the social problems of the time. New species – like the homosexual, the pervert, the masturbating child, the Malthusian couple, the hysterical woman – had literally been invented and come into being as organizing motifs for sexual problems and the spread of surveillance and regulation. The body had become a site for disciplinary practices and new technologies.

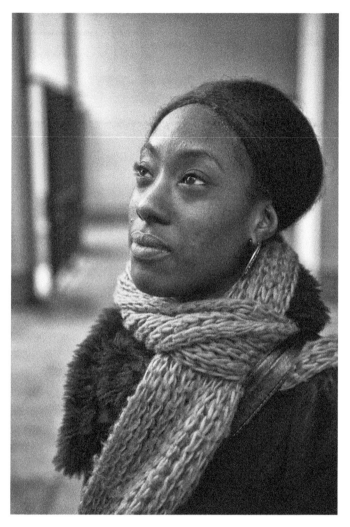

Plate 11.1 Isha Goodman, 20, former gang member who has turned her life around.

Source: Published in *The Observer*, 19 February 2012; *photo:* by Antonio Olmos for *The Observer*. Copyright Guardian News & Media Ltd 2012.

While uncovering exploitative crime against women and girls is to be welcomed, such media reports of sex crime can sometimes unduly raise public anxiety and lead to moral panics (see Chapter 20).

Feminist perspectives

Messerschmidt's (2000) notion of 'masculine practice' connects closely with how many feminists have understood sexual violence. Most sex offences, far from being pathological, are intentional behaviour chosen by men as part of their attempt to construct their masculinity as dominant and powerful. Likewise, sexual abuse is understood as an expression of masculinity, of men's desire to be in control and dominant, and it is intimately connected to normal relations within society.

Table 11.1 Recorded sexual crime by number of offences 1997 to 2010/11 and percentage change between 2009/10 and 2010/11, England and Wales

Number and Percentage charges

England and Wales, Recorded crime

Offence	1997	1998/99	1999/00	2000/01	2001/02	2002/03	2003/04	2004/05	2005/06	2006/07	2007/08	2008/09	2009/10	2010/11	% change 2009/10 to 2010/11
17 Indecent assault on a male	**3,503**	**3,683**	**3,614**	**3,530**	**3,611**	**4,132**	**4,110**	**1,003**	**347**	**76**	**209**	**158**	–	–	–
17A Sexual assault on a male aged 13 and over	–	–	–	–	–	–	–	1,316	1,428	1,450	1,323	1,161	1,208	1,287	7
17B Sexual assault on a male child under 13	–	–	–	–	–	–	–	1,227	1,394	1,237	1,121	1,004	1,054	1,125	7
19A Rape of a female	**6,281**	**7,132**	**7,809**	**7,929**	**9,002**	**11,445**	**12,378**	**693**	**61**	**25**	**145**	**170**	–	–	–
19C Rape of a female aged 16 and over	–	–	–	–	–	–	–	8,192	8,725	8,222	7,610	7,768	9,038	9,509	5
19D Rape of a female child under 16	–	–	–	–	–	–	–	3,014	3,153	2,853	2,422	2,537	2,909	2,880	–1
19E Rape of a female child under 13	–	–	–	–	–	–	–	970	1,388	1,524	1,487	1,658	1,964	2,235	14
Rape of a female	**6,281**	**7,132**	**7,809**	**7,929**	**9,002**	**11,445**	**12,378**	**12,869**	**13,327**	**12,624**	**11,664**	**12,133**	**13,911**	**14,624**	**5**
19B Rape of a male	**347**	**504**	**600**	**664**	**732**	**850**	**894**	**81**	**22**	**18**	**10**	**22**	–	–	–
19F Rape of a male aged 16 and over	–	–	–	–	–	–	–	444	438	413	332	317	368	392	7
19G Rape of a male child under 16	–	–	–	–	–	–	–	322	292	261	237	216	241	247	2
19H Rape of a male child under 13	–	–	–	–	–	–	–	297	364	458	430	408	564	671	19
Rape of a male	**347**	**504**	**600**	**664**	**732**	**850**	**894**	**1,144**	**1,116**	**1,150**	**1,009**	**963**	**1,173**	**1,310**	**12**
20 Indecent assault on a female	**18,674**	**19,524**	**20,664**	**20,301**	**21,789**	**25,275**	**27,240**	**5,152**	**1,215**	**267**	**768**	**575**	–	–	–
20A Sexual assault on a female aged 13 and over	–	–	–	–	–	–	–	15,087	17,158	16,883	15,793	15,500	15,694	16,358	4
20B Sexual assault on a female child under 13	–	–	–	–	–	–	–	4,391	4,647	4,245	3,984	3,665	4,149	4,301	4
21 Unlawful sexual intercourse with a girl under 13	**148**	**153**	**181**	**155**	**169**	**183**	**212**	–	–	–	–	–	–	–	–
21 Sexual activity involving a child under 13	–	–	–	–	–	–	–	1,510	1,950	1,936	1,836	1,650	1,819	1,773	–3
22 Unlawful sexual intercourse with a girl under 16	**1,112**	**1,135**	**1,270**	**1,237**	**1,328**	**1,515**	**1,911**	**436**	**138**	**67**	**33**	**51**	–	–	–
22B Sexual activity involving a child under 16	–	–	–	–	–	–	–	2,546	3,283	3,208	3,123	3,318	3,986	4,033	1

Code	Offence													% change
22A	Causing sexual activity without consent	–	–	–	–	–	–	–	239	224	217	151	129	167	29
70	**Sexual activity etc. with a person with a mental disorder**	–	–	–	–	–	–	104	139	163	127	131	124	**129**	**4**
71	Abuse of children through prostitution and pornography	–	–	–	–	–	–	99	124	101	108	116	134	152	13
72	Trafficking for sexual exploitation	–	–	–	–	–	–	21	33	43	57	52	58	67	16
74	**Gross indecency with a child**	1,269	1,293	1,365	1,336	1,654	1,917	1,987	398	120	64	149	121	–	–
	Most serious sexual crime	31,334	33,424	35,503	35,152	38,285	45,317	47,163	47,542	43,738	41,521	40,749	43,439	**45,326**	**4**
16	**Buggery**	645	566	437	401	355	287	247	73	35	49	36	36	49	–
18	**Gross indecency between males**	520	354	286	167	163	245	260	20	12	17	14	–	–	–
23	Incest or familial sexual offences	183	139	121	80	92	99	713	966	1,344	1,125	1,041	1,111	808	–27
24	Exploitation of prostitution	131	138	215	129	127	186	117	153	190	184	173	148	153	3
25	**Abduction of female**	277	240	251	262	291	403	86	36	21	4	4	4	4	4
27	Soliciting for the purpose of prostitution	1,107	973	1,028	1,655	2,111	1,944	1,821	1,640	1,290	1,216	1,071	1,190	826	–31
73	Abuse of position of trust of a sexual nature	–	–	–	12	417	678	792	682	361	328	195	185	146	–21
88A	Sexual grooming	–	–	–	–	–	237	186	322	313	274	313	397	310	–22
88B	**Other miscellaneous sexual offences**	10,327	9,476	8,647	9,735	9,873	11,593	11,363	10,209	8,848	–	–	–	–	–
88C	Other miscellaneous sexual offences	–	–	–	–	–	–	–	–	–	–	298	354	199	–44
88D	**Unnatural sexual offences**	–	–	–	–	–	–	–	–	–	–	5	15	12	–
88E	Exposure and voyeurism	–	–	–	–	–	–	–	–	–	–	7,530	7,516	7,202	4
	Other sexual offences	1,756	12,948	11,682	10,726	11,296	13,573	13,810	14,917	15,320	13,784	12,045	10,916	9,656	–12
	TOTAL SEXUAL OFFENCES	33,090	46,372	47,185	45,878	49,581	58,890	62,080	62,542	62,862	57,522	51,429	54,355	**54,982**	**1**

Source: http://www.homeoffice.gov.uk/publications/science-research-statistics/research-statistics/crime-research/hosb1011/

Chaplin et al. (2011) *Crime in England and Wales, 2010/11: Findings from the BCS and Police Recorded Crime* (HOSB:10/11), table 2.04, p. 43 in printed document.

Feminist sociological and socio-legal theories often link crime to masculinities (see Chapter 6). Important here are the workings of **patriarchies**: systems of male dominance that serve the interests of men. Power plays a key role in understanding sex offending, ranging from sexual violence to prostitution and pornography. Some US feminists such as Andrea Dworkin and Catharine MacKinnon have claimed that sexuality is organized by men for men and have denounced both 'heterosexuality' and heterosexual intercourse (for discussion, see Jackson and Scott, 1996).

The problem of violence against women includes several conceptually distinct yet overlapping concerns, which include rape, incest, battering, sexual harassment and pornography. English feminist sociologist Liz Kelly (1988) has argued that there is in fact a 'continuum of sexual violence', which ranges from the everyday abuse of women in pornographic images, sexist jokes, sexual harassment and women's engagement in compliant but unwanted marital sex, through to the 'non-routine' episodes of rape, incest, battery and sex murder. Kelly, with other feminists, highlights the research data suggesting most women have experienced some form of sexual violence. Sexual violence occurs in the context of men's power and women's resistance. Women are not passive victims. Feminist work has emphasized that they are 'survivors', with active agency, and that survival involves a rejection of self-blame, for once the abuse is made visible, it can be understood as precisely that, abuse.

Some recent feminist work departs from these kinds of studies by focusing on the role of women as perpetrators of violence and child abuse. Turton (2008), for example, shows that although child sexual abuse has been perceived as an almost exclusively male crime, a significant minority of cases involve women, typically mothers. Mothers' intimate care of young children's bodies, for example, can become abusive but such abuse is concealed through very powerful denial and harm-minimization strategies. This kind of work agrees that men are responsible for the vast majority of sexual offences but examines why some women can become involved and asks why protection agencies, police and criminologists have not always recognized these offences.

Rape as social control

Until the 1970s, the dominant way of understanding the crime of rape by society, the criminal justice system and criminology was that women were, at least in part, to blame for their assault. In the criminology literature at the time the concept of 'victim-precipitated' rape was in full currency (for discussion see Temkin and Krahe, 2008). It was argued that rape is most likely to occur in situations where the offender interprets the victim's behaviour as signalling availability for sexual contact. Such situations were said to include those in which a woman agrees to sexual relations but changes her mind, fails to strongly resist sexual overtures, or accepts a drink from a stranger. Even wearing 'provocative clothing' could be taken as a sign of sexual availability. Such a way of thinking about rape was eventually seen to encourage an array of 'rape myths' and attitudes, which according to some are still relevant in our current criminal justice system. For instance, Bohner et al. have identified four types of rape myth: '[B]lame the victim for their rape', by suggesting provocation; disbelieve claims of rape; offer mitigation for the offender; and make the claim that 'only certain types of women are raped' (2009: 19).

These myths are presumptions that women are tempting seductresses who invite sexual encounters, that women eventually relax and enjoy coercive sex, that men have urgent and uncontrollable sexual needs and that the typical rapist was a stranger or black man. In fact, the typical rapist is more likely to be a man acquainted or intimate with his victim, rather than a stranger or psychopath. More concerning perhaps is the evidence from researchers like Temkin and Krahe who suggest that these rape myths may be reproduced in the legal system: 'This reduction of "real rapes" to stranger assaults affects the way in which people, including those involved in the legal processing of rape complaints, evaluate and respond to rape victims' (Temkin and Krahe, 2008: 32). Therefore in cases of rape it can be very difficult for women to achieve justice and to hold men responsible for the harms they have perpetrated.

For example, there are contradictory societal expectations concerning rape. One view is that if a woman is raped, she should be too upset and ashamed to report it; the other is that she should be so upset that she would report it. Both these views exist, but it is the latter that is written into the law. Any delay in reporting is used against her. Furthermore, when she is in court she is expected to appear upset as a victim, but calm and controlled as a court witness. If in court she appears lucid as a witness, she is in danger of not coming across as a victim (for discussion, see Chapter 9). If she appears too upset, she runs the risk of being seen as hysterical and therefore not believable (Lees, 1996a, 1996b). Rape was a central issue for second-wave feminists who challenged the myths about its incidence, perpetrators, causes and consequences.

During the 1970s, feminist writers made a number of key arguments. First, Susan Griffin argued in a path-breaking article that all women inhabit a mental world where they are constantly in fear of being raped:

> I have never been free of the fear of rape. From a very early age, I, like most women, have thought of rape as part of my natural environment – something to be feared and prayed against like fire or lightning, I never asked why men raped; I simply thought of it as part of one of the many mysteries of human nature.
>
> (Griffin, 1971: 26)

This 'fear of rape' suggests the second argument: that men have a 'trump card' to play in keeping women in their place. Thus, Reynolds suggested that rape is a prime mode of social control:

> Rape is a punitive action directed towards females who usurp or appear to usurp the culturally defined prerogatives of the dominant role . . . [it] operates in our society to maintain the dominant position of males. It does this by restricting the mobility and freedom of movement of women by limiting their casual interaction with the opposite sex, and in particular by maintaining the male's prerogatives in the erotic sphere. When there was evidence that the victim was or gave the appearance of being out of place, she can be raped and the rapist will be supported by the cultural values, by the institutions that embody these values, and by the people shaped by these values – that is by the policy, courts, members of juries, and sometimes the victims themselves.
>
> (Reynolds, 1974: 62–8)

Stay in your homes; stay in suitable attire; stay loyal to your husbands; stay submissive in your manner – this is the message of rape to women.

Working outwards, then, from the actual impact of rape on women, the third argument starts to suggest what is happening. Susan Brownmiller, in her highly influential book *Against Our Will* (1975), put the thesis at its most blunt: 'From prehistoric times to the present, I believe, rape has played a critical function. It is nothing more or less than a conscious process of intimidation by which *all men* keep *all women* in a state of fear' (1975: 5; emphasis in original). Such a thesis was taken up by many feminists, notably Dworkin (1981), and used as the basis for viewing male sexuality as the root of all women's oppression. Other commentators were more cautious but still emphasized rape as a form of male power over women. Clark and Lewis, for example, stated that they are not 'anti-male' but that they were opposed to 'any social system erected on the assumption of inequality between kinds of persons such that power and authority accrue only to a pre-elected subset' (1977: 175).

Feminist views here were certainly shaped and borne out by history (Bourke, 2007). Marriage laws and rape laws developed alongside each other and reflected the view that women were the 'property' of men rather than autonomous individuals with their own legal rights. In the eighteenth and nineteenth centuries, a sexual offence against a woman or girl could be viewed as the 'violation' of the 'property' of her husband or father. Rape thus became the 'theft of sexual property under the ownership of someone other than the rapist' (Clark and Lewis, 1977: 116). Women – such as those who remained unmarried or those who were economically independent – who were outside the 'ownership' or 'protection' of such men were believed to put themselves at risk of sexual offences. It was only in 1991, after over 20 years of feminist campaigns on the issue, that rape within marriage (of a wife by a husband) was made formally illegal with the abolition of the marital rape exclusion clause. Until the comprehensive UK review of sexual offences in 2003 (discussed at the end of this chapter) rape was narrowly defined as the penetration of a vagina by a penis without the woman's consent – a definition that excluded the penetration of other parts of the body as well as excluding male rape. Prior to the 2003 review, UK rape legislation also used a notion of consent to a sexual act that placed a very unfair burden of proof on the victim and failed to include a consideration for coerced consent or submission other than under physical duress. Changes in the new Act were made to challenge the role of consent in rape trials indicating that, for instance, if intoxicated by alcohol or drugs, a woman may not be able to give appropriate consent to sexual acts. Thus in terms of the law, the 'consent defence' was weakened. Box 11.2 outlines the 2003 Sexual Offences Act's definitions of rape and assault by penetration – a new kind of offence that rightly broadens the category of sexual crime.

BOX 11.2 UK Sexual Offences Act, 2003

Rape

(1) A person (A) commits an offence if-
  (a) he intentionally penetrates the vagina, anus or mouth of another person (B) with his penis,
  (b) B does not consent to the penetration, and
  (c) A does not reasonably believe that B consents.

doing crime

(2) Whether a belief is reasonable is to be determined having regard to all the circumstances, including any steps A has taken to ascertain whether B consents.

Assault by penetration

(1) A person (A) commits an offence if-
    (a) he intentionally penetrates the vagina or anus of another person (B) with a part of his body or anything else,
    (b) the penetration is sexual,
    (c) B does not consent to the penetration, and
    (d) A does not reasonably believe that B consents.
(2) Whether a belief is reasonable is to be determined having regard to all the circumstances, including any steps A has taken to ascertain whether B consents.

Source: Office of Public Sector Information
http://www.opsi.gov.uk/acts/acts2003/ukpga_20030042_en_2#pt1-pb1-l1g1

Date rape

Changes to legal definitions of consent have placed a new emphasis on so-called 'date rape' or 'acquaintance rape'. Here, a sexual encounter might start out as consensual but then become coercive. Research evidence strongly suggests that many rapes occur in such settings and that most offenders and victims are acquainted in some way, however briefly. In Australia, for example, the 1996 Women's Safety Survey found that sexual assault by a boyfriend or a date accounted for 16.6 per cent of all sexual assaults that translated into around 24,000 separate incidents in the survey year (Russo, 2000). In England and Wales, Lovett and Kelly (2009) found in 77 per cent of the reported rape cases suspects were known to the victims. However, despite these figures, in sharp contrast to other kinds of sexual offences, victims of date rape can experience much lower levels of public support and also encounter outright media hostility for 'teasing' men, 'leading them on', being 'naïve' or even for placing false accusations. The dispersal of feminist movements and the rise of so-called 'post-feminism' has meant that such hostility often goes unchallenged, perhaps taking us back to old ways of 'blaming' female victims. Exceptions might involve cases where the rape was 'drug-facilitated' with the rapist making use of drugs such as Gamma-hydroxy butyrate (GHB) or Rohypnol, to incapacitate a victim. Here, intent to force sex is seen as much more clear-cut and the victim more obviously deserving of sympathy and redress.

Rape, war crime and genocide

Rape has a brutal global history bound up with conflicts, colonization and ethnic cleansing. In modern times, rape has been used as an instrument of war in the former Yugoslavia and Rwanda in the 1990s and most recently in the Sudanese province of Darfur, as documented by criminologist John Hagan (Hagan *et al.*, 2005, see also Allen, 1996; Barstow, 2000). Feminist legal theorists like Catharine MacKinnon who pioneered some of the original academic studies of rape in the 1970s are now active in this field (MacKinnon, 1998).

International criminal law has dealt with rape and sexual violence in different ways: as violation of the 1949 Geneva Conventions, the 1948 Genocide Convention, the 1984 Torture Convention, and a crime against humanity under the Nuremberg Charter. After the Second World War, the International Military Tribunal at Nuremberg declared rape to be a crime against humanity, but did not actually prosecute it. The Military Tribunal for the Far East (the Tokyo Tribunal) did convict Japanese officers of rape. Despite these legal precedents, rape has usually been treated by military and political leaders as a 'private crime' committed by individual errant soldiers or 'accepted' as part of war.

This changed dramatically in the 1990s. International Criminal Tribunals for the former Yugoslavia and for Rwanda both brought sexual violence charges. The Rwanda case (see Box 11.3)

BOX 11.3 Rwanda: rape recognized as an act of genocide

In 1998 the UN International Criminal Tribunal for Rwanda (ICTR) found former mayor, Jean-Paul Akayesu, guilty of nine counts of genocide, crimes against humanity and war crimes. The verdict was the first conviction for genocide by an international court; the first time an international court had punished sexual violence in a civil war; and the first time that rape was found to be an act of genocide to destroy a group.

The Rwanda Tribunal was initially reluctant to indict Akayesu for rape. When Akayesu was first charged in 1996, the 12 counts in his indictment did not include sexual violence – despite the fact that Human Rights Watch, and other rights groups, had documented widespread rape during the genocide, particularly in his area. A lack of political will among some high-ranking tribunal officials as well as faulty investigative methodology by some investigative and prosecutorial staff of the Rwanda Tribunal accounted for this omission initially.

During the Rwandan genocide, thousands of women were targeted by Hutu militia and soldiers of the former government Armed Forces of Rwanda on their genocidal rampage. Tutsi women were individually raped, gang-raped, raped with objects such as sharp sticks or gun barrels, held in sexual slavery or sexually mutilated. These crimes were frequently part of a pattern in which Tutsi women were subjected to sexual violence after they had witnessed the torture and killings of their relatives and the looting and destruction of their homes.

During the Akayesu trial Rwandan women testified that they had been subjected to repeated collective rape by militia in and around the commune office, including in view of Akayesu. They spoke of witnessing other women being gang-raped and murdered while Akayesu stood by, reportedly saying to the rapists at one point 'don't complain to me now that you don't know what a Tutsi woman tastes like'.

Source: Human Rights Watch

http://www.hrw.org/news/1998/09/02/human-rights-watch-applauds-rwanda-rape-verdict

doing crime

Plate 11.2 There is a long history of violence against women in films. Alfred Hitchcock's *Psycho* is considered to be a major depiction, and set into play a whole series of films in which women were brutally murdered (often in the bathroom!). This classic image features Janet Leigh in the famous scream shot.

Source: © Universal Studios.

was a landmark judgement in that it allowed rape to be prosecuted as an act of genocide on the grounds that it could be motivated by a desire to change the genetic basis of an ethnic group by enforced impregnation. In 1998 the treaty setting up the new International Criminal Court (ICC) expressly named crimes based on sexual violence as part of the court's jurisdiction. The ICC itself began operating in 2002.

Pornography

There is extensive debate within feminism on the issue of pornography. Some argue that pornography is central to women's oppression and must be subject to state controls (such as more intensive policing and more severe punishments for the creators, sellers and distributors). Similarly, others suggest that it is against women's interests and must be campaigned against. More recently and more controversially, pro-sex or libertarian feminists have argued that these views are outdated and that women's right to buy, view and enjoy pornography should be upheld.

Opponents of pornography argue that its connections between sex and violence reinforce masculinity and male power and depersonalize, objectify and degrade women. Their critique does not contend that there is a direct causal connection between media representations and behaviour, but rather takes issue with the fact much modern pornography celebrates violence and death as well as sex. The pornography these comments allude to is the highly extreme kind that involves rape, bestiality and children. Most people would wholly object to this kind of material.

However, it is not so easy to take this line on representations of women that are less obviously harmful, yet nevertheless contribute to a culturally sanctioned misogyny. One of the problems facing the feminist left is how far to take censorship while preserving democratic freedoms, since anti-pornography campaigns have attracted strong criticism from gay and lesbian groups because such legal regulation could be extended into other areas of sexual and social relations. There are also tensions between radical feminists and the perspectives of women who work as prostitutes or in the sex industry. For as Nicki Roberts, an ex-stripper, has argued,

Feminist anti-porn campaigners or the Whitehouse brigade [Christian moral campaigners]: it makes no difference to us. Both factions clamour for more repression and censorship at the hands of the state; both divert attention away from the real issue of women's poverty in this society; and both are responsible for the increased hounding and vilification of women who work in the sex industry.

(1986, cited in Edwards, 1990: 151)

The issues raised by these comments confront some of the real problems in contemporary feminism that concern the complexity of responses to justice, the law, freedom and inequality. There is no easy answer but one way forward is to understand that not all people are controlled or oppressed with the same tenacity, tyranny or consistency.

Criminologists have linked pornography to crime in a number of different ways. These include the coercive tactics, including trafficking, that might be used to force women and children to appear in pornographic images; the extent to which pornography directly or indirectly shapes sexual violence against women and children and the illegal distribution of pornographic images, especially over the Internet.

The instrumental and symbolic role of law in sex crimes

Laws may be seen as both instrumental and symbolic. The instrumental role is practical: it aims to bring about a specifically desired effect such as to stop rape. The symbolic role is one of latent concern – acting for example as a litmus paper for many moral panics and discourses that tap into a wide range of social anxieties. For example, it is now well documented that while, instrumentally, campaigns against commercialized prostitution in the nineteenth century certainly had real consequences in shifting public health and strengthening women's lives, they also symbolized the controversies over purity, immigration, 'dirty women' and 'the age of consent'. As a cultural symbol, prostitution seems to touch all the 'evils' of the modern world and often is seen to create a contradictory tension between the exploitation of women and the lust of men. Thus, for example, nineteenth-century feminists – in the USA, Australia, Canada, Europe and the UK – led movements for moral reform, chastity and temperance which attacked prostitution, the availability of contraception and the moral debauchery of men through drink. Many of these feminists were also evangelical Christians with a highly conservative moral agenda. Indeed, the debates that we witnessed in the latter parts of the twentieth century around pornography and sexual violence were largely repeats of debates that were present at the turn of the century. Historian Judith Walkowitz comments that these historical social purity campaigns tried to 'protect' women but also 'helped to spawn a hydra-headed assault against sexual deviation of all kinds' and that 'by ferreting out new areas of illicit sexual activity and defining them into existence, a new "technology of power" was created that facilitated control over an ever-widening circle of human activity' (Walkowitz, 1984: 130–1).

Likewise, attacks on and anxieties concerning the so-called slum sex code and upon young men at taxi-dance halls in the early twentieth century were often a way of attacking lower-class men, and raised social class issues (White, 1993). 'Perverts' of all kinds seem to have stalked the nineteenth and twentieth centuries, symbolizing an anarchic, non-reproductive, 'sick' kind of sex. Race often became an issue in battles over rape and lynching. Controversies over pre- and extra-marital sex reinforced patterns of the 'normal family'. In the late twentieth century, AIDS rapidly became the symbol not only of death, but also of promiscuity, permissiveness and perversions: it marked out the good and the bad. And at the start of the twenty-first century, a major concern over paedophile priests in the Catholic Church energized controversies around religion, sexuality, homosexuality and child abuse (Loseke, 2003a).

Hence while, instrumentally, these campaigns try to stop a particular form of behaviour; symbolically they reassert existing moral orders. Over and over again we find 'sexualities' being used in this way. Paraphrasing Mary Douglas's (1966) terms, we may say that sex is often equated with or symbolizes dirt and disorder, stuff out of place; and that a society needs to purify itself of all this. Sexual problems emerge when there is a perceived threat to social values, be they religious, familial, feminist or medical. Behind every sexual problem there is almost certainly a perceived threat to aspects of the moral order and a group of crusaders struggling to define boundaries.

Panics around sex crimes

As we have suggested sex crimes are a major social problem, with a history of generating anxiety and panic. Sometimes they enter public consciousness and reach levels of mass hysteria; sometimes we are hardly aware of them. And there are of course competing accounts of when and how they start to be noted and taken more seriously. Over half a century ago, the leading criminologist Edwin Sutherland summarized the passage of sex offence laws. His account still cannot be bettered:

> The diffusion of sexual psychopath laws has followed this course: a community is thrown into panic by a few serious sex crimes, which are given nation wide publicity; the community acts in an agitated manner; and all sorts of proposals are made; a committee is then appointed to study the facts and to make recommendations. The committee recommends a sexual psychopath law as the scientific procedure for the control of sex crime. The recommendation is consistent with the trend toward treatment policies in criminal justice in preference to policies of punishment.
>
> (Sutherland, 1950: 142)

Sutherland was writing about the diffusion of such laws around 1937 in the United States. Today, much of his analysis is seen as one possible (and possibly even cyclical) response. Punitive and rehabilitative models come and go: there are periods of silence and periods when sex crime is a great issue.

The feminist writer Jane Caputi, for example, has argued that sex crime starts to appear as a phenomenon with the famous and widely cited Jack the Ripper case in the late nineteenth century. It not only generated huge moral anxiety in its day, but also signalled 'the age of sex crime', in which serial killers and mass murderers become more and more common – in reality and in the mythology of the times. For instance, she suggests there were 644 serial sex killings in the United States in 1966 but 4,118 by 1982 (Caputi, 1988: 1–2). She cites many examples:

the 'Boston Strangler', 'Son of Sam', the 'Hillside Strangler' and the 'Yorkshire Ripper', as well as films that play to these fears: from the classics of M and *Psycho* to the more widespread teen slasher films such as the *Halloween* series. Her work outlines the creation of these fiends in the public minds, but at the same time shows how this is part of a wider issue of gender violence and aggression.

Taking a different view, sociologist Philip Jenkins has traced the differential responses to a hundred years of sex crimes from the late nineteenth century to current times. He suggests a different chronology:

> Originating in the Progressive era [early twentieth century], the imagery of the malignant sex fiend reached new heights in the decade after World War II, only to be succeeded by a liberal model over the next quarter of a century. More recently, the pendulum has swung back to the predator model: sex offenders are now viewed as being little removed from the worst multiple killers and torturers. And in each era, the prevailing opinion was supported by what appeared at the time to be convincing research. One reality prevailed until it was succeeded by another.
>
> (Jenkins, 1998: 2)

He does not see these stages as evolutionary and necessarily objective: rather, they 'have ebbed and flowed – we forget as well as learn' (p. 3). 'The nature of sexual threats to children was perceived quite differently in 1915 than in 1930, and the child abuse issue was framed quite differently in 1984 than in 1994' (p. 215). At the heart of his analysis lie vigorous campaigning groups: child-savers, feminists, psychiatrists and therapists, religious and moralistic groups, and, of course, politicians.

Jenkins claims that children are at very low risk from stranger homicide, making nonsense of the claims aired frequently in the 1980s that many thousands were killed each year by serial murders, pornographers or paedophile rings (1998: 10). Looking at figures for the United States between 1980 and 1994, he concludes that despite the claims made, strangers killed about 54 children per year, and about five of these victims were involved as part of a sexual assault.

In summary, then, sexuality appears to be a major device used to tap into all sorts of social anxieties, to generate panic, to denote deviance and to demarcate boundaries. Studies point to many different sources of these anxieties and boundary mapping, but they include anxieties over gender roles, heterosexuality, and the family; the importance of reproduction and pronatalism; concerns over the role of youth and childhood; race and racialized categories; the divisions between classes and 'class fears'; the nation-state itself; an overarching sense of moral progress and fears of decline; the very nature of ethical and religious systems; end of century/millennium fears; and even connections to the fear of death (for examples, see Bristow, 1977; Foldy, 1997; Hunt, 1998; McLaren, 1997; Showalter, 1990; Stein, 2001; Vass, 1986; Walkowitz, 1992; White, 1993).

The changing character of sex crimes

Just what can be designated a 'sex crime' changes all the time, and it will be interesting to examine a few illustrations briefly.

Homosexuality is an interesting case. For much of the nineteenth and twentieth centuries, it was against the law in most Western countries. Gradually it has become decriminalized over the past 30 years in those countries – though it does still remain illegal in some US states and in many parts of the world. Curiously, with the advance of a strong (and increasingly international) lesbian and gay movement, new issues have appeared such as universal lesbian and gay rights, including a universal age of consent and the inclusion of 'sexual orientation' in charters of human rights; and anti-discrimination laws, along with mandatory training in 'multiculturalism' and 'gay affirmative action', have become common in many Western contexts. 'Registered partnerships' – and sometimes marriages – for lesbians and gays along with the right of lesbians and gays to adopt and have children have become key foci of a growing international lesbian, gay, bisexual and transgender movement (Adam et al., 1999). New anti-gay crimes such as 'hate crimes' have been created and turned into social problems. A major reworking of the claims being made about homosexuality has been happening over the past 30 years; it can no longer be placed easily in a Western list of 'sex offences and crimes'.

Yet while all this is going on, there continues to be massive resistance to acceptance of homosexuality in many other countries worldwide. In most countries of Africa, Asia, Latin America or the Middle East, same-sex relations remain taboo: largely invisible, rarely discussed, officially non-existent, and embedded in religions, laws and beliefs that are deeply inimical to homosexuality. Even today, it is illegal in approximately 70 states in the world as well as being subject to the death penalty in seven. Indeed, the partial acceptance of homosexuality in parts of the West is often used as a major example of the West's decadence (Baird, 2001: 12).

Prostitution, too, is an interesting case. It is often not against the law per se, but it is regulated because of concerns over health risks and community safety. In the UK, after the Wolfenden Report of 1957, living on immoral earnings, keeping a brothel and soliciting by a 'common prostitute' became illegal; and subsequently in 1985, 'kerb crawling' became an offence. Prostitution is not in itself illegal in England and Wales, but the selling of sexual services in a street or public place is, along with any involvement of children. In the United States, it is legal in some states, regulated in others and outlawed in still others. Research on prostitution has also gone through many phases. Recent work has put male customers rather than female clients in the spotlight. A London study (Coy et al., 2007) investigates increases in reported rates of men paying for sex in the last ten years. It links the rise to a re-sexualization of popular culture, the rise of sexual consumption as a kind of recreation and the role of the Internet in facilitating access to sexual markets. Lap-dancing, pole-dancing and soft porn are now much more visible than they were. In 2000, one in 29 London men admitted buying sex in some form. More broadly, UK data on men arrested for 'kerb crawling' showed the average customer to be aged 35, in full-time work and with no criminal convictions. This raises issues about the flexible construction of masculine 'respectability' among other things.

Likewise, pornography is another form of sexual deviance that has changed over time. In the eighteenth century it was part of erotic subcultures involving men across classes (Gatrell, 2006) while in the nineteenth century it became a target for social purity campaigners. Today it remains a hotly contested issue, and although there have been many versions of obscenity law, these days the main issue concerning obscenity is closely linked to the purchasing and ownership of child pornography. Despite the laws introduced in the 1980s that made the production, sale, purchase and ownership of child pornography illegal, such activity has grown and developed with the advent of the Internet.

Sex crimes on the Internet

Recently, we have started to see the emergence of a new area of sex offences as more people come to use the Internet to make sexual contacts, buy sexual wares and view all kinds of websites that are saturated with every kind of sexual image you are ever likely to want (and not want) to see. All kinds of new potential criminal problems have emerged as a result: cyber-stalkers, cyber-rape, childhood security, paedophile abductions, camcorder sex, new forms of porn and ways of accessing it (alongside so-called cyborg sex and virtual sex). Such new forms are a largely uncharted area, and finding ways of regulating them through law and control agencies sees us with a new field of sex crimes just now in the making. In 1996 the Internet industry formed a self-regulatory body to facilitate the reporting of online crime and in 2001 the United Kingdom government set up the Task Force on Child Protection on the Internet, which led to the development of the Child Exploitation and Online Protection centre (CEOP) in 2006, a highly skilled multi-agency group with a remit to eradicate child sexual abuse online (for more discussion see Jewkes, 2007a). Alongside the new offences labelled in the Sexual Offences Act 2003, these controlling bodies provide some protection for children against exploitation, although this is a difficult task in a fast-moving, highly technological global environment.

BOX 11.4 Child pornography, globalization and the Internet

Another instance of globalization at work is the relatively recent arrival of a network of worlds linked through the Internet that caters for interests in child pornography and paedophilia. By most accounts, this is widespread, much condemned but hard to regulate, and has generated extensive public attention in the West.

In his study of child pornography on the Internet, Philip Jenkins shows just how difficult it is to regulate a fragmented network such as this. Although there are laws that make possession of pornographic pictures of anyone under 18 an imprisonable offence, other – often poorer – countries have much less stringent laws, and more pressures pushing children into these industries. Certainly, many of the images found on the Internet have originated in poorer, 'bandit' regions (the former communist world, parts of Asia and Latin America – and oddly, also Japan) where regulations are minimal. It may be hard to regulate in Western countries but it is even more difficult elsewhere. And as Jenkins comments, 'Lacking a global moral consensus, there will always be areas of unevenness, fault lines in moral enforcement, and the child pornographers are likely to survive in these cracks' (2001: 203).

Changes in the law concerning sexual offences in the United Kingdom

The 2003 Sexual Offences Act is seen by many as one of the most radical overhauls of sex offences legislation for over 50 years. From 1999 onwards, Tony Blair's Labour government conducted intensive reviews of existing legislation involving many organizations from lobby groups to children's charities. The reviews were set up with the following terms of reference:

- to provide coherent and clear laws which protect individuals, especially children and the more vulnerable from abuse and exploitation;
- to enable abusers to be properly punished;
- to be fair and non-discriminatory.

The resulting 2003 Act set out to broaden traditional notions of victims in these cases and shift the historical focus from (straight) women and children to include men, gay and lesbian people and those with learning and other disabilities. In practical terms, the Act addressed this by broadening the definition of rape (see Box 11.2) to include penile penetration of the mouth and anus as well as the vagina without consent and by introducing the new offence of 'assault by penetration' with an object or a part of the body. This means, for example, that women abusers can now be charged with this kind of penetrative offence. The Act also widened definitions of 'family' in relation to familial sexual offences to include not just blood relatives but also other family members living in the same household such as foster parents, foster siblings, step-parents, step-siblings and cousins.

In addition, the 2003 Act created several other new offences with the aim of shifting the previously accepted focus on physical, bodily assault to include other less physical but equally abusive behaviours, such as sexual grooming, administering a substance with intent (to facilitate a sexual act) and encouraging children to watch sexually explicit activity on video, television, webcams or any other media. A further key change here was the redefinition of consent and new kinds of responsibilities around this crucial aspect of any sexual activity. Before 2003, a defendant who was able to prove that they honestly believed that consent had been given – however unreasonable that belief might be – was likely to be acquitted (hence the historically low numbers of convictions in these kinds of cases as discussed earlier). Since 2003, defendants wishing to prove consent have to show that they have reasonable grounds to support their belief and must indicate what steps they took to elicit consent. The idea here is that consent must be active and not passive or assumed. An important exception here is that children under the age of 13 (and adults with certain kinds of learning difficulties in some cases) are deemed by law to be *unable* to give consent to sexual activity.

The 2003 Sexual Offences Act also changed police, court and community procedures for monitoring convicted sex offenders. The previous 1997 Sex Offenders Act had required these people's details to be recorded on sex offender registers. The new Act tightened procedures in a number of ways. Offenders must notify any change to their name or address within three days (as opposed to 14). If they stay at a UK address that is not their home for seven days or more, or if they spend more than three days abroad, they must notify police. These notification measures now apply to convicted foreign sex offenders visiting the UK. Certain registered offenders, such as suspected child sex tourists, can now be banned from travelling abroad at all if they are thought likely to endanger children as a result. A new 'risk of sexual harm order' can prevent someone from engaging in sexually explicit communication – including texting or emailing children – if they have been found to have done this at least twice before. Rehabilitation work with sex offenders is now coordinated by Multi-Agency Public Protection Arrangments (MAPPAs) involving the police, probation, local authorities and community organizations.

Overall, the 2003 Act aimed to create a new framework for defining and dealing with sexual crime that would reflect key shifts in late modern life, among them greater gender equality, more complex families, more emphasis on child protection and victims' rights, increased geographical mobility and huge changes in personal media technologies. Criminologists, sociologists and campaigning groups are now beginning to assess the impact of the 2003 Act. Table 11.1 shows that a significant number of offences against the new laws outlined above have been recorded – for example, incest or familial sexual offences (from 99 offences in 2002/3 to 808 in 2010/11), male rape (from 850 in 2002/3 to 1,310 in 2010/11) and the new offence of sexual grooming (from 0 offences in 2002/3 to 310 in 2010/2011). Although it still remains to be seen how effective the Sexual Offences Act 2003 is in controlling sex crime some early critique has already been voiced. For instance, Ost (2004) has indicated some of the difficulties involved in proving ulterior motives linked to sexual grooming while Thomas (2004) and Mcalinden (2006) have both challenged the effectiveness of the sex offenders' register as a means of preventing further sexual crime, arguing that the register can infringe offenders' rights. No doubt the causes and effects of the reframing of UK sexual offence laws will prove a rich seam for criminologists in the future.

Public reaction to the 2003 Act is difficult to gauge. Most people are probably unaware of the radical changes it made and many probably still feel that the courts are 'too soft' on sex offenders, particularly paedophiles. In the run up to the legal review, public feelings ran high following the murder of 8-year-old Sarah Payne by Roy Whiting, a known sex offender, in southern England in 2000. A high-profile tabloid-supported campaign pushed for the introduction of 'Sarah's law' as a means to publish details held on sex offenders' registers (modelled on New Jersey's 1994 'Megan's law' enacted after a similar case). In short, many say they want to be able, as a number of US residents are, to know if they themselves are living near a paedophile. During 2007 the Public Disclosure Scheme was piloted in four police areas and following evaluation has now been rolled out across all 43 police forces in England and Wales. This scheme allows parents and carers to ask if someone has a record of a child sexual offence. Such measures do raise complications, not least around the right to privacy and the high risk of vigilantism and similar actions that may follow with exposure of identity. Opponents also argue that this directs the focus once again on 'stranger danger' rather than on the very much more common dangers children face at the hands of those known to them – the very dangers that the 2003 Act attempted to address.

Public attitudes to sexuality are changing in key ways, as this chapter has indicated. These attitudes are often contradictory, however. Public feeling against paedophiles runs high yet arguably children, especially young girls, are sexualized to extraordinary degrees within everyday culture. The market in 'girl goods' is highly lucrative with high street stores selling make-up, mini-bras and thongs to the under 10s. Top Shop stocked a controversial badge stating 'I swallow' and Woolworths branded a girls' bed 'Lolita' though this was withdrawn after complaints. In a post-feminist culture where young female identity is seen as playful, ironic and sexually empowered it is difficult to counter this kind of hyper-sexualization (McRobbie, 2008). Yet efforts to reduce

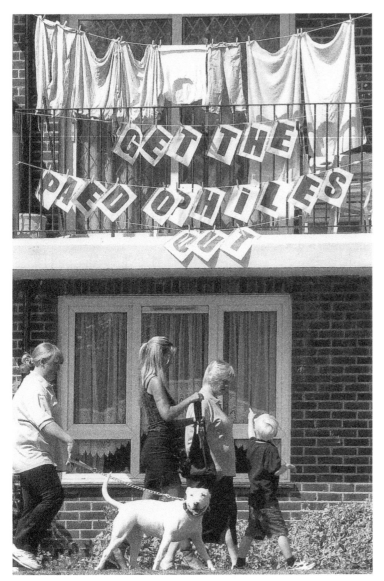

Plate 11.3 In the summer of 2000 in the UK there was hysteria against sex offences and paedophilia. In Paulsgrove estate, Portsmouth, people organized into Residents Against Paedophilia and went on the march.

Source: © PA.

what remain the most commonly reported kinds of sexual offence – abuse, assaults and rapes against girls and women – should be seen in this contradictory context.

Sex offences in global perspective

This chapter has largely focused on UK sex offences, though there are many similarities with other Western cultures. Other societies have very different laws and hence different patterns of offence. In some strongly Muslim societies (and Iran seems a central if changing case), the degree of surveillance over the lives of children and women on a day-to-day basis makes the possibility of any norm-violations (from masturbation to homosexuality) difficult indeed. Penalties are severe and executions not uncommon for homosexuality.

In 2008, the UK Home Secretary agreed to review the case of 19-year-old gay Iranian, Mehdi Kazemi, who claimed he would be executed if his claim for asylum was rejected forcing him to return to Iran. The teenager's case was taken up by gay rights activists across Europe. Kazemi moved to London in 2005 to study English but later discovered that his boyfriend had been arrested by the Iranian police, charged with sodomy and hanged. Human rights campaigners say that over 4,000 gay men and lesbians have been executed in Iran since the Islamic revolution of 1979 (BBC news website, 13 March 2008).

Honour killings take place in many Muslim communities around the world. Here, women may be punished by death (or raped) for actual (or even perceived) sexual (mis)conducts. Criminologist Aisha Gill (2006) argues that such acts use 'honour' to mask patriarchal violence.

Yet we are also now starting to sense the globalization of sexualities, in which the world becomes smaller and more interconnected: a major reordering of time and space in sexual relations may be taking place. Talk about 'sexual problems' moves across the globe, and in the process often becomes transformed and modified by local cultures. Traditional sexual customs become subject to rapid social change. Media and digitalization generate an information age haunted by the spectres of sexuality – from cybersex to cyber-rape. Postmodern values seem ascendant, giving priority to ideas of sexual difference and sexual choice. Global capital turns local sex markets into international ones. World sexual cultures become more and more interconnected. With all this, it should not be surprising to find that long-standing patterns of sexualities are becoming increasingly disturbed and disrupted (Altman, 2001).

Summary

1   Reported sex crime is increasing in the UK. The reasons for this are not clear but are likely to be linked to measures to encourage victims to report, a clampdown on interpersonal violence of all kinds and the broadening of legal definitions of sexual offences.

2   The conviction rates for sexual offences, especially rapes have not risen alongside the increased numbers of recorded crimes. One reason for this might be that changing legislation does not change social attitudes.

3   Sex crimes are not as common as many other offences but they remain under-reported, despite the measures listed above. Victims of sexual offences still face considerable personal and procedural difficulties, as well as public hostility (for example in cases of alleged date rape), when taking action against offenders.

4   Sociologists have understood sex crimes as closely connected to the structuring of gender and the male use of power. Rape is a prime example of this.

5   Moral panics are often linked to sex crimes. At different periods in history, these panics have focused on different kinds of crimes. Public attitudes to sexuality and sex crime can be highly contradictory. Globally, sex crimes can take very different forms in different countries.

6   In 2003 a major overhaul of the sex offences legislation took place in the United Kingdom in response to broad changes in late modern life around gender, sexuality, family, child protection, media, mobility and communication technology.

Critical thinking questions

1 Why are sex crimes seriously under-reported?
2 Discuss the factors that lead some men and a minority of women to commit acts of sexual violence.
3 Consider the processes by which sex crimes become identified as social problems.
4 Discuss the various policies for handling 'sex offenders' and consider which you think are most effective.
5 Why has there been so much interest in the problem of child sexual abuse and paedophilia in recent years?
6 Critically discuss changes made by the 2003 Sexual Offences Act in the UK.

Further study

Amnesty International (2001) *Crimes of Hate: Conspiracies of Silence*, London: Amnesty International. Useful review of the ways in which homosexuality remains a crime in many parts of the world.

Foucault, M. (1978) *The History of Sexuality*, Harmondsworth: Penguin. A highly influential study of the emergence of sexual categories and knowledge in modernity.

Holmes S. T. and Holmes, R. M. (2008) *Sex Crimes: Patterns and Behavior*, 3rd edn, Thousand Oaks, CA: Sage. A psychological approach to the profiling of sex offenders. Read for a contrast with the sociological view.

Jenkins, P. (1998) *Moral Panic: Changing Concepts of the Child Molester in Modern America*, New Haven, CT: Yale University Press, and (2001) *Beyond Tolerance: Child Pornography on the Internet*, New York: New York University Press. Two books that deal with issues of paedophilia and child abuse.

Kelly, L. (1988) *Surviving Sexual Violence*, Cambridge: Polity. One of many influential feminist texts on sexual violence.

Pearce, J. and Pitts, J. (2011) *Youth Gangs, Sexual Violence and Sexual Exploitation: A Scoping Exercise for the Children's Commissioner for England*, The University of Bedfordshire, Institute of Applied Research, www.childrenscommissioner.gov.uk/info/csegg1

Silverman, J. and Wilson, D. (2002) *Innocence Betrayed: Paedophilia, the Media and Society*, Cambridge: Polity. Connects moral panic theory, media and sex crimes into a very readable discussion.

Thomas, T. (2000) *Sex Crime: Sex Offending and Society*, Cullompton: Willan. A straightforward introduction to the field.

Useful websites

Office of Public Sector Information

http://www.opsi.gov.uk/acts/acts2003/ukpga_20030042_en_2#pt1-pb1-l1g1

For information on the 2003 Sexual Offences Act.

For information on the current UK government action plan to tackle all violence against women see:

http://www.homeoffice.gov.uk/crime/violence-against-women-girls/

Child sex offender disclosure scheme

http://www.homeoffice.gov.uk/crime/child-sex-offender-disclosure/

Child Exploitation and Online Protection Centre

http://ceop.police.uk/

CEOP works across the UK tackling child sex abuse and providing advice for parents, young people and professionals.

National Organization for the Treatment of Abusers

www.nota.co.uk

NOTA is a growing group comprising practitioners, managers and policymakers for the public, private and voluntary sectors. As a result, NOTA brings a wide variety of perspectives to interventions with sexual aggressors.

Child and Woman Abuse Unit

http://www.cwasu.org/

The Child and Woman Abuse Unit is based at London Metropolitan University and has a national and international reputation for its research, training and consultancy work. The unit exists to develop feminist research methodologies, theory and practice, especially in relation to connections between forms of sexualized violence.

The Fawcett Society

www.fawcettsociety.org.uk/

A UK women's rights organization that runs campaigns on sexual crime.

chapter 12

Crime, the Emotions and Social Psychology

Key issues

■ Why have the emotions been neglected in criminology?

■ Is crime seductive?

■ What is meant by 'fear of crime'?

■ How does resentment structure 'hate' crime?

■ What role does 'respect' play in violent encounters?

■ Does 'shaming' restore the balance of justice between offenders, victims and the community?

Introduction

It might seem obvious that human emotions play a significant part in the commission of crime, in punishment and in social control. Indeed, the relationship between emotion and crime has fuelled the creative imagination. To take an intense emotion – passion, for instance – *la crime passionel* has inspired great works of literature, theatre, art, symphonies and the opera. It is perhaps the tragedy of crimes of passion that has inspired the artistic imagination; they are offences committed by wretched but ordinary people, not otherwise inclined to transgress. Fuelled by one or more of a myriad of emotions – the wounds of betrayal, the hurt of infidelity, broken hearts, wounded pride, spoiled virtue, jealousy, envy, and many more, they are criminalized by their acts. Passion comes to overrule reason – usually with dire consequences for the offender and the victim.

In Shakespeare's tragic tale *Othello*, the enraged Othello 'the Moor' murders his wife, Desdemona, on account of her alleged adultery, and then kills himself in deep remorse when he realizes he has been deceived into believing in her infidelity. In Bizet's *Carmen*, the smitten soldier Don José kills his love, Carmen, after she has an affair with the handsome Escamillo. In 2002, the tragic story was recast as a 'Hip hopera' by MTV and New Line Television, starring Beyoncé. While in the world of popular music, crimes of passion have been acted out in numerous songs. 'Delilah', the hit by Tom Jones, is a classic example of betrayal with fatal consequences and in 1996 Nick Cave released an entire album of *Murder Ballads* (see Plate 12.1).

In this chapter we will examine how the emotions figure in criminology. We begin with describing how the emotions have been marginalized in much intellectual work, but have recently become a focal point across the humanities and social sciences.

Rediscovering the emotions

Although crimes of passion have inspired great artistic works and enthralled audiences for centuries, the subject of emotion has been only a peripheral interest within criminological inquiry and theory. Willem de Haan and Ian Loader, for instance, suggest that

> Many established and thriving modes of criminological reflection and research continue to proceed in ways that ignore entirely, or at best gesture towards, the impact of human emotions on their subject matter – if you doubt this, take a quick glance at almost any criminology textbook, whether of a conventional, radical or integrating bent.
>
> (de Haan and Loader, 2002: 243)

However, while the impact of human emotion on crime appears to be in the process of rediscovery in theoretical criminology, it has hardly been neglected in the past by research on crime and deviance. Many of these texts are amongst the foundational texts of social psychology,

Plate 12.1 Nick Cave's collection of murder ballads reveals the enduring popularity of blood, sex, melodrama and crime as themes in popular culture.

Source: *Murder Ballads* by Nick Cave and The Bad Seeds front cover image reproduced courtesy of Nick Cave & EMI.

doing crime

which can be defined as the systematic study of people's thoughts, feelings and conduct in social contexts. On this reckoning the emotions should not be reduced to psychological states, but as social and cultural practices that both come from within ourselves and from without – in larger structural processes that ritually shape how we feel and act.

Historically, indeed, a defining feature of Western thought is the way that emotion and reason have been regarded as opposing forces, with the emotional often seen as beneath the rational, as a sign of the lowly, primitive, natural and feminine. It has only been since the late 1970s that the sociology of emotions has become an established field within the discipline. Since then there have appeared several major perspectives on the emotions and social life (Hochschild, 1983; Kemper, 1978; Scheff, 1979), as well as the repositioning of the emotions in classical and contemporary social theory (Barbalet, 1998; Williams, 2001; Shilling, 2002), while feminists have explained how the marginalization of emotion has worked to subordinate the feminine, the body and intimate desires (Spelman, 1989; Jaggar, 1989; Ahmed, 2004). Taken together these developments suggest that criminology has much to gain from engaging with this resurgence of interest in the emotions across the humanities and social sciences. Nor should this be a one-way conversation. Criminological work has a crucial place in revealing the importance of emotions in shaping our inner worlds as well as broader social and cultural practices.

Status, stigma and seduction

The contemporary interest in crime and the emotions can usefully be traced back to Albert Cohen's (1955: 17) study of delinquent boys, which sought to demonstrate how 'psychogenic and subcultural factors' combined to produce delinquency through the humiliating 'status frustrations' experienced by working-class boys and the alienating differences of class-based value systems. In a series of insightful pieces Erving Goffman described how all encounters are guided by certain cultural scripts that establish the ground rules for interaction. His work captures how perceptions of social worth regulate human conduct. Famously, he argued that mental patients 'suffer not from mental illness, but from contingencies' (Goffman, 1962: 135) – people who may or may not have been experiencing some degree of mental distress, but have had the misfortune to end up in an asylum and then had to adjust their self-identities in line with the 'heavy machinery of mental-hospital servicing'. In Stigma, Goffman (1963) examined how people managed 'spoiled identity', the pain and shame associated with being considered less than human. Crucially, he emphasized that we all move between normal and troubled worlds, and each of us falls short some of the time, such that embarrassment (and the anxious expectation of it) clouds every social interaction.

In important ways, Goffman exposed in Stigma the very inappropriateness of the term 'deviance' to describe physical handicap, ethnic difference and numerous forms of social disaffiliation. Likewise, the sharp distinction drawn between deviant and conventional values in subcultural theory was also criticized by Matza (1964) who pointed out that juveniles inter-mittently drift into and out of delinquency. His focus on motivational will manages to grasp something of the immediate, intoxicating and alluring spell that delinquency casts, which he would later describe as the 'invitational edge' that deviancy offers (Matza, 1969: 111). It is this dizzying edge that Jack Katz (1988) attempts to capture in his seminal Seductions of Crime through concentrating on the experiential foreground of crime across a diverse range of acts that include juvenile 'sneaky thrills', armed robbery and cold-blooded, 'senseless' murder.

Each specific crime offers distinctive ways of overcoming the mundane routines of everyday life through presenting unique emotional attractions that provide 'a dialectic process through which a person empowers the world to seduce him to criminality' (Katz, 1988: 7). Whilst Katz's work has been influential (especially in cultural criminology) it has not escaped criticism on the grounds that it:

- disregards the wider social context in which all action takes place (O'Malley and Mugford, 1994; Young, 2007a);
- fails to secure 'serious distance' (implying that offending stories are taken at face value); and
- lacks any 'systematic explanation' of the various 'motivational' accounts (I. Taylor, 1999: 224).

Yet, as Hayward (2002: 83) suggests, these objections ignore 'the failure of "background" structural theories of crime to address the fundamental question of why (under shared social conditions) one person rather than another commits crime'. It is by exploring the relationships between crime, emotion and social psychology that some of these answers are to be found.

Conceptualizing emotions

Although there are ongoing debates over how to define exactly what are emotions, what they do and how they should best be studied (Williams, 2001; Strongman, 2003) there is now much agreement that *happiness, fear, anger* and *depression* are universal to all humans and are even said to be hardwired into human neuroanatomy (Kemper, 1987). Importantly, three of the four emotions are negatively tuned (Turner and Stets, 2005: 11) and we will be exploring how these primary emotions shape and colour other emotions like hate, shame, guilt, pride, wonder, resentment, nostalgia and dread amongst the many feelings encountered in our daily experiences. In his influential article Theodore Kemper (1987) argues that these secondary emotions are more socially constructed and arise from specific contexts where experiences are learnt. Guilt, for example, is derived from the primary emotion of fear and the social organization of punishment, religion or nationhood inducing some experience of shame, regret and sorrow. Table 12.1 summarizes his characterization of primary and secondary emotions, which provides a useful taxonomy of the emotions. Of course, it is important to recognize that there is considerable cultural and social variation in how these emotions are experienced, expressed and practised.

Table 12.1 Kemper's primary and secondary emotions

Primary emotions	Fear	Anger	Depression	Happiness
Emotions attached to primary emotions	Guilt	Shame	Ennui, sadness, resignation	Pride, loving, gratitude
Some combinations of primary emotions	Fear-anger: hate, jealousy, envy	Fear-happiness: wonder, awe, hope, shyness	Anger-happiness: vengeance, snobbery, contempt	Depression-happiness: nostalgia, yearning

Source: Adapted from Kemper (1987) and Turner and Stets (2005: 18).

We now turn from these broad conceptual issues to that emotional state which has received considerable criminological attention – fear. Indeed, it has become a well-worn observation that the problems posed by the fear of crime are potentially greater than crime itself and as we will see it was this discovery that prompted the plethora of studies on the topic.

Fear of crime

Fear is a complex human emotion. While fear is ubiquitous and felt by every living creature, the actual sources of dread are socially distributed. Different societies have developed different ways of living with the dangers that haunt them. Yet contemporary terms like the 'politics of fear', 'fear of crime', 'age of anxiety', 'risk society' and most recently 'liquid fear' (Bauman, 2006, see also Box 12.1) each suggest that we are living in times of such heightened insecurity that danger lurks everywhere. A number of important social changes are said to herald this new era and break with the past – the mass media now provide us with round-the-clock news of crisis, disaster and trauma; rising social mobility brings a greater range of experiences, expectations and troubles; technological innovations have brought with them immense global dangers; and since 9/11 'new' forms of terrorism further contribute to the cultural climate of fear (Carrabine, 2008).

Although research on the fear of crime was established in the late 1960s – paralleling the growth in more general criminological interest and policy concerns over victims of crime – it had moved to the centre of intense empirical, political and theoretical disputes by the 1980s. Today, the 'fear of crime' is an area of criminological inquiry that constitutes a 'sub-discipline in itself' (Lee, 2001: 468) and 'is probably the main legacy of endless, and endlessly repeated, national crime surveys which have consistently identified it as a social problem of striking dimensions' (Ditton *et al.*, 1999: 83). Few issues trouble the public in Europe and the USA more than crime. Surveys have repeatedly shown that worries over victimization surpass losing a job, ill-health, road accidents and indebtedness as issues of major concern (Farall and Gadd, 2004: 127).

BOX 12.1 Fears in motion

The trade in safety and security is highly lucrative. To take one example, there is the quite extraordinary phenomenon of the 'Sports Utility Vehicle' in the United States. This massive petrol-guzzling, quasi-military vehicle had at one point reached 45 per cent of all car sales in the USA and is sold as a 'defensive capsule'. It is portrayed in advertisements as offering immunity against the dangerously unpredictable urban life outside the protective armoured shell (Bauman, 2006: 143–4). According to Josh Lauer (2005) the SUV first emerged as a status symbol in the early 1980s with the introduction of the military Humvee (which stands for High Mobility Multipurpose Wheeled Vehicle) that was commissioned by the army to replace the jeep and came to popular attention during the first Gulf War. This prompted the development of a civilian version and the subsequent occupation of Iraq further heightened their popularity.

The massive civilian Hummer quickly become one of the most fashionable and popular vehicles in America and was embraced as an ultra-macho novelty vehicle yet with more than a third of its sales being to women drivers. Indeed, one television advert featured a woman driving a Hummer through city streets, with the tagline, 'Slip into something more metal'. Clearly there is something more going on here than an increased fear consciousness. The SUV is an expensive piece of 'high-end automotive jewellery' in which risk management is transformed into a symbol of conspicuous consumption (Lauer, 2005: 163–5). It is significant though that in the UK similar oversized, four-wheeled drive vehicles are frequently derided as 'Chelsea Tractors', which indicates their almost ridiculous remove from their original use amongst working farmers and the rural gentry (Carrabine, 2008).

Plate 12.2 Humvee on sale.

Source: Getty Images.

From the late 1960s in the USA initially, but later elsewhere around the world, interviewing citizens about their personal experiences of crime became commonplace. In addition to trying to obtain a more accurate view of victimization levels these national household crime surveys provide information on the public's beliefs and attitudes towards crime, policing, punishment and prevention. The British Crime Survey (renamed in 2011/12 as the Crime Survey for England and Wales, CSEW) was first carried out in 1982 and has been repeated at regular intervals since. Accompanying national surveys have been an increasing number of local crime surveys, which in the UK have been carried out in various places like Bristol, Sheffield, Merseyside, Islington and Edinburgh (Hale, 1996: 79). Typically fear of crime is often measured by responses to the question 'How safe do you feel walking alone in this area after dark?', or similar formulations, to which respondents are invited to reply by saying they feel 'very safe', 'fairly safe', 'a bit unsafe' or 'very unsafe'. The use of this question to uncover 'fear of crime' has been widely criticized, as it:

- fails to explicitly mention crime (Garafalo, 1979);
- cannot do justice to the emotional complexity of fear (Box *et al.*, 1988);
- ignores the fluidity of lived experiences (Goodey, 2005: 69); and
- through questionnaires respondents are 'forced to use the same language to express very different feelings' (O'Mahony and Quinn, 1999: 232–3).

doing crime

As Girling and her colleagues (Girling *et al.*, 2000: 13) emphasize, these studies tend to 'discover a lack of "fit" between expert knowledge and "lay" opinion' that have come to revolve around the question of whether fear is rational or irrational in an effort to distinguish between 'warranted' estimates of risks as opposed to debilitating misperceptions of threats by particular groups of the public. Home Office research continued to find that both women and the elderly were particularly 'irrational' given the distance between their high levels of expressed fear and their low levels of actual risk. The conclusion was that women and the aged were incapable of making rational sense of the risks they faced.

Feminists quickly challenged the assumed gendered stereotypes of women as fearful and men as fearless (see, *inter alia*, Goodey, 1997; Stanko, 1997; Gilchrist *et al.*, 1998; Sutton and Farrall, 2005). Betsy Stanko (1987, 1988) was an early critic and argued that this work could not adequately grasp women's experiences and fears of sexual danger. By using alternative research methodologies (like ethnographic studies, life histories and individual interviews) significant empirical evidence was unearthed that debunked 'the myth of the safe home' (Stanko, 1988) to reveal the extent of 'ordinary violence' women regularly face and manage across public and private domains (Stanko, 1990). Such work raises 'fundamental questions of whose standards are used as markers of a reasonable or rational fear' (Walklate, 1998: 409) and suggests there are some dubious conceptual assumptions behind conventional approaches to researching fear. In any case, the debate over whether the 'fear of crime' is rational or irrational is one that can never really be resolved, as it is difficult to state what a rational fear would look like (Sparks, 1992: 10). For women fear of sexual danger is a normal condition – a 'governing of the soul' (Stanko, 1997) – such that much criminological attention has now shifted to the issue of 'ontological security' (Giddens, 1991) in an effort to grasp how inner anxieties are structured in social space.

Urbanism, anxiety and the human condition

A rich seam of work has attempted to understand the ways fears and anxieties are locally constructed. Taylor (1996, 1997) has argued that the fear of crime has become a condensed metaphor, which attempts to capture broader concerns over the pace of socio-economic change. As he explains, the rise of defensive middle-class suburban social movements organized around crime prevention

> are activated not just by immediately presenting sets of problems in the specific locality (stories of aggressive young people and actual violence on the hitherto peaceful local High Street) but by deeper fears about joblessness and house prices, and (in the case of parents with suburban children) schooling 'for success', child safety, moral socialization . . . and a host of other increasingly agitated concerns.
>
> (Taylor, 1997: 66)

On this account, worries about crime are intimately bound up with the less easily grasped or articulated troubles generated by changes in economic, moral and social life (Taylor and Jameson, 1998).

This is a point further explored by Girling and colleagues (2000) in their study of public perceptions of crime in a prosperous English market town where they argue that

> people's responses to crime (in its association with other matters of concern to them) are both informed by, and in turn inform, their *sense of place*; their sense, that is, of both *the place* they inhabit (its histories, divisions, trajectories and so forth), and of *their place* within a wider world of hierarchies, troubles, opportunities and insecurities.
>
> (Girling *et al.*, 2000: 17; emphasis in original)

The importance of this work is that it attempts to situate people's fears in specific everyday contexts and in doing so it chimes with other recent developments that have highlighted how the individual's social location (Walklate, 1998) and inner personal senses of security (Hollway and Jefferson, 2000) shape perceptions of the wider world around them.

The introduction of psychoanalytical theory into the fear of crime debate offers much potential. Wendy Hollway and Tony Jefferson (1997, 2000) draw on the key psychoanalytical insight that anxiety is the price we pay for having a sense of self. Their work emphasizes that anxiety is a universal feature of the human condition and that dynamic 'unconscious defences against anxiety are a commonplace and constructive aspect of response to threats' (Hollway and Jefferson, 2000: 32). The specific unconscious defence mechanisms they focus on are **denial**, **splitting** and **projection** to explore how threats to the self are managed by these displacing activities. Their overall argument is that anxiety, as a pervasive but not fully formed emotion, lies behind much contemporary concern over fear of crime. Drawing on their research with people living on two council estates in northern England their analysis reveals quite varied and diffuse responses to the threat of crime. The differing responses are informed by individual biography, social location and unconscious defence mechanisms. As they put it 'a rampant "fear of crime" discourse which might on the face of it be thought to exacerbate fears, could actually serve unconsciously as a relatively reassuring site for displaced anxieties which otherwise would be too threatening to cope with' (Hollway and Jefferson, 1997: 263–4).

Hollway and Jefferson (2000: 31) have introduced a notion of human subjectivity that recognizes 'the non-rational, unintentional and emotional aspects of people's actions and experience' that had largely been neglected by criminologists. Nevertheless, sympathetic critics have contended that their approach is more about 'feeling than structure' (Walklate, 1998: 411) while others argue that to 'focus only on unconscious displacement tends to ignore both the conscious strategies and various circuits of communication' (Lupton and Tulloch, 1999: 515) adopted by their respondents. But replacing the rational, unitary subject with the anxious, fragmented subject need not dispense with a socially literate understanding of subjectivity (Carrabine, 2008).

It would be wrong to assume that people are constantly afraid – life would be unbearable if that were so – but the emotional intensity varies and we find imaginative ways of ignoring or adapting to precarious environments (Tuan, 1979: 9). As Walklate (2007a: 100) has succinctly put it, fear 'is not an ever present feeling or state of mind but burns differently in different contexts'. These different contexts will include our immediate social relations, broader external forces as well as our own anxious inner worlds, such that calls for a 'psychosocial criminology' (Jefferson, 2002a; Gadd and Jefferson, 2007) will involve paying greater attention to emotional life than criminologists have conventionally considered.

Hate crime

Perhaps one of the most explicit connections drawn between crime and a specific emotion in recent years concerns the emergence of the concept of 'hate crime' in the United States. The United States Federal Bureau of Investigation (FBI) defines hate crimes as offences that are 'motivated in part or singularly by personal prejudice against others because of a diversity – race, sexual orientation, religion, ethnicity/national origin, or disability'. While the term 'hate crime' is institutionalized in law in the United States – as in the Hate Crime Statistics Act 1990 – it has gradually become a site of legal intervention in Britain:

- The Crime and Disorder Act 1998 created a number of new racially and religiously aggravated offences.
- The Criminal Justice Act 2003 introduced tougher sentences for offences motivated by hatred of the victim's sexual orientation (this must now be taken into account by the sentencing court as an aggravating factor, in addition to race or religious hate motivation).
- The Racial and Religious Hatred Act 2006 made it a criminal offence to use threatening words or behaviour with the intention of stirring up hatred against any group of people because of their religious beliefs or their lack of religious beliefs.

The term 'hate crime' has also been adopted by the Metropolitan Police Service (MPS) – see also Plate 12.3 – and other police services, and the media, and has become firmly established in popular discourse. It is contestable, however, whether 'hate crime' does in fact manifest hate.

For many people, the term 'hate crime' arguably conjures up an image of a violent crime committed by extremists, by neo-Nazis, racist skinheads and other committed bigots – in other words, hate-fuelled individuals who subscribe to racist, anti-Semitic, homophobic and other bigoted ideologies. It is not surprising that many people think this way about hate crimes, because the media focus on the most extreme incidents – as is the case with crime reporting in general. The murder of Stephen Lawrence in south London in 1993, and the subsequent media coverage of

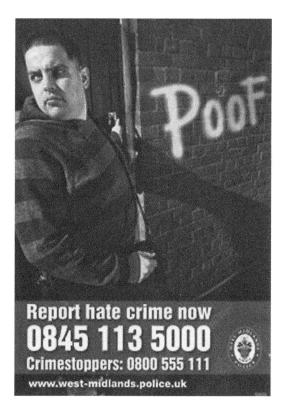

Plate 12.3 Campaign poster to combat hate crime.

Source: West Midlands Police.

Plate 12.4 *Daily Mail* extract, 1 May 1999.

Source: extract © Atlantic Syndication; *photo*: David Gaywood.

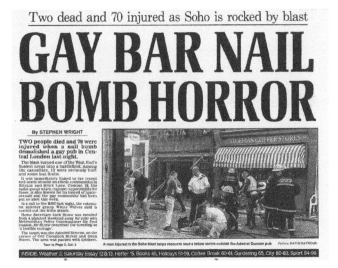

Two dead and 70 injured as Soho is rocked by blast

GAY BAR NAIL BOMB HORROR

By STEPHEN WRIGHT

the young men suspected of the murder and the racist views they expressed, provide a prime example. Other extreme incidents in Britain that quite understandably gained notoriety include the bombing in May 1999 of the Admiral Duncan, a 'gay pub' in Soho, London (Plate 12.4), in which three died and scores were injured. The young man convicted, David Copeland, had a history of involvement with racist organizations.

In the United States the brutality of the murder of James Byrd, an African American – who was beaten unconscious, chained to the back of a pick-up truck and dragged for miles along rural roads outside the town of Jasper, Texas, in June 1998 – attracted widespread media coverage. The brutality of the murder and the fact that the two perpetrators were members of a white supremacist organization evoked painful memories of **lynching** (see Box 12.2) and historical racial violence in the United States. The callousness of the attack on the young gay man Matthew Shepard, who was pistol-whipped and left lashed to a fence in freezing conditions to die later in hospital in Wyoming in October 1998, generated considerable debate about homophobic bigotry. The incident itself and its repercussions have been portrayed in the play and film *The Laramie Project*.

Paul Iganski (2006) demonstrated how in the UK the New Labour government's (1997–2010) specific concerns over racially aggravated offences – influenced to some extent by US legislation and debate – led to a gradual expansion of British law in this field, from race to religion, and also sexuality and disability. His account describes the many dilemmas surrounding such legislation: from the supporting arguments that crimes motivated by hate cause damage to the victim beyond the crime itself, that this additionally infects a wider community with fear and trauma, and constitutes an assault on the dominant values of society. Opponents criticize the legislation on the grounds that:

- ■ legislating against hate is indefensible as it suggests that hurting some kinds of people isn't quite as bad as hurting others (Jacoby, 2002);
- ■ it is a totalitarian response to prejudice as it punishes 'thought crime' in Orwellian fashion (Phillips, 2002); and
- ■ it treats equal crimes unequally, which goes against fundamental legal principles.

BOX 12.2 The politics of lynching

Lynching is a form of extrajudicial punishment involving public torture revived in the Southern United States as a response to the perceived loss of white male domination in the nineteenth century. The passage of the Thirteenth Amendment (1865) outlawed slavery and with emancipation former slaves became 'African Americans'. It has been argued that it was 'through the process of Reconstruction, the Union attempted to restore relations with the Confederate states' (Messerschmidt, 2007: 81) and it is in this context white male mob violence quickly arose as an attempt to reassert old hierarchies. For example, in May 1866, 46 African Americans were murdered when their schools and churches were set on fire by a white male mob in Memphis. Two months later, in July, 34 African Americans were killed in New Orleans at the hands of a white mob (Ayers, 1984).

The lynchings were explicitly violent and looked to ancient and medieval forms of aggravated death penalty, which included burning, castration, whipping as well as hanging. Indeed, the lynch mob insisted on punishments that were barbaric and the fact that they would outrage liberal sensibility was all part of their appeal. They were deliberately racialized and the lynch victim was often sought out as retribution for the alleged rape of a white woman by an African American man. The public lynching has been understood as a carnival critique of official criminal justice and total rejection of the law's commitment to equality while reasserting local understandings of caste superiority. As Garland (2007: 147) explains, public torture lynching communicated 'impassioned sentiments that could no longer be expressed in the official idiom of the criminal law' and inflicted 'a level of suffering that had long since been officially disavowed'. In Chapter 15 we will examine how punishment arouses powerful emotions that can appeal to cruel tendencies in the human condition.

Other academics, however, have considered why some groups appear to be deserving – through recognition within the legislation system – while others who suffer violent crime, such as victims of elder/domestic abuse, are often excluded from the hate crime debate (Morgan, 2002; Mason-Bish 2012).

The thrill of it all?

Given the range of victims of hate crimes, the variety of offenders involved and the different social situations in which hate crimes occur, there can obviously be no single explanation, and in any one incident there may be a range of explanations. However, one thing does appear to stand out: many incidents seem to be committed for the fun of it, for the kicks, for the excitement, as well as for other reasons. According to Jack Levin and Jack McDevitt (2002):

> Like young men getting together on a Saturday night to play a game of cards, certain hatemongers get together and decide to go out and destroy property or bash minorities. They want to have some fun and stir up a little excitement – at someone else's expense.

The payoff in such 'thrill-seeking hate crime', as Levin and McDevitt famously called it, is psychological as well as social:

> They enjoy the exhilaration and the thrill of making someone suffer. For those with a sadistic streak, inflicting pain and suffering is its own reward. In addition, the youthful perpetrators receive a stamp of approval from their friends who regard hatred and violence as 'hot' or 'cool'.
>
> (Levin and McDevitt, 2002: 67)

In a 'pick and mix' of bigotry, the victims of thrill-seeking hate crimes are often interchangeable.

Excitement is not the only emotion involved in so-called hate crime. Levin and McDevitt argue that resentment – to one degree or another – can be found in the personality of most hate crime offenders, and it takes many forms. There are individuals who, perhaps because of some personal misfortune, feel rejected by, estranged from and wronged by society. They look for someone to target in venting their anger.

For others, their bitterness is fuelled by a perceived or real threat to their economic security, and some strike at those they think are to blame: newcomers, immigrants, asylum seekers. Ray and colleagues (2003), drawing on research based in Greater Manchester, argue that much of the violence is related to the sense of shame and failure, resentment and hostility felt by young men who 'are disadvantaged and marginalized economically and culturally, and thus deprived of the material basis for enacting a traditional conception of working-class masculinity'. Such emotions, according to Ray et al., 'readily lead to violence only in the case of young men (and occasionally for young women) for whom resorting to violence is a common approach to settling arguments and conflicts' (2003: 112).

Self-esteem, shame and respect

The significance of **self-esteem** in violent encounters has been explored by Thomas Scheff and his colleagues. From their perspective, 'self-esteem concerns how we usually feel about ourselves. High self-esteem means that we usually feel justified pride in ourselves, low self-esteem that we often and easily feel ashamed of ourselves or try to avoid feelings of shame' (1989: 178). They propose that 'shame' is a primary emotion generated by the constant, incessant but commonly unacknowledged monitoring and negative evaluation of self in the eyes of others. As an emotion it is seen to be socially unacceptable.

Self-esteem, in short, is a 'summary concept', representing how well a person overall manages shame. People with high self-esteem have had sufficient experience of pride to outweigh their experience of shame; they can manage shame. However, when a person has had an insufficient experience of pride, then shame becomes a calamity for them. When they experience some form of humiliation, real or imagined, rather than acknowledging it, it is masked with anger. The person is then caught in a 'shame–rage feeling trap'. According to Scheff et al. (1989: 184),

> In our theory, rage is used as a defence against threat to self, that is, feeling shame, a feeling of vulnerability of the whole self. Anger can be a protective measure to guard against shame,

BOX 12.3 Reintegrative shaming

In his classic study *Crime, Shame and Reintegration* (1989), John Braithwaite emphasized the importance of the emotions in the restoration of justice between offenders, victims and the wider community. This work provided a powerful impetus to the 'restorative justice' movement in criminology and challenge to vindictive models of retributive punishment (described in more detail in Chapter 15). The book has decisively influenced studies of conflict, reconciliation and 'peace-making' as well as enabling accounts of the place of 'emotional work' in criminal justice institutions to emerge (e.g. Karstedt, 2002). His argument is that shaming the offence, and not the offender, will reintegrate the offender back into the community while giving victims a strong role in these reconciliation processes. Crucially though, the agents of shaming are not the victims, but the family and friends of the offender so that shame integrates rather than alienates. As he famously put it, the 'best place to see reintegrative shaming at work is in loving families' (Braithwaite, 1989: 56).

Braithwaite's arguments are closely allied to Scheff's work on shame (which suggests that one of the central features of life is our search for honour and the ways in which shaming plays a role in that search). Shame is linked to taking on the role of 'the other' (cf. Mead, 1934), and links to the pangs of conscience when confronted with the possibility of wrongdoing. We want and need the social approval of others. Shaming involves all social processes expressing disapproval that have the aim of inducing remorse in the offender. For Braithwaite, the shame that matters most is not that coming from officials such as the police, judges, courts or even victims, but that from the people we care most about. It is not stigmatizing in so far as it is aimed not at the offender per se but at the act the offender commits; the ultimate aim must be reintegration and he contends that reintegrative shaming is effective in complex societies as well as more traditional ones.

It is significant that Braithwaite developed his arguments from accounts of indigenous procedures of 'conferencing' in New Zealand and Australia, where he found that these community settings successfully combined shaming and reintegration. Critics worry whether these processes will be used against the most vulnerable groups in society or deployed only for trivial offences while conventional, custodial punishments continue to expand. It has been noted how the model of reintegrative shaming developed in Australia and currently exported around the world is one principally targeted at Aboriginal youth, intensifying police controls over this already marginalized population (Blagg, 1997). More recent Australian research has suggested that 'net-widening' may be a problem, and that more marginalized young people (including non-Aboriginal) are channelled away from youth conferencing into a youth 'justice system more punitive in its sentencing' (Cunneen and White, 2006: 107). The idealization of the family at the heart of the approach has been criticized for its reliance on defining 'others *as* others' (Ahmed, 2004: 199, emphasis in original) – those who have failed to live up to this ideal social bond – like single mothers, queer relationships and so forth. To be fair, Braithwaite has always recognized that shaming can be used tyrannically against unpopular minorities, but it is difficult to see how the communitarian politics that informs his thinking can oppose hostile collective sentiments when that is the community's will.

which is experienced as an attack on self. As humiliation increases, rage and hostility increase proportionally to defend against loss of self-esteem.

These arguments have also proven especially influential regarding the role of shame in restorative justice practices, where it is argued that the community conferences that lie at the heart of reintegrative shaming (Box 12.3) work not so much through the words said but through facial expressions, gestures and physical posture (Retzinger and Scheff, 1996). We now describe how the emotions are embodied in contemporary street cultures, where crime, hustling and violence have become a defining way of life for the ghetto poor.

Stories from the street

The issue of 'respect' is a key theme explored by Elijah Anderson in his book *Code of the Streets* (1999). He argues that for many inner-city youths in his study, a street culture has evolved what he calls a code of the streets – a set of informal rules governing public behaviour and the use of violence. It can be traced to the sense of hopelessness and to the alienation that the youths feel from mainstream society and its institutions, due to the joblessness and the pervasive racism they experience.

'Respect' is 'at the heart of the code' according to Anderson. Respect is about 'being treated "right", or granted the deference one deserves'. But gaining and maintaining respect has to be a constant endeavour:

> In the street culture, especially among young people, respect is viewed as almost an external entity that is hard-won but easily lost, and so must constantly be guarded. The rules of the code in fact provide a framework for negotiating respect. The person whose very appearance – including his clothing, demeanour, and way of moving – deters transgressions feels that he possesses, and may be considered by others to possess, a measure of respect. With the right amount of respect, for instance, he can avoid 'being bothered' in public. If he is bothered, not only may he be in physical danger but also he has been disgraced or 'dissed'.
>
> (Anderson, 1994: 82)

One key aspect of a person's demeanour to convey and hold respect is 'having the juice': projecting an image, a willingness to resort to violence, having the nerve to throw the first punch, to pull the trigger, and, in the extreme, not being afraid to die, and not being afraid of taking another's life if needs be, if someone 'gets in their face', if disrespected.

Respect is a scarce commodity. Deprived of achieving a sense of self-esteem through participation in the jobs market, and other institutions of mainstream society, 'everyone competes', according to Anderson,

> to get what affirmation he can of the little that is available. The craving for respect that results gives people thin skins. Shows of deference by others can be highly soothing, contributing to a sense of security, comfort, self-confidence, and self-respect. Transgressions by others that go unanswered diminish these feelings and are believed to encourage further

transgressions ... Among young people, whose sense of self-esteem is particularly vulnerable, there is an especially heightened concern with being disrespected. Many inner city young men in particular crave respect to such a degree that they will risk their lives to attain and maintain it.

(Anderson, 1994: 89)

Similarly, Bourgois (1995) describes in his In Search of Respect how the street identity cultivated by men from East Harlem, which involved limited social skills, assumed gender arrogance and intimidating physical presence, made them virtually unemployable – often appearing clumsy and illiterate before prospective female supervisors in Manhattan's booming service sector economy.

In an important critique of the underclass thesis, Carl Nightingale's (1993) ethnography of the black Philadelphian ghetto maintains that the culture of the ghetto is not only a product of alienation and isolation but rather a consequence of the desperate embrace of the American Dream:

Already at five and six, many kids in the neighbourhood can recite the whole canon of adult luxury – from Gucci, Evan Piccone, and Pierre Cardin, to Mercedes and BMW . . . from the age of ten, kids become thoroughly engrossed in Nike's and Reebok's cult of the sneaker.

(Nightingale, 1993: 153–4)

In ways that have clear echoes of Albert Cohen's earlier subcultural theory, Nightingale is arguing that structural exclusion is accompanied by an over-identification with mainstream consumer culture. As he explains:

Inner-city kids' *inclusion* in mainstream America's mass market has been important in determining those kids' responses to the economic and racial *exclusion* they face in other parts of their lives. And, indeed, kids' experiences of exclusion and of the associated painful memories has made their participating in mass culture particularly urgent and enthusiastic, for the culture of consumption has given them a seductive means to compensate for their feelings of failure.

(Nightingale, 1993: 135; emphasis in original)

The disturbing ambivalence at the heart of America's race relations is also captured in Naomi Klein's (2000: 76) discussion of companies like Tommy Hilfiger, whose marketing strategy is based on 'selling white youth on their fetishization of black style, and black youth on their fetishization of white wealth'. Jock Young (2007a: 51) has recently argued that these ghetto studies suggest that we need 'to return to the two stigmas which the poor confront, that of relative deprivation (poverty and exclusion from the labour markets) and misrecognition (lower status and lack of respect)'. Both of these are forms of humiliation, each generating powerful dynamics of resentment.

Humiliation, rage and edgework

At the beginning of this chapter it was observed that crimes of passion have fuelled the artistic imagination. We now turn to such crimes and draw from Jack Katz's analysis of the inter-relationship of emotion and crime in his book *Seductions of Crime* (1988). In the book Katz covers a range of criminal and deviant behaviours – the ways of the 'badass', the 'hardman', the 'cold-blooded killer' and white-collar criminal – but it is instructive to focus on cases of murder that Katz analyses using a variety of documentary sources. The incidents involving what Katz calls 'Righteous Slaughter' are impassioned acts committed in moments of rage – as is the case with many murders.

In the cases that Katz analyses, the victim-to-be inflicts a humiliation upon the killer-to-be: a wife caught by her husband *in flagrante* with another man; another tortured by her husband's infidelity; a man whose virility is challenged by his partner; a neighbour offended by another neighbour parking in front of their property. In each case, humiliation arises from the violation of a respected social role, such as husband, wife, virile male, property owner. The would-be killer's reaction to the humiliation, according to Katz's analysis, is 'a last stand defence of respectability'. Their mortal act is not calculated in a premeditated sense to restore their self-worth. It is instead experienced as a compulsion, driven by rage arising from the killer's emotional comprehension of the humiliation they have suffered.

Risk, excitement and routine

Jack Katz (1988) is drawing attention to the exciting, pleasurable and transgressive dynamics that are very much at the 'foreground' of criminal activity in an effort to critique the 'sentimental materialism' (as Katz, 1988: 313–17, terms it) of much liberal and radical criminology. British criminologists have also explored these issues. Matthews (2002) in his study of armed robbers, for instance, notes how during his interviews it was usually when his respondents were describing the actual robberies that the attractions of the crime become all too apparent. Similarly, Collison's (1996) research on masculinities and crimes connects these ideas to cultural consumption, risk-taking and drug use. For example, burgling a house is an activity laced with excitement but it is also riddled with risk. One of the respondents in his study described the dual-edged thrill and danger of getting caught, being assaulted by the homeowner, or the police, or later on the street, failing in front of male friends. As one 20-year-old put it: 'I always used to leave the room they was sleeping in till last . . . they never used to hear me for some reason . . . it was scary and exciting' (Collison, 1996: 443). Few stopped to calculate the risks but rather put their faith in a mystical sense of invincibility, or hope for a run of good luck, or sometimes used drugs to ease the sense of risk. It is useful to contrast these accounts though with Kearon and Leach's (2001) discussion of burglary where they describe the intense feelings of abjection that many victims of house theft experience.

What seems to be particularly important here, in terms of doing crime, is that this kind of 'edgework' (Lyng, 1990a, 2004) is deeply satisfying and seductive. Edgework has been described as a form of 'experiential anarchy' that is an 'experience that is much more real than the circumstances of everyday experience'. One British 19-year-old explained to Collison (1996: 435), that 'what I really want to do like to occupy my time, I'd like to jump out of planes like that, that's exciting to me, I couldn't afford things like that . . . so I just pinch cars, get chases, do burglaries and enjoy myself that way'. It is important to recognize that whilst this edgework may be an essential part of street life for underclass male youth, it also has routine features. For what comes across in all the narratives is how surprisingly ordinary this risk-taking is. But, and this is highly significant, these activities are not thought of in this way. They would be impossible to do if they were.

The important question here is why these activities are so exciting and seductive. In answering this question the crucial factor is drugs, not just in the sense of being able to 'get off your face' through ecstasy, amphetamines and LSD, but that they form a defining part of the irregular economy in poor communities for expendable male youth in Collison's (1996) study. For young underclass men the promised land is on the TV, and it should come as no surprise to learn that their favourite film was *New Jack City*, whilst real life here 'stinks'. In contrast, the drug economy provides these young men with their only realistic chance of fast living and the high life in Britain. Drug crime, like other forms of street crime, creates a space for acting out predatory forms of masculinity. Street-level drug dealing, whether this is on the corner or watched on film (and the two are frequently conflated) promises action and status success. According to Collison (1996: 441) forms of predatory street crime and excessive lifestyle among some young underclass males are not a simple response to poverty, they are attempts to 'munch' their way through consumer society and fill in the spaces of structure and identity, or in other words, to get a 'reputation as mad'.

Summary

1   Criminology has an important role to play in showing how the emotions shape our inner lives and broader social practices.
2   Fear and anxiety are central characteristics of modern living.
3   Human emotions play a central role in the criminal act.
4   The study of the emotional dynamics of crime illuminates why certain crimes occur.
5   The emotions can restore justice between offenders, victims and the wider community.

Critical thinking questions

1   Why have the emotions been marginalized in Western thought?
2   Why is 'fear of crime' an ill-defined term?
3   Why might 'hate crime' legislation be a totalitarian response to prejudice?
4   How could the arguments outlined in this chapter help us understand phenomena like 'road rage', 'lynch mobs' and 'queer bashing'?
5   What are the seductions of crime?
6   How does the 'search for respect' reproduce exclusion in North American ghettoes?

Further study

Anderson, E. (1999) *Code of the Streets: Decency, Violence and the Moral Life of the Inner City*, New York: W. W. Norton. A highly illuminating ethnographic exploration of the social and cultural dynamics of interpersonal violence in the inner city.

Bauman, Z. (2006) *Liquid Fear*, Cambridge: Polity. One of the most original sociological thinkers casts his eye over the fears and anxieties that haunt our current age.

Gadd, D. and Jefferson, T. (2007) *Psychosocial Criminology: An Introduction*, London: Sage. A lively demonstration of how a psychosocial approach sheds new light on the causes of many crimes, as well as challenging readers to rethink the similarities and differences between themselves and offenders.

Katz, J. (1988) *Seductions of Crime: Moral and Sensual Attractions of Doing Evil*, New York: Basic Books. An indispensable analysis of the sensual and emotional dynamics of crime.

Levin, J. and McDevitt, J. (2002) *Hate Crimes Revisited: America's War on Those Who Are Different*, Boulder, CO: Westview. An invaluable evaluation of the social, cultural, motivational and policy context of hate and crime.

Useful websites

American Psychological Association: 'Hate Crimes Today: An Age-Old Foe in Modern Dress'
http://www.apa.org/pubinfo/hate/homepage.html
A question-and-answer site shedding some clarification on the hate crime debate.

Hate Crime.org
http://www.hatecrime.org/
Information and links to related news articles concerning current events, political choices, and victims and further information.

National Gay and Lesbian Task Force: information on hate crime laws
http://www.nglft.org/issues/issue.cfm?issueID=12
NGLTF is the national progressive organization working for the civil rights of gay, lesbian, bisexual and transgender people.

Crime reduction
http://www.crimereduction.homeoffice.gov.uk/toolkits/fc00.htm
A typical Home Office site offering advice and information on how to tackle fear and disorder in the community.

chapter 13

Organizational and Professional Forms of Crime

Key issues

■ How easy is it to define and understand different forms of crime concerned with the pursuit of power and profit?

■ What kinds of activity have been engaged in by professional criminals in financial crime?

■ In what ways do the legitimate and illegitimate worlds of enterprise overlap?

Introduction

Various chapters of this book look at forms of crime where the emphasis is largely on the individual as criminal or victim (and sometimes both) and at locations of criminality and victimization, all of which are 'everyday' and generally occurring in the home or on the street.

This chapter is concerned with forms of crime originating with or enabled by the organizational and professional frameworks and status that perpetrators can draw upon. Different areas or worlds of activity, motives and consequences are identified and discussed – although it should become apparent that there is blurring and overlap between these categories. Broadly, this chapter covers:

- crime in the world of illegal enterprise – crime as an illegal profession;
- crime in the world of lawful professions – crime as abuse of legal professional status and resources;
- crime in the world of corporate-level business and commerce – crime as subversion or inversion of good corporate behaviour, producing negligence and/or illegality.

A final note before proceeding: as with so many other topics in this book, the range of possible issues and examples that could be covered here is enormous and all that can be provided is an indicative exploration.

Thinking about organizational and professional crime

In beginning to think about these rather different forms of crime, we are now talking about offending or deviance committed by or within organized structures, groups or associations. This is not to say we are concerned here only with 'criminal organizations', for clearly, individual employees or the self-employed commit crime at work or even engage in crime as their work. Certainly it is a mistake to assume that only those stereotypically perceived as 'criminals' or officially labelled as such commit criminal offences – as Karstedt and Farrall (2007: 1–2) have found:

> There is an area of criminal activity at the very core of contemporary society . . . committed by people who think of themselves as respectable citizens and who would certainly reject the label of 'criminal' for themselves. Politicians refer to them as the 'law-abiding majority', ignoring the fact that the majority do not abide by the law, or at least are highly selective about when to and when not to comply.

And indeed, in the UK as elsewhere in the world, politicians are among those professionals, such as lawyers, health care specialists, bankers and others, who have been known to abuse their positions of trust and authority.

While bearing all this in mind, what this chapter takes as the criteria for inclusion here are forms of crime that involve one or more of the following:

- a commitment to crime as a full-time activity – crime as a profession – working closely or loosely with others in criminal or legitimate networks;
- a benefit from and/or abuse of a professional and/or trusted position of some seniority or status – following from being an employee in an organization and/or recognition of qualifications by professional or other bodies (e.g. providing validation of specialist competence);
- a temporary or long-standing criminal association or organization for the pursuit of profit and/or power;
- a business or corporation that in part or whole 'goes wrong' and engages in crime or has actually been established as a legal organizational 'front' for criminal activity.

doing crime

Note that the case of 'everyday crime' at work, such as pilferage and fiddles, sometimes referred to as the 'hidden economy' or 'blue-collar crime', is discussed elsewhere (see Chapter 8; Mars, 2006).

Self-evidently, certain forms of crime depend on features of an organization – for example, planning, coordination, concealment, group membership and hierarchy. This applies to diverse examples of crime: for example, a 'project crime' (McIntosh, 1975) such as the raid on the Securitas cash depot in Kent in February 2006 when criminals posing as police officers kidnapped the depot manager and his family, tied up 15 staff members and made off with up to £50 million in cash (Souness, 2007); or the coordinated concealment of financial mismanagement, misappropriation and fraud, as in the case of the international energy giant Enron and the subsequent wave of financial scandals, to be dealt with later in this chapter. Other crimes may seem to be tied to individual activity – for example, the fraudulent lawyer or doctor – but when examined can be seen to rely on factors such as: the exploitation of systems, organizations and professional standing that all insulate the individual from suspicion or scrupulous investigation; abuse of trust and qualifications bestowed and supposedly guaranteed by professional associations; and victimization of clients and customers of services that are being offered.

Numerous studies have highlighted characteristics common to both illegitimate and legitimate profit-oriented organizations. These include:

- entrepreneurialism
- risk-taking
- rule-breaking
- specialist division of labour
- investment strategies
- managing evasion of unwelcome regulation
- avoidance of harmful scrutiny or control
- manipulation of financial systems and loopholes to avoid tax liabilities.

It can help to clarify what this chapter is focusing on if we note briefly what is excluded here. For example, youth crime may involve gangs and other more or less 'organized' groups (Wright, 2006; Hobbs, 2013; Newburn, 2002a; South, 1999a). However, the nature of organization in such cases is, in Britain at least, generally of a short-lived, immature and non-elaborated form. Where more complex structures do emerge, these may provide socialization into more established crime groups. These are readily seen as professional crime associations involved in control of territory for power and profit, and in illegal activity such as drug importation and dealing. In cases such as these, at least some of the characteristics listed above will apply, and indeed the tradition of study of youth gangs from Thrasher (1927) onwards has been partly typified by the search for the forms of structure and value systems that sustain involvement of certain youth in gangs, delinquency and crime (see Chapter 4) leading to criminal careers (Hobbs, 2013; South, 1999a). On the other side of the criminal justice fence, the incidence of crime and deviance in organizational contexts such as the police and prisons is important to note here, but it has simply made sense to refer to such crime – for example, corruption – in the chapters on these particular topics.

Crime in the world of illegal enterprise

Professional crime was seen by Sutherland (1937: 197) as based upon a craft that had been learned, and it was this achievement that defined the 'professional' thief (or safecracker or forger or whatever) as someone who had learned their trade and, like 'physicians, lawyers or bricklayers' (ibid.), developed a variety of abilities and skills. (Here we can see elements of learning theory and Sutherland's idea of differential association; see Chapter 5.) Of course, as many critics have pointed out, this is simply too neat and offers a rather romanticized notion of a career in crime, which in fact may provide little or no opportunity to learn skills or develop any expertise in a particular field of crime (Hobbs, 1994: 441; Ruggiero and South, 1995: 129–32). Nonetheless, the important point in Sutherland's work on 'the professional thief' was to draw attention to the idea of 'full-time crime'.

'Crime as a full time occupation can be traced to the decline of the feudal system in England, and to the need for those leaving the land to develop alternative forms of economic subsistence within the context of urbanization and the emergence of capitalism' (Roebuck and Windham, 1983). Full-time miscreants (Mack, 1964) were established in major metropolitan areas by the eighteenth century as the areas of the rich and the poor grew, and did so in ever-sharpening contrast. The business of the fence – a buyer and seller of stolen goods – was then, as now, a staple of the irregular and illegal economy of the city (Klockars, 1975; Sutton, 1998). Other forms of 'crime as business' were carried out by individualist criminal entrepreneurs or criminal 'firms' (Hobbs, 1988) – frauds, counterfeiting, robbery – but there are no signs in the history of British crime of large-scale organization and the comments by Low (1982: 195) concerning the underworld of Regency England are still largely applicable today: '[T]here were some big criminal entrepreneurs, but on the whole the criminal underworld was not organized, or even much influenced by its leading citizens: fortunately for the rest of society it remained essentially a community of small operators.'

In Britain today, criminal 'organizations' are probably more accurately described as semi-formal or informal associations of professional criminals (relatively small gangs, groups and networks) that remain small to medium-scale in the size and scope of their operations. They have been and remain subject to considerable flux and change in terms of membership and goals (Hobbs, 1995, 1997, 2013; Dorn et al., 1992). Nonetheless, it is, of course, the distinction of exhibiting some form of organizational capacity and modus operandi that means they are being discussed here and are the target of increasingly well-resourced and strategically directed policing agencies that are investing in better intelligence and smarter thinking to match the characteristics of modern organized crime.

> Criminal networks are becoming more fluid, extended and flexible, in part due to the use of specialist 'service providers' to assist with money laundering, logistics, documents, and other enablers. Meanwhile, the increased availability of information technology has both facilitated various crimes and spawned new forms of criminal activity.
>
> (SOCA, 2006/7)

Naturally, this complexity extends to the ways in which organized forms of crime have developed and operate in other countries and it would be foolish to believe that there is any kind of universal model. Indeed, a study of 40 criminal groups in 16 nations carried out by the United Nations Centre for International Crime Prevention (2000) found very different phenomena, quite different to the popular images of structured hierarchies and more in line with SOCA's view, exhibiting relatively loose structures based on dynamic and flexible networks.

Professional organized crime in Britain, 1930s–2000

The roots of modern professional organized crime in Britain lie in the 'hard man' gang culture of major cities such as Glasgow, Liverpool, Leeds, Birmingham and Newcastle (Freeman, 1996–7), the resilience of the illegal economies that prospered within but also assisted communities of poverty and marginality, and the enduring structure of the 'traditional neighbourhood family firm' (Hobbs, 2001, 2013; Samuel, 1981; Lea, 2002). In addition, social and population changes during and after the First World War were important: the dislocation of war in Europe brought refugees to Britain, some of whom settled into the criminal economies of survival and illegal opportunity; the old system of social class status, difference and deference was being eroded; and new opportunities for crime were emerging. Kohn (1992) explores these themes in relation to the emergence of subcultures of drugs and crime in the early twentieth century. However, as was the case with alcohol **Prohibition** in the United States from 1920 to 1933 and with the market for illegal drugs later in the century (see Chapter 12), where there is a prohibition of a commodity or service for which there is a demand, then an illegal supply, or the scope for corruption, will emerge (Nadelman, 1990). In Britain in the 1920s and 1930s, it was not the prohibition of alcohol sales but the illegality of street gambling, with resulting high profits for the bookmakers who could legally take bets at racecourses, that drew the attention of criminal groups. The gangs controlled the pitches, and rented them at extortionate prices to the on-course bookmakers, and the huge profits that rewarded the race course gangs created a violent marketplace where competing gangs vied for control (Hobbs, 2013: Shore, 2011).

During the Second World War, while community spirit and patriotism are seen as having helped Britain through 'the dark days of the Blitz' and the threat of invasion, a contrasting spirit of opportunism and profiteering was also evident, and illegal markets grew up around minor fiddling of ration allowances and a significant trade in state-controlled goods or commodities that were in short supply (Smithies, 1982; Thomas, 2003; Mannheim, 1965) and with the extension of rationing into the 1950s, competent criminals found that the post-war market hardly differed from its wartime equivalent.

However, it was London in the late 1950s and the 1960s that became the location and period most associated with a high-profile, and heavily mythologized, 'gangland' in Britain, epitomized by the operations of the Kray brothers in the East End of London and the Richardson Brothers who originated south of the river Thames (Pearson, 1973; Hobbs, 2013). The Krays cultivated celebrity and were photographed with show-business and sporting friends at charity events and at clubs in which they had an interest, and the somewhat less celebrity conscious Richardsons had legitimate business dealings in scrap metal and illegitimate expertise in long-firm fraud (Levi, 1981; and see Box 13.1), and were spreading their business interests beyond London before their arrest. However, the concept of organized crime was seldom invoked, and the phenomena remained in the public conciousness as something of Italian, American, essentially alien origin.

Plate 13.1 The hearse containing the body of the infamous gangster Reggie Kray arrives at Chingford cemetery, having travelled some 12 miles through London's East End past crowds of well-wishers, 11 October 2000. Kray was buried alongside his brother Ronnie to bring to a close a final chapter in the history of the London hardmen who were both imprisoned for murder in 1968.

Source: © Reuters 2000; *photo:* Jonathan Evans.

BOX 13.1 Long firm fraud

In a long firm fraud, the fraudsman simply sets up in business as a wholesaler, and places orders with suppliers with the intention of evading payment.

Initially payment is prompt in order to establish creditworthiness. Then larger orders are placed. When delivered, the goods are promptly sold for what they will fetch.

Primary objectives of a long firm fraud

- To establish credibility with manufacturers and suppliers.
- To obtain as many goods as possible over a credit period extended as long as possible.
- To make little or no payment to suppliers and creditors.
- To dispose of goods obtained with the minimum of delay.
- Abscond with the proceeds.
- Avoid identification and prosecution.

Source: Merseyside Police, Crime Prevention: Business Advice
http://www.merseyside.police.uk/html/crimeprevention/business/fraud/long-firm.htm

doing crime

In the 1960s and 1970s, affluence, consumerism, changing morality and new technologies expanded opportunities for criminal development and exploitation of various markets. Pornography, the counterfeiting of goods and VAT fraud were attractive and carried fewer risks than crimes such as armed robbery (Campbell, 1991). But the age of the criminal entrepreneur really arrived with the 1980s and the political promotion of a 'culture of enterprise' by the Conservative government of Margaret Thatcher (Hobbs, 1991). This is not to say that the market ideology of the new brand of conservatism 'caused' criminal enterprise, but many commentators agree that this was a period of significance in the reorientation of national values and the promotion of materialism. Suddenly, the wheeling and dealing culture of young men 'on the make' was a popular value system to aspire to, and markets – both legal and illegal – received a boost, domestically and internationally. Although women were also high achievers in this culture of aspiration, the impact in relation to crime was largely (though not exclusively – see the example below) a masculine matter (Newburn and Stanko, 1994; Messerschmidt, 1993; and see Chapter 14). While it was the so-called Big Bang of government-imposed deregulation in the financial operations of the City of London that changed the environment for business crime (see Carrabine *et al.*, 2002: 97; I. Taylor, 1999), the big bang that fuelled the new crime economy was undoubtedly the drugs 'explosion' of the 1980s (Dorn and South, 1987; and see Chapter 14). The central commodities here were heroin and cannabis, then later cocaine, ecstasy, LSD and amphetamines. In turn, the drugs economy has had its own influence on the global legal economy and its institutions (Castells, 1998; and see Chapter 7).

Writing at the end of the 1980s, the crime reporter Duncan Campbell (1991: 8) suggested that

> In a way, what has happened to British crime parallels what has happened to British industry. The old family firms . . . have been replaced by multinationals of uncertain ownership, branches throughout the world, profits dispersed through myriad outlets. . . . The 1990s [was] seen as a boom time for them, with the exploitation of a recreational western culture that wants its luxuries and its drugs. The legitimate businesses will run alongside the illegitimate ones.

Arguably this picture still holds. Some of the reminiscences of criminals such as safebreakers and thieves, recounted by Hobbs (1995), illustrate a world based on 'traditional' criminal crafts and skills that largely disappeared alongside a world in which manufacturing thrived and people worked in the same trades from generation to generation. The sharp contrast of the old with the new breed of criminal specialists is nicely relayed by the case of the 'female drug dealer who dresses smartly, uses a mobile phone and would not look out of place in a merchant bank or city finance house. Looking smart is part of her business method and she uses her gender to "fool" clients and police officers, who assume that as an attractive woman she is less competent' (Croall, 1998: 240; Hobbs, 1995: 25).

Ethnicity, outsiders and the organization of crime

The dominant US stance on organized crime can be seen as a reactionary response to immigration and urbanization which after the Second World War became institutionalized into a potent alien conspiracy theory (Woodiwiss and Hobbs, 2009). The classic, highly influential work on the Mafia as a highly organized and stratified empire of crime, spanning the United States from coast to coast, was Donald Cressey's *Theft of a Nation* (1969). However, this portrayal has been seriously questioned and the evidence upon which Cressey drew is now seen as discredited, as it relied heavily on the testimony of one key source whose reliability is doubted (Block, 1983). However, via American foreign policy and the policies of the United Nations, this notion of a hierarchically organized conspiracy has been adopted globally, and is frequently depicted by the image of an 'octopus of crime' with a controlling head and tentacles spreading out and embracing the nation (or the globe) (see Sterling, 1990, 1994). In fact, much subsequent criminological research has demonstrated the mythical nature of this creature and instead emphasized the diversity of cooperating and competing criminal organizations – sometimes referred to as 'disorganized crime' (Reuter, 1984). This reconceptualization does not suggest that such criminal groups do not exist or that they are incompetent or lacking in organizational skills or structures. Rather, it simply emphasizes a more realistic picture of the mixed and fragmentary character of the criminal economy than is provided by images of monolithic and monopolistic criminal conspiracies, and in particular the relationship between legal and illegal trading cultures (Hobbs, 2013).

Before the 1990s, with the exception of Italy, and to a lesser extent Germany (von Lampe, 2001), European states had considered themselves largely unaffected by organized crime (Paoli and Fijnaut, 2006). However, the end of the Cold War and the dismantling of internal borders as a result of the Schengen Implementing Convention in 1990 prompted concerns with a new threat from the East in the form of organized crime and a redefinition of their internal crime problem via the concept of organized crime. However, as in the USA in the 1960s, policy was not evidence-based but dominated by 'the strong opinions of experienced police officers, public rumours, sensational incidents and, of course, electoral interests' (Fijnaut, 1989: 76). Subsequently the 'New Evil Empire' of transnational organized crime was regarded in some quarters as a greater danger to international security than the communist threat of the Cold War era (Raine and Cilluffo, 1994; see Edwards and Gill, 2003).

Since the 1960s and particularly since the establishment of global law enforcement institutions in the 1980s and 1990s, other criminal networks and associations have been identified as operating on their own home territory and globally. So the picture of global organized crime groups now includes Colombian and Mexican cartels, Nigerian criminal networks, Japanese Yakuza, Chinese Triads, Russian Mafiyas, Jamaican Posses (Castells, 1998, ch. 3; Southwell, 2002; Paoli, 2003; Galeotii, 2003; Hill, 2003; Booth, 2001), and other 'big brands' that some scholars have dubbed 'Mafias' (Varese, 2011). Importantly, whatever form it takes, 'organized crime' is commonly regarded as a threat from beyond national borders, and reactions can be strongly fuelled by national anxieties and prejudices. For Britain this point is worth further consideration.

Although the term organized crime did not enter the UK's police or political lexicons until the 1990s, there are a number of notable examples of alien conspiracy theory in relation to Jewish 'white slavers', Chinese opium dealers and Maltese gangsters (Hobbs, 2013, ch. 4). However, the British 'underworld' of home-grown gangsters and robbers was regarded as a distinctly home-grown phenomenon derived from the detritus of the white working class, and policed by local police officers utilizing local knowledge (ibid).

Since the 1970s and 1980s, however, multi-ethnic Britain has produced criminal groups based on its own diverse ethnic communities, although as Ruggiero (2000) and others have shown, 'contrary to alien conspiracy theories the "outsiders" do not change the society. Rather the society and its existing structures provide the opportunities for crime and deviance, as well as the accompanying motivations and rationalizations' (Carrabine *et al.*, 2002: 90; see Ruggiero and Khan, 2006; Silverstone and Savage, 2010). Consequently the ebb and flow of both legal and illegal trade rather than the cosmopolitan nature of its participants provides some of the more relevant frameworks for unpacking the somewhat unhelpful category of 'organized crime' (Hobbs, 2013).

Organized crime as local and global

It is increasingly the case that even the most localized crime group can connect to the global stage (whether dealing in commodities from elsewhere or seeking to move profits out of the country), while 'current research indicates that even the classic "international" criminal organizations function as interdependent *local* units' (Hobbs, 1998: 419; emphasis added). Hence, today we must consider at least some, though not all, forms of organized crime activity in terms of both local dimensions (e.g. 'doing the job', distributing 'the goods') and international connections and resources (e.g. overseas demand for stolen works of art, for drugs such as ecstasy produced in the UK, for wildlife items – rare animals, birds, eggs; or overseas banks, lawyers, accountants and others that can help to launder profits or disguise the provenance of stolen goods). While a 'local' criminal project such as a raid on a warehouse or a lorry hijacking can still be seen as a familiar kind of venture, we also begin to see the complexity of the late modern criminal economy. We can give some sense of this 'big picture' in the following way.

After the organized terrorism attack on the World Trade Center in 2001, President Bush announced (on 24 September 2001) the intention of the United States to 'choke off' the sources of funding for terrorist groups by seizing or freezing their assets. This was a strong and easy political soundbite to make. However, if such a strategy is to be effective beyond the governmental borders of the United States, then it has to involve the banking systems of other countries because these are 24-hour, globally interlocking and mutually interdependent structures. This point may seem to take us into the territory of political crime and the financial criminals who help hide funds and indeed it does. But it is also a further reminder of the idea of 'glocalization'. Put simply, this is the proposition that the local matters to the global and vice versa. Leaving aside the specific nature of terrorist groups (we could talk instead of the assets of illegal arms traders, pornography distributors, drug traffickers, etc.) we need to recognize the enormous scale of the movement of murky money at the global level. The question that follows is: Where do these criminal profits come from? The following passage is taken from a report on money laundering prepared for the United Nations. It illustrates the interlocking global complexity and 'glocalized' nature of late modern criminal economies as well as the kinds of links and chains that transform illicit cash from the street into digital transactions on the legal, electronic financial markets.

> Sweatshops in big cities in the industrialized countries hire illegal aliens who are brought in by smuggling groups that may also deal in banned or restricted commodities, are financed by loan sharks who may be recycling drug money and make cartel agreements with trucking companies run by organized crime families, all in order to sell their goods cheaply to prestigious and eminently respectable retail outlets that serve the general public.

The masses of street peddlers in the big urban centres of developing countries sell goods that might be smuggled, produced in underground factories using fake brand-name labels or stolen from legitimate enterprises, thereby violating customs, intellectual property and larceny laws. They pay no sales or income taxes but make protection payments to drug gangs that control the streets where they operate. The drug gangs might then use the protection money as operating capital to finance whole-scale purchases of drugs or arms.

(Blum *et al.*, 1998)

While financial crime and money laundering have continued regardless of new efforts aimed at control, there has probably been some stimulation of other forms of criminal enterprise as a result. According to one analyst of the growing shadow economy of counterfeit goods,

The counterfeiting trade exploded in 2001 due to the terrorist attacks. Tightened banking regulations meant it was harder for criminals to store cash, so reinvesting it in a cash-generative business like counterfeiting makes sense. The War on Terror changed priorities in law enforcement, diverting attention away from 'harmless' crimes like counterfeiting and focusing Customs inspectors' attention on other threats.

(Phillips, 2006, 2005)

Fake fashion is a good example of how the apparently innocuous – a nice but cheap piece of designer label clothing from a market or temporary shop – connects to the local and global illegal and exploitative transactions underpinning the criminal economies described by Blum *et al.*

BOX 13.2 Counterfeit crime and the fake fashion economy

- Counterfeiting is a huge business – possibly 7 per cent or more of world trade according to Phillips (2006) and other sources (e.g. OSCE – the Organization for Security and Cooperation in Europe) – with transnational movement of illegal goods and cash, involving China, Taiwan, countries around the Mediterranean, all the way to sweatshops and factories doing 'work on the side' in many parts of the UK.
- It can involve exploited slave labour or high-tech pattern theft and copying.
- It has consequences for the legal workforce, undercutting prices and leading to loss of jobs (the majority being women in the clothing and fashion accessory industries), affects the profits of producers and investors which can damage confidence in the economy – knock-offs have knock-on effects.
- It is hard to detect – many people like to have a 'designer label' item even though they know it is a fake; others who have been fooled are reluctant to acknowledge this and complain.
- It is hard to prosecute – intellectual property rights are often at the core of the problem of what – if anything – has been stolen; the rights to designs and patterns, etc. have to be established and proven to be the subject of 'theft'.

Crime in the world of lawful professions

The American criminologist Edwin Sutherland was notable not only for his work on the idea of the professional criminal, but even more so for his elaboration of the idea of 'white-collar crime'. Sutherland first drew attention to this important concept in his address to the American Sociological Society in 1939, published the following year (Weisburd et al., 2001: 1–26). It is widely acknowledged that this was a major insight both theoretically and politically, and indeed it was once even suggested that were a Nobel Prize awarded for criminology, Sutherland would have been a worthy recipient for this contribution (Nelken, 1994a: 361). However, dispute around definitions arose almost straightaway. For a start, Tappan (1947) criticized Sutherland for attaching the term 'crime' to a variety of activities that did not necessarily break any criminal laws. To some extent this was, of course, Sutherland's point: the criminal law focuses downward on the poor, marginal and powerless, not upward on the affluent, mainstream and powerful. Yet the respectable middle and upper classes can engage in business and professional activities that can be far more financially or physically injurious to others, and with wider repercussions, than the offences for which working-class criminals are prosecuted and convicted. Furthermore, a factor of even greater importance for Sutherland (1949: 13) was that the crimes of respectable professionals violate the trust that society places in them: 'The financial loss from white-collar crime, great as it is, is less important than the damage to social relations. White-collar crimes violate trust and therefore create distrust: this lowers morale and produces social disorganization.'

Defining and identifying 'crimes' of the powerful

The application of the term 'crime' here is a signal about what may indeed not be legally 'criminal' but arguably should be, given its far-reaching seriousness. This is a tradition that has continued in critical criminology and does not mean that writers are ignorant of the law when they refer to, for example, the 'crimes' of the powerful (Pearce, 1976; Tombs and White, 2003; and see Chapter 6) but rather that they are drawing attention to biases in the law-making and criminal justice systems (Reiman, 2001). Such biases, and the incidence of hidden crimes of the powerful they disguise, remain highly controversial within criminology and related policy debates. Some writers have called for local and national crime surveys to include coverage of business crimes, consumer victimization and similar experiences (Tombs, 2000) and argued that methodological problems can be addressed. However as others, such as Spalek (2007: 7), have pointed out:

> there is little political incentive to include white collar offences in the British Crime Survey as their inclusion would mean an increase in the overall level of 'crime' and vicitimization recorded. This would place pressure on politicians to tackle this large area of social injustice, an area that . . . has traditionally attracted minimal state regulation since this has been viewed as imposing too many costs on business.
>
> (Snider, 2000)

One of the purposes of accruing power is to gain the privileges that it brings when used. In the case of crime and criminal justice, the use of power can redraw the line of legality and acceptability in the interests of some but not others and privilege their position so they stand above investigation and prosecution.

Definitions and breadth

A further definitional problem arises in relation to what Sutherland was actually including in his idea of 'white-collar crime'. As Nelken (1994a: 362; emphasis added) has pointed out, Sutherland's original concept

> is built on the *overlap* of (at least) three different types of misbehaviour (crimes). The first refers to any crime committed by a person of high status (whether or not in the course of their occupation); the second to crimes committed on behalf of organizations (by people of any status); and the third to crimes committed against organizations (whether or not these are carried out by people working in the same organization, another organization, or no organization at all). Sutherland focuses on that *area of overlap in which people of high status use organizations to commit crimes for their organizations* – against workers, consumers, or other organizations including competitors and the government.

In general, this area of 'overlap' (italicized in the preceding quotation) is useful as a guide to the discussion in this and the next section, but here we also focus on crimes committed by 'high-status' criminals on their own behalf. It is clearly wise to bear in mind the difficulty criminologists have had in providing hard-and-fast distinctions between white-collar and corporate criminality. It is also not entirely clear where all these definitional problems place those working within the public sector, for example, civil servants and politicians within the offices of national and local government. Here too, professionals qualified as specialists in law, management, medicine, accountancy, and so on work with autonomy and discretion, and with similar opportunities to their commercial-sector counterparts to connive at corrupt practices and derive benefits from fraud, bribery, theft and malpractice. Furthermore, in the world of 'politics as a profession', Cohen (1996b: 11) reminds us that the one thing as old as political power is political corruption:

> [T]he post-Watergate era has seen a quite unprecedented and uninterrupted series of public scandals about corrupt government in Western democracies. . . . In some cases, criminal activities (bribery, corruption, embezzlement, theft) were used for personal greed, in others for party political gain, in yet others to subvert basic and constitutional rules.

One Secretary-General of Interpol, Cohen notes, has remarked that 'it is becoming difficult to draw a clear line between what he called "normal" political business corruption and hard core, organized crime activity' (ibid.).

Of course, the mere fact that the criminological debate about the concept of white-collar crime is generally dated back to Sutherland's work does not mean that such crime was previously unknown! The business boom of Victorian England produced early versions of the banking frauds and stock swindles that became familiar in the 1980s (Robb, 1992). Further, from the nineteenth century onwards, the growth of commerce, of bureaucratic methods of organization and administration, of offices and their practices and technologies of accounting and filing, and of divisions of labour, all produced the infrastructure and conditions for the successful running of capitalism but also for the increasing diversity of criminal opportunity (Karstedt *et al.*, 2006).

Crime and the professions

We expect to be able to trust professionals, and this is the basis on which we 'entrust' them with our finances, our health, our security and personal information, or give permission to them to act upon our behalf in all manner of intimate ways and relationships. As mentioned, Sutherland noted the damaging consequences of the abuse of trust as a key feature of white-collar crime, and it is worth considering how these and other effects follow from examples of such crime.

The following discussion of some areas of professional practice illustrates both common themes within, and specific examples of, the criminality of trusted professionals. We can do no more than be indicative here, and readers should remember two important points about what follows. First, we are not saying that crime in the professions is so prolific that 'you can't trust anybody these days' (although this is a fairly common saying!). Second, however, we do emphasize that we are not just talking about 'a few bad apples', and the cases cited here should not be assumed to be extreme scenarios. As with the long history of police misconduct and corruption, we are talking about crimes and deviance that are largely hidden but quite widespread and deeply damaging.

Bankers as criminals

As Rawlinson (1998: 356) puts it,

> when money becomes a commodity in itself, subject to the vagaries of the market, banks find themselves caught up in the same competitive battles as other enterprises. Attracting customers becomes crucial, provoking banks into a less discerning concern over the quality of clients during straitened times.

The classic case of an outwardly legitimate and successful large-scale enterprise that actually harboured a wide range of illicit activity is that of the international but partly London-based Bank of Credit and Commerce International (BCCI) (Passas, 1995; Croall, 1998: 282–3; Punch, 1996). To operate as a criminal organization required the knowing involvement of many banking personnel, and the Governor of the Bank of England subsequently described BCCI as dominated by a 'criminal culture', although, as Spalek (2001) points out, the victims of the conspiracy also included numerous employees. Those who were part of the conspiracy reaped high profits, with the losers being ordinary savers and some commercial and public body investors who lost the funds of shareholders and taxpayers. Croall (1998: 282) notes that

> at his trial, one of the participants, Abbas Ghokal, was said to have run up a £795 million debt to the bank and to have been involved with a series of swindles, false documents, and a sham financial structure which funded his lavish lifestyle.

But BCCI is perhaps only the most prominent example of banking crime, and notable of course because its activities were exposed. Other financial institutions, such as those operating in tax havens like the Channel Islands, the Cayman Islands, Lichtenstein and elsewhere, offer services to those who wish to remove their funds from the attention of tax and other authorities and may make few enquiries and little distinction between 'clean' and 'dirty' money.

The case of Nick Leeson is probably at the other end of the scale of criminal ambition, for it was not Leeson's intention to criminally bankrupt Barings Bank, but this is what he managed to do by his uncontrolled dealing on the Singapore stock market and the consequences that emerged in 1995. Leeson's criminality lay in his concealment of enormous mounting losses and, as with a gambler believing their luck will change, his continued use of yet more of the bank's money in attempts to recoup his losses (Punch, 1999). But if Leeson was criminal in his actions, it could also be said that his managers back in London were guilty of incompetent oversight and rule-breaking themselves, 'sending sums of money to Leeson in Singapore for amounts that in some instances exceeded both the bank's assets as well as limits set by the Bank of England' (Gobert and Punch, 2003: 19).

Following this case and the huge publicity it generated (including a 1999 film of the story called *Rogue Trader* starring Ewan McGregor), it might have been assumed that a system failure of such proportions would be unlikely to occur again within a major bank. However in 2008, 31-year-old Jérôme Kerviel cost French bank Société Générale €4.9bn (£3.7bn) in a fraud involving four times as much money and probably the largest in financial history. This scandal hit France's second-largest bank, wiped out profits for 2007 and damaged European markets already fragile due to a credit crisis. Three main criminal charges followed – fraudulent falsification of banking records, use of such records and computer fraud. Like Leeson, Kerviel confessed to acting well beyond his 'limited authority' throughout 2007 and 2008, indicating that checks were inefficient or non-existent. According to the bank he was 'Aided by his in-depth knowledge of the control procedures resulting from his former employment in the middle-office, [and] managed to conceal these positions through a scheme of elaborate fictitious transactions'. While Kerviel was swiftly dismissed from his job, the offer of resignation by chief executive Daniel Bouton was rejected and instead he and the senior management were given a vote of confidence by the board of the bank. According to *The Guardian* newspaper, 'Roger Steare, professor of organizational ethics at Cass Business School in London said the SocGen scandal was further evidence of a "systemic deficit in ethical values" in the banking industry', adding that

> This latest rogue trader scandal is yet more evidence that while rules-based regulation and controls work for kids in the playground, it won't stop adults doing the wrong thing. The banking industry used to have a reputation for honesty, trust and prudence. This latest scandal, on top of the massive losses in credit markets, and the ongoing incidence of mis-selling to retail customers, indicates that there is a systemic deficit in ethical values within the banking industry.
>
> (Fiona Walsh and David Gow, 2008,
> http://www.guardian.co.uk/business/2008/jan/24/creditcrunch.banking)

doing crime

Health professionals as criminals

Medical practitioners have expertise and autonomy and can engage in the frauds and fiddles of white-collar criminality. In the United States a huge number of fraudulent claims are made to insurance companies for treatment that has not actually been carried out and, on a smaller scale, there have been a number of cases in the United Kingdom in recent years in which doctors and dentists have claimed payments from the National Health Service for visits to patients or for treatments that have not occurred. The same insulation from close scrutiny and the deep trust that society places in doctors can also be abused in the most extreme way, as was demonstrated in the case of Harold Shipman, a British GP working in Todmorden, Yorkshire, then later in Hyde in Greater Manchester. Over the course of 23 years, Shipman is believed to have murdered at least 215 of his patients. He had previously been convicted in 1976 of obtaining pethidine (a strong opiate-type drug) by forgery and deception, and later that year, in the name of a dying patient, he obtained enough morphine to kill 360 people. Nonetheless, he was simply given a stiff warning from the General Medical Council and allowed to continue to practice as a GP. Shipman was convicted in January 2000 and given 15 life sentences but committed suicide in 2004. Since this case, it has been proposed that all NHS trusts and the police should have investigation teams to check on doctors and nurses suspected of abuse and malpractice. The inclusion of nurses partly follows from the case of Beverley Allitt. Allitt was a British nurse who received 13 life sentences in May 1993 on being convicted of murdering four children and attacking nine others while working on a children's ward between February and April 1991. The subsequent Clothier Inquiry report noted that vital clues about what was happening were missed during the time she was employed at the hospital. But Allitt will not have been the first such case and has not been the last. In 2006, Benjamin Geen, a casualty nurse working in Oxfordshire, England, was convicted of two murders and grievous bodily harm to patients he caused to collapse with respiratory arrest and then helped to resuscitate because he enjoyed the excitement of the crisis and response. Part of Geen's modus operandi was to inject dangerous drugs he had stockpiled – something that was supposed to be far more difficult to do under measures introduced in the aftermath of the Shipman affair. Hesketh (2003) has referred to this kind of offending as 'medico-crime' and suggested it is time for a police and health professions protocol and the establishment of regional groups of specially trained police officers who would be better placed to carry out investigations in medical contexts. As Hesketh points out, just like any other member of the general public, health professionals can commit a huge variety of everyday crimes but there are also those that are particularly facilitated by their relationship with patients.

Health and pharmacy professionals deal on a daily basis with medicines that are themselves very valuable commodities and targets for theft. Historically and today, some professionals abuse their positions and divert medicines for personal use (usually stimulant or sedative drugs for recreation or for an addiction) (Strang et al., 1998). Of course, such drugs are also stolen in small-scale burglaries and larger-scale warehouse raids or lorry hijackings. Medicines may be stolen or diverted because they have great value in the illegal trade in drugs or may be profitably sold for their original medical use in Third World regions where they are scarce. The latter practice might actually occur because a Western government has declared a product unsafe for domestic consumption but is willing to allow or overlook the sale of the same product to other parts of the world (Dowie, 1979) – a phenomenon based on hypocrisy and creative interpretations of the law that extends to a range of hazardous goods (Harland, 1985). Braithwaite's (1984) and Abraham's (1995) studies of the pharmaceutical industry illustrate how the promotion of a benign image masks:

- price-fixing
- improper influence on regulatory systems
- industrial espionage
- knowing distribution of unsafe drugs
- and the 'dumping' of drugs that are not approved by Western countries in developing states desperate for medicines and with laxer regulations.

Medical and pharmaceutical deviance and malpractice come to light via public complaints, professional bodies and the courts but, as Jesilow *et al.* (1985) remarked over 20 years ago, this remains an understudied area – a fact that is all the more surprising given the importance of health care for everyone.

Lawyers and accountants as criminals

Like health professionals, lawyers and accountants are generally 'safe hands' and trustworthy, but occupy positions in which it is easy to act in unscrupulous fashion and abuse trust. Both types of professional can be employed by criminal organizations or themselves operate corruptly by, for example, inflating fees, forgery, pocketing money that should be passed on to clients, and engaging or colluding in frauds or even blackmail. The specialist expertise of accountants and lawyers and the high regard in which they are held as professions leave many opportunities for abuse of their position. For example, asylum seekers seeking advice and support concerning residence in the UK should use only services licensed by the Office of the Immigration Services Commissioner (OISC, established in 1999 under the Immigration and Asylum Act). However, as the National Criminal Intelligence Service reported in its 2003 Serious and Organized Crime Threat Assessment, 'a small number of corrupt solicitors and immigration advisors support the facilitation process by fraudulently completing asylum or work-permit applications for clients'. The OISC also noted that 'many are also involved in illegal activities such as document forgery and people trafficking' (McVeigh, 2003).

Accountants from the local high street to big names like KPMG have been scrutinized by accountancy academics like Sikka (2008; Association for Accountancy and Business Affairs) and found wanting in their conduct. KPMG, for example, has admitted in the USA to 'criminal wrongdoing' and paid a $456m fine in a major tax fraud case, while a UK tax tribunal found a tax avoidance scheme designed by the highly respected firm of Ernst and Young to be unacceptable. The scheme was described by a Treasury spokesperson as 'one of the most blatantly abusive avoidance scams of recent years' and could have cost the taxpayer over £300m per year but no prosecutions or inquiries have followed (Sikka, 2008).

The theme of connections between the local and the global is made by some of these examples. However, the examples of BCCI and the pharmaceutical industry also confirm the difficulty of establishing precise definitions of white-collar and corporate crime. BCCI was a case involving corrupt individuals within a corrupt organization that nonetheless somehow managed to operate as a legal, respectable and apparently competent institution for many years. Pharmaceutical companies have been the subject of various criminological studies and journalistic investigations exposing corporate criminality, but the question of the responsibility that the decision-makers within a company actually bear has proved to be far less straightforward than we might think (see Box 13.3).

Crime in the world of corporate-level business and commerce

Crimes of the powerful

Pearce's book *Crimes of the Powerful* (1976) was a Marxist critique of the bias of law, capitalism and control systems in favour of a ruling class and at the expense of the working class (see also Chapter 6). He used case studies from the United States to show how corporate interests had at times struck alliances with and made use of organized crime to suppress the labour unions, and how the law had been used to control the powerless through the criminalization of troublesome activity. In the same critical tradition within criminology, probably the most sustained and continually updated catalogue of examples of crimes of the powerful is the US overview by Jeffrey Reiman, nicely (and accurately) called *The Rich Get Richer and the Poor Get Prison* (2005, 7th edn; also discussed in Chapter 6). In a supplementary essay to the book, Reiman and Leighton (2003) focus on what they call 'the big crime story of 2002', which, for a change, was not 'the usual tale of murder and mayhem among the poor' but 'a long and complicated saga of corporate financial shenanigans that caused a significant drop in stock market prices'. The energy stocks corporation Enron, along with its compliant auditors Arthur Andersen (another example of accountants acting unprofessionally), were at the heart of scandalous revelations about unscrupulous and illegal business practices, but the case was soon followed by similar exposures at major companies such as Tyco, Xerox, AOL-TimeWarner, and by problems at some major US banks such as Citigroup.

While Enron boasted a remarkable record of growth and was symbolized by an impressive headquarters with a statue of the Enron symbol proudly displayed outside, in fact the enterprise was something of a house of cards and on 2 December 2001 was declared bankrupt – one of the largest bankruptcies ever, with debts over $31 billion. As Reiman and Leighton (2003) explain,

> Enron was subsequently accused of having perpetrated a massive 'disinformation' campaign, hiding the degree of its indebtedness from investors by treating loans as revenue, hiding company losses by creating new firms with company capital and then attributing losses to them and not to Enron, and encouraging company employees to buy and hold Enron stock while its executives apparently knew of its shaky condition and were busy selling off their own shares.

The culture of corrupt practice at Enron was not limited to US operations however. In 2007 three UK bank employees were convicted in the USA for wire fraud and received sentences of 37 months each in prison. The so-called 'NatWest Three', Giles Darby, David Bermingham and Gary Mulgrew, employees of a subsidiary of the UK NatWest bank, conspired with the Chief

Plate 13.2 Night view of the Enron sign at the company headquarters in Houston. Enron employees leave the building in downtown Houston, Texas, late on 7 February 2002. Under harsh questioning before Congress, former Enron corporation Chief Executive Jeffrey Skilling shouldered no blame for the bankrupt energy trader's collapse and said he had no reason to believe it was in financial trouble when he left in August 2001.

Source: © Reuters; *photo:* STR.

Finance Officer of Enron, Andrew Fastow, to defraud Greenwich NatWest of the true value of its holdings in a Cayman Islands investment company. The three bankers apparently made a profit of £1.1m each while Fastow and another Enron employee made even more.

While fraud and financial malpractice are one key area of corporate criminality, they are not necessarily the most injurious. Corporate negligence and management failing have also been held to be responsible for a variety of events in which great loss of life has occurred. In the UK, key cases from the late 1980s to today include the sinking of the *Herald of Free Enterprise* ferry; the King's Cross fire; and rail crashes at Clapham, Paddington, Southall, Ladbroke Grove, Hatfield, Potters Bar and Cumbria. Although public inquiries and academic studies can point to failings within the actions or inaction of organizations and individuals, the law in the UK has only recently introduced provision for the prosecution of a crime of corporate homicide or corporate manslaughter. After much promising and then stalling by the Labour government, legislation in this area finally came into force on 6 April 2008 as the Corporate Manslaughter and Corporate Homicide Act 2007 (see Box 13.3).

BOX 13.3 Timeline for legislation on corporate manslaughter and homicide

- Under the Conservative government, in 1996 the Law Commission produced a report, *Legislating the Criminal Code: Involuntary Manslaughter* that highlighted the ineffectiveness of the law in this area and published a draft bill that recommended the creation of an offence of 'corporate killing'.
- In 1997 the Labour Party manifesto promised to legislate on corporate manslaughter.

doing crime

- After Labour's 1997 election victory the then Home Secretary, Jack Straw, said that 'the new government believed those whose criminal negligence caused the deaths of innocent people should not escape punishment' (Bright, 2002: 6).
- The Confederation of British Industry has vigorously opposed plans for new legislation, arguing that it would be unworkable (Hodge, 2003: 3).
- But under current legislation, the Crown Prosecution Service is reluctant to bring corporate manslaughter cases because they are notoriously difficult to prove and win. 'There have only ever been five successful prosecutions and these have all been against small companies' (King, 2003: 10).
- Labour failed to follow up its manifesto commitment to legislate, but in 2000 did commence a wide consultation exercise about the proposed new offence. Not all those in the business world oppose action, and Ruth Lea of the Institute of Directors said in 2002, 'For business to look as if it is getting away with murder is extraordinary. It's common justice that if someone is killed through gross negligence that someone should be held responsible' (Bright, 2002: 6).
- In May 2003 the then Home Secretary, David Blunkett, announced the intention to publish a draft bill on reform of the law, but critics say this will concentrate 'virtually all the punishment on companies, rather than their managers and directors'.
- The history of demands for laws on corporate killing go back to at least 1965 when the bridge that Glanville Evans was working on collapsed and he fell into the River Wye. A prosecution failed, and since then, 'more than 31,000 people have been killed at work or through commercially related disasters such as train crashes. Safety reports have shown that management failures are responsible in most cases' (Hodge, 2003: 3).
- Gary Slapper, writing in the Times Online (18 July 2007: 1), welcomed the new Act noting that 'Globally, more people are killed each year at work than are killed in wars' and that this legislation makes prosecution and conviction an easier prospect than previously. This is not to say that the 'threshold of guilt' has been lowered – the Act

  criminalizes only an organization whose gross negligence has resulted in death. . . . The new law will apply not just to the UK's 2.3 million companies but to partnerships, other employers like trade unions, and to some non-commercial organizations. After much debate in Parliament, the new law will now also be applicable if the death of someone in custody resulted from gross negligence in the prison service or from those controlling police cells.

Transnational corporate crimes

With regard to business crime in a transnational context, Michalowski and Kramer (1987: 34) suggest that

  The increasing global reach of modern transnational corporations [TNCs] aggravates the difficulties of arriving at a satisfactory conception of corporate crime. TNCs at times engage in practices which, while they would be illegal in their home nations, are legal in a number of host nations.

Whether originating from legal or illegal sources, such crimes may have consequences related to social, health and economic as well as law enforcement issues in Britain or other countries.

The relocation by Western TNCs of high-pollution industries in less developed countries is notable here (Michalowski and Kramer, 1987: 37), resulting in the costs of crimes and offences against the environment and wildlife, and related damage to human health now and for future generations (Beirne and South, 2007; Croall, 1998: 280; and see Chapter 19).

Another example would be the enormous international catalogue of health and safety offences and breaches of regulations that have led to deaths and injuries as a result of what some have termed 'corporate violence' (Croall, 1992; Wells, 1993; Slapper and Tombs, 1999) and the crimes of toxic capitalism (Pearce and Tombs, 1998). As Pearce and Tombs (1998: ix) note, 'If the chemical industry has provided enormous material benefits, equally the costs have been enormous, even catastrophic', yet 'the destructive nature of the industry – the death, injury, ill-health, and environmental devastation which it causes – remains particularly poorly recognized and challenged.'

This latter idea raises an important question about the context of crimes of large-scale organizations, for despite the phrase coined by these authors, capitalism does not have a monopoly on such offending. The common characteristics of cost-cutting, negligence and under-investment in health and safety have featured as readily within the bureaucratic cultures of enterprises of communist and totalitarian states as they have in capitalist ones. In this respect, and in conclusion, when looking at large-scale, 'corporate' organizational crime, we can bring together the themes of:

- businesses operating to subvert or invert good corporate practice (see Gobert and Punch, 2003);
- the significance of transnationalization and globalization in respect of where crimes are committed and in terms of their effects; and
- the irony that we live in a world much improved by advances in science, industry and technology yet which now also suffers the multiple, unintended (though not always unforeseen) consequences, generating a constant awareness of the dangers of life in a 'risk society' (see Chapter 7).

Summary

1   Professional crime is changing, and while robbery and burglary will always be with us, new generations of career criminals seek to keep themselves at the cutting edge of developments. In the commercial, electronic and financial sectors, criminal entrepreneurs seek profitable loopholes and niches to exploit. At the same time an enormous amount of business is transacted involving prohibited goods and services (pornography, drugs and people smuggling).

2   Law enforcement agencies can respond only if they too keep at this cutting edge as indicated by investments in intelligence and specialist staffing to match the characteristics of modern organized crime.

3   Criminologists actually know relatively little about the workings of white-collar and corporate crime, and this has changed little since the early 1990s when Nelken (1994a: 367) noted that 'far more is needed on the modus operandi – the "how" of white collar crime (motivation, meaning, actions, decisions, alliances, escape routes, "techniques of neutralization" etc)'.

4   It remains as plain as ever that there is enormous disparity in the way that different crimes are treated and that a fair justice system would seek to rectify this through more effective investigation and prosecution of the crimes of the powerful.

5   Transnational crime is now a major challenge (Jameson *et al.*, 1998; Gros, 2003).

Critical thinking questions

1   **Professional criminals and organized crime groups are among the most popular subjects of novels, television programmes and films. Review a small sample and identify the key characteristics of the criminal careers and/or organizations featured.**

2   **Is 'greed' the explanation for both professional and corporate crime? If not, what else do we have to consider?**

3   **Draw or describe a hypothetical 'chain' that could link a crime (you choose) committed in Edinburgh to a contact in Rotterdam and an air ticket to the Cayman Islands.**

4   **If we accept the benefits of a more globalized society, do we have to accept the accompanying risks of globalized crime?**

5   **Check news reports and the websites of professional associations such as the British Medical Association or Solicitors Complaints Bureau for evidence about the misconduct or criminality of professionals.**

Further study

Croall, H. (2001) *Understanding White Collar Crime*, Buckingham: Open University Press. A key text reviewing studies and theories concerning white-collar and corporate crime.

Friman, H. R. and Andreas, P. (1999) *The Illicit Global Economy and State Power*, Oxford: Rowman and Littlefield. Contributors cover crime networks, links with states, the trades in drugs and in hazardous waste, and the wider global context.

Hobbs, D., Hadfield, P., Lister, S. and Winlow, S. (2003) *Bouncers: Violence and Governance in the Night-time Economy*, Oxford: Oxford University Press. Ethnography and analysis of licit and illicit aspects of the growing night-time economy, also discussing regeneration schemes, use of private security, and drug and alcohol problems in pub- and club-land.

Weisburd, D., Waring, E. and Chayel, E. (2001) *White Collar Crime and Criminal Careers*, Cambridge: Cambridge University Press. Longitudinal, quantitative study of the backgrounds and criminal careers of white-collar criminals, challenging some taken-for-granted assumptions.

Winlow, S. (2001) *Badfellas: Crime, Tradition and New Masculinities*, Oxford: Berg. A study of crime, culture, masculinity and community based on insightful ethnography and fieldwork.

Useful websites

Web of Justice

http://www.co.pinellas.fl.us/bcc/juscoord/eorganized.htm

This site provides numerous links to other websites concerned with crime, corruption and power.

United Nations

http://www.unodc.org/unodc/organized_crime.html

This UN site on organized crime provides a source about global developments in crime and control and links to national sites.

Nathanson Centre

http://www.yorku.ca/nathanson/search.htm

This site provides a searchable bibliographic database to help locate other relevant studies.

Criminal Justice Resources

http://www.lib.msu.edu/harris23/crimjust/orgcrime.htm

This site provides links to other sites both official – such as the FBI and Royal Canadian Mounted Police – and unofficial – such as journalist and community sites concerned with various forms of crime.

Association for Accountancy and Business Affairs

http://www.aabaglobal.org/

Paul's Justice Page

http://www.paulsjusticepage.com/

This site provides useful links and material concerning corporate crime and crimes of the powerful.

chapter 14

Drugs, Alcohol, Health and Crime

Key issues

■ How do drugs and alcohol contribute to crime?

■ What can history tell us about the legal and cultural status of drugs and alcohol?

■ Is drug use becoming more of a 'normalized' feature of everyday life?

■ How can we illustrate important connections between crime and health issues?

Introduction

In the past few years, senior politicians, police officers and other leaders have all done what might have once seemed unthinkable for such influential figures and called into question the dominant international approach to drug control – the idea of prohibition. For example, in 2011, the former UN Secretary-General Kofi Annan, former leaders of Colombia, Mexico and Brazil as well as writers, financiers, entrepreneurs and politicians, all contributed to a report arguing that 'repressive strategies will not solve the drug problem' and called for an end to the criminalization of drug use and exploration of alternative legal approaches that could weaken criminal organizations and promote health and treatment responses. In April 2012, the President of Guatemala, a country that has suffered from the consequences of drug trafficking as well as the fight against it for two decades, wrote an insightful analysis of some of the modern contradictions in policies and attitudes adopted toward drugs, intoxicants and some other natural products (see Box 14.1).

In the UK, familiar headlines suggest grounds for a rethink, for example:

Designer drug bans 'do more harm than good' (*The Observer*, 15 May 2011)

'Meltdown in the City: drug problems among traders reach record high' (*The Guardian*, 10 September 2011)

Western banks 'reaping billions from illegal cocaine trade' (*The Observer*, 3 June 2012)

Yet, the responses from governments in the UK and USA (regardless of political position) make their own headlines with a robust refusal to engage in a debate about all this. For example, in 2012 a new report by the House of Commons Home Affairs Select Committee 'said that after taking evidence from all sides of the drug debate, "now, more than ever" there is a case for a fundamental review of all UK drug policy' (*The Guardian*, 10 December 2012) prompting a reply from the Prime Minister in which he said:

I don't support decriminalization. We have a policy which actually is working in Britain. Drugs use is coming down, the emphasis on treatment is absolutely right, and we need to continue with that to make sure we can really make a difference.

This seems a familiar stalemate with commentators frequently asking why a rational debate is so hard to promote and pursue. Taverne (2010: 26), himself a former government minister, current member of the House of Lords and chair of the charity Sense about Science, puts the problem this way:

> Why do so many governments, including the UK's, continue to act irrationally? It seems to be from fear of public opinion – especially fear that they may be accused by influential sections of the popular press of being soft on crime.

> Yet there are good grounds for believing that these fears are misplaced. Some polls suggest that UK public opinion favours some easing of penalties for the possession of drugs. Furthermore, even where public opinion is hostile, experience has shown that policy changes based on evidence usually win support in the long run. Opinions can change, and some issues have little effect on how people vote.

A good example is the case of laws against driving having consumed more than a certain amount of alcohol. At first these were resisted and complained about by some motorists and lobby groups but this is now accepted and acknowledged as a sensible policy innovation.

Clearly, the 'drugs problem' remains one of the main headline crime and social policy stories of our times. As such, it can often be presented as if it is a relatively simple issue involving the supply of drugs, demand from different users and various kinds of associated crimes. In fact, it is, of course, a very complex subject in which problems of international politics, the legacy of history and the subcultures of use, as well as the economics of drug markets, law enforcement and provision of treatment services all interact.

By contrast, alcohol and its association with crime has been relatively neglected, although in fact it is probably of more real influence as a factor in crimes of violence and crimes on the road. Importantly, drugs and alcohol are also health issues yet criminology usually overlooks the significance of health as a factor in both influencing as well as reflecting the lives and behaviours of people (see Box 14.2).

This chapter therefore takes an innovative approach to these various subjects and adopts a holistic approach to the study of illegal and legal drugs in society.

BOX 14.2 Thinking about links between illegal drugs, alcohol, crime and health

Consider, for example:

- the link between intravenous drug use and AIDS/HIV or hepatitis C;
- the contribution of alcohol to crimes of violence – a problem not just for the police but also for providers of health care services;
- the fact that manslaughter deaths on the road caused by intoxication are recorded not just in the crime statistics but also in the mortality statistics;
- that offenders with mental health problems face additional difficulties and the courts and services face additional considerations in dealing with them;

- that alcohol may be a legal 'drug' but supplying alcohol to minors is illegal, and over-indulgence by young people can lead to health hazards and hospitalization;
- that medicine and, in particular, psychiatry are powerful systems of social regulation or social control.

Controlling illicit drugs and alcohol

Drugs and alcohol have been the subjects of varying forms of control. Their histories diverge from the early twentieth century, with alcohol remaining legal while drugs such as cannabis and opium became illegal.

In the eighteenth and nineteenth centuries it was largely the 'demon drink' that was seen as a problem for society, a threat to the health and morals of the individual and his or her family, and subversive of the good habits and social order of a civilized society.

BOX 14.3 Binge drinking and moral panics: historical parallels?

In the journal *History and Policy*, the historian Peter Borsay provides a thought-provoking comparison of concerns about the consumption of gin in an earlier period and about binge drinking today. The parallels provide material for discussion but there is also a debate to be had about how different life and society is today compared to then and what this means for patterns of consumption and intoxication. Borsay points out that patterns of consumption were affected by the differing levels of taxation on different kinds of alcoholic drink. *The debate about whether taxation has an effect on the amount that people drink is still a live one today and worth considering as a class or essay project.*

From the 1690s taxation changes favoured the distilling industry thereby encouraging consumption of a great deal of gin with some claiming that 'each inhabitant of the city was consuming roughly a pint of the substance a week'. This produced social or domestic problems and by 1751 changes in the economy, drinking behaviours and legislation meant consumption was falling. Hogarth's famous picture of this same year reflects concerns of the time.

So what parallels might be drawn between the news stories we are familiar with concerning binge drinking today and the alarm about the 'Gin Craze' of the eighteenth century?

> Firstly, the media play a critical role. The police and health professionals clearly have direct and regular contact with the phenomenon, but most older citizens make their acquaintance with binge drinking primarily through the media, especially TV and the newspapers. Certainly it is the media who control how we see it; it is they who create the visual and written images and texts that determine perceptions of the phenomenon.

Plate 14.1 'Gin Lane' (1751) by William Hogarth.

Source: Trustees of the British Museum.

Moreover, though we might like to think that the newspaper photographer or TV cameraman just point their lenses in a random way at the goings on, commonsense suggests that there is a good deal of calculation behind the production of the images.

Secondly, my impression from these images is that though young men are undoubtedly present it is young women that are the media's focus – scantily clad, sometimes roaming around in groups linked together by arms, other times staggering helplessly on their own, occasionally collapsed in the gutter vomiting.

Thirdly, where men are shown it is usually engaged in acts of bravado, damage to property, and inter-personal violence.

Fourthly, the setting is invariably urban rather than rural, city centre rather than suburban, and outdoors rather than indoors. Binge drinking is thus portrayed as a public and urban phenomenon.

Fifthly, pervading many reports is a sense of governmental inaction and complacency. The world is falling into chaos, but the state is doing little to address the problem. Indeed, where the government does act, it is to introduce measures such as allowing twenty-four hour drinking that, from a commonsense point of view, seem likely to inflame rather than relieve the problem.

Sixthly, one of the reasons given to justify the de-regulation of licensing hours is the example of Europe, where it is argued that permitting an all-day drinking culture encourages a more mature and civilized approach to alcohol consumption. However, such a line of argument simply fuels a xenophobic response in the media, where de-regulation is portrayed as yet another example of loss of autonomy and cultural identity as Britain is Europeanized.

Finally, though the media may project the crisis, behind it are a series of organizations, professional bodies and pressure groups drip-feeding information and statistics, and pursuing agendas which inevitably reflect their own take on politics and society.

Source: *History and Policy*, September 2007
http://www.historyandpolicy.org/papers/policy-paper-62.html

Drug politics and policy in the UK

During the nineteenth and early twentieth centuries, concerns about respectability and restraint were paramount for the new middle class; an emerging medical profession had ambitions to expand its influence and provide expert opinion; and the women's movement, religious groups and elements of working-class socialism all embraced a commitment to **temperance**. The agenda for control of intoxication – broadly defined – had emerged. New, scientific specialisms produced theories of 'disease' to explain a variety of conditions such as alcoholism and addiction but also, for example, homosexuality, insanity and criminality (see Chapter 3). New clinical terms such as 'narcomania' and 'morphinism' (see Berridge, 1999) reflected new approaches to knowledge, power, control of the body and the triumph of rationality over unreasonable desire (Turner, 1996). So we see medical treatment directed at the moral and mental health of individuals; the popularization of images of the drunkard or opium smoker as a broken body, degraded and enslaved; and the celebration of the moral values of abstinence and hard work.

In the early twentieth century, the agenda for drug control was partly shaped by a continuing commitment to controls by the law and the police. Some of the laws that came into force were the result of domestic concerns (Kohn, 1992) but from around 1912 to the 1920s the drug issue also became internationalized, with treaties and agreements being produced to define and categorize drugs and establish what was prohibited and what was permissible in legal trade for medical and research purposes (McAllister, 2000). Effectively, this is an early example of 'globalization' – a theme referred to in several chapters here. In Britain – but not, for example, the United States – a different form of control was also exercised through the medical profession. Following the Rolleston Committee report of 1926, doctors had won the right to prescribe drugs such as heroin and morphine to dependent users or 'addicts' and thereby 'maintain' them in a way that was aimed at enabling them to live as a useful citizen and keeping them from the criminal market for drugs. While on the one hand this was an early example of the medicalization of a social problem (Zola, 1972; Conrad and Schneider, 1992), it was also an important early precedent for the practice that in the 1980s became known as harm reduction.

The late 1960s and early 1970s saw increasing criminalization of drug dealers and drug users caught by the police in possession of prohibited drugs. At the same time, users seeking or directed to treatment services (the new Drug Dependency Units established from 1967) faced a tougher and more abstinence-oriented regime. This further medicalization of the problem developed under the direction of psychiatrists, emphasizing how drugs have frequently been associated with mental health and how this link is periodically reasserted by medical professionals and policymakers. (This link is returned to later.) From the 1980s the enormous challenges posed by an increase in use of heroin, then cocaine and crack, alongside mounting public health concerns about AIDS/HIV and hepatitis C, meant that harm reduction principles became very influential and shaped practice and services in the UK (Strang and Gossop, 2004, 2005; Stevens 2011). To some extent this was mirrored elsewhere, as in the Netherlands, but faced resistance in other countries such as the USA. While still a significant principle, harm reduction has been less politically favoured since the 2000s. In response to the increased availability of types of drugs not previously used recreationally and so-called new 'legal highs' a firmer extension of the prohibitionist approach was adopted. Thus GHB, GBL, ketamine, substituted cathinones (e.g. mephedrone) and substituted pyrovalerones (e.g. naphyrone) have all become controlled drugs in recent years (Measham and South, 2012). Interestingly, for criminologists familiar with the consequences of prohibition-inspired law enforcement, the emergence of legal highs and popular uptake of previously little known drugs can be linked to the suppression of availability of other previously favoured drugs. For example, in a discussion of the media and police attention paid to mephedrone since 2010:

> Key to mephedrone's extraordinary rise in Europe has been the recent success of crackdowns on ecstasy and cocaine supply: there was a drop in purity of cocaine seized by the police in England and Wales from over 60 per cent in 1999 to 22 per cent in 2009, and about half of ecstasy pills seized last year contained no MDMA, ecstasy's active ingredient.
> (Fleming, 2010)

BOX 14.4 Legal highs and the mephedrone panic

One of the biggest challenges for contemporary drug policy is how to respond to 'legal highs', a problem which emerged in the UK in 2009. 'Legal highs' developed from a catch-all term before 2009 referring to any uncontrolled drugs, to refer specifically to synthetic stimulants manufactured predominantly in China and the East and imported in increasingly large quantities to the UK from 2009 onwards. Although some seizures and public health concerns had been noted in Israel, Sweden and elsewhere a few years earlier, it was during the summer festival season of 2009 that the consumption of substituted cathinones, notably mephedrone, came to public and police attention in the UK. The reason for the emergence and rapid increase in popularity of unregulated synthetic stimulants appeared to be in part related to availability (they could be purchased from high street 'head shops' or ordered from internet retailers and delivered within hours) and price (at £10/g substantially cheaper than established street drugs), combined with disillusionment by more experienced drug users such as weekend party-goers and clubbers at the reduced purity/availability of street drugs such as cocaine and ecstasy at that time . . . A media furore unfolded, with politicians of all hues predictably eager for the assessment and control of apparently dangerous new drugs. This contrasted with liberal commentators criticizing the rapidity of control and the unnecessary widening of the net of prohibition . . . Meanwhile, in the absence of an established body of scientific research on these substances – details of prevalence of use, drug-related harms and drug-related deaths remained hotly disputed . . . Whilst demand for mephedrone has continued after its control, what is less apparent is evidence of displacement to other, currently unregulated 'legal highs'.

Source: Measham and South (2012: 700–1).

Measham and Moore (2008) have argued that recent trends amount to the 'criminalization of intoxication' per se through 'proactive prohibition' and as this has been accompanied by a reduction in funding for harm reduction approaches (Hunt and Stevens, 2004) the focus of resources available to support work with recreational users has been directed toward law enforcement rather than education. 'Treatment' remains a priority as part of the government's 2010 *Drug Strategy: Reducing Demand, Restricting Supply, Building Recovery*, in which the Home Secretary Theresa May argues in her Foreword (p. 2) that: 'A fundamental difference between this strategy and those that have gone before is that instead of focusing primarily on reducing the harms caused by drug misuse, our approach will be to go much further and offer every support for people to choose recovery as an achievable way out of dependency.'

As Monaghan (2012: 30) observes:

The first New Labour strategy emerged in 1998 followed by an updated version in 2002 and a successor document in 2008. The Coalition Government published their version in 2010. Over this 12 year period a creeping moralisation has re-emerged in social policy

doing crime

that has at its heart a specific desire to change the behaviour of specific 'problematic' populations without fully appreciating the underlying causes. This has filtered down into drug policy.

Recent trends have seen efforts made to increase the availability and take-up of treatment alongside an increase in powers to impose penalties for refusing or breaking treatment orders and for repeated offending. Of course, as ever, the issue is not really that simple. In some cases, treatment as a 'cure' or 'solution' is possible and achieved but in many cases treatment and forms of long-term support and intervention, whether by counselling or maintenance with drugs such as Methadone, are required and can also be effective (Bean and Nemitz, 2004; Stevens 2011).

Overall though, it is the law enforcement agenda that has remained at the centre stage of policy since the 1980s and it has been strengthened, focusing on national and international large-scale traffickers (Dorn *et al.*, 1992; Dorn, 2004; Matrix, 2007) and on links between drug trafficking and professional organized crime groups (see Chapter 13). Money laundering of the profits derived from drugs is a large-scale and complex business in itself, and has become a higher enforcement priority following concerns among police and intelligence agencies that such funds help to support terrorist groups (Levi and van Duyne, 2005).

Prohibition and control remain the dominant message yet there is still considerable energy and effort expended on debates about the best way to 'deal' with 'the drugs problem'. For some, it is not self-evident that prohibition of drugs is necessary, and far from evident that it is a successful policy. So various positions compete: proposals for legalization or decriminalization (see Box 14.5), **harm reduction**, stepping up the eradication of drug crop cultivation and anti-smuggling efforts, zero tolerance approaches to use, more effective treatment, and so on. Thus, in the early twenty-first century we can see increased *contestation* about drugs. This is easy to see in the changes of emphasis in government proposals for their drug strategies and in the criticisms these often attract.

BOX 14.5 Legalization/decriminalization: pros and cons

The debate about the 'decriminalization' or 'legalization' of drugs is both old and new. It is old in the sense that drugs that were once legally available have come to be controlled, but at the beginning of the twentieth century there were debates about whether this was best done by the methods of policing or those of medicine (Lee and South, 2003; Berridge, 1984). In the United States, after the 1914 Harrison Act law enforcement became the dominant approach, while in the United Kingdom, after acceptance of the Rolleston Committee report published in 1926, medical management was allowed but within the framework of legal control.

In terms of the recent debate (Inciardi, 1999), the supporting argument for the legalization option is that presently illegal drugs cause less harm than legal drugs: it is their illegality that is responsible for related harm (e.g. through adulteration; through the committing of crime to obtain drugs; and because of the profitability of illegal supply, hence the growth of major crime groups and the incentive to commit violence or murder to protect profits). A counter-argument is that legal drugs are widely available, illegal drugs are not: the health, social and crime-related consequences of the widespread legal availability of drugs are therefore unknown. The decriminalization/legalization arguments are unlikely to gain government support in the foreseeable future because of the powerful influence of international prohibitionist agreements and assumptions that this would be politically unpopular with the voting public. However, some research studies and independent inquiries (Runciman, 2000; RSA 2007) have suggested that in fact there is room for greater flexibility in the interpretation of these treaties than governments have generally acknowledged, and so a careful yet more imaginative 'middle way' may be possible. In preparing their report on drug policy matters, published as 'Drugs – facing facts' (RSA, 2007: 295), the Royal Society of Arts working party commissioned a survey – one of the largest so far undertaken – from YouGov and found that 'a clear majority of people indicated that they would be happy to see the personal use of "soft" drugs such as cannabis either made legal or the penalties for their possession lowered'. The authors qualify this by noting that such results need to be treated cautiously but this does suggest that public opinion is not as hardline and fixed as politicians seem to assume.

The anomaly of alcohol control

Among the concerns of social reformers in the nineteenth century, the abuse of alcohol loomed large. It is therefore intriguing that the control of alcohol went in the opposite direction to that of other drugs. During the First World War, regulations under the Defence of the Realm Act introduced both the first legal controls over cocaine and opium and also the alcohol licensing laws, which restricted the opening times of public houses and considerably tightened up the regulations relating to the sale, purchase and consumption of alcohol. However, thereafter drugs became subject to ever-increasing and widening controls but alcohol availability was liberalized. War-time restrictions were barely enforced, and while the Licensing Act 1921 signalled that alcohol was an intoxicant that needed some regulation, throughout the twentieth century it became, as the Royal College of Psychiatrists (1986) put it, 'our favourite drug'. Outlets multiplied, from beyond the pub to the corner shop and now the supermarket and cross-Channel hypermarkets, and drinking patterns changed, with women greatly increasing their consumption since the 1980s (Alcohol Concern, 2008). For all this, the legal status of alcohol does not mean it has no connections with crime. Entirely to the contrary: for example, because there is value in avoiding the higher taxation on alcohol imposed in Britain, smuggling from across the Channel is profitable; and alcohol is a serious intoxicant associated with crime in various ways. This is returned to below.

However, it is drugs that have had the higher profile in relation to crime and social problems. Therefore, the following questions arise:

■ Where do drugs come from? Is this a local, national or global issue?
■ How much of a problem do drugs pose? How many people take drugs and who says it's 'a problem' at all?
■ What are the connections between drugs and crime?

BOX 14.6 What is heroin?

Heroin (medical name diamorphine) is one of a group of drugs called 'opiates' which are derived from the opium poppy.

Opium is the dried milk of the opium poppy. It contains morphine and codeine, both effective painkillers. Heroin is made from morphine and in its pure form is a white powder.

The main source of street heroin in the UK is the Golden Crescent countries of South West Asia, mainly Afghanistan, Iran and Pakistan.

Today street heroin usually comes as an off-white or brown powder. For medical use heroin usually comes as tablets or injectable liquid. A number of synthetic opiates (called opioids) are also manufactured for medical use and have similar effects to heroin (e.g. methadone, a drug which is often prescribed as a substitute drug in the treatment of heroin addiction).

Source: Edited from: Drugscope, the UK library and information resource on drugs (http://www.drugscope.org.uk/resources/drugsearch/drugsearchpages/heroin.htm)

Plate 14.2 Opium poppy (*Papaver somniferum*).

Drugs as a global issue

The opium trade in the nineteenth century

The original international opium traffickers were the great colonial traders such as Britain and the Netherlands (McAllister, 2000: 9–39). In the nineteenth century, Britain invested heavily in the export of opium from India to China, and although opium became a profitable commodity for China itself (Berridge, 1999: xxvi), originally the country was a victim of market exploitation by the British Empire. Britain wanted certain luxury goods that China produced but needed to balance the trade and did so via the export of opium. When China sought to close its ports to this importation, Britain went to war against China on two occasions (1839–42 and 1856–8) to secure the future of its profits. This history partly explains why domestic control over opiate use in Britain was so limited at this time.

The drugs trade in the late twentieth and early twenty-first centuries

Since the end of the 1970s and the early 1980s, changes relating to the geopolitics of opium production and to international trafficking routes have been significant. The British opiate market of the 1960s was primarily fed by a combination of leakage of pharmaceutically produced drugs from the legal prescribing system and then by 'street heroin' produced and distributed from the Golden Triangle region of Southeast Asia (Ruggiero and South, 1995). However, by around 1980 what became known as the Golden Crescent area (including Afghanistan and Pakistan) was producing most of the heroin reaching Britain. Since the start of the military occupation of Afghanistan the production of opium has continued to rise – even when affected by conflicts, limitations on land use or poor weather conditions (such as drought), opium cultivation is a very attractive crop for farmers in terms of the financial return, a source of revenue for the Taliban and produces profits for organized crime groups involved in the global drugs distribution business.

Corruption, crime and political opportunism all combine to consolidate and protect the bases of the 'narco-economy'. In response to this problem it has sometimes been suggested that opium production in Afghanistan could be licensed and the drug be produced for the medical market. However, as others point out,

- there is currently no shortage of opium legally produced for medical purposes and indeed there has been overproduction since 2000;
- there is a real difference between the conditions of stability and security in places like Tasmania and Turkey where some licit cultivation takes place and the conditions of failed infrastructure and lawlessness in Afghanistan (Rolles, 2007);
- even if some or all of the opium grown could be diverted to legitimate use, this would do little or nothing to diminish the demand for illegal opium-based products and the incentives to farmers and traffickers to engage with the criminal market would remain.

Alongside increasing availability, the fact that heroin produced from these sources can be smoked and does not need to be prepared for injection has been a contributory factor in the widespread upsurge in heroin use from the 1980s onward. In retrospect, the 1980s was a watershed decade (Dorn and South, 1987). The explosion of the international heroin trade was quickly followed by the growth of the cocaine market, with Colombian crime groups initially aiming production at demand in the United States but by the end of the 1980s also targeting Europe (Streatfeild, 2002; Ruggiero and South, 1995; see also Chapter 7). Money laundering, corruption of police and customs officials, the stimulation of local drugs micro-economies based on drug supply and demand, and the profits from acquisitive crime generated to pay for drugs all followed, while the price of drugs has largely proved to be inflation-resistant.

Drug trafficking is truly global and can be found to involve organizations in most nations and with varying degrees of size and complexity. While local markets will depend on individual

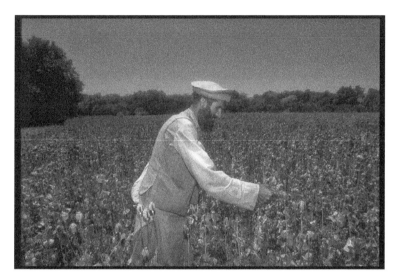

Plate 14.3 Pod-picker working in opium poppy field in Jalalbad, Afghanistan.

Source: Getty Images.

dealers or groups there is also a more elusive tier of what can be called 'upper level trafficking'. Desroches (2007: 829) suggests that there is, in fact:

> no clear consensus as to what constitutes upper level drug trafficking. Terms used in the literature include upper level and higher level drug traffickers, importers, smugglers, middle-level dealers, distributors, suppliers, wholesalers, drug-brokers, go-betweens, and facilitators.

What does seem important is that flexibility and, in many cases, the small size of the core of key personnel, with expendable contacts and networks at the periphery and extending outward, make these illegal businesses particularly hard for law enforcement agencies to effectively penetrate and close down (Dorn *et al.*, 2005). Desroches's (2007: 838–9) review of the literature on upper level trafficking groups notes that:

> Illicit enterprises are required to engage in risk management strategies in order to protect their assets from seizure and their personnel from arrest and conviction. Because the risks they confront are varied and pervasive, higher level traffickers employ a sophisticated modus operandi that include a number of security and risk management measures that function to protect them against theft or robbery, diminish losses through bad loans or police seizures, shield clients from competitors, protect themselves from would-be informants, and insulate themselves from arrest and conviction. These include the following:

- working within a small network of trusted associates
- relying on kinship, friendship, and ethnic bonds
- maintaining secrecy and operating on a need-to-know basis
- delegating or contracting high risk activities to lower level operatives
- maintaining information networks to stay abreast of what is happening in the drug scene

- operating with multiple couriers, transportation routes, safe houses, etc. so that drug seizures and arrests of underlings will not result in unsustainable losses
- using credit carefully and paying one's debts
- paying associates and employees well; and treating people with respect.

A cross-cultural view

All of this is, however, looking at drug use and trade from a very Western viewpoint with particular policy and legal preoccupations and cultural biases. There are, of course, other ways of looking at drugs and what they mean to people. This is to acknowledge that if we jettison Western preconceptions and adopt a more cross-cultural perspective, we will find that in some countries or cultures, drugs are not a 'problem' but can be:

- a long-established socio-cultural asset
- a form of support
- the basis for socialization
- and for belief-systems.

In some other contexts where drugs *have* become a destructive force this may have followed from Western influences (e.g. the intrusion and activities of organized crime groups). Drug use per se is far from predictive of problematic behaviour or problematic social outcomes and various forms of 'traditional' drug use have their roots in practices that are hundreds, if not thousands, of years old, for example, the use of opium by rural dwellers in India or coca chewers in Bolivia and Peru. In many such examples the substances involved are sacred to those who practise them and international conventions aiming to prevent their use could be argued to be unreasonably ethnocentric (Coomber and South, 2004, 2014).

Are drugs 'a problem'?

Certainly governments, the media and the public see drugs as a major threat to society. Even the strongest supporters of liberalization or legalization would acknowledge that drugs cause harm to individuals, families and the wider community, although their argument is that these harms and problems follow from the criminalization of drugs and drug users, and the inadequacy of support services

Of course, the 'problem' status of drugs can also be seen in terms of the labelling or social constructionist position (see Chapter 6) that this is a result of the application of labels and processes of stigmatization representing the agenda of moral entrepreneurs and agents of control rather than a rational policy. The effect of stigmatization may also be to enable or cause drug users to affirm their identities as deviant, rebellious and members of subcultures differing from 'straight' society (Young, 1971). On the other hand, there are arguments that the moral and cultural landscape has changed and that drugs have come out of the subcultures and on to the dance-floor. In fact, we are probably talking about two different landscapes. For the homeless heroin user, stigmatization and their distance from mainstream society remain highly important in influencing their sense of identity, lifestyle and opportunities (Green *et al.*, 2005). For today's recreational drug users, official definitions of propriety and of prohibitions seem to be increasingly ignored or subverted, and new scripts and meanings about both the place of drugs in everyday life as well as the places where leisure and intoxication take place, are being changed and created – whether the consumption involves cannabis, ecstasy, amphetamine or alcohol (South, 2004; Measham, 2004).

According to one argument, use of at least some kinds of drugs has now become *normalized* for many young people (Parker *et al.*, 1998). But is this true? And, if so, what does this mean? One position is that although 'normalization' does not mean that everyone is now a drug user, nonetheless, it is now non-acquaintance with drugs or drug users that has become 'the deviation from the norm'. The idea of 'social supply' is not new – users of drugs sharing or selling drugs at non-profit rates with other users known to them is an obvious way of reducing costs and increasing the sociable element of drug experiences. However, it may be becoming an even more common pattern, especially in relation to drugs like cannabis or ecstasy (Coomber and Turnbull, 2007; South, 2004).

The opposing argument is that drug use has not become a 'normal' activity for the majority of young people: prohibitions, peer-group resistance, parental attachment and preference for alternative expressive activities remain central to their lives. Both arguments (Parker *et al.*, 1998; Shiner and Newburn, 1999; South, 1999b) would seem to have some validity across late modern societies, and MacDonald and Marsh (2002) usefully suggest that a process of 'differentiated normalization' may be occurring, with some young people remaining anti-drug abstainers, some being frequent recreational users, and some serious, problematic drug users.

As Measham (2004: 221) notes,

> The normalization thesis adopted six key indicators of change: drug availability or offers; drug trying or lifetime prevalence of use; current or regular drug use; future intentions in use; being 'drugwise'; and the cultural accommodation of the illicit.

Measham then points out that one of the limitations of the debate generated by this thesis was the emphasis placed on quantitative indicators to the neglect of what was arguably the most important indicator of 'normalization' – 'the wider cultural accommodation of drug related attitudes and behaviours amongst drug using and non-drug using groups of young people and in society more generally'.

While some studies suggest that drug use has been in decline or has stabilized, others suggest that at least some forms of drug use are increasing. Whatever the composition of the market, the spending power involved is enormous for what is still a supposedly illegal and hard-to-access market – 'Home Office estimates of the scale of the drug trade, between £4bn and £6.6bn in 2003–04, suggested the amount spent on drugs each year was equal to 33% of the tobacco market and 41% of that for alcohol' (Travis, 2007; Matrix, 2007).

Apart from surveys, we can also look at law enforcement statistics about drugs and crime but must also recognize that these are limited in what they can tell us. Realistically, such statistics can reflect only what is known, that is drug offences and related crimes that have been detected, seizures made and convictions secured in the courts – although some extrapolations can be made from current trends. Drugs offences are not reported in the same way that robberies or burglaries are (see chapters 9 and 10) – the participants in a drug sale will not report their transaction and are unlike, for example, the victim of a robbery who will probably be quick to involve the police and their insurance company. Statistics suggesting seizures of large amounts of drugs may be seen as an indicator of enforcement success. Alternatively, they could be interpreted as evidence of the success of traffickers because it takes only a few large seizures to inflate law-enforcement

BOX 14.7 Statistics on drug misuse – England, 2012

Key facts

Drug misuse among adults (16–59 years)

In England and Wales:

■ In 2011/12 an estimated one in three adults (36.5 per cent) had ever taken an illicit drug in their lifetime (around 12 million people), 8.9 per cent of adults had used an illicit drug in the last year (nearly 3 million people) and 5.2 per cent of adults had used an illicit drug in the last month (an estimated 1.7 million people).

As in previous years cannabis was the most commonly used type of drug in the last year; in 2011/12, 6.9 per cent of 16–59 years had used cannabis in the last year followed by powder cocaine (2.2 per cent) and ecstasy (1.4 per cent).

■ In 2009/10 it was estimated that there were 306,150 opiate and/or crack users in England. This corresponds to 8.93 per thousand of the population aged 15–64.

Drug misuse among young adults (16–24 years)

In England and Wales:

■ In 2011/12 an estimated 37.7 per cent young adults have ever taken an illicit drug (around 2.5 million people), 19.3 per cent had done so in the last year (nearly 1.3 million) and 11.1 per cent in the last month (an estimated 0.7 million).

Drug misuse among children (11–15 years)

In England:

■ There has been an overall decrease in drug use reported by 11–15 year olds since 2001. The prevalence of lifetime drug use fell from 29 per cent in 2001 to 17 per cent in 2011.
■ There were also decreases in the proportion of pupils who reported taking drugs in the last year; from 20 per cent in 2001 to 12 per cent in 2011.

Source: © 2013, Reused with the permission of the Health and Social Care Information Centre. All rights reserved.

doing crime

'performance indicator' figures but a drop in seizure statistics does not necessarily mean there has been a drop in importation and dealing. In most countries, police and customs agencies generally feel unable to realistically claim much more than a 10 per cent interception rate. In the UK, seizures of heroin, cocaine and cannabis seem to have been increasing in recent years.

BOX 14.8 Seizures of drugs

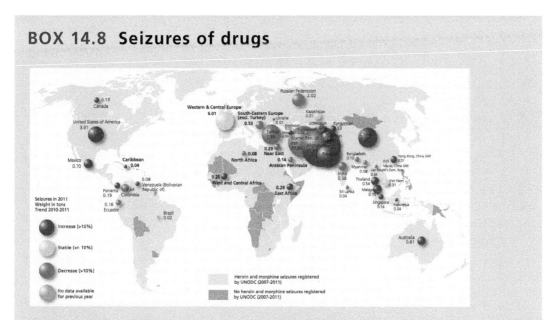

Figure 14.1 Map of global seizures of heroin and morphine, 2011.

Source: United Nations Office on Drugs and Crime (UNODC) (2013).

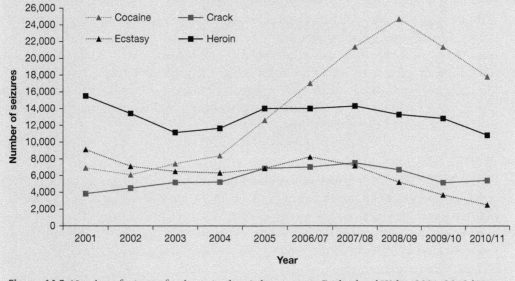

Figure 14.2 Number of seizures for the main class A drug types in England and Wales, 2001–2010/11.

Source: Coleman (2011).

Overall, the numbers of seizures made are affected by police activity and changes in recording practices and police powers, such as the introduction of cannabis warnings. Therefore, the number of drug seizures made and quantity of drugs seized should not be taken as measures of drug prevalence in England and Wales. This is addressed in the Drug Misuse Declared publications, based on results from the British Crime Survey.

- There were 212,784 drug seizures by the police and the UK Border Agency (UKBA) in England and Wales in 2010/11, a 5 per cent decrease on 2009/10.
- Class A seizures decreased by 15 per cent between 2009/10 and 2010/11, to 35,246. Class B seizures fell by 4 per cent to 175,218, while class C seizures rose by 16 per cent to 7,516.
- Cocaine was again the most commonly seized class A drug in 2010/11, with 17,689 seizures, a 17 per cent decrease on 2009/10. The second highest seized class A drug was heroin at 10,812, a 16 per cent decrease from 2009/10.
- The majority of class B seizures were for cannabis. The 167,381 seizures in 2010/11 compared to 176,830 in 2009/10, a 5 per cent decrease.
- The number of seizures of other class B drugs increased to 2,722 in 2010/11 from 377 in 2009/10. This is largely due to mephedrone and other cathinone derivatives being made controlled substances in April 2010.

Drugs are used by many different people and in many situations. Here are typical findings from national and local surveys carried out in the UK:

In general
- Drug use has increased significantly in recent years. This includes *increases in use of medicines and an increase in cigarette smoking, alcohol consumption* as well as illegal and other socially unacceptable drugs, especially among young people.
- Illegal drug use is only an occasional activity for most people.
- Most illegal drug use is experimental or on a relatively controlled, recreational basis.
- Most people who use drugs – be it legal or illegal substances – do not come to serious harm.
- Recent trends mean that soon the majority of parents of school-aged children in many areas will have tried illegal drugs when they were young.

Age of use
- Use of drugs (other than medicines) tends to become significant by the age of 14 for many young people, and both numbers using and quantities consumed increase throughout the remaining teenage years.
- Most young people moderate their use of, or completely stop using, illegal drugs and moderate their alcohol use by their mid- to late twenties when they 'settle down' and take on adult responsibilities.
- A small, but significant, number of people continue to use illegal drugs, and particularly cannabis, into their thirties. Many of these people are parents.

Drugs and crime

The most evident examples of drugs and crime activity can be distinguished at two levels:

- street-level drugs offenders, including the activities of users sufficiently dependent that they become involved in crime to generate funds, or those already engaged in criminality who are then initiated into drug use;
- the activities of professional crime groups involved in organizing drugs distribution.

There is a small industry producing research on the drugs–crime connection but for all this – or perhaps because of the variety of studies and different kinds of evidence – there is no single conclusion about the nature of this relationship. Of course, there is no dispute about the fact of an association between drugs and crime but there is disagreement about how direct or mediated the link may be. It is obviously clear that the very illegality of drugs will make their possession and supply an offence but thereafter matters are less straightforward. Put simply: Does drug use lead to crime or does involvement in a criminal lifestyle lead to drug use?

Heroin and crack users with a serious addiction may be committing a considerable amount of acquisitive crime to fund their habit (Bennett *et al.*, 2001) but, at the same time, as Seddon (2002) argues, a link between drugs and crime is in fact only found among a minority of drug users – the 3 per cent or so of illicit drug users who are termed 'problem' users. Within this group, the association is primarily between use of heroin and/or crack cocaine and commission of certain economic/property offences (especially drug selling, shoplifting, burglary and other theft). For others, the route to drug use may be through involvement in an array of routes into delinquent and criminal lifestyles (Auld *et al.*, 1986; Hammersley *et al.*, 1989; Pudney, 2002), and drugs are just one commodity bought and sold in the pleasure markets of the late modern illicit economy (South, 2004; Hobbs *et al.*, 2003).

BOX 14.9 Data on drugs offences in the UK

Home Office data on 'Offenders dealt with' show a consistent rise in the number of persons found guilty, cautioned or 'dealt with by compounding' for drugs offences under the Misuse of Drugs Act. In 1998/99, the total number of drug offences was 136,000 rising to 232,000 in 2010/11 (Chaplin *et al.*, 2011: 45). Some 199,000 of these offences in 2010/11 (86 per cent) related to possession offences and of these, 160,000 (81 per cent) were specifically cannabis-related possession offences.

Source: Measham and South (2012); Chaplin *et al.* (2011).

Criminal groups and the drug market

A 2007 Home Office report on organized crime and its profits and costs to society observed:

> That the UK illicit drugs market is dominated by organised criminal groups is well known. The industry is typically characterised by a vertically disintegrated supply chain: drugs are imported in bulk to the UK, sold onto different middle market groups (where numerous transactions may occur), before being sold to dealers and then the final user. The source country varies depending on the drug in question. For heroin the largest supplier is Afghanistan, and for cocaine it is Colombia. The researchers assume that the entire market is organised. Although there are some exceptions – for example some cannabis is grown and consumed by the same person – these instances make little difference to the total organised crime market size.

There is, by now, a very extensive international literature on drug trafficking and related serious, organized crime. The drugs market provides opportunities for entrepreneurial criminals to trade in a highly profitable commodity. In many ways, such illegal enterprise will have characteristics not dissimilar to those of legal businesses, albeit that while disagreements and contract disputes in the legal market may be resolved via the courts, increasingly the illegal drugs market may use violence and even murder as a form of dispute resolution and contractual enforcement.

This understanding of the entrepreneurial mix in the market is important and has replaced the once prevalent and more limited notion of a simple 'pyramid' model of the market, familiar in police intelligence at one point (Broome Report, 1985). This model assumed the dominance of drugs trafficking organizations by a 'Mr Big' or several such hidden hands and was shaped less by evidence of market structure and more by an expectation that the hierarchical organization of police detective work reflected a hierarchy of criminal organization. In other words, at divisional level, local police countered local dealers and related crime; force-wide drug squads were more intelligence led and pursued middle-level dealers; while regional crime squads and their 'drugs wings' targeted drug crime operating nationally and internationally (Bean, 2002: 123). The idea of the mixed, fluid and relatively open market is more useful, and even where major cartels can be pointed to – such as that led by Pablo Escobar in Colombia in the 1980s – these are operating in competitive markets, accompanied by significant levels of corruption and violence. Indeed, research suggests that the fragmentary, flexible, temporary and ad hoc nature of some forms of transnational crime, such as heroin and cocaine trafficking and smuggling of humans, means that 'traditional' crime organizations such as Triads and La Cosa Nostra are of declining significance (Zhang and Chin, 2003). The example of the involvement of Vietnamese gangs in the UK cannabis trade shows how relatively easy it is for new entrants to flourish in a flexible trade and market.

Controlling drugs

Efforts to exercise control have been reflected in a long series of legislative Acts (see Box 14.10) and through an increasing emphasis on drugs as a problem for everybody: a community issue requiring action from within the school curriculum, from housing associations and local government housing departments, and from health services (Lupton *et al.*, 2002). The response and organization of law enforcement agencies have become increasingly specialized and sophisticated through the decades, from local drugs squads to national agencies and international cooperation.

BOX 14.10 Timeline: UK legislation and influences on the control of drugs

1908 The Poisons and Pharmacy Act regulates sale of cocaine.

1912 The Hague Convention (International Opium Convention) requires signatory nations to limit opiate use, manufacture and trade to medical purposes; close opium dens; and implement laws against unauthorized possession and/or sale.

1916 The Defence of the Realm Act, Regulation 40B controls the possession of cocaine.

1920 The Dangerous Drugs Act implements the Hague Convention; this is mainly concerned with opium but also introduces some controls on cannabis.

1925 The Dangerous Drugs Act amends the 1920 Act and restricts the import and export of coca leaf and cannabis.

1926 The Rolleston Committee Report (Interdepartmental Committee on Morphine and Heroin Addiction) recommends that the prescribing of morphine and heroin be allowed where it is part of a therapeutic programme of maintenance for the incurably addicted or of gradual withdrawal.

1951 The Dangerous Drugs Act consolidates previous Acts.

1961 The First Brain Committee Report (Interdepartmental Committee on Drug Addiction) fails to detect signs of change and feels that new controls on heroin and cocaine are unnecessary.

1965 The Second Brain Committee Report discusses a significant increase in drug use and recommends that doctors 'notify' the Home Office about addicts in treatment, and restrictions on the availability of heroin and cocaine prescriptions.

1967 The Dangerous Drugs Act implements the Brain recommendations and introduces police powers to stop and search individuals and vehicles for drugs.

1968 The Medicines Act regulates the production and distribution of medicines, e.g. whether they are available only on prescription, or without a prescription but only from a pharmacist, or generally available from any shop.

1971 The Misuse of Drugs Act – still the main legislation (with subsequent amendments) covering controlled drugs, divided into three classes:
Class A, e.g. heroin, cocaine, LSD, opium;
Class B, e.g. amphetamines, barbiturates and, previously, cannabis, which has (from 2004) moved to –
Class C, also including, for example, steroids, various tranquillizers and stimulants.

1979 The Customs and Excise Management Act – which complements the 1971 Act, penalizing trafficking in controlled drugs.

1986 The Drug Trafficking Offences Act introduces provisions for seizure of the assets of traffickers unless they can be proved to have no connection with the profits of drug crime (importantly, the burden of proof was moved from the prosecution to the defendant); it also made the sale or supply of certain drugs paraphernalia illegal (e.g. cannabis pipes).

1988 The Road Traffic Act makes it an offence to drive if unfit owing to drink or drugs. The police can stop those they suspect of being under such influence and request saliva, urine or blood samples to test.

1994 The Drug Trafficking Act updates the 1986 Act.

1997 The Crime (Sentences) Act introduces minimum sentences of seven years for those convicted of a Class A drug trafficking offence for the third time.

1998 The Crime and Disorder Act introduces a new Drug Treatment and Testing Order (DTTO).

2000 The Criminal Justice and Courts Act introduces a new sentence of Drug Abstinence Order.

2005 Drugs Act introduces new powers relating to intention to supply a controlled drug, drug offences searches, and detention of suspected drug offenders; includes mushrooms containing psilocin, etc., as Class A drugs.

Sources: originally adapted from the Runciman Report (2000), J. Cohen (2002) and updated for this edition.

Alcohol and crime

The principal focus of concern about alcohol and crime is the contribution it makes to levels of violence in society – whether hidden in the household or highly visible on the streets. In 2005 a report from the Faculty of Public Health of the Royal Colleges of Physicians in the UK pointed out that:

> In England and Wales, alcohol is thought to play a part in approximately 1.2 million violent incidents – almost half of all violent crimes, with devastating health consequences for victims, their family, friends and the wider community. While health, police and other public services deal with the consequences of alcohol-related violence, such staff are also victims.
> (http://www.fphm.org.uk/resources/AtoZ/bs_alcohol_violence.pdf)

Raistrick *et al.* (1999: 55) have summarized a wide body of research and noted several other connections between alcohol and crime:

- Intoxication may tip the balance between contemplating crime and committing it.
- Alcohol use may be a financial motive for crime.

■ Alcohol problems can produce a home environment in which anti-social and abusive behaviour occurs, such as domestic violence, child abuse and cruelty towards animals.

As we saw earlier, there is a long history of public anxiety about binge drinking, alarm about rowdy and violent behaviour on the streets, and desire to prohibit drink because of its effect on morals or its encouragement of socializing with 'bad company'. According to the early criminologist Cesare Lombroso (see also Chapter 4),

> Alcohol . . . is a cause of crime, first because many commit crime in order to obtain drinks; further, because men sometimes seek in drink the courage necessary to commit crime, or an excuse for their misdeeds; again, because it is by the aid of drink that young men are drawn into crime; and because the drink shop is the place for meeting of accomplices, where they not only plan their crimes but squander their gains . . . it appears that alcoholism occurred oftenest in the case of those charged with assaults, sexual offences, and insurrections. Next came assassinations and homicide; and in the last rank those imprisoned for arson and theft, that is to say, crime against property.
>
> (Lombroso, 1911/1968: 95–6)

However, it is not as clear as Lombroso implies that alcohol 'causes' crime; rather, it appears to have an effect in relation to crime (Alcohol Concern, 2001; All Party Group on Alcohol Misuse, 1995; *The Lancet*, 1999; Man *et al.*, 2002; McMurran and Hollin, 1989: 386; Raistrick *et al.*, 1999; Dingwall, 2005):

■ Data from the British Crime Surveys and other sources consistently show that heavy drinking and drunkenness are linked with aggression and violence.
■ Facial injuries and wounds to the victim are associated with heavy drinking by the assailant (although the victim may also have been drinking).
■ Drinking and driving is the leading cause of death among young people aged 15–24.
■ The British Medical Association suggests that the offender or victim had been drinking in 65 per cent of murders, 75 per cent of stabbings, 70 per cent of beatings and 50 per cent of fights or domestic assaults.
■ One-third of people are intoxicated when they are arrested.
■ Heavier users of alcohol are more likely to have criminal records and to admit to criminal acts than those who are moderate drinkers or non-drinkers.
■ Even when alcohol and committing crime can be shown to be related it is difficult to point to a causal direction, i.e. which came first – the drinking or the crime?

Alcohol consumption obviously has an effect on the drinker, but it is easily understood that social contexts and psychological factors influence how these effects are experienced and manifested. Similarly, understanding the role of alcohol (or indeed other drugs) in relation to the committing of crimes needs sensitivity not just to the interaction between pharmacology and physiology, but also to immediate social context and wider cultural norms. As with the idea that users 'learn' how to interpret and 'enjoy' drug effects (Becker, 1963), so it is the case that belief about how alcohol is 'supposed' to affect behaviour, alongside the influences of context and culture, is as important in shaping behaviour as the amount of alcohol consumed (Borrill and Stevens, 1993; Pearson, 1992; Deehan, 1999).

Images of alcohol use on television, in films and in advertising promote an association with desirable lifestyles, fun, sex and success, with obvious connections to the culture of the carnivalesque and seductions of crime (Presdee, 2000; Katz, 1988) that have been discussed in relation to youth offending, hedonism and susbstance use (Collison, 1996). Such advertising is designed to appeal to both young men and young women. Use by the latter has been increasing steadily since the 1980s. Nonetheless, it is particularly in relation to masculinity that the association between alcohol consumption and offending, including violence, has been seen as a serious problem (Graham and Wells, 2003).

The economic boom of the night-time economy (Hobbs *et al.*, 2003) has assisted the regeneration of some inner-city areas and has created opportunities for employment and leisure in the 24/7 city but has also led to developments of criminological interest: a new arena for masculine play and power, to be enjoyed but also fought over; the proliferation of venues legally selling alcohol and where drugs are illegally easily available; development of protection rackets and turf wars between criminal entrepreneurs; increases in alcohol-related injuries requiring medical attention; and in relation to control, the growth of the use of bouncers and private security as the feudal forms of regulation of the night-time life of the city (see also Chapter 18).

Whether alcohol use is related to disorder and violence in the community or in the home, there are many avenues to explore for explanations of links. The complexity of this task is indicated by the intertwining of alcohol dependence, offending and imprisonment, and indications of mental illness and social exclusion (see Box 14.11).

BOX 14.11 Offenders, alcohol and mental health

- One study revealed that 63 per cent of men and 39 per cent of women serving prison sentences had been hazardous or harmful drinkers in the year prior to incarceration (Singleton *et al.*, 1997).
- As many as 90 per cent of prisoners have a mental illness and/or substance misuse (including alcohol) problem (Department of Health, 2001).
- People who are dependent on alcohol are more likely to be homeless on release from prison than those who are not (Revolving Doors Agency, 2002).

Source: Alcohol Concern website.

Drugs, alcohol, crime and community: a public health issue

Drug users have a likelihood of facing more health problems than the general population (Neale, 2004; Stevens, 2011), some of which follow from methods of use (e.g. infections, tetanus, hepatitis) and some from the problematic past histories and current lifestyles commonly found among heavy drug users. The National Association for the Care and Resettlement of Offenders (NACRO, 2001: 15) has suggested that 'background research into the relationship between health and youth crime is far from extensive', but 'That which exists . . . suggests a high correlation between substance misuse, adverse mental health and a range of other health-related problems on the one hand, and offending by children and young people on the other.' While this correlation is worrying by itself, it becomes doubly so when the problems of **rehabilitation** and reoffending are considered. The Prison Reform Trust (2004: 1) has pointed out how frequently alcohol and drug problems or dependence are found among those sentenced to prison and how difficult it is for such individuals to then re-establish themselves in society and find appropriate support:

> Nearly two-thirds of sentenced male prisoners (63 per cent) and two-fifths of female sentenced prisoners (39 per cent) admit to hazardous drinking prior to imprisonment which carries the risk of physical or mental harm. Of these, about half have a severe alcohol dependency. It is common for prisoners who have alcohol problems also to have drug problems. Just over a quarter of male prisoners and about a fifth of female prisoners who are hazardous drinkers are dependent on at least one type of illicit drug.

Connecting crime and health issues

In a broader sense, while the impact of crime on the psychological and social health of victims of crime has been acknowledged (see Chapter 9), it has probably not been well understood. Research by the Public Health Alliance (McCabe and Raine, 1997) found that

> The effects of the fear of crime, rather than crime itself, on the health of individuals and communities has been largely underestimated. In particular, the impact of 'incivilities' on well being is not well recognized . . . both victims of crime and non-victims identified a deterioration in their quality of life and adopted a range of coping mechanisms likely to be detrimental to health, in particular increased use of alcohol, smoking and use of both licit and illicit drugs.

Contemporary criminology has largely overlooked health as a variable of relevance but, at the same time, public health has also tended to neglect violence and assault as relevant. As Shepherd and Farrington (1993: 89–90) observe, 'Until recently, assault has not been treated as a public health problem, despite the fact that it is a major threat to health and a major cause of disparities in health between richer and poorer segments of the community.' Shepherd and Lisles (1998: 355) found that overall, and consistent with the findings of the British Crime Survey, 'about four times more incidents [involving violence and assault] come to the attention of [Accident and Emergency Departments] than are recorded by the police'. Such data are a potentially important source of information about violent crime (Hobbs *et al.*, 2002: 354) that goes unreported in criminal justice statistics.

In a valuable review of the literature, Robinson *et al.* (1998) identified several categories of connections between health and crime, including:

- the impacts of crime and fear of crime on physical and psychological health;
- the health needs of victims;
- costs to the health services.

Crime-related injury and victimization lead to health problems and the need for services. However, costs to the health services (and hence wider society) do not solely result from care of the injured. In recent years, violence against health service staff in Britain has increased significantly, and so worrying is this trend that the National Health Service (NHS) has made a key policy commitment to reduce violence against its employees. Further, as is familiar to any viewers of prime-time hospital and police drama series, the emergency services are repeatedly exposed to events such as major accidents or to physical and emotional damage to victims, which in turn contribute to mental ill-health and post-traumatic stress for emergency service staff (Brayley, 2001). Hence, the costs of crime and violence to society are felt directly and indirectly in personnel and financial costs to health and related services.

Crime, public health and social inequalities

With reference to violent crime and health inequalities, a study by Shepherd (1990: 293–4) shows that the assault rate was higher the greater the ranking of the area of residence in terms of social and material deprivation. More recently, Hope (2001) has investigated the positive correlation between social deprivation and crime victimization. On a national scale, data from the British Crime Survey for 2000 reflect higher 'concern' about crime among deprived groups – the poor, those in unskilled occupations, residents in inner-city and council estate areas – and also reports that those who considered themselves to be in poor health or who had a limiting illness or disability had heightened levels of concern about crime (Kershaw *et al.*, 2000: 47–9, table A7.9).

The importance of public health and its relevance for crime and victimization issues were given serious emphasis by the Acheson Report (1998: 53) on health inequalities. This report observed that both fear of crime and violence and victimization can have damaging consequences for health. It noted the simple but significant (yet frequently neglected) point that increased risk of ill-health *and* of crime victimization are highest among those already most disadvantaged. Furthermore:

> Although the evidence is incomplete, the link between income inequality, social cohesion and crime has important policy implications. It suggests that crime prevention strategies which only target the perpetrators and victims of crime and the high crime areas in which both groups live, will not achieve a significant reduction in crime unless they are accompanied by measures to reduce income inequality and promote social cohesion.
>
> (Acheson, 1998: 54)

Hence, public health is sometimes described as 'social medicine', and its aims can be seen to coincide with much work in criminology concerned with the effects of social exclusion – for example, strategies for health improvement that require reductions of inequalities and of poverty, of pollution, of sources of ill-health and transmittable disease in the community, and of crime and victimization.

Public health as social policing

Public health can be seen as a benign system of inspection, information gathering, regulation and intervention but also, precisely because of these characteristics, can be understood in the sense developed by Foucault (1975) as part of the dispersal of disciplinary power throughout the major institutions of modern society. Public health therefore has a role in the 'policing' of our health and of services and businesses that have an impact on our health, deploying various professionals such as health visitors, nutritionists and environmental health officers (who focus on pollution, food purity, hygiene in food stores and so forth; on 'food crime' see Croall, 2007). Public health is also about preventing disease and illness and promoting reduction of harm. So, to return to drug misuse and AIDS/HIV, the public health approach adopted in the United Kingdom has been far more effective than the US emphasis on a response by the criminal justice system (Stimson, 1995). It is also important to see that in the contemporary context of public policy, multi-agency strategies and initiatives have come to occupy a central place.

The idea of recognizing physical and mental health as relevant to understanding crime is receiving interest in various ways. But of course this is not a new development. As earlier chapters indicate, it can be 'functional' to society to identify, blame and stigmatize those who are 'tainted' or 'misfits': the vagrant, the imbecile, the pariah marked by disease, from the leper of the Middle Ages to the AIDS victim today. Religious, moral and medical judgements have long created categories of risk and danger and techniques for redemption, rehabilitation or treatment (Cohen, 1985). Since the nineteenth century, the medical profession – in particular, psychiatry – has come to be the secular successor to religion as the arbitrator of status as 'healthy' or 'sick', and has acquired the power to exercise forms of authority that can be hard to challenge. Some writers, both sociologists of health and medicine (Zola, 1972; Conrad and Schneider, 1992) and criminologists (Cohen, 1985; Sim, 1990), have drawn attention to the power of medicine as a form of social control.

Medicine as a form of social control

Medical and psychiatric interventions as social control

Antidepressant drugs such as tranquillizers have been seen by some as a pharmaceutical tool that society uses to pacify women discontented with the drudgery and limitations of domestic life. The medicalization of female deviance, the drive to normalize women's behaviour according to particular ideals of femininity and the tendency of medical professionals to over-prescribe mood-altering drugs for women are common practices (Ettore, 1992). In the United States, significantly more women than men receive prescriptions for antidepressants, tranquillizers and sedatives. Within prisons (see following section), the use of psychotropic drugs on male inmates is often justified with reference to 'problems of institutional control', while female inmates tend to be drugged in the name of 'treatment' in an attempt to correct their deviant behaviour in a psychological–social–physiological manner. Such drugs in prison have been described as a 'liquid cosh', their use being a soft technique of control and prison management (Sim, 1990).

Proposals to 'modernize' mental health legislation have been subject to recurrent debate about how to balance protection of the rights of the mentally ill individual versus the public who may possibly be 'at risk'. This is not a subject where the science is infallible, the risk easy to determine or the principles involved clear-cut. For example, the idea that someone may be examined and then placed in some form of incarceration based on 'the opinions of others regarding the likelihood that they would behave dangerously at some point in the future' (Farnham and James, 2001: 1926) obviously lends itself to controversy and dispute. How reliable can prediction of future behaviour be? There is an important debate here. Society rightly expects government to act to minimize harm to citizens and provide protection from dangerous people but some may see such proposals as a 'conscious deception', employing diagnoses with little credibility (ibid.). Others – politicians, members of the general public, pressure groups representing victims of violent, disordered offenders – might argue that public safety is always the overriding priority.

Medicalization of control in prisons

The use of psychotropic drugs to control inmates in institutions is far from new. In the nineteenth and early twentieth centuries, those committed to prisons or asylums might be given 'sleeping draughts' to 'modify' their behaviour. Following the Second World War, the emergence of the multinational drug industry produced large-scale manufacture and availability of powerful new drugs with sedative or other behaviour-modification properties (McAllister, 2000). Particularly from the 1970s, as prisons experienced crises of disorder and protest, the demand for enhanced security meant that medical management of prisoners took on new significance. In the United States there is similar evidence of use of psychotropic drugs in prisons since at least the 1970s. These offer a 'quick, cheap and effective' aid to the warehousing of increasing numbers of inmates in cramped conditions.

Diagnosis and medication may vary in relation to gender and ethnicity, and in one UK study, Genders and Player (1987) found that large doses of antidepressants, sedatives and tranquillizers were prescribed to women in prison, who received proportionately five times more medication as men. Around ten years later, a 1998 Parliamentary debate gave rise to concerns that strong tranquillizing drugs are routinely prescribed to young women prisoners who mutilate themselves, and are also used as pacifiers and substitutes for illegal drugs despite the side effects of their own addictive potential (Hansard, 22 October 1998: col. 1400).

Critics also argue that psychiatric medicine and the criminal justice system operate with ethnocentric assumptions or racist stereotypes that are introduced into medical or legal judgements. Hence, African and Caribbean psychiatric in-patients are more likely than whites to be defined as 'aggressive', placed in secure units and subjected to invasive forms of treatment such as intramuscular medication and electroconvulsive therapy. During the 1980s a number of cases involving black prisoners in Britain raised concerns about the nature of their psychiatric assessments, the inappropriate and/or inadequate medical treatment they received, the question of force-feeding, the use of drugs as a technique for control, and their certification as mentally ill, leading to transfer to a mental hospital, thereby influencing the criteria for eligibility for release.

However, yet again there are two sides to the issue, for one very important criticism of the prison system is that far too many people with mental health problems and other illnesses are held in totally inappropriate prison conditions when they should be in hospital settings.

Medicine and the criminal justice system

The medical and allied health professions have come to play an increasingly central role in the criminal justice system:

- Medical experts are called to give evidence at criminal trials, though not without controversy: psychiatric diagnoses once credible may now be criticized, for example the idea of homosexuality as a dangerous perversion. Since 2003, medical evidence about the statistical improbability of more than one infant death occurring in a family has been seriously questioned, leading to several convictions for murder being overturned, prosecution cases failing and, since 2004, steps have been taken to reopen a number of past cases.
- The courts may receive psychiatric reports on offenders to help determine their fitness to stand trial and their comprehension of their actions and the consequences.
- Secure hospitals run as psychiatric and therapeutic institutions are the 'prisons' for those who cannot, for various reasons, be sent to traditional jails, but these institutions also perform valuable therapeutic functions.
- The police employ 'police surgeons' – that is, medically qualified staff (usually contracted local GPs) – to provide health assessments and care for those held in custody.
- Prisons have medical wings with dedicated health care staff now incorporated into the NHS.
- Psychiatric nurses in secure institutions need to employ therapeutic techniques but also are effectively jailers and may need to use techniques of restraint and coercion. The majority will work to high standards, but, as with prison officers, there are cases of serious abuse of power and patients.
- In relation to drug offenders, as already indicated, the criminal justice and health systems are increasingly linked, with the latter seen as offering those willing to take the opportunity a diversionary route away from crime and from punishment by the criminal justice system.

As others have suggested, there are some crime matters that might be more helpfully seen as public health matters. The policing and regulation of drug misusers is an obvious candidate. Alcohol services have frequently and justifiably complained that when compared to the priority and funding attached to dealing with illegal drug problems, they have been the neglected Cinderella services. Yet, as we have seen, alcohol is as relevant to a strategy for reducing crime and victimization as illegal drugs. Of particular note here is the increasing significance of the night-time economy, fuelled by the economics of the successful leisure industry and welcomed by local and national government as a contributor to urban regeneration. This high-profit industry also produces high profits for the Treasury as highly taxed alcohol sales boom. Yet there is a clear tension between this development and certain concerns on the crime reduction and policing agendas, as late-night 'binge' drinking is associated with public disorder and violence; local residents' fear of crime and victimization is increased, and the new leisure landscape is increasingly 'policed' not by public police but by private security and bouncers (Hobbs et al., 2003).

Summary

1   In this chapter we have described the history of controls and policy concerning alcohol and illegal drugs. We have discussed the complex relationships between alcohol, drugs and crime, and also examined the widening availability of drugs and alcohol.

2   The idea that drug use is becoming 'normalized' can be seen as an important but debatable proposition. Certainly, though, for some intoxicant consumers, a mix of alcohol and illegal drugs has become a regular menu of choice. This has important implications for education about 'drugs' but also for health.

3   The chapter has adopted a holistic approach and addressed not only crime and control matters but also the health implications of rising alcohol and drug use, broadening out to also consider other dimensions of the link between health and crime, such as mental health problems and social deprivation.

4   The introduction of health issues into criminological consideration is overdue and also draws attention to the role of health professionals as gatekeepers and controllers. The specialism of public health can be seen as social medicine but also as a form of surveillance and control. This function is explored in relation to debates about the role of psychiatrists.

5   Health services and therapeutic/control interventions also extend into the prison system and are part of new forms of diversion into treatment for drug-using offenders appearing before the courts.

Critical thinking questions

1   Consider the debates about decriminalization versus the prohibition of drugs. What is the evidence on both sides?

2   Can you provide examples of how 'good intentions' in the criminal justice and health systems have produced 'bad outcomes'?

3   Consider the growth of the night-time economy and its implications for crime and disorder.

4   Read this chapter alongside Chapter 13 and review the links between drugs and major crime from the local to the global.

Further study

Berridge, V. (1999) *Opium and the People*, rev. edn, London: Free Association Books. The 'classic' social history of the place of opium in English life in the nineteenth century, its legality and the development of moves toward control.

Measham, F. and South, N. (2012) 'Drugs, Alcohol and Crime', in M. Maguire, R. Morgan and R. Reiner (eds) *The Oxford Handbook of Criminology*, 5th edn, Oxford: Oxford University Press. An authoritative overview of key criminological issues relating to alcohol and drugs.

Monaghan, M. (2012) 'The Recent Evolution of UK Drug Strategies: from Maintenance to Behaviour Change?' *People, Place & Policy Online*, 6/1: 29–40. A detailed overview of how UK-based drugs policy has shifted emphasis and approach.

South, N. (ed.) (1995) *Drugs, Crime and Criminal Justice*, 2 vols, Aldershot: Dartmouth. A comprehensive overview of key issues relating to drugs and crime.

Stevens, A. (2011) *Drugs, Crime and Public Health: The Political Economy of Drug Policy*, London: Routledge.

Useful websites

Drugscope
http://www.drugscope.org.uk/
An invaluable site with access to an online encyclopaedia about drugs and to Drugscope's library.

Alcohol Concern
http://www.alcoholconcern.org.uk/
This site provides links to many other useful sites and a good overview of key issues surrounding alcohol.

part 4　Controlling Crime

chapter 15

Thinking about Punishment

Key issues

- What are the main theoretical positions on crime control?
- In what ways is punishment morally justified?
- What are the aspects of social control involved in punishment?
- How does the punishment of women challenge mainstream thinking?

Introduction

This chapter provides an overview of criminological thinking on punishment, which can be simply defined as 'a legally approved method designed to facilitate the task of crime control' (Garland, 1990: 18). However, the fact that punishment causes pain, suffering and harm raises important ethical dilemmas. Consequently the punishment of offenders requires moral justification for, as Nicola Lacey (1988: 14) points out, the power to punish derives from the legal authority of the state to do things that would otherwise be 'prima facie morally wrongful' (see also Box 15.1). Moral philosophy is the contemporary branch of thinking that concerns itself with distinguishing between the age-old questions of identifying what is 'right' and 'wrong' and establishing 'good' and 'evil' through defining what ought to be the proper goals of punishment. Such questions are explicitly normative in that they ask what aims and values a system of punishment must fulfil if it is to be morally acceptable.

Of course, most judges or magistrates passing a sentence do not justify their decisions in the language of moral philosophy and if pushed they would tend to do so quite simply through recourse to 'what the law prescribes, what the Court of Appeal or the Magistrates' Association recommends, or what the local bench has agreed upon' (Walker, 1991: 6). Yet this can only, at best, amount to a principle of ensuring consistency – it does not explain why it is 'right' to punish in any meaningful sense or what greater 'good' might be achieved through inflicting more harm. Consequently, justifications of punishment are firmly rooted in broader moral and political philosophies that often conflict.

A second distinctive perspective can be regarded as a sociology of control for while it does attend to the uses of punishment it does so through considering the wider aspects of social control to reveal the 'deeper structures' of penal systems (Cohen, 1984). Although there is a tendency to evade complex normative issues this approach nevertheless does 'raise basic questions about the ways in which society organizes and deploys its power to punish' (Duff and Garland, 1994: 22). The difference can be put simply through using Barbara Hudson's (1996: 10/2003: 10) distinction which maintains that the philosophy of punishment deliberates on how things *ought* to be whereas the sociology of control tells it like it really *is* through explaining why particular societies adopt specific modes of punishment.

Although the principles of each philosophical justification will be emphasized it is important to recognize that the different rationalities coexist in uneasy hybrid combinations. As Nigel Walker (1991: 8) puts it, in 'practice Anglo-American sentencers tend to be eclectic reasoning sometimes as utilitarians but sometimes, when they are outraged by a crime, as retributivists'. Similarly while there are competing forms of sociological explanation, which often fundamentally differ over how the same issues should be interpreted, the overall argument is that punishment, as a social institution, is an inherently complex business that needs to be approached from a range of theoretical perspectives, as no single interpretation will grasp the diverse meanings generated by punishment. Indeed, the problem of punishment is also one of the most enduring in political theory and has developed into an established subdiscipline of moral philosophy.

BOX 15.1 Why punish?

The following passage from the Russian novel *Resurrection* by Leo Tolstoy originally published in 1899 is widely quoted by philosophers:

> He asked a very simple question: 'Why, and by what right, do some people lock up, torment, exile, flog, and kill others, while they are themselves just like those they torment, flog, and kill?' And in answer he got deliberations as to whether human beings had free will or not; whether or not signs of criminality could be detected by measuring the skull; what part heredity played in crime; whether immorality could be inherited; and what madness is, what degeneration is, and what temperament is; how climate, food, ignorance, imitativeness, hypnotism, or passion affect crime; what society is, what

its duties are – and so on . . . but there was no answer on the chief point: 'By what right do some people punish others?'

(Tolstoy, cited in Matravers, 2000: 1)

Tolstoy's question asks what justifies the deliberate infliction of suffering on those who do wrong? As we will see, modern philosophical thinking treats punishment as a crucial element in the classic liberal problem of how the individual should relate to the state. Ultimately, liberal theories are concerned with individual rights and freedoms. On this basis punishment is justified 'in so far as it protects the freedom of individual citizens to go about their lives safe from the threat of crime' (Duff and Garland, 1994: 3), while individual rights are advocated as essential defences against the abuse of power by the state.

Philosophical justifications

Every time a court imposes a sentence it emphatically declares, in both a physical and symbolic sense, the sovereignty of the political power to which it owes judicial authority. Most criminologists would argue that as a consequence of this

> close proximity between the power to punish and the wider power to *rule*, it has become an axiom of political theory that the act of judicial sentencing requires to be justified by reference to some greater moral or ethical principle than merely the will of either the sentencer or the *de facto* law-giver.
>
> (Brownlee, 1998: 34; emphasis in original)

There are a number of competing justifications, which are rooted in opposing ideas over what the purpose of punishment should be. They fall into two distinctive groups. Those that see the aim of punishment as the prevention of future crimes are generally referred to as **reductivist**, and those that look to the past to punish crimes already committed are typically known as **retributivist**. In practice, however, most criminal justice systems fashion quite contradictory justifications so that the different rationalities often uncomfortably coexist and tensions between the two perennially arise. For instance, in criminal justice it is recognized that the pursuit of crime prevention (as a general good) must be subject to the specific constraints of procedural justice so that the innocent are not deliberately punished nor the guilty excessively punished (Duff, 1996: 3). These perennial tensions between the crime control and due process orientations of criminal justice are often compared to pendulum shifts between two competing values, with neither quite extinguishing the other, but a changing balance between them.

Reductivist principles

Reductivism justifies punishment on the grounds of its alleged future consequences. These arguments are supported by the form of moral reasoning known as utilitarianism. Although the origins of utilitarian thinking can be found in the fifth century BC in Plato's dialogues with Protagoras, a Thracian philosopher (Walker, 1991: 142), this moral theory was most famously advanced by Jeremy Bentham (1748–1832) as he argued that moral actions are those that produce 'the greatest happiness of the greatest number' of people. For punishment to reduce future crimes the pain and unhappiness caused to the offender must be 'outweighed by the avoidance of unpleasantness to other people in the future – thus making punishment morally right from a utilitarian point of view' (Cavadino and Dignan, 2002: 34). By pointing to a future or greater 'good' reductivist principles focus on the instrumental 'ends' of punishment. In doing so, utilitarian justifications of punishment make two further important appeals: 'that human well-being matters and that moral rules ought to be evaluated in light of their effect on human well-being' (Matravers, 2000: 5).

Utilitarian philosophy establishes what is good to do on the grounds of social usefulness and it judges actions by their consequences. It stipulates that 'the good' is human happiness, not some abstract metaphysical property, like the idea of 'natural rights', which Bentham famously dismissed as 'nonsense on stilts' or an empirically unknowable object, as in the will of God. Bentham's intention was to establish the law on a rational basis, which for him meant the facts of pleasure and pain rather than the vague fictions of natural rights – ideas driving much social reform in the nineteenth century (Carrabine, 2006: 192–3). The utilitarian justification of punishment is that the wrong experienced by the offender is outweighed by the compensating good effects for overall human well-being. The avoidance of further crime can be achieved through a number of strategies, such as:

- deterring potential criminals;
- reforming actual criminals; or by
- keeping actual or potential offenders out of circulation.

Deterrence

Deterrence is based on the idea that crime can be discouraged through the public's fear of the punishment they may receive if they break the law. For Bentham and contemporary thinkers a distinction is drawn between *individual* and *general* deterrence. Individual deterrence is said to occur when someone finds the experience of punishment so unpleasant that they never wish to repeat the infraction for fear of the consequences.

There is a long history of governments introducing severe punishments through claims that harsher penalties will produce special deterrence effects. The results, however, are modest at best. For instance, the introduction of 'short, sharp, shock' regimes into detention centres for young offenders in England and Wales by the Conservative government in the early 1980s 'proved to have no better post-release reconviction scores than centres operating the normal regime' and, likewise, the popular American 'boot camps' of the 1990s, based on the aggressive training regimes of US marines, 'have not been shown to be at all effective in discouraging reoffending' (Dunbar and Langdon, 1998: 10).

In addition to these empirical doubts over the effectiveness of such strategies there are also more general moral objections raised against individual deterrence as it can.

■ be used to justify punishing the innocent as what matters is the communication of the penalty (Duff, 1996: 3);
■ allow for punishment in excess of that deserved by the offence; and
■ is primarily concerned with offences that might be committed in the future, rather than the offences that have actually been committed (Hudson, 1996: 27/2003: 25).

Individual deterrence then is of little value as a moral justification for penal policy. On the other hand, general deterrence seems to offer a more plausible justification. This is the idea that offenders are punished, not to deter the offenders themselves, but to discourage other potential offenders. There can be little doubt that the existence of a system of punishment has some general deterrent, but it is important to recognize that the effects are easily overestimated. In recognition of these difficulties reductivists can also justify punishment on the basis of reform or rehabilitation.

Reform and rehabilitation

The term 'reform' is generally used to refer to the nineteenth-century development of prison regimes that sought to change the offender through a combination of hard labour and religious instruction, whereas 'rehabilitation' describes the more individualized treatment programmes introduced in the twentieth century in conjunction with the emergence of the welfare state (Garland, 1985). Both are based on the idea that punishment can reduce crime if it takes a form that will improve the individual's character so that they are less likely to reoffend in the future.

When the 'rehabilitative ideal' was at its height in the 1950s and 1960s it was strongly informed by positivist criminology, which viewed criminal behaviour not as freely willed action but as a symptom of some kind of mental illness which should be 'treated' like an illness. From around the mid-1970s it became widely assumed that whatever reform measures were chosen the research showed that 'nothing works' (Martinson, 1974). This message became accepted, less because of its validity, but more because it suited the mood of the times, in which there was a general move to the political right on both sides of the Atlantic and a widespread backlash against any form of welfarist solutions to social problems.

However, there are indications that rehabilitation is undergoing something of a revival as there have been recent attempts to find 'what works' (McGuire, 1995; Hollin, 1999; Crow, 2001). Few now maintain the appropriateness of 'medical' models of punishment, or claim that science can provide a cure for all criminality (though see Plate 15.1 and Box 15.2 for the turn to cognitive behavioural therapy (CBT) in recent probationary practice). Rehabilitation programmes are now seen as measures that might 'facilitate change' rather then 'coerce a cure' (Cavadino and Dignan, 2002: 38). Aside from the question mark over the effectiveness of rehabilitation programmes there are important moral objections raised by the very assumption that criminals need reform – a view criticized in Aldous Huxley's *Brave New World* (1994, first published in 1932) and Anthony Burgess's *Clockwork Orange* (1962), and, as is seen later in the chapter, by the criminologist Stan Cohen (1985) who offers a dystopian vision of an oppressive control net that intrudes into practically every aspect of our lives (see also Box 15.4).

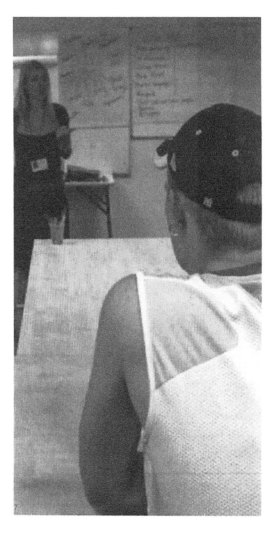

In Essex this year, we more than met all performance measures for accredited programmes.

People completing their programme requirement amounted to 126% of target.

Changing the habits of a lifetime...

IT IS ALWAYS POSSIBLE for skilled staff to prepare a detailed analysis of what has led someone to commit crime. The resulting document can often chart a life of misery, penury, sometimes abuse, often neglect, possibly mixed with plain bad luck, and plain bad management.

Diagnosis is only the beginning, however. Afterwards comes the hard stuff.

The individual needs to take on the responsibility for what they've done. They have to want to stop doing it. They must believe that it is possible. Then they need to find a way to change what is often solidly entrenched behaviour.

Anyone who has tried to kick a smoking habit will know of the denial, the resistance, the procrastination, and then the massive effort it takes to make the changes necessary for cutting it out altogether.

Looking at the distorted attitudes and thinking, learned over a lifetime, that must start changing before any serious move away from crime can occur, it is easy to appreciate that ours is a more complex task.

Programmes have been crafted to tackle the ingrained thinking, and achieve under-standing of what are complicated issues for anyone. Cognitive Behavioural techniques, combined with good groupwork skills, are important in achieving gradual change that will stick. Internalising the issues is vital.

When people understand their own motives, their own trigger points, and then learn the practical skills for changing their responses, success is possible.

Plate 15.1 This image is taken from a typical Probation Service report and highlights the current faith in cognitive behavioural techniques. Note the emphasis on individual responsibility, distorted thinking and internalized issues in an effort to define crime as a symptom of entrenched unacceptable behaviour.

Source: Essex Probation Service Annual Report 2005–6.

controlling crime

BOX 15.2 A short history of probation

The search to find alternatives to imprisonment has taken many twists and turns over the past century or so. From the introduction of probation in the late nineteenth century, through to an increasing use of fines, to the more recent expansion of community penalties in the 1960s and 1970s there has been a quest to find less expensive, but still demanding, forms of non-custodial sentence (Worrall and Hoy, 2005). The origins of probation, which remains the main form of supervising offenders in the community, lay in religious missionary work and humanitarian concerns over the plight of the poor. For example, the Church of England Temperance Society played an active role in the courts by promoting the moral reform of offenders through abstinence from alcohol in the late Victorian era. Religious sensibilities played a prominent role in the campaign for a probation law in Britain, which came to fruition in the 1907 Probation of Offenders Act. This legislation allowed for the informal supervision of offenders in the community, in place of other punishment, if they seemed likely to reform.

It was not until the 1950s that probation services everywhere in Britain were provided by salaried, trained specialists rather than by a mixture of professional social workers and well-meaning amateurs. Throughout its history probation has been marked by a diverse mix of justifications and has encompassed a range of concerns: a way of reducing rising prison populations; a method of reducing crime or drunkenness; a means of saving souls from damnation by divine grace; and/or a way of easing personal and social problems experienced by offenders (Vanstone, 2007: 19). Especially important to the emerging professionalization of the probation service were the influence of psychological ideas and the facilitation of change through therapeutic work. This new approach adopted the old term 'casework' (which in its original use by the Charity Organization Society meant simply 'work on cases') to denote a process of one-to-one work in which the offender's needs and motivations were characteristically hidden behind a 'presenting problem', which could be revealed through a process of insight that involved working back to childhood to understand problematic behaviour (Whitehead and Statham, 2006: 56).

Most probation officers were trained as social workers and for much of the mid-twentieth century probation officers worked according to a 'treatment model' where probation was seen as a social service designed to prevent further crime by changing the offender's conduct. The demise of the 'rehabilitative ideal' in the 1960s and 1970s undermined the 'treatment model' on which probation in the post-war era had come to rest and gave rise to the pessimism of 'nothing works'. Critics from across the political spectrum were uniform in discrediting probation. Marxist criminologists argued that the treatment model of probation was paternalistic and coercive; pragmatists argued that it simply did not work; conservatives insisted that it was too soft and should be replaced by tougher sentences.

Over the last decade or so there has been something of a renaissance in probation under the 'What Works?' agenda where cognitive behavioural programmes have been optimistically embraced (see Plate 15.1). These programmes are based on the assumption that offenders commit crimes because of misperceptions and cognitive-behavioural therapy targets specific unacceptable behaviours and seeks to modify these by correcting distortions in the way offenders think about their crime. The programmes cover a range of specific problem behaviours like anger management, drink driving and sex offending. Critics though have argued that enthusiasm for the cognitive-behavioural approach should not result in the neglect of providing basic literacy and social skills, nor should the wider social problems leading people into crime be ignored (Worrall and Hoy, 2005).

The history of probation is one characterized by a diverse mix of political, religious and social concerns, but for many commentators the setting up of the National Offenders Management Service (NOMS) in 2004 has effectively ended the existence of an 'autonomous probation service with a distinctive ethos and primary task to work, in the main, with offenders in the community' (Whitehead and Statham, 2006: 3). The complaint is that NOMS brings probation into much closer alliance with the prison system and this fatally compromises the traditional identity and role of the probation service. It was not just this merging of these two agencies with very different cultures and ways of dealing with offenders that was controversial but the principle that 'all the functions of the Probation Service in a given geographical area could be transferred to a private or voluntary sector bidder' (Raynor, 2007: 1087). For critics this was yet further evidence of New Labour's unstinting faith in the ability of the private sector to reform public services and fundamental rejection of welfare policies. As the Coalition government has found its feet and implemented public expenditure cuts NOMS remains the executive agency of the Ministry of Justice responsible for commissioning and providing 'offender services' in prison and in the community.

Incapacitation

The idea that an offender's ability to commit further crimes should be removed, either physically or geographically (through locking them up, removing offending limbs or killing them) is generally referred to as incapacitation. In contrast to other justifications of punishment the logic of incapacitation appeals to neither changing the offender's behaviour nor searching for the causes of the offending. Instead it advocates the protection of potential victims as the essence of punishment, as opposed to the rights of offenders. Many contemporary criminal justice strategies currently subscribe to the doctrine of incapacitation. In part, this is because it fills the void created by the collapse of rehabilitation and the associated argument that 'nothing works' in the 1970s, but also because it claims to offer a means of social defence through removing offenders from society and thereby eliminating their capacity to commit further crimes.

Examples of current criminal justice sentencing policy that are informed by the logic of incapacitation include the 'three strikes and you're out' penalty and selective incapacitation, both of which usually involve long periods of incarceration. More generally, incapacitation has become the main philosophical justification for imprisonment in countries that subscribe to the notion that 'prison works' as it takes many persistent and serious offenders off the streets and thereby, it is claimed, reduces the crime rate (Murray, 1997).

The model for this approach is what is known as the American 'prison experiment' where there has been a dramatic growth in the prison population over the last few decades (Mauer, 2001). For instance, in 1970 there were 196,000 prisoners in state and federal prisons in the United

States, but by the turn of the century the figure exceeded 2 million and it has been estimated that if current US trends continue, '30 per cent of all black males born today will spend some of their lives in prison' (Garland, 2001: 6). Critics argue that the 'experiment' has been funded by the diversion of public expenditure from welfare to the prison, while the level of violence, particularly among the young and disadvantaged, continues to devastate life in many North American cities (Currie, 1996) while others point to the alarming racial dimension to this strategy of containment (Wacquant, 2001). Over a decade ago it was revealed that one in nine African American males aged 20–29 is in prison at any one time, and that a staggering one in three is either in prison, on probation or parole (Mauer, 1997).

The question of why the United States has embarked on such a divisive social policy of mass incarceration has received considerable attention. It is clear that the prison explosion has impacted disproportionately on young, less educated African American men and has deepened already entrenched inequalities. Many are critical of the idea that the cause is simply due to an increase in crime committed by that particular population. Bruce Western's (2006) analysis of national datasets reveals that despite the huge increase in the incarceration rate of black men in the last quarter of the twentieth century, they were less involved in crime in 2000 than in 1980. Moreover, the data suggest that the racial disparities in imprisonment for drug offenders (the 'War on Drugs' is often said to be the key driving force fuelling penal expansion) are not primarily due to race differences in offending. Indeed, the actual evidence suggests that the current prison boom is not a simple and straightforward response to crime, given that crime rates were *declining* before the massive prison expansion even began (Gilmore, 2007). It is to broader cultural, institutional, political and structural forces that recent scholarship has turned so as to grasp the factors shaping criminal justice policy (see Wacquant, 2009; Alexander, 2010; Tonry, 2011; and Lynch, 2012 for different theoretical explanations).

Retributivist principles

In its simplest form, retributivism is the view that wrongdoers should be punished because they deserve it, irrespective of any future beneficial consequences and this principle dates from antiquity. For instance, the Code of Hammurabi is among the first written legal codes and enshrined the phrase 'an eye for an eye' in 1750 BC in Babylon, which is based on the concept of *lex talonis* – the 'law of retaliation'. This principle was developed by the Enlightenment philosopher Immanuel Kant (1724–1804) into a highly influential critique of utilitarian justifications of punishment, which use offenders 'merely as means' rather than fully recognizing their humanity so that the innocent can be deliberately punished if it is expedient to do so. For Kant the duty to punish was a **categorical imperative** that restored the moral equilibrium – a view that led him to famously declare that even on the dissolution of society 'the last murderer remaining in prison must first be executed' (cited in Walker, 1991: 77).

Kant introduced a crucial distinction between what it would be *good* to do on the grounds of utility and what we have a *right* to do (Murphy, 1994: 49). Missing this important distinction between desire and duty reveals the illiberal consequences that can flow from utilitarian reasoning as there will be times when the individual is sacrificed for the general welfare of the many, with torture being perhaps the most controversial example (see Box 15.3). In Kantian terms justice

BOX 15.3 The torture debate

The debate on torture gathered force in the wake of the 'War on Terror' with the treatment of 'unlawful combatants' at Guantanamo Bay and the humiliating practices experienced by Iraqi prisoners at Abu Ghraib each revealing the extent to which torture has become commonplace in the post 9/11 climate, while Britain's denial that its territories have been used for 'extraordinary rendition' (where suspects are moved to 'interrogation centres' in third-party countries where they are held outside the law) has also been challenged by human rights investigators (Doward, 2008: 3). Nevertheless, much of the emphasis is now on what has been termed 'preventive investigational torture', that is where torture is used to obtain information to thwart terrorist attacks and several justifications have been advanced to support this position (Dershowitz, 2002; Bagaric and Clarke, 2005; Greenberg, 2006). In one way or another each draws on Bentham's utilitarian reasoning and his justifications were invoked by the police and other security agencies around the world long before the 9/11 attacks (see Morgan, 2000; and for an account of the origins of modern torture, see Welch, 2007).

Bentham, however, seemed to be aware of the dangers of torture – even if there are short-term advantages (such as extracting information that saves hundreds of lives); in the long run torture fatally undermines the principles and legitimacy of liberal democracy itself. Much of the current debate though rests on what has been described as the 'ticking bomb' scenario. This is used to show how torture can be morally justified:

> Apart from a few orthodox Kantians, there is hardly a soul who would not have to concede that in an extreme enough situation, in which hundreds of lives could be saved by using force to extricate the information needed to find and defuse a ticking bomb from the person responsible for placing it, if no other means were available, severe force could, and possibly even should be used to extract the information.
>
> (Kretzmer, 2007: 123)

As Slavoj Žižek (2002: 5–6) wrote in response to these ideas that torture can be justified by keeping within 'reasonable' bounds, this is the worst kind of 'liberal illusion', not least since the ticking bomb scenario is deceptive: in the vast majority of cases torture is not carried out to find ticking bombs, but for quite different reasons (to punish enemies, or to psychologically break prisoners, or to terrorize an entire population, etc.). As he explains, a 'consistent ethical stance has to reject such pragmatic-utilitarian reasoning'.

Others have maintained that an absolute prohibition on torture has to be made. Any relaxation on prohibition will, it is argued, inevitably lead to the use of torture in wide-ranging situations that are completely removed from these 'ticking bomb' scenarios (Kretzmer, 2007: 124). Torture does not obtain truth, it will make most ordinary people say anything the torturer wants. The evidence from history is that torture forces innocent civilians to confess to fantastical crimes, and that the tortured eventually accept the view that they are guilty (Roper, 2004; Thurston, 2006).

is an issue of doing right rather than what would be good to do. Nevertheless, it was the increasing attraction of utilitarian justifications in the nineteenth and twentieth centuries that led to retributivism falling from favour as it appealed to archaic and reactionary feelings of revenge, yet one of the more striking developments of the last 30 years has been the revival of retributivist ideas under the guise of 'just deserts'.

Just deserts

During the 1950s and 1960s the penal system was generally understood to be an important element in the welfare state's programme of social engineering that would prevent crime through deterring potential offenders, incapacitating actual offenders and it was hoped that treatment programmes would rehabilitate offenders. As we have seen, by the mid-1970s the institutions of the welfare state were under serious attack from all shades of the political spectrum not simply because of their perceived failure but also because of their moral costs. In addition to neo-conservative critics (Wilson, 1975) liberal thinkers also began to reassert the importance of justice over utility and of individual rights against the claims of the state (Rawls, 1972; Dworkin, 1978). One important 'manifestation of this moral shift was that theorists began to focus on the rights of the guilty as well as those of the innocent' (Duff and Garland, 1994: 10). This gave birth to a prisoners' rights movement that chimed with broader conceptions of civil rights so that the need to protect prisoners and others from the arbitrary and discretionary powers of state bureaucracies became paramount (Fogel, 1975).

It is in this context that the 'new retributivist' arguments emerged and formulated the principle of 'just deserts', which insists that offenders should only be punished as severely as they deserve in reaction against the unfair excesses of rehabilitation and the 'get tough' incapacitative drive from conservatives. The leading advocate of this movement, Andrew von Hirsch (1976), proposed that greater consistency and certainty should lie at the centre of the criminal justice system with punishment fitting the crime rather than the person. Key elements here are *proportionality* – the offender should be sentenced according to what the act deserves; and *denunciation* – condemnation of the offence through restoring the moral equilibrium whilst expressing social disapproval.

These principles, in certain important respects, recall the classical criminologist Cessare Beccaria's (1738–94) arguments for due process in the criminal justice system and are based on a similar understanding of the social contract, which is supposed to apply equally and fairly to everyone. Retributive punishment is thereby regarded as ensuring that offenders do not profit from their wrongdoing. Yet, as critics have argued, the fundamental flaw in this line of thinking is that it is only applicable if social relations are just and equal, otherwise there is no equilibrium to restore. It is the case, however, that offenders tend to be already socially disadvantaged so that punishment actually increases inequality rather than reducing it (Cavadino and Dignan, 2002: 42).

Hybrid compromises

So far we have been setting out the fundamental philosophical justifications and discussing their respective limitations, yet it is important to emphasize that in practice most criminal justice systems combine these differing rationales in uneasy combinations. For instance, it is generally acknowledged that the 'just deserts' approach to criminal justice proposed by liberals critical of rehabilitation in the 1970s had by the 1980s become co-opted by the political right (Hudson, 1987). The clearest indication of this is the strategy pursued by the Conservative government which culminated in the Criminal Justice Act 1991. This piece of legislation repeatedly emphasized the principle of 'just deserts' as the aim of criminal justice with a greater stress on proportionality in sentencing, yet at the same time the Act designated community penalties (discussed in more detail below) as 'punishment in the community' in an effort to reinforce the tough 'law and order' image of the government.

Shortly after the legislation was introduced the Conservatives appeared to abandon 'just deserts' in an effort to further strengthen their punitive credentials in favour of another hybrid combination of incapacitation and deterrence – famously declared by the then Home Secretary Michael Howard, in his insistence that 'prison works'. For some critics the 'populist punitiveness' of John Major's Conservative government continued under New Labour (Carrabine et al., 2000: 194–6). One indication of this is the insistence that imprisonment should not be only reserved for serious offenders but is also suitable for persistent petty offenders. This directly contradicts the principle that punishment should fit the crime and it was reported that when Jack Straw was Home Secretary he explicitly stated that he wanted to end the 'just deserts' philosophy through arguing that 'it is time to make the sentence fit the offender rather than the offence' (Cavadino and Dignan, 2002: 53). Others have argued that 'penal populism' has enabled various governments to rely less on the experience of civil servants and academics in the formulation of criminal justice policy and instead politicians seek to tap into what they believe to be the general public's appetite for tough punishment (Pratt, 2007).

Clearly the fundamental justifications can exist in different combinations but to explain why these uneasy compromises might be more than simply passing fashions it is to sociological forms of explanation that we need to turn.

BOX 15.4 Restorative justice: a new justification for punishment?

Some criminologists are now arguing that restorative justice brings fresh and more just relationships between offenders and victims. The arguments are based partly on the principle of reparation in that those who offend should do something to repair the wrong they have done, and in so doing acknowledge the harm they have caused. Although reparation can take many forms and has a long history (see Box 15.2), such as paying a fine (through the courts) to compensate a victim or carrying out unpaid work that will benefit the community, there is an important sense in which there is a recognition of the rights of victims to have redress for the harm they have suffered. It is partly as a result of these developments that restorative justice has gained momentum as an alternative to modern Western systems of punishment.

Over the last 20 years the principles of restorative justice have moved from the margins of criminology to the centre of lively debates not only in the discipline but also in criminal justice policy. The origins of restorative justice are diverse and yet all arise from disillusionment with modern systems of criminal justice. Its supporters include penal abolitionists, social theologians, postcolonial critics and the victims movement who are united in their efforts to redefine justice as a process of shoring up rifts in communities through helping the victim and offender overcome their trauma through forms of 'reintegrative shaming' (Braithwaite, 1989). Scandinavian penal abolitionists (Christie, 1977) have been arguing since the 1970s that state punishment is oppressively authoritarian and ought to be based on an alternative concep- tualization of 'redress' that disperses decision-making amongst a much more heterogeneous community (de Haan, 1990). Another important set of developments has been the 're- discovery' of distinctive indigenous systems of justice. For instance, 'family group conferences' arose through Maori criticism of the dominant Western juvenile justice system that had stripped the community of responsibility for dealing with its young, whereas 'sentencing circles' were revived in the Yukon Territory, Canada, and are 'an updated version of the traditional sanctioning and healing practices of Canadian Aboriginal peoples' (Bazemore and Taylor-Griffiths, 2003: 78).

Although there have been scattered mediation schemes in England and Wales since the 1970s, the Crime and Disorder Act 1998 and the Youth Justice and Criminal Evidence Act 1999 formally introduced elements of restorative justice as a mainstream response to youth offending in a number of different ways, including family group conferences based on the New Zealand model, reparation orders for offenders aged 10 and older, and consultation with victims before any reparative intervention is organized (Gelsthorpe and Morris, 2002: 246). Most recently the Ministry of Justice has announced plans to embed restorative justice more coherently in the criminal justice system of England and Wales (Ministry of Justice, 2012c), while the development of various schemes in the country are analysed by Joanna Shapland and her colleagues through detailed case studies (Shapland et al., 2011).

Restorative justice is not without its critics who point out that there are few safeguards to protect the most vulnerable groups from the pious moralizing of reintegrative shaming. Making offenders face up to their wrongdoing can lead to some serious abuses of power, as critics suggest:

> The potential for coercion and even bullying of young people, outnumbered and outwitted by a 'room full of adults', none of which has direct responsibility to safeguard and promote the best interests of the child and, moreover, where there may be a collusion of interests on the side of the victim, must be recognized and must be actively prevented by the 'good practice' of participants (as there are few built-in legal or procedural safeguards).
>
> (Haines and O'Mahony, 2006: 119)

This absence of accountability compounds the lack of protection for the offender in terms of appeals to legal process and due rights (Ashworth, 2003); while a former supporter has become highly sceptical of the claims made by the more evangelical advocates (Daly, 2002). Others argue that only human rights can guarantee fair treatment in restorative justice approaches (Hudson, 2005: 66). Fundamental issues remain over whether restorative justice challenges or casts the net of social control deeper into the community (see Cunneen and Hoyle, 2010, for contrasting perspectives on these debates).

Sociological explanations

Instead of asking questions over punishment's effectiveness or justification, sociologists 'attend to the ways in which penal policy is determined by political forces and the struggle of contending interests, rather than by normative argument or relevant empirical evidence' (Duff and Garland, 1994: 32). In exploring the deeper role punishment plays in society a number of competing perspectives can be identified. Each is informed by a social theory that can be traced back to the 'founding fathers' of sociology as authors tend to adopt a Durkheimian approach or a Marxist position and then critically disregard other ways of thinking. What this chapter will now do is set out the main sociological explanations of punishment that are derived from the work of Durkheim, Marx, and Foucault before discussing feminist critiques of these 'malestream' perspectives.

Although these diverse approaches cannot simply be bolted together to form the definitive sociological statement on punishment, as there are fundamental differences of interpretation, there is an important sense in which sociology reveals the complex and multifaceted dimensions of punishment as a social institution that otherwise remain hidden. Nevertheless, the overall argument follows David Garland's (1990: 2) insistence that criminologists must develop 'a more pluralistic approach' to capture the 'richness of meaning' generated by punishment.

Durkheim and social solidarity

The distinctive contribution of Émile Durkheim (1858–1917) lies in the way that he examined the relationships between crime, law and punishment to reveal the mechanisms that create and sustain **social solidarity**. This sociological approach is often referred to as functionalism, as he argued that whatever aspect of social life is being studied it must be approached from the perspective of discovering what role it performs in preserving social stability and promoting moral consensus. Although his ideas have been dismissed for their inherent conservatism, there is an important sense in which he draws attention to the functions punishment plays in maintaining social order in the face of rapid economic change and political upheaval.

Durkheim's theory of punishment is initially advanced in his most famous book *The Division of Labour in Modern Society* (1893/1960) and is then extended in the article 'Two Laws of Penal Evolution' (1901/1984) to give a more nuanced understanding of historical change. In *The Division of Labour* he develops his classic theory on the emergence of specialized work in modern societies through distinguishing between simple, pre-industrial societies in which there is little division of labour and more advanced societies, where people perform complex, specialized tasks.

At the core of his work is a concern with social solidarity, by which he means the shared conventions, meanings and moralities that hold societies together. In each type of society he saw punishment playing an important role in the creation of solidarity and he goes so far as to say that 'passion is the soul of punishment' as it arouses furious moral indignation and a ritualized expression of social values against those who had violated the sacred moral order. Even though modern 'penal systems may try to achieve utilitarian objectives, and to conduct themselves rationally and unemotively', the strength of Durkheim's account is how it reveals that 'at an underlying level there is still a vengeful, motivating passion which guides punishment and supplies its force' (Garland, 1990: 31).

Punitive passions and degradation rituals

There is an important sense in which Durkheim draws attention to the expressive qualities of punishment, how 'all healthy consciences' come together to reaffirm shared beliefs through dutiful outrage that constructs a 'public wrath' (Durkheim, cited in Giddens, 1972: 127). In the controversial work of the German philosopher Frederich Nietzsche (1844–1900) an altogether more sinister account of punitive sentiments is offered in his *Genealogy of Morals* where he argues that punishment gratifies sadistic and cruel tendencies in the human condition. He explains that to 'witness suffering does one good, to inflict it even more so – that is a harsh proposition, but a fundamental one, an old, powerful, human all-too-human proposition . . . in punishment there is so much that is *festive!*' (Nietzsche, 1887/1996: 50; emphasis in original). In his history of ethics Nietzsche (ibid.: 46–7) sought to expose how the Judaeo-Christian and liberal traditions of compassion, equality and justice are products of brutal and cruel processes – how they 'have long been steeped in blood' and 'not even with old Kant: the categorical imperative gives off a whiff of cruelty'. Of course, modern penal systems refute any association with cruelty, humiliation, malice and sadism, but Nietzsche insists that these passions continue to exist even though we are now in what the psychoanalyst Sigmund Freud (1856–1939) would call **denial** as 'the pleasure in cruelty' barely troubles 'even the most delicate hypocritical conscience' (ibid.: 49).

A less disturbing account of punitive passions is outlined by the Chicagoan social psychologist George Herbert Mead (1863–1931). Mead followed Durkheim by maintaining that there was a close relationship between punishment and social solidarity, but his account differs in that he argued that the collective hostility toward a criminal had the effect of 'uniting members of the community in the emotional solidarity of aggression' (Mead, 1918: 591). Mead did not regard this intense emotion as healthy but believed that it promoted a number of harmful consequences. As Claire Vallier (2002a: 31) puts it, 'the spirals of rage emanating outwards from a heinous crime were traumatising rather than healing'.

The Durkheimian tradition has continued to provide insightful analyses of how penal rituals provoke symbolic and emotive effects. For instance, the Danish sociologist Svend Ranulf argued that criminal law developed as a consequence of middle-class moral indignation (Barbalet, 2002), while Harold Garfinkel (1956a: 420–4) insisted that the rituals of the courtroom should be understood as a 'degradation ceremony' as 'moral indignation serves to effect the ritual destruction of the person denounced' by defining the accused as an enemy of all that is good and decent in society – a view subsequently developed by Pat Carlen (1976) in her analysis of *Magistrates' Justice* (see also Chapter 16). More recently, Philip Smith (2008) has ambitiously sought to reinterpret every significant penal institution – from public executions, through the panopticon and guillotine up to the electric chair and supermax prisons – through a neo-Durkheimian framework.

The legacy of the Durkheimian tradition has been summarized by drawing attention to the fact that in modern penal systems there is a crucial division

> between the *declaration* of punishment, which continues to take the form of a public ritual and which is continually the focus of public and media attention, and the *delivery* of punishment that now characteristically occurs behind closed doors and has a much lower level of visibility.
>
> (Garland, 1991: 125; emphasis in original)

Plate 15.2 Two women shout abuse at a police van transporting Maxine Carr from Peterborough on 18 September 2002. Carr was arrested and charged with attempting to pervert the course of justice over a police investigation into the murder of two young girls in Soham, Cambridgeshire.

Source: © Reuters; *photo:* Ian Waldie.

Plate 15.3 A boy stands next to a banner as he awaits the departure of Ian Huntley from Peterborough Magistrates' Court on 10 September 2002. Police mounted a heavy security operation outside the court after hundreds of protestors turned up the previous month when Maxine Carr, Huntley's girlfriend, was charged with perverting the course of justice.

Source: © Reuters; *photo:* Darren Staples.

So while Durkheim and his contemporaries identify the function of modern punishment in reassuring public sentiment they have rather less to say about the form it takes – issues that are addressed in the following perspectives.

Marx and political economy

Marxist analyses of punishment not only address a whole range of themes ignored by Durkheim, but also reinterpret many of those that Durkheim does consider. Karl Marx's (1818–83) legacy to sociology was to insist that societies must be understood in terms of how economic structures condition social practices. Consequently, Marxists tend to consider punishment in relation to economic structures and examine the class interests served by penal practices. In marked contrast to Durkheim, they argue that punishing offenders for breaking laws maintains and reinforces the position of the ruling class, rather than benefiting society as a whole, and that punishment as a social institution plays an important political role as a repressive state apparatus.

One of the earliest Marxist analyses of punishment was carried out by the German Marxist scholar Georg Rusche. It was later written up with the assistance of Otto Kirchheimer and published in 1939 through the exiled Frankfurt School of Social Research in New York, as *Punishment and Social Structure*. It is a work that charts the changing deployment of penal methods from the Middle Ages up to the early decades of the twentieth century. Rusche and Kirchheimer's analysis highlights the relationships between the form that punishments take and the economic requirements of particular modes of production. They argued in a much-quoted passage that:

> Every system of production tends to discover punishments which correspond to its productive relationships . . . it is self-evident that enslavement as a form of punishment is impossible without a slave economy; that prison labour is impossible without manufacture or industry, that monetary fines for all classes of society are impossible without a monetary economy.
>
> (Rusche and Kirchheimer, 1939/1968: 5–6)

These arguments have subsequently been criticized on the grounds of what is known as economic determinism as they excessively (and eventually incoherently) rely on the concept of 'labour market' to explain forms of punishment.

Nevertheless, they emphasize what other commentators have called the principle of **less eligibility** as vital to the management of inequality in capitalist societies, by which they refer to 'the standard of living within prisons (as well as for those dependent on the welfare apparatuses) must be lower than that of the lowest stratum of the working class' (Rusche and Kirchheimer, 1939: 108). Their basic thesis has been developed by Dario Melossi and Massimo Pavarini (1978) who argue that the reason why the prison has developed as the response to crime in capitalist societies is because of the development of wage labour, which crucially has put a price on time. An important consequence of which is that it now seems natural that criminals should pay for their crimes by doing time, since workers are rewarded for their labour by the hour. Although this argument does rightly emphasize the importance of economic relations on penal practices, it does so in a way that minimizes the significance of other crucial factors. This political economy approach has recently been revived in Alessandro de Giorgi's (2006) ambitious attempt to provide a materialist explanation for the development of new technologies of control since the 1970s up to the present day.

Punishment, ideology and class control

In contrast, other Marxists have stressed the role of punishment in ideological class struggles and the maintenance of state power rather than labour market conditions and systems of economic production. The elements of such an interpretation are present in the work of the Russian legal theorist E. B. Pashukanis (1924/1978) as he argues that the penal sanctions of capitalist societies articulate bourgeois mentalities and ideological conceptions relating to the commodity form: an exchange transaction, in which the offender pays a debt and concludes the contractual obligation through serving a prison sentence (a clear influence on Melossi and Pavarini, 1978). In this manner the ideological content of capitalist societies and bourgeois values (like fair trading and liberty) are reaffirmed in spite of the harsh realities that exist in such societies (such as inequality and impoverishment).

As Garland (1990: 118) argues, this account is developed by the social historian Douglas Hay (1975) in his analysis of eighteenth-century criminal law, drawing attention to its dual functions of ideological legitimation and class coercion. In particular, he regards the expansion of capital punishment as a 'rule of terror' on the part of the landed aristocracy over thousands of landless poor, with the exercise of clemency (where the lord of the manor speaks to fellow gentry on behalf of a tenant at risk of severe punishment) regarded by Hay as a central factor contributing to the culture of deference still in evidence today among rural peasantry. Writing from within a humanistic tradition of Marxism, E. P. Thompson contends that the law can function ideologically to legitimate the existing order, but that

> people are not as stupid as some structural philosophers suppose them to be. They will not be mystified by the first man who puts on a wig . . . If the law is evidently partial and unjust, then it will mask nothing, legitimize nothing, contribute nothing to any class's hegemony.
> (Thompson, 1977: 262–3)

The clear implication is that the law is an 'arena for class struggle' rather than the exclusive possession of a ruling class (Thompson, 1977: 288). However, critics of this form of Marxist analysis point out that the criminal law and penal sanctions command a wide degree of support from the subordinate classes (the very population said to be controlled and regulated by such mechanisms of class rule) and that such practices afford a degree of protection previously unrealized (Fine, 1985). Nevertheless, one of the strengths of Marxist analysis is that it invites us to think of punishment not as a simple response to crime but as an important element in 'managing the rabble' (Irwin, 1990: 2) – matters that are now considered in the work of Michel Foucault who, for some, marks a decisive break with Marxism.

Foucault and disciplinary power

Over the past 30 years or so the French philosopher Michel Foucault (1926–1984) has cast an enormous influence over criminology – even though he was rather scathing of the discipline. His work can be located in a tradition begun by Nietzsche, who was highly sceptical of Western rationality, and continues in the disenchanted sociology of Max Weber (1864–1920) who wrote pessimistically of an 'iron cage' of rationality and bureaucracy that will ultimately imprison us all. Foucault's *Discipline and Punish* (1977) is not simply a detailed analysis of the emergence of the prison in the nineteenth century (see Chapter 18) but is also an account of how power operates in the modern era. The book opens with a striking juxtaposition of two entirely different styles of punishment that illustrate the fundamental transformations that had taken place in penal practices, namely the disappearance of the public spectacle of violence and the installation of a different form of punishment by the early nineteenth century, which is captured in a bland listing of the rules from an institutional timetable used in a Paris reformatory (see Chapter 4).

On a broader scale these developments are illustrative of how power operates in modern society and he sets himself the ambitious task of 'writing the history of the present' (Foucault, 1977: 31). One influential commentator has summarized Foucault's argument in the following way:

> the 'Great Incarcerations' of the nineteenth century – thieves into prisons, lunatics into asylums, conscripts into barracks, workers into factories, children into school – are to be seen as part of a grand design. Property had to be protected, production had to be

standardised by regulations, the young segregated and inculcated with the ideology of thrift and success, the deviant subjected to discipline and surveillance.

(Cohen, 1985: 25)

The new disciplinary mode of power which the prison was to represent belonged to an economy of power quite different from that of the direct, arbitrary and violent rule of the sovereign. Power in capitalist society had to be exercised at the lowest possible cost, both economically and politically, while its effects had to be intensified and extended throughout the social apparatus. Although his work continues to be influential, as we will see in the next section it has been criticized for:

- its 'appalling' historical inaccuracies (Braithwaite, 2003: 8);
- 'impoverished' understating of subjectivity (McNay, 1994: 22);
- preference for 'ascetic description' over normative analysis (Habermas, 1987: 275); and for
- not being able to tell the difference between prison and life outside.

The punitive city and surveillance society

It is more than a little ironic that at the very moment when Foucault's (1977) analysis of the 'Great Incarcerations' was published many Western societies seemed to be radically reversing the institutional response to deviance through processes of **decarceration** and the use of alternative sanctions in the community. Community corrections came to be regarded as a more humane and less stigmatizing means of responding to offenders, while treating mental illness in the community was generally seen as preferable to the asylum. However, a number of authors were sceptical and argued that treatment in the community amounted to malign neglect, with the mentally ill left to fend for themselves in uncaring environments (Scull, 1977). In criminology, Stan Cohen (1979b, 1985) has maintained that the development of community corrections marks both a continuation and an intensification of the social control patterns identified by Foucault (1977). This 'dispersal of discipline' thesis insists that there is now a blurring of where the prison ends and the community begins (see Box 15.5) with an accompanying increase in the total number of offenders brought into the system.

While Cohen (1985) chronicled the recruitment of friends, relatives and neighbours into the web of surveillance through curfews, tracking and tagging that now pervade the 'punitive city' (Cohen, 1979b) a debate ensued over the applicability of Foucault's ideas to contemporary patterns of punishment (Bottoms, 1983; Nelken, 1989; I. Taylor, 1999). Other developments since the 1990s include the rapid expansion of electronic, information and visual technologies, all of which greatly enhance the surveillance capacities of the state (see Chapter 20 on crime and the media). Today, surveillance operates in so many spheres of daily life that it is impossible to avoid – a situation well described in the following passage:

Most of our social encounters and almost all our economic transactions are subject to electronic recording, checking and authorization. From the Electronic Funds Transfer at Point of Sale (EFTPOS) machine for paying the supermarket bill or the request to show a barcoded driver's license, to the cellphone call or the Internet search, numerous everyday tasks trigger some surveillance device.

(Lyon, 2001: 146)

BOX 15.5 A vision of social control

Stan Cohen wrote this over 25 years ago – does it still sound like the future?

Mr and Mrs Citizen, their son Joe and daughter Linda, leave their suburban home after breakfast, saying goodbye to Ron, a 15-year-old pre-delinquent who is living with them under the LAK (Look After A Kid) scheme. Ron will later take a bus downtown to the Community Correctional Centre, where he is to be given two hours of Vocational Guidance and later tested on the Interpersonal Maturity Level scale. Mr C. drops Joe off at the School Problems Evaluation Centre from where Joe will walk to school. In his class are five children who are bussed from a local Community Home, four from a Pre-Release Facility and three who, like Ron, live with families in the neighbourhood. Linda gets off next – at the GUIDE Centre (Girls Unit for Intensive Daytime Education) where she works as a Behavioural Contract Mediator. They drive past a Threequarter-way House, a Rape-Crisis Centre and then a Drug-Addict Cottage, where Mrs C. waves to a group of boys working in the garden. She knows them from some work she does in RODEO (Reduction of Delinquency Through Expansion of Opportunities). She gets off at a building which houses the Special Parole Unit, where she is in charge of a 5-year evaluation research project on the use of the HIM (Hill Interaction Matrix) in matching group treatment to client. Mr C. finally arrives at work, but will spend his lunch hour driving around the car again as this is his duty week on patrol with TIPS (Turn In a Pusher). On the way he picks up some camping equipment for the ACTION weekend hike (Accepting Challenge Through Interaction with Others and Nature) on which he is going with Ron, Linda and five other PINS (Persons In Need of Supervision).

Source: Cohen (1985: 224–5).

Likewise urban fortress living has quickly moved from a dystopian vision (Cohen, 1985) to become a reality, particularly in Los Angeles (Davis, 1992, 1999) so that contemporary surveillance is both inclusionary, offering a sense of safety, security and order for some city dwellers, and exclusionary for others, prohibiting certain teenagers from entering panoptic shopping centres while planners develop sadistic street environments to displace the homeless from particular localities. John Fiske (1998) has further analysed the video surveillance of the American city to reveal how it is a rapidly developing control strategy focused on the young black male and is a disturbing instance of the totalitarian undercurrents in late modern democracies. Whereas Ray Coleman and Joe Sim (2000: 636) have argued that the deployment of CCTV in city centres is not simply a crime prevention technology but is a troubling response to 'gaps left by a series of legitimation deficits around policing and in urban governance generally' (see the recent edited collection by Ball et al., 2012, for a sense of the range of commentary on surveillance in these times of 'post-privacy').

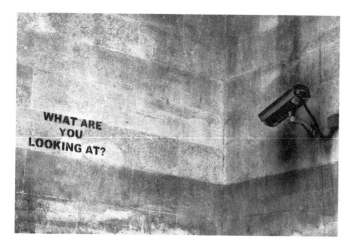

Plate 15.4 Banksy's 'What are you looking at?', Marble Arch, London.

Source: iStockphoto.

Feminist challenges

It will be clear that these main philosophical and sociological traditions have largely ignored the punishment of women and it is only in the last 30 years or so that studies of the control of women have appeared. Nevertheless, it is important to emphasize that the study of gender continues to be marginalized and, as Ngaire Naffine (1997: 5) argued, criminology remains a male-dominated discipline consisting largely of academic men studying criminal men, while she maintained that the 'costs to criminology of its failure to deal with feminist scholarship are perhaps more severe than they would be in any other discipline'. A clear instance of this is the widespread finding that when women are punished, this is as much about upholding conventional gender stereotypes as penalizing criminality (Carlen, 1983; Edwards, 1984; Howe, 1994).

Moreover the control of women indicates processes of **transcarceration**, which is defined as the movement of offenders between different institutional sites (Lowman *et al.*, 1987). Feminist studies have shown how there is a continuum of regulation in women's lives that encompasses the penal system, mental health and social welfare systems through to informal social (and anti-social) controls (Cain, 1989; Smart, 1995). The overall picture that emerges from this work is a more nuanced understanding of disciplinary control once the variable application to women and men is considered. For instance, it is clear that women are much more likely to be controlled by psychiatry and social work while men are more readily incarcerated. It would seem that gender divisions are as fundamental to structuring punishment as those of class and race.

Feminist jurisprudence

Underpinning proposals for a 'feminist jurisprudence' (Carlen, 1990; Daly, 1989; Naffine, 1990) are two main premises. The first, is that legal categories which are supposedly gender-neutral, instead reflect male dominance (Mackinnon, 1987); the second, and much more controversial among feminists, is that there is a kind of reasoning, characteristic to women, that is excluded from criminal justice decision-making (Hudson, 2003: 180). While feminist scholars continue to emphasize the need to bring women's experiences and voices into criminological and legal theorizing, there is widespread dispute over whether there is a universal 'female voice'.

The idea that women have a distinctive form of moral reasoning that is more concerned with finding solutions to specific and concrete problems than men, who are more concerned with the application of general abstract rules, is primarily associated with the work of Carol Gilligan in her book In a Different Voice (1982). She termed the female moral style 'the ethic of care' in contrast to the male 'logic of justice' and argued that both voices should have equal weight in moral reasoning, but in practice 'women's voices were misheard or judged as morally inferior to men's' (Daly, 2002: 65). Consequently, feminist criminologists have called for legal processes to admit expert witnesses with specific feminist viewpoints to qualify masculine constructions of crime and punishment (O'Donovan, 1993; Valverde, 1996).

This concept of feminist moral reasoning is controversial. Carol Smart (1989) has argued that it advances a view of men and masculinity as beyond culture and history, which serves to distort women's experiences. At the same time the work appears to want to replace one unitary view of the world, the male view, with another unitary and, ultimately, distorting, female view. Sandra Walklate (2001: 167) further explains that this 'desire to replace one world view with another fails to remove feminism from the traps of both essentialism (men and women are naturally and fundamentally different) and determinism (people, men nor women, have no choice)'. Overall, Smart's work is sceptical as to whether it is possible or even desirable to strive for a way of thinking through the law that represents all women's (or even all men's) experiences.

Nevertheless, these debates effectively demonstrate that criminologists need to examine crime and punishment from a gendered perspective. This point has been put in the following way:

> Feminist criminology has prospered by focusing on the plight of women – women victims and potential victims and women offenders – and instead avoided the arguably more pressing work of bringing feminist analyses to bear on the old penological question of the rehabilitation of (largely male) offenders, especially violent offenders.
>
> (Valverde, 2012: 248)

There are no easy answers, and while gender differences are important, there is no consensus over what these actually are and how these might shape practices of punishment, treatment and control. Mariana Valverde (2012: 247) also makes the telling point that those 'of us who popularized phrases such as "the medicalization of women's deviance" in the 1980s do not find it easy now to turn on a dime, intellectually, to protect psychiatric services for women in conflict with the law from austerity campaigns and budget cuts'. In this regard, it is important here to acknowledge the findings of the Corston Report (2007) which addresses psychiatrization and the particular vulnerabilities and different needs of female offenders and their neglect in the criminal justice system and penal policy (see also Chapter 18). But the overall point is that there remain some problematic tendencies in theoretical work that excels in critique, but flounders in the painful world of practice.

Summary

1 The power to punish derives from the legal authority of the state to do things that would otherwise be prima facie morally wrongful. Consequently, the pain, suffering and cruelty caused by punishment require some form of moral justification.

2 This chapter has reviewed a number of competing philosophical positions that seek to legitimate the harm (e.g. deterrence, retribution, rehabilitation, etc.) through to forms of moral reasoning that define what ought to be the proper goals of punishment.

3 In contrast sociological approaches to punishment have tended to consider the wider aspects of social control. Here the deeper structures of penal systems are excavated to show how penal policy is determined by political forces rather than by abstract philosophical argument or relevant empirical evidence.

4 The chapter has also described how the punishment of women challenges conventional thinking and reviewed the arguments surrounding feminist moral reasoning.

Critical thinking questions

1 Compare the differences between reductivists and retributivists over how punishment should be justified and how much punishment ought to be inflicted.

2 In what ways, if any, is the current American prison 'experiment' a 'totalitarian solution without a totalitarian state' (Bauman, 1995: 206)?

3 Why might punishment provoke solidarity and hostility among the public?

4 How does the principle of 'less eligibility' continue to inform contemporary practices of punishment?

5 In a pamphlet for a prisoners' rights campaign Michel Foucault (quoted in Eribon, 1992) once remarked that '[T]hey tell us that the prisons are overcrowded, but what if the entire population is over imprisoned?' What do you take to be the implications of this assertion?

6 Can you make a case for feminist jurisprudence?

Further study

Brooks, T. (2012) *Punishment*, London: Routledge. A new textbook approach to the philosophy of punishment covering classic and contemporary theories in wide-ranging fashion.

Cavadino, M. and Dignan, J. (2007) *The Penal System: An Introduction*, 4th edn, London: Sage. An indispensable guide, which provides an accessible overview of the field.

Garland, D. (1990) *Punishment and Modern Society: A Study in Social Theory*, Oxford: Clarendon Press. This is an authoritative discussion of sociological explanation, save for feminist challenges to the discipline.

Hudson, B. (2003) *Understanding Justice*, 2nd edn, London: Sage. A wide-ranging and accessible guide.

Scott, D. (2008) *Penology*, London: Sage. A basic but imaginative introduction to the field.

Simon, J. and Sparks, R. (2012) *The SAGE Handbook of Punishment and Society*, London: Sage. A state of the art collection featuring many of the leading authors writing perceptively on their topics and defining the field of study.

Smart, C. (1995) *Law, Crime and Sexuality*, London: Sage. A book giving insight into feminist analysis in this area.

Walker, N. (1991) *Why Punish?*, Oxford: Oxford University Press. A lively introduction to philosophical positions.

Useful websites

Restorative Justice online

www.restorativejustice.org

Excellent resource providing access to thousands of publications on restorative justice.

The Home Office: Publications: A Guide to the Criminal Justice System in England and Wales

http://www.homeoffice.gov.uk/rds/cjspub1.html

Publications available online, on the criminal justice process in England and Wales.

Criminal Justice System

http://www.cjsonline.org/home.html

This is another site that has useful information on the criminal justice process in England and Wales.

Crown Office and Procurator Fiscal Service

http://www.crownoffice.gov.uk/

This site has information on the Scottish criminal justice system plus a selection of other links for reference.

Criminal Justice System Northern Ireland

http://www.cjsni.gov.uk/

A site on the criminal justice process in Northern Ireland.

Proceedings of the Old Bailey

http://www.oldbaileyonline.org/

A fully searchable online edition of the largest body of texts detailing the lives of non-elite people ever published, containing accounts of over 100,000 criminal trials held at London's central criminal court.

chapter 16

The Criminal Justice Process

Key issues

- What are the key stages of the criminal justice process?
- How are criminal cases socially constructed by the criminal justice process?
- What happens when the process goes wrong?
- What do we mean by 'justice', and how 'just' is the criminal justice process?
- How do different social groups experience the criminal justice process?

Introduction

Questions about crime and questions about the control of crime are not easily separated and they may be best understood as two sides of the same coin (see Chapter 6). Patterns of recorded crime, types and numbers of offenders brought to justice, and the constitution of prison populations are largely determined by the actions of various criminal justice gatekeepers to report, detect, judge and punish criminal activities. These gatekeepers include the press and the public, and also the people and professionals working in the criminal justice system including the police, lawyers, magistrates, juries and judges. This chapter provides an overview of the key stages of the criminal justice process in the United Kingdom, and it describes the roles and responsibilities of the key actors and institutions involved: the police, the Crown Prosecution Service, the Probation Service and the judiciary. It looks at the historical development of the criminal justice system, the main gatekeeping decisions that underpin the working of each area, the related social constructions of criminal cases, and the principles and realities of justice that ensue from this.

Historical context

Historians and sociologists have examined how and why criminal justice processes and allied forms of and ideas about the control of deviancy underwent significant changes at a particular point in time in the development of Western nations (see, for example, Ignatieff, 1978; Rothman, 1971; Foucault, 1977). For instance, in his book *Visions of Social Control* (1985), Stanley Cohen examines transformations in what he called 'the master patterns' of the social control apparatus from the pre-modern to the modern period. As Chapter 15 shows, many of these key transformations can be seen clearly in the changing principles and practices of punishment. Yet, there were other major shifts associated with this – namely the increasing involvement of the modern state in the development of a centralized, rationalized and bureaucratic system of crime control, and the associated professionalization and expansion of criminal justice experts. These changing patterns were evident in developments in British criminal justice in the nineteenth century, most notably in the formation of its adversarial trial system populated by lawyers, judges and juries, and in the emergence of a full-time, professional police force and other specialized criminal justice professionals (Emsley, 1996; Rawlings, 1995). Across this period, policing, prosecution and other activities within the courtroom gradually came to be seen as the preserve of specialized formal agencies and professionals working for the state.

Changes in the 'master patterns' of social control towards the increasing centralization, professionalization and formalization of criminal justice meant that criminal cases were no longer regarded as a predominately private affair between the victim(s) and the perpetrator(s) of crime. As Nils Christie (1977) has argued, forms of crime and deviance that were once largely regulated and managed informally by communities and individuals had, by the nineteenth century, become the official 'property' of the state. Criminal trials thus became a contest between the state (as prosecutor) and the offender (as defendant), and, as we shall see, the very spatial, organizational and procedural framework of the courts underlines this point. The opposing parties (defence and prosecution), the judge, the structural position of the experts, the construction of 'a case' and the conduct of trials are based on very formalized criminal procedures, ceremonies and rules of legal relevance. Within this system, both victims and offenders become marginalized and disempowered. They enter the courts as non-professional outsiders, reduced often to only passive spectators, lacking knowledge and input into courtroom procedures and process (for more information about victim participation in the criminal justice process, see Chapter 9).

Overview of criminal justice institutions in the UK

Institutions formally developed for the control of crime and delinquency such as the police, courts and prisons can be found in virtually all countries, albeit with different names and involving different laws and procedures. There is also some variation in the legal and crime control system within the United Kingdom itself. For instance, the political processes involved in the devolution of Scotland from England and Wales has brought about a number of key changes, as well as continuities, to the criminal justice system in the Scottish context (see McAra, 2005). The age of criminal responsibility is 12 in Scotland and 10 in England and Wales and Northern Ireland. Here, as in all Western nations, and many others, young offenders are generally dealt with in specialist forums. Under the Scottish Children's Hearings System, lay panel members consider and make decisions on the supervision and welfare needs of the child. Scotland's public prosecution service also has different roles and responsibilities as compared to those in England and Wales. Unlike the Crown Prosecution Service (CPS) in England and Wales (described below), the Procurator Fiscal Service in Scotland has a wider responsibility for directing the investigation and prosecution of crimes and in diverting offenders from court by issuing a warning. Additionally, once the case comes to court, a 'not proven' verdict can be given in Scotland, which it cannot in England and Wales. In Northern Ireland, the Criminal Justice Review Group was set up in 1998 under the Good Friday Agreement to undertake a wide-ranging review of Northern Irish criminal justice. It made 294 recommendations for change in areas as diverse as the prosecution service, courts, the judiciary, youth conferencing, community safety, victims and witnesses, law reform and international cooperation.

In the UK as a whole, criminal justice institutions have undergone considerable scrutiny and reform in recent years. This is partly a result of the perception of 'new' security problems like terrorism but it is also related to a shifting political environment (e.g. politicians' desire to display their 'toughness on crime', and EU harmonization) and to the ongoing drive towards efficiency in the public sector. The increasing politicization of crime since the 1970s has contributed to a significant growth in the UK law and order budget, rising from 3.3 per cent of total government expenditure in 1978–9 to 5.5 per cent in 2008–9 – where just under £35 billion was spent (Crawford et al., 2009). Until 2007, criminal justice in England and Wales was under the administration of the Home Office but, following a high-profile reorganization, most responsibility for the criminal justice system was passed to a new government agency – the Ministry of Justice (MoJ), and Home Office management of migration issues was moved to the new Border Agency. The MoJ became responsible for criminal law and sentencing, reducing reoffending, and for prisons and probation. It also oversees the Magistrates' Courts, the Crown Court, the Appeals Courts and the Legal Services Commission. The Attorney General's Office continues to provide legal advice to government and oversees the Crown Prosecution Service (CPS), which, as will be described below, is responsible for the prosecution of nearly all criminal cases in England and Wales.

Officially, the MoJ aims to: 'protect the public and reduce reoffending, and to provide a more effective, transparent and responsive criminal justice system for victims and the public . . . [and] also provide fair and simple routes to civil and family justice' (http://www.justice.gov.uk/ about/moj). While this rhetoric seems entirely reasonable, the reality is that the public are not always protected, reoffending rates remain staggeringly high, and the criminal justice system is not always effective, transparent or responsive. As we will see throughout this and other chapters, the criminal justice process involves numerous conflicting values, aims and interests, such as convicting the guilty versus protecting the innocent from wrongful conviction; ensuring just processes versus achieving just outcomes; protecting the rights of defendants versus meeting the needs of victims (Chapter 9); enforcing the law versus maintaining order (Chapter 17); and delivering punishment (Chapter 15) without imposing disproportionate cost with consequent harm to other public services.

Key stages of the criminal justice process

There are several key stages of the criminal justice process through which suspects are processed – from being charged by the police to being sentenced by a judge (Figure 16.1). As Chapter 3 shows, as a result of non-reporting by the public and non-recording by the police, many crimes do not enter into the criminal justice process at all. Even if crimes are recorded by the police, not all of them are processed up to the CPS or into the courts. In this sense, the criminal justice process can be seen to act like a filter whereby only some cases proceed fully through the process. This is a necessary function of the criminal justice process as it reduces the likelihood of wrongful conviction but it also means that some cases that should be processed are mistakenly filtered out.

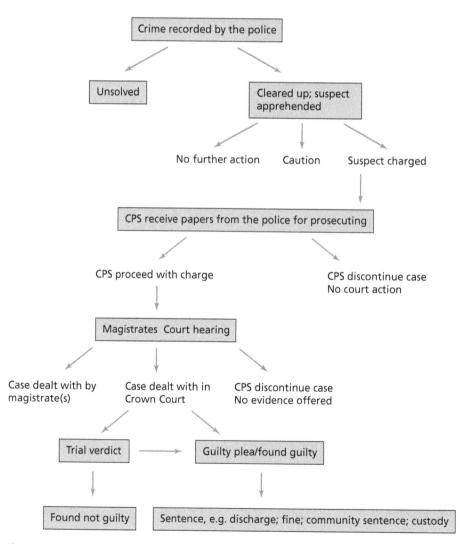

Figure 16.1 Main stages of the criminal justice process in England and Wales.

The filtering, or 'attrition', of criminal cases out of the criminal justice process is the result of the decisions made by the various actors in the process. Some of the most important questions for criminologists to ask, therefore, are how these decisions are made and what effects they have upon justice. As will be demonstrated in the following sections, the decisions made by criminal justice professionals, magistrates and juries are not based completely on the objective evidence of a case but they are highly influenced by social stereotypes, prejudices and biases that tend to favour some suspects and defendants over others. These biases have contributed to a number of high-profile miscarriages of justice and to the disproportionate representation of some groups in the official criminal population.

BOX 16.1 Attrition rates around the world

One way of measuring the effectiveness of criminal justice systems is to examine the attrition rates of selected types of crime as they proceed through the system. In effect, this measure reflects which proportion of cases entering the system are resolved, closed or dispensed with by criminal justice agencies. Levels of attrition can be measured at a number of points within the criminal justice process – for example, the number of police-recorded cases that are actually prosecuted, or the number of recorded or prosecuted cases resulting in a conviction.

According to the United Nations Survey of Crime Trends, for the period 1980–2000, a conviction was likely to be achieved in one out of every four cases of homicide and one out of every eight cases of robbery. There were, however, considerable regional differences. In sub-Saharan Africa, for example, a conviction was obtained in only one of every 18 cases recorded by the police. In Latin America, where fewer prosecutions are initiated, the ones that did occur were more likely to result in a conviction (about one in seven cases). In the European Union, a conviction was obtained in every two recorded cases. The attrition rates for robbery show a slightly different picture. On average, only one in every 40 cases of reported robbery in Africa resulted in a prosecution for the period 1990–2000. In Latin America and the Caribbean, one conviction was recorded for approximately every 15 reported cases. Both North America and the European Union show one conviction for every nine cases of reported cases of robbery, just above the global average.

Source: http://www.unodc.org/pdf/crime/forum

The police

The police are by far the most researched group in the criminal justice system (Brown, 1996). They are also, perhaps, the most significant, because of their position as the initial gatekeepers in the criminal justice process. Although police have a statutory responsibility to record all crimes, they retain considerable discretion about whether and how to deal with possible offences that come to their attention. Reports from the public may be disbelieved, considered trivial or deemed not to concern a criminal offence. Since the adoption of the National Crime Recording Standard (NCRS) by all police forces in England and Wales in 2002, there have been increases in the overall proportion of crimes recorded by the police but, according to British Crime Survey figures, in 2010/11 only 41 per cent of all offences were reported and recorded by the police. Put another way, this means that less than half of crimes against individuals and their households end up in the recorded crime count, although it does tend to be more minor crimes that are not recorded. Despite the NCRS there also remains considerable variation in the police recording rates between different force areas and offence types (see Chapter 17). The number of offences 'discovered' by the police themselves, although generally low, are also subject to changes in law-enforcement priorities and activities. More proactive or 'priority oriented' policing, or high-profile planned operations against a particular type of offence (e.g. drugs or burglary) will inevitably bring about an increase in arrests and thus the discovery and recording of new offences in the targeted areas. Conversely, numbers may fall if there is a withdrawal of police interest in a particular type of crime or area.

Even if a suspect is detected and charged, police retain significant discretion over the processing of the case, and police arrest does not always lead to prosecution. In general, around one in four suspects are released from pre-charge detention with no further action (NFA), and many suspects (especially young people and minor offenders) continue to be dealt with outside the court system. If, for example, suspects admit their guilt, the police may use cautioning or, since the Criminal Justice and Police Act 2001, they may issue a Fixed Penalty Notice. Although there are national standards that set out the formal criteria for police use of prosecution, penalty and caution (based on evidential sufficiency or public interest), police **working rules** and cultures have continued to significantly shape the exercise of police discretion and case outcomes (see Chapter 17).

The influence of the initial decisions taken and the way in which information is gathered, sifted through and written up to become a 'case' by the police also endures through the process to influence later decisions made by magistrates, judges and juries. Indeed, a number of studies of police investigations (e.g. Sanders, 1977; Erickson, 1981; McConville et al., 1991) have shown how initial investigations and the way in which police officers construct their case notes provide the essential basis for the way in which the case will proceed through the rest of the criminal justice process or not. William Sanders's (1977) classic study of detectives, for instance, shows how case notes inevitably simplify the actual criminal event. Crimes take place in three-dimensional space, occur over time, and often involve a number of people doing different things all at once, but police officers must choose what details to include or exclude, how to present the chosen details, emphasizing particular elements and downplaying others. It is this initial police construction of case notes that is passed to the CPS.

The Crown Prosecution Service

Created under the Prosecution of Offenders Act 1985 as part of wider criminal justice reform in England and Wales, the CPS consists of salaried lawyers whose task is to review cases passed to them by the police and to decide whether prosecution commenced by the police should continue into the courts. The CPS also looks at the appropriateness of charges, makes decisions on matters of law and conducts prosecutions in court. The CPS was introduced into the system because the police were seen as too close to the case and inclined to proceed under a crime control model even when there was insufficient evidence against the suspect, or to ignore vital clues they considered irrelevant to the case for prosecution. The argument was that a new prosecuting agency would encourage greater impartiality, efficiency and consistency in the approach to prosecution. As well as the CPS, other bodies such as Customs and Excise, the Inland Revenue, the Serious and Organized Crime Agency, and the Department of Trade and Industry also bring prosecutions in the UK.

In principle, the CPS as a public prosecution service exists to provide effective scrutiny of cases, to secure consistency in decision-making, and to filter out weak prosecution cases from the criminal justice process. Their decision on whether to prosecute an offender is guided by the Code for Crown Prosecutors (2004), which sets out the two crucial tests of the case: 'evidential sufficiency', and 'public interest'. First, the CPS must be satisfied that there is a 'realistic prospect of conviction' (i.e. whether magistrates or jury are more likely than not to convict) on the available evidence. Second, Crown prosecutors must consider whether it is in the 'public interest' for a prosecution to be brought. The main public interest factors considered to mitigate *against* prosecution include:

- The likelihood of a small or nominal penalty
- The offence was committed as a result of a genuine mistake
- The loss or harm was minor
- There has been a long delay since the offence
- A prosecution will adversely affect the victim's physical or mental health
- The defendant is elderly or at the time of the offence suffering from significant mental or physical illness.

On the other hand, public interest factors considered to necessitate prosecution include:

- The likelihood of a significant sentence
- Use of a weapon or violence threatened
- Premeditated or group offence
- Victim particularly vulnerable, put in fear, or suffered personal attack, damage or disturbance
- Offence motivated by racial, sexual, religious, disability or political discrimination
- Likelihood of repetition.

To many observers, the independence of Crown prosecutors is the key to effective control of police discretion. In practice however, typically fewer than one in ten cases sent to the CPS by the police are discontinued (Home Office, 2002a: table 6.2). The low discontinuance rate could of course be due to the strength of the cases provided by police but commentators have pointed out that working relationships and shared assumptions between the CPS and the police may also be relevant factors. In the process of case construction, according to McConville *et al.* (1991), the independence of the CPS is limited because of:

- its reliance on the information given to them by the police (Crown prosecutors cannot realistically go through all paperwork or listen to all taped interviews);

- its organizational position (they are on the same side as the police and state in the adversarial trial system); and
- its operational philosophy (to ensure that the prosecution policy is carried out efficiently).

Prosecution decisions are also taken in a working context that brings the CPS into contact not just with the local police but also with victims and magistrates. Any attempt to understand practical decision-making must, therefore, take into account the organizational, operational and cultural contexts in which the CPS make decisions. As Doreen McBarnet (1981: 100), drawing on the seminal work of Aaron Cicourel (1968), argues in her study in the Scottish context, cases for prosecution and convictions in court are highly socially constructed:

> [S]trong and weak cases do not miraculously appear after an incident ready formed like tablets of stone on Mount Sinai. They are the product of a process of construction in which both the technical skills of lawyers and the structural opportunities and limitations offered by the legal system play their part in shaping what facts get into the courts and just how strong or weak a case can be independent of the incident in question.

The judiciary and the courts

In liberal democracies (unlike authoritarian regimes – see Chapter 22), the doctrine of the separation of state powers dictates that there has to be a degree of separation of functions between the three essential bodies of the state: the legislature, the executive and the judiciary. For example, the judiciary, which adjudicates upon crimes and conflicts between state institutions, between state and individual, and between individuals, is meant to be independent of political influence in its interpretation of the law and judgements on cases. In practice, however, the separation of powers has never been absolute, and the imprecision of the doctrine has sometimes led to different interpretations of the meaning of, or even acrimonious debates about, judicial independence from government (e.g. over sentencing policies and practices).

Three sets of decision-makers have evolved in the judiciary through the past ten centuries in England and Wales: magistrates, judges and jury. Criminal cases are dealt with in either the magistrates' court or the Crown Court. Magistrates tend to deal with more minor 'summary' offences where, in the vast majority of cases, an offender has pleaded guilty. Crown Courts, on the other hand, rule upon more serious and ambiguous cases and sentence offenders to custody. When defendants are aged under 18, their cases are generally dealt with in the specialist youth courts.

There are about 30,000 lay magistrates and about 140 district judges (formerly known as stipendiary magistrates) in England and Wales (www.judiciary.gov.uk). In contrast to district judges, who are full-time legally trained professionals that normally sit alone in larger urban magistrates' courts on serious cases where guilt needs to be established, lay magistrates (also known as Justices of the Peace) are unpaid volunteers who sit part-time on local benches. They are advised on points of law by professional Clerks of the court, and they are meant to represent an important lay element in the criminal justice process as representatives of the general public. Yet, in practice, the composition of the lay magistracy is unbalanced, rather less in terms of gender than of age, race and class whereby magistrates tend overwhelmingly to be composed of older middle-class white men and women (Morgan and Russell, 2000). How this affects the quality of justice is subject to debate but there is evidence to suggest that some defendants (especially those from an African or Caribbean background) consider magistrates' courts to be biased towards the prosecution, are more likely to opt for trial by jury and believe that the Crown Court, because of its jury system, offers a fairer and fuller hearing with a higher chance of acquittal (Hedderman and Moxon, 1992; Fitzgerald, 1993). This is not to say that juries or professional judges have escaped criticism. Judges, for example, are commonly seen as out of touch with 'what ordinary people believe'. This is shorthand for the view that the majority of judges are drawn from a public-school educated elite who impose excessively lenient sentences – even though the actual sentencing patterns and high imprisonment rates in Britain reflect a rather different reality (see Chapter 18).

The vast majority (around 95 per cent) of criminal cases are, nonetheless, dealt with entirely in magistrates' courts. The remaining cases are passed to the Crown Court to be heard before a judge (who decides on the sentence) and a jury (who decide on guilt). Crown Courts are presided over by full-time judges who also hear appeals against conviction in a magistrates' court and decide on sentences in the more serious cases referred from magistrates' courts. The jury system has by many been hailed as a symbol of participatory democracy. This is because the involvement of the public in the criminal justice process arguably gives people confidence in its fairness, ensures that unpopular or unjust laws cannot be enforced, and operates as a defence against the oppressive use of state power. The right to be tried by 12 of one's peers has also been described as a fundamental right (Darbyshire, 1991), although it is hard to draw any meaningful conclusions about the democratic credentials of a country by the presence or absence of a jury system. For example, Germany and the Netherlands do not have a jury system in criminal cases, while Belgium and France use it only in serious cases. Critics of the jury system suggest that jury trials are costly and time-consuming. There are also many trials in which juries fail to prevent wrongful convictions – from the high-profile cases of miscarriages of justice (see below) to the more routine successful appeals against convictions. Critics also argue that juries may not actually be very representative of society and that trials for some crimes (such as major frauds) may be too complex for juries to follow (see Findlay and Duff, 1988). More recently, there has been much resistance to continuing government attempts to restrict the right to trial by jury, and, according to a public survey conducted on behalf of the Bar Council and the Law Society in 2002, most of those surveyed believe a jury of 12 individuals is most likely to reflect their own and society's views and values, and that they would get a fairer trial from a jury than from a judge (www.dca.gov.uk/criminal/auldcom).

BOX 16.2 Adversarial versus inquisitorial approaches to criminal justice

The system of justice in England and Wales is sometimes referred to as an 'adversarial system' of justice. This is different from an 'inquisitorial' system of justice, as found in some other countries. In the adversarial system the magistrate(s) or jury decide on a verdict, having heard two opposing presentations of the case. The prosecution and defence parties present their case as they see fit and tactically cross-examine witnesses. Not guilty pleas result in a contest (hence the term 'adversarial') between the two parties arguing over the facts of a case. This might be contrasted to the inquisitorial approach adopted in many continental European countries, where there is a continuing judicial supervision of the process from the beginning of the investigation to the decisions in sentencing. In an inquisitorial system a judge is involved in the preparation of evidence by the police and in how the various parties are to present their case at the trial. The judge questions witnesses while prosecution and defence parties can ask supplementary questions. The influence of the judge in the trial process tends to reduce the level of contest between the two parties. In contrast, the English judge will usually have little knowledge about the case before the trial; he or she will not have been engaged in supervising any investigation, taking statements from witnesses or the accused, or making bail decisions. Nor, except in rare circumstances, would he or she be consulted over decisions to release from prison (Home Office 2000a: ch 4; Uglow, 2002).

Lawyers and the adversarial system

In practice, the vast majority of cases processed through the criminal justice system are routinely resolved through a guilty plea. In the magistrates' courts, over 90 per cent of defendants on summary trial plead guilty. Most of these cases involve relatively minor matters that almost always end in a fine. A contested trial in a magistrates' court is very rare, and it is therefore not surprising that the nature of most courtroom appearances has been described as a 'routine, boring, ritual, unproblematic processing of cases' (Carlen, 1976). Even in the Crown Court, the rate of guilty pleas is around 60 per cent (Sanders et al., 2010). However, if cases are processed into the Crown Court, and if the defendant pleads not guilty, the highly adversarial nature of the UK court system springs into being.

In the UK (and the USA), the criminal justice process is an adversarial one in which two sides (the defence and the prosecution) present their sides of the story to attempt to convince the jury of their view of the defendant's innocence or guilt. Most of us are familiar with the adversarial nature of British justice from the plethora of crime dramas that we see on our TV screens. Here, defence and prosecution stories are told by professional lawyers who represent either the state (the prosecution) or the accused (the defence). As lawyers are paid to work for their client or by the state, it is not necessarily a just outcome that they desire, rather lawyers want to win the case for their side (McConville et al., 1991). This means that courtrooms and their proceedings are sites for dramatic storytelling where, like in any good drama, lawyers use props (evidence) and make moral judgements about the characters involved (victims, witnesses and defendants) in order to tell convincing stories. As will be elaborated below, a number of sociological studies of trials indicate that the cogency and credibility of the stories told by lawyers can trump evidential details of a case and contribute to biased judgements and even miscarriages of justice.

The Probation Service

The Probation Service (now part of the National Offender Management Service (NOMS) alongside the Prison Service) plays a key role in the criminal justice process at the sentencing stage in the United Kingdom. It assists magistrates and judges in their sentencing decisions through the provision of pre-sentence reports and bail information reports. It is also responsible for supervision of offenders in the community. In the area of youth justice, the Crime and Disorder Act 1998 established Youth Offending Teams (involving, for example, the police, social services, education, probation and health services) to assess young offenders in order to reduce youth offending within a context of wider problems (from poor parental supervision and domestic violence or abuse, to truancy, school exclusion, substance misuse or mental health problems), and to enforce community sentences for young offenders.

Probation, or the practice of releasing offenders from court with some kind of condition that they behave themselves in future, has been central to the history of community sentences (Raynor and Vanstone, 2002; May, 1991). Originally set up as a community response to offending in the nineteenth century (as 'police court missionaries'), the Probation Service became a formalized agency of full-time professionals under the Probation Offenders Act 1907. Against a background of emerging psychological and environmental explanations of crime and human behaviour (see Chapter 4), the original role of probation practitioners was to 'advise, assist and befriend' the offender (e.g. through one-to-one supervision and practical help). However, as rehabilitative ideals increasingly came under attack and the debate over 'toughened-up' community-based penalties (e.g. intensive probation, inclusion of more demanding conditions, curfew) intensified in the latter half of the twentieth century, the role of the Probation Service in delivering public protection, risk management and 'proper punishment' in the community remains highly contentious. David Smith (2005), for example, argues that under the slogan of 'Enforcement, Rehabilitation and Protection' the work of the Probation Service has been rebranded in ways that have distanced it from social work in terms of its purposes and values.

Taken together, these institutions in the criminal justice process have the main responsibility for administering justice and managing and controlling the official criminal population up to the point of sentencing. The decisions and activities at any one point in the criminal justice process have a cumulative effect at a later stage of the process. Of course, crime and its control have never been the concern of criminal justice professionals alone. Statutory organizations working in the areas of public health, education and housing at central and local government level have, for example, developed services and multi-agency partnerships around particular notions of 'anti-social behaviour', crime prevention and community safety (Newburn, 2002b; McLaughlin and Muncie, 2000). Penal establishments have been built with private money and run by the private sector (Matthews, 1989), and recent proposals by the Coalition government aim to privatize probation services for minor offenders and offences. Charities and voluntary groups have also been very much involved with crime and treatment-related work since at least the nineteenth century (Cox, 2003). Prostitutes, abused children, child abusers, vagrants, drug and alcohol users, mentally disordered offenders, battered women, ex-prisoners and many other groups have all been the subject of specific charitable campaigns by organizations ranging from the Female Mission to the Fallen to Women's Aid, from the Temperance Movement to Alcoholics Anonymous, from the Howard League for Penal Reform to the National Association for the Care and Resettlement of Offenders (NACRO). All this suggests that different elements of civil society, broadly defined, also play a major part in the definition, detection, and reform of criminals.

The nature of justice

So what kind of justice does the British criminal justice process deliver? There are at least three approaches to interrogating whether criminal justice is 'just': by examining the procedural safeguards enacted to prevent unjust prosecution and conviction (i.e. **procedural justice**); by looking at the substantive outcomes of the criminal justice process (i.e. **substantive justice**); and by analysing the negotiations and social interactions of the actors involved in the routine production of justice within the criminal justice system (i.e. **negotiated justice**).

Procedural justice

The criminal justice process, alongside the military, is the most explicit coercive institution of government. It is therefore crucial in a liberal democracy that police and courts interfere with the liberties of citizens only within the constraints of law and not through any arbitrary exercise of their power. This in essence is the rule of law – that is, the sovereignty or supremacy of law above every individual. For those caught up within the criminal justice process, principles of legality and equality before the law demand that a person's legal rights are protected, that there are checks and balances upon judicial power, and that justice is administered according to standards that are fair, publicly known and seen to be just. Formal independence of the courts from the state is an essential check on the power of executive government, and independence from the other criminal justice agencies is also meant to make the courts a neutral forum, which is a key aspect of 'due process' of law.

The concept of procedural justice is brought to bear in a number of stages of the criminal justice process. For example, arrested persons should be informed as to what the charges are and be given the opportunity to defend themselves. Evidence gathered by the police should be reliable and acquired, in most cases, by lawful means. Proceedings should normally be conducted in open court so that justice is seen to be done. There should also be clear standards of proof and strict rules and formal procedures of evidence to ensure that evidence admitted into court is of an admissible nature and is fairly presented (see Ashworth, 1998; Sanders and Young, 2007).

When legal rules and procedures are ignored or only partially applied, injustice in the form of abuse of power or wrongful conviction can, and does, occur. Wrongful convictions can result from police malpractice or error, because the prosecution withholds evidence, the trial judge is biased, or from faulty forensic evidence (Greer, 1994). The cases of the 'Birmingham Six', the 'Guildford Four' and the 'Maguire Seven' are among the most publicized examples of miscarriages of justice in the UK. In each of these cases, the defendants were wrongfully convicted and served long prison sentences for alleged Irish Republican Army (IRA) terrorist actions but their convictions were eventually quashed by the Court of Appeal following years of campaigning by relatives, friends and public figures for a review of their cases (Rozenberg, 1993). Andrew

Plate 16.1 The Birmingham Six with Chris Mullen, MP, outside the Old Bailey in London after their convictions were quashed, 14 March 1991. Left to right: John Walker, Paddy Hill, Hugh Callaghan, Chris Mullen, MP, Richard McIlkenny, Gerry Hunter, William Power.

Source: © PA Photos 2003; *photo:* Sean Dempsey.

Ashworth (1998: 14) summarizes the abuses of power by the police and other deficiencies within the criminal justice process that were exposed by these cases: the concoction or falsification of evidence by police officers; oppressive questioning and violence by the police; non-disclosure of vital evidence by forensic scientists and/or by the prosecution to the defence; slow and cumbersome appeal procedures; and a general reluctance to accept that the police had not told the truth.

By the early 1990s, public confidence in the police and the justice system had eroded to such an extent that a Royal Commission was appointed (Royal Commission on Criminal Justice, 1993). Attempts have since been made to introduce stronger legal safeguards for defendants, and the Criminal Cases Review Commission was created under the Criminal Appeal Act 1995 to investigate miscarriages of justice and to refer cases back to the Court of Appeal. The Human Rights Act 1998 also incorporates rights protected under the European Convention on Human Rights into domestic law and has since been used to mount a number of challenges to the criminal justice system (concerning, for example, the right not to incriminate oneself, and the rights of prisoners). Critics, however, have pointed to recent legislative developments that give extensive powers to the state as a result of the aftermath of the terrorist attacks on the United States on 11 September 2001. For example, the UK Prevention of Terrorism Act 2005 has been criticized by Human Rights Watch for empowering the state to impose clandestine restrictions on terrorism suspects (including indefinite 'house arrest' for those placed under Control Orders)

BOX 16.3 Miscarriages of justice

Some of the most high-profile 'miscarriages of justice' in Britain concerned alleged Irish Republican Army (IRA) terrorist suspects who were imprisoned for up to sixteen years on false confessions and dubious evidence in the early 1970s before being released. The wrongful convictions focused on the cases of the 'Birmingham Six' (for two explosions in Birmingham which resulted in 21 deaths); the 'Guildford Four' (for explosions in Guildford and Woolwich); and Judith Ward (for several explosions, including one on an army bus). After years of campaigning, all their cases went to successful appeals, and ten of the eleven people concerned in these cases were released in 1991–2 and given compensation (the eleventh had already died in prison). It was subsequently revealed that the suspects had been assaulted by the police, intimidated with further threats of severe violence, deprived of sleep, and relentlessly questioned. Some 'confessed' or signed confessions that were fabricated by the investigating officers. The police were also found to have withheld vital information from the courts.

Another notorious case is that of the 'Cardiff Three', convicted in 1990 of the murder of a Cardiff prostitute. Their convictions were also overturned by the Court of Appeal (in 1992) on the grounds that the interrogations amounted to bullying and oppression by the police, and that the interviews should have been excluded from evidence. This case is particularly significant because it occurred some years after the implementation of the Police and Criminal Evidence Act 1984 (PACE), which put in place regulation of pre-trial investigation and routine tape-recording of police interviews. This perhaps suggests that the officers did not think that their approach was unacceptable. (For information concerning PACE, see Box 17.4.)

on the basis of 'reasonable suspicion' that is subject only to delayed and non-transparent judicial review. They argued that: 'The lack of procedural safeguards seriously undermines the right to a fair trial, the presumption of innocence and the right to an effective defence' (http://hrw.org/backgrounder/eca/uk). The 'state of exception' (Agamben, 2005) generated by the widespread fear of terrorism under the current 'war on terror' provides impetus and justification for the further expansion of secretive policing and emergency powers and a concomitant erosion of procedural safeguards for individuals suspected, but not proven, of being involved in terrorist activity (see chapters 17 and 21).

In addition to the formal checks and balances provided by the nature of the law and the structure of legal oversight, it must be taken into consideration that criminal justice professionals also work within particular social and institutional contexts. These contexts have been shown to have built-in cultural assumptions about how and which cases should be constructed and about how critical questions that may embarrass other actors in the system are to be automatically filtered out of view. As Maurice Punch (2003: 188) points out in relation to the systemic failures of criminal justice:

> What raised the miscarriages of justice to the system level was the collusion of other actors in the system – supervisory officers who did not intervene when violence occurred, senior

officers who signed 'dodgy' statements, forensic specialists who went to work uncritically (and even unprofessionally), prosecutors who did not probe sensitive areas in the material given to them, judges who turned a blind eye to discrepancies in evidence and the Home Office which forestalled an appeal for so long.

Seen in this light, miscarriages of justice are neither rare nor exceptional. Instead, error may be an inbuilt feature of the criminal justice system, which may be part of the reason why the many attempts to reform it have ended in failure (Naughton, 2007).

So far, by looking at some clear examples of where the criminal justice process 'goes wrong', we have concentrated on unsafe convictions and miscarriages of justice where the innocent are imprisoned. Critics would argue however that the process also fails to deliver justice where it does not prosecute and/or convict people who should be prosecuted and convicted. The repeated failure to convict the murderers of Stephen Lawrence due to police incompetence and 'institutional racism' (see Chapter 17) can be seen as one such example. Other instances include the extremely low and declining conviction rate for reported rape cases (falling, for example, from around a 32 per cent conviction rate in 1977 to a staggeringly low 5.6 per cent in 2002), which has been identified by many feminists and criminal reform groups as a serious 'justice gap' (Kelly et al., 2005). As a result of such issues, victims and their families may feel let down or angry with the criminal justice process, and there is substantial evidence to suggest that victims' treatment by criminal justice agencies, and the court experience itself, can also produce a sense of unfairness, bewilderment and trauma (Shapland et al., 1985). Indeed, the criminal justice process can create a form of 'secondary victimization' that compounds and exacerbates the pain and trauma produced by criminal victimization (see Thiel, 2013; and Chapter 9).

Substantive justice

'Unjust' or ineffective outcomes may arise even when legal rules are formally adhered to and when supposedly 'neutral' criteria in criminal justice decision-making are applied. A classic example is the differential impact of a fine on offenders with and without the financial means to pay it. Furthermore, concerns have continually been raised, both from within criminology and from within social movements (such as the feminist movement and anti-racist activist groups), that existing criminal justice policies and procedures are inequitable by having the effect of punishing a higher proportion of one social group than another.

Gender

The question of whether male and female offenders are treated differently in the criminal justice system has been subject to much criminological debate. The so-called 'chivalry hypothesis' – that is, that the police, courts and other agencies extend greater leniency towards all women – has been disputed by most empirical studies (Eaton, 1986; Carlen, 1983; Daly and Bordt, 1995; Player, 1989; and see Chapter 6). Instead, there is evidence to suggest that the opposite is true: that some female offenders and delinquents may be 'doubly punished', both for breaking the law and transgressing their gender roles, and are often disciplined under notions of penal care and welfare that in fact tend towards longer and more invasive sentences (Gelsthorpe, 1989; Cain, 1989; Allen, 1987; Steward, 2006; but see Hedderman and Hough, 1994).

Other feminists have questioned the discourses of equality of treatment in which women are treated 'the same as men'. They have asked whether this is always appropriate to the circumstances surrounding women's offending or to the resources and treatment they may need to help reintegrate back into society or to avoid reoffending (Hudson, 1993; Naffine, 1995). As Mary Eaton (1986: 97) concludes in her seminal research study of a magistrate's court:

> Hillbury Court treats men and women equally, i.e. they receive similar sentences when they appear in similar circumstances. However, men and women rarely appear in similar circumstances – the differences in their recorded criminal involvements are as marked as the differences between the sexes in other areas of life. Formal equality within the strictly defined area of the court does not affect the substantial inequality of women and men who appear before the court.

Structural inequalities mean that as a group, women have, historically, always been poorer than men (occupying more menial jobs, combining periods of paid employment with periods of unpaid childcare, earning less during their working lives therefore having fewer savings and reduced pensions, and so on). Indeed, studies suggest that increases in women's prosecutions and imprisonment rates in Britain and elsewhere can be explained by a rise in specific crimes – almost all related to continuing and worsening levels of female poverty, including benefit fraud, prostitution, irregular migration and drug-related offences (Carlen, 1998; Pantazis, 1999; Hedderman, 2004; Lee, 2007a). Some men and women – for example, young black men, minority ethnic women, homosexuals and those belonging to minority faith groups – are also more likely to experience more forms of marginalization than others. It follows, therefore, that adopting legal safeguards and giving equal treatment to all men and women who appear before the court in similar circumstances may satisfy the court's procedural criteria of justice but this does not in itself achieve 'just' or effective outcomes.

Ethnicity

A majority of studies have consistently shown that black people (especially young black males) are over-represented throughout the criminal justice process, with proportionately many more being:

- stopped and searched (black people are about seven times more likely to be stopped and searched than whites according to Ministry of Justice, 2010);
- arrested by the police (Bucke, 1997; Home Office, 2005c);
- prosecuted in court (Home Office, 2005c; Phillips and Brown, 1998); and
- sentenced to prison once in Crown courts (Hood, 1992; Kalunta-Crumpton, 1999).

Whether these variations are due to any direct discrimination against minority groups in the criminal justice process (as both Hood's and Kalunta-Crumpton's sentencing studies have shown) or a combination of other factors (e.g. deprivation and class, urban living and ensuing patterns of offending, suspects entering not guilty pleas, or not showing appropriate signs of 'remorse') has been subject to intense debate. Quantitative research methods have been used to assess whether race or ethnicity has a separate or independent effect on decision-making over and above any other factors such as age, class, plea or area of residence (see, for example, Hudson's (1989) survey of sentencing decisions where she uncovers 'residual discrimination' against African and Caribbean males in more mundane offences). Yet, there are difficult methodological problems in attempting to isolate the variable of 'race' from other variables, meaning it is very problematic to accurately measure the extent of racial discrimination at particular stages of the criminal justice process (see Reiner, 1993). Nonetheless, enduring stereotypes related to the association of particular types of people with offending certainly influence decision-making throughout the criminal justice process. While adopting legal safeguards and ensuring procedural justice may have some impact on the worst excesses of 'institutionalized racism' within the criminal justice system, this does not address the underlying racist constructions of criminality or the associated exclusionary and intensive monitoring processes of some minority ethnic groups (Bosworth et al., 2008; Phillips and Bowling, 2012; and see Chapter 17).

Negotiated justice

A third approach to understanding the nature of criminal justice is to consider the actual ongoing negotiations and social interactions of the various people involved in the routine production of justice. In principle, the trial is the focal point of the ideology of democratic justice, and it is generally portrayed as making rational decisions within the overall values of the rule of law. The court is where the process of justice is not only carried out but also put on public display (for instance, all UK adult criminal courts have public galleries). But we should be cautious in accepting trial outcomes in terms of only their public transparency – there are elements in the management and organization of the courts and trials that directly contradict and undermine justice. As Uglow (2002) has argued,

> Offenders are processed and disposed of as efficiently as possible in terms of time and resources. Key performance indicators relate to such issues as cost per case, the time taken between first appearance in magistrates' court and committal or between committal and trial or the backlog of cases for a particular court . . . This leads to pressure to speed up cases and to the negotiation of outcome. The defendant's role can be reduced to passivity especially where there are on-going professional relationships between the defence and prosecution lawyers, the police, probation services, court administrators and judges. Thus there is a divergence between the official and articulated ideals of the courtroom and the organizational reality that exists behind them.

As suggested above, most cases processed through the criminal justice system are routinely resolved through a guilty plea. Yet, pleading guilty is not always a freely made decision. A number of classic sociological studies in 1960s and 1970s Britain and the United States have examined the interactional, informal and bureaucratic aspects of the production of a guilty plea (Bottoms and McClean, 1976; Skolnick, 1966; Baldwin and McConville, 1977; Carlen, 1976). A particularly contentious issue is the use of plea bargaining between prosecution and defence. In the US context, the widespread use of explicit 'pleas' or negotiations over the charge and sentence is seen to facilitate smooth functioning of the justice system because it means there is no risk of complete loss at trial for either side in the adversarial courtroom drama. However, such bargaining has been criticized for the pressure it places on innocent people to plead guilty and the fact that it penalizes those who exercise their constitutional right to trial. From a different perspective, some critics have also argued that plea bargaining allows offenders to escape appropriate punishment for their crimes. Although explicit plea bargaining over sentences with the judge is not permitted in England and Wales, some form of 'sentencing discount' does exist for an early guilty plea, and plea sometimes determines both the length and the type of sentence (Sanders and Young, 2007). In the context of negotiated justice, it is perhaps inevitable that some innocent people will plead guilty. According to a research study commissioned by the Royal Commission on Criminal Justice, over 10 per cent of those who pleaded guilty in the Crown Court claimed to be innocent (Zander and Henderson, 1993).

When a case is contested in court, studies conducted from a micro-sociological perspective have highlighted how the negotiation of justice is framed and judicial order maintained through the control of formal rules and symbolic boundaries in courtroom interaction. The use of a high level of ritual in the formal procedures of the court and the complex legal language and gestures by court professionals to 'cool out' defendants and to systematically deny them a speaking part, has been well documented (Cicourel, 1968; Parker *et al.*, 1989; Dell, 1971; Rock, 1993). Pat Carlen (1976), for example, has shown how control in court is achieved through manipulation of 'situational rules'. The court team – magistrates, judge, clerk of court, police, lawyers, probation officers – render defendants as 'dummy players' by ruling that any challenge he or she poses to the ritual, administration or legitimacy of the law is 'out of place, out of time, out of mind, or out of order'. All this reflects the imbalance between the power and resources available to the prosecutor/state as opposed to the individual accused (see Chapter 9). The very spatial organization of the court carries this powerful symbolism on: the elevated bench, private access to judge's chambers, the judge's costume and throne-like chair, the defendant in the dock, and the public at the back of the court who are allowed to observe but not to participate. Carlen also suggests that the organization of space is such as to impede communication, especially for those who are not part of the routine cast (including both the victim and the accused, as well as their families and supporters). Communication rules and distances in court are much greater than people normally use for disclosure of private or traumatic incidents, and, as already mentioned, communication is largely conducted and carefully managed by lawyers. Additionally, most talk in the courtroom involves either interrogation or monologue, both of which would be deemed extraordinary or even resented if they occurred in everyday conversation.

Of course, sociologists have long been interested in the regular everyday 'drama of interaction' and in the social rules that underpin this. In his seminal book, *The Presentation of Self in Everyday Life* (1959), Erving Goffman examines peoples' ongoing efforts to create specific impressions of themselves in the minds of others, especially through the use of 'performances' that utilize particular props, costumes and rituals to support their authenticity. In the courtroom setting, the dramatic and ritualistic elements of the spatial, presentational and linguistic conventions powerfully contribute to the sense of the authority of the court and towards establishing the authoritative version of the events to both the court itself and to the outside world. This enables the court to send a powerful signal to society that justice has been done, thereby maintaining

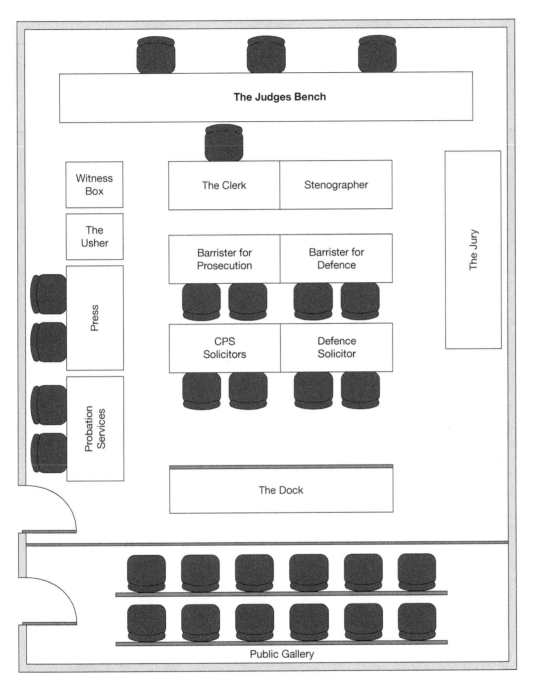

The Judges Bench

Witness Box

The Usher

Press

Probation Services

The Clerk

Stenographer

Barrister for Prosecution

Barrister for Defence

CPS Solicitors

Defence Solicitor

The Dock

The Jury

Public Gallery

Figure 16.2 Layout of and main actors in the Crown Court.

social order by making it less likely that the public would take things into their own hands in the form of, for example, vigilantism.

Stigma, recidivism and reintegration

The dramatic and authoritative symbolism of the courtroom also works to strip offenders of their dignity as a prelude to judicial punishment, and this has been thoroughly explicated and analysed by the sociologist Harold Garfinkel (1956a, 1956b). He wrote about the 'degradation ceremonies' through which an entire community formally stigmatizes an individual and destroys their former identity: 'Any communicative work between persons, whereby the public identity of an actor is transformed into something looked on as lower in the local scheme of social types, will be called a "status degradation ceremony".' The ceremonial order of the court proceedings represents one particular and very powerful form of 'status degradation ceremony' in the modern context. As Garfinkel suggested, the trial is a process of recasting the defendant away from their own identity and into a stereotyped and stigmatized social role (mugger, hooligan, drunk, vagrant). The trial becomes a degradation ceremony that reduces the defendant to a lower status. While, through this process, broader patterns of social authority and power are demonstrated to the offender and to wider society, it also has a powerful labelling effect.

John Braithwaite (1989), in his ground-breaking work into the effect of feelings of shame upon criminal offending and reoffending, draws on Garfinkel and labelling theory to show how court-based degradation ceremonies can create a criminal 'master status' which pushes offenders into deviant subcultures that, in turn, provide the conditions for reoffending (see Chapter 6). Through the state taking control of prosecution, excluding victims, and by conducting trials in legalistic and adversarial ways, Braithwaite also shows how the modern criminal justice and trial system has the effect of blinding offenders from the effects of their actions upon others. This, he argues, inhibits the development of feelings of shame which is an essential factor preventing offending. Braithwaite thus proposes an alternative system to the trial process called 'reintegrative shaming ceremonies' whereby offenders and their victims are brought together in non-legalistic mediated contact outside of the formalized court system. Here, the offence (but not the offender) is degraded and offenders come to see the adverse effect that their crime has had upon the victim, provoking feelings of shame and an apology. Following apology, the mediator encourages a gesture of forgiveness from the victim which effectively invites the offender back into the moral (and actual) community, inhibiting status degradation, secondary deviance and further offending (see Braithwaite and Mugford, 1994). Forgiveness also provides the foundation for both parties to come to an agreement on a form of restorative action that the offender should undertake in order to provide some redress for the offence (see Chapter 15).

Restorative forms of justice that aim to restore or repair the damage done by the offence (rather than modern punitive justice systems that predominately punish), and alternatives to court-based trial systems like reintegrative shaming ceremonies, have been adopted in the UK criminal justice process since the 1970s in piecemeal fashion – and have been widely used for white-collar criminals (see Braithwaite, 2003). More recently, under the Crime and Disorder Act 1998 and the Youth Justice and Criminal Evidence Act 1999, elements of restorative justice have became a more mainstream response to youth offending in the UK – at least for minor offenders and offences. Although not without its critics (see, for example, Haines and O'Mahony, 2006), evaluations of reintegrative shaming types of procedures for juvenile offenders generally show that victims experience greater satisfaction and feel less likely to be victimized again as compared to those whose cases are processed in mainstream courts, and that rates of offender recidivism are markedly reduced (Dignan, 2005). Despite such positive evidence, in a world where criminal justice professionals (particularly lawyers) have strong vested interests, where crime has become so highly politicized, and political parties compete with one another to be 'tough on crime', the use of alternatives to the mainstream criminal justice process remains partial and always fragile.

The futures of criminal justice

Some critics have argued that by the end of the twentieth century it was the criminal justice system itself that was put on trial. Although the criminal justice agencies in the United Kingdom have enjoyed an unprecedented period of growth in overall resources and powers, the official crime rate, up until 1995, had escalated to unparalleled levels, and:

> The sheer number of individuals entering and re-entering the system was threatening to paralyse the functioning of the courts . . . Spiralling rates of re-offending were increasing levels of victimization and the public's fear of crime and growing intolerance generated demands for more police officers, tougher policing strategies and harsher sentences, which in turn thrust even more people into the system . . . To cap it all, a series of high profile miscarriages of justice undermined public confidence in the ability of the criminal justice system to identify the guilty and protect the rights of the innocent.
>
> (McLaughlin and Muncie, 2000: 170)

Against this background of 'failure to deliver', some Home Office statements have even conceded, in classic Durkheimian fashion (Chapter 5), that a certain level of crime is normal and inevitable and that it is unrealistic to expect any set of policies to drastically reduce the crime rate (Young, 1992: 104). Globalization presents another set of challenges to criminal justice. Criminal justice systems around the world may be converging through the impact of the power and spread of neo-liberal economics, cultural interdependency, policy and technology transfer, and international human rights conventions (Garland, 2001b). Yet, as Janet Chan (2005: 342) has argued, the convergence of criminal justice policy (e.g. the dominance of situational crime prevention, risk-based sentencing, zero tolerance policing, or the privatization of prisons) is not always a positive development, 'whereby, for example, the "exporting" of inappropriate criminal justice policy from powerful nations to others is a controversial area'. At the same time, however, criminal justice systems remain highly sensitive to distinctive national cultures and politics, and are subject to localized difference, negotiation and resistance that inhibit the full-scale globalization of crime control systems (Newburn and Sparks, 2004). Yet, regardless of this, there is little doubt that contradictions and tensions in the criminal justice system in terms of its values, interests, stated aims and actual practices will continue long into the future.

Summary

1 Official statistics on crime do not indicate 'real' amounts of crime but rather they show how events are defined and processed by social control agents. The key stages of the criminal justice process include discovery of the offence by the victim, reporting to and recording by the police, charge, prosecution, conviction and sentence.

2 A number of institutions and decision-makers are involved in the key stages within the criminal justice process in England and Wales: the police, the Crown Prosecution Service, the judiciary and the Probation Service. Their decisions and activities at any one point in the criminal justice process have a cumulative effect at a later stage of the process.

3 Unsafe convictions and miscarriages of justice whereby the innocent are imprisoned are clear examples of cases in which the criminal justice process has gone wrong. Victims may also feel let down by the criminal justice process when it fails to prosecute and/or convict those who should be prosecuted and convicted.

4 There are at least three approaches to understanding the nature of criminal justice: by examining procedural safeguards (procedural justice), the substantive outcomes (substantive justice), and the negotiations and social interactions involved in the routine production of justice (negotiated justice).

5 There are some viable alternatives to the existing mainstream criminal justice process, some of which have made some inroads into the process in the UK, including various forms of restorative and reparative justice, and reintegrative shaming-based approaches.

Critical thinking questions

1 What are the key stages of the criminal justice process and what factors affect whether a case proceeds to the next stage or is filtered out of the criminal justice process? How can we ensure that the decisions taken at each stage are fair and just?

2 Examine how biases and stereotypes enter into the criminal justice process and consider how they contribute to constructing the official criminal population.

3 What are the relative advantages and disadvantages of adversarial and inquisitorial justice systems? Which system provides the most just and equitable form of justice and why?

4 Find out about the gender, age and ethnic composition of the lay magistracy in your local area (the Magistrates' Association website is a useful starting point). How does it compare with the national picture? Do you think that a more balanced lay magistracy would necessarily deliver better justice?

Further study

Braithwaite, J. (1989) *Crime, Shame and Reintegration*. Cambridge: Cambridge University Press. A brilliant and influential examination of modern criminal justice systems and their effect upon both victims and offenders which proposes a viable alternative to mainstream criminal justice.

Davies, M., Croall, H. and Tyrer, J. (2005) *An Introduction to the Criminal Justice System in England and Wales*, 3rd edn, Harlow: Longman. A very useful introductory text on the key components, policy and practice issues in the criminal justice system in England and Wales.

McBarnet, D. (1981) *Conviction: Law, the State and the Construction of Justice*, London: Macmillan. A pioneering socio-legal study of the routine construction of justice in court.

McConville, M. and Wilson, G. (2002) *The Handbook of the Criminal Justice Process*, Oxford: Oxford University Press.

Sanders, A., Young, R., and Burton, M. (2010) *Criminal Justice*, 4th edn, Oxford: Oxford University Press. Two accessible and useful texts which synthesize and review the key concepts, debates and controversies in criminal justice.

Useful websites

Home Office
http://www.homeoffice.gov.uk
The government ministerial office responsible for policing and related social control activities in England and Wales.

Ministry of Justice
http://www.justice.gov.uk
The government ministerial office responsible for key elements of the justice system including the courts and prisons in England and Wales.

Crown Prosecution Service
http://www.cps.gov.uk
Website of the organization that undertakes the prosecution of offenders on behalf of the government.

World Factbook of Criminal Systems
http://www.ojp.gov/bjs/abstract/wfcriminal justice.htm
This factbook provides narrative descriptions of the criminal justice systems of 45 countries around the world.

Criminal Justice System
http://www.criminaljusticeonline.org
This is another site that has useful information on the criminal justice process in England and Wales.

Crown Office and Procurator Fiscal Service

http://www.crownoffice.gov.uk/

This site has information on the Scottish criminal justice system plus a selection of other links for reference.

Criminal Justice System Northern Ireland

http://www.criminal justicesni.gov.uk/

A site on the criminal justice process in Northern Ireland.

chapter 17

Police and Policing

Key issues

- What is the difference between the police and policing?
- What are the roles and functions of the police?
- Whose interests do the police serve?
- Why do we need effective systems of police accountability?
- What is the future for policing?

Introduction

The **police** exercise their state-sanctioned authority over citizens and they regulate conflicts between them. This means that **policing** is inherently controversial and inevitably contested. It is a delicate social institution that requires effective mechanisms of accountability and a certain level of legitimacy in the eyes of the public whom it bears down upon. In this context, the police should be analysed in terms of 'what they do' and 'how they do it' but they should also be discussed critically by looking at 'who they do it for' and 'what they do but shouldn't'. This chapter will plot the history of policing, discuss the roles, cultures and functions of the police, look at mechanisms of accountability, and examine some recent changes in policing.

Historical origins and continuities

To understand the development of police and policing, it is helpful to distinguish between them. As Robert Reiner (2000: 1–2) argues:

> 'police' refers to a particular kind of social institution, while 'policing' implies a set of processes with specific social functions. 'Police' are not found in every society . . . 'Policing', however, is arguably a necessity in any social order, which may be carried out by a number of different processes and institutional arrangements. A state-organized specialist 'police' organization of the modern kind is only one example of 'policing'.

The development of the police is tied intimately to the development of modern state systems, and the very concept of 'police' has its roots in the notion of the good order and administration of the early city-states (Emsley, 1996b). In modern democracies, police rely upon consensus, legitimacy and legal authority in order to carry out their work effectively. Yet they are also empowered and licensed by the state to use force upon their publics. In authoritarian states, police are more explicitly arms of the state whereby they tend to exercise pure force rather than operate through consent and legitimacy. The past police states of Nazi Germany or the Soviet Union are extreme examples.

In modern democracies like Britain, the professional police officer that we are familiar with today developed from an initially highly variable and localized mosaic of 'policing'. In the fourteenth century, for example, towns and villages were generally policed by community-based systems of the 'watch', local constables and private 'thief-takers'. Constables and thief-takers would chase down lawbreakers for reward money. One infamous group of thief-takers, Jonathon Swift and his men, would frequently commit the crimes that they then solved for a reward, including the return of property stolen by themselves. Constables performed a wide array of broader policing functions in service of the monarch, such as collecting taxes, regulating alcohol production and weights and measures. They, like thief-takers, were consequently not at all popular with local communities that predominately lived poor subsistence lives and were unable to pay reward money (Emsley, 1996; Rawlings, 2008).

By the seventeenth century this haphazard and often corrupt system of policing began to weaken under calls for a more standardized and rational system of criminal justice (see Chapter 4). Yet even by the late eighteenth and early nineteenth centuries there was significant suspicion amongst the public about the formation of a state-based 'standing police force' – not least because of fears of Continental systems of police spies and police states. Nonetheless, the Bow Street Runners, a London detective agency, was formed in the 1720s, and, by the late eighteenth century, following a number of large-scale public riots, the 1792 Middlesex Justices Act established seven constabularies in London – each staffed by a magistrate and a number of constables and watch men. It was not however until the 1820s when Sir Robert Peel, a committed advocate of the benefits of a public police force, became Home Secretary and introduced the 1829 Metropolitan Police Act, that the 'new police' – the modern 'bobby' – began.

The 'new police' were to be highly visible, work under strict military-style discipline and bureaucracy, use only the minimum of force, and be responsible to the Home Secretary yet independent from direct government control. Combining this with recruiting most police officers from the working classes, Peel assumed would prevent the new police being seen as spies or direct arms of the state and, by being highly visible, their presence on the streets of the metropolis would prevent crime. However, with increased anxieties about fast-growing cities and slums full of deprived, anonymous and potentially 'dangerous classes', there was a gradual extension of the powers of the new police in order to increasingly regulate city life (Emsley, 1983; Petrow, 1994).

Not every section of society was affected by the new police in the same way. The police were often called upon to enforce a law that favoured one social group over another – for example, evicting tenants, enforcing masters' terms of employment, or maintaining order at the growing numbers of workers' demonstrations of the time. A variety of new legislative powers, by-laws and regulations designed to cope with the problems generated by the mass influx of the rural poor to the industrializing cities tended to direct police attention to particular social groups such as the poor and homeless, youths, beggars, Gypsies, travelling hawkers and prostitutes (Emsley, 2005). In effect, enforcing new statutes (e.g. over vagrancy or street trading) meant that police work increasingly impinged upon the lives of the poor – those Vic Gatrell et al. (1980: 335) describe as the '30 per cent or more at the base of the social pyramid'.

The introduction of street patrolling predictably led to an increase in the number of arrests for minor misdemeanours, especially for drunkenness and disorderly behaviour by men. Again, it was in those poor working-class districts that men were to be found indulging in customs and pastimes such as Sunday drinking, cockfighting and street gambling that offended middle-class Victorian perceptions of public morality and which the new police were directed to control (Storch, 1976). The working class thus became a section of society that John Lee (1981) has termed 'police property'.

The consequence was that the new police did not receive an easy welcome from a large section of the public and they would only gain acceptance over time. According to some historians, working-class hostility to the police continued well into the second half of the nineteenth century, as evidenced in, for example, the numbers of assaults on the police (Storch, 1975; Weinberger, 1981). Other accounts of policing in some working-class neighbourhoods related to the feud-like relationships between the police and young people in the inter-war years (Cohen, 1979b; Pearson, 1983). As Eugene McLaughlin (2007: 4) points out, a great deal of cultural and political work had to take place in order for 'this most "un-English" of institutions to be first of all sheltered from popular resentment and gradually transformed into one which could be celebrated as "a very English institution . . . a reassuring symbol of all being well and tranquil in the world"'.

During the 1950s public support for the police in Britain reached its highpoint (Reiner, 2010). The cosy image of the helpful and much admired English bobby was idealized in a BBC television series Dixon of Dock Green from this period. The 'Dixonian policing model' is still routinely evoked as a form of shorthand to define the traditional values of English policing, national unity, cultural cohesion, neighbourliness and law and order. Nevertheless, distrust of the police and allegations of abuse of discretionary police powers remained, and remain, in large sections of the population living at the base of the social pyramid.

Police use of excessive force, widespread 'stop and search' operations, excessive surveillance and apparently unnecessary armed raids, especially in Britain's black and minority ethnic communities, have continued to be controversial (see Bowling et al., 2008; Keith, 1993; Cashmore and McLaughlin, 1991; Thiel, 2009). Take, for example, police use of 'stop and search' powers. In 2009–10, black people were recorded as being seven times more likely to be stopped and searched than white people (Ministry of Justice, 2010: 34). Moreover, insensitive policing was seen to have played a pivotal role in triggering the urban riots that occurred in Britain in the early and mid-1980s (Scarman, 1981), and it was the fatal shooting by the police of Mark Duggan in Tottenham, London, that sparked the beginnings of the large-scale 'summer riots' in England in 2010. Preliminary results from one major study (Lewis *et al.*, 2011) show that police–community tensions was one key factor underlying the spread of rioting from Tottenham into the many other UK inner-city areas. The simultaneous 'over policed and under protected' (Macpherson, 1999: 312) nature of particular sections of British society has serious implications, especially against a background of the continuing revelations about police misconduct and miscarriages of justice.

Policing protest

In the nineteenth century, police powers had clashed with legitimate protest in conflicts over, for instance, workers' rights, pay and poverty, and sometimes in opposition to the police

Plate 17.1 Kettling at the G20 protests.

Source: Getty Images.

controlling crime

themselves (Emsley, 2005). Given that protests were highly moral, appealing to 'the common good' (e.g. defending communities or challenging unjust laws), the policing of public protest was – and still is –highly problematic.

P.A.J. Waddington (2000) describes how the policing of legitimate protest rests on a very delicate moral balance between upholding the legitimate right to protest and controlling the limits of protest. If legitimate protests are policed heavy-handedly, the police are brought into moral disrepute. Yet, in the late twentieth and early twenty-first centuries, police have been involved in a number of often violent confrontations with various trade union and social movements concerned with, for instance, jobs and workers' rights, the building of new motorways, export of live animals, and demonstrations against multinational capitalism and world poverty. Indeed, there are many examples of police in both authoritarian states and democracies using tear gas, pepper sprays, water cannons, plastic bullets and baton charges to disperse protesting crowds with a view to restoring a particular form of 'order'. All this highlights the important fact that 'Public order policing is irreducibly political; it is a highly visible representation between state and citizen' (Waddington, 2000: 171), and it raises sharply the question of whose order police maintain (see also Jefferson, 1990; McLaughlin, 2007).

The UK police have recently developed a tactic called 'kettling' to control order at public protests. Here, protestors are rendered immobile through being surrounded by and hemmed in by a wall of police officers (see Plate 17.1). These practices have come under question in terms of their legitimacy and legality. Her Majesty's Chief Inspectorate of the Constabulary (2009) has questioned the 'paramilitary tactics' of recent protest policing for undermining public trust in the police, and called for a fundamental overhaul of British protest policing. This was not least spurred on by the highly publicized death of Ian Tomlinson during anti-war protests at the G20 Summit in London in 2009 (see Box 17.1).

The proliferation of mobile telephones with visual recording devices and the huge expansion of mass media platforms on the Internet, means however that the police themselves are being increasingly watched. In one analysis, Greer and McLaughlin (2010) show how 'citizen journalists' using mobile phone filming at the G20 protests effectively challenged police activity to cover up the misconduct of some of their officers (see also Chapter 20). While public order policing has always rested on a fragile moral balance, in a world of hand-held video technology and mass access to media, it is being brought under increasing scrutiny.

Plate 17.2 A demonstration by hunger marchers is broken up by mounted London police, 13 November 1932.

Source: © Mary Evans Picture Library; *photo:* Achille Beltrame in *La Domenica del Corriere*.

Spooks and spies

One of Robert Peel's aims for the new police was that they would be highly visible and identifiable, and thus avoid being perceived as state spies. However, due to the rise in the nineteenth century of Irish Fenian (the forerunner to the IRA) terrorism, a secretive undercover policing unit, the Special Irish Branch of the Metropolitan Police, was established in 1883. The Special Branch, as they came to be known, style of undercover policing occurred not only in Britain; almost all Western democracies have both a uniformed and a secret police force (Bayley and Weisberg, 2009). Jean Paul Brodeur (1983) suggests that the Special Branch style of policing can be conceptualized as 'high policing', which differs from usual uniformed 'low policing' because it tackles political crimes such as terrorism and espionage that threaten the state and political order, as opposed to the street crimes investigated by 'low policing'. As political crimes can have devastating consequences, 'high policing' is concerned primarily with intelligence collection so that it is able to pre-empt and prevent potential devastation.

The UK Special Branch monitors political groups that threaten the state, mostly those it deems terrorist or extremist. To do this, the Special Branch operates in secret, infiltrating, spying on and subverting these groups. A graphic example of their modus operandi emerged in the media in 2011 when seven Special Branch officers were exposed infiltrating various political campaign groups as part of a unit called the Special Demonstration Squad. One of these officers, Mark Kennedy, had spent seven years undercover with an environmental group and, under his false identity, he had been an agent provocateur who had carried out crimes, been arrested and even testified in court. Two other undercover officers had sexual relations and fathered children with members of the infiltrated groups. Like the policing of public protest, these activities bring the political nature of policing into sharp focus. Since the 9/11 attacks in the USA, and the 7/7 bombings in the UK, there has been a large-scale increase in high policing activity (see Chapter 21). In the UK, this activity has been targeted mostly at British Muslim communities, leading some to claim that British Muslims have become a 'suspect community' effectively living in a police state (Pantazis and Pemberton, 2009).

Police roles and functions

Historically and in the contemporary context, the image of public police has been predominantly one of crime fighter. On this view, the primary police roles involve the prevention of crime, the detection of criminals and the preservation of order. The question of whether the police actually have an effect on crime is however a vexed one and not easily answered. There are major problems in interpreting the rise and fall of recorded crime rates (see chapters 3 and 16) but there is little evidence to suggest that any police strategy alone can reduce overall rates of crime (Audit Commission, 1993; Eck and Maguire, 2000).

Increasing visible patrols is a measure popular with the public but, unless this increase were to a level of saturation that many might find an uncomfortable intrusion on their lives, then the chances of the police being 'in the right place at the right time' would be somewhat slim. Indeed, one study estimated that a patrolling officer in London was likely to pass within 100 yards of a burglary in progress only once every eight years, and even then might not know that the offence was taking place and would be even less likely to be able to catch the perpetrator (Clarke and Hough, 1984: 6–7).

An alternative strategy to police patrol or response to calls from the public that is increasingly popular in the UK and USA is 'hot-spot' policing whereby police officers focus in on a single problem (e.g. drug dealing) in a single location. Although there is evidence that this may reduce crime in the immediate area, there is lingering concern that such intensive police efforts may merely work to displace crime to other locales. Targeted police operations appear to have only limited long-term impact on, for example, drug-dealing activities and drug availability, and some local drugs economies continue to flourish (Lupton et al., 2002; Edmunds et al., 1996; Jacobson, 1999). In addition, such concentrated police efforts cannot occur in all locations at all times, so their use will necessarily be limited.

The most prominent example of intensive 'hot-spot' policing in action is the so-called 'zero tolerance' strategy in New York City from the mid-1990s (see Box 17.2). The strategy is based on the principle that by clamping down on minor street offences and incivilities, more serious offences will be curtailed. This often translates into more intensive policing operations against visible crimes such as under-age smoking or drinking, obstruction by street traders, public urination, graffiti writing, and the arrest or moving on of beggars, prostitutes, pickpockets, fare dodgers, 'squeegee merchants', abusive drunks and litter louts for instance (Burke, 1998; Silverman, 1999). Many politicians and senior police officers have argued that the approach is a success, reducing rates of robbery and murder. Critics, however, question the precise reasons for any decline in crime rates and also the overall efficacy of the zero tolerance strategy. Indeed, there are question marks over the social and ethical costs involved in this moral 'street cleaning'

BOX 17.2 Zero tolerance policing in New York

The New York Police Department (NYPD) approach incorporated some of the ideas derived from Wilson and Kelling's (1982) 'Broken windows' theory, but it became associated with the term 'zero tolerance'. Zero tolerance policing (ZTP) conveyed a policy of tough enforcement on the street, constant police pressure with high visibility, vigorously tackling 'disorder', focusing on minor offences (e.g. fare dodging, begging, urinating in public places, graffiti), 'crime mapping', and targeting of 'hot spots' as well as hounding frequent offenders. Zero tolerance policing has been credited for reducing crime in New York, including serious and violent crime, improving quality of life and 'reclaiming' parts of the city (subway stations, parks and areas around public buildings). However, critics have argued that crime was already falling in New York before the introduction of ZTP and that crime fell in many other cities that did not propagate ZTP. In San Diego, using largely a community-oriented approach that was the antipathy of ZTP, crime also dropped. Zero tolerance and the notion of 'fixing broken windows' can lead to intolerance, exclusion and demonisation of out-groups. It has been argued that the assertiveness of ZTP could turn into police aggression, and there were examples of excess violence by the police. There was also a steep rise in citizen complaints about abuse of authority, discourtesy, use of obscene language, and other infractions that indicate a brazen force.

Source: Punch (2007: 17–20).

(see, for example, Duneier, 1999), and over whether it is ever possible to disentangle the effect of good police work from broader changes in the economic and social context (Bowling, 1999; Greene, 1999).

The detection or 'clear-up' rate (i.e. the proportion of cases in which a suspect is identified and charged) has been used by many as the standard indicator of police effectiveness in crime-fighting. In Britain, detection rates have been generally falling across almost all crime types, albeit at different rates. About one in four recorded crimes are ever 'cleared up' by the police. Clear-up rates also vary significantly according to the types and locations of offences. Those types of offence where there is a high likelihood of the victim being able to identify the offender (e.g. violence against the person), or because knowledge of the offence directly identifies the offender (e.g. possession of drugs), will inevitably have higher detection rates than others (e.g. burglary). In 2010–11, for example, detection rates varied from 13 per cent for burglaries, 21 per cent for robbery, 44 per cent for violent crimes, to 94 per cent for reported drug offences (Taylor and Chaplin, 2011).

In practice, most police work is mundane and not actually directly crime-related. Research consistently shows that a high proportion of police time is spent carrying out tasks that do not involve crime control – for example, calming disturbances, negotiating conflicts and responding to a wide range of emergencies from car crashes to finding lost children (see Audit Commission, 1993; Shapland and Hobbs, 1989). Indeed, classic studies of the police role in the 1960s and 1970s in the United States (Bittner, 1967; Cumming *et al.*, 1965) and in Britain (Banton, 1964;

controlling crime

Cain, 1973) point to most police work being service-based performing the role of a 24-hour 'social service' (Punch and Naylor, 1973).

In the contemporary context, the balance between the crime-fighting and the service roles of the police remains a highly contentious issue and subject to intense policy debate. The important point is that the police officer is not, and never has been, simply a law enforcement officer. As the first major sociological study of police in Britain, that by Michael Banton (1964), suggests, police officers might better be called 'peace officers'. Police most commonly resolve problems or disputes by forms of 'peacekeeping' intervention that do not rely on law enforcement: 'the most striking thing about patrol work is the high proportion of cases in which policemen [sic] do not enforce the law' (1964: 127).

Police culture

An understanding of how police officers see the world and their role in it is crucial to an analysis of what they do, how they do it, and the broader political ramifications of their work. The authority that the police exercise in compelling compliance from the public is underwritten by the fact that police officers, along with the military, are 'monopolists of force in civil society' (Bittner, 1974). Police work is distinguished from other work by its capacity to legally exercise coercive force. This has an important effect on police occupational culture and, consequently, on how police work is done.

Egon Bittner's (1970) early study of the police shows how having licence to use force means that police regularly impose power to effectively undertake their tasks. Out on the street, police have a large autonomy to do this, and such autonomy allows them to adapt to an array of tasks they are called upon to perform. This, however, allows malpractice to creep into police practice. Bittner thus uncovers a paradox in police work: although police are bound by professional codes, legal rules and bureaucracy, once on the street these codes are too inflexible to adapt to the plethora of police tasks. Officers thus rely on the informal rules of their occupational culture to get the job done.

'Cop culture' also evolves ways to manage other peculiarities of the job. In another early sociological study, Jerome Skolnick (1966: 44) argues that police occupational subculture develops in response to 'two principle variables, danger and authority, which should be interpreted in the light of a "constant" pressure to appear efficient'. And, in a more recent study of the Los Angeles Police Department, Steve Herbert (1997) graphically describes a murky world where every day the officers face danger and dishonesty in ambiguous conflict situations. As a consequence of this, the LAPD draw a stark line between good and evil and right and wrong, placing themselves on the side of good. Herbert argues that they espouse such a clear-cut morality precisely because of the moral ambiguities of their job and because they cannot actually be very effective in preventing crime.

It should be emphasized however that the police culture is neither monolithic nor unchanging. It varies according to the views of police leaders, department styles, the power structure of the community policed, different patterns and problems of the policing environments, and specific situations (see Westmarland, 2008). Some elements of the police occupational culture are shared by front-line officers and managers alike, although there is evidence that points to internal differences and tensions between 'street cops' with their sense of professionalism based on experience and grounded knowledge, and 'management cops' with a more bureaucratic and education-based notion of police professionalism (Ianni and Ianni, 1983; Holdaway, 1983).

Nevertheless, there are some general characteristics of the occupational culture that are common to the police in modern liberal democracies. In a summary of the literature, Robert Reiner (2000) suggests that cop culture is characterized by the following core features:

1   *Suspicion*: a product of the need to keep a look out for trouble and because some people continually lie to them. Police need to see through dishonesty to achieve their sense of mission and consequently suspicion becomes a strong element of their subculture.
2   *Isolation/solidarity*: police officers tend to mix mostly with other officers due to their strong subculture and unorthodox work hours that inhibit out-of-work interaction with non-police. Police also need to be able to rely on one another in the face of adversity and danger, and so they develop a strong solidarity between them.
3.   *Moral and political conservatism*: 80 per cent of UK police are politically conservative, which is tied into the problematic morality they live through.
4.   Old-fashioned *machismo*: police have an action centred, boozing culture akin to traditional working-class masculinity.
5.   *Pragmatism*: police do not have the time or resources to debate the philosophical detail of crime fighting, rather they need to make quick snap decisions on the spot, often looking toward short-term goals of getting through their shift.

This macho, moralizing, action-oriented culture is, Reiner argues, paradoxical, considering that most police work is 'boring, messy, petty, trivial and venal' (ibid.: 89). Much police work is not thus seen as 'real' police work by the police. Moreover, knowledge of how to do police work is viewed by officers as honed through practice at the 'sharp end' out on the streets (see Manning (1979) on the need to become a 'good practical copper'). Taken together, these features mean that officers hold strong views on which 'types' of people in which circumstances might mean trouble. These stereotypes emerge partly from the attitudes of wider society but are embellished through police experience of dealing with largely young, underprivileged men.

Given the ambiguous nature and vast array of circumstances of everyday police work, police discretion is inevitable and sometimes desirable. There is a need to make choices at every level about priorities; a need to interpret general legal rules in specific enforcement situations; a need to resolve the conflict between demands for high productivity and due process; and a low visibility of street-level policing from the point of view of managerial scrutiny. The problem is that police discretion may be exercised in discriminatory ways. A series of biases involving not only police stereotypes shaped by the occupational culture but also elements of the law, organizational deployment and managerial practices, cumulatively produce patterns of bias on lines of class, gender and ethnicity (Brogden *et al.*, 1988: 146–50; McConville *et al.*, 1991), filling the criminal justice system with some social groups and not others (see Chapter 16). Critics have argued that the enduring stereotypes embedded in the occupational culture have also resulted in discrimination within the police – against black police officers (Holdaway, 1996;

Holdaway and Barron, 1997), female officers (Halford, 1993; Anderson *et al.*, 1993; Martin, 1996) and gay or lesbian officers (Burke, 1993).

The extent to which police culture and practices can be altered is debatable, and attempts at reform have led to rather mixed results in Britain and elsewhere (Foster, 1989; Skolnick and Bayley, 1986; Chan, 1997; Crank, 2004; Foster *et al.*, 2005). Others have highlighted the need to consider the changing dynamics of occupational socialization and the ways in which 'each generation of officers both re-enacts police culture and renews it at the same time' (McLaughlin, 2007: 57).

None of this is to suggest a complete correspondence between police attitudes and behaviour. As Reiner (2010) points out, a number of observational studies of police work have shown that officers may talk tough and express class and race stereotypes but regularly fail to enact in practice the attitudes they have articulated in the canteen or in interviews. Indeed, an important distinction has been made between 'cop culture' – the orientations implied and expressed by officers in the course of their work – and 'canteen culture' – the values and beliefs exhibited in off-duty socializing (see Waddington, 1999). In other words, just like all of us, what the police say is not necessarily what they do. Nonetheless, stereotypes and tacit assumptions about particular types of offenders undoubtedly influence police activity.

BOX 17.3 The Stephen Lawrence murder and the Macpherson Inquiry in Britain

On 22 April 1993, Stephen Lawrence, a young black teenager, was murdered in an unprovoked attack carried out by white assailants. The police investigation into his death was grossly inadequate and the racist nature of the attack given little attention. A long campaign by Stephen's family and supporters called for an official inquiry into the police handling of the case, failure to follow up important information available at the start of the investigation, and lack of success in providing evidence that could lead to the prosecution of identified suspects. The call for an inquiry was resisted by the Metropolitan Police and rejected by Conservative Home Secretaries. In 1998 the new Home Secretary, Jack Straw, asked Sir William Macpherson, a former High Court judge, to chair an official inquiry into the case. Sir William examined three specific allegations against the police: that they were incompetent, racist and corrupt. Macpherson (1999) did not find evidence of corruption but firmly concluded that the police investigation had been 'marred by a combination of professional incompetence, institutional racism, and a failure of leadership by senior officers'. Individuals had failed, but so had the system; and the micro-processes of conduct in the Lawrence case exposed the institutionalized shortcomings of the Metropolitan Police.

Naturally, comparison was made with the report prepared by Lord Scarman into the riots in 1981, which had found evidence of racism within the police and made important recommendations concerning police–community relations and the need for racism awareness training for the police. Macpherson's reminder of the intervening lack of progress in improving police recruitment of minorities and changing police culture has been disturbing. Perhaps more significantly, he went further than Scarman and argued that racism was a problem that could be viewed as pervasive throughout the Metropolitan Police (and, by implication, throughout the police service nationally). The report referred to the idea of institutional racism to describe this state of affairs, defining it in the following way:

> The collective failure of an organization to provide an appropriate and professional service to people because of their colour, culture or ethnic origin. It can be seen or detected in processes, attitudes and behaviour which amount to discrimination through unwitting prejudice, ignorance, thoughtlessness and racist stereotyping which disadvantage minority ethnic people. ... Often this arises out of uncritical self-understanding born out of an inflexible police ethos of the 'traditional' way of doing things. Furthermore such attributes can thrive in a tightly knit community, so that there can be a collective failure to detect and to outlaw this breed of racism.
>
> (Macpherson Report, 1999: para. 6.34)

Police accountability

What can be done to ensure that the police do the job required of them in an efficient and equitable manner? This in essence is the meaning of **police accountability**. To whom are the police accountable, and do mechanisms set up to control police actions actually work? There are four main models of rendering police accountable for their actions: legal, political, public and managerial accountability.

Legal accountability

The law provides control over police actions by laying down particular limits to police powers and how they can be exercised, although, as suggested above, out on the streets the law tends to be used as a flexible resource rather than a concrete guide to policing. In Britain the landmark Police and Criminal Evidence Act 1984 (PACE) gave new powers to the police but at the same time incorporated more controls over their use. These include requirements to tell suspects why they were being arrested or stopped and searched, and to record the incident (see Box 17.4 on PACE). However, critics argue that this form of accountability is indirect, retrospective and limited (Lustgarten, 1986; Brogden et al., 1988; McLaughlin, 1994; Macpherson, 1999; Scarman, 1981). Indeed, the continuing police misconduct and the miscarriages of justice that have taken place since the implementation of PACE (see Chapter 16) provide a clear reminder of the limited effectiveness of legal control of police actions.

BOX 17.4 The 1984 Police and Criminal Evidence Act (PACE)

The 1984 Police and Criminal Evidence Act (PACE) sets out the powers of the police and the procedures they must follow in relation to investigation of offences, arrest and detention.

- ◼ It aims to regulate police practices by balancing police powers with safeguards for suspects.
- ◼ It originates in the report of the 1981 Royal Commission on Criminal Procedure, which formalized various existing powers as a general power 'to stop and search people or vehicles' where an officer has reasonable grounds for suspecting possession of stolen or prohibited items.
- ◼ It introduces new safeguards regarding the questioning of suspects: the requirement to tape-record the interview and to have a complete account of the entire interview.
- ◼ It allows the suspect the right to have a solicitor present and to say nothing to the police. This measure helps protect against self-incrimination and, coupled with audio (and possibly in the future video) recording, safeguards against the police seeking false confessions.

Since its introduction PACE has however regularly come under pressure from competing legislation and political interference. For example, the Criminal Justice and Public Order Act 1994 to some degree curtails the right to silence, and Section 44 of the Terrorism Act 2000 nullified 'reasonable suspicion' for stops and searches in areas deemed at risk of terrorist attack or as producing terrorists.

Political and public accountability

Given the selective nature of police work (i.e. responding to a near-infinite amount of crime with finite resources), police choices about which laws to uphold, against whom, and by what means are inevitably political decisions (Brogden *et al.*, 1988: 161). Under the model of political accountability, control over police operations is to be taken by political institutions in a democracy 'on behalf of the people'. The Police Act 1964 established a 'tripartite' structure of control in England and Wales (with the exception of London, where the Metropolitan Police Authority was not established until 1999), comprising the chief constable, the Home Office and the Police Authority. The precise relationship between Police Authority, chief constable and the Home Office has been subject to considerable debate (Jefferson and Grimshaw, 1984; Reiner and Spencer, 1993; Jones and Newburn, 1996), and, in practice, most police authorities were less than equal partners with their chief constables, unable to exert effective control over policing policies. Partly as a consequence, in 2012, Police Authorities were replaced by Police and Crime Commissioners (PCCs) elected by and directly responsible to the public and who have the power to appoint and dismiss chief constables. Here, political accountability has shifted to a more direct form of public accountability. However, the very low turnout by the public to vote for PCCs (fewer than 15 per cent of the public voted) indicates that PCCs are likely to be accountable to only a small proportion of their publics rather than the public as a whole.

Managerial accountability

Finally, since the 1980s, government has been at the forefront in pressing for a fundamental shake-up of the police working practices, managerial structures and processes. Government set national policing objectives and quantifiable performance indicators to facilitate inter-force comparisons, explicit costing of activities, adaptation to a competitive environment characterized by market relations, service contracts and agency status, as well as standardizing recruitment, equipment and training (Savage et al., 2000: 26–30; McLaughlin and Muncie, 2000; McLaughlin and Murji, 2001).

The police have also been subject to inspection and regulation via a number of ever-growing quasi government bodies ('quangos') including a revamped Her Majesty's Inspectorate of Constabulary (HMIC), the Audit Commission, a 'Best Value' rolling audit that applies to all public services, the National Policing Plan, the National Intelligence Model, and the (now defunct) National Policing Improvement Agency. Under a broader trend of managerialism in all public services, the police are compelled to rationalize the purpose and scope of their activities, to provide detailed information about the costs, resource use and evidence of police effectiveness, and to be responsive to market conditions. All of this has placed police work under the spotlight as never before and, since the global recession in 2007 and ensuing cuts in public spending, cost effectiveness has come under ever-increasing scrutiny.

In addition to these accountability mechanisms there are also special mechanisms set up to deal with police abuse of power. The Police Complaints Authority (PCA) was set up in Britain in 1985 and involved a degree of external oversight in the handling of police complaints but was seen by many complainants as an ineffective and compromised body (Maguire and Corbett, 1991). As Sanders and Young (2002: 1065) argued, many people with grievances are deterred from activating the formal complaints procedure and instead prosecute or sue the police. These civil claims increased in number throughout the 1980s and 1990s, in some cases involving the award of significant punitive damages against the police. The PCA gave way to an Independent Police Complaints Commission (IPCC) under the Police Reform Act 2002. Although most complaints continue to be dealt with by the police, the IPCC, staffed by civilians, has the power to directly investigate or supervise complaints which are more serious or are considered to involve issues of public confidence (e.g. deaths in police custody, serious corruption, miscarriages of justice, racist conduct) (see McLaughlin, 2007: 175–9). The IPCC has come under much criticism however. For example, in 2008, 100 lawyers resigned from the IPCC advisory committee in protest of their disillusionment with the commission.

Police deviance and criminality

There is a long history of police deviance and malpractice in Britain and elsewhere (Mollen Commission, 1994; Sherman, 1974; Punch, 1985; Hinton and Newburn, 2009). As Maurice

Punch (2003: 171–2) argues, many of the cases that have been exposed impinge on fundamental abuses of the rule of law, due process and human rights:

> In Spain there was a secret unit (GAL) that carried out the murders of ETA members (i.e., Basque separatists) associated with terrorism. The former Minister of the Interior and a number of police officers have been jailed in relation to this clandestine policy . . . In South Africa testimony before the 'Truth Commission' revealed close cooperation between the police and the underworld in attacks on ANC (African National Congress) members during the period of the apartheid regime (Truth and Reconciliation Committee 1999). . . . In New York the Mollen Commission (1994) revealed that corruption and violence seemed to go together. Suspects were 'tuned up' (severely beaten) by officers. Some police officers were closely involved with drug dealers, had themselves become drug users and were prepared to do dirty work for the dealers (including 'riding shotgun' for them and even committing murders).

In Britain, research and official inquiries have found evidence of a range of corrupt activities in police work, including: opportunistic theft; acceptance of bribes to lie on oath; providing tip-offs to criminal associates; destroying evidence; planting of drugs or stolen property on individuals; illegal searches; involvement in violence; participation by police officers in drug dealing, and protection of major drug operations (see Newburn, 1999). More recently, the Leveson Inquiry into press standards (see Chapter 20) investigated a number of police officers for phone hacking and selling confidential information to the tabloid press. Most officers facing criminal or disciplinary procedures tend to be from the lower ranks but there have also been cases involving some senior officers (Her Majesty's Inspector of Constabulary, 1999).

In 1998 the then Commissioner of the Metropolitan Police, Sir Paul Condon, acknowledged that there may have been up to 250 corrupt police officers serving in his force at this time, suggesting that an unknown number of criminal investigations may have been seriously compromised. In response, a special squad of anti-corruption investigators, including accountants and private surveillance experts, was established to target officers believed to be implicated not only in accepting bribes but also in offences that included planning and carrying out armed robberies, large-scale drug dealing, and violence against the public. Such a high-profile response to police corruption is reminiscent of the campaign of Sir Robert Mark, the reforming chief of the Metropolitan Police in the 1970s, who was charged by government with rooting out corruption, especially in specialized units such as the Obscene Publications Squad and the Drugs Squad.

Why does police misconduct matter? Police deviance often arouses in the public a sense of disillusionment and betrayal. After all, citizens expect public officials to be impartial, trustworthy and dependable. This is particularly true of the police, who enforce many laws at their own discretion, and who have the power to use legitimate force and deprive people of their freedom. Police deviance therefore undermines public confidence in the police, reducing the legitimacy of their authority. This is a serious criminological issue because lack of police legitimacy, due to both practice (what they do) and process (how they do it), has been shown to make it less likely that people will cooperate with the police or follow the law (Tyler, 1990).

In some cases, police misconduct has also led to the imprisonment of innocent people while the guilty remain unpunished. Indeed, public confidence in the police has been damaged by continuing revelations about their involvement in the suppression of evidence, leading to wrongful convictions and gross miscarriages of justice, as well as involvement of some officers in routine rule-bending in order to secure convictions (see Reiner, 2010). In the 1980s for example, the now-disbanded entire Regional Crime Squad of the West Midlands Police in Britain was found to have fabricated evidence, physically and psychologically abused suspects, and written false criminal confessions (Walker and Starmer, 1999; and see Chapter 16).

Part of the problem is that police association with lawbreakers (e.g. informants) and contact with sources of temptation (such as large sums of money, especially in drug cases) are in fact intrinsic to policing. Indeed, police rule-bending and rule-breaking can be seen not only as a problem of the deviant cop slipping into bad ways (i.e. the 'rotten apple' metaphor), but perhaps as an indication of systemic failures (the alternative metaphor of 'rotten orchards') (Punch, 2003). Such failures are inextricably related to the nature of police organizations (e.g. the low visibility of police work), the character of occupational culture (internal solidarity, rule-bending, 'cutting corners'), and the particular opportunities and pressure for results presented by the environment that is policed – particularly in high-profile cases. The false conviction of Barry George in 2001 for the murder of the British TV presenter Jill Dando, can be seen as one such high profile case that produced an unsafe conviction. George was later released on appeal following seven years' imprisonment.

Changes and futures of policing

The uniformed police officer on patrol and responding to calls from the public has a remarkable consistency in modern British history. Yet, at the same time, both the police and the broader balance of policing is constantly altering and adapting in response to changing social conditions, technologies and political philosophies. This chapter has been mostly concerned with the public police but, as the history of policing demonstrates, the idea that the 'public police' are the natural and only holders of certain powers and responsibilities relating to crime is a recent one. In fact, the notion of a 'public monopoly' over policing is and always has been a fiction (Garland, 1996; Jones and Newburn, 2002: 133; Zedner, 2005). The public 'police' should not be assumed to be the providers of everything that might be described as 'policing'.

Privatization and pluralization

Since the 1960s and 1970s there has been a growing input of private security in policing (South, 1988; Hobbs *et al.*, 2003). The history of private provision is, of course, much longer, going back to private associations and patrols in the nineteenth century, and continuing through the establishment of private guard companies before the Second World War. Yet, in more recent decades, trends in political ideology have encouraged the increasing use of the private sector and the 'downsizing' of non-essential staff in the public sector, thereby replacing many formally in-house staff by contracted security. Patrols of public spaces and use of security companies to escort and guard prisoners, for instance, have replaced jobs previously undertaken by police or prison officers.

The policing of public but privately owned space by private security – the 'mass private property' of shopping malls and 'megaplexes' (Shearing and Stenning, 1987) – has also changed the street-level face of policing. To some commentators, this 'rebirth of private policing', where order maintenance functions shift from state agencies to the 'free market' supplied by security firms, has fundamentally changed our conceptions of policing as a state-centred activity (Sheptycki, 1995).

To some critics, the privatization of policing institutions and processes indicates that security itself has become commoditized – bought and sold in the marketplace like any other commodity (Spitzer, 1987). One problem is that the consumption of that commodity (e.g. in the form of bolts, alarms, electronic surveillance and street patrols) may not produce a corresponding feeling of security. Instead, the opposite may happen: 'the more we enter into relationships to obtain the security commodity, the more insecure we feel' (Spitzer, 1987: 50). Furthermore, there is the problem of a highly inequitable system of security in which the rich can buy protection from private police and retreat behind 'gated' enclaves (see Davis, 1992, on Los Angeles), while the poor cannot afford this protection and may tend to be policed rather than protected (Bayley, 1994).

The expansion of private security has led to the development of a transnational crime control industry of some significance. As Button (2002: 25) notes, there is now a large global security market containing some very sizeable companies that operate on an international basis (for example Group 4 Falck, Securitas, Securicor and Wackenhut). Group 4 Falck, for instance, in 2011 operated in 125 countries, had a £7.5 billion turnover, and employed 657,000 staff worldwide, providing services from guarding and the management of prisons to the provision of ambulance and firefighting services.

In line with these changes, Ian Loader (2000; see also Walker, 1999) has offered a classification of the contemporary landscape of the plurality of policing:

■ policing by government – Home Office police forces and agencies including the National Crime Squad;
■ policing through government – services supplied by contractors (private security) but on behalf of government;
■ policing above government – transnational developments in cooperation, intelligence-sharing and strategy, such as Europol and Interpol;
■ policing below government – officially endorsed activities such as communities engaged in Neighbourhood Watch, as well as officially discouraged vigilantes and other extra-legal 'popular justice' groups.

Managerialism and risk

Developments in the New Public Management of state services has meant that the police are expected to achieve performance targets and have had to reorient their culture around an explicit mission of service delivery under an ethos of consumerism that mimics the private sector. This is tied up with the fact that we now live in a society obsessed with calculation and the prediction of risk (Beck, 1992; Garland, 2003), and because the police have become a key element in the risk-reduction matrix (Feeley and Simon, 1994).

To reduce crime risks, the police must act pre-emptively, and, to do this, 'knowledge work' has become essential. Knowledge about offenders and offences is used to prevent potential crime risks from occurring, rather than the more traditional police action of responding to crimes after they have been committed. Pre-emptive policing of this kind can be seen in traditional 'high policing' activities; in the cases of hot-spot and zero tolerance policing described above; and, in Britain, with the increasing dominance of 'Intelligence-led' (ILP) and 'Problem Oriented' (POP) policing models. In both models, the police attempt to prevent the most visible and worrying crimes by identifying particular areas, offenders and/or victims, and then putting situational controls in place (street lighting, increased patrol, CCTV, locks and bolts) (see Tilly, 2008; and Chapter 8). The ethos of ILP and POP is a plural approach whereby the police work in partnership with a raft of other agencies in order to prevent crime, including local councils, schools, neighbourhood communities, social workers and health services (see Maguire and John, 2006).

In the Canadian context, Ericson and Haggerty (1997) argue that the police have become 'knowledge brokers' in a 'risk society'. Police now process information into a number of 'systems' for a range of commercial and government agencies and community organizations to act upon, rather than only for criminal prosecution and punishment. The consequence is that the new 'entrepreneurial police' may increasingly take on

> the role of (a) accrediting and managing a consumer-driven 'mixed economy' of security and policing services; (b) developing specialist 'products' to 'trade' on the national and international security market; (c) professionalizing core competencies in criminal investigation, prosecution and forensics; and/or (d) co-coordinating confidential information flows between a range of private and public institutions.
>
> (McLaughlin, 2007: 97)

This emphasis on police knowledge work is also central in the development and practice of transnational policing. For instance, the main tasks of Europol (the European police force) and Interpol (the International police force) include collecting and analysing intelligence, preparing situation reports and crime analyses, and maintaining a central database for various crime categories (Sheptycki, 1998; Bowling, 2009). These changes in the nature of police work have altered police officers' experiences and thus led to alterations in their cultures. James Sheptycki (1998) argues that as many aspects of police work become more technical and office-based, the cultures of these officers differ sharply from those out on the street. Indeed, in terms of the increasing trend towards pre-emptive knowledge work, Sheptycki points to the possibility of a data-mining cop-culture in which ever-increasing surveillance becomes a standard aspect of their occupational orientation. In this context, the expanding surveillance capacity of the transnational 'high policing' enterprise in the name of a global 'war' on drugs and terrorism is also a concern. Moreover, a number of criminologists have asked to whom transnational policing agencies are accountable when they operate often in secret, above any single government, and outside of public control (see Loader, 2002; Bowling, 2009).

Despite these shifts in the logic, philosophy and practice of British policing in particular and Western democratic policing in general, there has in the UK and USA, been a return to the Peelian policing vision of policing in the form of community or neighbourhood policing. In 2008 the

Neighbourhood Policing Programme (NPP) was implemented across the whole of Britain. Neighbourhood policing teams, composed of police officers and Police Community Support Officers (PCSOs), regularly patrol, on foot or bicycle, small local beats. PCSOs wear police-like uniforms but do not have the power of arrest. The philosophy of the NPP is that by being in the community on a daily basis the teams are seen by and get to know local community members and respond to their most worrying crime concerns by working with the communities to reduce crime and thereby bring about a sense of community 'reassurance'. In the spirit of Peel, neighbourhood police also aim to prevent crime by simply being visible. Research has shown however that neighbourhood policing has, at best, only very mild effects on crime itself, but it does appear to reduce fear of crime and increase public support for the police (Skogan and Steiner, 2004; Quinton and Morris, 2008).

Policing and the police in democratic nations has expanded, pluralized and altered its practices, and sometimes reinvented older ones. Developing from a patchwork of various policing agents and agencies in the nineteenth century, policing became increasingly standardized under the control of a centralized state. Since the 1970s, however, policing has, to some degree, shifted back towards a more pluralized and mosaic set of institutions. Yet, no matter how the futures for policing in the twenty-first century map out, the issue of police powers, accountability, and the control of public police and alternative forms of policing will remain high on the criminological agenda.

Summary

1   The police are distinguished from other public services by their specific capacity to exercise legitimate coercive force. Notwithstanding the popular image of the police as crime fighters and their role in preventing crime, detecting criminals and maintaining order, a great deal of everyday police work is not crime related.

2   Historically and in the contemporary context, a series of biases involving the social functions of police, elements of the law, police occupational culture and organizational deployment have produced patterns of bias in police work on lines of class, gender and ethnicity.

3   Police accountability matters, because police work is about the exercise of authority and the regulation of conflicts in society, which is highly controversial and contested. There are four models of rendering police accountable for their actions: legal, political, public and managerial accountability.

4   Police rule-bending and rule-breaking can be seen not only as a problem of individual deviance but also as an indication of systemic organizational and cultural patterns. Police deviance is related to the nature of police organizations, the character of occupational culture, and the particular opportunities and pressure presented by the environment that is policed.

5   Contemporary policing is also carried out by a variety of individuals, groups and techniques.

Critical thinking questions

1 Robert Peel's vision for modern policing was one in which the police commanded authority through consent. Do the police today actually have this kind of consent and authority? If not, what might be the consequences?
2 'Bad apples' or 'rotten barrels'? Discuss in relation to police deviance.
3 What might be the drawbacks of an increasingly pre-emptive and forward-looking police force?

Further study

Banton, M. (1964) *The Policeman in the Community*, London: Tavistock. A pioneering sociological study of the police based on an analysis of field diaries of a sample of Scottish police officers, observation, and interviews (both in Britain and in the USA).

Emsley, C. (2010) *The Great British Bobby: A History of British Policing from 1829 to the Present*, London: Quercus. A very accessible introduction to the history of the 'new police' and the changing social and political contexts in England from the eighteenth century to the present.

Reiner, R. (2010) *The Politics of the Police*, 4th edn, Oxford: Oxford University Press. An excellent text covering the history of the police, the sociology of policing, and the law and politics of the police in the UK.

McLaughlin, E. (2007) *The New Policing*, London: Sage. A stimulating text on the contemporary developments and key debates in policing, security and crime control in the UK and USA.

Newburn, T. (ed.) (2008) *Handbook of Policing*, Cullompton: Willan; and

Newburn, T. (ed.) (2005) *Policing: Key Readings*, Cullompton: Willan. Two comprehensive collections of classic and contemporary readings that examine the issues, debates and recent transformations in many key areas of the police and policing.

Useful websites

UK Police Service
http://www.homeoffice.gov.uk/police/
This site provides links to official police forces – both regional and non-regional – and related organizations.

Police Complaints Authority
http://www.pca.gov.uk/
The PCA is an independent body set up by the government to oversee public complaints against police officers in England and Wales, plus the National Crime Squad, National Criminal Intelligence Service, British Transport, Ministry of Defence, Port of Liverpool, Port of Tilbury, Royal Parks and UKAEA police.

State Watch
http://www.statewatch.org/
A non-profit-making voluntary group founded in 1991; the site provides useful police policy documentation and investigative case studies in Europe.

chapter 18

Prisons and Imprisonment

Key issues

■ What are the international differences in rates and types of imprisonment?

■ Why has incarceration become the dominant response to crime?

■ Is the prison system in crisis?

■ What are the causes of prison unrest?

Introduction

Imprisonment provokes profound questions of justice to the extent that the use of penal institutions provides a stark barometer of the condition of democracy in any society. This point has long been recognized, for as de Tocqueville observed in the 1830s while 'the United States gives the example of the most extended liberty, the prisons of that same country offer the spectacle of the most complete despotism' (Garland, 1990: 11). Prisons continue to be the most controversial institutions in modern penal systems and occupy a central place in popular sentiment and political rhetoric on punishment, even though in no jurisdiction in the world are the majority of convicted offenders actually sent to prison (Sparks, 2002: 202). Imprisonment is a social practice that generates deep-seated disputes, and there is considerable consensus that the penal system in England and Wales has been in a state of ever-deepening crisis since the 1960s.

Whilst few informed commentators would deny that the penal system has serious, if not irreversible, problems, perhaps the key question is: How is it able to maintain a semblance of order for most of the time in the face of grave and often intractable difficulties? Instead it makes more sense to view the penal 'crisis' as an enduring feature of the last few decades, which is composed of several interweaving components that compromise not only the ability of the state to maintain order but also challenge moral sensibilities on what the purposes of imprisonment might, or ought to, be. In other words, the severe problems in prisons that are the subject of this chapter are as much moral and philosophical matters as practical and material ones.

Comparing penal systems

The penal crisis, at a very basic level, can be regarded as simply too many offenders and too few prison places, which has given rise to overcrowding, understaffing, decrepit conditions and poor security. Yet a prison sentence continues to be the harshest penalty available to the courts of England and Wales. On 2 November 2012 some 85,450 prisoners were held in 138 UK prisons, while in 1992–93 the average prison population was 44,628 (Prison Reform Trust, 2012: 4). Over two decades the UK prison population has almost doubled. This steep rise was ostensibly caused by a combination of new indeterminate sentences for public protection (IPP), the lengthening of sentences, and increasing breach of licence proceedings by those 'on licence, leading to their recall to prison' (Ministry of Justice, 2012a: 5). All of this stands in stark contrast to the situation in the immediate post-war era. In 1946 there were only about 40 UK prisons, approximately 15,000 prisoners, and around 2,000 staff (Morgan, 2002: 1117), at which point there began a steady rise followed by the dramatic increase in the mid-1990s (see Figure 18.2).

The reasons for this striking increase are complex and even though conclusions drawn from international comparisons should always be treated with caution, it is clear that England and Wales consistently uses imprisonment to a greater extent than practically every country in Western Europe. For instance, in 2012, 153 persons were incarcerated per 100,000 population in England and Wales, compared to 102 in France, and 71 in Norway (International Centre for Prison Studies, 2012). Such crude comparisons also indicate that England and Wales lie some way behind the global leaders in imprisonment – Russia, the USA, China and South Africa – as well as most of the countries in Eastern Europe (see South and Weiss, 1998, and Cavadino and Dignan, 2005 for further comparative analyses of penal systems).

There are more than 10.1 million people held in prisons throughout the world. Yet almost half are found in just three countries – the USA (2.29 million), China (1.65 million plus an unknown number of pre-trial detainees and prisoners in 'administrative detention') and Russia (0.81 million), while the numbers are growing across all five continents (Walmsley, 2011: 1). As commentators have noted it is truly striking how three countries at the extreme ends of cold-war politics, with 'such dramatically different histories, cultures and patterns of crime, should hold, as it were, gold, silver and bronze positions in the world league table of numbers of prisoners' (King, 2007: 98).

In this chapter we will be primarily concerned with documenting the problems to be found in the English and Welsh prison system. Scotland and Northern Ireland each have their own separate systems, though much of what we discuss extends beyond national boundaries. In order to appreciate the problems of the present it is vital that the concerns of the past are first outlined, as these issues continue to shape contemporary penal systems.

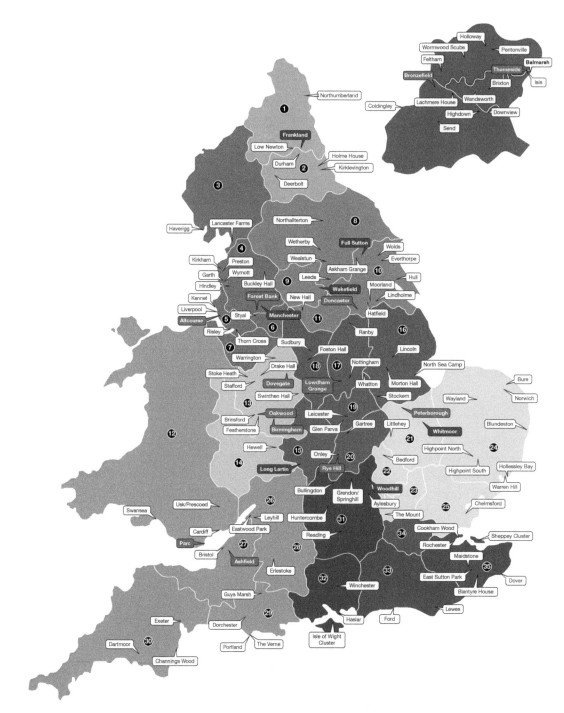

Figure 18.1 Probations and prisons map.

Source: National Offender Management Service: http://www.justice.gov.uk/downloads/contacts/hmps/prison-finder/prisons-map.pdf

the criminological imagination

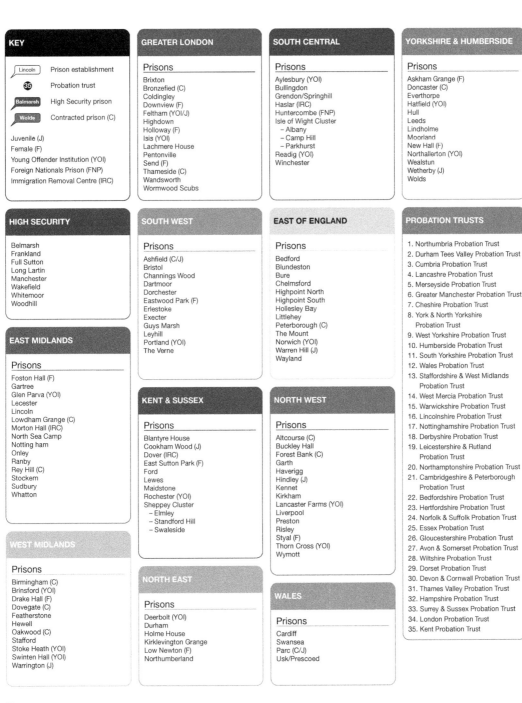

KEY

Lincoln	Prison establishment
35	Probation trust
Belmarsh	High Security prison
Wolds	Contracted prison (C)

Juvenile (J)
Female (F)
Young Offender Institution (YOI)
Foreign Nationals Prison (FNP)
Immigration Removal Centre (IRC)

GREATER LONDON

Prisons

Brixton
Bronzefied (C)
Coldingley
Downview (F)
Feltham (YOI/J)
Highdown
Holloway (F)
Isis (YOI)
Lachmere House
Pentonville
Send (F)
Thameside (C)
Wandsworth
Wormwood Scubs

SOUTH CENTRAL

Prisons

Aylesbury (YOI)
Bullingdon
Grendon/Springhill
Haslar (IRC)
Huntercombe (FNP)
Isle of Wight Cluster
 – Albany
 – Camp Hill
 – Parkhurst
Readig (YOI)
Winchester

YORKSHIRE & HUMBERSIDE

Prisons

Askham Grange (F)
Doncaster (C)
Everthorpe
Hatfield (YOI)
Hull
Leeds
Lindholme
Moorland
New Hall (F)
Northallerton (YOI)
Wealstun
Wetherby (J)
Wolds

HIGH SECURITY

Belmarsh
Frankland
Full Sutton
Long Lartin
Manchester
Wakefield
Whitemoor
Woodhill

SOUTH WEST

Prisons

Ashfield (C/J)
Bristol
Channings Wood
Dartmoor
Dorchester
Eastwood Park (F)
Erlestoke
Execter
Guys Marsh
Leyhill
Portland (YOI)
The Verne

EAST OF ENGLAND

Prisons

Bedford
Blundeston
Bure
Chelmsford
Highpoint North
Highpoint South
Hollesley Bay
Littlehey
Peterborough (C)
The Mount
Norwich (YOI)
Warren Hill (J)
Wayland

PROBATION TRUSTS

1. Northumbria Probation Trust
2. Durham Tees Valley Probation Trust
3. Cumbria Probation Trust
4. Lancashre Probation Trust
5. Merseyside Probation Trust
6. Greater Manchester Probation Trust
7. Cheshire Probation Trust
8. York & North Yorkshire
   Probation Trust
9. West Yorkshire Probation Trust
10. Humberside Probation Trust
11. South Yorkshire Probation Trust
12. Wales Probation Trust
13. Staffordshire & West Midlands
    Probation Trust
14. West Mercia Probation Trust
15. Warwickshire Probation Trust
16. Lincolnshire Probation Trust
17. Nottinghamshire Probation Trust
18. Derbyshire Probation Trust
19. Leicestershire & Rutland
    Probation Trust
20. Northamptonshire Probation Trust
21. Cambridgeshire & Peterborough
    Probation Trust
22. Bedfordshire Probation Trust
23. Hertfordshire Probation Trust
24. Norfolk & Suffolk Probation Trust
25. Essex Probation Trust
26. Gloucestershire Probation Trust
27. Avon & Somerset Probation Trust
28. Wiltshire Probation Trust
29. Dorset Probation Trust
30. Devon & Cornwall Probation Trust
31. Thames Valley Probation Trust
32. Hampshire Probation Trust
33. Surrey & Sussex Probation Trust
34. London Probation Trust
35. Kent Probation Trust

EAST MIDLANDS

Prisons

Foston Hall (F)
Gartree
Glen Parva (YOI)
Lecester
Lincoln
Lowdham Grange (C)
Morton Hall (IRC)
North Sea Camp
Notting ham
Onley
Ranby
Rey Hill (C)
Stockem
Sudbury
Whatton

WEST MIDLANDS

Prisons

Birmingham (C)
Brinsford (YOI)
Drake Hall (F)
Dovegate (C)
Featherstone
Hewell
Oakwood (C)
Stafford
Stoke Heath (YOI)
Swinten Hall (YOI)
Warrington (J)

KENT & SUSSEX

Prisons

Blantyre House
Cookham Wood (J)
Dover (IRC)
East Sutton Park (F)
Ford
Lewes
Maidstone
Rochester (YOI)
Sheppey Cluster
 – Elmley
 – Standford Hill
 – Swaleside

NORTH WEST

Prisons

Altcourse (C)
Buckley Hall
Forest Bank (C)
Garth
Haverigg
Hindley (J)
Kennet
Kirkham
Lancaster Farms (YOI)
Liverpool
Preston
Risley
Styal (F)
Thorn Cross (YOI)
Wymott

NORTH EAST

Prisons

Deerbolt (YOI)
Durham
Holme House
Kirklevington Grange
Low Newton (F)
Northumberland

WALES

Prisons

Cardiff
Swansea
Parc (C/J)
Usk/Prescoed

Please note:
This map is for illustration only. Probation Trust boundaries are shown on the main map. The map also gives an indication of prison locations.
The inset map shows the prison locations for London.
Last update July 2013. More prison and probation information can be found on the internet under Organization & MCIMS Map

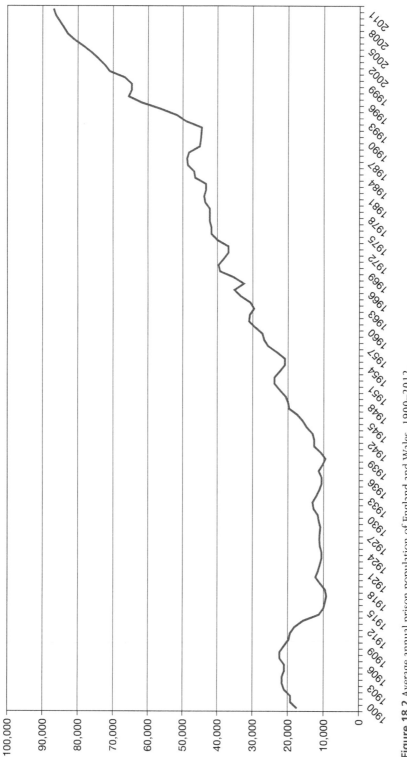

Figure 18.2 Average annual prison population of England and Wales, 1900–2012.

Source: Prison Population Statistics, 2012 note for Parliament.

Origins of imprisonment

Before the eighteenth century, imprisonment was only one, and by no means the most important, element in systems of punishment. Throughout pre-industrial Europe courts drew upon a much wider range of sentences than is possible today. The range of penal measures included aggravated forms of the death penalty, such as breaking on the wheel (with bodies left to rot on the device as warnings to the living), through to minor sanctions like warnings not to repeat the offence. In between lay a diverse variety of more and less serious forms of corporal punishment (such as mutilation, branding and whipping), forms of public shaming (such as the pillory), forms of bondage (such as galley servitude, transportation and the workhouse), banishment, fines, and a host of other minor prohibitions (Spierenburg, 2005).

The historian Ralph Pugh (1968) has described how in medieval England imprisonment came to serve three main uses:

- custodial (detaining those awaiting trial or sentence);
- coercive (forcing fine defaulters and debtors into making good their misfortune); and
- punitive (as punishment in its own right).

These legal distinctions continue to be significant, yet it is important to recognize that the main purposes of the medieval prison were custodial and coercive, with sentences likely to have been corporal or capital and it was not uncommon 'for a person to be sentenced and hanged or flogged on the same day' (McConville, 1998: 118).

However, as feudal systems of existence began to break down, with the advent of mercantile capitalism, large numbers of people migrated from rural areas to burgeoning towns and cities. This new population was viewed as being composed of vagrants, beggars, robbers and the unemployed so that during the sixteenth and seventeenth centuries there began to emerge a range of secular institutions (that are the precursors of modern imprisonment) across Europe, which sought to confine the growing numbers of poor, homeless and dispossessed citizens. From the 1500s bridewells, workhouses and transportation to colonies came to complement conventional forms of corporal and capital punishment, as a means of distinguishing the 'deserving' from the 'undeserving' poor and fuelling colonial expansion (see the timeline in Box 18.1 for historical details of the developments discussed in this chapter).

Nevertheless, it was eighteenth-century Enlightenment critics that promoted the prison as the generalized response to crime, as opposed to the public spectacles of suffering that were losing their legitimacy in England as well as other parts of Europe (Spierenburg, 1984, 1998b). Whilst there are competing explanations as to why the prison came to be the dominant response to crime from the end of the eighteenth century, which are discussed below, it is important to emphasize that for much of the eighteenth century the bridewells, workhouses and local gaols were characterized by disorder and neglect. It was this widespread squalor, disease and corruption that a number of penal reformers, including John Howard and Elizabeth Fry, campaigned to end. They were opposed to the indiscriminate mixing of men and women, the lack of segregation between the tried and the untried, the open sale of alcohol, the gambling and the generally filthy conditions, where diseases like typhus were rife. Many of the institutions were also run as private enterprises for profit – and there is evidence that many bridewells had become lucrative brothels (Zedner, 1995).

BOX 18.1 Timeline: key developments that created the modern penal system

1166   The Assize of Clarendon, legislation by Henry II that sought to establish a gaol in every English county, a task completed by the thirteenth century.

1556   The first bridewell was converted from a little used royal palace in London (known as Saint Bridget's well) into the earliest recorded 'house of correction'.

1717   The Transportation Act, provided for the considerable expansion of transportation to the colonies (which had begun over a century earlier).

1779   Hulks introduced, which were broken-down transportation ships (also referred to as 'floating hells') moored at river banks that acted as penal warehouses in the light of losing the American War of Independence.

1779   The Penitentiary Act, included proposals for improved diet, paid labour in prisons and the building of two 'ideal penitentiary houses'.

1823   The Gaol Act imposes new classification system involving the separation of men and women.

1838   A separate juvenile prison established at Parkhurst.

1852   Transportation abandoned and government introduce Australian 'ticket of leave' scheme, the precursor of parole.

1865   Prison Act formally amalgamated the gaol and house of correction.

1868   Public ceremonies of execution end.

1877   Prison Act brings control of local prisons under central government and a Prison Commission established under the charge of the Home Secretary.

1895   The Gladstone Committee on Prison reports and recommends rehabilitation and treatment as priorities for the prison system rather than simply punishing offenders.

Influenced by religious piety and Enlightenment reason, the reformers advocated the benefits of classification, isolation and sanitation. Howard's widely publicized description of the abuses and distress encountered in these institutions and his comprehensive proposals for change, combined with the effects of the American War of Independence of 1776, which left the government with nowhere to send those sentenced to transportation, lay behind the 1779 Penitentiary Act. These two developments led central government to build new prisons known as 'penitentiaries' in an effort to reform and allow 'repentance' of the convicted and deter any others (Harding *et al.*, 1985). The Act promoted a new vision of imprisonment that would unite the punitive and reformative through hard labour and religious instruction in a system where prisoners were classified into groups, while profits from their labour paid prison staff.

During the nineteenth century it was increasingly assumed that only the state could be entrusted with preventing neglect and creating reformatory systems of prison discipline through solitary confinement, surveillance and the daily grind of the treadmill. This assumption led to the 1863 Penal Servitude Act and the 1865 Prison Act (which abolished the distinction between gaols and houses of correction to create a 'new' institution known as 'prison') and culminated in the nationalization of the prison system in 1877 which brought prisons under centralized state control.

Why prison?

The question that needs to be answered is why the prison became the dominant response to crime across Europe and North America from the end of the eighteenth century. Until the 1970s the explanation would have been that imprisonment represents an enlightened, humanitarian, progressive response over the barbarism of earlier epochs. This Whig view of history emphasized how early forms of punishment, based on vengeance, irrationality and cruelty had been replaced by informed, professional and expert intervention and would celebrate the zeal of benevolent reformers in explaining why contemporary penal systems exist. However, this interpretation has been widely challenged by a range of 'revisionist' histories of the 'Great Incarcerations' (Cohen, 1985).

The earliest work that looked behind the rhetoric of reformers and asked why particular punishments gain prominence during certain historical periods is provided by George Rusche and Otto Kirchheimer (1968). As Chapter 15 shows, their argument is informed by a Marxist understanding of social relations and highlights the relationships between the form of punishment and the economic requirements of particular modes of production. For instance, they argue that the prison emerged with the advent of industrial capitalism as a means of creating a submissive and regulated workforce.

Their account has been criticized for the way in which it provides a one-dimensional explanation of penal relations that prioritizes the significance of the labour market at the expense of other factors. A more sophisticated account is Michael Ignatieff's (1978) analysis of the birth of imprisonment. He rejects economic functionalism and argues that incarceration was a response to the crisis in class relations wrought by the Industrial Revolution as it served to establish the legitimacy of the law and was understood as an element of a larger vision of securing popular consent in an increasingly unequal, class divided society.

However, the most influential 'revisionist' history of imprisonment is Michel Foucault's *Discipline and Punish* (1977), which argues that the emergence of the prison does not mark a more humanitarian form of punishment. Instead it represents an attempt to punish more efficiently and extensively in order to create a disciplined society, through the techniques of surveillance, classification and examination perfected in the new institutional spaces (e.g. Bentham's Panopticon). The originality of Foucault's argument lies in the importance he attaches to the relationship between power and forms of knowledge.

The emergence of the prison is just one instance of the dispersal of new forms of knowledge and Foucault's project is to examine how domination is achieved and how individual subjectivity is socially constructed. The prison has always been a failure, as it does not reduce crime, yet the reason why it persists is because it stands at one end of a continuum in which surveillance and regulation have become normalized throughout society. Foucault coins the phrase 'carceral archipelago' to describe the chain of people processing institutions (like asylums, barracks, factories and schools) that stretch out from the prison to imply that Western liberal democracies are intimately bound up with forms of oppression.

Although 'revisionist' histories continue to be influential, a number of critics have found fault with the way in which:

- all social relations have been described in the language of domination;
- complex processes are oversimplified;

- the instrumental aspects of punishment are exaggerated; and
- the wide social support for punishment is ignored (Garland, 1990).

Moreover, there is a failure to consider the punishment of women, which problematizes thinking about the role and development of incarceration. For instance, why women are more likely to be treated as 'mad' rather than 'bad' poses questions that conventional and revisionist historians are unable to answer.

In addition, feminist historians and criminologists have demonstrated how the ideological practice of institutional confinement began much earlier for women than for men. Mary Bosworth's (2000) analysis of the Hôpital de la Salpêtrière – the main hospital–prison complex for women in Paris from 1656 up to 1916 – indicates that many of the practices commonly held to originate in nineteenth-century penitentiaries in fact emerged far earlier in the seventeenth and eighteenth centuries. Likewise, Sherrill Cohen (1992) emphasizes how the existence of separate institutions for women across Europe from the sixteenth century onward, such as Magdalene houses for 'repentant' prostitutes, combined penitence, religious instruction and reformative labour in ways that anticipated developments in the nineteenth century.

It was also the case that women made up a considerable percentage of the population of bridewells. It has even been estimated that for much of the seventeenth and eighteenth centuries in London the number of women confined in bridewells was often greater than the number of men (Matthews, 1999: 14), while Victorian responses frequently 'drew attention to "crimes of morality" committed by women, such as prostitution or public drunkenness' (Zedner, 1991: 309). Clearly the lessons to be learnt from 'herstory' are not only that the confinement of women in the early modern period challenges conventional and revisionist chronologies, but also that women were central to the burgeoning practices of institutional exclusion, segregation and control.

The modern prison estate

Imprisonment in England and Wales continues to be dominated by this Victorian legacy. Nevertheless, it is important to recognize that there are now a range of institutions that can be grouped under two main types. First, there are local prisons and remand centres whose primary task is to receive and deliver prisoners to the courts, and to allocate those serving sufficiently long enough sentences to the second set of institutions. These are young offender institutions and adult training prisons, which are further subdivided into closed and open institutions for men and women. This subdivision reflects a prisoner security classification and the level of security that institutions provide. All prisoners are classified A, B, C or D according to a scheme devised in 1966 by Lord Mountbatten (Home Office, 1966) following a series of notorious prison escapes that pushed the issue of security to the top of the political agenda.

Mountbatten's recommendations have done much to shape the penal system of today. Category A prisoners are those 'whose escape would be highly dangerous to the public or police or to the security of the state' and whilst Mountbatten thought that such prisoners would probably be no more than 120, a more recent estimate puts the figure at some 700 (Morgan, 2002: 1143). Category D prisoners are those 'who could be trusted under open conditions' (Home Office, 1966). Category B and C prisoners are those held in closed conditions providing more or less security. Trial and remand prisoners are, with the exceptions of those provisionally categorized as A, all assumed to be Category B.

The allocation of sentenced Category A prisoners has been the subject of a long-running controversy. Mountbatten called for the concentration of all Category A prisoners into one single-purpose maximum security fortress that would not only ensure that high-risk prisoners were to be kept in secure surroundings but that security could be relaxed in other regimes. This proposal was quickly rejected on the basis that concentrating all high-risk prisoners within a single fortress would mean that maintaining order and providing a constructive regime would be near impossible in a prison composed of 'no-hopers'. Instead a policy of 'dispersal' was adopted, in that maximum security prisoners should be spread around amongst a few high-security prisons. There are currently five 'dispersal' prisons plus a further five that have high-security arrangements and it is becoming increasingly common for institutions to have multiple functions.

It is fair to say that whilst the **dispersal policy** might have solved the problem of perimeter security, it has intensified the problems of internal control. For within the prison system the presence of a small number of maximum security prisoners affects the vast majority of other prisoners who are subjected to custodial regimes to a greater extent. It is also important to recognize that the system of classification maintains a sharp differentiation between dispersal prisons, training prisons and local prisons, to the extent that the latter have come to bear the brunt of the chronic overcrowding, squalid conditions and understaffing that characterize some of the dimensions of the prison crisis, whilst the dispersal and training prisons have to a large extent been protected. The crisis is composed of the following sets of interrelated issues:

- an expanding prison population;
- overcrowded and decrepit conditions;
- authority and legitimacy deficits; and
- severe social consequences.

Contemporary crises

The expanding prison population

In order to make sense of the increases in the prison population it is instructive to consider longer-term trends. It is clear that since the 1950s the growth in the prison population has consistently kept ahead of available space in penal institutions. This is in marked contrast to the inter-war era, when prisons were routinely half full. For instance, in 1928 there were only just over 11,000 prisoners in a system that could offer 20,000 cells. By 1938 the number of prisoners remained around the 11,000 mark, but many prisons had been closed on the grounds that they were no longer required (Stern, 1993: 24).

This is a striking difference to the post-war era, in which there was a fivefold increase in recorded crime (from 280,000 in 1938 to 1,334,000 in 1965). During this period the courts' proportionate use of imprisonment actually decreased (with the fine replacing probation as the main form of sentence), yet the prison population tripled – from 11,100 in 1938 to 32,500 in 1968 (Bottoms, 1987: 181). As illustrated by Figure 18.2, even though the prison population rose modestly during the 1980s, and reached a peak at around 50,000 in 1988–89, it then declined in the early 1990s to around 45,000. Between 1993 and 1998 it increased rapidly by some 47 per cent to reach 65,300 and then declined slightly only to increase from January 2001 and reach a new peak of 71,220 in June 2002 (Home Office, 2002a). In March 2006 the prison population in England and Wales stood at 77,004, a rise of 2,603 on the year before (Prison Reform Trust, 2006: 4), and in February 2008, the population reached a record of 81,681 with the Prison Service declaring the system 'full' for the second time in eight months and court cells used to confine the overflow (Ford, 2008: 1). The soaring rise in the prison population is all the more remarkable as it has taken place against a backdrop of steadily declining crime rates, however measured, since the mid-1990s (Simmons et al., 2002). Moreover, since 2008, this rising trend has continued unabated, spurred on not least by the 900 people imprisoned for involvement in the 2011 UK riots.

At a basic level the increase is due to the courts sending more people to prison and passing longer custodial sentences when passing judgement. Andrew Millie and his colleagues (2005: 108) have argued that prison growth is a combination of factors, including:

- a more punitive climate of opinion;
- a more punitive legislative framework;
- sentencing guidelines that counteract leniency;
- some changes in patterns of offending; and
- sentencers' perceptions of changes in patterns of offending.

Nevertheless, it is important to recall that there has been a policy of **bifurcation** operating across criminal justice policy since at least the mid-1970s (Bottoms, 1977), which enables governments to pursue both 'soft' and 'tough' sentencing options simultaneously. For instance, in mid-1980, 22 per cent of prisoners were serving sentences of over four years, but by mid-2000 this figure stood at 46 per cent of adult male prisoners (Home Office, 2001: 76). These changes are partly explained by the introduction of parole in 1967 and subsequent developments in its use (see Morgan, 2002: 1130–2), but the important point to note is that long-term prisoners dominate life in most training prisons and consequently preoccupy prison administrators, with important consequences for the remaining prisoners.

Overcrowding and conditions

Prison overcrowding is predominantly a post-war phenomenon and even though there have been episodic attempts to expand the prison estate, for the most part these efforts have been insufficient to stave off serious overcrowding in the system. The problem is partly explained by the inflexibility of prison space, but there have been, and remain, clear policy preferences to concentrate overcrowding in local prisons and remand centres so that resources can be used to optimize the regime in training prisons and make best use of the facilities available there. The rationale behind this policy is the assumption that for prisoners serving short sentences there is too little time to achieve results. For example, at the end of the last century 'roughly 80 per cent of local prisons and around one-third of all prisons were overcrowded by more than 20 per cent (with the worst handful being of the order of 70 per cent overcrowded' (Sparks, 2001: 213–14). During 2010–11 an average of 20,211 prisoners were held in overcrowded accommodation, accounting for 24 per cent of the total prison population (Prison Reform Trust, 2012: 4).

The effects of overcrowding contribute to a sense of crisis in many ways. Most obviously the problem of numbers has a deleterious impact on conditions, and it is beyond doubt that prisoners who begin their carceral career, as most do, in a local prison will typically find themselves in the midst of the worst conditions that the penal system can inflict where overcrowding has been a daily feature of life within many of these institutions for over three decades. The problem of numbers has to be located in the context of dilapidated physical conditions in which prisoners are contained, combined with poor sanitation, scarcely edible food, decaying cramped cells, clothing shortages and brief, inadequate family visits. Compounding this wretchedness is the severely restricted and oppressive regimes that are imposed since there is neither the space, facilities nor resources to provide prisoners with a range of training, work and educational opportunities when there are too many prisoners to cope with. Currently two-thirds of the prisons in England and Wales are overcrowded, with nearly a quarter of people in prison being held in overcrowded accommodation, either doubling up in cells designed for one occupant or being held three to a cell in spaces designed for two people (Ministry of Justice, 2012b).

Authority and managerialism

The crisis of authority (Cavadino and Dignan, 2002: 200–5) refers not only to the long and bitter industrial relations between prison staff and management, but also to major changes in the philosophy and organizational form of prison administration. In the post-war era there has been a shift in the source of authority in prisons from a highly personalized form of charismatic power, embodied in the prison governor, to systems based on bureaucratic rules and procedures. Further organizational changes have also meant that the Prison Service, formerly a Department of State within the Home Office, became a semi-autonomous executive agency in 1993 and privatization (the contracting out of public services to the private sector) is now an important and controversial feature of the penal landscape. Indeed, since the early 1990s many of the newly built and privately managed prisons have been local prisons, which tend to have better regimes and facilities than the 'traditional locals' – suggesting that there is now a two-tier local prison system with the old prisons bearing 'the brunt of overcrowding and reduced regimes' (Morgan and Liebling, 2007: 1118).

It is highly debatable, however, whether these organizational changes have been able to tackle the continuing crisis of authority as there are clearly deep and long-standing legitimacy problems in the Prison Service caused in some respects by the demise of rehabilitation in the 1970s as the guiding purpose of penal practice. The subsequent turn to managerialist issues in the 1980s and 1990s only served to undermine a sense of mission to the service, save for meeting narrow management objectives and performance indicators. It is also highly significant that the definitive statement on the causes of prison riots in the English context emphasized the importance of **legitimacy** in securing the acquiescence of the confined (Woolf and Tumim, 1991). In particular, the implication is that there are variable conditions which render it more or less likely that prisoners will accept, however conditionally, the authority of their custodians.

Social consequences

Youth custody

It is no coincidence that the modern youth justice system emerged at the middle of the nineteenth century, at the same time as 'adolescence' and 'juvenile delinquency' were 'discovered'. The deep ambivalence of the Victorians toward children was played out in the various discourses surrounding childhood – children were simultaneously idealized, worshipped and protected as well as being feared, exploited and regulated (Hendrick, 1990). During this period many social reformers and philanthropists directed their energies toward 'saving' and 'protecting', demanding that young people should be removed from the 'adult' prison population and placed in separate institutions. The Youthful Offenders Act 1854 provided the basis of the reformatories for the 'dangerous classes', and legislation three years later established 'industrial schools' for the 'perishing classes' (Hebdige, 1988: 21).

The Children Act 1908 was a major piece of legislation that created juvenile courts, barred under-14s from prison and created 'borstals' to cater for 16–21-year-olds (a 'juvenile-adult' category) based on welfare principles. The Children and Young Persons Act 1933 further underlined the move toward welfare through prohibiting capital punishment for those under 18, and reorganized the reformatory and industrial schools into 'approved schools' which provided young offenders with education and training, while remand homes kept juveniles apart from adults. In the post-war period the dramatic rise in crime and prison overcrowding contributed to continuing changes in penal policy as legislation introduced the detention centre in the 1950s that was intended to provide a brief, unpleasant custodial experience for young offenders, but while their development was slow they would return under the guise of a 'short, sharp, shock' in the 1980s.

The Children and Young Persons Act 1969 proved to be a high-water mark in the welfare era and introduced the principle of diversion. The general aim was to keep young offenders out of the youth justice system or, only where it was absolutely necessary, to send them to juvenile court for 'care' and to 'treat' young offenders rather than punish them. These developments have provoked considerable debate among criminologists over their 'net widening' effects and intensification of disciplinary power (Cohen, 1985). The Act also abolished the system of approved schools and remand homes and replaced them with 'community homes', and it was intended that detention centres and borstals should be phased out and replaced by 'intermediate treatment'.

However, in 1970 a Conservative government replaced a Labour administration that refused to fully implement the Act and became blamed for failing to deal with rising juvenile crime while the emphasis increasingly switched from a 'welfare' approach to one of 'justice' by all sides in the debate. As the 1970s progressed it became obvious that a process of bifurcation, or a 'twin-track approach' (Bottoms, 1977), was occurring with custodial sentences increasing for serious juvenile offenders while the use of cautions was adopted for less serious offenders.

The election of a Conservative government in 1979 that took a pledge to 'stand firm against crime' saw the return of traditional criminal justice values in the Criminal Justice Act 1982, but also saw borstals and indeterminate sentences replaced by 'youth custody' – with the institutions becoming known as Youth Custody Institutions. As Lorraine Gelsthorpe and Allison Morris (2002: 240) argue, the 1980s witnessed 'a period of "law and order" and "crime control", with policies which were designed to reassert the virtue and necessity of authority, order and discipline'. Widespread concerns over increases in juvenile crime in the 1990s were fuelled by joyriding in deprived council estates, widespread publicity over persistent young offenders and the murder of James Bulger by two 10-year-old boys. This forced the main political parties into rethinking their positions on crime and punishment into what has become known as 'populist punitiveness' (Bottoms, 1995).

One of the consequences was a fierce controversy over whether the principle of *doli incapax* should be upheld. This refers to the age of criminal responsibility; in England and Wales it is 10 years, and children under that age cannot be found guilty of a criminal offence. Children between 10 and 13 were presumed to be *doli incapax* (incapabale of criminal intent) and despite vehement opposition from the Home Secretary the principle was 'upheld on the grounds that there is wisdom in protecting young children against the full rigour of the criminal law' (Gelsthorpe and Morris, 2002: 241). Nevertheless, the age of criminal responsibility is unusually low in comparison with most of Western Europe, where offenders under the 14 are usually dealt with by civil proceedings.

There is considerable debate over whether the New Labour government elected in 1997 ushered in a 'new youth justice' (Goldson, 2000). Certainly there were many new proposals and activities in the Crime and Disorder Act 1998 and the Youth Justice and Criminal Evidence Act 1999. These are too numerous to detail here (see Goldson and Muncie, 2006, for an overview), but significantly include the setting up of the Youth Justice Board, the creation of Youth Offending Teams; and the restructuring of the non-custodial penalties available to the youth court (including elements of restorative justice – see Chapter 15). Some have argued that New Labour virtually 'invented' the concept of 'Anti-Social Behaviour' and have shown that it was intimately bound up with the government's politics of crime and disorder (Tonry, 2004).

Child custody is the most controversial sanction available and while the use of it had fallen by the end of New Labour's third administration – from a peak of over 3,000 in 2007/8 to 1,643 at the end of August 2012 (Prison Reform Trust, 2012: 38) – more children are locked up in the UK than in most other countries in Europe. Recent years have seen a series of reports by penal reform groups and children's pressure groups criticizing the damaging consequences of child custody and highlighting the plight of very young children (Glover and Hibbert, 2009), the overuse of remand (Gibb and Hickson, 2009), the impact of learning difficulties (Talbot, 2010) and multiple inequalities (Jacobson et al., 2010). According to the last report most of the children who were sentenced to custody were repeat offenders – and it is the persistence of their offending, rather than the seriousness of the specific offences for which they were sentenced, which explains the use of custody in many cases.

Gendered prisons

It has been estimated that women, on average, make up about 4 per cent of the total prison population (Walklate, 2001: 169). Since imprisonment is largely experienced by young adult men, most criminologists argue that the organization and culture of the prison system reflects this dominance to the extent that there are very different regimes for male and female prisoners. For instance, the tendency has been to define women prisoners as mad or sad rather than bad, and the regimes have reinforced traditional stereotypes of motherhood and domesticity (Carlen, 1983; Bosworth, 1999).

Since there are far fewer women in prison this has serious consequences, as there are only 17 or so geographically disparate institutions, which makes it both extremely difficult to sustain relationships with friends and family whilst compounding the marginalization of women in the system. However, this has begun to change as the drastic increases in the female prison population over the last decade, and a series of scandals, have pushed the issue of women's imprisonment to the forefront of policy debates.

For instance, the dramatic rise in the numbers of women in prison can be seen in the increase from an average of 1,560 in 1993 to 4,248 in 2006, with an all-time high of 4,672 reached in May 2004 (HM Prison Service, 2008: 1). Between 2000 and 2010 the women's prison popu-

BOX 18.2 Alternatives to prison

Some alternatives to prison have quite considerable histories, while others have been introduced only relatively recently. Anne Worrall (1997) identifies three distinctive groupings. 'Self-regulatory' penalties involve some form of public shaming that is assumed to be sufficient to deter offenders from further lawbreaking. 'Financial' penalties generally tend to be paid to the central administration of a criminal justice system, though it is possible, and some would argue desirable, for some form of compensation to be paid to the victim. 'Supervisory' sentences have increased in number since the 1970s and involve elements of rehabilitation (through education and welfare programmes), reparation (through unpaid work in the community) and incapacitation (through curfews and electronic tagging).

The use of alternatives to prison gathered force as part of a **decarceration** movement (see also Chapter 15) in the 1970s when various non-custodial sentences came to be regarded as a more humane and less stigmatizing means of treating offenders. Equally importantly, many governments were keen to find less expensive, but equally demanding, alternatives to imprisonment in the face of growing economic problems facing welfare states. Many proponents have since argued for displacing the use of specific parts of the prison system (e.g. juvenile detention), while others have concentrated on advocating alternative community-based sanctions. The overall pattern has been one of expansion, with such penalties accompanying rather than being an alternative to an increasing prison population.

BOX 18.3 Timeline: key dates in youth custody

1838 The first separate juvenile prison established at Parkhurst.

1901 A penal reformatory to house young offenders opens at Borstal, Kent, a name that in time would come to be applied to all institutions for young offenders.

1908 The Children's Act creates a separate system of juvenile justice.

1948 Criminal Justice Act promotes wider use of borstals, though more punitive detention centres would come to prominence in the 1950s.

1969 The Children and Young Persons Act 1969 introduces the principle of diversion based on the ethics of 'care' and 'treatment'.

1982 Borstal training replaced by youth custody and the ideological reintroduction of the 'short, sharp shock' in detention centres.

1999 Youth Justice and Criminal Evidence Act is a key element in New Labour's restructuring of juvenile justice.

2003 The Anti-Social Behaviour Act and Criminal Justice Act introduce a whole raft of provisions extending legislation over young offenders.

lation increased by 26 per cent (Prison Reform Trust, 2012: 30). Most of the rise is due to the significant increase in the severity of sentences. For example, in the Crown Court in 1991 only 8 per cent of women convicted of motoring offences went to prison, by 2001 that figure had increased to 42 per cent. Similarly, women convicted of theft or handling stolen goods at the Crown Court are now twice as likely to go to prison as in 1991, while in the magistrates' courts the chances of a woman receiving a custodial sentence has risen sevenfold (Prison Reform Trust, 2006: 14).

The sense of crisis in women's prisons extends far beyond numbers. Since the mid-1990s the media have widely reported on the shocking practices of manacling mothers in labour; degrading methods of drug testing; Holloway prison, the largest prison for women, was deemed too filthy to inspect by the Chief Prisons Inspector; and in 2002 more women killed themselves in prison than ever before. It remains the case that prisons, 'even the most reformed ones, produce damage and diseases, in varied forms and intensity they produce damaged and ill people' (Gallo and Ruggiero, 1991: 278). Although women make up only 4 per cent of the prison population 20 per cent of prison suicides from January to August 2004 were women, with nearly half of all self-harm incidents involving women (Scraton and Moore, 2004: 35–6).

Half of all women in prison are on prescribed medication such as antidepressants or anti-psychotics, and two-thirds have children under the age of 16, which has been estimated at some 24,000 children (Kennedy, 2004: 285). One in four women in prison have spent time in local authority care as a child, while over half have suffered domestic violence, and one in three has experienced sexual abuse (Prison Reform Trust, 2006: 15). The then government's *Strategy for Women Offenders*, published in 2000, recognizes that the 'current system does impact differently on women and men' (cited in Scraton and Moore, 2004: 36). For instance, Pat Carlen (1998: 10) has argued that women's imprisonment 'incorporates and amplifies all the anti-social modes of control that oppress women outside the prison' and that the very rationales for reducing the imprisonment of women have been subverted and are now used to lock up more women through processes of 'carceral clawback' (Carlen, 2002).

In recognition of women's complex underlying needs Baroness Corston (2007) produced a government-commissioned review of *Women with Particular Vulnerabilities in the Criminal Justice System*. Corston made 43 recommendations to the then government for necessary and positive changes to policy, and while initially the government responded positively, the original optimism has proved to be short-lived and progress has stalled on many fronts (Santa-Olla, 2011: 27). It is clear that instead of punishment being used as a sanction 'of last resort, women's prisons appear to have become stopgap providers of drug detox services, social care, mental health assessment and treatment and temporary housing – a refuge for those who have slipped through the net of local services' (Prison Reform Trust, 2011: 1) and in many ways underlines Wacquant's (2010) argument that changes in justice and welfare are interlinked in neo-liberal states. The problems of women's justice are multifaceted and are unlikely to be solved by sending so many women to prison.

Ethnicity, nationality and racism

The picture presented by the statistics is that prisoners in England and Wales are dispropor-tionately young, poor, members of ethnic minorities, with few occupational skills, or academic qualifications, and are likely to be suffering from psychiatric distress (Sparks, 2001: 215–16).

Recent figures indicate that at the end of September 2012, one in four of the prison population, 21,747 prisoners, was from a minority ethnic group, which compares to one in ten of the general population (Prison Reform Trust, 2012: 34). There are a number of reasons for this over-representation. One key factor is nationality, and it has been noted that 12 per cent of the UK prison population comprises foreign nationals (a growing trend observed across Europe), whilst another is that the relative youthfulness of ethnic minorities compared to the white population means that over-representation is all the more likely to occur (Morgan and Liebling, 2007: 1121).

Foreign national prisoners in the UK come from 157 countries, but over half are from just ten countries (Jamaica, Poland, the Irish Republic, Romania, Nigeria, Pakistan, Lithuania, India, Somalia and Vietnam) – the total number of foreign nationals in prison nearly doubled (99 per cent) between 2000 and 2010, which compares to a 20 per cent increase in British nationals (Prison Reform Trust, 2012: 36). Over the last two decades there has also been significant legislative activity leading to the criminalization of immigration, or 'crimmigration', which has further complicated the picture (see Box 18.4) and has largely escaped criminological attention (exceptions include Aliverti, 2012; Bosworth, 2012; Cecchi, 2011; De Giorgi, 2010; Lacey, 2008; Welch and Schuster, 2005).

Coretta Phillips and Ben Bowling (2007: 445) have argued that the historical context for understanding 'race relations' in prisons must acknowledge the strong support for the National Front among many prison officers in the 1970s, combined with much evidence of brutality and harassment (Gordon, 1983), that led to the introduction of policies to combat racism in the early 1980s. Elaine Genders and Elaine Player (1989) have provided substantial evidence of racial discrimination within prisons. For example, they found that the best jobs were regularly allocated to white prisoners, as prison officers believed that Afro-Caribbean prisoners were arrogant, lazy and anti-authority. More recently, the official inquiry into the racist murder of Zahid Murabek in March 2000 by his white racist cellmate, in Feltham Young Offenders Institution, found that institutional racism pervaded Feltham, which led to the Prison Service inviting the Commission for Racial Equality to carry out a formal inquiry into racism in prisons. The report identified 20 'systemic failures' by the Prison Service to prevent the murder (Commission for Racial Equality, 2003).

The government initially resisted the demand by Mubarek's family for a full public inquiry, and an independent public investigation into the murder was set up only after the House of Lords ruled that human rights law justified the family's campaign for such a report. The three volume report (available at www.zahidmubarekinquiry.org.uk) heard evidence of a persistent culture of racism not only at Feltham, but of similar patterns of racial prejudice throughout the prison system. It heard, for instance, reports of 'gladiator games' where officers were accused of putting white and black prisoners in a shared cell and then placing bets on how long it would take before violence would break out between them (Temko, 2006: 5).

It has also been argued that the brutal deaths of individuals from ethnic minorities while in prison custody are similar to the deaths of African/Caribbean prisoners in police custody, as there is 'a tendency for prison staff to overreact to disruptive behaviour by African/Caribbean prisoners, whereby the stereotype of "Big, Black and Dangerous" seems to predominate in determining their response' (Bowling and Phillips, 2002: 208). It is beyond doubt that racism and racial discrimination structure daily life in prison. Recent research reveals a complex pattern of interactions in the 'multicultural prison' where the intersections of ethnicity, masculinity, class and neighbourhood forge social relations inside (Phillips, 2012).

Plate 18.1 Zahid Mubarek was killed by Robert Stewart in March 2000 in a racist attack in Cell 38, which they shared at Feltham Young Offenders Institution. Official reports have since found evidence of a persistent culture of racism not only at Feltham, but also similar patterns of racial prejudice throughout the prison system.

Source: Photonews Service Ltd Image Library.

BOX 18.4 Immigration removal centres

There are currently 12 immigration removal centres in the UK, which are used as 'temporary detention' for those 'who have no legal right to be in the UK but have refused to leave voluntarily' (UK Border Agency, 2013: 1). The increased reliance on the criminal law to enforce immigration statutes has also been accompanied by a growth in new legislation, which now effectively makes any breach of immigration rules a crime (Home Office, 2010: 26). Although there has been a long-standing tradition of criminalizing such breaches, the last 15 years have seen a heightened intensity around the 'immigration issue' and especially the abuse of the asylum system, leading to not only more legislation but also the vigorous application of existing powers to detain and deport offenders (Aliverti, 2012: 420). (And, since the 2007 Act, all new UK detention centres are privately run.)

Since the passage of the UK Border Act 2007, any foreign national from outside the European Economic Area (EAA) sentenced to 12 months or more in prison, or whose sentence over the past five years adds up to 12 months, has been subject to mandatory deportation. EEA nationals are held to the same rules of expulsion if sentenced to 24 months. Any non-British national sentenced to prison can be considered for deportation. Some foreign offenders are now routinely given deportation orders by judges and magistrates as part of their criminal sentence, others are given it while serving their sentence once their case is considered by the UK Border Agency. In an effort to manage the increased population the UK Border Agency and National Offender Management Service (NOMS) devised a new system known as 'Hubs and Spokes' in 2009.

In this new arrangement, individual prisons become 'hubs' while 'spoke' prisons would channel their foreign prisoners to these 'hubs' where a set of UK Border Agency staff process their paperwork. As Mary Bosworth (2012: 126) explains, this practice has created 'a significant new role for the prison, binding it to border control and in the process, altering its process and effect' where it is now involved in 'identifying and creating citizens', while the 'discards from this system, the "non-citizens", are the product and target of immigration detention'. Consequently, immigration removal centres are destinations for people en route to an airport, but they are increasingly holding men and women for over six months, where the pains of detention are compounded by the absence of citizenship. Following much criticism the UK Border Agency was abolished in 2013, with its work returning to the Home Office, but the controversies around immigration removal centres are certain to continue.

BOX 18.5 Prisoners and rights

The modern prison was born in the late eighteenth century, and since then it has been justified according to the utilitarian aims of deterrence, incapacitation and rehabilitation, or the retributive principles of just desert, hard labour and less eligibility. Each of these often conflicting goals has come to dominance at some point over the last 200 years, and they have been combined in uneasy compromises ever since. Throughout Europe up until the eighteenth century trials were usually held in secret, with the accused often unaware of the specific details of the case against them, while torture was routinely used to extract confessions. As Foucault (1977) emphasized, this intense secrecy stood in stark contrast to the sheer visibility of punishment as a public spectacle. Although the legal rights of the accused (rights to a fair trial, innocent until proven guilty, due process constraints and so forth) have since become regarded as essential defences against arbitrary and oppressive practices, the convicted are still tainted by the feudal doctrine of 'civil death', which was based on the assumption that the proven criminal was an 'outlaw' without any legal rights (Tappan, 1954: 99).

Many critics have argued that prisons have remained 'lawless agencies' (Greenberg and Stender, 1972) and that in 'Britain . . . the law for most purposes tends to stop at the prison gates, leaving the prisoner to the almost exclusive control of the prison authorities' (Zellick, 1974: 331). The continuing irony is that while there is a complex web of rules and regulations surrounding a prisoner's daily life, the institution itself possesses enormous discretion with the rule of law practically non-existent. The authorities enjoy considerable power over the confined as the rules themselves are not only extensive and vague but prisoners are often unaware of their specific content. Indeed, they are frequently denied access to the mass of standing orders, circular instructions and service standards that supplement the statutory rules.

controlling crime

The formal rules do not, in any case, provide a code of legally enforceable rights for prisoners, and the courts have generally been reluctant to intervene in prison life even when prisoners have had solid grounds for challenging decisions.

Such factors reveal the continuing legacy of 'civil death' and compound the arbitrary character of prison regimes because legal authority offers no defence against the highly discretionary power of the custodians. Lord Denning's (1972) ruling in *Becker* v. *Home Office* that the Prison Act did not give 'any colour of right' to a prisoner confirmed the long-standing judicial view that prison managers should be left to manage and that prisoners are unreliable troublemakers. Hence his comment that if 'the courts were to entertain actions by disgruntled prisoners, the governor's life would be made intolerable' as the 'discipline of the prison would be undermined' (cited in Schone, 2001: 72). However, the last thirty years have seen some important developments in prison law and the emergence of some judicial recognition of prisoners' rights (detailed in Carrabine, 2006, and van Zyl Smit, 2007).

It is important to put this judicial activism into sociological perspective. Although many of these cases have been hard won, their actual impact on prisoners' lives has been very selective, and this highlights the difficulties of relying on the legal establishment to defend and define rights (Carrabine, 2006: 202–3). The successes have been restricted to residual individual liberties such as correspondence with lawyers, access to courts, disciplinary hearings and release procedures – all matters which the judiciary are confident in dealing with. In contrast, the courts have not intervened in controversial administrative issues, such as transfers, segregation and living conditions which have a debilitating effect on prisoners. The fact that the courts have had such a negligible impact on most areas of prison life is partly explained by the long-standing scepticism towards natural rights in English political life, while the continuing deference to parliamentary sovereignty ensures that 'the statutory regime governing prisons in England is concerned, not with the definition of the prisoners' legal status or the creation of legally enforceable rights, but with clarifying lines of political control and accountability' (Lazarus, 2004: 251).

The recent debates over extending the right to vote to prisoners exemplify many of the issues at stake. Britain is unusual in banning prisoners from voting rights, and the European Court of Human Rights ruled in 2005 that the ban is a breach of human rights. The ban is a relic from the era when imprisonment for a felony meant 'civic death', which included the loss of property and the removal of civic rights, including the right to vote, which were based in property. Today most people do not see the right to vote as an issue of property rights, but an issue intrinsic to adulthood. However, in the House of Commons the Prime Minister David Cameron stated that he felt physically sick at the very notion of extending the right to vote to prisoners, sentiments shared by many in the opposition. The reasoning is that when a citizen commits a crime against society they forfeit the right to take part in deciding how it should be governed. In February 2012, MPs voted by 234 to 22 to keep the blanket ban, in response to a government proposal to give the vote to offenders sentenced to a custodial sentence of less than four years. The latest bill on prisoners' votes offers a number of options, including keeping the no-votes status quo – in defiance of the European Court. It will be considered in detail by a parliamentary committee before a final version comes before MPs. There is little chance of any change before the 2015 general election, and it is clear that the issue is being passed on to the next government to handle.

Prison sociology

Prisoner subcultures and 'mind games'

Much of the classic literature in sociology (for example, Clemmer, 1958; Sykes, 1958; Goffman, 1961; Mathiesen, 1965; Cohen and Taylor, 1972/1981) arises from monograph research on life in prisons. These studies have illuminated the day-to-day routines and struggles within these institutions. Although this early work was preoccupied with prisoner subcultures and how they mitigated against the pains of imprisonment, especially in American penitentiaries, more recent British sociological writing tends to emphasize the complexity of responses to confinement. This varies a great deal according to the category of prison, the quality of its regime, and the shifting patterns of stratification.

For example, Richard Sparks and his colleagues (1996: 176–81) have indicated in their study of two long-term dispersal prisons (where one might expect the presence of well-developed subcultures) that simple analogies based on class structures, with 'gangsters' portrayed as the 'ruling class' and 'nonces' as a 'lumpenproletariat' are seriously misleading. Instead, a rather more fluid pattern of competing groups (based on ethnic or regional affinities as much as on 'business' interests) was more in evidence than the rigid separation of roles and group solidarity that was a defining characteristic of the classic subculture research.

As Rock (1996: 40) puts it, with reference to a woman's prison, there is not one prisoner world but several. This point is developed by Carrabine (2004) in his discussion of the culture of a local prison, whose captive membership is constantly in flux as new prisoners arrive to be allocated elsewhere, others are returning from dispersal prisons under 'transfers', yet more will be seeing out short-term sentences, whilst there will always be those deemed as 'unsuitable' for training prisons – the 'old lags' who have been imprisoned on many previous occasions. This argument suggests that it is not only that antagonisms, friendships and influence constantly have to be renegotiated amid the frantic pace of daily change and upheaval on the wings and landings of local prisons, but that it is the staff occupational culture that also plays a pivotal role in shaping institutional interactions, not least because prison officers spend a far greater proportion of their working lives in the same place than either the prisoners or their managers.

Another illustration of sociological analysis is provided in Kathleen McDermott and Roy King's (1988) discussion of the 'mind games' played on the wings and landings of five English prisons. They provide a number of game metaphors to illustrate the various degrees of conflict between prisoners and staff. For example, one of the most basic prison rituals is going to the lavatory, and this is one of the many routine degradation rituals faced in prisons as the toilet was then a bucket in the cell (the practice of 'slopping out' was said to have officially ended in April 1996, although there continues to be evidence that prisoners do not have adequate access to toilets).

Consequently, one way of making do is through what McDermott and King (1988: 360) call *pass the parcel*. This refers to the ways in which excrement is wrapped up in parcels and thrown out of a window. It is partly functional as it relieves prisoners from spending time with the stench. Yet it is also a gesture of anger, as it has to be cleared up by someone else and using prison clothing as the wrapper brings the issue back to the authorities, where it belongs. However, the game is not played by the staff, as they do not clear up the mess – they organize prisoners to do this and ultimately the prisoners also suffer through clothing shortages.

Survival games continue when prisoners are permitted outside their cells where their encounters with staff, prisoners and arbitrary rules that govern their lives increase. For staff to survive they have to develop skills to both avoid an assault in the heat of the moment, and in the longer term to avoid reprisals in a future riot. Prison staff are often in the situation where they have to bear the brunt of prisoners' frustrations but are powerless to relieve them, and they tend to play the *sloping shoulders game* where an officer passes on a prisoner's request to a superior, invariably away from the landing, so that the officer is not immediately turning down the request. Meanwhile, prisoners are involved in *charades*. This is usually played by sex offenders who are anxious to avoid the label 'nonce'. For example, one prisoner was called this by another prisoner in their study, and though the sex offender knew he would lose, he challenged the prisoner to a fight. This earned him **respect** and an avoidance of the more severe beating he would have later received from a group of prisoners in his cell or in the recess.

Prison riots and the problem of order

Few would deny that prisons are dangerous places, and whilst violence is often described in terms of the characteristics of individual prisoners, such an understanding leaves much unexplained (Edgar *et al.*, 2003). The level of violent incidents in prisons indicates that intimidation, assaults and abuse form part of the everyday routine, whereas riots and disturbances are much rarer and pose a '*special problem* of the occasional complete or near-complete breakdown of order' (Sparks *et al.*, 1996: 2; emphasis in original).

Riots and disturbances can be further distinguished in the sense that a riot involves the authorities losing 'control of a significant number of prisoners, in a significant area of the prison, for a significant amount of time' (Useem and Kimball, 1989: 4), whereas a disturbance is a step down from a riot as there are fewer prisoners involved and the administrators do not lose control of any part of the institution, but it can still involve collective protest over conditions, through refusing to eat or stopping work for example. Whilst these definitions can be criticized for their vagueness they do have the advantage of highlighting the ways in which the problem of order is a daily feature of institutional life, for even though major riots are rare events they do not abruptly occur in an otherwise tranquil vacuum but they have multifaceted causes.

Moreover, the term riot is a pejorative one summoning images of frenzied mob violence and historians have indicated how the label has been used by ruling elites to discredit the revolutionary crowd in European history (Rudé, 1964). Prison riots are disturbing, complex and diverse events that raise profound questions over human action, social structure, historical context and political reasoning. In Bert Useem and Peter Kimball's (1989) examination of nine prison riots in the United States they provide a fresh understanding of prison disorder because it introduces the issue of legitimacy as crucial to structuring institutional stability. Their argument is that well-managed prisons instigate conformity, whereas breakdowns in administrative control render imprisonment illegitimate in the eyes of the confined, providing the background for riots to occur.

This study anticipates Lord Woolf's conclusion that the 25-day occupation of Strangeways prison in Manchester, England, during April 1990 was due to widely shared feelings of injustice, and the explicit argument is that there are variable conditions under which the confined accept or reject custodial authority (Woolf and Tumim, 1991). It is difficult to underestimate the significance of Woolf's report as it not only marks a decisive break with previous government understandings of prison unrest but is universally regarded as the most important examination of the UK prison system in the last 100 years. The recipe of reform he advocated was widely understood as one which would take the prison system out of the nineteenth century and into the twenty-first.

The concept of legitimacy locates the understanding of prison riots in the broader problem of order familiar to social and political theorists. By doing so it establishes that there are no simple answers to the question of why prisoners rebel in the ways that they do (Carrabine, 2004, 2005). In fact, it raises the pressing issue of how such matters as age, class, gender, race, religion and sexuality challenge a universalizing notion like legitimacy. Perhaps the unsettling conclusion to be drawn from this case study on prison riots is that they ought to happen more often. Explaining why they do not involves recognizing that prisons typically generate diverse forms of social order in spite of frequently illegitimate distributions of institutional power and severe crises outlined earlier in this chapter. Ben Crewe (2007: 143) has argued that in the UK prisoners are increasingly encouraged to self-govern and 'assume responsibility for the terms of their own incarceration, in a way that represents neither direct coercion nor autonomous consent'. As Richard Sparks and his colleagues (1996) pointed out over fifteen years ago, there is some considerable variation in the ways that prisons achieve a semblance of order and that these matters are sociologically complex.

More recently Jonathan Jackson and his colleagues have discussed the relevance of procedural justice to the production of legitimacy in British prisons and explored how the perspective can inform policy developments aiming to improve the experience, and integration, of black and minority ethnic prisoners (Jackson et al., 2010). Such work chimes with a renewed focus on ethnographic research in prisons which has focused on how penal power has been reshaped in these late modern times (good examples include Crewe, 2009; Drake, 2012; Mann, 2012; Phillips, 2012). In doing so these studies provide fresh insights into the dynamics of life in prison and give a sense of the diversity of prisoner experiences, while being attuned to the broader social meanings of imprisonment.

Summary

1   Prisons are one of the most controversial institutions in modern penal systems and occupy a central place in popular sentiment and political rhetoric on punishment.
2   The chapter has reviewed a number of competing explanations of the historical reasons why the prison became the dominant response to crime across Europe and North America from the end of the eighteenth century.
3   The account of the modern prison estate that followed demonstrated how there are a range of interrelated issues that contribute to a sense of crisis in the system, with grave social consequences.
4   The chapter has also included illustrations of sociological analyses of prison life in relation to 'mind games' and the problem of order.

Critical thinking questions

1   In what ways does gender challenge historical and contemporary accounts of imprisonment?
2   What are the key components of the prison crisis?
3   Why does youth custody involve elements of rescue, rehabilitation and repression?
4   Can you explain why the prison system is orderly most of the time?

Further study

Cavadino, M. and Dignan, J. (2007) *The Penal System: An Introduction*, 4th edn, London: Sage. The best criminological introduction to imprisonment, which covers the central issues in a broad and lively fashion.

Jewkes, Y. (ed.) (2007) *Handbook on Prisons*, Cullompton: Willan. An excellent edited collection of essays written by many of the leading academics in the field as well as professionals who have worked in and around prisons.

Matthews, R. (1999) *Doing Time: An Introduction to the Sociology of Imprisonment*, Basingstoke: Macmillan. This is a more detailed sociological account of imprisonment.

Stern, V. (1993) *Bricks of Shame*, London: Penguin. This is a compassionate and thought-provoking examination of the institution.

Useful websites

The Home Office
http://www.homeoffice.gov.uk
Provides access to a wide range of information on the criminal justice service generally.

The Home Office: Publications
http://www.homeoffice.gov.uk/rds/pubsintro1.html
Provides access to a wide range of publications.

HM Prison Service
http://www.hmprisonservice.gov.uk/
Contains news, reports, statistics and prison rules for prisons in England and Wales.

Scottish Prison Service
http://www.sps.gov.uk
Contains news, reports, statistics and prison rules for prisons in Scotland.

Prison and Probation Ombudsman
http://www.ppo.gov.uk/
The Prisons and Probation Ombudsman provides access to annual reports and publications.

Report of Her Majesty's Chief Inspector of Prisons
http://www.homeoffice.gov.uk/justice/prisons/index.html
A link to a report by the Inspector of Prisons can be found here along with further information on the Inspectorate.

Howard League for Penal Reform
http://www.howardleague.org/
Information, links and publications on penal reform.

National Association for the Care and Resettlement of Offenders (NACRO)
http://www.nacro.org.uk/
This site has information on penal reform and lists relevant publications.

Prison Reform Trust
http://www.prisonreformtrust.org.uk/
Information on the Prison Reform Trust, which aims at creating a just, humane and effective penal system.

Youth Justice Board for England and Wales
www.youth-justice-board.gov.uk.
Contains information on policies, news, press releases and details of youth offending teams.

***The Guardian*: Prisons**
http://www.guardian.co.uk/prisons
The *Guardian*'s coverage of prison issues is an excellent resource.

***The Observer*: Special Reports**
http://www.observer.guardian.co.uk/crimedebate
This offers further critical commentary on prison issues.

The Zahid Mubarek Inquiry
www.zahidmubarekinquiry.org.uk
This site is a link to the final report.

International Centre for Prison Studies
http://www.prisonstudies.org/
This site also maintains the indispensable World Prisons Brief.

UK Border Agency, Immigration Removal Centres
http://www.ukba.homeoffice.gov.uk/aboutus/organisation/immigrationremovalcentres

part 5 **Globalizing Crime**

chapter 19

Green Criminology

Key issues

- What is a 'green criminology' and what can be identified as 'green crimes'?
- How are green crimes identified and 'criminalized'?
- What are the social costs of 'green crimes'?
- How do social movements shape reactions and responses to green crimes?

Introduction

Green criminology is concerned with crimes and harms affecting the environment, the planet and the associated impacts on human and non-human life. Since the early 1990s it has developed into a fertile area of study bringing together a range of research interests and theoretical orientations (see e.g. South and Brisman, 2013; Beirne and South, 2007; Sollund, 2008; White, 2010). Green criminology is not based on any single theory or school of thought but is better seen as an evolving *perspective* (South, 1998b: 212–13). It can be defined as:

> a framework of intellectual, empirical and political orientations toward primary and secondary harms, offences and crimes that impact in a damaging way on the natural environment, diverse species (human and non-human) and the planet.

In terms of criminological lineage it most clearly arises from within the tradition(s) of critical criminology but, at the same time, it actively seeks inter- and multi-disciplinary engagement. It can be seen as *a body of work* but also as *an active network* of interested individuals sharing and debating ideas.

This approach can cover several major themes, topics and problems. These include (but this is not an exhaustive list):

- pollution and its regulation;
- corporate criminality and its impact on the environment;
- health and safety in the workplace where breaches have environmentally damaging consequences;
- involvement of organized crime and official corruption in the illegal disposal of toxic waste;
- the impact and legacy of law enforcement and military operations on landscapes, water supply, air quality and living organisms populating these areas – human, animal and plant;
- as well as forms of law enforcement and rule regulation relevant to such acts (South and Brisman, 2013; Lynch, 1990; South, 1998b: 214; Eman et al., 2009).

Relevant work has been underway for some time but may have adopted different names or labels. For example, 'environmental criminology' has been proposed by White (2008) but this term has suffered the drawback of being too easily confused with its longer established usage to describe crime patterns and features of the urban environment. However, a leading expert has recently suggested the latter might be better described as 'Socio-spatial criminology' with one reason for this name change being to avoid confusion with 'the important emerging field of "green" criminology' (Bottoms, 2012: 451). Other terms include:

- 'eco-crime', suggested by Walters (2010) as a way of covering 'existing legal definitions of environmental crime, as well as sociological analyses of those environmental harms not necessarily specified by law';
- 'conservation criminology' (Gibbs et al., 2010);
- eco-global criminology (White, 2010).

But criminologists most frequently employ the term 'green criminology' to describe the study of ecological, environmental or green crime or harm, and related matters of speciesism (see Beirne, 2009) and of environmental (in)justice.

The plundering of the earth's resources has only recently been thought of as a crime but there is increasing recognition of the problems of wasteful over-consumption and exploitation. In their approach to these issues, criminologists may adopt either a

- *legal-procedural approach* to environmental issues, retaining a traditional focus on violations of enacted environmental law (including civil and regulatory violations), or
- a more *critical* or *socio-legal approach* examining environmental harms that are not statutorily prohibited but regarded as equally or more damaging than some actions that are legal offences.

Various typologies have been offered to deepen our understanding of environmental crimes and harms. These are important as ways of identifying and organizing clusters of issues and problems.

Distinguishing between *primary* and *secondary* green crimes: this is a simple but suggestive way of differentiating clusters of harms and crimes by classifying some as:

resulting directly from the destruction and degradation of the earth's resources

and others as:

crimes or harms that are symbiotic with or dependent upon such destruction and efforts made to regulate or prevent it.

Purely as an illustrative exercise, we can identify four main primary green crimes or harms in which the environment and non-human species as well as humans are harmed, damaged or degraded through human actions – all of which, to add a positive note, have become the subject of some national and international legislative efforts to protect and intervene in recent years:

1. Crimes and harms of air pollution
2. Crimes and harms of deforestation
3. Crimes and harms against animals
4. Crimes and harms of water pollution

Secondary or symbiotic green harms and crimes can arise from the exploitation of conditions that follow after environmental damage or crisis (e.g. illegal markets for food, medicine, water) and/or from the violation of rules that attempt to regulate environmental harm and to respond to disaster. These can include numerous major and minor practices whereby states violate their own regulations (either by commission or omission) and in so doing contribute to environmental harms.

As another set of distinctions, White (2008: 98–9) has developed a threefold 'brown', 'green' and 'white' typology. 'Brown' issues are defined in terms of urban life and pollution (e.g. air pollution, disposal of toxic/hazardous waste, oil spills, pesticides, pollution of beaches and water catchments, stormwater pollution). 'Green' issues refer to conservation matters and 'wilderness' areas (e.g. acid rain, biodiversity loss, habitat destruction, invasive species introduced via human transport, logging practices, ozone depletion, toxic algae and water pollution). 'White' issues refer to the impact of new technologies and various laboratory practices (e.g. animal testing and experimentation; cloning of human tissue; environmentally related communicable diseases; food irradiation; genetically modified organisms; *in vitro* processes; and pathological indoor environments).

The development of critical thinking around green issues in criminology has produced case studies and theory that connect to and interweave with aspects of philosophy, political science, sociology, economics, the arts and the environmental sciences. These interdisciplinary possibilities are exciting but it may still not be obvious to everybody how environmental challenges relate to criminology in the traditional sense.

One starting point here is to remember that, as shown in earlier chapters, 'traditions' in criminology have always been in a state of invention and re-discovery, revival and renewal – and a green criminology both builds on past developments such as those concerning corporate crime and victimization, while identifying new directions. This was noted by Zahn (1999: 2) in her 1998 Presidential Address to the American Society of Criminology:

> pollution of our rivers and oceans is causing global mass extinctions and a significant reduction in biodiversity. The impacts for life on this planet are far-reaching. Particulate pollution annually kills . . . four times [more people than] . . . homicide. . . . With more focus on environmental crime will come a new definition of victims to include species other than humans and a definition of offenders to include those who pollute for convenience . . . [and] for profit. Just as Sutherland's white-collar crime expanded our crime paradigm (1949), . . . environmental crime will change it in the future.
>
> (Zahn, 1999: 2)

Criminology constantly questions the 'taken-for-granted' nature of definitions and classifications of crime and deviance. It asks whether existing laws and labels are appropriate and it makes alternative proposals about where concern and regulation should be directed. In the case of a green criminology it is argued that a wide range of actions imperil the planet as well as the future of humanity and other species, and these crimes and harms need to be recognized and responded to.

Example – the case of climate change

To take the best-known and most pressing issue of this nature, consider the case of climate change.

Climate change will shift the patterns and transactions of both local and global life: it will simultaneously encourage and impede mobility, lead to the revaluation of resources and the restructuring of markets, and as one outcome (among many) also reshape the causes and consequences of some forms of crime and conflict (Fussey and South, 2013; South, 2012). Abbott (2008), for example, suggests that increasing temperatures, rising sea levels and weather volatility could, by 2050, have led to

- resource wars over food and water;
- the plight of up to 200 million 'environmental refugees' fleeing devastation;
- an inflation of ethnic tensions and conflicts;
- the prospect of the police and border services of countries closing down rather than opening up borders;
- violent protests against polluters.

Our globalized society is hugely dependent on energy, communications and travel but both climate change and energy crises could have significant effects on these and the sociologist John Urry (2008) has suggested control of oil and gas could lead to regional warlords emerging and conflicts erupting over access to resources while familiar systems of communication break down and standards of living decline.

BOX 19.1 An unusual forecast for climate change and crime

Kristof (2008) has written in *The New York Times* that 'climate change will have consequences that will be difficult to foresee but will go far beyond weather or economics'. For example, climate scientists expect economic problems and crop failures to occur in some poor countries and this is a pattern that can lead to violence and political upheaval. But drawing on a study published in the respected *Review of Economic Studies* (Miguel, 2005) Kristof goes on to point out how climate, culture and human activities – including forms of crime and deviance – can interact:

> Here's a forecast for a particularly bizarre consequence of climate change: more executions of witches. As we pump out greenhouse gases, most of the discussion focuses on direct consequences like rising seas or aggravated hurricanes. But the indirect social and political impact in poor countries may be even more far-reaching, including upheavals and civil wars – and even more witches hacked to death with machetes.

In rural Tanzania, murders of elderly women accused of witchcraft are a very common form of homicide. And when Tanzania suffers unusual rainfall – either drought or flooding – witch killings double.

The implications from this study are that if climate change produces more drought years in Tanzania and other countries where witches are commonly identified as scapegoats for problems, then victimization and murder of these women will rise. This is not new says *The Times*'s story and echoes how scapegoats have been sought down the centuries in times of social panic and economic crisis: 'There is evidence that European witch-burnings in past centuries may also have resulted from climate variations and the resulting crop-failures,' says Kristof (2008).

(See also the discussions of labelling theory (Chapter 6) and Box 20.2 on 'Classic moral panic theory'.)

Why should climate change be of interest to criminologists?

Although the case described in Box 19.1 may seem a particularly unusual possible consequence of climate change, there are many other ways in which climate change has been seen as potentially criminogenic (i.e. a cause of crime).

If climate change causes drought, flooding, crop failure and social unrest all this may lead to scarcity of food, water and goods and to disruption of supply chains. Scarcity is often managed by rationing and increasing prices. These are classic factors that can lead to corruption, illegal diversion of goods, illicit markets, profiteering, food riots and security challenges for policing and distribution agencies. These impacts may be most devastating in parts of the world that are already poor and now developing but they will also have consequences along the distribution chains and in terms of how the populations most affected try to respond. The impacts will also be differentiated in terms of power and, as Wachholz (2007: 161) has suggested, climate change will have a bearing on women's vulnerability to male violence because:

> The asymmetries in social, political and economic power that exist both between and within countries are influencing how individuals experience, respond to, and recover from the environmental hazards and the natural disasters that climate change brings in tow. . . . In this sense . . . climate change must also be understood as a social process that is situated within the context of unequal distributions of power and privilege.

Climate change will also produce differentiated social vulnerability in other ways, for example, in terms of access to water and food (Bohle et al., 1994). In 2010, food protests in Mozambique provided an illustration of how the interaction of changing weather patterns in different agricultural regions and influences on the commodity markets that transcend borders can lead to conflict and crime. Following a period of price increases for bread as well as for water and electricity supply, grocery stores were robbed and riots broke out. The rising price of bread reflected the fact that local crop production could not meet demand and this could no longer be easily supplemented by purchase from abroad because wildfires had destroyed parts of the grain belt of Russia during the hottest summer heatwave for a century, leading to export bans from that country. At the same time, international commodity speculators were engaging in what the World Development Movement has called 'gambling on hunger in financial markets' (Patel, 2010: 31).

Such conditions have further consequences. Food crises and starvation could push many refugees onto the road of migration to countries that are not so seriously affected such as those in Europe (McKie, 2009). Migration can lead to further damage and despair: losing a home, sense of belonging, being vulnerable and without shelter – all can mean people become victims caught up in human trafficking or in conflicts, often being waged over the riches of the earth. Such conflicts, in turn, displace more people as well as damaging local environments and dependent species.

Globalization and the risk society

Environmental degradation is nothing new but it was really only in the latter years of the twentieth century – as pollution and its effects accelerated and the impacts of human behaviour such as use of pesticides and dumping of waste began to be understood – that global awareness of the seriousness of this issue began to grow. It is now apparent that any understanding of the natural environment and its problems must be global in scope – and so must our responses. This can be thought of in terms of the process of globalization that we have discussed elsewhere in this book (see especially Chapter 7).

We may also see these problems as part of what the German sociologist Ulrich Beck (1992) called 'the **risk society**', whereby *modern industrial societies create many new risks – largely manufactured through modern technologies – that were unknown in earlier human history*. Of course, past societies were risky and dangerous places too: whole populations could be wiped out by major earthquakes, floods or plagues. But Beck argues that new kinds of risks appear with the development of the industrial world that are not 'in nature' but are 'manufactured'. These are associated with the many new technologies that generate new dangers to lives and to the planet itself. These dangers are humanly produced, may have massively unforeseen consequences, and may take many, many thousands of years to reverse. For Beck and like-minded commentators, these 'manufactured risks' are taking us to the edge of catastrophe, posing 'threats to all forms of life on this planet' and presenting us with an 'exponential growth of risks and the impossibility of escaping them'.

Risk is associated with a society that tries to break away from tradition and the past, and where change and the future become more valued. All these changes – from the railway to the computer, from genetic engineering to nuclear weapons – have consequences that we cannot easily predict. The emergence of '**green crimes**' is part of these new risks, bringing new patterns of crime which could not have been easily foretold a century or so ago.

BOX 19.2 A brief history of environmental degradation

Pre-1500	Global extinctions of whole species – up to 90 per cent were lost at the end of the Permian and Cretaceous periods; many large mammals lost; some species through overhunting. Microbe movements leading to epidemics; long-term natural climate changes.
1500–1760	European ecological expansion and capitalist growth starts to lead to rising resource shortage and land degradation; demographic movements and ecological transformation of the Americas.
Modern: 1760–1945	Capitalist industrialization, urbanization, concentration, ecological expansion and colonialization . . . local resource exhaustion, urban air, soil and water pollution, change in rural environments and forest loss, some global extinction of species and some contribution to global warming
Contemporary	Global warming, marine depletion, water in short supply, deforestation, desertification, soil exhaustion, overspills, hazardous waste, acid deposition, nuclear risks, decline of the global ecosystem comes with Western growth and consumption, industrialization and expansion of the developing economies of the world, new risks from technology and warfare.

Sources: Harrison and Pearce (2000);
Held *et al.* (1999: 391).

Green criminology and harms against the environment

Green criminology takes 'harm' as a central concept and addresses violations of what have been variously termed 'environmental morality', 'environmental ethics' and 'animal rights' (Beirne and South, 2007: xiii). In so doing, it aims to uncover sources and forms of harm caused by the unjust exercise of power and the persistence of social inequality. Of particular interest is how certain forms of harm are denied, overlooked or excused (see Cohen, 2001, for insights into these processes). This kind of perspective is similar to the social harm approach described by Hillyard *et al.* (2004: 1) and involves 'a focus on all the different types of harms which people experience from the cradle to the grave'. A green criminology counts among its avenues of investigation the 'why, how and when' of the generation and control of such harms and related exploitation, abuse, loss and suffering. Gender inequalities, racism, speciesism and classism are all key categories for such an approach.

Harms, connections and consequences

An important aspect of green criminology is the way that it directs attention to cases and causes of harms, crimes and conflicts, and related connections and consequences that are usually overlooked or neglected in criminology. For example, although it is now a commonplace feature of criminology to find reports on transnational organized crime, it has been relatively rare until recently to find these placing a significant emphasis on environmental resources, including wildlife crime and trafficking. However, this features as a whole chapter in a 2010 report on *The Globalization of Crime* from the United Nations Office on Drugs and Crime, which notes in particular (p. 149) how

> The trafficking of environmental resources is a key challenge for some developing countries. Many emerging economies are based on exporting raw materials, but under-resourced governments may lack the capacity to regulate the exploitation of these assets. Rather than promoting economic progress, poorly managed natural wealth can become a cause of bad governance, corruption or even violent conflict.

One phenomenon of relevance here has been called the 'resource curse' of developing countries rich in mineral, plant and wildlife 'wealth' which has led to the exploitation of their environment in damaging and harmful ways. This exploitation contributes to what Wenar (2008: 2) has described as a 'system of global commerce' built upon laws and agreements that are 'little more than a cloak for larceny' generating both legal and illegal trades in diamonds, timber and wildlife. These trades may bring little or no return to indigenous peoples but do produce huge profits for organized crime groups, corrupt governments and unethical corporations. In addition, there is a longer-lasting and profound effect of intergenerational ecological injustice (Weston, 2012). This offends one of the key principles of sustainability:

> that we look at the earth and its resources not only as an investment opportunity, but as a trust passed to us by our ancestors for our benefit, but also to be passed on to our descendants for their use. This notion conveys both rights and responsibilities. Most importantly, it implies that future generations have rights too. These rights have meaning only if we the living, respect them, and in this regard, transcend the differences among countries, religions, and cultures.
>
> (Weiss, 1992: 19–20)

Both human rights (see Chapter 22) and the principle of environmental sustainability are entwined and need to be upheld across national, religious and cultural divides.

The case of the Democratic Republic of Congo (DRC) is a now well-known example of a country affected by the 'resource curse'. Rich in mineral resources, including gold, the country has suffered ceaseless conflict involving several other countries for nearly two decades. According to a UN expert panel, this had led to 'highly organized and systematic exploitation' (UN, 2002: 10, para. 52) involving rebels and government forces, with both profiting from the trades in mineral ores and subjecting civilians to massacres, rape and extortion, using forced labour and coercing children into the role of soldiers. Taylor (*The Guardian*, 3 September 2011: 30) reports cases of rape victims in eastern DRC being forced to work in conditions of slavery in mines producing coltan, gold and tin ore, used for mobile phones, laptops and jewellery.

The mining practices adopted also adversely affect the food chain and water supply of other species and plant life. Species harms and violations also occur because the tantalum/coltan mining areas also cover national parks that are home to the endangered mountain gorilla (Nellemann *et al.*, 2010). Here ground clearance for mining has led to the gorilla population halving in recent years as their food supply has been disrupted or lost; at the same time, the displacement of the human local population has led to their impoverishment and to hunting gorillas to slaughter for 'bush meat' to consume and to sell to miners and rebel armies.

Harms to the planet and its inhabitants: a typology

The case for a reappraisal of traditional notions of harms and crimes, offences and injurious behaviours has been made by many and examples are found throughout this book. From the perspective of a green criminology, the argument is that we must re-examine the role that societies play in damaging our shared environment. By this we should mean all constituent parts of society, from corporations and governments to ordinary people in their everyday lives. So as well as examining the crimes of the powerful it is important to emphasize the role that ordinary acts carried out by ordinary people play in damaging and over-exploiting the natural environment and other species in unsustainable ways. The criminologist Robert Agnew (2013) has written about these 'ordinary acts that contribute to ecocide' (see Box 19.3).

BOX 19.3 Ordinary acts of everyday life that contribute to ecocide

Robert Agnew (2013) writes that:

> These ordinary acts have several characteristics: they are widely and regularly performed by individuals as part of their routine activities; they are generally viewed as acceptable, even desirable; and they collectively have a substantial impact on environmental problems.

Many specific acts meet these requirements; the most notable include living in a large, suburban home, heated and cooled to comfortable levels; using a gasoline-powered automobile for most transportation; frequently purchasing consumer products; and regularly consuming meat. These . . . 'ordinary harms' . . . contribute to ecocide by increasing air, water, and soil pollution; destroying natural habitats and animal life; depleting natural resources; and helping to cause climate change (Worldwatch Institute 2010). . . .

. . . The United States (US) leads the world in the commission of ordinary harms. For example, US residents comprise only 5% of the world's population but account for 32% of all global expenditures on consumption. If everyone lived at the same level as US citizens, the world could sustain only 1.4 billon people (the current population is 6.8 billon) (Worldwatch Institute 2010). . . .

Ordinary harms have not only been neglected by mainstream criminologists, but by many green criminologists as well – who more often focus on the environmental harms committed by states, corporations, and organized criminal groups. . . . The focus on these latter harms is readily understandable given the tremendous damage they cause. . . . But ordinary harms also cause great damage. Furthermore, a full understanding of environmental harm requires that we consider both the actions of individuals and larger groups, for they are symbiotically related. Ordinary harms committed by individuals provide much incentive for those state and corporate behaviors that contribute to ecocide, such as deforestation and the generation of electricity in coal-powered plants. At the same time, states and corporations encourage and facilitate the commission of ordinary harms.

Source: Agnew (2013: 58–72).

To return to the four clusters of environmental harms and crimes identified earlier.

Harms and crimes of air pollution

Fossil-fuel burning releases about 6 billion tons of carbon into the air each year, adding about 3 billion tons annually to the 170 billion tons that have settled since the Industrial Revolution. The rate of growth in carbon emissions is around 2 per cent per year. Harms and crimes here result from pollution of the air by cars and planes, as a result of wars, burning of corporate waste, and those responsible are governments, big business and ordinary consumers.

Walters (2013: 136) writes that

> The link between air pollution and premature death has been widely established. . . . It is estimated that twice as many people today suffer from lung disease and asthmatic conditions caused by air pollution than they did twenty years ago. . . . Furthermore, it is important to perceive of the harms created by air pollution in a broader global context . . . it is most often the poorest people on the planet that experience the worst effects of pollution. An estimated 65% of all annual deaths resulting from air pollution occur within the slums and poverty stricken areas of developing countries.

BOX 19.4 World Resources Institute

There are numerous sources for information and statistics about environmental change. A key source used here is the World Resources Institute, a non-profit, independent organization. Their website is: http://www.wri.org/

Advice on pollution prevention from the UK government Environment Agency points out that

> Businesses and individuals are responsible for complying with environmental regulations and for preventing pollution of air, land and water. Many thousands of pollution incidents occur each year, originating from factories, farms, transport activities and even homes. Each incident is an offence and can result in prosecution as well as environmental damage. However, most cases are avoidable.
>
> (Environment Agency: General Guide to the Prevention of Pollution, http://publications.environment-agency.gov.uk/PDF/PMHO0501BFOX-E-E.pdf)

As with many other kinds of crime or cases of non-criminal breaking of rules or regulations, the failure to take measures to avoid the problem is significant. Non-compliance with good practice and efforts aimed at prevention can follow from short-term assumptions about cost-saving and familiar narratives of denial – 'whatever I do won't matter or make a difference', 'no one will catch me', 'others are more guilty of this than me', and so on, and because there have always been problems with the inadequacy of resources for enforcement of such rules and laws it is possible that offenders will remain undetected or not prosecuted (du Rees, 2001). At the same time, support for sanctions can wax and wane illustrating how vulnerable to political values and the social construction of public agendas environmental law actually is.

Harms and crimes of deforestation

Here harms and crimes are caused by those involved in the destruction and misuse of forest and woodland environments and traditional lands. However, both raising awareness and implementing policy changes targeted at environmental harms can make a difference and in recent years it has been reported that the net rate of forest loss across the planet has been slowing down as efforts have been made to reduce logging in areas like the Amazon and as major growth economies like China have adopted tree planting plans on a large scale. However as the UN Food and Agriculture Organization (FAO) emphasizes, despite this 'slowdown', the *rate of loss* of forest continues to be 'alarming' (Richard Black, Environment correspondent, BBC News online, 25 March 2010). The world has lost half of its forests over the past 8,000 years and, just in the latter part of the twentieth century, between 1960 and 1990, about 20 per cent of the world's tropical forest was lost. Between 70 and 95 per cent of the earth's species live in the world's disappearing tropical forest. The world is becoming increasingly urbanized – 37 per cent of people in 1970 lived in urban areas, which is projected to rise to 61 per cent by 2030. At the same time, millions of hectares of fertile land are lost every year due to soil degradation meaning there is less land to grow food while more is needed to feed people.

Reporting on his fieldwork in the Amazon, the green criminologist Tim Boekhout van Solinge says that land taken over for the logging industry and/or to be used for farming can often lead to disputes about who rightfully owns the land. In turn this can lead to violent conflicts over land use:

> In Brazil's rural and forested areas, it is quite common for loggers and farmers to use gunmen, *pistoleros*, who use or threaten to use violence against traditional communities when disagreements over land tenure occur. Other victims have included human rights and environmental activists. . . . While these murders received much international attention, most of the violence that occurs in the Amazon in the context of deforestation and land conflicts goes virtually unnoticed.
>
> (Boekhout van Solinge and Kuijpers, 2013: 199)

These environments and their inhabitants also suffer at the hands of those who exploit natural resources without regard to questions of justice about ownership and rights, supplying illegal markets that are based upon the sale of valuable and sometimes irreplaceable natural commodities. The expanding and controversial area of bio-prospecting, bio-patenting and **biopiracy** is also relevant (see also discussion in Chapter 10), representing a global market for the products of ancient and tropical forests or other remote regions as well as the commercial appropriation and reinterpretation of indigenous knowledge previously preserved by passage from generation to generation (South, 2007). Bio-patenting or biopiracy yields enormous profits for Western corporations yet little or no return for the inhabitants of the source sites. Depletion of resources could also have consequences of immediate and long-term effect for global health as experts note that:

> Medicines for HIV and cancer could be lost because plants used in their preparation are facing extinction. . . . Deforestation and over-collection now threaten the survival of up to 400 key plant species, according to a survey by Botanic Gardens Conservation International. The at-risk plants include yew trees whose bark is used in cancer drug Paclitaxel and autumn crocus which helps to fight leukaemia. . . . More than 50 per cent of drugs prescribed by doctors are derived from chemicals first identified in plants.
>
> (Powell, 2008: 12)

Harms and crimes of species decline and animal abuse

According to a report from the United Nations Convention on Biological Diversity (2010: 26), across the world today all species for which we have trend-based data,

> are, on average, being driven closer to extinction. . . . Among selected vertebrate, invertebrate and plant groups, between 12% and 55% of species are currently threatened with extinction. Species of birds and mammals used for food and medicine are on average facing a greater extinction risk than those not used for such purposes. Preliminary assessments suggest that 23% of plant species are threatened.

Of course, because we don't actually know how many species there are on the planet (and many are microbial), we cannot say with scientific certainty how many species are being lost each year but one thing we do know is that human actions are accelerating and causing processes of loss of biodiversity rather than this simply happening through natural extinction (see Box 19.5). Significant contributors to the disruption of habitats and loss of sustainability include various forms of urban and industrial development but it is also the case that another key source of harmful impact is the major international wildlife trafficking business. Organized crime networks as well as legitimate firms trade in all kinds of species, and criminal and unethical commercial operators also trade in the body parts of various prized species. This is a global market, trading across borders around the world. South and Wyatt (2011: 546, drawing on Burgener et al., 2001; emphasis added) define such trade, wildlife trafficking and illegal wildlife trade, in the following ways:

> Trade encompasses collection, harvesting, possession, processing, acquiring or transporting of wildlife for the purpose of purchasing, importing, exporting, selling, bartering or exchanging. Wildlife trafficking or the illegal wildlife trade is the specific name of the green crime that involves the illegal trade, smuggling, poaching, capture or collection of endangered species, protected wildlife . . . derivatives or products thereof.

Sollund (2013: 319) suggests definitions using terms such as 'harvesting' and 'poaching' are anthropocentric as they imply that animals can be the property of humans, indistinguishable from crops, plants and natural resources, and this denies them rights that should be attributed to them and respected. Sollund therefore suggests the term 'abduction' (i.e. to carry away by force), rather than 'harvesting' or 'poaching'. But whatever the terminology, this is now big business and the UNODC (2010: 149) report on the globalization of crime notes that factors such as widespread poverty and conflicts in Africa alongside the high prices that exotic animal products, such as elephant ivory and rhinoceros horn, attract has encouraged poaching on a large scale. In Southeast Asia different forces of supply and demand are seeing species under threat because of the high prices that are paid for items used for traditional medicines or as food, decorative products or exclusive pets. The skin and bones of tigers are sought after but becoming ever rarer and hence more expensive as there are thought to be only around 3,200 still surviving in the wild.

BOX 19.5 World Wide Fund for Nature – WWF

For more information on species loss see the website of the World Wide Fund for Nature: http://wwf.panda.org/about_our_earth/species/problems/

National and international laws exist to protect animal and plant species but apart from the under-resourcing of enforcement noted above there are other reasons why such laws can be ineffective. Among these can be genuine ignorance of restrictions, or historical and culturally grounded motives for denial, as well as rejection of any reasons why such restrictions should apply or be necessary. Laws exist in many countries to protect animals from exploitation and cruel deaths in, for example, cases of dog-fighting, badger baiting and other 'animal spectacles' organized for entertainment and profit but such laws do not apply everywhere. These are complex cases and law alone may not be sufficient to combat what can be highly profitable trades or embedded cultural ideas and practices.

Harms and crimes of water pollution and resource depletion

Around one billion people across the world, mainly in developing countries, lack safe drinking water and this may reach 2.5 billion by 2025. On a daily basis, almost 40,000 men, women and children die from diseases directly related to drinking polluted water. Yet elsewhere, in advanced societies with water readily available through purification and pipe systems, this precious resource has become another commercial product at the heart of a huge industry based on the bottling of water to meet a culturally created consumer demand that is, according to Gleick (2010: 116), 'an act of economic, environmental and social blindness'. So, while many go without, others package and sell the products of the earth and its ecosystems into commodities, a point noted by cultural criminologists such as Jeff Ferrell (2004: 167) who are critical of what they see as patterns of profligate hyper-consumption that are contributing to environmental destruction.

Freshwater **ecosystems** are in decline everywhere. Some 58 per cent of the world's reefs and 34 per cent of all fish may be at risk due to overfishing, poaching and non-sustainable fishing techniques, as well as pollution (see Box 19.6). Poaching remains a problem today, as it has for centuries, but not merely in the sense of being an offence against property owners. Poaching can also represent inequalities of resource distribution and employ methods that are damaging or highly destructive to stocks and other species. It can also have links to more serious forms of organized crime because of the high end-price of particular delicacies, which may be gathered by exploited and impoverished gatherer-poachers paid pittance wages or rewarded with addictive drugs. The legal gathering of popular seafood such as cockles can also be associated with the exploitation of cheap labour provided by illegal immigrants working for unscrupulous gangmasters, as was revealed in the case of the tragic deaths of 21 Chinese cockle pickers in Morecambe Bay in 2004. The growth of markets for all kinds of foods has prompted other unwelcome impacts on human workers and local environments – the intensification of supply of prawns to meet enormously increased global consumer demand being a good example (see O'Brien, 2008). Indeed another important subject of interest for a green criminology is the production, supply and consumption of food and how crimes and harms intersect with the food chain at various points (see Croall, 2013).

BOX 19.6 Case study: Gulf of Mexico oil spill and BP

On 20 April 2010 a deepwater oil well operated by BP, lying on the sea bed in the Gulf of Mexico, exploded with the immediate effect of killing 11 people and injuring 17 others. But the wider impact was that with oil leaking at a high rate of (according to some estimates) around 40,000 barrels a day, it was soon evident that the spill was a huge risk to both sea and land environments as well as local populations and businesses. The oil would pollute and destroy fauna and flora and affect more than 100 miles of shoreline in Louisiana.

Declared the worst ecological disaster in US history, the damage was then compounded by the chemical dispersants used to neutralize the slick: more than 3.5 million litres of chemicals combined with crude oil in turn posed their own severe threat to public health. This is a good example of how our industrial capabilities can cause problems which are then addressed by attempts at a scientific solution or 'technical fix' but which, in turn, can then cause further problems. (See the discussion of the risk society in this chapter.)

The crisis began with the explosion of the Deepwater Horizon rig about 50 miles offshore but thereafter, as is often the case with green crimes and similar corporate crimes, the matter of who was to blame and who might be held responsible was not entirely clear-cut. Although the BP Chief Executive Tony Hayward stepped down under pressure later in 2010 and BP can certainly be blamed for incompetence, fraudulent sidestepping of safety rules, or for hiring unprofessional contractors to carry out some extraction and maintenance operations, the

Figure 19.1 Map showing BP oil spill in the Gulf of Mexico.

broader matters of attribution of 'blame' and identification of 'cause' of this disaster are complicated and relate to our dependence on oil. More critical commentators have also blamed US political and business interests, seduced by the cheap petrol and high tax revenue provided by BP while the oil industry's major safety watchdog in the USA was accused of bending to the power of the oil industry and failing to regulate drilling and other operations: 'Halting offshore operations of any particular company would improve safety, but reduce tax revenues by $13bn annually' (Macalister, 2010). Ultimately however, it is consumer addiction to oil that provides the background to this disaster. As the US imports 10 million barrels of oil a day it was probably always doubtful that any US administration would seriously fall out with the oil industry, and despite short-term anger expressed by politicians and local residents, fuelled by some media outlets (see Chapter 20 on the media and moral outrage), the long-term relationship between government and big oil seems likely to continue as one of co-dependence.

Economic impact
- The government asked for $20 billion in damages from BP and BP's share price fell.
- Local industries, such as fishing were threatened. There was a ban on fishing in the water.
- Tourism declined.

Environmental impact
- Plants and animals were completely covered in the oil. Seabirds, sea turtles and dolphins have been found dead.
- Oil that entered wetland areas meant recovery would be slow.
- Fish stocks were harmed, and productivity decreased.

The size of the oil spill was one of the largest America had seen. However because the oil entered warm waters, organisms in the water helped to break down the oil. The overall effect may be less than *Exxon Valdez* oil spill in 1989 which happened in colder water.

Source: http://www.bbc.co.uk/schools/gcsebitesize/geography/
wasting-resources/waste_pollution_rev5.shtml

Secondary or symbiotic green crimes

Aside from direct (primary) damage and destruction caused to environments and species, we can also refer to symbiotic (secondary) green crime as growing out of illegal or negligent government or corporate activity, which can even include the flouting of rules set by such bodies themselves to regulate environmentally sensitive activities.

For example, while states condemn 'terrorism' they may actually employ terrorist-type methods when in conflict with opposing groups. A particularly notorious example is the 1985 sinking of the Greenpeace flagship *Rainbow Warrior* in Auckland harbour, New Zealand. This was a crime of terrorist violence carried out by commandos from the French secret service. In this operation, sanctioned at cabinet level within the French government, 22 kilos of explosive was used to blow up the Greenpeace ship as an expression of French anger over its use in protest activities against French nuclear tests in the Pacific. Miraculously, of the crew of 13 on board at the time of the blast, only one was killed (Day, 1991: 281–4). In his book *The Eco-wars*, Day (1991) charts a variety of similar state-sponsored acts of violence and intimidation against environmental activists or groups. His comments on these and the *Rainbow Warrior* affair are highly relevant to the idea of a criminology that takes environmental issues and politics seriously:

> The most unusual aspect of the Rainbow Warrior affair was that, to some degree at least, the murder mystery was solved. Although justice was not done, the truth came out. There have been many other acts of state terrorism linked with the anti-nuclear war but it is seldom possible to prove that they are linked directly to government officials. Indeed, if the agents had not been caught red-handed, there is no doubt that Greenpeace activists would have been scoffed at for pointing the finger at the French government. Their accusation would have been dismissed as just one more lunatic fringe conspiracy theory. Why, after all, would the French government worry about the activities of a small-scale anti-nuclear protest group? Surely only a total paranoid would believe that violent action was necessary to stop such a group. The answer is that when it comes to nuclear issues the French – and the governments of *all* nuclear powers – *are* paranoid. In every case where a government has committed itself to nuclear weapons or nuclear power, all those who oppose this policy are treated in some degree as enemies of the State.
>
> (Day, 1991)

Waste dumping, victims and organized crime

The limited or ineffective regulation of waste dumping, especially in advanced Western industrial nations, has created a highly profitable domestic and international trade in illegal disposal and dumping of hazardous toxic waste. Both weak and serious regulation can lead to illegal and dangerous disposal of waste – the former because rules are easily flouted and the latter because the costs of legitimate disposal can encourage illicit practices and services to deal with difficult waste. This has manifested itself in various forms of corporate organized crime, sometimes – perhaps even frequently – with tacit state acknowledgement (Ruggiero and South, 2010; Szasz, 1986; Scarpitti and Block, 1987; Van Duyne, 1993). Toxic and general waste dumping is an increasingly significant crime and, as Simon (2000: 639) points out, some waste-dumping activities are particularly devastating because most of the people who suffer the consequences of waste polluting their living environments are among the 'least powerful people on the face of the earth, poverty-stricken people of color, . . . powerless to resist the environmental deviance of multinational firms'. Many studies have drawn attention to this environmental victimization of communities of the poor and powerless due to the frequency with which their locations may be the sites of, for example, polluting industry, waste-processing plants or other environmentally hazardous facilities (Bullard, 1994; Williams, 1996; Lynch and Stretesky, 2001).

As with so many crimes, environmental crimes and harms have a strong link to inequalities. Indeed, we can speak of *environmental racism* as the pattern by which environmental hazards are perceived to be greatest in proximity to poor people, and especially those belonging to minorities. Historically, factories that spew pollutants have been built in and near districts inhabited by the poor, who often work there. As a result of their low incomes, many could afford housing only in undesirable localities, sometimes in the very shadow of the plants and mills. Although workers in many manufacturing industries have organized in opposition to environmental hazards, they have done so with limited success, largely because the people facing the most serious environmental threats have the least social power to begin with. As with many crimes then, there are identifiable victims who are often from less advantaged groups. We can see this happening globally and locally.

Developing nations as 'dump sites'

Since the mid-1970s, most Western countries have toughened up anti-dumping and pollution laws and regulations. It would be naive, however, to suppose that such problems have been mitigated, let alone eradicated, by tougher laws. What the regulations in advanced Western nations have done is to create an international trade in dumping. Toxic waste defined as unsuitable for landfill burial in the West may be shipped to developing countries that do not have similar regulatory laws, or lack enforcement resources, or who welcome such waste because its disposal yields profit, paid for in needed foreign currency. This whole combination of factors is conducive to corruption. In many cases, the export of such waste would not normally be granted export licences by North American or West European regulatory agencies, and the proper procedure should be for such waste to be reprocessed to reduce its toxicity before disposal. This is, however, potentially very expensive, and hence the waste may be moved illegally. Toxic waste does not seem to be a problem so long as we can find somewhere else to dump it other than our own back yard.

Local communities as dump sites

Environmental discrimination is a fact of life for many poor communities. Restrictions on housing opportunities (often through discriminatory practices) have led to all manner of environmental hazards. Thus, black communities in the USA often find their housing situated right next to 'garbage dumps, hazardous-waste landfills, incinerators, smelter operations, paper mills, chemical plants, and a host of other polluting industries' (Bullard, 1990: xiv); 'industries often follow the simplest opportunities and dump their stuff in economically poor and politically powerless black communities'. Moreover, as already stated, the disposal of waste generally, and toxic waste in particular, as well as the siting of controversial high-pollution industries, are also displaced or 'regionalized' in another way: by exporting them to the developing world. Here the environmental victims may still remain largely hidden or forgotten, at least until catastrophe occurs.

Such 'toxic tragedies' (Cass, 1996) are commonplace internationally, frequently exhibiting characteristics such as: difficulty of prosecution due to problems in drawing together evidence that can tie commercial operations to specific illegal offences; cases of corruption; and strong industry 'profit-at-all-costs' motivations (Cass, 1996: 110–12). In the latter case, the rationality of a business enterprise may lead to deliberate choice of criminal activity due to the low chance of detection, difficulty of proof of guilt and options for 'fixing' cases should they come to the attention of rule- or law-enforcers or even the courts (Cass, 1996: 112, drawing on Sutherland, 1949). Within this general pattern may be found what Gobert and Punch (2003: 27) refer to as 'crime facilitative industries in which one can discern a recurring and disproportionate pattern of criminal activity. Persons with a criminal record may be attracted by the opportunities provided by these industries, seeing in them the potential for remunerative illicit business.' Gobert and

BOX 19.7 Green crimes affecting local communities

Love Canal is an area near Niagara Falls, USA. In 1978 and over the next two years, the story of past dumping of hazardous toxic waste in the area emerged. This was a very serious story because of what had been built on the land after the dumping. In the 1940s, Love Canal was an abandoned navigation channel, and for years a company called Hooker Chemical had simply disposed of thousands of drums of toxic chemical waste directly into the canal (Szasz, 1994: 42).

In 1952 the canal was covered up. A year later, the Hooker company sold the land to the Niagara Falls Board of Education. A school was built. Developers built homes and 'unsuspecting families' moved in. In the 1970s, after heavy rains, chemical wastes began to seep to the surface, both on the school grounds and into people's yards and basements. Federal and state officials confirmed the presence of eighty-eight chemicals, some in concentrations 250 to 5,000 times higher than acceptable safety levels. Eleven of these chemicals were suspected or known carcinogens; others were said to cause liver and kidney ailments (ibid.).

The Love Canal case received massive media attention and for a while highlighted the fact that damaging the environment with no regard for future generations was not illegal or a crime. New US laws had already been drafted, though, and in 1979 stricter federal regulations were introduced (though many were then reversed by the Reagan administration, see Snyder, 1991: 226–7; Vogel, 1986). At the same time, the US Environmental Protection Agency estimated that 80 per cent of waste was being disposed of 'improperly, inadequately or illegally' (Szasz, 1994: 44).

Punch draw on the work of Huisman and Niemajer (1998) to identify some of the features that may make elements of the Netherlands' waste disposal business prone to rule-bending and criminal opportunism. It seems highly likely that the same features will be found more broadly across international boundaries:

> Companies are paid prior to delivery and, as a result, are easily tempted to take on contracts they cannot possibly fulfil. They then will turn to illegal methods for satisfying their obligations. The firms involved are typically small and run by managers with a dominant managerial style but few qualifications. By providing high rewards and/or by establishing dependency relationships, managers who are averse to regulation and unions are nonetheless able to create a loyal workforce. At the same time these managers will strive to forge good contacts with government officials, employing professional consultants to advise them on how to portray an image of being environmentally friendly . . . Behind this façade the companies will consciously and systematically violate the law.

Mandel (1999: 66) describes the business of such violators as 'deadly transfers' of 'unsanctioned hazardous materials', unwanted and frequently toxic waste moved from regulated spaces to sites where weak or no opposition will be encountered and from developed to developing nations as part of a global industry. For Mandel, this occurs in a 'disorderly world' which poses a number of problems for the development and application of law relevant to the environment.

The making of green crimes: criminalizing environmental harms

A major part of criminology is concerned with the study of law-making – criminalization. Although environmental crimes highlight a new field of criminalization in the making, its roots lie in the recent past. In most industrialized countries, health statutes and criminal laws usually date from the late nineteenth and early twentieth centuries.

Early pollution legislation

Think of Western Europe in the 1940s and 1950s. Each nation was committed to a programme of reconstruction and reindustrialization. The aim was to build a better post-war world, and indicators of economic growth suggested that this was a possibility, not a dream. However, in major cities across Europe, centres of growing populations, expanding transport systems and new enterprises, as well as in regions of high industrial concentration, a new social problem was being produced. In itself, of course, this 'new' problem – pollution – was hardly unfamiliar to these cities and regions. The industries of the nineteenth century – mining, smelting, refining, and so on – all changed the landscape and affected air quality, with health consequences for local populations. It was the scale and severity of pollution that were new. For example, in London in 1952 the number of deaths caused by the 'killer smog' (which sounds like a science-fiction fantasy but was actually dense atmospheric pollution) caused public alarm and calls for action, leading to the Clean Air Act 1956. With the opening up of Eastern Europe it slowly became apparent that such problems were even greater in some areas there (Carter and Turnock, 1993). (For further discussion of the problem of pollution and the right to 'atmospheric justice' see Walters, 2013.)

The international context and environmental legislation

Legislation in various forms has gained pace internationally since the mid-twentieth century, and the 1972 United Nations Conference on the Human Environment is generally credited with giving rise to further enhanced awareness of the need for environmental regulations. It led to a Declaration and an Action Plan with 109 recommendations in six broad areas (including human settlements, natural resource management, pollution, educational and social aspects of the environment, development, and international organizations), a programme to manage the 'global commons' and establishment of a UN environment programme. Subsequent world conferences have been held at Rio in 1992 (formally the UN Conference on Sustainable Development) which set out a series of principles to inform agreements about how to balance economic growth and sustainable development but subsequent meetings up to the Rio+20 conference held in 2012 (i.e. 20 years later) have made little or no further progress in arriving at any such global agreements.

Although the field of international and domestic environmental law is now well established the laws in place are by no means secure or implemented consistently and it is worth emphasizing that the practical problems that such law turns upon are criminological matters such as offences and enforcement. International treaties depend on compliance and regulation, and conflicts will increasingly be fought over environmental resources. The environment and the other species that share the planet are victims of violence, theft and exploitation, in need of protection and – just as in the fight against other forms of crime – will require specialist policing and intelligence services and the enforcement of agreements and rules.

At present, it seems that late-modern societies are set on a path of behaviour that is – and is likely to remain – detrimental to the environment and, according to some commentators, worthy of description as 'ecocide' and requiring legally recognized instruments of protection and response. Indeed some have called for 'ecocide' to be recognized as a 'crime against humanity' (Higgins, 2010; South, 2010 Higgins *et al.*, 2013).

The criminalization of environmental offences

There are many legal and policy issues raised by green crimes. Various populations may be exposed to hazardous waste and emissions but cases attempting to establish liability and responsibility for this have often proved unresolvable in courts of law.

The question of how we should respond to green crimes does not have easy answers. The use of criminal and civil law, and of effective enforcement strategies, leads to a debate about *criminalization* as an effective tool for regulation. Although there are now many international laws in place, the case against this approach alone is that (1) there are frequently legal problems in getting to the stage of bringing a prosecution, and (2) if this does happen, pollution cases are notoriously difficult to prove in terms of culpability and 'knowing intent'; (3) even if a prosecution is brought and is successful, penalties are usually modest relative to the damage done: if the corporation is fined, it will absorb such costs and/or simply pass them on to consumers. Attempts to identify and sanction key responsible individuals have only had rare success (Geis and Di Mento, 1995; Ridley and Dumford, 1994).

Potentially more effective is Braithwaite's (1989) notion of 'shaming' (see also Chapter 9). Adapted for present purposes, this is an argument based on the proposition that corporate image is a more vulnerable target for censure and sanctions than corporate assets. Bad publicity and the projection of a negative image about offending businesses can hurt public relations, profits and share prices. The argument would be that being a bad corporate citizen is bad news for a company; it hurts community relations and finds disfavour with government and with other businesses in the same sector that desire a clean image. In some respects this view carries a degree of realism and sophistication in its strategy that are lacking in the 'get tough' enforcement and 'let's cooperate' compliance models. However, this is also an argument with its own limitations, not least in that it may be naive about the extent to which corporate business really cares about 'image', or conversely it may well underestimate how hard business will fight to undermine critics (Rowell, 1996). It is also a view that may overestimate the extent to which the general public actually care about what corporations do, especially if their offences are committed in another country, and particularly if this is in the developing world.

Environmental justice and social movements for resistance and change

The call for social and environmental justice has been taken up within a wide network of activists engaged in 'toxic struggles' (Hofrichter, 1993), who employ strategies similar to those of the civil rights, anti-war and anti-nuclear movements. As Hofrichter (ibid.: 4) defines the idea, environmental justice

> is about social transformation directed toward meeting human need and enhancing quality of life – economic equality, health care, shelter, human rights, species preservation and democracy – using resources sustainably. . . . Environmental problems . . . remain inseparable from other social injustices such as poverty, racism, sexism, unemployment, urban deterioration, and the diminishing quality of life resulting from corporate activity.

This emergent and strengthening environmental justice movement has provided the 'conceptual starting point' for the exploration of ideas such as environmental racism and victimization, and the need for an environmental victimology (Williams, 1996; Hall, 2012).

Numerous political and pressure groups now exist across the world, addressing environmental issues and questions on a daily basis. Some do so in the spirit of positive advocacy to 'defend the planet'. Others believe that it is more pressing and equally just to 'defend a way of life' and 'business as usual' and that the environment can continue to support populations and societies without the need for radical change. Pro-environment groups range from the extreme (those that embrace terrorism), and the controversial (e.g. those adopting a philosophy that places animal life as of equal or greater importance than human life), to the more local forms of NIMBYism (Not In My Back Yard!) through to various 'new social movements' and middle-range versions of the conservation-minded members of the political left, centre and right (Paehlke, 1995; Szasz, 1994).

The importance of the feminist critique of masculine violence against the environment and non-human species and parallels with male violence against women and children (Sollund, 2013), as well as the emergence of networks of black activists in the USA working against environmental damage to their communities (Bullard, 1990), are expressions of protest that a forward-looking criminology should take note of. At the same time, the significance of a 'backlash' against green concerns should not be underestimated (Rowell 1996).

The green criminology agenda

The limited project outlined here – to suggest some foundations for a green criminology – is only one aspect of the need to reformulate scientific and social thought generally in the direction of 'thinking green'. Beck argues that too often we think of environmental issues simply 'as matters of nature and technology, or of economics and medicine' (Beck, 1995: 25) – we fail to think socially, sociologically – and criminologically – about these matters.

Green issues connect with changes in the world we live in now and, perhaps even more importantly, the world the next generation will inherit. Social and economic conflicts arising from resource scarcity or exploitation, as well as climate change phenomena, present major challenges for human rights, civil society and species preservation in many parts of the world. As outlined at the start of this chapter, climate change may be both criminogenic and a stimulus to control and security measures. Future conflicts and crimes could increasingly revolve around environmental resources. The development of public health improvements, the growth of environmental protection legislation, and the resources put into regulation, inspection and prosecution, all demonstrate social commitment to environmental protection. From the local activism of community groups through issue-prioritizing bureaucracies to the breadth of international law, there are powerful pressures at work and tools available for environmental action. How long this may be the case is, however, a different question.

A green criminology has the potential to provide not only a different way of examining and making sense of various forms of harm and crime, responses and controls (some well known, others less so) but can also make explicable much wider connections that are not generally well understood. In a world of talk about global security and human rights we should reflect that such goals will never be fully realized unless we can protect and preserve the planet that we all share.

Summary

1   As part of the many ways in which criminology is developing, diversifying and maturing in the twenty-first century, there has recently been the growth of a green criminology that focuses upon crimes against the environment.
2   These crimes may come about simply because of the violation of international agreements and laws about the environment; or they may come about through various forms of exploitation, corruption and associated state or corporate crimes which find ways of avoiding or abusing such legislation.
3   Green crimes are a feature of a global risk society and need to be located in such a framework.
4   At this early stage in its development, a green criminology has four main tasks:
    (a) to document the existence of green crimes in all their forms and to evolve basic typologies and distinctions such as that between primary and secondary green crimes;
    (b) to chart the ways in which the laws have been developed around this area, and to assess the complications and political issues generated;
    (c) to connect green crimes to social inequalities;
    (d) to assess the role of green social movements (and their counter-movements involved in a backlash) in bringing about such change.

Critical thinking questions

1 Do we really need a 'green criminology'? Is it just another field of study that is really part of white-collar and organizational crime – another instance of the crimes of the powerful that does not really need its own special 'field' of study?

2 Look up green social movements, such as Greenpeace, on the Web, and explore some of the latest campaigns and issues. (See the 'More Information section' at the end of the chapter.) In the light of what you have read in this chapter, can you see where there is a potential for both primary and secondary green crimes?

3 Can 'animals' or 'non-human species' be said to have rights?

4 How does a green criminology use ideas like 'risk society' and 'globalization'?

5 Consider the relationships between living in a deteriorating environment and social class, gender and race.

Further study

Farrall, S., French, D. and Ahmed, T. (eds) (2012) *Climate Change: Legal and Criminological Implications*, Oxford: Hart.

South, N., Eman, K. and Meško, G.(2014) 'The Growth of Green Criminology', *Encyclopedia of Criminology and Criminal Justice*, Gerben Bruinsma and David Weisburd (eds), p. 440, New York: Springer Verlag.

South, N. and Brisman, A. (eds) (2013) *The Routledge International Handbook of Green Criminology*, London: Routledge.

White, R. (ed.) (2012) *Climate Change, Crime and Criminology*, New York: Springer Verlag.

Gorazd, M., Kangaspunta, K., South, N. and White, R. (eds) (2013) 'Green Criminology', special issue of *Crime, Law and Social Change*, 59 (3).

Ruggiero, V. and South, N. (eds) (2010) 'Green Criminology', special issue of *Critical Criminology* (the journal of the Critical Criminology Division of the American Society of Criminology), 18 (4), pp. 245–323.

Adam, B., Beck, U. and Van Loon, J. (eds) (2000) *The Risk Society and Beyond*, London: Sage.

Beck, U. (1992) *Risk Society*, London: Sage. The now classic and key statement of the emergence of a risk society, though it is far from being an 'easy read'.

Beck, U. (2000) *World Risk Society*, Cambridge: Polity Press.

Worldwatch Institute (2004) *State of the World: 2004. A Worldwatch Institute Report on Progress toward a Sustainable Society*, London: Earthscan. Published annually, this collection of essays focuses on a range of environmental dangers in global perspective. Chapter 9 of this edition discussed 'Controlling international environmental crime'.

Carson, R. (1962) *Silent Spring*, Boston, MA: Houghton Mifflin. This book about the dangers of chemical pollution helped launch the environmental movement in the United States and elsewhere.

Useful websites

Worldwatch Institute
www.worldwatch.org
Produces useful annual reports covering a range of issues relevant to a criminology concerned about the environment, see State of the World reports on the website.

Europe and Environmental Crime
http://europa.eu.int.comm/environment/crime/
The pages of the European online site that deals with the environment and crime.

Earthscan from Routledge
http://www.routledge.com/sustainability/
Provides resources and books giving information about the state of the environment.

Friends of the Earth
http://www.foe.org/

Greenpeace
http://www.greenpeace.org/international_en/
The two major activist websites.

chapter 20

Crime and the Media

Key issues

- Do the media cause violence?
- Have moral panics outlived their criminological usefulness?
- Why do we fear crime while consuming it so avidly?
- What are the main forms of crime on the Internet?
- How are 'extreme media' reshaping cultural boundaries?

Introduction

The relationships between crime and the media have long been the subject of intense debate. In particular, a preoccupation with the supposed harmful effects of popular culture on public morality has been a recurring theme in social commentary since at least the sixteenth century – when it was argued that popular songs were especially dangerous as they all too often presented criminals as heroes (Barker and Petley, 1997: 7). As we will see, debates over the harmful effects of the media are driven by a powerful combination of class antagonism, generational fear, social change, symbolic decline and technological development.

Yet at the same time the media, and popular culture more generally, are fascinated with crime – whether this be as diverse forms of 'entertainment' in such staples as cop shows, crime novels, comics and films or as 'news' in television documentaries, newspaper articles and broadcast bulletins – to the extent that maintaining a distinction between 'fact' and 'fiction' is becoming increasingly difficult. This is partly as a consequence of the rapid growth in 'reality' TV that blurs the 'boundaries between fact, fiction, and entertainment' (Carrabine *et al.*, 2002: 129) in such programmes as *Crimewatch*, *Police Camera Action*, *Car Wars* and, more recently, *Street Wars*. In addition, the live broadcasting of spectacular events on rolling news programmes have become common, such as the O. J. Simpson car chase and subsequent trial, while the enormity of the destruction of the World Trade Center on September 11 owed much to the fact that the graphic images were televised around the world so that initial reactions were formed 'within established media interpretative frames (including the plots and images of countless Hollywood movies)' (Stevenson, 2003: 1).

This blurring of boundaries is captured well in the following passage:

> Today, as criminals videotape their crimes and post them on YouTube, as security agents scrutinize the image-making of criminals on millions of surveillance monitors, as insurrectionist groups upload video compilations (filmed from several angles) of 'successful' suicide bomb attacks and roadside IED (improvised explosive device) detonations, as images of brutality and victimization pop up on office computer screens and children's mobile phones, as 'reality TV' shows take the viewer ever deeper inside the world of the beat cop and prison setting, there can be no other option but the development of a thoroughgoing *visual* criminology.
>
> (Hayward, 2010: 2; original emphasis)

It is significant that Keith Hayward has highlighted the need for a visual criminology that can grasp what is new about global cultural processes, where the power of images plays a key role in shaping the social imaginary (see also Box 20.1). Of course, the 2011 protests and revolutions in the Middle East were also characterized by distinctive forms of cyber-organizing through social media like Facebook, Twitter and YouTube that helped shape grassroots political activism while also enabling new forms of surveillance dedicated to countering dissent.

BOX 20.1 Visual criminology

The last few years have seen a remarkable visual turn in criminology and the radical claim, made by cultural criminologists, is that a 'decisive moment' has now been reached – where it is no longer possible to divorce crime and control from how they are visually represented – and they urge an end to the distinction made between 'real' crime and the 'unreal' image (Ferrell and Van de Voorde, 2010: 36). Yet, ever since the birth of the camera in the nineteenth century photography has been accused of breaching the divide between public worlds and private selves, transforming the very act of looking and giving rise to a whole series of characterizations of this condition: the society of spectacle, the politics of representation, the gendered gaze, and so forth, are amongst the better known. Indeed, photography was a vital element in the construction of the modern criminal subject and has since become central to the dynamics of celebrity, criminality, desire, fame, trauma and voyeurism that continue to shape social practices in significant and often disruptive ways.

From its earliest days the status of photography as a medium drew from both its ability to authentically record the truth and to present a radically new way of seeing the world.

Photography promised a visual record of the way things really are, an encyclopedic inventory to be 'put at the service of science, commerce, physiognomy, empire, and art' (Solomon-Godeau, 1991: 171). Photojournalism originated in war reporting, and provided a sobering counterpoint to the official battlefield art produced by 'war artists', which tended to glamorize combat. War photography revealed to many the horrors of conflict and has since become integral to news reporting. All the characteristic photographic practices now associated with the documentary tradition were well established by the 1860s: aside from war photography, historical sites, sacred places and exotic natives each became subjects of the lens as colonial empires expanded.

Cesare Lombroso's criminal anthropology is the best-known example, to criminologists at least, of how photography was used to classify bodies into distinguishable types in this era. Alan Sekula (1989) and John Tagg (1988) have each argued that the photographs taken for police and prison records should be understood in relation to the boom in portraiture, whereby people were encouraged to measure the respectable citizen against the criminal body and visualize social difference. It was not until the 1880s that a French bureaucrat, Alphonse Bertillon, developed 'anthropometric' techniques to systematically record and identify offenders. His filing card system helped transform what had been an uneven and inconsistent practice into a disciplinary technology that rapidly expanded and remains pivotal to contemporary biometric databases devised to identify and classify increasingly mobile populations.

At the beginning of the twenty-first century a plethora of new tools – including biometrics, DNA analysis, digital imagery, surveillance systems and computer databases – provide new ways of representing, and watching, criminals and suspects. Jonathan Finn (2009) has described how the development of police photography in the nineteenth century laid the foundations for contemporary identification practices, including several that have been established after the terrorist attacks of September 11, 2001. Contemporary law enforcement agencies, he argues, position the body as potentially criminal in his analysis of the use of visual representation in police practices. The collection and archiving of identification data – which today consist of much more than photographs or fingerprints – reflect a reconceptualization of the body itself.

Phil Carney (2010: 27) has also examined how artists have played with the relationship between 'celebrity and desire in the criminal identification photograph', from Andy Warhol's 'Most Wanted Men' series of silk screens in 1964, through Marcus Harvey's enormous painting of Myra Hindley's infamous mug shot initially shown at the *Sensations* exhibition in 1997, to the more recent work of Neil Hepburn and Russell Young that superimposes the faces of model Kate Moss and musician Pete Doherty on the mug shots of the child killers Myra Hindley and Ian Brady to comment on contemporary tabloid culture. Others have argued that the documentary photography tradition offers much that a visually attuned criminology can learn from (Ferrell and Van de Voorde, 2010; Carrabine, 2012). Not least since contemporary practitioners have become increasingly aware that they have certain social responsibilities towards the subjects they photograph, while remaining committed to anthropological exploration, moral commitment and political reform.

Blurring boundaries

Nevertheless, it is important to emphasize that the popular fascination with crime has a long history and that the boundaries between fact and fiction have always been fairly fluid. For instance, scholarship on crime writing in the seventeenth and eighteenth centuries (Davis, 1983; Gatrell,1994; Rawlings, 1992) examines how the flourishing commercial trade in crime and execution reports (in such genres as criminal biographies, gallows speeches and trial reports) vicariously mapped for readers a transgressive underworld, with their popularity owing as much to the development of new printing technologies and improved means of book distribution as a lens 'that brought into focus much of what was most disturbing, and most exciting, about contemporary experience' (Gladfelder, 2001: 5). It is this complex dynamic between the popular fascination with crime and the heightened anxieties of crime the media are said to arouse that is one of the issues explored in this chapter.

The transformations in media technology wrought by print, telegraph and wireless communication that gave birth to the electronic age from the mid-twentieth century have been described by some commentators as a phenomenon of **mediatization**. This is defined as a powerful force eroding divisions between 'fact and fiction, nature and culture, global and local, science and art, technology and humanity' to the extent that 'the media in the twenty-first century have so undermined the ability to construct an *apparent* distinction between reality and representation that the modernist episteme has begun to seem somewhat shaky' (Brown, 2003: 22; original emphasis). In other words, the advent of postmodernity has meant that it is becoming increasingly impossible to distinguish between media image and social reality (Osborne, 1995: 28). It should call for a close relationship between the fields of cultural analysis, social theory, criminology and media studies, but cross-disciplinary scholarship still remains limited (Brown, 2011: 413). These are provocative arguments that have profound consequences for how criminologists should understand the relationships between crime and the media.

In criminology three distinctive approaches can be identified. The first assesses whether the media 'through depictions of crime, violence, death and aggression' can be said to 'cause' criminal conduct (Kidd-Hewitt, 1995: 1) in what has been called the 'ill effects' debate (Barker and Petley, 1997). The second examines how crime news unjustly stereotypes groups (Cohen, 1972) in the orchestration of moral panics (Hall et al., 1978) and thereby heightens public fear of crime. The third and more recent development attends to a broader consideration of how crime and punishment have been consumed (Carrabine et al., 2002), imagined (Young, 1996) and represented (Sparks, 1992) in popular culture, which begins on the basis that there are a diverse range of media forms to excavate as opposed to the singular preoccupation with news content found in earlier critical media studies (Cohen and Young, 1973). This chapter will begin by reviewing these three approaches and conclude with a discussion of crime in cyberspace. The Internet provides an especially challenging site for criminologists to investigate as it is 'frequently depicted as a dark virtual domain inhabited by a mixture of dissenting computer hackers, organized criminals, extremist political groups and purveyors of pornographic images' (Thomas and Loader, 2000: 1). In a remarkably short space of time the Internet has transformed social relations and criminologists have been quick to chart the many forms of crime, danger and deviance accompanying the digital revolution.

Media effects, popular anxieties and violent representations

The question of whether media representations of violence have damaging effects upon audiences is one of the most researched issues in the social sciences and despite the amount of time and money spent on the topic no clear evidence for or against such behavioural claims has yet been produced (Livingstone, 1996). Given that several thousand studies have failed to reach convincing conclusions, it is not only reasonable to suppose that 'the wrong question is being asked' (Brown, 2003: 108) but that the agnostic verdicts also expose the limits of 'empirical social science' (Reiner, 2002: 396).

Most of the **'effects' studies** are based on banal and outmoded understandings of science whereby a group of subjects typically undergo various forms of exposure to a media stimulus (such as a film, programme, or video extract) in an approximation of laboratory conditions and some aspect of their behaviour is measured in relation to attitudes before and after the experiment. Critics argue that:

■ the artificiality of such experiments fatally compromises them (Surrette, 1998: 122–3);
■ they fail to 'place "effects" in their social contexts' (Murdock, 1997: 69);
■ there is a spurious 'psycho-logic' in the studies as they rely on 'mechanistic fairy-tales about how audiences process messages' (Vine, 1997: 125).

None of these critics deny that the media have 'effects', as the point of the media is to communicate, but that the problem is assuming that the relationship is simple and straightforward while misunderstanding the ways in which media socially construct reality.

Nevertheless, in public opinion the overwhelming view is that there is a direct causal link between media violence and real violence, and it is this 'common sense' assumption that drives the dominant research tradition rather than challenging the question itself. In doing so it is important to recognize that the 'effects' debate is as old as popular culture, with the most recent controversies surrounding 'video nasties', computer games and the Internet. As Sheila Brown (2003: 27) argues the 'debate gathered force through high profile cases exemplified in the UK by the murder of Liverpool toddler James Bulger (Smith, 1994) by two young boys who were famously alleged to have viewed video nasties'. In trying to explain the appalling murder police speculated that the boys had copied scenes from *Child's Play 3* (1991), a film rented by the father of one of the boys a month before the murder. The judge thought that 'violent video films may in part be an explanation' (cited in Schubart, 1995: 222) and the *Sun* newspaper launched a campaign to burn all copies of the film – even though it was never actually proved that either child had ever seen the video. Clearly, it is the appeal of such simple and convenient mythologies that demands explanation.

One way of approaching the issue is to consider who is supposed to be at risk from the supposed harmful effects of the media. As Martin Barker and Julian Petley (1997: 5) argue, it is not 'the "educated" and "cultured" middle classes, who either don't watch such rubbish, or else are fully able to deal with it if they do so', instead 'those who are most "affected" are the young, especially the working-class young'. They go on to explain how in the nineteenth century the music hall and lurid stories in 'penny dreadfuls' were blamed for inciting hooliganism, while almost since its inception the cinema has been accused of encouraging 'copy cat' crime. These arguments correspond with Pearson's (1983) 'history of respectable fears', which demonstrates how popular anxieties in the present often rely on idealized images of the past and are driven as much by generational fear as class antagonism in the creation of moral panics over social problems.

The following passage summarizes the limitations of blaming a medium for a particular crime:

> There are two major difficulties with drawing direct causal links between media images and forms of social behaviour. The first is that they're unprovable (which results in people falling back on unhelpful appeals to 'common sense', and ignoring that correlation is not the same thing as causality). The second is that making such links draws attention away from the real causal factors of the behaviour in question, factors whose roots lie deep in the socialisation process (or lack of it) and which raise uncomfortable questions about the kind of society in which we live.
>
> (Petley, 2009, cited in Wykes, 2010: 379)

It is important to emphasize that in refusing to ask different questions the complex issues of how the media represent violence have yet to be adequately addressed in criminology and it is on such matters that future research should be directed. For instance, one question might be how the 'eroticisation of violence and the spread of pornography as an industry' have altered the 'newsworthiness of sex crimes' and redefined 'acceptable behaviour' (Osborne, 1995: 43) while the press coverage of rape trials continues to distort and demean victims (Lees, 1996b; Meyers, 1997). As Brown (2003: 114–15) suggests, criminologists need to appreciate 'the many faceted ways in which violence is inscribed within media representations'. A focus on the diverse meanings generated by violence might also explain 'why the audience of a splatter movie react with laughter instead of fear when faced with violence, blood, mutilations and killings' (Schubart, 1995: 218).

This last point suggests we need to place violent representations in broader cultural context. Indeed, so ingrained are disturbing images (incest, rape, cannibalism, torture, murder, and so on) in the masterpieces of Western literature and art that literary critics have suggested that these great works have endured precisely because they enable readers to indulge in the most taboo of fantasies from safe distances (Fielder, 1982; Schechter, 2005; Trend, 2007). Grotesque violence is deeply embedded in human storytelling:

> Shakespeare and Marlowe understood that violence and horror were crowd-pleasers, as did Robert Louis Stevenson and Charles Dickens (whose *Uncommercial Traveller* includes a story about a man who makes his wives into meat pies). Even so rarefied a writer as Henry James appreciated the appeal of the sensational, framing his own most popular story – the supernatural chiller 'The Turn of the Screw' – with a scene in which a group of friends are swapping spook-stories by the fireplace. When one of the party announces that he knows a tale that can top all the others for sheer 'ugliness and horror and pain,' his listeners can't wait to hear it. 'Oh, how delicious!' cries one of the ladies, nicely summing up the titillating pleasure afforded by such nasty diversions.
>
> (Schechter, 2005: 8–9)

More unsettling is Stephen Eisenman's (2007) argument that there is a powerful cultural force, which he calls the 'pathos formula', that is central to Western culture and aesthetics. Here victims of cruelty are shown to actively participate and even take pleasure from their own destruction (his examples range from the dreaming eyes of saints in Renaissance paintings, as they await death by torture, to the way that the Abu Ghraib prison torture scenes were explicitly sexualized and organized to be photographed). Such arguments suggest that the desire for disturbing imagery and horrific stories is not a pathological departure from social norms. Rather, it is *the* norm (Trend, 2007: 12). Confronting why this is so is the crucial criminological question here.

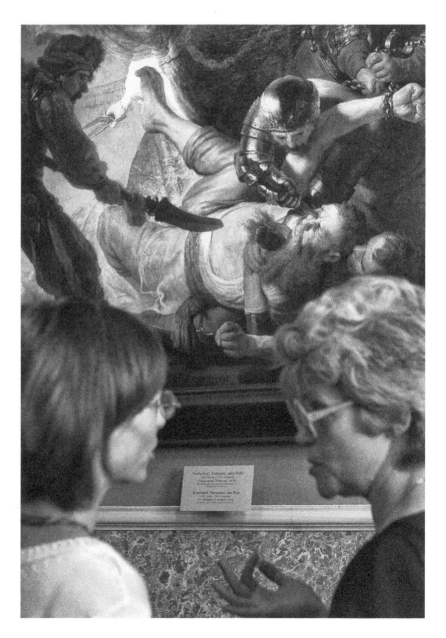

Plate 20.1 Visitors viewing Rembrandt's 'The Blinding of Samson'.

Source: Alexander Drozdov/AFP/Getty Images.

globalizing crime

Dramatizing crime, manufacturing consent and news production

Investigating the ways in which the press and broadcast news report crime is now an established field in criminology, and owes much to the pioneering work of critical scholars in the 1960s and 1970s who sought to unmask the ideological role of the media. The central issue is not whether the media cause troubling 'copy cat' behaviour by young people, but rather how the media promote damaging stereotypes of social groups, especially the young, to uphold the status quo. As Chapter 6 shows, Stan Cohen's (1972) formulation of moral panic has proved to be highly influential as the argument is that demonizing deviants serves to reinforce boundaries of normality and order (see Box 20.2). In fact, there is evidence to suggest he initially intended the term to be 'a modest and descriptive one' (Sparks, 1992: 65) as he subsequently cautioned against being 'obsessed with debunking' (Cohen, 1985: 156) and in his more recent work he is concerned with explaining the apparent public indifference to media images of distant suffering through forms of **denial** (Cohen, 2001). Nevertheless, it is important to recognize that in his and Jock Young's (1971) early studies there was a strong Durkheimian emphasis on how societies are able to cohere through uniting in moral indignation against deviant groups.

In this regard both Cohen and Young saw the media's need to maintain circulation in competitive markets through the 'ethos of "give the public what it wants" involves a constant play on the normative worries of large segments of the population; it utilizes outgroups as living Rorschach blots on to which collective fears and doubts are projected' (Young, 1973: 316). Moreover this process was only possible through 'exaggerating grossly the seriousness of events' (Cohen, 1973: 228). As Young (1974: 241) then explained, 'newspapers select events which are *atypical*, present them in a *stereotypical* fashion and contrast them against a backcloth of normality which is *overtypical*' (Young, 1974: 241).

The emphasis on how the media distort reality was subsequently developed through a neo-Marxist understanding of ideology by Stuart Hall and his colleagues at the Birmingham Centre for Contemporary Cultural Studies in their *Policing the Crisis: Mugging, the State, and Law and Order* (1978). In this book the somewhat vague Durkheimian notion of social control is replaced by a more rigorous concern with state power. Hall *et al.* (1978) introduced Gramsci's (1971) concept of hegemony to understand the timing of the moral panic that emerged in the early 1970s around mugging as an important element in securing consent at a time of political crisis. These have proved to be controversial arguments, and their analysis has been criticized for claiming that the criminality crisis over mugging was contrived by ruling elites to deflect attention away from the economic crisis facing the British state, while others accuse the authors of ignoring the impact of crime on the working class (Young, 1987).

Nevertheless, the overall legacy of this approach is that it is a sustained attempt to analyse the 'social production of news' to reveal the ways that the media 'inculcate and defend the economic, social, and political agenda of privileged groups' (Herman and Chomsky, 1988: 302). More recent studies have qualified the conspiratorial determinism of these earlier accounts, but crucially they do not reject the view that political forces and economic constraints 'limit access to the production, distribution and consumption of information' (Schlesinger and Tumber, 1994: 8). Robert Reiner (2002: 404–6) defines this work as 'cultural conflict' as it highlights the struggles that take place on newsroom floors between journalists, editors, owners and sources.

et while these accounts might portray a more fluid and contingent picture of news duction, they do not fundamentally change the role of crime news. It has been argued that in the final instance the 'news media are as much an agency of *policing* as the law-enforcement agencies whose activities and classifications are reported on' (Ericson *et al.*, 1991: 74; original emphasis). In other words, they 'reproduce order in the process of representing it' (Reiner, 2002: 406). In addition, journalists are 'better seen as bureaucrats than as buccaneers, [and] begin their work from a stock of plausible, well-defined, and largely unconscious assumptions' (Curran and Seaton, 1994: 265). These studies continue to argue that the organizational requirements of news production reinforces a tendency towards the standardized and ideological nature of news content so that the state is able to secure consent for its actions.

BOX 20.2 Classic moral panic theory

Developments in the American sociology of deviance (which are discussed in chapters 5 and 6) combined with the British statistician Lesley Wilkins's (1964) understanding of 'deviancy amplification' laid the groundwork for analysing mediated moral panics. In both Stan Cohen (1972/2002) and Jock Young's (1971) pioneering work there was an emphasis on the much-publicized conflicts between youth subcultures and establishment forces in the 1960s. Cohen's study uses the notion of deviancy amplification to explain how the petty delinquencies of rival groups of mods and rockers at seaside resorts were blown up into serious threats to law and order. Identifying a number of stages in the social reaction he divides the media inventory of the initial skirmishes into three phases: exaggeration, prediction and symbolization.

First, the media exaggerated the numbers involved, the extent of the violence and the damage caused. The seriousness of the events was further distorted by the use of sensational headlines, melodramatic reporting and unconfirmed rumours presented as objective fact. Second, predictions in the inventory period implicitly assumed that what had happened would inevitably happen again with even more devastating consequences. Third, the media coverage involved a form of symbolization where key symbols acquire semiotic power: 'a word (Mod) becomes symbolic of a certain status (delinquent or deviant); objects (hairstyle, clothing) symbolize the word; the objects themselves become symbolic of the status (and the emotions attached to the status)' (Cohen, 1972/2002: 40). One of the consequences of symbolization is that it leads to sensitization. Here, otherwise unconnected events are linked into a pattern by various moral entrepreneurs (judges, the police, politicians and so forth) and understood as symptomatic of the same underlying menace. Calls for action are stepped up, leading to further marginalization and stigmatization in a deviancy amplification spiral, punitive legislation is rushed through parliament and new control measures proliferate.

Cohen goes to some length to situate the moral panic over mods and rockers in social context. In particular, the hostile reaction revealed much about how post-war social change was being experienced – the new affluence and sexual freedom of teenage youth cultures in the 1960s fuelled jealousy and resentment amongst a parental generation who had lived through hungry depression, world war and subsequent austerity. Although there is an implicit

globalizing crime

social psychology here that recognizes there are real problems at stake, the actual object of anxiety is displaced by a more diffuse fear or a mystification of the dangers posed. Thus he insists that moral panics are a product of 'boundary crises' (the term is Ericson's, 1966). They occur when a society has some uncertainty about itself. This ambiguity is resolved through ritualistic confrontations between the deviant group and the community's official agents, whose duty it is to define where the boundaries lie and how much diversity can be tolerated. In effect they clarify the normative contours at times when the boundaries are blurred. In this way moral panics tend to occur when society is undergoing rapid change, when the need to define boundaries is particularly acute.

Current debates

However, some have come to argue that in today's news environment of digital, satellite and cable technologies with news coming in many different forms, including 'serious', 'soft', 'hard' and 'popular', delivered online as well as in traditional print and global broadcasting, with increasing concentration of media ownership, new approaches to 'the complex and more differentiated field of news production' (Cottle, 2003: 16) will need to be developed. One example is the growth in 'alternative media' exemplified in the network of Independent Media Centres or IndyMedia (http://www.indymedia.org) that came to prominence during the demonstrations in Seattle against the World Trade Organization summit meeting there on 30 November 1999 to provide an outlet for the anti-capitalist movement. It has since expanded into 'the most thorough working-out on the Internet of the conditions and processes of alternative media projects' (Atton, 2003: 53). Other news sites featuring what has been described as 'participatory journalism' include OhmyNews and Wikinews in further efforts to democratize the media landscape. Stuart Allan (2006) has shown how the emergence of blogging alongside the rise of the 'citizen journalist' reporting on the South Asian tsunami, London bombings and Hurricane Katrina (often involving technologies like digital cameras and mobile phones) are shaping journalistic practice in some quite surprising and profound ways.

These developments are symptomatic of the 'new visibility' (Thompson, 2005) and recent work has been drawn to how these technologies in the hands of ordinary citizens have changed public perceptions of policing in these new media environments (Greer and McLaughlin, 2011). Andrew Goldsmith (2011) has, for example, examined how the prevalence of mobile phone cameras and the capacity of video-sharing platforms like YouTube and social networking sites such as Facebook have enabled many to share images of apparent police misconduct with mass audiences, often challenging official versions of events. He focuses on two important cases, the death of Ian Tomlinson in London in April 2009 during the G20 protests and the death of Robert Dziekanski at Vancouver airport in October 2007. In both examples, amateur video footage captured police wrongdoing and triggered public controversies that have had far-reaching implications.

Critics have become wary of using the notion of moral panic as it is often used indiscriminately and 'applied to anything from single mothers to working mothers, from guns to Ecstacy, and from pornography on the Internet to the dangers of state censorship' (Miller and Kitzinger, 1998: 221) and have insisted that the concept is 'deeply in need of revisiting and revamping' (McRobbie, 1994: 198). In order to 'revamp' moral panic theory a number of authors (Carrabine, 2008; Critcher, 2011; Jewkes, 1999; Hier, 2008; Thompson, 1998; Ungar, 2001) have recently turned to the concept of 'risk society', as formulated by the theorist Ulrich Beck (1992) to understand contemporary anxieties and insecurities. For instance, it has been argued that the increased frequency of dramatic moral narratives in the mass media in the 1990s is partly a response to the increased pressures of market competition, but is also a key means by which

> the at-risk character of modern society is magnified and is particularly inclined to take the form of moral panics in modern Britain due to factors such as the loss of authority of traditional elites, anxieties about national identity in the face of increasing external influences and internal diversity.
>
> (Thompson, 1998: 141)

Chas Critcher (2003: 164), one of the co-authors of *Policing the Crisis*, has conceded that it may well 'be useful to rethink moral panics as discourses about risk' in his overview of the topic. More recently he has made a strong case for a political economy of moral panics as a form of moral regulation (Critcher, 2011).

Nevertheless, one of the main problems with the classic formulations and the recent attempts to refine the concept of moral panics is captured in Richard Sparks's (2001: 199) telling criticism that these authors remain committed to a 'style of analysis which treats the detailing of media "contents" or "mythologies" (depending on methodological preference) as a largely self-sufficient activity, and which tends to enter grand and mostly unsustainable generalizations about their hold on public opinion or their ideological predominance'.

Of course, this is not to suggest that investigating media representation is unimportant but to caution against assuming a straightforward relationship between state power, media content and public opinion. In his recent paper exploring the hidden political dimensions of moral panic theory Stan Cohen (2011) has argued that the concept is inherently normative and calls for a more nuanced understanding of the forces at work. Yet, it is also important to emphasize that the news is only one source of information about crime and that there is a 'complex intertextuality of media forms' (Brown, 2003: 24) that include film, drama, documentary, radio, fiction, 'true crime' and 'reality TV' that media audiences commute between in their daily lives. It is to this diversity that we now turn.

Imagining transgression, representing detection and consuming crime

There is a sense in which stories of transgression are central to every culture's imagining of its origins, while the process of discovery is often said to be a universal function of all narrative fiction. For instance, 'detective fiction has been compared with the myth of original sin, the first loss of innocence in the Garden of Eden, and the myth of Oedipus, whose discovery of his origins is also a discovery of his crimes' (McCracken, 1998: 51). In Gladfelder's (2001: 7) discussion of literary scholarship on the rise of the novel from the mid-seventeenth century he explains how commentators were 'unsettled from the outset by the genre's concentration on the experience of a range of socially disruptive figures familiar from the network of criminal narrative: socially climbing servants (as in *Pamela*), illegitimate and outcast children (as in *Tom Jones*), runaway and fortune-hunting adventurers (as in *Robinson Crusoe*)'. Yet it is the pleasures and dangers posed by transgression and 'Otherness' that make such narratives so seductive for readers. We will return to the ambiguity provoked by criminal texts below for it is important to begin by offering a glimpse of the diversity of crime narratives that can be encountered through television viewing, cinema-going and reading popular fiction.

To take popular fiction, the detective story is one of the most studied **genres**, as its origins are usually traced from Edgar Allen Poe's 1841 short story 'The Murders in the Rue Morgue'. Here the narrative is organized around the intellectual genius of a detective hero, Auguste Dupin, who reconstructs the scene of a crime and catches the guilty party through the clues and traces left behind and it was this innovation that Conan Doyle was to translate into a commercially successful formula in his Sherlock Holmes stories, the first of which appeared in 1887 (Bennett, 1990: 212). However, in accounting for the development of detective fiction we need to recognize its rich social meanings, rather than simply celebrate the individual genius of a particular author. In exploring these developments, Carrabine (2008: 104–9) draws on the work of the literary critic Walter Benjamin (1892–1940) to examine how the 'private eye' of detective fiction complements the 'panoptic eye' of disciplinary power, through rendering social relations totally legible to the gaze of power as it has been argued that the classical detective story embodies the totalitarian aspiration of a transparent society rendered visible through the exercise of power and the registration of knowledge (Moretti, 1990: 240).

Yet, one of the central themes that begins to emerge in the early twentieth century, and continues up to contemporary representations of crime on television, at the cinema and in literature, concerns the 'ambivalent but central place of the city in modern sensibility and the place of the individual moral agent in the face of social organizations too extensive to direct or comprehend' (Sparks, 1992: 36). In other words, a far more ambiguous and complex set of relationships obtain between the city, crime and detection. A sense of the range of narratives is given in Table 20.1, which is taken from Reiner's (2000) discussion of media representations of policing and will allow the reader to compare and contrast the ways in which class, power and place structure the various stories.

In his discussion of the concepts of narrative and genre, Nick Lacey (2000: 229) argues that the 'TV cop programme is one of the most interesting genres broadcast on television' as it 'is a genre that is continually being "reinvented" as new variations are tried in an attempt to replace tiring cornerstones of the schedules'. Moreover, there is an important sense in which 'detective fictions might be considered to be phenomena which bear the imprint of their times' (Sparks, 1993: 99). This position is developed by Charlotte Brundson (1998: 225) when she argues that the genre 'in its many variants, works over and worries at the anxieties and exclusions of being British and living here, now'.

Another important development she identified has been the move towards the 'medicalization of crime' in the genre with the focus shifting away from the police as the solvers of mysteries to forensic pathologists and criminal psychologists (Brundson, 1998: 242). Examples of this genre hybridity include *Cracker* (1993–), *Dangerfield* (1995–99), *Silent Witness* (1996–), *Waking the Dead*

Table 20.1 Law enforcement stories

TYPE	HERO	CRIME	VILLAIN	VICTIM	SETTING	POLICE ORGANIZATION	PLOT STRUCTURE
Classic sleuth	Grey-celled wizard (usually amateur)	Murder by person(s)/method unknown	Personal motive – outwardly respectable	Exceptionally murderable	Respectable upper-class, often rural	Honest, well-meaning, rule-bound plods	Order – crime – red herrings – deduction – order restored
Private eye	Self-employed. Motive: honour. Skill: dedication, moral intuition	Greed and/or passion murder. Mystery not crucial	Apparently respectable and/or professionals. Several cross-plotting	Not always clear. Client (i.e. apparent victim) often morally dubious	Respectable upper-class façade masking corruption, and underworld links	Brutal, corrupt, but may be tough and efficient	Moral disorder – private eye hired – blows, brawls, bullets, broads and booze – use of moral sense – 'solution' – moral disorder continues normally
Police procedural	Routine cops, using footwear, fingerprints and forensic labs	Murder, usually for gain. Whodunnit less important than how apprehended	Usually professional and not sympathetic	Ordinary, respectable folk. Weak, guileless innocents	Cross-section of urban life, including cops' home	Team of dedicated professionals. Hierarchical but organic division of labour restored	Order – crime(s) – one damn thing after another – use of police procedures – order restored
Vigilante	Lone-wolf cop or amateur	Bestial behaviour by habitual, not necessarily economic, criminal	Psychopathic. Unsympathetic even if 'analysed'	Tortured innocents, though gullible	Urban jungle, ruled by naive, incompetent elite	Rule-bound bureaucrats v. wise street cops	Rampage in urban jungle – ruthless chase – elites try to restrain vigilante – defiance – 'normal' jungle life restored
Civil rights	Professional, dedicated, legalistic cop	Mystery to allow hero to exhibit professionalism	Usually personal motive, with modicum of sympathy to justify concern for rights	Respectable/ influential: strong pressure for 'results'	Unequal society. Money and status 'talk'	Servants of power	Unfair order – crime – innocent accused – professionalism – solution – fairer order

Undercover cop	Skill is courage + symbiosis with underworld: ability to 'pass'	Organized racket	Professional organized structure. Leader unknown (or proof required)	Ordinary citizens	Underworld	Team of professionals to give hero back-up	Order – crime – infiltration – hero's rise in racket – solution – combat – order
Police deviance	Honest 'loner' cop	Police brutality or corruption	Other law-breaking cops	Suspects or ordinary citizens	Police station + underworld	Rotten basket, or bad apples	Police deviance – investigation – control of deviance or of investigator
Deviant police	Rogue cop or Freudian fuzz	Police protagonist's brutality or corruption	Professional crooks who 'invite' his brutality or corruption	Suspects, processed by protagonist, or general public	Police station + underworld	Generally honest but bad apple(s)	Temptation – fall of protagonist – chance of redemption – redemption/death
Let 'em have it	Elite gangbusters	Organized racket	Known gang (maybe unknown leader)	Ordinary folk	Underworld v. overworld	Tough combat unit	Order – rackets – battle – victory – order
Fort Apache	Team of routine cops	'Raids', skirmishes with ethnic minority enemy	Ghetto toughs, and renegade or foolish whites	Ordinary folk	Police outpost in hostile enemy territory	Beleaguered minority. Camaraderie broken by discipline and deviants	Cold war – incident – threat of all-out war – troublemakers neutralized – cold war
Police community	Routine patrol cops: very human	Many petty misdemeanours. Tempt cop to cynicism	No specific person. Real villain is despairing cynicism	Ordinary citizens. Many are unsavoury 'assholes'	Police station/car, contrasted with city jungle and domestic tensions	Brotherhood, 'family' of disparate types	Picaresque. Will cop save or lose his soul?
Community police	Routine patrol bobby: very human	Petty, if any	Prodigal son, if any	Ordinary folk. Salt-of-the-earth types	Organic integrated community	Microcosm of larger community. Non-divisive hierarchy and specialization	Order – everyday human problem – police use moral wisdom + social bonds – order restored

Source: R. Reiner (2000) The Politics of the Police, 3rd edn, Oxford: Oxford University Press, pp. 150–2.

(2000–) and *Wire in the Blood* (2002–), which are part of a broader diversification of the police procedural formula in an effort to increase and keep audiences in an increasingly competitive television market. This influence can be seen in how the American producer of CSI: *Crime Scene Investigation* (2000–) 'had demanded a show so stylistically different that a channel-surfing audience would be forced to stop and view the unusual looking images' (cited in Lury, 2005: 38). Competition for TV audiences in an era of hundreds of cable and satellite channels has meant that primetime programming has had to develop distinctive visual styles and elaborate story arcs to seduce viewers (Carrabine, 2008). The CSI franchise has received much attention among criminologists as it seeks to assert the reliability of scientific expertise and forensic technology in detection (Leishman and Mason, 2004; Gever, 2005; Cavender and Deutsch, 2007).

Meanwhile, the landmark HBO television series *The Wire* (2002–8) received much acclaim for how it pursued rich sociological themes; in the words of William Julius Wilson, who, at a Harvard seminar in 2008, and worth quoting at length, unequivocally states that:

> it has done more to enhance our understandings of the challenges of urban life and urban inequality than any other media event or scholarly publication, including studies by social scientists . . . *The Wire* develops morally complex characters on each side of the law, and with its scrupulous exploration of the inner workings of various institutions, including drug-dealing gangs, the police, politicians, unions, public schools, and the print media, viewers become aware that individuals' decisions and behaviour are often shaped by – and indeed limited by – social, political, and economic forces beyond their control.
>
> (cited in Penfold-Mounce *et al.*, 2011: 152)

Indeed, it has been argued that the series can be understood as a form of social-science fiction that stimulates the powers of the sociological imagination for television viewers by detailing the human complexity of social situations in ways that differ markedly from their narration in CSI.

Crime in cyberspace

We now turn to a key media technology that has so far been discussed only briefly, as the Internet is part of an information revolution that has crucial implications for representations of crime as well as offering opportunities for committing and being a victim of crime. The Internet is a global network of interconnected computers, and while rumours that 'it started life as a sinister US military experiment may be somewhat exaggerated . . . a computer network called ARPANET run by the US Defense Department from 1969 was a primary component of the super-network which would eventually become the internet, and the US Government was definitely interested in a network that could withstand nuclear attack' (Gauntlett, 2000: 4).

For some commentators 'the criminal reality of the Internet is not the all engulfing "cyber-tsunami", but, like the terrestrial world, a large range of frequently occurring small-impact crimes' (Wall, 2001: xi). The types of activity that might be regarded as criminal include:

■ accessing, creating and distributing child pornography;
■ websites espousing misogynist, homophobic or racist hate;

- copyright violations of intellectual property rights through 'digital piracy';
- electronic harassment (including spamming, stalking and extortion); and
- hacking (encompassing simple mischief through to political protest).

However, Douglas Thomas and Brian Loader (2000: 2) have encouraged us to regard 'cyber-crime as a significantly new phenomenon' as the processes of economic globalization, which are being facilitated by the Internet and web-based information and communication technologies (ICTs), not only provide the conditions for the lucrative expansion of international information markets but also raise, as Manuel Castells (1996, 1998) argues, the prospect of globally organized criminal networks.

The new ICTs not only make it much easier for criminals to bypass national boundaries but also offer 'more sophisticated techniques to support and develop networks for drugs trafficking, money laundering, illegal arms trafficking, smuggling and the like' (Thomas and Loader, 2000: 3). Yvonne Jewkes (2003: 20–1) suggests that cybercrimes can be classified into two categories: 'new crimes using new tools' – these are crimes like hacking and sabotage through viruses – and 'conventional crimes' using ICTs, which include fraud, stalking and identity theft. She acknowledges that there are a number of additional activities that are not strictly illegal but would be considered harmful to some users, including certain forms of pornography and unsolicited email in the form of 'spam'. Her discussion provides a useful characterization of some of the most serious crimes and harms posed by ICTs, which we now briefly outline.

Types of cybercrime

As we will see in more detail below, most public concern over the Internet centres on *child pornography* and the dual problems of illegal pornography of minors, and children accessing sites with pornographic content (Chatterjee, 2001). However, it has been argued that, ironically, it was online pornography that fuelled the rapid growth of the Internet and illustrated its commercial promise (Di Filipo, 2000; Wall, 2001), while demands for tougher sanctions have provoked fierce debate about censorship and, it is argued, reveal 'much about the fear of technological advancement and about authorities' inclination to police *people* under the guise of policing crime' (Jewkes, 2003b: 22; original emphasis).

The use of the Internet to perpetuate *hate crime* especially from groups on the political far right – including neo-Nazi, White Aryan Resistance, Ku Klux Klan and anti-gay groups – remains largely unregulated with several thousands of sites preaching violence and intolerance. As Brown (2003: 164) suggests this 'immediately deflates the claims of those who see in the cyber a global community, for the "community", as in the real world, is itself the focus of political and pathological hatred'.

A major consequence of the information and communications revolutions is that they have significantly undermined *intellectual property rights*. The best-known case is that of Napster, the free music download service that was forced to suspend operating in 2001 when the Record Industry Association of America took it to court for copyright infringement. The numerous peer-to-peer file-swapping services that have since emerged suggest that 'digital piracy' will continue to undermine record company profits – it was estimated some time ago that 'something like

4 million people are online at any moment down-loading and sharing music tracks from which the companies derive no royalties whatsoever' (McNaughton, 2003: 6).

Other research has found that online file sharers 'actually buy more music, up to four and a half times more in legal downloads' (Wall and Yar, 2010: 261). In a nuanced study of the more routine and mundane aspects of online counterfeit crime James Treadwell (2012) has shed fresh light on how organized crime is being transformed by new technological advances in the cyber-bazaar. Nevertheless, media corporations continue to prosper as they develop new business models that work with, rather than against, 'the download generation' (Hayward, 2012: 455). The phenomenal case of Apple and the plethora of iPods, iPads, iPhones and iTunes demonstrate how markets expand and respond to technological innovations. Indeed, James Allen-Robertson (2013) has argued, through detailed intricate histories of illicit Internet piracy networks, how they have shaped our relationships with media objects and transformed digital distribution.

There are a number of forms of *electronic harassment*, which range from 'spamming' (unsolicited commercial email) to online personal defamation, stalking, extortion and identity theft. Social networking sites like Facebook, Bebo and MySpace are especially open to identity theft, with one study finding that 44 per cent of adults who had a profile allowed their profile to be seen by anyone and 25 per cent of users had posted personal data about themselves on their profiles, including their home address, telephone number or email address (Smith, 2010: 278). *Hacking* is an activity that involves breaking into computer systems and networks to 'embrace so many different virtual acts of sabotage, intrusion, infiltration, and "theft", or "fraud" that a unifying definition is not immediately apparent' (Brown, 2003: 157–8). The threats posed by hacking and malware have changed considerably over the years, to the extent that our understandings of what they do and how they do it will also need to continually evolve (see Furnell, 2010, for a good overview).

Rinella Cere (2003) has examined the role of 'hacktivism' in circulating information and gathering support for radical politics and the anti-capitalist movement. She considers the uprising of the indigenous people, the Zapatistas, against occupation by a tyrannical government in Chiapas, Mexico, which began on 1 January 1994, as the first political struggle to become a 'cyberwar' and contends that 'despite the difficulties of access and attempts at sabotage by the Mexican state, the Internet has succeeded in the promotion of passionate discussion not just about the struggle in Chiapas, but more widely about the failures of global capitalism and market-driven neoliberalism around the world' (Cere, 2003: 155). The more recent story of the whistle-blowing website WikiLeaks, which was founded in 2006, released details of operating manuals at Guantanamo Bay in 2007, Sarah Palin emails in 2008 and the massive document leak dubbed 'Cablegate' in 2010, has opened up an important set of questions over the power of information itself (Gournelos, 2012).

Meanwhile, the issue of *state surveillance* of citizens has been a rather under-reported aspect of the new ICTs, but one which was brought into sharp focus by the events of September 11, 2001, and in particular use of the 'Echelon network', a US intelligence search system that was, it is claimed,

> used to monitor communications traffic (especially Internet and mobile phone communi-
> cations) of European citizens, politicians and military personnel; a sophisticated 'eaves-
> dropping' device that is justified on grounds of terrorism and crime, but has been found

routinely to intercept valuable private commercial data (Hamelink, 2000). In addition, listening devices called 'carnivores' have been installed at several ISPs [Internet service providers] to monitor email traffic.

(Jewkes, 2003b: 30–1)

The implications of these monitoring activities have been understood as 'one element of the creeping normalization of surveillance that embraces CCTV cameras, electronic databases, "smart" identity cards, digital fingerprinting and all manner of other innovations presented in the name of technological progress' (Jewkes, 2003b: 34). For instance, the *commercial surveillance* of consumers on the Internet is an additional and rapidly growing phenomenon, ranging from the so-called Cookies (client-side persistent information), which give extensive tracking capacities to companies eager to exploit data on individuals, to the data processing company Internet Profiles (I/PRO), which provides information on how well and by whom sites are used. I/PRO's clients are said to include Yahoo!, Compuserve and Netscape among others (Lyon, 2001: 102). Concern has also been expressed over the way formerly distinct databases have increasingly merged, forming potent assemblies of data that may impact significantly on the life chances of its subjects (Lyon, 2009). As Miller (2011) suggests, there is now no more 'social forgetfulness' for our virtual 'presence' leaves disembodied bits of our personas across online space that are always out there to be trawled, mined and profiled by organizations ranging from credit and consumer agencies to anonymous surveillance companies.

David Lyon (2003) has assessed the consequences of increased surveillance in the aftermath of 9/11 – where consumer data merged with that collected by policing and security forces. As with other developments, 9/11 did not prompt the introduction of communications interceptions as it is one of the oldest methods of surveillance used by military intelligence agencies, but 'not long after 9/11 it became clear that forms of business analysis were being retooled for anti-terrorist purposes' (Lyon, 2003: 119). Indeed, Edward Snowden's exposure of how the US National Security Agency systematically collects and mines data from Internet companies demonstrates how advanced this merger between commercial and security information practices has become. These, and other, themes are developed by Finn (2009) in his account of contemporary law enforcement practices, which shows how identification data can be interpreted and reinterpreted according to highly variable and sometimes dubious conceptions of crime and criminality.

The links between military power and surveillance technologies are also developed by Stephen Graham (2006: 266) in what he describes as the US 'Revolution in Military Affairs' in the urban battlespaces of the Middle East and other areas of the global South that 'embed stark biopolitical judgements about the varying worth of human subjects'. Drawing on the category of *homo sacer* (see Box 20.3, which has the philosopher Slavoj Žižek's classic account of the term) denoting 'bare life' he explains how

those deemed to be 'abnormal' within surveilled and simulated urban space-times and ecologies in global south cities will, as examples of what Agamben (1998) has called 'bare life', be exposed to increasingly autonomous surveillance systems designed to sustain continuous, automated and cyborganized state violence.

(Graham, 2006: 266)

BOX 20.3 Bare life and sovereign power

When Donald Rumsfeld designated the imprisoned Taliban fighters 'unlawful combatants' (as opposed to 'regular' prisoners of war), he did not simply mean that their criminal terrorist activity placed them outside the law: when an American citizen commits a crime, even one as serious as murder, he remains a 'lawful criminal'. The distinction between criminals and non-criminals has no relation to that between 'lawful' citizens and the people referred to in France as the 'Sans Papiers'. Perhaps the category of *homo sacer*, brought back into use by Giorgio Agamben in *Homo Sacer: Sovereign Power and Bare Life* (1998), is more useful here. It designated in Roman law, someone who could be killed with impunity and whose death had, for the same reason, no sacrificial value. Today, as a term denoting exclusion, it can be seen to apply not only to terrorists, but also to those on the receiving end of humanitarian aid (Rwandans, Bosnians, Afghans), as well as the Sans Papiers in France and the inhabitants of the favelas in Brazil or the African American ghettoes in the USA.

Concentration camps and humanitarian refugee camps are, paradoxically, the two faces, 'inhuman' and 'human', of one sociological matrix. Asked about the German concentration camps in occupied Poland, 'Concentration Camp' Erhardt (in Lubitsch's *To Be or Not To Be*) snaps back: 'We do the concentrating, and the Poles do the camping.' . . .

The logic of *homo sacer* is clearly discernible in the way the Western media report from the occupied West Bank: when the Israeli Army, in what Israel describes as a 'war' operation, attacks the Palestinian police and sets about systematically destroying the Palestinian infrastructure, Palestinian resistance is cited as proof that we are dealing with terrorists. This paradox is inscribed in the very notion of a 'war on terror' – a strange war in which the enemy is criminalized if he defends himself and returns fire with fire. Which brings me back to the 'unlawful combatant', who is neither enemy soldier nor common criminal. The al-Qaida terrorists are not enemy soldiers, nor are they simple criminals – the USA rejected out of hand any notion that the WTC attacks should be treated as apolitical criminal acts. In short, what is emerging in the guise of the Terrorist on whom war is declared is the unlawful combatant, the political Enemy excluded from the political arena.

This is another aspect of the new global order: we no longer have wars in the old sense of a conflict between sovereign states in which certain rules apply (to do with the treatment of prisoners, the prohibition of certain weapons, etc.). Two types of conflict remain: struggles between groups of *homo sacer* – 'ethnic–religious conflicts' which violate the rules of universal human rights, do not count as wars proper, and call for a 'humanitarian pacifist' intervention on the part of Western powers – and direct attacks on the USA or other representatives of the new global order, in which case, again, we do not have wars proper, but merely 'unlawful combatants' resisting the forces of universal order.

Source: Žižek (2002: 1–3). This article first appeared in the
London Review of Books (23 May 2002), www.lrb.co.uk

Taken together these activities strongly suggest that criminologists need to be at the forefront of debates questioning what constitutes cybercrime and recommending suitable responses to the harm generated in cyberspace.

Child pornography

Much public concern is focused on the Internet where the problems of children viewing obscene imagery and the harms posed by child pornography itself dominate attention. Criminologists recognize that there are many difficult moral questions surrounding pornography, but would emphasize that there are different kinds of content found on websites and its varying legal status:

> The majority of internet based pornography is adult consensual pornography, whether it is soft-core sexual imagery or even hard-core imagery depicting penetration and other sexual acts. Although subject to moral strictures, its consensual nature leaves it largely non-contentious within most western jurisdictions, and with some caveats, within the boundaries of law. Even 'extreme' pornographic materials depicting acts on the borders of consensuality are unlikely to be prosecuted so long as the acts are consensual . . . It is only where there is clear evidence of violence against one or more parties by the other that an investigation may take place, and then usually only after a formal complaint has been made to the police.
>
> (Wall, 2007: 107–8)

However, it is the fear that children will be unwittingly exposed to such material that exercises much alarm and has led to the growth of Internet filtering software that is at best only partially effective in blocking access to explicit content – suggesting that there are no easy technological or legislative remedies here given the supply of and demand for illicit material.

The difficulties faced by the police in their attempts to tackle the trade in abusive images of children have been well described (Jewkes and Andrews, 2005) as has the phenomenon of online 'grooming' (O'Connell et al., 2004) – whereby adults deceive children into sexual conversation and interaction. When considering the problems posed by online child pornography it is important to recognize, however, that although the abuse is not new, and there is a long history of commercial production (O'Toole, 1998), the Internet has transformed the ways it is produced, distributed and consumed (O'Donnell and Milner, 2007; Quayle, 2010).

Extreme media

Although much public concern has focused on child pornography recent years have seen contemporary anxieties centre on the role of the Internet in the 'pornographication' of mainstream Western culture (McNair, 2010). Much of the literature is American and is concerned both with the sheer size of the porn industry in the country, which generates more revenues than Hollywood and all the major league sports combined (Williams, 2004: 2), and the way that a porn aesthetic has become 'chic' across the worlds of advertising, art, cinema, fashion, journalism, literature and popular music videos.

According to one recent estimate there are some 420 million Internet porn pages, 4.2 million porn websites, and 68 million search engine requests for porn every day (Dines, 2010: 47). In the words of one of the leading critics of this phenomenon there are two benchmarks that need to be considered:

> First, imagine what we could call the cruelty line – the measure of the level of overt cruelty toward, and degradation of, women in contemporary mass-marketed pornography. That line is heading up, sharply. Second, imagine the normalization line – the measure of the acceptance of pornography in the mainstream of contemporary culture. That line also is on the way up, equally sharply.
>
> (Jensen, 2007: 16)

The first point concerns the increase in 'hard-core, body-punishing sex in which women are demeaned and debased' (Dines, 2010: xi), while the second focuses not so much on what men are doing to women, as what women are doing to themselves.

In her best-selling book *Female Chauvinist Pigs: Woman and the Rise of Raunch Culture*, Ariel Levy (2005) depicts a bleak picture of American women who embrace the sex industry and celebrate the 'pornification' of other women, and themselves, through their sexual objectification. She regards 'raunch culture' as the outcome of two anti-female trends: the acceptance of patriarchal definitions of what it is that women want sexually and how they should perform to get it, and the intrusion of market forces into private lives. Rosalind Gill (2007: 103) has identified a postfeminist sensibility based on sexual confidence and autonomy, where 'raunch culture' is understood as a shift 'from an external, male judging gaze to a self-policing narcissistic gaze' in a new sexualized culture that is changing the boundaries between public and private spheres.

New forms of 'public intimacy' are developing in a 'striptease culture', which is preoccupied with self-revelation and confessional exposure in ever louder and more mediatized ways (McNair, 2002). These debates on the spread of sexual images in the public sphere and the abundance of easily available pornography have been recently developed in Europe by a number of edited collections. These include *Pornification: Sex and Sexuality in Media Culture* (Nikunen et al., 2007), *Mainstreaming Sex: The Sexualization of Western Culture* (Attwood, 2009) and *Everyday Pornography* (Boyle, 2010) which each explore the complex and contradictory ways in which the commodification of sex is occurring in popular culture.

Accompanying the sexualization of mainstream media, much attention has recently been given to those images thought 'to exist at the fringes of culture which are seen as increasingly extreme' (Attwood, 2011: 18). In the English context these concerns crystallized in the 2008 Criminal Justice and Immigration Act, which makes it a criminal offence to possess what it defines as 'extreme pornographic images'. Before this point it had been an offence to produce or distribute material likely to 'deprave and corrupt' a viewer, but now it is the consumer who faces prosecution if found guilty – which represents a significant legal change and is intended to install a 'censor inside the head of the individual subject' (Petley, 2012: 150).

The extreme porn debate condenses a range of anxieties about the increasing sexualization of society and the role played by media technologies in enabling the dissemination of this material. A telling example is how the term 'pornography' has been used to describe a recent cycle of horror films including *Saw* (2004), *Hostel* (2005) and *Wolf Creek* (2005), which have been dubbed 'torture porn' on account of their gruesome depictions of torture, mutilation and nihilistic cruelty (Edelstein, 2006). At the same time Jean Baudrillard (2005) coined the term 'war porn' to describe the infamous Abu Ghraib photographs taken by American troops in Iraq (see also Carrabine, 2011).

These different uses of the term suggest a crisis over the meaning of 'porn', and indicate that it may be less concerned with images of sexual pleasure than with various attempts to make a spectacle of the body. This is a theme developed by Steve Jones and Sharif Mowlabocus (2009: 622) who discuss how numerous 'representations of body rupture have become immensely popular in western culture' across a broad range of factual and fictional media where scenes of 'opening up' the body are now commonplace. What unites these otherwise diverse images is their focus on extreme experiences and the visceral sensations they provoke. Likewise Feonna Attwood (2011: 19) has also situated these extreme forms of representation in a 'broader cultural trend towards the depiction of humiliation, suffering and terror', which raises pressing new questions on 'the ways in which the body, technology and the self are represented and experienced in contemporary Western societies'. It is by examining these wider processes we can understand why it is that the boundaries of the forbidden, taboo and illicit have reconfigured in recent times.

Summary

1   The popular fascination with crime has a long history and the supposed harmful effects of the media on morality have been a recurring theme in social commentary.
2   This chapter has assessed whether the media cause violence through representations of violence and concluded that such arguments rest on idealized images of the past and are driven by a combination of generational fear and class antagonism.
3   In addition we have outlined the extent to which the news media produce negative stereotypes of social groups and discussed the arguments around the concept of moral panic.
4   Much criminological attention has focused on the news media. In this chapter we have also examined a broader range of narratives about criminality found in popular culture and considered how stories of transgression are central to storytelling.
5   The chapter has also addressed the diverse forms of criminal conduct found on the Internet and concluded with a discussion of the recent concerns over extreme media.

Critical thinking questions

1   What do you understand by the term mediatization?
2   Why do present-day anxieties rely on idealized images of the past?
3   Do you think that the concept of moral panic has outlived its usefulness?
4   In what ways, if any, does cybercrime challenge conventional thinking about crime?
5   Why should the mainstreaming of pornography be a criminological issue?

Further study

Carrabine, E. (2008) *Crime, Culture and the Media*, Cambridge: Polity. Develops many of the ideas presented here as well as covering some of the long-standing debates in the field.

Greer, C. (2008) *Crime and Media: A Reader*, London: Routledge. An edited collection that gathers together an impressive range of classic and key readings.

Jewkes, Y. (2010) *Media and Crime*, London: Sage. Second edition of a lively and accessible introduction to the material.

Rafter, N. and Brown, M. (2011) *Criminology Goes to the Movies: Crime Theory and Popular Culture*, New York: New York University Press. Brings a fresh way of looking at cinema from a criminological perspective and reveals much about how theories of crime circulate in mass-mediated worlds.

Sparks, R. (1992) *Television and the Drama of Crime*, Milton Keynes: Open University Press. An influential examination of 'cop shows' that draws on social theory, media studies and criminology in an innovative fashion.

Valverde, M. (2006) *Law and Order: Images, Meanings, Myths*, New Brunswick, NJ: Rutgers University Press. A North American contribution that draws on examples from film, television and the press to offer a wide-ranging study.

Useful websites

Independent Media Centre
www.indymedia.org
Daily articles produced by a collective of independent media organizations and journalists.

Media Studies.Com
http://www.newmediastudies.com
A website for the study of new media, with articles, reviews, guides and other resources.

'Media Panics' podcast
http://britac.studyserve.com/home/lecture.asp?ContentContainerID=124
A discussion on 'Moral Panics: Then and Now' by Stan Cohen, Stuart Hall and David Garland at the British Academy in March 2007.

Political Violence, Terrorism and Counter-terrorism

Key issues

- What are the key problems concerning the definition of terrorism?

- How have criminologists engaged with the issue of terrorism?

- Has research given us any useful answers for why people carry out terrorist acts?

- What are the main approaches to countering terrorism and what are the key controversies and debates that accompany them?

Introduction

Since 9/11 there has been an unprecedented increase in academic interest in terrorism. According to the British newspaper *The Guardian* (2008), only a mere 100 academic articles focused on terrorism in 2001. By 2007 this had grown to over 2,300 per year. As Ranstorp notes in his review of terrorism research since 9/11:

> Prior to 9/11, the size of the academic community interested in and committed to building a sustained body of knowledge remained resiliently very small but academically diverse

. . . Literally overnight with 9/11 the field of terrorism studies catapulted from the relative periphery into the absolute vortex of academic interest and policy concern worldwide.

(Ranstorp, 2007: 3)

Despite centuries of focusing on transgressive behaviour, criminology has been rather slow to engage with this rapid growth of academic interest in terrorism. Instead, recent studies have been most noticeably informed by the disciplines of political science, international relations, social psychology and geography. However, given the multidisciplinary inclinations of sociology, sociologically informed criminology can add much to our understanding of terrorism. Moreover, because mainstream criminology has shifted attention away from aetiological concerns over the last half-century, possibly the greatest contribution of the field can be found in the analysis of counter-terrorism, particularly the role of policing, surveillance and criminal justice responses.

This chapter is organized around three key areas of discussion relating to terrorism and counter-terrorism. Underpinning each of these discussions is the larger question of the contribution of a sociologically informed criminology to our understanding of these issues. The chapter will first look at the conceptual and definitional debates surrounding terrorism. This will include attention to the pejorative, politicized and selective definitions of terrorism and the similarities and differences to more 'conventional' forms of criminality. The chapter will then examine some of the ways in which terrorist activity has been understood before analysing the practice of counter-terrorism and the role of criminology in understanding these activities.

Defining terrorism

What exactly does terrorism mean? Brian Jenkins (2000) suggests that 'terrorism' refers to 'the use or threat of violence to create an atmosphere of fear and alarm and thus bring about a political result'. Eugene McLaughlin (2006) suggests that 'terrorism' is 'an essentially pre-meditated political act . . . [the intention of which is] to influence . . . policy by creating an atmosphere of fear or threat, generally for a political, religious or ideological cause'. Such definitions extend the meaning of terrorism beyond actual violence to include the *suggestion* that any violence might occur. Furthermore, because terrorism has many intended audiences, the role of 'atmosphere' is crucial here. Such audiences may include a range of actors including politicians in a position to cede to terrorist demands, the public who may fear victimization, and the groups terrorists rely on for support and resources.

Despite its popular usage in political discourse and media coverage, there is no internationally agreed legal definition of terrorism. As Cooper (1977) famously stated, 'we can agree that terrorism is a problem, but we cannot agree what terrorism is'. Much of this disagreement is because 'terrorism' may be deployed as a relative, emotive, pejorative or ideologically driven label. Thus, any meaningful analysis of terrorism must first address the thorny issue of how terrorism is conceptualized and defined.

The subjectivity of the 'terrorist' label is often articulated by the simplistic notion of the *terrorist versus freedom fighter* cliché. Although this does much to highlight the moral relativism of terrorist action, beyond this, it is close to conceptually useless. As Weinberg (2005: 2) correctly argues, the maxim 'simply confus[es] the goal of terrorism with the activity'. Terrorist goals and activities are often distinct and it is helpful to delineate them. For example, some groups, such as the former Liberation Tigers of Tamil Elan – the 'Tamil Tigers' (LTTE) – may be categorized as essentially guerrilla groups that occasionally resort to terrorist tactics as part of a repertoire of strategies (see O'Duffy, 2007). Elsewhere, criminal gangs have, on occasion, resorted to more recognizable terrorist tactics, as the case of Brazilian street gangs shooting down police helicopters with shoulder-mounted missiles illustrates (Fussey et al., 2011). Both of these examples invite one to separate each group's goals and the strategies used to achieve them. Failure to separate activities and goals also makes it difficult to grasp the nuances and complexities of more lengthy terrorist campaigns and how strategies and activities evolve over time. For example, the long campaigns of the Italian *Brigate Rosse* and the Red Army Faction in Germany both became increasingly violent and more focused on murder over time. At what point would members of each group stop being freedom fighters and become terrorists?

There are numerous other difficulties associated with the broader issue of defining terrorism. Like 'criminality', the label of terrorism denotes a wide range of extremely different activities. Of the 303 people charged under UK terrorism legislation between 9/11 and December 2012, for example, more than half related to activities of an arguably non-violent nature. These include the 'encouragement of terrorism', 'membership of a proscribed organisation', breaching a Control Order or withholding information that might prejudice an investigation (Home Office, 2012).

Why define terrorism?

Struggles for definition are thus important on a number of levels. Definitions of what constitutes legitimate or illegitimate violence are highly contested and ideologically constructed. Moreover, the 'terrorist' label is a potent means to delegitimize the activities of particular groups and justify intensive law enforcement responses that may not be deemed acceptable or proportionate under other circumstances.

For example, the heightened visibility of international mass-casualty terrorism on 9/11 led to calls for a more joined-up globalized response. Yet this was not matched by a shared understanding of the problem. The role of the United Nations Security Council (UNSC), the major arbitrator of global security activities, provides a clear example of this tension. Prior to 9/11 the UN had avoided disagreements over the definition of terrorism by passing resolutions that not only avoided the term 'terrorism', but also intentionally focused on specific activities such as aircraft hijacking. Ongoing mid-twentieth-century de-colonial struggles would have made universal agreement on what was legitimate and illegitimate violence impossible during this period. In the wake of the 9/11 attacks, however, the UNSC hurriedly passed Resolution 1373 mandating all member states to 'tak[e] additional measures to prevent and suppress . . . any acts of terrorism' (UNSC, 2001). This was ordered without specifying with any clarity or consensus what 'terrorism' actually meant. Countries thus were required to counter terrorism, but not informed of what terrorism is, thus problematically providing a mandate without a definition. Among the many problems with this approach is the possibility that, under the mantle of counter-terrorism, states may justify repressive measures against forms of political expression or against minor infractions. The UN then subsequently attempted to rectify this omission via UNSC Resolution 1566, passed with unanimity in 2004, which defines terrorism as,

Criminal acts, including [those] against civilians, committed with the intent to cause death or serious bodily injury, or taking of hostages, with the purpose to provoke a state of terror in the general public or in a group of persons or particular persons, intimidate a population or compel a government or an international organization to do or to abstain from doing any act, and all other acts which constitute offences within the scope of and as defined in the international conventions and protocols relating to terrorism, are under no circumstances justifiable by considerations of a political, philosophical, ideological, racial, ethnic, religious or other similar nature.

(UNSC, 2004)

Here, the words 'under no circumstances justifiable' are particularly striking. Critics have argued this statement removes any legal 'just cause' from political violence. This definition thus potentially labels violence aimed at overthrowing repressive regimes as terrorism. Many events including anti-Apartheid struggles in South Africa and aspects of the 2011 'Arab Uprising' could be classed as terrorism under this definition.

For these reasons many contemporary definitions of terrorism have been criticized for being too 'bottom up', focused on individuals and groups, rather than concentrating on 'top-down' forms of state repression (see Chapter 22). One of the main controversies surrounding the definition of terrorism, then, is not only that it is too broad but that it also ignores the most significant and abundant form of political violence: that committed by states. In response, a key development in the study of terrorism has been the development of 'critical terrorism studies', which places increased attention on the role of the state as an arbitrator of insecurity (see Jackson et al., 2009).

In many ways, this renewed focus on the crimes of the powerful reflects some of the conceptual shifts in criminology over the last 40 years or so. For example, in his book *Becoming Deviant*, David Matza (1969) argued against the depoliticized nature of much criminological thought, such as that expounded by positivists: 'among their most notable achievements, the criminological positivists succeeded in what would seem impossible. They separated the study of crime from the workings and theory of the state.'

In short, throughout the early part of the twentieth century criminology had separated crime from politics. Matza's target was not simply the biological positivism of Lombroso but also the sociological positivism of the Chicago School and later subcultural theory. The radical criminology of the early 1970s thus began to shift the focus of academic criminology in part to crimes of the powerful and, recently, this tradition has been picked up in criminological analyses of political violence, particularly with relation to state crime (see Chapter 22).

Overall, it is now widely recognized that normative and moral considerations shape definitions and judgements of what constitutes terrorism – just as they shape definitions of crime. In turn, the passing of time and social change can moderate or sharpen these influential ways of thinking about these actions. These shifts – and, as a corollary, the difficulties of achieving a stable long-term definition of terrorism – are illustrated by the way terrorism has been differently conceived across modernity. For example, during the French Revolution (1789–99), one of the key events of early modernity, 'terror' had a very different meaning. Then it was associated with anti-monarchist violence, and seen by many as instrumental in protecting the nascent republic (Hoffman, 2006). In this context, terrorism was something used to *protect* democracy, a meaning very different to that ascribed to today's political usage of the term. Throughout the nineteenth and twentieth centuries terrorist tactics, actions and labels have been applied to ever-changing sets of conflicts. During the 1880s, for example, Russian anti-Tsar anarchists frequently resorted to the use of political assassinations. In the post-World War Two period, tactics and actions defined as terrorism have been an integral part of political conflicts between those pursuing goals of independence from those perceived as colonialist or occupying powers (see for example the histories of Algeria, Northern Ireland, Palestine). From the 1960s, European far left and far right groups such as the Red Brigades, Baader Meinhoff, and ethno-nationalist groups such as *Euskadi Ta Askatasuna (ETA)* and the Provisional Irish Republican Army (PIRA) became more prominent. During the 1980s, the label of narco-terrorism emerged and also state action supporting groups pursuing politically motivated violence. Examples of the latter include US support of the 'Contras' in Nicaragua, the French government's bombing of the Greenpeace ship the *Rainbow Warrior*, and Iranian sponsorship of Hezbollah.

The new millennium brought attempts to distinguish a 'new terrorism' that was deemed to hold distinctive features from that which preceded it. Drawing on the historian Laqueur's (1999) concept of 'The New Terrorism', Giddens (2005) argued that in a globalized world there are several key differences between 'old' forms of terrorism and 'new' forms of terrorism. These are:

'Old' terrorism (e.g. ETA, PIRA)

- tight local organization
- local political objectives
- relatively low levels of violence
- relative restraint regarding tactics
- threat to specific authorities (e.g. specific government).

'New' terrorism (e.g. al Qaeda)

- loose global network
- located in failed or failing states (e.g. Afghanistan)
- high levels of violence
- less restraint regarding tactics
- threat to strategic interests of the West and to the notion of cosmopolitan society
- use of high-tech communication to coordinate its actions and promote its cause.

Yet such typologies have their problems. Local features associated with the 'old terrorism' remain prominent in contemporary conflicts. As Burke's (2011) meticulously researched work on violence in post-Taliban Afghanistan demonstrates, parochial concerns are often dressed in the language of internationalist Jihadi struggle, but these are generally shaped by local dimensions. Similarly, the argument that post-millennium terrorism is somehow less discriminating is also inexact. Terrorist targeting preferences are largely guided by ideology and some positions, such as right-wing extremism, have rarely been discriminating in their targeting of civilians (such as the 'nail bomber' David Copeland's trio of bomb attacks in London's Soho, Brick Lane and Brixton in 1999). It is also worth remembering that seemingly new trends in terrorism are often not that new at all.

Whilst there are many features of the 9/11 attacks that are noteworthy and shocking, mass-casualty terrorism, aviation-based attacks and suicide tactics are hardly new. For example, in 1974 Samuel Byck attempted to hijack a passenger plane with the intention of flying it into the White House and killing President Nixon. The nineteenth-century anarchists operated in small 'cells' situated throughout Europe, and planted bombs in public areas including on trains and in transport stations. Further back, Silke (2003) identifies how the Sicarii ('knife men') often used suicide attacks in their attempt to oust the Roman occupation of Judea during the Jewish Revolt of 66 CE.

Overall, defining terrorism is a problematic enterprise. With the potential breadth of the concept, along with its ideological, pejorative and moralistic connotations, it is unlikely that broad consensus will ever be reached. For example, Schmid and Jongman (1988) surveyed 109 different definitions of terrorism and found as many as 22 different aspects. Such conceptual complexity demonstrates the impossibility of generating agreement over what constitutes 'terrorism'. To McLaughlin (2006: 434), too many variations exist for terrorism to be a meaningful term,

> There is a strong argument that we should not [use the terms 'terrorism' and 'terrorist']. Both . . . are polemical and a pathologizing device which makes rational discussion of the causes of political conflict impossible . . . [It] is more fruitful to recognize that there is a continuum of politically motivated and enacted violence.

Others such as Honderich (2002) argue that we should keep the term but use it more carefully. In particular, we should signal the fact that not all politically inspired acts of anti-state violence are illegitimate and that terrorism is a feature of most modern conflicts. In many ways, problems over the ideological and subjective constructions of terrorism reflect those that have accompanied the struggles to define what crime is. For example, many criminologists have recognized that the way transgressive behaviours become labelled as criminal are the product of social (Maguire, 1997), legal (Lacey, 2007) or ideological (Sumner, 1994) constructions.

Understanding terrorist action

Researching terrorism

The recent growth of interest in terrorism has produced many theories and ideas seeking to explain why people become (and stay) involved in terrorist activity. Before exploring some of these explanations in more detail it is worth sounding a brief note of caution. Despite, or perhaps because of, the animated and emotive nature of the subject, there is little agreement among terrorism scholars as to what leads people to engage in illegitimate political violence. Debates over terrorism generally produce plenty of heat, but very little light. There are a number of reasons for this discord. Terrorist events are extremely rare. It is therefore extremely hard to distil trends and generalized principles of (terrorist) action from very infrequent events. Moreover, and notwithstanding a few notable exceptions (Hassan, 2001; Horgan, 2009), the field of terrorism studies rests on extremely sparse empirical evidence.

In a comprehensive survey of 1990s research, for example, Silke (2001) identifies that less than 13 per cent of research outputs contained any substantive empirical basis. Silke's (2008) later, post-9/11, examination of this issue indicates that the proportion has reduced further still. Such observations reflect an exacerbation of a long-term trend in the field, as Schmid and Jongman (1988: 17, cited in Silke, 2009: 36) observed years before al Qaeda existed:

> much of the writing in the crucial areas of terrorism research . . . is impressionistic, superficial, and at the same time . . . venturing far-reaching generalizations on the basis of episodal evidence. . . . There are probably few areas in the social science literature on which so much is written on the basis of so little research.

One of the key problems here, then, is that much research on terrorism is neither empirical nor does it engage with primary sources. Of course, restrictions on researcher access alongside the sensitivity of the topic have rendered the field notoriously difficult to research. Despite some valuable (though limited) research being carried out on terrorist prisoners and on former terrorists, the field as a whole still suffers from a lack of empiricism and remains heavily reliant on the regurgitation of existing material and on secondary analysis.

An added difficulty is the narrow focus of most terrorism research. Anglophonic analyses have dominated the field with 73.5 per cent of journal contributors hailing from the United States or United Kingdom. These relatively narrow conceptual and methodological approaches to terrorism have not significantly altered in the post-9/11 period (Silke, 2008). Furthermore, the administrative and policy-oriented basis of much research in this area has attracted criticisms of short-termism, of uncritically accepting hegemonic definitions of terrorism, and a tendency to view terrorism in oversimplistic and non-dynamic ways (*inter alia* Jackson *et al.*, 2009).

One additional difficulty with terrorism research has been the over-reliance on media sources. For example, one of the most commonly used datasets throughout the 1980s and 1990s was the International Terrorism: Attributes of Terrorist Events (ITERATE) database, which was composed of publicly available materials documented in global press reports. Whilst the examination of media sources is a recognized form of social science research, it normally tells us more about the media itself than the events being reported (see Chapter 20). In this context it is likely that the most 'newsworthy' terrorist acts (for example, those targeting European and North American citizens) would be over-represented in the database. Media values also change over time, so longitudinal evaluations (comparisons over a long period of time) would be flawed if this dataset were used.

Explaining terrorism: rediscovering positivism

The velocity of terrorism studies' growth also generated a further problem: previous learning (and its shortcomings) has been routinely ignored. Many 'new' theories are repeatedly presented that have been previously offered – and challenged – many years before. This process of reinvention is perhaps most prominent in analyses of individually focused explanations of terrorist action. This particularly concerns attempts to focus on the psychological – or, even, the pathological – 'abnormality' of terrorists, or of the quest to identify deterministic factors that 'radicalize' terrorists, all of which draw heavily on the discredited assumptions of positivist criminology (see Chapter 4). Since the 1970s such claims have periodically resurfaced to argue that terrorists hold distinct psychological and physiological characteristics (see Horgan, 2003 for an overview). Whilst many of these claims sometimes acknowledge the role of environmental settings, they have generally not withstood scrutiny.

Here, many of the criticisms aimed at positivistic explanations of more conventional criminality also apply. These include the shifting notions of transgressive behaviour over time and place alongside changes in social norms and legal categories; the fact that 'transgressive' characteristics (such as aggression) often lead to success in conventional and legitimate activities (for example in sport or business); and failure to account for why many others holding the same traits and conditions, or immersed in similar environments, never engage in transgression. As such, the *absence* of violence is a crucial yet neglected site of enquiry. These arguments and counter-arguments have existed for over 200 years. In the case of terrorism, an additional set of arguments exists. In particular, the realities of living as a terrorist, as noted above, are not conducive to stable lifestyles. As Taylor and Horgan (2006: 6) note,

> loyalty in the face of continuing hardship and unrelenting commitment to the greater ideological cause and movement are qualities that go hand in hand with being a member of an illegal, underground organization.

Another problem with the 'unstable terrorist' thesis is that victims and targets are largely selected on a rational, strategic and tactical basis. Often, these selections are based on ideological grounds (Drake, 1998; Fussey, 2011). This stands opposed to the more 'individualistic' approach of many psychopathic or more general criminal murderers such as those motivated by anger, personal gain or fantasy (see Fussey and Richards, 2008). Another aspect of this issue is the fact that many terrorists do not experience their violence first-hand (Horgan, 2005; Taylor and Horgan, 2003). As Silke and Taylor (2000) illustrate in their study of the PIRA volunteers, some individuals are emotionally equipped to plant explosive devices and conduct violence from a distance, yet are unwilling to engage in more intimate and proximate 'punishment beatings'. Such incidences do not point to terrorists as unstable actors who are psychologically disturbed.

In recent years it has become commonly accepted that 'abnormality' or psychopathology are unconvincing explanations of terrorist action. As Martha Crenshaw famously stated more than 30 years ago 'the outstanding common characteristic of terrorists is their normality' (1981: 390). Indeed, the ability to undertake complex tasks under extreme pressure is a distinct advantage and not one well suited to psychotic or otherwise unstable individuals. As Hassan's (2001) qualitative study of over 250 potential and failed Palestinian suicide bombers and their handlers, and Sageman's (2004) analysis of violent Jihadi extremist networks relate, most perpetrators they encountered had very conventional lifestyles and no signs of psychopathology at all.

Considerable difficulties therefore limit the identification and likelihood of individualistic, 'interior', features of terrorist action. As a result, terrorist action has begun to be more helpfully and realistically conceptualized as a 'process', whereby the manifest attack represents the execution of its final stage (see *inter alia* Horgan, 2005). As Taylor and Horgan (2006) argue, individuals do not emerge as 'fully fledged' terrorists. They become terrorists through their involvement in terrorism and related activities and environments. In their analysis of individual pathways into, and migration across, different terrorist activities Taylor and Horgan (2006) further argue that involvement is heavily mediated by ideological and political exposure.

Beyond the individual

Individual accounts of terrorist action – and, particularly, the idea that terrorists are somehow very distinct from the communities they are drawn from – are therefore problematic. More recently there has thus been an increased interest in the social and environmental contexts of terrorist activity. Many of these analyses have been informed by political science. These include studies arguing that groups escalate their violent activities when in competition with others for constituencies of support (see della Porta, 1995, for the case of the Italian Red Brigades, and Bloom, 2005, for Palestinian suicide bombing during the 'Second Intifada'). Other studies have emphasized peer group and other close social interaction as an important part of the process of becoming involved in terrorist activity. For example, a tiny number of refugee camps around Hebron, Jenin and Nablus have provided the majority of 'martyrs' during the most intensive period of suicide bombing of the entire Israel–Palestine conflict (the Second Intifada, approximately from 2000 to 2002). In one case, a football team from Hebron ('The Jihad Mosque') supplied Hamas with eight martyrs. Six of the eight attackers were next-door neighbours (Ricolfi, 2005). Such events are not easily explained by recourse to individual psychology or psychopathology but rather, more likely, to their collective experiences of suffering and humiliation (Sarraj, 1997).

Another manifestation of research emphasizing small/peer-group dynamics developed into one of the most significant debates over the last 10 years within the field of terrorism studies, the so-called 'Sageman vs Hoffman debate'. Ostensibly this is a debate around degree of leadership and structural coherency of al Qaeda activity. In brief, former Pakistan-based CIA Officer Marc Sageman (2008) presented what he called the 'leaderless jihad' or 'bunch of guys' theory, arguing al Qaeda operated through unstructured, self-starting and distanciated terrorist groups. For Sageman (2008), al Qaeda recruitment has occurred in four distinct 'waves'. The first wave comprised the recruitment of Afghan Arab militants who fought the Soviets in the 1980s. The second wave involved middle-class people drawn to global Jihadi struggle in the 1990s, often part of European diasporas and educated in Western universities. The third, recruited after the fall of the Taliban in 2011 and motivated by invasions of Afghanistan and Iraq, became inspired by the actions of former recruits and formed more fluid and disconnected networks. Sageman (2008: 33) argues that the fourth wave involves those motivated by reactionary, revivalist, principles 'built on the belief that the world has decayed into a morass of greed and moral depravity'.

By contrast, Hoffman (2008) argued that these recent al Qaeda-related activities operated through more structured and guided sets of arrangements. At the heart of this debate, however, is the issue of methodology, with Hoffman reserving particular hostility for Sageman's approach to research, stating his analyses would have been 'rigorous had he employed [the] essential and basic tools of social science research and built on core theoretic[al understandings] of social and terrorist networks' (2008: 138).

More sociologically informed analyses of terrorism draw on broader processes – particularly issues of migration, social change and the alienation these may inspire – in their analyses of terrorist action. Particularly prominent among such approaches are notions of anomie (Durkheim, 1897/2002) and strain (Merton, 1938) to explain the prominence of middle-class and affluent terrorists. For example, in an outstanding study of the development of al Qaeda,

Burke (2007) argues that the high levels of middle-class suicide attackers in Afghanistan can, in part, be attributed to a combination of a well-developed higher education system and a chronic shortage of employment opportunities. Individuals would become highly educated and then enter a situation where they could not apply these skills nor find meaningful, if any, employment. Here, the way in which the individual mediates broader social and environmental processes is important.

Notwithstanding potential problems with constructing simple typologies of complex, dynamic and international processes, opportunities exist to explore the relevance of sociological analyses of anomie to Sageman's (2008) 'second wave'. More recently, sociologically informed criminological analyses have drawn on Cohen's (1955) subcultural theory – specifically the subversion of conventional mainstream values and the 'delight' in deviance (1955: 26) – as a way of explaining Sageman's post-2001 'third wave' recruitment into al Qaeda-inspired groups (Cottee, 2011).

In sum, sociologically informed analyses of terrorist action have enabled new ways of thinking about the issue. However, such approaches are not without their problems. Most notably, the generality of analysis makes it difficult to explain different levels and intensities of involvement within groups. Another issue affecting much research on terrorist involvement is that we only have a very partial view of who becomes involved. Terrorism is a clandestine activity. It is rare and only very small numbers of people are convicted. Moreover, in many cases the principle reason people become involved in terrorist activity is because they are *selected* among several aspirant candidates. Some groups, such as the Provisional Irish Republican Army (PIRA) and, in a completely different context, Hamas, were never short of willing recruits. Instead, it was the organization that channelled the flow of recruits due to issues such as ability, security and the impact of their status. For example, in the Palestine–Israel conflict, there is much evidence that wealthy recruits are more likely to be selected for suicide missions because they have a greater impact. Handlers may assume, for example, if a doctor commits a suicide mission, it will have more resonance, and conveys a more powerful sense of sacrifice, than if it was carried out by an unskilled labourer (see Zoroya, 2002; Pape, 2005). Thus, high numbers of middle-class suicide bombers are not necessarily driven by issues of wealth or strain, but by the realpolitik of the organization's aims and strategies.

Differentiating crime and terrorism

Whilst some useful research, analysis and theory on terrorism does exist within the criminological canon, as noted above, criminologists have been slow to engage with the study of terrorism. One of the reasons for this, aside from the aforementioned difficulties of conducting empirical work in this area and the comparative rarity of events, is that there are arguably key differences in the motivations, activities and ambitions between criminality and terrorism.

Some criminologists have sought to resolve this problem and apply their ideas about crime to terrorism by imagining that these differences simply do not exist. This approach is particularly prominent among rational choice approaches to crime control. For example, Clarke and Newman (2006: 5–6) who sought to apply their ideas about burglary to al Qaeda argued, '[t]he supposed differences between crime and terrorism therefore rarely stand close scrutiny and . . . are of marginal importance'. For them, human action is reduced to 'the outcome of an interaction between motivation and opportunity' (ibid.: 7). Such thinking is also found in other models of terrorist behaviour that seek to reduce complex human actions to basic trade-offs between opportunities, gains and potential costs.

There are many difficulties with these approaches. Chief among these is the way complex and dynamic activities are reduced into over-deterministic models of how potential terrorists may behave. But, as Adey (2008) puts it, people are not rational billiard ball-like objects that act in solely logical ways. Moreover, terrorist and politically violent activity is intrinsically infused with human values and generally underpinned by a sense of grievance (*inter alia*, Horgan, 2005; Silke, 2008). It is therefore difficult to conceive of terrorist activity operating in an objective, rational and value-free context. Instead, affective, emotional, ideological and other factors all exert themselves.

Other differences between crime and terrorism also exist. For example, ostensibly similar acts, such as murder, can be performed very differently depending on whether terrorist or criminal motivations are at play. In one study of murder in Northern Ireland between 1974 and 1984, for example, Lyons and Harbinson (1986) identify how 85 per cent of non-political murders occurred in the home. This dropped to 6 per cent for politically motivated murders. Clearly, numerous circumstances affect the behaviour of those at risk from being victims of the latter, not least the likelihood of greater preparedness (hence senior PIRA members installed steel internal doors and shatterproof glass in their homes). Although the outcome of the offences may be similar, the divergent means of perpetrating them suggests that different approaches are required to understand their dynamics. In spite of these potential differences, criminology has perhaps had greatest utility in examining the way terrorism is tackled.

Countering terrorism

The debates over the issues covered thus far – defining and explaining terrorist action – have important implications for the way in which terrorism is tackled. For example, clarity on what is and what causes terrorism has significant implications for the appropriateness, effectiveness and acceptability of counter-terrorism strategies. As the above discussion highlights, proper scrutiny of how the terrorism label is applied provides a corrective against the 'illiberal practices of liberal regimes' (Bigo and Tsoukala, 2008). It enables questions to be asked about the proportionality of counter-terrorism measures.

Since 9/11 the landscape of counter-terrorism practice has become ever more crowded. In the USA, the 'Homeland Security' model has seen the creation of new and potent centralized counter-terrorism organizations. The UK has also experienced a proliferation of counter-terrorism agencies and actors but, reflecting the 'responsibilization' of crime control more generally (see Garland, 1996), a number of similar roles and responsibilities were devolved to both the local state and non-state actors and agencies. The post-9/11 period has thus seen a significant intensification, diversification and pluralization of counter-terrorism provision. As the architect of the UK's overarching counter-terrorism strategy, 'CONTEST' (COuNter-TErrorism STrategy), explained, there was a conscious attempt to induce greater interdependence across different actors and institutions in order to effect 'reduced state dominance of the security environment' (Omand, 2010: 14). Such sentiments have been echoed in the Institute for Public Policy Research's major review of UK national security in the twenty-first century, where reduction of state dominance over security policy and provision is portrayed as generating a greater reliance on 'partnership working . . . with the private sector, with community groups and with local government and citizens as individuals' (Institute for Public Policy Research, 2009: 4).

Thinking about counter-terrorism

There have been a number of explanations of this shift towards the diversification of counter-terrorism practice. In some respects this process can be located in broader neo-liberal trends occurring across other forms of social control and criminal justice (see Chapter 15) where the functions and responsibilities of the state become devolved to non-state actors such as the private sector (see Coleman and Sim, 2000). In other respects, the Madrid train bombings of 2004 and the 2005 '7/7' London bombings have exerted a particular influence on counter-terrorism practice. These attacks, both perpetrated by 'home-grown terrorists', led to terrorism, and particularly al Qaeda-inspired militancy, becoming increasingly viewed as a domestic security problem. In the UK this shift is reflected in the doubling of the domestic intelligence service MI5's budget following the '7/7' attacks (Manningham-Buller, 2011). Writing before 9/11 Didier Bigo (2001) presciently identified a broader process of collapsing distinctions between once distinct 'internal' and 'external' security realms, within which such changes in counter-terrorism may be located.

This apparent shift towards diversified and non-state provision of counter-terrorism has many significant implications. In the first instance, there is a tension where many traditional manifestations of terrorism aspire to coerce the state. Yet a number of post-9/11 national counter-terrorism strategies devolve the responsibility for protection 'down' towards non-state actors, agencies and institutions. At the same time, and in contrast to more conventional forms of violence and criminal transgression, the state constitutes the definitive 'risk holder' in relation to terrorism.

These processes also hold multiple significant conceptual and theoretical implications. Increasing numbers of organizations have been drawn into the practice of combating terrorism and, in doing so, have brought different logics, practices and assumptions about transgressive behaviour and how to deal with it. This in turn has led to a proliferation of 'expert knowledge' and many new ways of anticipating different risks and threats. The involvement of diverse agencies, discourses, logics and forms of regulation within counter-terrorism practice has been explained through many different theoretical approaches. Particularly prominent here has been the work of Michel Foucault and his concepts of 'dispositif' ('a thoroughly heterogeneous ensemble consisting of discourses, institutions, architectural forms, regulatory decisions, laws, administrative measures, scientific statements, philosophical, moral and philanthropic propositions' (Foucault, 1980: 194)) and 'governmentality' (the 'art of government', a complex and diffused relations of power where the central state has little presence nor 'this unity, this individuality . . . this rigorous functionality, nor . . . this importance' (Foucault, 1991: 103)) (for uses of these concepts see Aradau and van Munster, 2007; Mythen and Walklate, 2006; Amoore, 2009; Adey and Anderson, 2012; Fussey, 2013).

Yet, for all the focus on non-state organizations, the state remains a highly prominent actor in the practice of counter-terrorism. For example, militaristic responses, such as the 'Global War on Terrorism' (see Chapter 22) are driven by the state, as are many judicial and police-based forms of counter-terrorism. Given its growth and diversification, it would be difficult to provide a detailed analysis of all its components and features within one chapter. Instead, the remainder of this chapter will outline some of the key themes and debates associated with contemporary forms of counter-terrorism.

Judicial responses

The 9/11 attacks stimulated a rash of rapid law-making in many countries, giving the police and criminal justice agencies unprecedented powers to tackle terrorism. Prominent examples include the US Providing Appropriate Tools Required to Intercept and Obstruct Terrorism (PATRIOT) Act and the UK's Anti-terrorism, Crime and Security Act, both passed within months of 9/11 and both containing controversial provisions. In the UK, some of the most controversial aspects allowed for suspects to be held without charge indefinitely pending deportation (part 4 of the Act). The difficulty here was that other legislative obligations, namely the Human Rights Act, prohibited the deportation of people to countries where they may face torture. This impasse led to 16 suspects (known as the 'Belmarsh detainees') being held indefinitely and without trial, a measure seen by civil liberties campaigners as an abandonment of *habeas corpus*, the centuries-old right to a fair trial in a court of law. Such events illustrate some of the many tensions and contradictions that exist between anti-terrorism laws and more conventional criminal statutes.

This particular provision was successfully challenged by the Law Lords (now Justices of the Supreme Court) leading to the creation of terrorist 'Control Orders' under the Prevention of Terrorism Act 2005. In essence, Control Orders (now replaced by ostensibly similar 'Terrorism Prevention and Investigation Measures') are essentially a form of ASBO (see Chapter 18) where restrictions (typically home curfews and limits on association and Internet usage) can be placed on suspects without the need to bring criminal charges (or requisite evidence) against them.

Such events highlight a number of further debates surrounding anti-terrorism law. The first is the way conflict exists *within* the state (in this case between the government and the House of Lords) over the most appropriate way of legislating against terrorism. A second debate concerns the way counter-terrorism legislation is increasingly pervading the non-criminal 'civil' sphere. A third area of contention questions the necessity and proportionality of anti-terrorism laws. For example, most of those charged with terrorism-related offences in the UK over the last decade have been charged under legislation that was in place before 9/11, particularly the Terrorism Act 2000. In addition, many terrorist suspects are charged under very old criminal (non-terrorist) legislation including conspiracy to murder (Criminal Law Act 1977), the Explosives Substances Act of 1883 and the Offences Against the Person Act of 1861. For example, Abdallah el-Faisal – an extremist preacher widely regarded to have had a radicalizing influence on Germaine Lindsay, the most lethal of the '7/7' suicide bombers – was convicted, imprisoned and later deported through the 150-year-old criminal offence of 'soliciting murder'.

Policing terrorism

Perhaps most significantly, legislation has afforded the police considerable and often controversial powers to tackle terrorism. In the UK, perhaps the most vocal debate across public, media and political discourses has centred on two issues: the use of 'stop and search' powers and the length of time a terrorist suspect can be detained without being charged.

Particularly controversial here has been the recently scrapped Section 44 of the Terrorism Act 2000, that allowed police officers to stop individuals for terrorism-related matters in designated zones without requiring the grounds of 'reasonable suspicion'. The entire Greater London urban area was one such designated zone. According to the UK government's former independent reviewer of terrorism legislation, Lord Carlile, Section 44 did not generate a single arrest for terrorism-related offences despite being used to authorize over 200,000 searches each year (Carlile, 2011). Lord Carlile also criticized 'excessive' use of the power by the British Transport Police and London's Metropolitan Police Service. Many of these excesses included searches of children (some as young as 6 years old), octogenarians, peaceful protesters, railway enthusiasts and photographers. Moreover, there is some evidence that Section 44 powers were applied disproportionately to black and Asian youths (Human Rights Watch, 2010).

It is important to note, however, that stop and search strategies are not solely aimed at catching potential terrorists 'in the act', but also serve a preventative and intelligence-gathering function. However, as Hillyard (1993) argued in a study of policing of Britain's Irish minorities, such approaches remain highly controversial, risk alienating large sections of the population and undermine the consent of populations to be policed in this manner. Moreover, the removal of 'reasonable suspicion', and thus more objective criteria, into the decision to stop suspects elevates the role of discretionary policing. As Reiner (2007c) noted, research into policing has repeatedly demonstrated how increasing police discretion has a consequence of raising the likelihood that an officer's background prejudices begin to inform operational decision-making.

Another area of controversy has centred on the length of time the police are allowed to detain suspected terrorists without charging them. Many in the police and government security agencies have argued that, because terrorist offences are exceptional, additional time for questioning, evidence gathering and case building is needed. In the UK this has translated into legal right for the police to detain terrorist suspects for 28 days without charge. Moreover, the former Labour government shared this belief and twice attempted to extend the limit, once to 90 days and more recently to 42 days (as part of parliamentary debates for The Terrorism Bill 2006 and The Counter-terrorism Bill 2008 respectively).

Despite clear support from some sections of the government and the police, pre-charge detention remains one of the most controversial anti-terrorist police powers. Although significant differences in legal systems make simple international comparisons difficult, the UK provision of 28 days appears to significantly exceed limits set in other European countries. For example, of those European countries that have experienced sustained terrorist campaigns over the last 40 years, Germany has a limit of two days pre-charge detention, in Italy it is four, and it is five days in both Russia and Spain (Liberty, 2010). Others have criticized the excessive length of pre-charge detention on operational as well as civil libertarian grounds. For example, in a government-commissioned major review of counter-terrorism powers, Lord Macdonald QC argued that despite having the power to do so, the police had not detained anyone for more than 14 days since 2007. For Macdonald (2011: 4) this 'hardly speaks of pressing need' to have such a long period of detention without charge.

Intelligence

Despite the academic, public, political and media attention placed on judicial and policing approaches, the related yet clandestine field of intelligence work has been long regarded as the most effective method of tackling terrorism (Wardlaw, 1982; Bamford, 2004; Gill and Phythian, 2006). Intelligence work has traditionally been divided into two broad areas, 'human intelligence' (HUMINT, for example, the pursuit of individuals or use of informants) and 'signals intelligence' (SIGINT, for example, the use of codes, communications and data). In recent years, however, intelligence work has become more complex with the distinctions between HUMINT and SIGINT becoming less clear. Intelligence work has been further complicated by a proliferation of both old and new sources of intelligence. This includes online sources of intelligence (CYBINT) and the growing importance of geo-spatial information (GEOINT).

Traditionally, different institutions have been responsible for different aspects of intelligence work. The UK, for example, has three main intelligence agencies: Government Communications Headquarters (GCHQ) which focuses on SIGINT, the Security Service (MI5) which tackles domestic threats and the Secret Intelligence Service (MI6) responsible for tackling overseas risks. In the US the National Security Agency (NSA) focuses on SIGINT, domestic threats are tackled by the Federal Bureau of Investigation (FBI) and the Central Intelligence Agency (CIA) take the lead in challenging overseas risks. However, the aforementioned processes of proliferating sources of intelligence, increasing complexity of intelligence work and the collapsing distinction between internal and external security have meant that these institutional boundaries have become increasingly blurred in recent years.

This increased opacity, growth and complexity have generated a number of consequences. The growth and overlap of intelligence functions have increased the importance of coordination and collaboration between agencies, an area of significant tension and contestation in the past. For example, throughout the twentieth century MI5 was relatively uninvolved with what we would today consider to be terrorist activity. Instead, its activities were shaped by international politics and were targeted towards German and then Soviet espionage activities (Andrew, 2009). After two decades of PIRA attacks on the British mainland, however, MI5 eventually took over the lead responsibility for intelligence gathering from the Metropolitan Police Special Branch in 1992, a move that caused considerable acrimony between the organizations.

The post-9/11 period has seen a number of efforts designed to unify intelligence agencies. In the UK, for example, many diverse organizations – including GCHQ, MI5, MI6, TRANSEC (part of the Department for Transport that specializes in counter-terrorism and other major security concerns) and the Metropolitan Police's SO15 Counter-Terrorism Command – have become cloistered within the Joint Terrorism Analysis Centre (JTAC). JTAC currently holds multiple functions, although it principally focuses on sharing information across institutional boundaries and generating consensual guidance on intelligence analysis for the central government (Omand, 2010). Contrary to the diversification of practice in other areas of counter-terrorism or in the intelligence community, the post-9/11 period has been characterized by attempts at convergence and drawing together previously autonomous agencies into potent clandestine coalitions.

A second consequence of the growth and complexity of intelligence work concerns the extent and prioritization of information. Contrary to depictions in popular culture or conspiracy theory, intelligence agencies are far from omniscient. Some forms of intelligence are more amenable to merging and 'mining' than others. As Edward Snowden's revelations over the way the NSA accesses data from ICT companies such as Microsoft, Apple, Google, Facebook, Yahoo and others, communications and other SIGINT data constitutes a particularly fertile area for such surveillance activities. However, such potency is not necessarily replicated in other areas of intelligence work. With regard to HUMINT, for example, Wilkinson (2008) noted it may take up to 40 different intelligence officers to monitor and decipher information from one suspect in a 24-hour period. As a result, intelligence agencies are not capable of acting on all information and need to make judgements over which information is significant and what should be prioritized. Mistakes are inevitable and often become seen as high-profile intelligence failures. For example before they carried out their attacks two '7/7' bombers, Mohammed Siddique Khan and Shehzad Tanweer, and Boston Marathon bomber Tamerlan Tsarnaev, passed across the respective consciousness of MI5 and the FBI. In Tsarnaev's case the FBI appeared to have ignored intelligence sent from overseas agencies whereas MI5 were aware of Khan and Tanweer but considered them to be involved in only low-level criminality and thus failed to prioritize their cases. As well as drawing significant criticism towards intelligence agencies such events connect with broader critiques of the intensification of counter-terrorism activities. For example, Fussey (2007) has argued that extending counter-terrorism activities does not necessarily enhance security and, through data overload, may actually undermine it. Sufficient surveillance and information-gathering capabilities already exist in many instances. What is missing is the ability to reflexively analyse the value of collected information, something that often becomes more problematic as increasingly potent and numerous forms of surveillance become deployed.

Surveillance

Surveillance has been a consistent feature of urban settings dating back to antiquity (Dandeker, 1990) and, as Fussey and Coaffee (2012) note, during modernity it became an integral ordering feature of societies. Indeed, the integration of surveillance, particularly its technological forms, into contemporary life has led many scholars to suggest we are now living in a 'surveillance society' (Norris and Armstrong, 1999). There have been many sociologically informed attempts to understand the contemporary ubiquity of surveillance. Particularly prominent have been accounts that stress the 'top-down' coercive nature of surveillance. These include the overused Orwellian metaphor of 'Big Brother' and neo-Marxist or other interest-based accounts of surveillance as a means of creating or reinforcing socio-economic inequalities (Coleman, 2004). Also prominent has been the application of Foucault's (1977) panoptic metaphor to examine the diffusion of surveillance practices and the way subjects may self-regulate in response to perceived ubiquity of control. Most recently, French sociologist Bruno Latour's (2005) Actor Network Theory has been increasingly influential in understanding how technology is neither neutral nor passive. Instead, these accounts argue that, like humans, technology may exert its own agency and play an active role in shaping social relations and practices.

Surveillance is central to counter-terrorist activities and cuts across many practices including intelligence work, policing and the trend towards fortified urban environments. The immediate post-9/11 period saw a rapid intensification in the scale, potency and intensity of surveillance networks. For example, significant resources were poured into the analysis and connection of data held on individuals ('dataveillance') and existing surveillance assets – such as surveillance cameras initially deployed to prevent low-level criminality – became increasingly co-opted for counter-terrorism purposes. There has also been a noticeable growth in the cohesion and technologization of counter-terrorist surveillance strategies since 9/11 (Lyon, 2003a). For example, aviation security has placed greater reliance on passenger screening data and on technological interventions such as bodyscanners, whilst in more public spaces, police in New York City have expressed a desire to use imaging technology to replace 'stop and frisk' activities with 'walk and scan' processes.

Perhaps the most familiar form of counter-terrorist surveillance has been the use of public space cameras to capture images of suspects in the aftermath of an attack. The use of cameras in this way tells us much about the potential effectiveness and the hidden social costs of surveillance. Contemporary terrorist attacks such as those in Washington (2001), London (2005), Mumbai (2008), and Boston (2013) were swiftly followed by evocative 'visual epitaphs' (Carrabine, 2008) of suspects on their way to carry out atrocities.

Such images help to create a strong and potent association between surveillance, public safety and protection from terrorism. In turn, such events have often been followed by calls for greater numbers of surveillance cameras and capabilities (e.g. *The New York Times*, 2013a). Whilst surveillance cameras have been successful in a number of counter-terrorism operations (such as the identification and capture of David Copeland during his 1999 nail-bombing campaign in London), questions remain over their effectiveness. Fussey (2007), for example, argues that cameras may have greater utility in tackling right-wing extremists (such as Copeland) – often characterized as single actors targeting public settings and intent on escape afterwards – but that this success does not translate over all forms of terrorism. For all of the emotive imagery of the perpetrators of 9/11, '7/7', Mumbai and Boston, surveillance cameras remained impotent observers at the time. The London '7/7' bombers were identified through more traditional detective approaches (e.g. forensic examination of corpses) and cameras very rarely catch someone 'in the act'.

The debate around the social benefits and harms of surveillance is often characterized as a trade-off between liberty and security. Yet numerous critics have challenged this dichotomy and argued it represents a narrow and impoverished way of understanding the wider issues at hand. As the above examples demonstrate, increased surveillance capabilities do not necessarily translate into enhanced security. Intensified surveillance infrastructure may also impose broader social harms beyond just liberty and privacy too. These include an overall decline in levels of trust (Wood et al., 2006) and surveillance 'creep' (Marx, 2002) from one function to another. In an example of the latter, one of the first public uses of Automatic Number Plate Recognition (ANPR, ALPR in the USA) cameras was in the financial district of London following PIRA bombings during 1990, 1992 and 1993. These cameras failed to identify a single terrorist and were instead used to identify drivers of untaxed vehicles (Coaffee, 2009). Whilst potent surveillance technologies may be permissible, proportionate and acceptable when tackling serious offences such as terrorism, it is unlikely they remain so when applied to more mundane transgressions.

Another key surveillance cost not articulated in the 'security versus liberty' paradigm is a process defined by David Lyon (2003b) as 'social sorting'. Here, surveillance and monitoring technologies and techniques are used to 'sort' subjects into categories which may impact severely on an individual's life chances, rights to mobility, and access to credit and services. Whilst such processes are commonplace in the commercial realm (e.g. credit scoring) they are also increasingly present in counter-terrorism activities. These include being placed on 'no-fly' lists or being categorized as worthy of additional scrutiny due to an individual's past travel or financial activities. Key debates here relate to the lack of accountability of those conducting sorting activities, the way some activities are entirely innocent but become categorized as suspicious, and the difficulty of challenging or changing unfair categorizations (see Lyon, 2003b).

Perhaps the most significant social cost of surveillance is that it does not impact upon everyone equally. It is those on the margins of society and already disadvantaged or members of poorly defined 'suspect populations' that feel the impact of surveillance most heavily. Critics have long noted the way surveillance camera operators may rely on 'hunches' and preconceived stereotypes of suspicious subjects when targeting individuals for monitoring (Norris and Armstrong, 1999). However, the decision to encircle two areas of Birmingham containing large British Muslim populations with 190 surveillance cameras (many of them covert) during 2008–10 represents a particularly problematic case of crude categorical suspicion underlying contemporary counter-terrorist surveillance practices (see Box 21.1 and Fussey, 2013).

However, categorical suspicion is not confined to the actions of the police. Recent terrorist attacks (and incidences of civil disorder) have seen the increasing use of public mobile phone camera footage and social media websites as investigation tools. In the aftermath of the Boston marathon attacks categorical suspicion was generated from below. Twitter users falsely identified missing student Sunil Tripathi as one of the suspects, an act leading to threats and abuse to his family. Reddit – a user-generated social media site – hosted pictures of the bombers to which contributors wrongly named scores of individuals as suspects. In the words of Reddit's owners, these activities amounted to 'online witch hunts and dangerous speculation which spiraled into very negative consequences for innocent parties' (*The New York Times*, 2013b).

BOX 21.1 Surveillance cameras in Birmingham track Muslims' every move

Counterterrorism police have targeted hundreds of surveillance cameras on two Muslim areas of Birmingham, enabling them to track the precise movements of people entering and leaving the neighbourhoods.

The project has principally been sold to locals as an attempt to combat antisocial behaviour, vehicle crime and drug dealing in the area. But the cameras have been paid for by a £3m grant from a government fund, the Terrorism and Allied Matters Fund, which is administered by the Association of Chief Police Officers.

About 150 automatic numberplate recognition (ANPR) cameras have been installed in Washwood Heath and Sparkbrook in recent months. Birmingham's two predominantly Muslim suburbs will be covered by three times more ANPR cameras than are used to monitor the entire city centre. They include about 40 cameras classed as 'covert', meaning they have been concealed from public view.

. . .

Police sources said the initiative, code-named Project Champion, is the first of its kind in the UK that seeks to monitor a population seen as 'at risk' of extremism.

When the cameras become operative, residents will not be able to drive into or leave the two neighbourhoods without their movements being tracked.

Officials maintain the cameras will prove useful for tackling a whole range crime. The areas were ringfenced for intense surveillance in 2007 after a police investigation into a suspected plot to kidnap and kill a British soldier in the area.

The Safer Birmingham Partnership, a joint initiative between police and the local authority which will run the cameras, expressed 'regret' there had not been fuller consultation. Senior SBP officials said they only became aware that the cameras were paid for by counterterrorism funds as a result of *Guardian* inquiries.

. . .

Steve Jolly, a local activist leading a campaign to have the cameras removed, called on the deputy prime minister to intervene: 'Nick Clegg has made a real point of emphatically drawing attention to the surveillance society and promising to stop unnecessary infringements of privacy,' he said. 'I think we should hold him to his word, and say, "Look at what is happening in Birmingham – are you going to allow it to go ahead?"'

Source: *The Guardian* (4 June 2010). Copyright Guardian News & Media Ltd 2010.

Fortified urbanism

Drawing on notions of situational crime prevention, rational choice and routine activity theory, urban spaces have been progressively 'target-hardened' against terrorism. Influenced by Oscar Newman's (1972) notion of 'defensible space', the intention is to manipulate the built environment to reduce the possibilities for, and the impact of, terrorist activities. Some of these measures are fairly explicit whilst others are subtle and conceal their true function, yet their forms exert a significant impact on the vibrancy, diversity and vitality of the urban realm. Discreet architectural interventions have long been used to exert subtle forms of social control in the city, including street furniture designed to make it impossible to sleep on, the use of sprinklers in parks where the homeless may congregate (Davis, 1990) or siting a building's hot air vents on rooftops to deny warmth to nearby rough sleepers (Raco, 2003). Typically, anti-terrorist target-hardening strategies involve a number of repeated themes. Prominent among them is the control of traffic flows and parking to restrict the access of vehicles carrying bombs ('hostile vehicle mitigation'), often involving strategically sited (reinforced) plant pots, signs or street furniture designed to withstand high-speed collisions (see Plates 21.2 and 21.3).

Plate 21.1 Subtle hostile vehicle mitigation techniques: a sign physically preventing vehicles reaching Arsenal FC's Emirates Stadium, London.

Photo: Pete Fussey.

Buildings in high-risk areas are often constructed with shatterproof glass (flying glass is the principal cause of casualties in terrorist attacks), and access points to particular areas or even entire neighbourhoods may be restricted. High-risk areas often have very few places where packages could be concealed: litter bins are removed and manhole covers welded shut (see Coaffee, 2009). Critics have noted a number of sociological implications of such measures including the retreat of the wealthy into 'padded bunkers' (Davis, 1990), architectures of fear (Ellin, 1997) and proliferating 'architectures of enmity' (Amoore, 2009) that restrict the unstructured and unpredictable encounters that characterize the richness of urban life (Jacobs, 1961). Other critics argue that urban spaces are becoming increasingly militarized, partitioned into fortified enclaves and reinforced by intensive policing and regimes of technological surveillance (Coleman and Sim, 2000; Graham, 2004; Bauman, 2004). In one of the most thorough examinations of these phenomena, Stephen Graham (2010) argues that many countries are experiencing a 'new military urbanism'. Drawing on the work of Foucault (2004), Graham argues that this process is driven by a 'boomerang effect' where militarized counter-terrorism measures are applied and finessed in conflicts overseas and then reimported into Western cities, whereby: 'Techniques and technologies of colonial urban warfare and repression travelled back and forth between colonial frontiers and European metropolitan heartlands' (Graham, 2010: 11–12).

Thus physical anti-terrorism techniques and architectures of occupation (Weizman, 2007), are perfected in spaces such as Baghdad's Green Zone and eventually become commonplace in London and New York. Other critics have identified additional factors driving the militarization of public space in the name of anti-terrorism. In particular, recent academic attention has turned to the role of 'mega-events' and other urban spectacles as testing grounds for intensive forms of security. For example, Fussey et al. (2012) identify how the recent 2012 Olympic Games saw London host surveillance drones, surface-to-air missiles, large troop deployments and warships in one of Europe's most densely populated spaces.

Plate 21.2 Explicit hostile vehicle mitigation techniques: Jersey barriers at Westminster, London.

Photo: Pete Fussey.

Preventing radicalization

One controversial form of counter-terrorism has been the use of community-focused initiatives designed to prevent individuals from becoming violent radicals. In the UK this approach became known as the 'Prevent' strategy, something the government committed £140m a year to at the end of the last decade (Briggs, 2010). The Prevent strategy has been through a number of iterations. Its launch in 2006 was quickly followed by an enormous increase in expenditure and an extension of the programme beyond grass-roots community organizations, to include multiple public organizations such as universities, schools and health care providers.

Since their inception, radicalization prevention strategies have been designed for numerous purposes including 'capacity building' of moderate Muslims to enable more radical narratives to be challenged; establishing forums for disaffected youths to cathartically express non-violent forms of radicalism; and building trust in and legitimacy of the police within communities. Yet this breadth of purpose led to significant ambiguity and inconsistency in the delivery of these strategies and drew criticism from across the political spectrum.

Among the many complaints were criticisms that Prevent strategies were rooted in a romanticized belief of recreating cohesive self-policing communities that have never existed. Others complained that the emphasis on terrorism was overstated and Prevent strategies hijacked existing and less controversial community development policies. Another problem concerned the way that, as noted earlier in the chapter, 'radicalization' or 'pathways to radicalization' have been envisaged in rather deterministic and linear ways that do not reflect the complex, diverse and dynamic nature of violent activity. Moreover, for all the talk of preventing 'extremism' more generally, attention was overwhelmingly placed on Muslim communities and largely ignored 'radicalization' among other groups, such as the far right. This partiality led the Institute of Race Relations (2009: 6) to claim these strategies were 'in effect, constructing the Muslim population as a "suspect community"'. Indeed, although strenuously denied by the government, the most potent criticism of the Prevent strategy has been that it operated as a type of Trojan Horse: a seemingly benign vehicle that enabled state agencies to penetrate local communities for intelligence-gathering purposes. Another difficulty affecting Prevent strategies has been the conflicting roles occupied by the police. Trust between the police and some communities is difficult to establish and easily lost following excessive use of stop and search or tensions that follow counter-terrorist raids (see Thiel, 2009).

Summary

1   Terrorism is a contested concept shaped by ideological, normative and moral considerations.
2   Despite the proliferation of academic commentary on terrorism, little primary research exists.
3   Pathologized explanations of terrorism bear little scrutiny.
4   There has been an increasing merger of crime control and counter-terrorism practices since 9/11 which has raised important questions over the governance, proportionality and acceptability of security measures.

Critical thinking questions

1 Why is it important to understand the problems of defining terrorism?
2 What do criminologists have to offer the study of terrorism?
3 In what ways does the supposed balance between liberty and security limit our understanding of the costs and benefits of counter-terrorist practices?

Further study

Fussey, P. (2007) 'Observing Potentiality in the Global City: Surveillance and Counterterrorism in London', *International Criminal Justice Review*, 17 (3): 171–92. Analyses the use of surveillance technology in relation to terrorist attacks in London.

Graham, S. (2010) *Cities Under Siege: The New Military Urbanism*, London: Verso. A comprehensive study of the use of military hardware and techniques in civilian urban settings.

Hoffman, B. (2006) *Inside Terrorism*, New York: Columbia University Press. A primer on terrorism.

Horgan, J. (2005) *The Psychology of Terrorism*, London: Routledge. Rapidly seen as a classic in the field of psychological explanations of terrorism.

Human Rights Watch (2010) *Without Suspicion: Stop and Search under the Terrorism Act 2000*, New York: Human Rights Watch. A comprehensive critique of the use of stop and search in relation to terrorism.

Jackson, R., Breen Smyth, M. and Gunning, J. (2009) *Critical Terrorism Studies: A New Research Agenda*, London: Routledge. A key text in the field of critical terrorism studies.

Thiel, D. (2009) *Policing Terrorism: A Review of the Evidence*. London: The Police Foundation. A comprehensive overview of the policing of terrorism in England and Wales.

Vertigans, S. (2011) *The Sociology of Terrorism: People, Places and Processes*, London: Routledge. A rare sociological analysis of terrorism.

Useful websites

Foreign Affairs: security analysis
http://www.foreignaffairs.com/topics/Security
Analysis of US foreign policy and global affairs with detailed analysis of security issues and recent events.

MI5
https://www.mi5.gov.uk
Presentation of security issues from a UK government and security service perspective.

American Civil Liberties Union
http://www.aclu.org/keep-america-safe-and-free-0
A civil liberties NGO perspective on counter-terrorism in the USA.

Liberty: counter-terrorism legislation
https://www.liberty-human-rights.org.uk/human-rights/terrorism/index.php
An overview of UK counter-terrorism law and its accompanying debates.

State Crime, War Crime and Human Rights

Introduction

In order to maintain social order and protect their populations, modern states make laws, employ police, and provide for armies and military weaponry. In Max Weber's (1958/1970) words, states claim the monopoly of the legitimate use of violence in the enforcement of their order. Yet, by monopolizing violence, states hold the capacity to put that to deleterious effect in the violent control of human life and the promotion of one idea of social order over another. Indeed, the extraordinary levels of violence and human suffering that have occurred as a result of crimes committed by nation-states make more traditional street crimes pale into insignificance by comparison. In both war and peacetime, states of all kinds – democratic, dictatorial and colonial

– have instigated and overseen mass robbery, injury, murder, rape and environmental devastation on a grand scale in acts ranging from illegal wars to genocide, slavery and colonialism. This chapter explores a number of these crimes of states, examining how they are organized, legitimized and carried out. It considers why the criminological imagination has most often failed to consider state crimes, and it examines how otherwise law-abiding people can be drawn into carrying out extreme levels of state-sanctioned violence.

The denial of contemporary barbarism

The classic figureheads of European sociology in the nineteenth and twentieth centuries were preoccupied with understanding modernizing societal development which they generally saw as placing societies on a path towards increased peace, stability and civilization. Émile Durkheim (1893/1960) maintained that a 'cult of the individual' had developed in which individual human life had become sacred, and Norbert Elias (1939/1978) argued that bodily emotions and violent activity were placed under increasing social control in the 'civilizing processes' of European society. A level of proof for these assertions can be found with the massively declining rates of homicide across Europe from the sixteenth to the nineteenth centuries (see Chapter 2). We also know that public execution, torture and inhumane detention were all gradually outlawed with the development of modern European criminal justice systems from the eighteenth century (see Chapter 15). More humane ways of engaging in international conflict also occurred between states with the development of notions of 'civilized warfare' and 'rules of war' that were agreed upon by many nations at the end of the nineteenth and beginning of the twentieth centuries in the signing of the Geneva and Hague Conventions and the establishment of the League of Nations (see Box 22.1).

BOX 22.1 The Geneva and Hague Conventions

The Geneva and Hague Conventions established international laws and agreements to govern state conduct in war and they provide the backbone to International Humanitarian Law. The Conventions are upheld and enforced by the United Nations Security Council and the UN Charter which binds all members of the UN to the Conventions. The Geneva Convention originates in an 1864 rule that established agreement for a neutral body to provide aid to battlefield casualties in war zones (and from which the Red Cross was formed). Another provision in 1906 legislated for the humane treatment of prisoners of war and prohibited targeting civilians in war. The Hague Conventions of 1899 and 1907 drew on the earlier Geneva Conventions but also established an international court – the Permanent Court of Arbitration – and they developed international rules governing the use of particular types of weaponry in war, prohibiting most forms of chemical warfare. The Conventions were codified in the Nuremberg trials of Nazi war criminals following the Second World War where they were ratified by 194 countries.

Taken at face value, modernization was a force for humane civilization and the pacification of society. However, revisionist historians and post-colonial theorists have challenged these claims by pointing to the existence of, for instance, the European slave trade and European colonialism – which were ongoing at the very time of modernization and the birth of European sociology (see, for example, Agozino, 2003; Goody, 2007). Claims about the civilizing nature of modern states have also been challenged by the twentieth century itself. Despite the development of rules of war and, following the Second World War, the signing of the Declaration of Human Rights, the historian Eric Hobsbawm (1994) argues that with the onset of the First World War, the world paradoxically descended into barbarism – a barbarism that, by the 1990s, had become so normal that it was hardly noticeable.

In addition to the approximately 50 million deaths that occurred as a result of the Second World War (Roberts, 1999), a barbaric normality can be seen in the sheer numbers of people killed, robbed and injured by states in wars and internal conflicts since. In his spine-chilling book about the contemporary normalization and denial of state crimes, *States of Denial*, Stanley Cohen writes:

> In the half-century since the end of the Second World War, some 25 million people have been killed, mostly civilians and by their own governments, in internal conflicts and ethnic, nationalist or religious violence. Civilian fatalities have climbed from the 5 per cent of war-related deaths at the turn of the century to more than 90 per cent in the 1990s. About 50 million people were forced to flee their homes. In 1998, more than 2,000 people every month were killed or maimed by land-mine explosions. It is impossible to even estimate the numbers injured and disabled, tortured and raped, during these conflicts.
>
> (Cohen, 2001: 287)

Cohen asks why it is that criminology, while expending much time and effort to understand relatively minor crimes like drug-taking or anti-social behaviour, stands by and lets mass atrocity go on with little comment. He argues that by ignoring or denying state crimes, this effectively allows them to flourish. He also raises the question that if much criminology is motivated by a desire to curb human suffering, how is it that the same criminology has largely ignored crimes of states? Cohen's answer is to suggest that both states and societies engage in a number of forms of justification and denial of atrocity that has the effect of facilitating, legitimating and normalizing state crimes.

States engage in 'spirals of denial' (Cohen, 1993) in order to hide and forget their illegal activities. States may first try to employ 'total denial' by suggesting that an atrocity simply 'didn't happen'. This has been done, for instance, by the Turkish state with respect to its total denial of the Armenian genocide resulting in the deaths of between 1 and 1.5 million Armenians during 1915–17 (Hovanissian, 1986). Total denial effectively blocks any kind of interrogation or conversation about the events, allowing states to silence their critics, hide from prosecution, and forget their activities. If total denial is exposed, states may then engage in 'partial denial' by admitting that something did happen but 'what happened was really something else'. Examples of this include the USA's renaming of civilian deaths in the war in Iraq as 'collateral damage' or in their reframing of the use torture in the 'war on terror' as intended to stress but not to cause psychological and physical damage (see Box 22.2).

BOX 22.2 A new paradigm for twenty-first century torture

Stanley Cohen (2006) argues that in order to use torture in the twenty-first century 'war on terror', the USA has had to publicly justify its practices both to itself and to the international community. The USA thus debated the use of torture openly and widely in its media, but this, according to Cohen, was a form of 'mock honesty' that reframed torture in order to make it seem like a legitimate practice. The new forms of 'Torture lite' legitimated by the USA included hooding, beating, shaking, sleep and noise deprivation, the use of stress positions, and 'water boarding'. These practices, according to US military officials, were not physically or psychologically damaging brutality but they merely induced stress. Moreover, they were said to be carried out on 'unlawful combatants' and not prisoners or prisoners of war, and they thus fell outside of the Geneva Convention. Cohen argues that renaming and reframing torture in this way allowed not only legal protections for the USA to use torture but it also enabled a partial denial of their activities which has led the way for a new twenty-first century paradigm of normalized torture.

Plate 22.1 The scandal surrounding Abu Ghraib military prison near Baghdad, Iraq, involved evidence of acts of torture and abuse committed by US military personnel against Iraqi prisoners during 2004.

Faced with criticism for their partial denial, states engage in neutralization of their activities by suggesting that 'what happened was justified'. Just like the juvenile delinquents studied by Sykes and Matza in the 1950s (see Chapter 5), Cohen suggests that states use various 'techniques of neutralization' to justify their activity. These include the 'denial of injury', 'denial of responsibility' and 'denial of the victims' humanity'. In the case of torture in the war on terror, it is claimed by the US that because no one is seriously physically injured, there can be no victim. States will also 'condemn their condemners' and 'appeal to higher loyalties' in order to neutralize their crimes, for instance, by claiming that their practices are protecting the 'greater good' of Western civilization from an evil enemy and are thus necessary and legitimate. As we shall see below, wars, invasions and colonialism are usually justified by states as for the 'greater good' of civilization. Yet, in the light of the twentieth-century barbarism described above and the colonialism, slavery and genocides described below, the actual civility of modern states is highly questionable.

In our contemporary multi-mediated world, spirals of denial may, however, be increasingly difficult to maintain. The Internet provides open access to unrivalled amounts of information about state activities, websites like WikiLeaks are committed to exposing cover-ups, and camera phones can transform citizens into journalists (see Chapter 17). These features may be unravelling the spirals of denial which, combined with globalization and the proliferation of human rights organizations, are major reasons for the increasing attention that is now paid to state crime by criminology. The Allied war on terror and the questionable legality of war in Iraq have also been significant factors for the growing interest in state crime (Rothe, 2009). On the other hand, as Cohen (1993) maintains, a number of 'bystander effects' will likely continue to restrict the amount of focus, criminological or otherwise, on state crimes. These include:

- a lack of identification with geographically and socially distant victims;
- a general inability to be able to conceive of effective interventions to prevent state atrocity; and
- a sense of diffused responsibility where everybody asserts that everybody else should do something about a problem rather than themselves, resulting in no action by anybody.

BOX 22.3 Normalization of the terror bombing of civilians

Ronald Kramer (2010) describes how the killing of innocent civilians through state-sanctioned terrorism has become a normal feature of contemporary conflict. He traces the beginning of this process to the large-scale 'area bombing' from air planes and artillery during the Second World War which culminated in the USA's atomic bombing of the Japanese towns of Hiroshima and Nagasaki in 1945, killing between 150,000 and 220,000 people directly and countless others over time. Following the Second World War, only the losers of the war – individual Germans and Japanese – were tried for war crimes in the Nuremburg trials, leaving US terror bombing free from any sanctions. This was effectively a moral silence that helped enable the USA to murder 2–3 million Koreans in the 1950s and between 2 and 4 million Vietnamese in the 1970s – a process of state-sanctioned terrorism that Kramer suggests continues into the present day with the 'collateral damage' from US military bombing campaigns in Iraq, Pakistan and Afghanistan.

Types of state crime

Although there are scattered examples of criminological attention paid to state crime from the 1970s onwards – mostly notably in the human rights-based approach to crime developed by Herman and Julia Schwendinger (1970/1975) – it was not until William Chambliss's presidential address to the American Society of Criminology in 1989 that state crime emerged as a clearly articulated topic of criminological interest. Here Chambliss developed the concept of 'state-organized crime' which he described as: 'acts defined by law as criminal and committed by state officials in the pursuit of their job as representatives of the state' (1989: 184). State-organized crime did not include criminal acts that benefited only individual officeholders (unless they were official state policy) but it was official behaviour embedded in organizational pressures to achieve a state's goal while simultaneously attempting to maintain its legitimacy. Examples include state complicity in piracy, drug and arms smuggling, money laundering and state-organized assassinations and murders. This concept, while bringing state crime more firmly into criminological consciousness, was criticized however for what was seen as too narrow a focus on crimes defined as such by law and which ignored most types of war crime. Consequently, in 1995, drawing on a more human rights-based approach, Chambliss broadened and internationalized his definition of state-organized crime to include 'behaviour that violates international agreements and principles established in the courts and treaties of international bodies' (1995: 9). Based on this later definition, three major types of state crimes can be identified:

- war crimes;
- crimes against humanity; and
- repressive state crimes.

War crimes and crimes against humanity are those proscribed by the Geneva and Hague Conventions which have, since its establishment in 2002, been enforced by the International Criminal Court in The Hague. These laws are intended to govern the actions of states during conflicts, although crimes against humanity also prohibit the peacetime crimes of slavery and colonization. Major war crimes include genocide, illegal invasion, torture, the ill-treatment of prisoners of war and battlefield casualties, and the deliberate targeting of civilians in war. Yet, as suggested above, despite the legal rules and institutions enacted to control and prevent war crimes, such crimes regularly occur. Even genocide – defined by the United Nations General Assembly as the 'deliberate and systematic destruction, in whole or in part, of an ethnic, racial, religious, or national group', is not simply a crime of the past – as exemplified most starkly by the Holocaust during the Second World War – but it has continued to happen throughout recent history including in Bosnia and Rwanda in the 1990s and in Sudan in the 2000s.

'Repressive state crimes' are those crimes outlawed by international human rights law which governs states' actions toward their own populations during peacetime. The most regular offenders of repressive crimes are authoritarian dictatorships bound to one-party rule, including: the Soviet Block under communism where approximately 2.7 million people died in the Gulag forced labour camps alone; or in the current absolutist state of Saudi Arabia where women's rights or rights to political expression are fiercely suppressed. Authoritarian states put limits on citizen's rights as a matter of routine and they tend to be incredibly repressive towards those that try to challenge their autocratic rule. The totalitarian and militarized state of North Korea, for instance, has been shown by human rights organizations such as Amnesty International to regularly engage in extra-juridical killings, arbitrary arrest, false imprisonment and torture of its own citizens.

While rarely so severe, democratic states may also limit their citizens' human rights. This tends to occur especially during times of emergency when fears over security can dominate over the liberty of citizens. This has happened in the contemporary UK and USA where the threat of Islamist terrorism has led to the enactment of domestic legislation that limits freedom of expression, rights to privacy and protection from arbitrary arrest, including the US Patriot Act and the UK Terrorism Act 2006 (see Chapter 21). Pantazis, and Pemberton (2009) go as far as to argue that UK counter-terrorism laws and the state activity accompanying them have cast

British Muslims as a 'suspect community' who have become subject to illegal surveillance and internment. Fuelled by the fear of Islamist terrorism, this 'state of exception' (Agamben, 2005) has also provided the impetus for what a number of criminologists argue has been the illegal invasion of Iraq, illegal ill-treatment of combatants and civilians there, and the illegal transformation of the Iraqi economy (see Kramer and Michalowski, 2005)

Crimes against humanity: colonialism and slavery

Some of the largest and most notable state crimes in history include the European slave trade and Western European colonization of parts of Africa, Australasia, the Americas and the Middle East. While slavery was prohibited by most nations by the mid-nineteenth century and many colonies gained independence following the Second World War, the effects of slavery and colonization continue to have a profound influence on contemporary state crimes and social injustices, and a number of colonies that have since become settler nations have all but wiped out indigenous peoples and their cultures.

From the sixteenth century the British state began a long reign of colonization which, by the early twentieth century, led to the British ruling over around one-fifth of the world's population and a quarter of the world's land, colonizing North America, the Indian subcontinent, Australia, large parts of East and West Africa, and more. In North America, Australia and New Zealand, the British created permanent settlements in order to exploit the sea and land for products to trade, and these colonies of course remain today. In India and East Africa, on the other hand, British settlement was smaller and temporary, exploiting, for example, India's very advanced textile industry which provided many of the skills and resources for the British Industrial Revolution. In Africa, one of the major resources that the British took were human slaves who were transported predominately to Caribbean and North American colonies to be forced to work on the plantations. Estimates vary but it is generally agreed that around 11 million people were transported from Africa by the Europeans during the Atlantic slave trade, with between 1.5 and 2 million dying during the voyage alone (Thomas, 1997).

The murder, subjugation and exploitation of indigenous peoples are characteristic features of the history of a number of today's settler nations like the USA, Canada and Australia. The Australian criminologist Chris Cunneen (2008) explains how between 1492 and 1892, 90 per cent of the entire Native American population was wiped out through being murdered, starved and frozen to death. And, in Australia, mixed race children and the children of aboriginals were taken by the state from their parents to be 'civilized' in squalid Christian boarding schools where sexual abuse was common. Many of these children were told that their parents were dead, and this type of state-sanctioned kidnapping went on in Canada right until the 1980s. Cunneen conceptualizes these activities as 'ethnocide' in which, under a supposedly rational and humanitarian claim to be civilizing 'savage' indigenous peoples, the aim was to completely erase indigenous cultures from the colonies.

For these activities to have occurred, the rule of law that was brought by and applied to white European settlers had to be suspended for the natives. Colonial policing and justice tended therefore to be composed of two separate systems – a modern rational criminal justice system for white Europeans; and a violent militarized system for the others who were deemed irrational

BOX 22.4 State crime in the Belgian Congo

Indigenous peoples of the colonies were dominated by the rule of Western states through non-juridical and violent forms of social control resulting in the death and ill-treatment of tens of millions. In Belgium-ruled Congo between 1885 and 1908, around 10 million indigenous peoples are estimated to have died at the hands of their colonists through starvation, exhaustion, disease and murder. Tony Ward (2005) describes how the Congolese people were terrorized under the orders of King Leopold II's militarized violence. Drawing on Merton's (1938) strain theory, Ward argues that the Belgians, facing economic recession, innovated through the use of extraordinary violence to terrorize the Congolese into frantically harvesting rubber and ivory for the international market. With economic gain in mind, the moral and financial costs of the Belgians' actions were pushed to the background and extreme violence became a routine feature of everyday life to the point at which most of the ivory and rubber, and many of the Congolese labour force, were almost totally destroyed, emptying the Congo of the resources that King Leopold II so desperately desired.

and thus unable to be controlled through Modern systems (Agozino, 2003). It was only in the 1990s that settler nations began to unravel their spirals of denial and publicly admit that they had committed numerous state crimes against indigenous peoples. Yet, despite this, sizable proportions of indigenous groups in Australia, New Zealand, Canada and the USA continue to be subject to high levels of state control and live at a disadvantage to the settlers. In Colin Samson's (2003) ethnographic research with the Innu peoples of Labrador in Canada, he describes how the once nomadic people that drew much of their cultural identity from their attachment to hunting have been forced by the Canadian state to live on government-built settlements and banned for many years from their traditional hunting grounds and practices. Corresponding with this, alcohol and solvent abuse became rife, and rates of suicide, premature death, ill-health and mental illness increased massively. A highly disproportionate number of Innu have also found themselves at the imposition of the colonist criminal justice system with its very different assumptions about crime, punishment and culpability to those found in Innu culture.

The legacy of slavery also continues into the present day in terms of the huge over-representation of black people in Western criminal justice systems – most notably in the USA. Loic Wacquant (2001) explains the over-representation of African Americans in the US prison system as a direct legacy of slavery which laid the foundations for African Americans' disadvantaged social and economic position, and subsequent ghettoization, in the contemporary USA. This over-representation also underpinned the dehumanizing discourses on non-white peoples that were developed to justify slavery and colonialism and which still linger on in contemporary US thought, arguably fuelling discrimination by its police and criminal justice system (see, for example, Bosworth, 2010).

The dehumanizing and violent legacy of colonialism also lingers on in colonies that have won their independence from European settlers. This is a theme explored by the influential post-colonial writer Frantz Fanon who examines how the hierarchical symbolism and extreme violence of colonial domination becomes inculcated into the psyche of colonial peoples to the detriment of their countries following independence. In *The Wretched of the Earth* (1967), Fanon describes how, usually through the means of violent revolution, indigenous elites take control of the post-colony and govern through the violent and kleptocratic colonial systems that had formed their colonial consciousness. Having little legitimacy in the eyes of much of the rest of the population, however, the elites are violently challenged by other indigenous groups, resulting in cycles of violence and civil wars. Much of Fanon's work is based on his experience of Algeria and its independence from the French in the 1960s, but a process similar to what he describes can also be seen in a number of African countries including Rwanda where, in 1994, fixed by its colonial past, a bloody genocide occurred killing 80,000 people (see Box 22.5).

BOX 22.5 Colonial foundations and the 1994 Rwandan genocide

Colonized by the Germans in 1894, Rwanda was given to Belgium following the First World War. In order to administer their new colony, the Belgians awarded power to a 'comprador class' – the Tutsis – a minority indigenous group who would help Belgium rule over the majority Hutu population. The Tutsis and Hutus were not separate tribal or ethnic groups but more accurately viewed as social classes where Tutsi were peoples who owned livestock and Hutu were those who did not. The two groups shared a similar culture, spoke the same language, often intermarried and lived in the same neighbourhoods, and a Hutu could become a Tutsi if they could afford to buy livestock (Strauss, 2006). The Belgians, however, in order to justify their rule, installed a symbolic system based on the hierarchy of ethnicity whereby they, the white Europeans, stood at the top as the natural leaders, the Tutsi in the middle, and the Hutu at the animal-like nadir of the hierarchy (see Mason, 1970). The two groups were later issued with identity cards that stated their 'ethnicity', and difference was further exacerbated by the separate economic situations imposed on the two groups by the Belgians, and through educating Tutsis in the Belgium schooling system in Rwanda.

In 1962, Rwanda gained independence from Belgium. The subsequent democratic elections brought the subordinate but majority Hutu into power. Because the elections were primarily based on the Hutu party trying to gain Hutu votes, ethnicity was given further spin and meaning by the Hutu party. By the 1990s, escalating economic and political crisis led to a civil war in Rwanda where Hutu hardliners in government attempted to cling on to power by further fuelling race hate propaganda toward the Tutsis, and it was amid this that the Hutu president was killed when his plane was shot down in 1994. From then on, for the next 100 days, in what has been called 'the twentieth century's fastest genocide' (Strauss, 2006: 41), hardliners in government ordered the deaths of all Tutsis – including women, children and unborn babies, and any moderate Hutus who were married to or tried to protect the Tutsi. Around 800,000 Tutsis, almost three-quarters of the Tutsi population, were slaughtered by large marauding groups of Hutus wielding guns, machetes and sticks (Prunier, 1995). Tutsi

Plate 22.2 A Rwandan child wearing military boots he found wandering the closed part of Mugunga refugee camp places an abandoned helmet on a stick, August 1995. Both the helmet and boots belonged to Rwandan soldiers, who discarded their uniforms when they fled Rwanda.

Source: © PA.

property was looted and burnt, and countless numbers of women were gang raped and their sexual organs mutilated (Mullins, 2009).

In these acts, the Hutu had hit back against the Tutsi who had ruled and dominated them during colonialism. They reversed the colonist discourse of domination, relegating Tutsis to the bottom of the hierarchy and dehumanizing them with labels such as 'cockroach', 'snake', 'rats' and 'dogs'. In terms of Fanon's (1967) post-colonial theory, these symbols of domination can be seen as a psychological outcome of the pattern of modern Western domination that had been set by European colonization.

Genocide: a crime of obedience

Any large-scale state crime like the ethnocide of indigenous peoples, the bombing of civilians, or the genocide of entire groups like in 1990s Rwanda, while ordered and organized by state leaders and military officials, is also reliant on the cooperation of regular soldiers, police and civilians in order to sustain and carry it out. It has been suggested, for instance, that one-third of the Hutu population were involved in the genocide of the Tutsis (Strauss, 2006), and it can be assumed that another sizable proportion stood by. Additionally, in Europe by the end of the Second World War, six million Jews had been exterminated by the Nazis, as well as five million others – including Polish immigrants, gypsies, homosexuals, and the physically and mentally handicapped. The scale of the Nazi genocide was so vast that it also could not have been undertaken without a very high level of organization involving a sizable proportion of the German population. The question this raises, then, is why and how do populations of normally law-abiding people become involved in atrocity? Are they somehow different to normal populations, or does something special happen in these situations to awaken a savage brutality that usually lies dormant?

Raphael Lemkin, the Jewish lawyer who coined the concept of genocide, like most others at the time thought that the Nazi Holocaust represented a reversion of the German people and state to a form of pre-modern barbarism that was an ugly aberration on modern civilization. Additionally, Theodor Adorno and his colleagues (1950) at the Frankfurt School claimed that the many Germans who assisted the Holocaust must have been unusually authoritarian as a result of strict, disciplinarian upbringings. While these ideas found favour at the time and, indeed, continue to offer palatable explanations to modern sensibilities, a number of studies suggest that populations that assist genocide are not psychologically or morally different to any other modern citizenry and that, in the case of the Holocaust at least, it was actually the social organization of modern civilization that lay at the heart of organizing mass murder.

Hannah Arendt (2006/1963) examines the trial of the high-ranking Nazi officer Adolf Eichmann who had ordered the deaths of tens of thousands of people during the Holocaust. Eichmann's own explanation for his activities was that he was simply doing his job, and Arendt shows that he was not particularly anti-Semitic. She also cites Israeli psychiatric reports that found him not to be psychologically disturbed in any major way. Indeed, Arendt suggests that Eichmann seemed to be quite an agreeable man, although one who found it difficult to think for himself and who had an unhealthy willingness to please his superiors. She concludes that Eichmann's case represents the 'banality of evil', that is that good people often do terrible things simply as a result of wanting to be accepted by those around them and carrying out orders – the implication being that we all have the propensity to engage in evil.

BOX 22.6 Stanley Milgram's 'Behavioural study of obedience'

Hannah Arendt's (2006/1963) claims about 'the banality of evil' are bolstered by a series of experiments carried out by the social psychologist Stanley Milgram in the 1960s. In his 'behavioural study of obedience' (1963), experimental subjects are arranged to meet a scientist for an experiment that they are told is to test the effect of punishment on learning. The scientist assigns the subject to the role of teacher, instructing them to administer a series of tests of learning to another subject who is assigned the role of learner but who is actually an actor. Both learner and subject are taken to a separate room where the learner is wired up to an electric device while saying that he has a heart condition. The subject is taken back into the main room and given a mild but actual electric shock so as to be convinced of the supposed reality of the shocks. The subject is then instructed by the scientist to give an electric shock to the learner each time he gets a question wrong, and that the shocks will rise progressively in 15 volt increments up to a maximum of 450 volts. As the subjects increase the number of volts in response to incorrect answers, the learner can be heard initially groaning, asking to be let out, and then shouting, until 300 volts are reached when the learner goes silent – implying the possibility that he has had a heart attack and died.

Despite the learner going silent, and regardless of the numbers of volts on the machine being accompanied by signs indicating the higher-level volts as being 'Intense', 'Extreme Intensity' and, finally, 'Danger: Severe Shock', Milgram found that a staggering 98 per cent of subjects carried on the electric shocks until they had reached 300 volts – and 65 per cent carried on through the full range of shocks until they had reached 450 volts – continuing to shock the learner long after he had fallen silent. Many subjects were visibly anxious in doing this, protesting and arguing with the scientist, and some having panic attacks and even seizures, yet the vast majority carried on the shocks, being compelled only by the words of the scientist who would simply urge them to continue and tell them that the experiment was painful but not fatal. When asked if we ourselves would administer these shocks, most of us put ourselves into the 2 per cent that refused to go to 300 volts, yet the reality is that 98 per cent of us would continue until the learner has gone silent. This further illustrates the 'banality of evil' – suggesting that even in peacetime, devoid of Nazi propaganda and of any real sanction, most people will do what they are told by those in authority regardless of the potentially atrocious outcomes of doing so.

Modernity and the Holocaust

Building on the work of Arendt, the sociologist Zygmunt Bauman (1989) argues that modern social organization routinely produces the perfect conditions for obedience, and it was these conditions that lay at the heart of the German population's involvement in the Holocaust. Bauman suggests that 'Without modern civilization and its most central essential achievements, there would be no Holocaust' (ibid.: 87). The central achievements of modern civilization are:

- First, a division of labour, which during the Holocaust enabled German soldiers and civilians to psychologically divorce themselves from the outcomes of their activities. Each person was simply doing just one small task in the division of labour and thus no single person could be individually responsible for the atrocities. Here, organization itself obliterated personal responsibility meaning that the Germans were not compelled to reflect on their actions and so could easily deny their wrongdoing.
- Second, bureaucratization, which when applied to a killing system meant that the 'objects' of production in the division of labour were deemed not as people but as rational units or

numbers, thereby dehumanizing the victims and placing them outside of the normal human moral universe. Those working in the bureaucracy, just like Adolf Eichmann, became thoughtless followers of rules concerned with achieving the technical outputs of the bureaucratic system rather than any moral outcomes.

- Third, the repetition and routine characteristic of bureaucratic work, which had the effect of making the act of violence become a routine and thus normal. Indeed, if that routine were to be abandoned, Bauman suggests that this would put an individual's past action under question as they would then have to face up to their own wrongdoing. In such a situation it becomes psychologically easier to simply carry on, in denial of the outcomes of one's activity.
- Lastly, instrumental rationality, in which rational methods are employed to achieve 'progress' rather than any moral, spiritual or aesthetic guides to behaviour. This had torn the German people away from their own notions of right and wrong, and led them into working only for the greater good of the organization.

In the end, Bauman argues, the highly rational organizational system resulted in irrational outcomes as the Jews could have been used effectively as slave labour to aid the war effort, and ghettoizing, transporting and killing them was a very expensive undertaking. The Nazi bureaucracy however lost sight of this because it functioned so well at its ultimate task – mass murder.

Bauman's analysis is a cautionary one that reminds us of the violent possibilities of modern state power and warns us against seeing the Holocaust as the result of a *lack* of social order. It was, he argues, the result of social order – and a specific type of modern social order that we still live within and so the Holocaust could happen again. Despite the strength of his argument, other twentieth-century genocides put aspects of Bauman's thesis into question. For example, the Rwandan genocide occurred not through a factory system with a highly organized division of labour, but was carried out much more directly in large marauding groups. Here, there could be little bureaucratic distancing of oneself from the killing because it was so direct and bloody. Yet, just as it would be a mistake to view the Holocaust as an aberration of modern civilization, it would also be a mistake to see the Rwandan genocide as resulting from some kind of anomic barbarism. Scott Strauss's (2006) research shows how the post-colonial Rwandan state was, like the Nazi state, highly centralized and organized with a physical geography that facilitated state authority to reach deep into Rwandan society. In another study into the Rwandan genocide, Smeulers and Hoex (2010) describe how regionally based and militarily controlled groups of young Hutu men, the Interahamwe, trained, armed and funded by the Hutu state, began the killing and later organized its expansion by compelling the Hutu public to either kill or be killed. They argue that the fear produced by the Interahamwe compelled the public into joining in the killing which eventually, over the 100 days of the genocide, became a routine and normal part of life.

Of course, as Milgram's experiments illustrate, a threat to one's life is not a necessary ingredient to compel publics into carrying out state-sanctioned violence – official authority and a sense of duty can be enough (see also Browning, 1998). These crimes of conformity that characterize genocide and many other state-sanctioned mass atrocities represent somewhat of an enigma to a criminology that almost solely focuses on crimes of deviance. In this context, it has been said that criminology has much work to do to in order to develop effective theoretical tools to understand state-sanctioned atrocity (see Jamieson, 1998). Indeed, the most enlightening analyses of state crimes have grown from sociology and social psychology such as in the above-mentioned works of Milgram and Bauman. In another important social psychological work, *Crimes of Obedience* (1989), Kelman and Hamilton examine the My Lai massacre that occurred during the Vietnam War in 1968 when a platoon of US soldiers massacred some 400 civilians. From this case and that of a number of other sanctioned massacres they identify three general conditions that enable crimes of obedience:

- 'Authorization' – told by those in authority to do something, almost regardless of the outcomes, people tend to follow orders sometimes resulting in murderous activity;
- 'Routinization' – when people commit violence or ill-treatment on many occasions, day in, day out, it becomes taken for granted, which inhibits people's reflection on the morality of their activity; and
- 'Dehumanization' – the humanity of enemies is always linguistically re-categorized so as to exclude people from the human moral universe, enabling their ill-treatment.

These three conditions of crimes of obedience can be seen as general features of mass state violence throughout history, including genocide, ill-treatment of combatants and civilians, and colonial domination.

Conceptual and definitional issues

Despite the usefulness of international laws and treaties to aid criminologists to conceptualize and begin to understand various forms of state-organized crime, a number of criticisms have arisen. The first concerns the conceptual problems generated by isolating state activities from interests and influences that lie outside the state itself.

'State–corporate crime'

Kramer and Michalowski (1993) argue that, in reality, state crimes and corporate crimes are rarely committed by states or corporations alone but that they work in conjunction. They thus propose the concept 'state–corporate crime' as a more effective and novel way of imagining both state crime and corporate crime. This, they split into two parts: 'state-initiated' and 'state-facilitated' corporate crime.

- 'State-initiated corporate crime' occurs when states direct, initiate or approve corporate misconduct, such as in the privatization of the post-war Iraq economy described in Box 22.7, or the 1986 space shuttle *Challenger* disaster where risky and negligent decision-making by state-controlled NASA and the corporate-controlled Morton Thiokol led to the explosion of the space shuttle killing seven astronauts.

■ 'State-facilitated corporate crime' occurs when governments fail to regulate corporate activity and misconduct, usually as a result of shared interests between states and corporations. State-facilitated crimes of this type most commonly include government failure to enforce various laws and regulations that result in unnecessary death or injury. Examples of this include the explosion of the Imperial Food Products chicken processing plant in North Carolina in 1991 where 25 workers were killed and another 56 seriously injured (see Aulette and Michalowski, 1993). In the UK, the government's failure to effectively regulate and interrogate drug test results by large pharmaceutical companies in the 1990s can be seen as state-facilitated crime. This occurred, for instance, with the suppression of clinical trial data that had indicated a link between some anti-depressant 'wonder drugs' and increased levels of suicide among adolescent users (see McGoey and Jackson, 2009).

Plate 22.3 The space shuttle *Challenger* just moments before its explosion.

Source: © PA.

BOX 22.7 State–corporate crime and the liminality of war

State–corporate collusion in crime is nothing new but it is a normal part of modern state building (see Chambliss, 1989; Kramer *et al.* 2002; Tilley, 1985). During the Second World War, for example, major corporations such as IBM, General Motors and Ford all sold products to the Nazis. Indeed, as Vincenzo Ruggiero (2010) argues, war tends to open up ungovernable lawless spaces in which corporate crime can flourish, and he shows how this has occurred recently in the privatization of the post-invasion Iraqi economy where large US and UK companies including Halliburton and Aegis have secured huge profits. Dave Whyte (2007) describes this as the 'neo-liberal colonization' of Iraq whereby an overriding neo-liberal ideology based on free markets, private owners and an expanding economy is the new regime that is being imposed on Iraq by Allied states and their corporations. Whyte shows how, in 2004 alone, $48.7 billion of seized Iraqi oil revenue went to US firms in the form of reconstruction contracts but, due to the erratic and chaotic nature of war, poor record keeping means that the total amount of money seized or on what it has been spent simply cannot be known with any certainty.

Social harms perspective

The second main criticism of legally based conceptualizations of state crime derive from the observation that because states hold the power to make laws and have the ability to criminalize certain actions, they also thereby have the power to avoid the criminalization of their own activities. Recent examples of this include the Allied invasion of Iraq which, although deemed by the then UN Secretary General Kofi Annan as violating international law and the UN Charter, was justified by the Allies on the grounds of self-defence and humanitarian intervention (see Sands, 2005). Cohen (2006) points to a similar process of legal reconstruction by the USA in terms of their legal and moral justifications for the use of torture in the war on terror (see Box 22.2). This ability of powerful states to shield off criminal labels and sanctions combined with their power to criminalize the actions of others has led some to argue that criminologists should avoid any legal basis for the definition of state crime. Writers including Raymond Michalowski (1985) and Paddy Hillyard and colleagues (2004) argue that a more enlightened criminology should focus on 'social harms' rather than state-defined crimes. A progressive 'peace-making' criminology would, Hillyard *et al.* (2004) suggest, explore activities that are socially injurious regardless of whether they are deemed criminal or not. This perspective introduces a number of additional 'state harms' into any conceptualization of state 'crime', which may include state-facilitated poverty and inequality, differential health and life expectancy, and state failure to protect minorities from hate crimes.

'Crimes of globalization'

Building on the social harms perspective, Friedrichs and Friedrichs (2002) developed the concept 'crimes of globalization'. By this they mean the mass social harms caused by the imposition of global finance onto the people of developing nations through the direction of international financial organizations such as the World Bank and the International Monetary Fund. Here, financial institutions, in return for financial help, impose 'structural adjustments' onto developing economies, often rapidly, by, for instance, privatizing state assets, opening up economies to cheap imports and devaluing currency. Loans may also be provided to countries that struggle to pay them or even their interest back meaning that spending on other services such as health, education or employment falls off, injuring and impoverishing populations. In West Africa, for example, over 70 per cent of surplus goes to the West to pay off loans – essentially locking much of West Africa into a cycle of poverty (Agozino, 2003).

Only a small number of Western nations control the major international financial organizations. The USA, for example, holds over 16 per cent of voting rights in the World Bank – despite the Bank being formed of 184 member countries. International financial organizations also tend to regulate themselves with no independent oversight. For these organizations, expansion of global capital often takes precedence over what happens to the people and their nations, and it is commonly through them that Western corporations move into the developing world to exploit the resources. According to Friedrichs and Friedrichs (2002) this is a 'crime of globalization' and one initiated largely by powerful Western states. In another example of crimes of globalization, Rothe *et al.* (2008) describe how structural adjustments imposed on the Rwandan economy in the 1980s provided the economic basis for the flourishing of the 1994 genocide. They suggest that currency devaluation, rapid inflation and government debt caused the mass unemployment of young Tutsi men which encouraged them to join the Interahamwe – the militarized regional groups that started and organized the genocide.

With crimes of globalization no actual laws are broken but the actions of international financial organizations working in concert with large transnational corporations and under strong neo-liberal ideologies, can be seen to produce widespread social harms that may thus be the subject of criminological investigation. Whether the social harms perspective widens the view of criminology too far and into the realm of other academic disciplines like development studies and sociology is subject to debate. However, as a result of state power to set agendas and organize what we, both criminologists and the general public, perceive as criminal or harmful activities, many very harmful activities do avoid criminalization and moral censure. Crimes of globalization and social harms perspectives can thus be useful for a criminology of state crime – reframing the criminological imagination in a way that enables the problematic and injurious effects of state activities to be identified and understood.

Summary

1   Three main forms of state-organized crime can be identified in relation to international humanitarian law: 'war crimes', 'crimes against humanity' and 'repressive state crimes'.

2   Following the global ratification of international laws prohibiting state crimes after the Second World War, the killing of innocent civilians, torture and ill-treatment of combatants, and the violent repression of oppositional political groups have expanded to extraordinarily high levels in the twentieth and twenty-first centuries.

3   Despite the innumerable occurrences of robbery, death and injury of civilians at the hands of states, criminology has until very recently largely ignored state crimes – partly because of the capacity of states to deny, hide and legitimate their crimes.

4   Large-scale state-sanctioned atrocities like genocide always involve otherwise peaceful and law-abiding populations undertaking mass violence. Populations engage in mass violence and ill-treatment simply by being ordered to do so by those in authority, illustrating the 'banality of evil' and the criminogenic nature of modern organizational systems.

5   Because states have the capacity to legally reconstruct their activities and they rarely operate in isolation from corporate interests, some criminologists question the efficiency of using legally based definitions of state crime. Concepts like 'state–corporate crime', 'crimes of globalization' and the 'social harms' perspective have been proposed as better alternatives.

Critical thinking questions

1   **Through what processes has the ill-treatment of both civilians and combatants become a normalized aspect of contemporary conflicts?**
2   **Is torture ever justifiable, even if it takes the form of 'torture lite'?**
3   **What is the 'banality of evil'?**
4   **What does criminology gain or lose by adopting a 'social harms' perspective on state crimes?**

Further study

Chambliss, W., Michalowski, R. and Kramer, R. (2010) (eds) *State Crime in the Global Age*, Cullompton: Willan. Written and edited by the leading state crime scholars, this book develops conceptual approaches to state crime and discusses a number of contemporary examples of state crime, particularly those committed by democratic states in the 'war on terror'.

Green, T. and Ward, P. (2004) *State Crime: Governments, Violence and Corruption*, London: Pluto. An excellent introduction to conceptual issues surrounding the understanding of state crimes, providing clear examples and justifications for a criminology of state crime.

Rothe, D. (2009) *State Criminality: The Crime of all Crimes*, Lanham, MD: Lexington Books. Also provides an excellent introduction to conceptualizing state crime and develops helpful typologies to understand how and why various types of states tend to commit particular kinds of crimes.

Salvesberg, J. (2010) *Crime and Human Rights: Criminology of Genocide and Atrocities*, London: Sage. A very concise and clear introduction to genocide and war crimes which explains and develops understanding of 'crimes of conformity'.

Useful websites

International State Crime Initiative
http://statecrime.org/
A cross-disciplinary community of scholars working to further the understanding of state crime, their website contains useful and up-to-date information about contemporary state crime and state crime research.

Universal Declaration of Human Rights
http://www.un.org/en/documents/udhr/index.shtml

Amnesty International
www.amnesty.org.uk
The worldwide movement campaigning for internationally recognized human rights.

Human Rights Watch
www.hrw.org
Produces regular reports into human rights abuses around the world.

Stanley Milgram's 'Behavioural study of obedience'
http://v.youku.com/v_show/id_XMTQzMzQ2MjI0.html
Original film footage of Stanley Milgram's experiment into obedience to authority, arguably one of the most profound works of twentieth-century psychology.

chapter 23

Criminological Futures

Key issues

- This chapter poses questions about the futures of crime, control and criminology.
- It reviews links between past, present and future.
- The expansion of the criminological horizon is discussed.
- Criminology is an exciting, ongoing but continually 'unfinished' project.

Introduction

Criminology addresses a wide range of problems, issues and challenges to society. It investigates, and theorizes about, crime and control developments that threaten and protect the social, moral and economic orders of life that we take for granted. Most of these challenges are familiar and long-standing, but the various media (factual and fictional) and their audiences are most interested in sensational or new developments – hence the fascination with serial murderers and the success of numerous recent films depicting futuristic scenarios of crime, chaos and control. There is a contrast here between the ordinary and everyday forms of crime that have a practical importance for people and that are easily grasped as local threats versus the large-scale, globally cumulative, financially significant but somehow less tangible forms of crime that are generally harder to grasp as 'our problems'. Loader and Sparks (2007: 94) make a similar point noting that:

> A concern with the implications of macrolevel developments for criminological theory and research . . . is not now (any more than at any other time) simply a licence for

preferring the novel, the fashionable, and the sweeping over the grounded, the empirical, and the local, nor for disengaging from intricate and detailed problems of policy and politics wherever we happen to encounter them.

In drawing this book to a close, we seek to reflect on the current and future state of crime and control and to briefly explore how we can take a sociological approach to the public issues and private troubles that are cast about on the changing landscape of 'criminology'.

Visions of the future?

One starting question is whether we can identify different views about the 'futures' of crime and control, as distinct from views about the 'futures' of criminology. In some respects, for example, we might reasonably predict that whatever the future nature of crime and control, different but already existing varieties of criminological theory and method will be applied and developed further. So, one 'future' of criminology could simply be 'more of the same' but with interesting and important diversifications.

On the other hand, a more dramatic vision might assume that some of the 'big changes' in crime, control and criminology referred to in earlier chapters will see further amplification, eventually resulting in 'paradigm changes' (Kuhn, 1962) in the field of study, or, at the very least, profound changes and innovations in the types and characteristics of different criminological perspectives. In some ways this may be the vision of the future we want to hear about because our fascination with the future is largely based on an assumption that it will somehow be dramatically different (whether appealingly or appallingly so).

However, the future arrives only slowly and, in reality, the idea that criminology may look a great deal different in the future than it does today may not be easily supported. This is because if we look back over the twentieth century, for all the different changes in crime (and, equally importantly, in perceptions of crime), developments in understanding have – by and large – been the products of new variations on existing criminological themes and traditions. The fact that this history is full of references to 'breaks' and 'breakthroughs', new insights and new criminologies, and so on, partly reflects criminology's amnesia (Young, 1979) about the past, as old ideas and perspectives are recycled, combined, reinvented and renamed. To be sure, much that was overlooked or required serious and overdue attention has been attended to – the development of the feminist perspective being a notable example. Similarly, debate between critical commentators and crime science adherents moves the field along, while the expansion of awareness about how criminological ideas follow through into policy and practice – sometimes with unintended consequences – provides its own lessons for a maturing subject (see e.g. Chancer and McLaughlin, 2007). Yet, the criminological kaleidoscope remains a mechanism with familiar patterns of problems, methods and theories that receive an occasional 'shake-up' to produce variations on the familiar and, every now and then, the strikingly 'new' criminological image that shapes the view of new possibilities for a new generation.

From this starting point, looking to the futures of crime, control and criminology could be a modest project that extrapolates from some current trends and considers how they may develop. This is nonetheless an important exercise, and we follow up the idea in this chapter, although readers of this book should by now feel quite well positioned to do some of this 'futurology' themselves. Our discussions of crime, control and criminology have indicated relevant dominant characteristics and trends, and so, with a little use of the criminological imagination, readers can assess for themselves whether certain kinds of crime or theory are in ascendance or decline.

Persistence of the past

As in any speculative exercise, it is worth remembering that the future is not just about 'the new' but also about the persistence of 'the old'. 'The poor are always with us', goes the saying, but so are the rich, so there are certainly persuasive reasons (based on existing evidence and theory) to assume that some current patterns of crime will simply continue as they are. At the same time, some currently insignificant areas of crime may become important in ways that we *cannot easily predict*, while others that are currently neglected will attract more attention because of social and demographic changes that we *can predict*. For example, on the one hand, in the UK (though not in the USA) early twentieth-century concerns about links between drugs and crime had largely evaporated by the end of the 1920s (Parssinen, 1983), and thereafter for the following decades, right into the late 1950s, there was little evidence that could have provided the basis for a prediction about the worldwide scale of the drugs and crime industry that emerged from the 1970s and 1980s (Measham and South, 2012). On the other hand, there are a host of previously neglected issues that have come to greater prominence in recent years as social attitudes and tolerance have changed, media and professional attention has increased, and the law has begun to catch up – issues such as child abuse, domestic violence, animal cruelty, and abuse of elder people spring to mind in this context.

Extension of current trends

Generally, the extension of current trends into the near future might run as follows. Left, liberal and right political perspectives tend to arrive at a consensus about future trajectories of crime even if they differ strongly about the causes and remedies. However, in terms of how policy is made and then implemented it is striking that in the UK and USA even historically familiar differences about appropriate responses to crime have faded and convergence has produced look-alike political promises, police powers and penal crises. All of this represents a trend worth watching.

There may be broad agreement that an increase in the number of those finding themselves among the socially excluded, within marginal groups in society, is likely to lead to more property crime, burglary, shoplifting, theft from the person, and similar crimes. A consumer culture, fuelled by diversity of choice, advertising and aspiration, aims to create, meet and stimulate the needs and desires of all, but it is only those with the necessary income (legal or illegal) who can be full consumers. Surrounded by the signs and symbols of consumerism, the obsessions of materialism and the fetishism of designer-label fashion, the argument that feelings of relative deprivation can provide criminal motivation is a powerful one. A culture of narcissism (Lasch, 1979) values appearances, experiences, hedonism and disposable possessions yet still leaves people feeling unfulfilled, empty, in search of more. The mountain of aspirations for people to climb just gets bigger and higher. Writers from different perspectives within criminology, from Merton's theory of adaptation to those interested in the 'seductions of crime' and a cultural criminology, have been interested in this kind of scenario.

As Sutherland (1949) suggested so many years ago, the focus of the criminal justice agencies will be upon those offenders at the bottom of the social pile rather than those in positions of advantage who are committing crimes of more economic or social seriousness. Unless the future brings radical or revolutionary social change (Lea, 2002), this is unlikely to look much different. The crimes of the middle and managerial classes are likely to follow, at least in the West, current trends – with respectable employees, professionals and employers being both victims and perpetrators of crime. As we saw in Chapter 13, the pressures of domestic and global competition, the continued erosion of the bases and virtues of trust, and the inability of late modern market capitalism to regulate corporate activity, are all factors contributing to such trends.

Drug-related crime shows little sign of abeyance, although (as discussed in Chapter 14), at least at the levels of users and small dealers, it is likely to remain unclear whether involvement in drug cultures leads to criminality or involvement in crime cultures leads to drug use and dealing. This is important for a 'future' in which both the illicit economy and the drugs trade are among the major growth industries for the two will increasingly fuel each other. Regardless of this particular debate, the profits of drug distribution will continue to stimulate significant developments in criminal organization, further diversification into legitimate commerce, and intrusion into political processes via corruption, economic influence (Castells, 1996) and the funding of military and terrorist activities. The local as well as the global dimensions of drug trafficking are complex and enormously resistant to legal controls, quasi-military interventions or development aid efforts (Mena and Hobbs, 2010). Criminal and legitimate enterprises blur with increasing significance (Naím, 2005; Ruggiero, 1996; Punch, 1996); global politics and financial swings can affect patterns of both legal and illegal trade and migration (Jamieson et al., 1998). The breakdown of borders and the power of instant global communication have encouraged and enabled more transnational crimes such as fraud, terrorism and extortion, directed against governments and corporations as well as individuals.

Armed conflicts in the Middle East, in Eastern Europe, in Africa and Asia remind us that crimes of war and violations of human rights are affecting hundreds of thousands of people on a daily basis (Chapter 22; and see Cohen, 2001). Similarly, crimes against the environment such as pollution and environmental exploitation, and resulting problems such as damage to public health and victimization of local populations, are now matters for international crime and control agendas to take seriously (Chapter 19).

In this representation of trends, we clearly seem to have moved from a world of the past where crime was generally seen as a local problem to a new landscape requiring understanding of the global contours of crime. However, we must not romanticize or produce a cosy caricature of the past. Some forms of crime have always relied on cross-border markets. There is nothing new to the international dimension of crimes of war; the cross-continental slave and then drugs trades, while legal in earlier centuries, were forerunners of today's major international crimes; the development of international travel and means of communication has a long history, always facilitating crime along the way.

We tend to assume that the past rested on more solid foundations, where the differences and continuities between localities and the nation-state were well established, and tradition was a serious social force. Yet across the West, wars and occupations, conflicts between labour and capital, the rise and decline of empires, and so on, have all meant that the securities and certainties of the past may have been more insecure and elusive than we sometimes think. The path from the past to the future may simply be one of 'continuity of change'. Nonetheless, today, globalization and glocalization, 'McDonaldization' and 'postmodernization', 'wars in the name of peace' and 'terrorism in the name of religion', may all mean that the world around us is experiencing such change at a faster pace. Does all this create new contexts and conditions for crime?

The present into the future

Criminological thinking – present and future?

Most commentators would agree that the past thirty–forty years have seen major transformations in the nature of crime control as a result of a remarkable increase in post-war crime rates. A substantial escalation in crime had at least three consequences for 'thinking about crime' (Carrabine, 2004).

First, it gave rise to intense debate on the left between neo-Marxist 'idealists' and social democratic 'realists', and, on the right, the return to biological positivism and folk demonism. Somewhere in between, according to current 'criminological classifications', comes the development, by officials associated with the Home Office and various academics focusing on the crime prevention agenda, of an 'administrative criminology' that has come to regard crime as a normal, if regrettable, outcome of everyday life. From a certain vantage point, all of this mix, dispute and competition makes sense in terms of how a 'postmodern' vision of the future of criminology might develop (South, 1997). The old-fashioned grand theoretical overviews that promised certainty of explanation (such as Marxism and functionalism) have been replaced by the fragmentation of narratives and a story of the collapse of deference, the embrace of difference and the disguising of difficulty.

Second, crime both in the popular imagination and in personal experience became a central feature of public concern and cultural consumption. Moreover, certain kinds of 'hidden' crime, such as domestic violence, child sex abuse and rape, became more visible, while forms of corporate, white-collar and state crime have periodically attracted sustained attention in ways that would have been unimaginable thirty years ago. Yet it remains the case that crimes of the powerful and those committed in the home are under-represented in recorded crime figures and, as feminist research has consistently demonstrated, violence against women is widespread and exists throughout the class structure.

The third consequence of the increase in crime from the 1960s onward was the politicization of 'law and order'. From the 1970s, forms of government based on welfare state models of economic management and responses to social problems came under attack and were replaced by, first, New Right administrations, for example in Australia, Britain, New Zealand and the United States, and then by otherwise traditionally left–liberal governments that combined their revised philosophies with free market principles and traditional conservative values. Following the 9/11 and then 7/7 bombings in New York and London political parties have given prominence to anti-terrorism policies and commitments to increased security measures. In all this history of political realignment, the overt politicization of crime and control was, and is likely to remain, fundamentally key to vote-winner strategies and social policies. For the future, the subject of crime and its control can only become even more a matter of political significance.

Criminological futures?

While bearing in mind our earlier caution about the persistence and power of the past it is worth considering how new 'ways of thinking' might emerge in criminology. An optimistic view might take the national and global promotion of the human rights agenda as a key starting point, albeit with realistic acknowledgement of the barriers facing this project (Cohen, 2001). Nonetheless, the gains of movements and success of some proliferating legislation concerned with human rights, civil liberties, acknowledgement of the victimization of minorities, women and children, and the protection of the environment, might all be achievements we can project into 'one' future of responses to crime and violations. On the other hand, these developments based on rights and universalism are already matched by many other trends in the politics, practice and criminology of risk control that translate into technologies and techniques that are rather less liberal in their implications.

Risk and risky populations as the future focus of control?

It is understandable that society should aim to prevent crime – but do we want to be able to do so by the use of a 'science of criminology' that can predict from an early age who will, and who will not, be a good or bad citizen?

A common feature in much recent development in theories of crime, control and criminal justice is the prioritization and pursuit of earlier prediction of risk in order to enhance response. The idea of 'the present' as one of increasing precariousness and risk is worth further examination if we assume it will remain influential into the future. This is not only because of its current wide influence but also because it is now attracting some serious criticism.

The importance of the risk analysis arguments, originally associated with the idea of actuarial justice (see Chapter 7) or a 'new penology', is that this is 'in part the product of a societal accommodation to routinely high volumes of crime, as well as of the refinement of professional practices for monitoring, surveillance and aggregate management' (Sparks, 2000: 131). In other words, the causes of crime are no longer seen as important. Instead, probabilities are central for a form of actuarial justice that 'does not see a world free of crime but rather one where the best practices of damage limitation have been put in place' (Young, 1999b: 391).

It is clear that writers on risk have identified a new trend in crime control. Crime has become a risk to be calculated, by offender and potential victim, rather than a deviation from civilized conduct caused by individual pathology or faulty socialization – the hallmarks of traditional criminology. Instead, the new criminologies of everyday life see crime as an outcome of normal social interaction (Garland, 2001b).

A different (sociological) future?

Influentially, David Matza (1969: 1) once warned of the dangers of imposing order where none existed – but this was during an era when the scepticism characteristic of the sociology of deviance briefly held sway over the unimaginative rigidity of 'traditional' criminology. As late as the 1980s in the UK, teaching or researching about criminology was principally associated with the Cambridge University Institute of Criminology, the Oxford University Centre for Criminology, and the Home Office. However, the study of deviance was hosted by departments of sociology, and was encountered by students alongside the full range of sociological concerns, including education, housing, race and gender, with sociological theory and methodology lodged at the core of both undergraduate and postgraduate study.

The subsequent and extraordinary growth of criminology as a taught subject in the UK should be linked to the commodification of higher education, a phenomenon that has gone hand in hand with the expansion of the university sector following the shrinkage that took place during the Conservative administration of the 1980s. As a direct consequence of this expansion there has been an explosion of criminology degrees, lectureships, departments, journals, conferences, publishers and the invention of 'a criminological tradition'. Along the way, the sociological content of much criminology was drained, leading to the establishment of a false dichotomy in some varieties of British criminology that seek to set out a simplistic aetiology of criminal action. By contrast sociologically trained researchers have long laboured to present crime and its control as a complex, messy, dull, exciting, pleasurable and painful set of experiences, and while criminology is a 'rendezvous discipline' (Downes, 1988) it has traditionally met under the sociological clock. The pace of social change will require thinking outside the criminological box in order to cope with, for example, the impact of the market on social relations (Harman, 2009: 325–8), the increased securitization of policing (Fussey et al., 2011), the recalibration of hedonism in the wake of post-industrialism (Winlow and Hall, 2006) and the privatization of formal control (Hobbs et al., 2003), as well as many other related developments fostered by neo-liberalism (Hall, 2012). Scholars should consider the impact of housing policies and consequent markets on the emergent cultures of the post-industrial working class (Hobbs, 2013: ch. 10), and extend the emerging interest in consumerism (Hall et al., 2008; Hayward, 2004) and its impact on property relations, communality, and our understanding of nihilistic violent predation in the suites as well as the streets, all the time acknowledging the role of the law in negotiating market behaviours.

More broadly, engagement from across the entire range of the social sciences is vital if we are to understand the interactions between global cultures and toxic bazaars (Ruggiero and South, 1995) whether dealing in stocks, drugs or people. Scholars of crime and control will need to understand how global diasporas and cross-border migrations feed the legal and illegal markets (Turner and Kelly, 2009) that are integral to 'countergeographies of globalization' (Sassen, 1998) and how all these relate to environmental changes and impacts on food and water supply and security (South, 2012; Fussey and South, 2012; South and Brisman, 2013).

A crossroads?

Criminology and its relationship to sociology are now at a crossroads. Where once the linkages had been strong – especially in studies of deviance – today that is no longer the case. The separation has occurred as criminology has successfully established itself as an autonomous, independent academic subject that no longer sees itself as a subfield of the legal, medical or social sciences. Some regard this remarkable expansion of criminology and move away from the more basic disciplines as a sign of success and a proud achievement, others are more ambivalent and warn of the dangers growing isolation will bring (Carrabine, 2013).

From the outset many of the leading figures insisted that criminology is not a discipline, and the entire National Deviancy Conference movement can be seen as a form of 'anti-criminology' which has gradually had to 'absorb the implications of its own creations' (Cohen, 1988: 16). One influential definition has it that criminology is a 'rendezvous subject', where various branches of learning gather around a shared substantive theme, sometimes overlapping, more often moving past one another in different directions (Rock, 2011: 20). On this reading criminology is simply a meeting point for the traffic in ideas between researchers schooled in the more fundamental disciplines of economics, history, law, philosophy, psychology and sociology.

For some, contemporary criminology has all the organizational trappings of an academic discipline but one with no intellectual core around which the diverse approaches and speciality areas can cohere. It has a 'subject matter but no unique methodological commitment or paradigmatic theoretical framework' (Savelsberg and Sampson, 2002: 101) and the worry is that an 'independent criminology' will further 'fragment into distinct specialisms' with an increasingly inward focus resulting in 'negative consequences for collective learning' (Garland, 2011: 312). Criminology's growing isolation from the more basic disciplines comes with great costs; as it disengages from them it has opened itself up to greater government intrusion and runs the risk of losing true academic status as a university subject. Writing in the US context, Andrew Abbott (2001: 134) has noted how 'status differences' work to keep certain hierarchies in place: 'Criminology departments hire from sociology departments, but seldom vice versa.'

It is not simply that criminology has divorced itself from sociology in the United States. Sociology has also 'pulled away from criminology, particularly as taught and studied at elite institutions' (Short, with Hughes, 2007: 632). The expansion of an applied, vocational criminology has adversely impacted on the subject's intellectual status and, according to some, has hastened the demise of the specialism in the sociology departments of leading research universities (Garland, 2011: 311). Despite the centrality of research on crime and deviance in many of these departments in the first half of the twentieth century, a certain disdain for the subject matter has subsequently long been in evidence. The tensions between the disciplines are captured in the following account, describing how courses in:

> criminology and criminal justice split off from sociology, where they were regarded – along with [courses in] marriage and the family – as waifs, tolerated because they kept enrolments high. Their later structural independence demonstrated clearly enough that the problems they addressed often were considerably more significant than the more esoteric menus offered by their parent discipline. Indeed, as sociology has tended to wane, criminology and criminal justice studies have flourished.
>
> (Geis and Dodge, 2002: xliii)

This passage captures the kind of populist, lowbrow regard in which criminology is held by some sociologists.

Clearly we are against the increasing 'independence' of criminology from sociology, but it is worth asking just what a sociological criminology should look like? Here the pioneering American sociologist Edwin Sutherland's (1924: 3) definition of criminology as a body of knowledge that regards crime as a social phenomenon, which studies the 'processes of making laws, of breaking laws, and of reacting toward the breaking of laws' remains unsurpassed. It raises three deceptively simple questions: Why are laws made? Why are they broken? What should be done about this? Yet it is a formulation calling for an 'intellectual perspective that lies outside the ideology and interests of those who run the crime-control system and the academics they hire to help them' (Cohen, 1988: 9). Crime and punishment are bound up with wider social processes and while there will always be contested views of what criminology is, these are state-defined categories and practices, which intimately tie criminology to government in quite troubling ways (Garland, 2011: 305). One of the central tasks of a sociological criminology, then, is to identify these links and the problems that flow from them, even as the relationships change and become more obscure.

None of this is to say that sociology is the only discipline criminology should be seeking a renewed relationship with; there are no doubt productive encounters to be had with its other constitutive disciplines. In the effort to establish its own disciplinary credentials, criminology has lost some of its intellectual energy and it is worth remembering that it has nearly always been animated and enlivened by ideas imported from elsewhere. The metaphor of 'rendezvous subject' is a well-used one, and it is the traffic in multidisciplinary approaches that has sustained post-war British criminology but which has also left it prone to a bewildering eclecticism and disorganized fragmentation. Under these circumstances the growing separation of criminology from sociology is to be resisted; instead a renewed focus on how dialogues across many disciplines can be facilitated is the way forward (see also Carrabine, forthcoming).

Criminology has many problems but none is so great that it requires us to abandon the subject (Smart, 1990). Rather, renewal is one of the strengths of the field (South, 1997). The study of criminology is exciting and challenging. As Muncie et al. (1996: xxiv) have argued, there is and always will be an inherent tension in criminology between those who seek continually to challenge and expand the traditional boundaries of criminological discourse and those who remain content to operate within criminology's self-imposed constraints. Ultimately, 'Criminology will always appear to be in a process of "becoming". Its work will never seem to be complete' (ibid.).

Further study

Bosworth, M. and Hoyle, C. (eds) (2011) *What is Criminology?* Oxford: Oxford University Press.
Carrabine, E. (2013) 'Criminology, Deviance and Sociology', in J. Holmwood and J. Scott (eds) *History of Sociology in Britain*, Basingstoke: Palgrave.
Carrabine, E. (forthcoming) 'Criminology and the Sociological Imagination', in J. Frauley (ed.) *C. Wright Mills and the Criminological Imagination: Prospects for Creative Enquiry*, Aldershot: Ashgate.
Hobbs, D. (2013) *Lush Life: Constructing Organized Crime in the UK*, Oxford: Oxford University Press.

Glossary

actuarialism Probability calculations and statistical distributions to measure risk and which underpin correctional policies.

alcohol prohibition In the United States, the 'Volstead' Act (1919) prohibited the sale and production of alcohol, leading to the 'bootlegger business', i.e. the illegal production and distribution of alcohol for consumption in secret venues, providing profits for organized criminal groups. Prohibition was repealed in 1933.

anomie A condition where norms are confused or break down. There is a lack of normative regulation, which could lead to deviant behaviour. Merton produced a typology of responses to anomie.

area offence rate All recorded offences in a particular area.

area victimization rate Level of offences against a particular group in a particular area.

bifurcation Refers to the dual-edged approach to crime control whereby tougher measures are used for more serious offenders while less severe measures are used for ordinary offences.

biopiracy A term given to the practices of some companies that have asserted the right of ownership over genetic materials taken from living organisms.

capitalism An economic system in which the production of goods depends on private investment and the making of profit.

categorical imperative A principle of moral philosophy derived from the Enlightenment thinker Immanuel Kant, who insisted that certain duties are absolute and unconditional.

classicism The Enlightenment view of crime that stresses free will and rationality and the corresponding rationality of the justice system.

collective efficacy The extent to which a community exerts informal control over a given local area through cohesion and mutual trust.

colonialism A process by which some nations acquired others as colonies and exercised economic, political and cultural influence.

community safety Policy initiatives to reduce crime through local partnerships involving the police and other community agencies.

concentric zone theory (or **zonal theory**) Holds that city centres are business districts bordered by a ring of factories, followed by residential rings with housing that becomes more expensive the further it stands from the noise and pollution of the city's centre.

constitutive criminology A postmodernist theoretical perspective on crime in contrast to a modernist one.

continuum of sexual violence Ranges from the everyday abuse of women in pornographic images, sexist jokes, sexual harassment and women's engagement in compliant but unwanted marital sex, through to the 'non-routine' episodes of rape, incest, battery and sex murder. (Note: this is not meant to be a continuum that simply moves along lines of severity of the act.)

control theory Holds that delinquent acts result when an individual's bond to society is weak or broken. There are four bonds: attachment, involvement, commitment and belief.

cultural criminology Uses mainly qualitative and cultural methods to study mostly urban subcultures with a focus on image, representation and style.

cultural property Movable or immovable property of great importance to the cultural heritage of every people.

dark figure A term used to refer to the hidden figure of unreported or unrecorded crime.

data mining A process to uncover patterns and match information within and across large datasets.

decarceration The process that refers to the deliberate move away from imprisonment as the central penal sanction towards the use of alternative sanctions, usually in the community.

defensible space Idea that it is possible to modify the built environment to reduce the opportunity for crime and to promote community responsibility.

denial A term that refers to feelings and the ideas attached to them that are not necessarily available to conscious awareness, but handle the dangerous and threatening aspects of our inner and outer worlds. For example, when husbands and wives fail to see the signs of their partner's infidelities, or when we do not notice the symptoms of illness in those we love. This is when denial acts as an unconscious defence mechanism to protect us from disturbing and upsetting realities.

determinism According to the positivist school, people become criminals through factors largely out of their control – be they biological, psychological or social.

deterrence Based on the idea that crime can be discouraged through the public's fear of the punishment they may receive if they break the law.

differential association Crime is basically learned in the same ways as everything else. Edwin Sutherland's theory came ultimately to be presented as nine propositions (given in the text of Chapter 5).

discourses Bodies of ideas and language, often backed up by institutions.

dispersal policy Introduced in the wake of a series of prison escapes in Britain in the 1960s, so that maximum security prisoners are spread around a few high-security prisons.

ecology of crime Idea that crime is linked to the (urban) environment in predictable ways.

ecosystem The system composed of the interaction of all living organisms and their natural environment.

'effects' studies Seek to establish whether the media cause crime through representations of violence.

emotion A mental state involving how a person feels rather than thinks.

Enlightenment thinking Thought that emerged during the eighteenth century in the West and that championed rationality, science and progress, alongside the importance of the individual and the tolerance of different beliefs.

epistemological Relating to the theory of knowledge.

ethics A set of principles guiding research practice, especially where human participants are involved.

ethnography A research approach in which the researcher participates – overtly or covertly – for a lengthy period of time in the daily lives of those being studied, and listens, observes, asks questions and collects whatever data are available.

evaluation research Research aiming to assess the impacts of a policy intervention.

evidence-based policy Policy clearly shaped by research evidence.

experimental criminology Research that aims to test out theories in the criminal justice field and make policy recommendations based on 'hard' evidence of what works.

feminist criminology A criminology that puts women at the centre of the analysis.

forensic science Scientific techniques to investigate crime and criminality.

free will According to the classical school, people possess reason. This means that they can calculate the course of action that is in their self-interest. This in turn gives them a degree of freedom.

functionalist perspective A theory that looks at the ways in which societies become integrated as their various parts perform various functions.

gatekeepers Individuals or agencies who can aid or inhibit a researcher's access to a particular research field.

genres One of the ways in which differences between narratives can be defined through identifying the conventions that other texts in the same grouping share.

geo-data personal, local or global geographical data often involving a combination of data from different sources such as digital maps and databases.

globalization of crime The increasing interconnectedness of crime across societies.

green crimes Crimes against the environment.

green criminology A reappraisal of more traditional notions of crimes, offences and injurious behaviours and an examination of the role that societies (including corporations and governments) play in generating environmental degradation.

harm reduction As an alternative to insistence on abstaining from drug use, this is an approach to working with users to minimize the possibility of serious harms such as AIDS or overdose.

hierarchy of victimization A concept that captures the unequal status that victims experience in the crime discourse and in their treatment by criminal justice agencies. Those at the top are regarded as innocent and deserving of help and sympathy, those at the bottom less so.

human rights Rights that belong to all people.

humiliation The experience of a loss of respect or self-esteem.

industrialization Mass production of manufactured goods and a means of organizing workers, employers and finance.

just deserts A justification for punishment which insists that offenders should be punished only as severely as they deserve. It was a reaction against the unfair excesses of rehabilitation and the 'get tough' drive from conservatives during the 1970s.

labelling theory Highlights social reaction and suggests that crime may be heightened by criminal sanctions.

late modernity One of many concepts used to characterize a new emerging social order after modernity and capitalism.

legitimacy In the context of prisons, is the process whereby institutional power gains a moral grounding through prisoners consenting to the authority of staff and regimes.

less eligibility A penal doctrine that maintains that offenders should endure harsher institutional regimes than the poorest free citizens.

lynching A form of extrajudicial punishment involving public torture, revived in the Southern United States as a response to the perceived erosion of white male domination in the nineteenth century. The lynchings were explicitly violent and included burning, castration and whipping as well as hanging. They were deliberately racialized and the lynch victim was often sought out as retribution for the alleged rape of a white woman by an African American man.

McDonaldization The principles of the fast food industry become increasingly applied to all of social life.

mapping Processes by which spaces are defined and represented.

marginalization A state in which people live on the edge of society and outside the mainstream with little stake in society overall.

mediatization refers to the process whereby the rapid expansion of the media has undermined distinctions between image and reality.

Megan's law Named after Megan Kanka, a 7-year-old girl from New Jersey who was sexually assaulted and killed by a convicted sex offender living in the same street.

mixed methods A new approach to social research which seeks to combine qualitative and quantitative methods.

money laundering Concealing the origins of money gained illegally by moving it through a series of banking transfers to 'clean' it.

moral panic The heightened awareness of certain problems relating to crime at key moments.

negotiated justice The construction of cases, negotiations (e.g. between the defence and prosecution) and social interaction involved in the routine production of justice.

neutralization, techniques of A series of strategies through which the individual's 'bond' to society is weakened, hence making that individual more likely to commit crime.

night-time economy Production and consumption of night-time recreational services.

'normalization' Although not everyone is now a drug user, nevertheless (the argument runs) it is now non-acquaintance with drugs or drug users that has become the deviation from the norm. The drugs in question are usually those associated with leisure cultures, such as cannabis, ecstasy, amphetamines or cocaine. Others reject the idea: particularly for the majority of young people, persisting prohibitions, peer-group resistance, parental attachment and preference for alternative activities remain central to their lives. Both arguments appear to have some validity.

occupational culture The values, norms, perspectives and informal rules that can inform the conduct of those engaged in a particular occupation (in the context of this book, the police). It has many variations and can change according to particular situations and the interactional processes of each encounter.

output The means by which the findings of a research project are disseminated and circulated.

paradigm A general view of how the world works.

participant observation A qualitative research method in which the researcher observes and interacts with people, often in everyday settings.

partisan One-sided; adhering to a particular cause.

pathologization The linking of criminality, or other behaviours, to physical or bodily attributes.

patriarchies Systems of male dominance that serve the interests of men.

police A state-organized institution with specific powers and a mandate to prevent and investigate crime or disorder.

police accountability The institutional arrangements made to ensure that the police do the job required of them.

policing A set of activities aimed at maintaining security and the social order through surveillance and the threat of sanctioning. It can be carried out by a variety of people and techniques.

positivism In criminology, 'positivism' highlights (a) scientific methods in the study of crime; (b) the importance of criminal types; and (c) theories of cause or aetiology.

postmodernism Grand or absolute truths are challenged, and in their place we find partial and limited truths: a much less certain and more provisional view of the world is in the making.

prediction studies Criminological research aiming to forecast the future conduct of persons under certain conditions.

primary and secondary deviance The distinction between original and effective causes of deviance: primary deviation arises from many sources and is minor and insignificant; secondary deviation is pivotal because stigma and punishment make it so.

primary and secondary victimization Primary victimization refers to the direct impact of crime on the victims while secondary victimization refers to additional negative impact resulting from the way others (especially criminal justice agencies) respond to them and the crime.

procedural justice Formal adherence to legal rules and safeguards throughout the criminal justice process and the impartial application of neutral criteria in criminal justice decision-making.

Prohibition *See* **alcohol prohibition**.

projection A psychoanalytical concept describing one of the many unconscious defensive mechanisms by which we protect ourselves from the troubling contents of our inner worlds. It is the process by which we impute something that is actually within oneself on to some other person or object. Projection protects against danger by investing another person or object with the qualities we feel we do not have. It is also the principal psychological mechanism involved in such phenomena as racism, sexism and homophobia.

property crime Stealing and dishonestly obtaining or damaging another's property, which includes both tangible goods and intangible property.

public criminology Draws on human rights, social justice and public policy agenda to raise public awareness of crime issues and to argue against indifference, intolerance and inequality; and to provide opportunities for political and practical action in broad arenas of public policy concern.

qualitative research A form of investigation in which researchers gather data about people's beliefs, impressions and understandings.

quantitative research A form of investigation which seeks to quantify and measure social trends.

record linkage Identifying records that relate to the same entity across a range of sources (also referred to as data linkage).

reductivist Refers to justifications of punishment that regard the prevention of future crimes as the moral basis on which to base systems of punishment.

rehabilitation Based on the idea that punishment can reduce crime if it takes a form that will improve the individual's character so that they are less likely to reoffend in the future. It tends to view criminal behaviour not as freely willed action but as a symptom of some kind of causal factor, whether this be economic, social or personal.

relative deprivation A perceived disadvantage arising from a specific comparison.

repeat victimization Occurs when the same location, person, household, business or vehicle suffers more than one crime event over a specified period of time.

research design A research plan which sets out key questions to be investigated, methods to be used, timeframe, possible problems and how the proposed work will relate to other relevant studies and related fields.

respect Deference, esteem and regard.

retributivist Justifications of punishment that insist that only the crimes of the past should be punished.

rights Claims supported by some justification.

risk society Beck's idea that modern industrial societies create many new risks – on a global scale and largely manufactured through modern technologies – that were unknown in earlier days. Examples include nuclear war and environmental pollution.

secondary deviance *See* **primary and secondary deviance**

secondary victimization *See* **primary and secondary victimization**

self-esteem A positive opinion about oneself.

self-report studies Studies of crime and other social issues which use interviews or question-naires to gather personal experiences of offending and/or victimization.

shame A painful emotion arising from an awareness of inadequacy, guilt or dishonour.

social construct The ways in which people shape reality.

social crime A term used by social historians to refer to the criminalization of 'everyday' practices, especially those connected to work, customary rights and the economy.

Social Darwinism The social application of Darwinian evolutionary theory.

social psychology Analyses the relationships between individuals and society, examining how individuals relate to each other and to the networks in which they operate.

social solidarity A key element of Durkheim's sociology, it refers to the sources of integration that preserve social stability and promote moral consensus in the face of rapid economic change and political upheaval.

space Locations and places where social life is lived and imagined.

splitting A psychoanalytical concept describing one of the defence mechanisms with which we deal with the inner and external worlds. It is a way of dealing with anxiety by splitting the threat into two, 'good' and 'bad', elements.

subcultures Groups with a distinct image and set of beliefs that seem to set them apart from mainstream culture.

substantive justice Just and effective outcomes of criminal justice decision-making that take into account social inequalities and their impact on different social groups.

survey Systematic data collection about the same variables or characteristics from a number of respondents or cases.

symbolic, laws Laws that act to highlight (symbolize) key issues. They may serve as a litmus test for many moral panics and discourses that tap into a wide range of social anxieties.

temperance The commitment to abstinence from alcoholic drink, associated in particular with early twentieth-century social and religious movements.

transcarceration The movement of offenders between different institutional sites, state agencies and correctional programmes, so that the network of social control is expanded rather than reduced.

transgression The act of overstepping boundaries or limits established by rules, laws, principles, custom, convention or tradition.

urban flight Movement out of inner cities by middle- and working-class groups – a movement partly driven by beliefs about crime.

urbanization The creation of large-scale urban societies linked to industrialization, migration and population growth.

victimology An area of study that is concerned with the victim of crime. Often described as a subdiscipline of criminology.

working rules Rules that those following a particular occupation – in this case, that of police officer – internalize so that they become the effective principles that guide their decisions and actions.

References

Abbott, A. (2001) *Chaos of Disciplines*, Chicago, IL: University of Chicago Press.

Abbott, C. (2008) *An Uncertain Future: Law Enforcement, National Security and Climate Change*, Oxford: Oxford Research Group.

Abercrombie, N. (1996) *Television and Society*, Cambridge: Polity.

Abraham, J. (1995) *Science, Politics and the Pharmaceutical Industry: Controversy and Bias in Drug Regulation*, New York: UCL/St Martin's Press.

Acheson, D. (1998) *Health Inequalities*, London: Department of Health.

Adam, B., Beck, U. and Van Loon, J. (eds) (2000) *The Risk Society and Beyond*, London: Sage.

Adam, B. D., Duyvendak, J. W. and Krouwel, A. (eds) (1999) *The Global Emergence of Gay and Lesbian Politics*, Philadelphia, PA: Temple University Press.

Adey, P. (2008) 'Airports, Mobility, and the Calculative Architecture of Affective Control', *Geoforum*, 1: 438–51.

Adey, P. and Anderson, B. (2012) 'Anticipating Emergencies: Technologies of Preparedness and the Matter of Security', *Security Dialogue*, 43 (2): 99–117.

Adler, F. (1975) *Sisters in Crime: The Rise of the New Female Criminal*, New York: McGraw-Hill.

Adler, P. A. and Adler, P. (1998) 'Forward: Moving Backward', in J. Ferrell and M. Hamm (eds) *Ethnography at the Edge: Crime, Deviance and Field Research*, Boston, MA: Northeastern University Press.

Adorno, T. W., Frenkel-Brunswik, E., Levinson, D. J. and Sanford, R. N. (1950) *The Authoritarian Personality*, New York: Norton.

Agamben, G. (1998) *Homo Sacer: Sovereign Power and Bare Life*, Stanford, CA: Stanford University Press.

Agamben, G. (2005) *State of Exception*, trans. K. Attell, Chicago, IL: University of Chicago Press.

Agnew, R. (2013) 'The Ordinary Acts that Contribute to Ecocide: A Criminological Analysis', in N. South and A. Brisman (eds) *Routledge International Handbook of Green Criminology*, London: Routledge.

Agozino, B. (2003) *Counter-Colonial Criminology: A Critique of Imperialist Reason*, London: Pluto.

Ahmed, S. (2004) *The Cultural Politics of Emotion*, Edinburgh: Edinburgh University Press.

Albrecht, H.-J. (2000) 'Foreigners, Migration, Immigration and the Development of Criminal Justice in Europe', in P. Green and A. Rutherford (eds) *Criminal Policy in Transition*, Portland, OR: Hart Publishing.

Albrow, M. (1990) *The Global Age*, Cambridge: Polity.

Alcohol Concern (2000) *Britain's Ruin*, London: Alcohol Concern.

Alcohol Concern (2001) www.alcoholconcern.org.uk/

Alcohol Concern (2008) 'Women and Alcohol – A Cause for Concern?' Factsheet, December. London: Alcohol Concern.

Alexander, M. (2010) *The New Jim Crow: Mass Incarceration in the Age of Colorblindness*, New York: The New Press.

Aliverti, A. (2012) 'Making People Criminal: The Role of the Criminal Law in Immigration Enforcement', *Theoretical Criminology*, 16 (4): 417–34.

All Party Group on Alcohol Misuse (1995) *Alcohol and Crime: Breaking the Link*, London: Alcohol Concern.

Allan, S. (1999) *News Culture*, Buckingham: Open University Press.

Allan, S. (2006) *Online News: Journalism and the Internet*, Berkshire: Open University Press.

Allen, B. (1996) *Rape Warfare: The Hidden Genocide in Bosnia-Herzegovina and Croatia*, Minneapolis: University of Minnesota Press.

Allen, H. (1987) *Justice Unbalanced*, Milton Keynes: Open University Press.

Allen-Robertson, J. (2013) *Digital Culture Industry: A History of Digital Distribution*, Basingstoke: Palgrave.

Altman, D. (2001) *Global Sex*, Chicago, IL: University of Chicago Press.

Alubo, S. O. (1994) 'Death for Sale: A Case Study of Drug Poisoning and Deaths in Nigeria', *Social Science and Medicine*, 38 (1): 97–103.

Alvesalo, A. and Tombs, S. (2002) 'Working for Criminalization of Economic Offending: Contradictions for Critical Criminology?', *Critical Criminology*, 11 (1): 21–40.

Amir, M. (1971) *Patterns of Forcible Rape*, Chicago, IL: University of Chicago Press.

Amnesty International (2001) *Crimes of Hate: Conspiracies of Silence*, London: Amnesty International.

Amoore, L. (2009) 'Algorithmic War: Everyday Geographies of the War on Terror', *Antipode: A Radical Journal of Geography*, 41: 49–69.

Anderson, E. (1994) 'The Code of Streets', *Atlantic Monthly*, 5: 80–94.

Anderson, E. (1999) *Code of the Streets: Decency, Violence and the Moral Life of the Inner City*, New York: W. W. Norton.

Anderson, N. (1923) *The Hobo: The Sociology of the Homeless Man*, Chicago, IL: University of Chicago Press.

Anderson, R., Brown, J. and Campbell, E. (1993) *Aspects of Sex Discrimination within the Police Service in England and Wales*, London: Home Office Police Research Group.

Anderson, S., Kinsey, R., Loader, I. and Smith, C. (1994) *Cautionary Tales: Young People, Crime and Policing in Edinburgh*, Aldershot: Avebury.

Andrew, C. (2009) *The Defence of the Realm: The Authorized History of MI5*, London: Allen Lane.

Aradau, C. and van Munster, R. (2007) 'Governing Terrorism through Risk: Taking Precautions, (un)Knowing the Future', *European Journal of International Relations*, 13 (1): 89–115.

Archer, J. (1990) *By a Flash and a Scare: Incendiarism, Animal Maiming and Poaching in East Anglia, 1815–1870*, Oxford: Clarendon.

Arendt, H. (2006/1963) *Eichmann in Jerusalem: A Report on the Banality of Evil*, New York: Penguin.

Arnot, M. and Usborne, C. (eds) (1999a) *Gender and Crime in Modern Europe*, London: UCL Press.

Arnot, M. and Usborne, C. (1999b) '"Why Gender and Crime?" Aspects of an International Debate', in M. Arnot and C. Usborne (eds) *Gender and Crime in Modern Europe*, London: UCL Press.

Arrigo, B. (1997) 'Review of Stuart Henry and Dragan Milovanovic's Constitutive Criminology', *Theoretical Criminology*, 3: 392–6.

Arrigo, B. and Milovanovic, D. (eds) (2010) *Postmodern and Post-structuralist Theories of Crime*, Farnham: Ashgate.

Ashworth, A. (1986) 'Punishment and Compensation: Victims, Offenders and the State', *Oxford Journal of Legal Studies*, 6: 86–122.

Ashworth, A. (1993) 'Victim Impact Statements and Sentencing', *Criminal Law Review*, pp. 498–509.

Ashworth, A. (1998) *The Criminal Process*, 2nd edn, Oxford: Oxford University Press.

Ashworth, A. (2003) 'Is Restorative Justice the Way Forward for Criminal Justice?', in E. McLaughlin, R. Fergusson, G. Hughes and L. Westmarland (eds) *Restorative Justice: Critical Issues*, London: Sage.

Ashworth, A. (2004) 'Social Control and "Anti-Social Behaviour": The Subversion of Human Rights?', *Law Quarterly Review*, 120: 263–91.

Atton, C. (2003) 'Organization and Production in Alternative Media', in S. Cottle (ed.) *Media Organization and Production*, London: Sage.

Attwood, F. (2009) (ed.) *Mainstreaming Sex: The Sexualization of Western Culture*, London: I. B. Taurus.

Attwood, F. (2011) 'The Paradigm Shift: Pornography Research, Sexualization and Extreme Images', *Sociology Compass*, 5 (1): 13–22.

Attwood, F. and Smith, C. (2010) 'Extreme Concern: Regulating "Dangerous Pictures" in the United Kingdom', *Journal of Law and Society*, 37 (1): 171–88.

Audit Commission (1993) *Helping with Enquiries: Tackling Crime Effectively*, London: HMSO.

Audit Commission (1996) *Streetwise: Effective Police Patrol*, London: HMSO.

Auld, J. (1973) 'Cannabis: The Changing Patterns of Use', *New Society*, September: 568–70.

Auld, J., Dorn, N. and South, N. (1986) 'Irregular Work, Irregular Pleasures: Heroin in the 1980s', in R. Matthews and J. Young (eds) *Confronting Crime*, London: Sage.

Aulette, J. and Michalowski, R. (1993) 'Fire in Hamlet: A Case Study of State–Corporate Crime', in K. D. Tunnell (ed.) *Political Crime in Contemporary America: A Critical Approach*, New York: Garland.

Ayers, E. (1984) *Vengeance and Justice: Crime and Punishment in the Nineteenth-century American South*, New York: Oxford University Press.

Back, L. (1996) *New Ethnicities and Urban Culture: Racisms and Multiculture in Young Lives*, London: UCL Press.

Bagaric, M. and Clarke, J. (2005) 'Not Enough Official Torture in the World? The Circumstances in which Torture is Morally Justifiable', *University of San Francisco Law Review*, 39.

Baird, V. (2001) *The No-Nonsense Guide to Sexual Diversity*, London: New Internationalist/Verso.

Baldwin, J. and Bottoms, A. E. (1976) *The Urban Criminal*, London: Tavistock.

Baldwin, J. and McConville, M. (1977) *Negotiated Justice*, London: Martin Robertson.

Bales, K. (1999) *Disposable People: New Slavery in the Global Economy*, Berkeley: University of California Press.

Bales, K. (2005) *Understanding Global Slavery*, Berkeley: University of California Press.

Ball, K., Haggerty, K. and Lyon, D. (eds) (2012) *Routledge Handbook of Surveillance Studies*, London: Routledge.

Ballinger, A. (2000) *Dead Woman Walking: Executed Women in England and Wales, 1900–1955*, Aldershot: Ashgate/Dartmouth.

Bamford, B. (2004) 'The United Kingdom's "War against"', *Terrorism and Political Violence*, 16 (4): 737–56.

Banton, M. (1964) *The Policeman in the Community*, London: Tavistock.

Barak, G. (ed.) (1994) *Media, Process, and the Social Construction of Crime: Studies in Newsmaking Criminology*, New York: Garland.

Barak, G. (2001) 'Crime and Crime Control in an Age of Globalization: A Theoretical Dissection', *Critical Criminology*, 10 (10): 57–72.

Barak, G. (2007) 'Doing Newsmaking Criminology from within the Academy', *Theoretical Criminology*, 11 (2): 191–207.

Barbalet, J. (1998) *Emotion, Social Theory and Social Structure: A Macrosociological Approach*, Cambridge: Cambridge University Press.

Barbalet, J. (2002) 'Moral Indignation, Class Inequality and Justice: An Exploration and Revision of Ranulf', *Theoretical Criminology*, 6 (3): 279–97.

Barclay, G. and Tavares, C. (2002) *International Comparisons of Criminal Justice Statistics 2000*, Home Office Statistical Bulletin 05/02, London: Home Office.

Barker, M. and Petley, J. (eds) (1997) *Ill Effects: The Media/Violence Debate*, London: Routledge.

Barrie, D. and Broomhall, S. (eds) (2011) *A History of Police and Masculinities, 1700–2010*, Abingdon: Routledge.

Barstow, A. L. (2000) *War's Dirty Secret: Rape, Prostitution, and Other Crimes Against Women*, Cleveland, OH: Pilgrim Press.

Barthes, R. (1975) *The Pleasure of the Text*, New York: Hill and Wang (originally published in French, 1973).

Barton, A. (2005) *Fragile Moralities and Dangerous Sexualities: Two Centuries of Semi-penal Institutionalisation for Women*, Aldershot: Ashgate.

Barton, B. F. and Barton, M. S. (1993) 'Modes of Power in Technical and Professional Visuals', *Journal of Business and Technical Communication*, 7 (1): 138–62.

Baudrillard, J. (2005) 'War Porn', *International Journal of Baudrillard Studies*, 2 (1), http://www.ubishops.ca/baudrillardstudies/vol2_1/taylor.htm (accessed 22 April 2012).

Bauman, Z. (1989) *Modernity and the Holocaust*, Cambridge: Polity.

Bauman, Z. (1992) *Intimations of Postmodernity*, London: Routledge.

Bauman, Z. (1995) *Life in Fragments: Essays in Postmodern Morality*, Oxford: Blackwell.

Bauman, Z. (1998) *Globalization: The Human Consequences*, Cambridge: Polity.

Bauman, Z. (2004) 'War, Terror and the City', paper presented at the Institute of Contemporary Arts, London, 22 October.

Bauman, Z. (2006) *Liquid Fear*, Cambridge: Polity.

Baumgartner, F., De Boef, S. and Boydstun, A. (2008) *The Decline of the Death Penalty and the Discovery of Innocence*, Cambridge: Cambridge University Press.

Bayley, D. H. (1994) *Police for the Future*, New York: Oxford University Press.

Bayley, D. and Weisburd, D. (2009) 'The Role of the Police in Counter-terrorism', in D. Weisburd, L. Mock, I. Hakimi, T. Feucht and S. Perry (eds) *To Protect and to Serve: Policing in an Age of Terrorism*, New York: Springer.

Baylis, J. and Smith, S. (eds) (1997) *The Globalization of World Politics*, Oxford: Oxford University Press.

Bazemore, G. and Taylor-Griffiths, C. (2003) 'Conferences, Circles, Boards, and Mediations: The "New Wave" of Community Justice Decisionmaking', in E. McLaughlin, R. Fergusson, G. Hughes and L. Westmarland (eds) *Restorative Justice: Critical Issues*, London: Sage.

Bean, P. (2002) *Drugs and Crime*, Cullompton: Willan.

Bean, P. and Nemitz, T. (2004) *Drug Treatment: What Works?*, London: Routledge.

Beattie, J. (1975) 'The Criminality of Women in Eighteenth-Century England', *Journal of Social History*, 8: 80–116.

Beattie, J. (1986) *Crime and the Courts in England, 1660–1800*, Oxford: Clarendon Press.

Beck, U. (1992) *Risk Society: Towards a New Modernity*, London: Sage.

Beck, U. (1995) *Ecological Politics in an Age of Risk*, Cambridge: Polity.

Beck, U. (2000) *World Risk Society*, Cambridge: Polity.

Becker, H. S. (1963) *Outsiders: Studies in the Sociology of Deviance*, New York: Free Press.

Becker, H. S. (1967) 'Whose Side Are We On?', *Social Problems*, 14: 239–47.

Behlmer, G. K. (1982) *Child Abuse and Moral Reform in England, 1870–1908*, Stanford, CA: Stanford University Press.

Beirne, P. (1993) *Inventing Criminology: Essays on the Rise of 'Homo Criminalis'*, Albany: State University of New York Press.

Beirne, P. (2009) *Confronting Animal Abuse*, Lanham, MD: Rowman and Littlefield.

Beirne, P. and South, N. (eds) (2007) *Issues in Green Criminology*, Cullompton: Willan.

Bellamy, R. (ed.) (1995) *Beccaria: On Crimes and Punishments and Other Writings*, Cambridge: Cambridge University Press.

Bennett, T. (1990) 'Knowledge, Power, Ideology: Detective Fiction', in T. Bennett (ed.) *Popular Fiction: Technology, Ideology, Production, Reading*, London: Routledge.

Bennett, T., Holloway, K. and Williams, T. (2001) *Drug Use and Offending*, Findings 148, London: Home Office.

Bentham, J. (1789/1970) *An Introduction to the Principles of Morals and Legislation*, ed. J. H. Burns and H. L. A. Hart, London: Athlone.

Benton, T. (1984) *The Rise and Fall of Structural Marxism: Althusser and His Influence*, Basingstoke: Macmillan.

Berger, P. (1963) *Invitation to Sociology: A Humanistic Perspective*, Garden City, NY: Doubleday.

Berridge, V. (1984) 'Drugs and Social Policy: The Establishment of Drug Control in Britain, 1900–1930', *British Journal of Addiction*, 79: 1.

Berridge, V. (1999) *Opium and the People*, revised edn, London: Free Association Books.

Best, J. (1990) *Threatened Children: Rhetoric and Concern about Child Victims*, Chicago, IL: University of Chicago Press.

Best, J. (2001) *Damned Lies and Statistics*, Berkeley: University of California Press.

Biggs, S., Phillipson, C. and Kingston, P. (1995) *Elder Abuse in Perspective*, Buckingham: Open University Press.

Bigo, D. (2001) 'The Möbius Ribbon of Internal and External Security(ies)', in M. Albert, D. Jacobson and Y. Lapid (eds) *Identities, Borders, Orders: Rethinking International Relations Theory*, Minneapolis: Minnesota University Press.

Bigo, D. and Tsoukala, A. (eds) (2008) *Terror, Insecurity and Liberty: Illiberal Practices of Liberal Regimes*, London: Routledge

Bishop, R. and Robinson, L. (1998) *Night Market: Sexual Cultures and the Thai Economic Miracle*, London: Routledge.

Bittner, E. (1967) 'The Police on Skid Row: A Study in Peacekeeping', *American Sociological Review*, 32: 699–715.

Bittner, E. (1970) *The Functions of the Police in Modern Society; A Review of Background Factors, Current Practices, and Possible Role Models,* Chevy Chase, MD: National Institute of Mental Health, Center for Studies of Crime and Delinquency.

Bittner, E. (1974) 'Florence Nightingale in Pursuit of Willie Sutton: A Theory of the Police', in H. Jacob (ed.) *The Potential for Reform of Criminal Justice,* Beverly Hills, CA: Sage.

Blagg, H. (1997) 'A Just Measure of Shame: Aboriginal Youth and Conferencing in Australia', *British Journal of Criminology*, 37 (4): 481–501.

Block, A. (1983) *East Side-West Side: Organizing Crime in New York, 1930–1950,* Newark, NJ: Transaction.

Blok, A. (1972) 'Social Banditry Reconsidered', *Comparative Studies in Society and History*, 14: 495–505; reprinted in A. Blok, *Honour and Violence,* Cambridge: Polity, 2001.

Blomley, N. and Sommers, J. (1999) 'Mapping Urban Space: Governmentality and Cartographic Struggles in Inner City Vancouver', in R. Smandych (ed.) *Governable Places: Readings on Governmentality and Crime Control,* Aldershot: Ashgate.

Bloom, M. (2005) *Dying to Kill,* New York: Columbia University Press.

Blum, J., Levi, M., Naylor, R. and Williams, P. (1998) *Financial Havens, Banking Secrecy and Money Laundering,* New York: United Nations Office for Drug Control and Crime Prevention.

Boekhout van Solinge, T. and Kuijpers, K. (2013) 'The Amazon Rainforest: A Green Criminological Perspective', in N. South and A. Brisman (eds) *Routledge International Handbook of Green Criminology,* London: Routledge.

Bohle, H., Downing, T. and Watts, M. (1994) 'Climate Change and Social Vulnerability: Toward a Sociology and Geography of Food Insecurity', *Global Environmental Change*, 37.

Bohner, G., Eyssel, F., Pina, A., Sieber, F. and Tendayi, V. G. (2009) 'Rape Myth Acceptance: Cognitive Affective Behavioural Effects of Beliefs that Blame the Victim and Exonerate the Perpetrator', in M. Horvath and J. Brown (eds) *Rape: Challenging Contemporary Thinking,* Cullompton: Willan.

Booth, M. (2001) *The Dragon Syndicates: The Global Phenomenon of the Triad,* New York: Carroll and Graf.

Borger, J. (2001) 'U.S. Lets Fight against Smog Disappear into Thin Air', *Guardian*, 9 August: 12.

Boritch, H. and Hagan, J. (1990) 'A Century of Crime in Toronto: Gender, Class, and Patterns of Social Control, 1859 to 1955', *Criminology*, 28 (4): 567–600.

Borrill, J. and Stevens, D. (1993) 'Understanding Human Violence: The Implications of Social Structure, Gender, Social Perception and Alcohol', *Criminal Behaviour and Mental Health*, 3: 129–41.

Bosworth, M. (1999) *Engendering Resistance: Agency and Power in Women's Prisons,* Aldershot: Dartmouth.

Bosworth, M. (2000) 'Confining Femininity: A History of Gender, Power and Imprisonment', *Theoretical Criminology*, 4 (3): 265–84.

Bosworth, M. (2010) *Explaining U.S. Imprisonment,* New York: Sage.

Bosworth, M. (2012) 'Subjectivity and Identity in Detention: Punishment and Society in a Global Age', *Theoretical Criminology*, 16 (2): 123–40.

Bosworth, M. and Flavin, J. (eds) (2007) *Race, Gender and Punishment: From Colonialism to the War on Terror,* New Brunswick, NJ: Rutgers University Press.

Bosworth, M., Bowling, B. and Lee, M. (2008) 'Globalization, Ethnicity and Racism: An Introduction', *Theoretical Criminology*, 12 (3): 263–73.

Bottoms, A. (1977) 'Reflections on the Renaissance of Dangerousness', *Howard Journal of Criminal Justice*, 16: 70–96.

Bottoms, A. (1983) 'Neglected Features of Contemporary Penal Systems', in D. Garland and P. Young (eds) *The Power to Punish,* London: Heinemann.

Bottoms, A. (1987) 'Limiting Prison Use: Experience in England and Wales', *Howard Journal of Criminal Justice*, 26: 177–202.

Bottoms, A. (1995) 'The Philosophy and Politics of Punishment and Sentencing', in C. Clarkson and R. Morgan (eds) *The Politics of Sentencing Reform,* Oxford: Clarendon Press.

Bottoms, A. E. (2007) 'Place, Space, Crime and Disorder', in M. Maguire, R. Morgan and R. Reiner (eds) *Oxford Handbook of Criminology,* 4th edn, Oxford: Oxford University Press.

Bottoms, A. E. (2012) 'Developing Socio-spatial Criminology', in M. Maguire, R. Morgan and R. Reiner (eds) *Oxford Handbook of Criminology*, 5th edn, Oxford: Oxford University Press.

Bottoms, A. E. and McClean, J. D. (1976) *Defendants in the Criminal Process*, London: Routledge and Kegan Paul.

Bottoms, A. E. and Wiles, P. (2002) 'Environmental Criminology', in M. Maguire, R. Morgan and R. Reiner (eds) *Oxford Handbook of Criminology*, 3rd edn, Oxford: Oxford University Press.

Bourdieu, P. (1984) *Distinction: A Social Critique of the Judgement of Taste*, London: Routledge.

Bourgois, P. (1995) *In Search of Respect*, Cambridge: Cambridge University Press.

Bourke, J. (2007) *Rape: A History from 1860 to the Present Day*, London: Virago.

Bowling, B. (1998) *Violent Racism: Victimization, Policing and Social Context*, Oxford: Clarendon Press.

Bowling, B. (1999) 'The Rise and Fall of New York Murder', *British Journal of Criminology*, 39 (4): 531–54.

Bowling, B. and Phillips, C. (2002) *Racism, Crime and Justice*, Harlow: Longman.

Bowling, B. and Ross, J. (2008) 'The Serious Organised Crime Agency: Should We Be Afraid?', *Criminal Law Review*, pp. 1019–34.

Bowling, B., Parmar, A. and Phillips, C. (2008) 'Policing Minority Ethnic Communities' in T. Newburn (ed.) *The Handbook of Policing*, 2nd edn, Cullompton: Willan.

Box, S. (1983) *Power, Crime and Mystification*, London: Routledge.

Box, S. and Hale, C. (1984) 'Liberation/ Emancipation, Economic Marginalization or Less Chivalry', *Criminology*, 22: 473–97.

Box, S., Hale, C. and Andrews, G. (1988) 'Explaining Fear of Crime', *British Journal of Criminology*, 28: 340–56.

Boyd, S., Chunn, D. and Menzies, R. (eds) (2002) *Toxic Criminology: Environment, Law and the State in Canada*, Halifax: Fernwood.

Boyle, K. (ed.) (2010) *Everyday Pornography*, London: Routledge.

Boyle, K., Hadden, T. and Hillyard, P. (1975) *Law and State: The Case of Northern Ireland*, London: Martin Robertson.

Bozovic, M. (ed.) (1995) *The Panopticon Writings of Jeremy Bentham*, London Verso.

Braga, A. and Weisburd, D. (2010) *Policing Problem Places: Crime Hot Spots and Effective Prevention*, Oxford: Oxford University Press.

Braithwaite, J. (1984) *Corporate Crime in the Pharmaceutical Industry*, London: Routledge.

Braithwaite, J. (1989) *Crime, Shame and Reintegration*, Cambridge: Cambridge University Press.

Braithwaite, J. (2001) 'Crime in a Convict Republic', *Modern Law Review*, 64 (1): 11–50.

Braithwaite, J. (2002) *Restorative Justice and Responsive Regulation*, Oxford: Oxford University Press.

Braithwaite, J. (2003) 'What's Wrong with the Sociology of Punishment', *Theoretical Criminology*, 7 (1): 5–28.

Braithwaite, J. and Mugford, S. (1994) 'Conditions of Successful Reintegration Ceremonies', *British Journal of Criminology*, 34 (2).

Brajuha, M. and Hallowell, L. (1986) 'Legal Intrusion and the Politics of Fieldwork: The Impact of the Brajuha Case', *Urban Life*, 14: 454–78.

Brantingham, P. J. and Brantingham, P. L. (1991) *Environmental Criminology*, revised edn, Prospect Heights, IL: Waveland.

Brayley, N. (2001) 'Coping with the Effects of Traumatic Stress', *PCW Review*, 4: 24–5.

Briggs, R. (2010) 'Community Engagement for Counterterrorism: Lessons from the United Kingdom', *International Affairs*, 86 (4): 971–81.

Bright, M. (2002) 'Fury over Delay to "Corporate Killing" Law', *Observer*, 21 July: 6.

Bright, M. (2003) 'Youth Hit Hardest by Wave of New Laws', *Observer*, 13 April: 9.

Bristow, E. J. (1977) *Vice and Vigilance: Purity Movements in Britain since 1750*, Totowa, NJ: Rowman and Littlefield.

British Institute for Brain-Injured Children (2005) *Ain't Misbehavin: Young People with Learning and Communication Difficulties and Anti-Social Behaviour: A Report*, Bridgewater: BIBIC.

Brodeur, J.-P. (1983) 'High Policing and Low Policing: Remarks about the Policing of Political Activities', *Social Problems*, 30 (5): 507–20.

Brogden, M. and Nijhar, P. (2000) *Crime, Abuse and the Elderly*, Cullompton: Willan.

Brogden, M., Jefferson, T. and Walklate, S. (1988) *Introducing Policework*, London: Unwin Hyman.

Bromley, R. D. F. and Nelson, A. L. (2002) 'Alcohol-related Crime and Disorder across Urban Space and Time: Evidence from a British City', *Geoforum*, 33 (2): 239–54.

Brooks, T. (2012) *Punishment*, London: Routledge.

Broome Report (1985) *Working Party on Drugs Related Crime*, London: Association of Chief Police Officers.

Brown, C. (1984) *Black and White in Britain: The Third PSI Survey*, London: Policy Studies Institute.

Brown, J. (1996) 'Police Research: Some Critical Issues', in F. Leishman, B. Loveday and S. Savage (eds) *Core Issues in Policing*, Harlow: Longman.

Brown, J. and Heidensohn, F. (2000) *Gender and Policing: Comparative Perspectives*, Basingstoke: Macmillan.

Brown, L. R. et al. (eds) (2004) *The State of the World: 2004. A Worldwatch Institute Report on Progress toward a Sustainable Society*, London: Earthscan.

Brown, S. (1994) *Whose Challenge? Youth, Crime and Everyday Life in Middlesbrough*, published report to Middlesbrough City Challenge Partnership, Middlesbrough: Middlesbrough City Challenge.

Brown, S. (1998) *Understanding Youth and Crime: Listening to Youth?*, Buckingham: Open University Press.

Brown, S. (2003) *Crime and Law in Media Culture*, Buckingham: Open University Press.

Brown, S. (2005) *Understanding Youth and Crime: Listening to Youth*, Maidenhead: Open University Press.

Brown, S. (2011) 'Media/Crime/Millenium: Where Are We Now? A Reflective Review of Research and Theory Directions in the 21st Century', *Sociology Compass*, 5 (6): 413–25.

Browning, C. (1998) *Ordinary Men: Reserve Police Battalion and the Final Solution in Poland*, New York: Harper.

Brownlee, I. (1998) *Community Punishment: A Critical Introduction*, Harlow: Longman.

Brownmiller, S. (1975) *Against Our Will: Men, Women and Rape*, New York: Simon and Schuster.

Brundson, C. (1998) 'Structure of Anxiety: Recent British Television Crime Fiction', *Screen*, 39 (3): 223–43.

Bucke, T. (1997) *Ethnicity and Contacts with the Police: Latest Findings from the British Crime Survey*, Home Office Research Findings 59, London: Home Office.

Budd, T. (1999) *Violence at Work: Findings from the British Crime Survey*, London: Home Office.

Budd, T. and Mattinson, J. (2000) *The Extent and Nature of Stalking: Findings from the 1998 British Crime Survey*, Home Office Research Study 210, London: Home Office

Bullard, R. (1990) *Dumping in Dixie: Race, Class and Environmental Quality*, Boulder, CO: Westview Press.

Bullard, R. (1994) *Unequal Protection: Environmental Justice and Communities of Color*, San Francisco, CA: Sierra Club Books.

Bulmer, M. (1984) *The Chicago School of Sociology: Institutionalization, Diversity, and the Rise of Sociological Research*, Chicago, IL: University of Chicago Press.

Burgess, A. (1962) *A Clockwork Orange*, London:

Burke, J. (2011) *The 9/11 Wars*, London: Penguin

Burke, M. E. (1993) *Coming Out of the Blue*, London: Cassell.

Burke, R. H. (ed.) (1998) *Zero Tolerance Policing*, Leicester: Perpetuity Press.

Burke, R. H. (2001) *An Introduction to Criminological Theory*, Cullompton: Willan.

Burt, C. (1925) *The Young Delinquent*, London: University of London Press.

Bushway, S. and Weisburd, D. (2005) *Quantitative Methods in Criminology*, Aldershot: Ashgate.

Button, M. (2002) *Private Policing*, Cullompton: Willan.

Byrne, P. J. (1993) *Criminal Law and Colonial Subject: New South Wales, 1810–1830*, Cambridge: Cambridge University Press

Cain, M. (1973) *Society and the Policeman's Role*, London: Routledge and Kegan Paul.

Cain, M. (ed.) (1989) *Growing Up Good: Policing the Behaviour of Girls in Europe*, London: Sage.

Calder, A. (1991) *The Myth of the Blitz*, London: Cape.

Campbell, A. (1981) *Girl Delinquents*, Oxford: Basil Blackwell.

Campbell, A. (1984) *The Girls in the Gang: A Report from New York City*, Oxford: Blackwell.

Campbell, A. (2007) 'Global Disasters Rocket by 60% in Just a Decade', London Metro, 13 December: 15.

Campbell, D. (1991) *That Was Business, This Is Personal*, London: Mandarin.

Campbell, D. (1994) *The Underworld*, London: BBC Books.

Caputi, J. (1988) *The Age of Sex Crime*, London: Women's Press.

Carlen, P. (1976) *Magistrates' Justice*, London: Martin Robertson.

Carlen, P. (1983) *Women's Imprisonment: A Study in Social Control*, London: Routledge and Kegan Paul.

Carlen, P. (1988) *Women, Crime and Poverty*, Buckingham: Open University Press.

Carlen, P. (1990) *Alternatives to Women's Imprisonment*, Buckingham: Open University Press.

Carlen, P. (1996) *Jigsaw: A Political Criminology of Youth Homelessness*, Buckingham: Open University Press.

Carlen, P. (1998) *Sledgehammer: Women's Imprisonment at the Millennium*, Basingstoke: Macmillan.

Carlen, P. (2002) 'Carceral Clawback: The Case of Women's Imprisonment in Canada', *Punishment and Society*, 4 (1): 115–21.

Carlen, P. and Worrall, A. (eds) (1987) *Gender, Crime, and Justice*, Milton Keynes: Open University Press.

Carlile, Lord (2011) 'Reflections on UK Counter-terrorism Legislation', Paper presented at Royal United Services Institute, London, 11 July.

Carline, A. (2011) 'Criminal Justice, Extreme Pornography and Prostitution: Protecting Women or Promoting Morality?', *Sexualities*, 14 (3): 312–33.

Carney, P. (2010) 'Crime, Punishment and the Force of Photographic Spectacle', in K. Hayward and M. Presdee (eds) *Framing Crime: Cultural Criminology and the Image*, London: Routledge.

Carrabine, E. (2004) *Power, Discourse and Resistance: A Genealogy of the Strangeways Prison Riot*, Aldershot: Dartmouth.

Carrabine, E. (2005) 'Prison Riots, Social Order and the Problem of Legitimacy', *British Journal of Criminology*, 45 (6): 896–913.

Carrabine, E. (2006) 'Punishment, Rights and Justice', in L. Morris (ed.) *Rights: Sociological Perspectives*, London: Routledge.

Carrabine, E. (2008) *Crime, Culture and the Media*, Cambridge: Polity.

Carrabine, E. (2011) 'Images of Torture: Culture, Politics and Power', *Crime, Media, Culture*, 7 (1): 5–30.

Carrabine, E. (2012) 'Just Images: Aesthetics, Ethics and Visual Criminology', *British Journal of Criminology*, 52 (3): 463–89.

Carrabine, E. (2013) 'Criminology, Deviance and Sociology' in J. Holmwood and J. Scott (eds) *History of Sociology in Britain*, Basingstoke: Palgrave.

Carrabine, E. (forthcoming) 'Criminology and the Sociological Imagination', in J. Frauley (ed.) *C. Wright Mills and the Criminological Imagination: Prospects for Creative Enquiry*, Aldershot: Ashgate.

Carrabine, E., Lee, M. and South, N. (2000) 'Social Wrongs and Human Rights in Late Modern Britain: Social Exclusion, Crime Control and Prospects for a Public Criminology', *Social Justice*, 27 (2): 193–211.

Carrabine, E., Cox, P., Lee, M. and South, N. (2002) *Crime in Modern Britain*, Oxford: Oxford University Press.

Carson, R. (1962) *Silent Spring*, Boston, MA: Houghton Mifflin.

Carter, F. and Turnock, D. (1993) *Environmental Problems in Eastern Europe*, London: Routledge.

Cashmore, E. and McLaughlin, E. (1991) *Out of Order? Policing Black People*, London: Routledge.

Cass, V. (1996) 'Toxic Tragedy: Illegal Hazardous Waste Dumping in Mexico', in S. Edwards, T. Edwards and C. Fields (eds) *Environmental Crime and Criminality: Theoretical and Practical Issues*, New York: Garland.

Castells, M. (1996) *The Rise of Network Society*, Oxford: Blackwell.

Castells, M. (1998) *End of Millennium*, Oxford: Blackwell.

Cavadino, M. and Dignan, J. (2002) *The Penal System: An Introduction*, 3rd edn, London: Sage.

Cavadino, M. and Dignan, J. (2005) *Penal Systems: A Comparative Approach*, London: Sage.

Cavadino, M. and Dignan, J. (2007) *The Penal System: An Introduction*, 4th edn, London: Sage.

Cavender, G. and Deutsch, S. (2007) 'CSI and Moral Authority: The Police and Science', *Crime, Media, Culture*, 3 (1): 67–81.

Cecchi, D. (2011) 'The Criminalization of Immigration in Italy: Extent of the Phenomenon and Possible Interpretations', *Italian Sociological Review*, 1 (1): 34–42.

Centre for Contemporary Cultural Studies (1980) *Women Take Issue*, London: Hutchinson.

Centre for Contemporary Cultural Studies (1982) *The Empire Strikes Back*, London: Hutchinson.

Cere, R. (2003) 'Digital Counter-cultures and the Nature of Electronic Social and Political Movements', in Y. Jewkes (ed.) Dot.cons: Crime, Deviance and Identity on the Internet, Cullompton: Willan.

Chambliss, W. (1976) 'The State and Criminal Law', in W. Chambliss and M. Mankoff (eds) Whose Law, What Order?, New York: Wiley.

Chambliss, W. (1989) 'State-Organized Crime', Criminology 27 (2): 183–208.

Chambliss, W. J. (1989/1994) 'State Organized Crime', in N. Passas (ed.) Organized Crime, London: Dartmouth.

Chambliss, W. (1995) 'Commentary by William J. Chambliss', Society of Social Problems Newsletter, 26 (1): 9.

Champion, D. J. (2005) Research Methods for Criminal Justice and Criminology, 3rd edn, Upper Saddle River, NJ: Prentice Hall.

Chan, J. (1997) Changing Police Culture: Policing in a Multicultural Society, Cambridge: Cambridge University Press.

Chan, J. (2005) 'Globalisation, Reflexivity and the Practice of Criminology', in J. Sheptycki and A. Wardak (eds) Transnational and Comparative Criminology, London: Glasshouse.

Chancer, L. and McLaughlin, E. (2007) 'Public Criminologies: Diverse Perspectives on Academia and Policy', Theoretical Criminology, 11 (2): 155–73.

Chandola, T. (2001) 'The Fear of Crime and Area Differences in Health', Health and Place, 7 (2): 105–16.

Chaplin, R., Flatley, J. and Smith, K. (eds) (2011) Crime in England and Wales, 2010/11: Findings from the BCS and Police Recorded Crime, HOSB: 10/11 http://www.homeoffice.gov.uk/publications/science-research-statistics/research-statistics/crime-research/hosb1011/

Chatterjee, B. (2001) 'Last of the Rainmacs: Thinking about Pornography in Cyberspace', in D. Wall (ed.) Crime and the Internet, London: Routledge.

Chatterton, P. and Hollands, R. (2003) Urban Nightscapes: Youth Cultures, Pleasure Spaces and Corporate Power, London: Routledge.

Chesterton, A. (1928) Women of the Underworld, London: Stanley Paul.

Chivite-Matthews, N. and Maggs, P. (2002) Crime, Policing and Justice: The Experience of Older People, Home Office Statistical Bulletin 8/02, London: Home Office.

Choo, C. (2001) Mission Girls: Aboriginal Women on Catholic Missions in the Kimberley, Western Australia, 1900–1950, Nedlands: University of Western Australia Press.

Christie, N. (1977) 'Conflicts as Property', British Journal of Criminology, 17 (1): 1–15.

Christie, N. (1986) 'The Ideal Victim', in E. A. Fattah (ed.) From Crime Policy to Victim Policy, Basingstoke: Macmillan.

Christie, N. (2000) Crime Control as Industry, 2nd edn, London: Routledge.

Cicourel, A. (1968) The Social Organization of Juvenile Justice, New York: John Wiley.

Clancy, A., Hough, M., Aust, R. and Kershaw, C. (2001) Crime, Policing and Justice: The Experience of Ethnic Minorities, Findings from the 2000 British Crime Survey, Home Office Research Study 223, London: Home Office.

Clapson, M. (1998) Invincible Green Suburbs, Brave New Towns: Social Change and Urban Dispersal in Post-War England, Manchester: Manchester University Press.

Clapson, M. (2003) Suburban Century: Social Change and Urban Growth in England and the United States, Oxford: Berg.

Clark, A. (1987) Women's Silence, Men's Violence: Sexual Assault in England 1770–1845, London: Pandora.

Clark, L. and Lewis, D. (1977) Rape: The Price of Coercive Sexuality, Toronto: Women's Press.

Clarke, J., Hall, S., Jefferson, T. and Roberts, B. (1976) 'Subcultures, Cultures and Class', in S. Hall and T. Jefferson (eds) Resistance through Rituals: Youth Subcultures in Post-war Britain, London: Routledge.

Clarke, R. V. and Hough, M. (1984) Crime and Police Effectiveness, London: Home Office.

Clarke, R. V. and Brown, R. (2003) 'International Trafficking in Stolen Vehicles', Crime and Justice: A Review of Research, 30: 197–227.

Clarke, R. and Newman, G. (2006) Outsmarting the Terrorists, Westport, CT: Praeger Security International.

Clemmer, D. (1958) The Prison Community, New York: Rinehart.

Clifford, M. (ed.) (1998) *Environmental Crime: Enforcement, Policy and Social Responsibility*, Gaithersburg, MD: Aspen.

Cloward, R. and Ohlin, E. L. (1960) *Delinquency and Opportunity: A Theory of Delinquent Gangs*, New York: Free Press.

Coaffee, J. (2009) *Terrorism, Risk and the Global City: Towards Urban Resilience*, Farnham: Ashgate.

Cohen, A. K. (1955) *Delinquent Boys: The Culture of the Gang*, Glencoe, IL: Free Press.

Cohen, J. (2002) *Understanding Drugs and the Law*, London: Drugscope.

Cohen, P. (1972) 'Subcultural Conflict and Working Class Community', *Working Papers in Cultural Studies*, 2: 5–52.

Cohen, P. (1979) 'Policing the Working Class City', in B. Fine, R. Kinsey, J. Lea, S. Picciotto and J. Young (eds) *Capitalism and the Rule of Law*, London: Hutchinson.

Cohen, R. and Kennedy, P. (2000) *Global Sociology*, Basingstoke: Macmillan.

Cohen, S. (ed.) (1971) *Images of Deviance*, Harmondsworth: Penguin.

Cohen, S. (1972/2002) *Folk Devils and Moral Panics: The Creation of the Mods and Rockers*, London: MacGibbon and Kee.

Cohen, S. (1973a) 'Mods and Rockers: The Inventory as Manufactured News', in S. Cohen and J. Young (eds) *The Manufacture of News*, London: Constable.

Cohen, S. (1973b) 'The Failures of Criminology', *The Listener*, 8 November: 622–5.

Cohen, S. (1979a) 'Guilt, Justice and Tolerance: Some Old Concepts for a New Criminology', in D. Downes and P. Rock (eds) *Deviant Interpretations*, Oxford: Martin Robertson.

Cohen, S. (1979b) 'The Punitive City: Notes on the Dispersal of Social Control', *Contemporary Crises*, 3 (4): 341–63.

Cohen, S. (1980) 'Symbols of Trouble: Introduction to the New Edition', in *Folk Devils and Moral Panics*, 2nd edn, London: MacGibbon and Kee.

Cohen, S. (1984) 'The Deeper Structures of the Law, or "Beware the Rulers Bearing Justice"', *Contemporary Crises*, 8: 83–93.

Cohen, S. (1985) *Visions of Social Control: Crime, Punishment and Classification*, Cambridge: Polity.

Cohen, S. (1988) 'Against Criminology', in S. Cohen (ed.) *Against Criminology*, Oxford: Transaction Books.

Cohen, S. (1993) 'Human Rights and Crimes of the State: The Culture of Denial', *Australian and New Zealand Journal of Criminology*, 26 (1): 87–115.

Cohen, S. (1996a) 'Human Rights and Crimes of the State', in J. Muncie, E. McLaughlin and M. Langan (eds) *Criminological Perspectives: A Reader*, London: Sage.

Cohen, S. (1996b) 'Crime and Politics: Spot the Difference', *British Journal of Sociology*, 47 (1): 1–21.

Cohen, S. (1997) 'Intellectual Scepticsm and Political Commitment', in P. Walton and J. Young (eds) *The New Criminology Revisited*, Basingstoke: Macmillan.

Cohen, S. (2001) *States of Denial: Knowing about Atrocities and Suffering*, Cambridge: Polity.

Cohen, S. (2006) 'Neither Honesty Nor Hypocrisy: The Legal Reconstruction of Torture', in T. Newburn and P. Rock (eds) *The Politics of Crime Control: Essays in Honour of David Downes*, Oxford: Oxford University Press.

Cohen, S. (2011) 'Whose Side Are We On? The Undeclared Politics of Moral Panic Theory', *Crime, Media, Culture*, 7 (3): 259–75.

Cohen, S. and Taylor, L. (1972/1981) *Psychological Survival: The Experience of Long-Term Imprisonment*, Harmondsworth: Penguin.

Cohen, S. and Young, J. (eds) (1973) *The Manufacture of News*, London: Constable.

Cohen, Sherrill (1992) *The Evolution of Women's Asylums since 1500: From Refuges for Ex-prostitutes to Shelters for Battered Women*, Oxford: Oxford University Press.

Coleman, C. and Moynihan, J. (1996) *Understanding Crime Data: Haunted by the Dark Figure*, Buckingham: Open University Press.

Coleman, K. (2011) *Seizures of Drugs in England and Wales, 2010/11*, 2nd edn, HOSB: 17/11, 9 November, London: Home Office.

Coleman, R. (2004) 'Reclaiming the Streets: Closed Circuit Television, Neoliberalism and the Mystification of Social Divisions', *Surveillance and Society*, 2 (2/3): 293–309.

Coleman, R. and Sim, J. (2000) '"You'll Never Walk Alone": CCTV Surveillance, Order and

Neo-liberal Rule in Liverpool City Centre', *British Journal of Sociology*, 51 (4): 623–39.

Collard, A. with Contrucci, J. (1988) *Rape of the Wild: Man's Violence against Animals and the Earth*, London: Women's Press.

Collier, R. (1998) *Masculinities, Crime and Criminology: Men, Heterosexuality and the Criminal(ised) Other*, London: Sage.

Collison, M. (1995) *Police, Drugs and Community*, London: Free Association Books.

Collison, M. (1996) 'In Search of the High Life: Drugs, Crime, Masculinity and Consumption', *British Journal of Criminology*, 36 (3): 428–44.

Commission for Racial Equality (2003) *The Murder of Zahid Mubarek: A Formal Investigation by the Commission for Racial Equality into HM Prison Service of England and Wales, Part 1*, London: CRE.

Conklin, J. (1994) *Art Crime*, London: Praeger.

Conrad, P. and Schneider, W. (1992) *Deviance and Medicalization*, St Louis, MO: Mosby.

Coomber, R. and South, N. (2004) *Drug Use and Cultural Contexts 'Beyond the West'*, London: Free Association Books.

Coomber, R. and Turnbull, P. (2007) 'Arenas of Drug Transactions: Adolescent Cannabis Transactions in England – Social Supply', *Journal of Drug Issues*, Fall.

Coomber, R. and South, N. (2014) 'Fear and Loathing in Drugs Policy: Risk, Rights and Approaches to Drug Policy and Practice', in B. Labate and C. Cavnar (eds) *Prohibition, Religious Freedom, and Human Rights: Regulating Traditional Drug Use*, Heidelberg: Springer.

Cooper, H. (1977) 'What is a Terrorist? A Psychological Perspective', *Legal Medical Quarterly*, 1 (1): 16–32.

Corbett, C. (2003) *Car Crime*, Cullompton: Willan.

Cornish, D. and Clarke, R. (eds) (1986) *The Reasoning Criminal*, New York: Springer.

Corston, J. (2007) *The Corston Report: A Review of Women with Particular Vulnerabilities in the Criminal Justice System*, London: Home Office.

Cote, S. (ed.) (2002) *Criminological Theories: Bridging the Past to the Future*, Thousand Oaks, CA: Sage.

Cottee, S. (2011) 'Jihadism as a Subcultural Response to Social Strain: Extending Marc Sageman's "Bunch of Guys" Thesis', *Terrorism and Political Violence*, 23 (5): 730–51.

Cottle, S. (ed.) (2003) *Media Organization and Production*, London: Sage.

Cowie, J., Cowie, V. and Slater, E. (1968) *Delinquency in Girls*, London: Heinemann.

Cox, P. (2002) 'Race, Delinquency and Difference in Twentieth Century Britain', in P. Cox and H. Shore (eds) *Becoming Delinquent: British and European Youth, 1650–1950*, Aldershot: Ashgate.

Cox, P. (2012) *Bad Girls in Britain: Gender, Justice and Welfare, 1900–1950*, Basingstoke: Palgrave.

Cox, P. and Shore, H. (eds) (2002) *Becoming Delinquent: British and European Youth, 1650–1950*, Aldershot: Ashgate.

Coy, M., Horvath, M. and Kelly, L. (2007) 'It's Just Like Going to the Supermarket: Men Buying Sex in East London', Report for Safe Exit, London: CWASU.

Craine, S. (1997) 'The "Black Magic Roundabout": Cyclical Transitions, Social Exclusion and Alternative Careers', in R. MacDonald (ed.) *Youth, the 'Underclass' and Social Exclusion*, London: Routledge.

Crank, J. (2004) *Understanding Police Culture*, Cincinnati, OH: Anderson.

Crawford, A. (2002) *Crime and Insecurity: The Governance of Safety in Europe*, Cullompton: Willan.

Crawford, A., Jones, T., Woodhouse, T. and Young, J. (1990) *Second Islington Crime Survey*, London: Middlesex Polytechnic.

Crawford, R., Emmerson, C. and Tetlow, G. (2009) *A Survey of Public Spending in the UK*, London: Institute for Fiscal Studies.

Crenshaw, M. (1981) 'The Causes of Terrorism', *Comparative Politics*, 13: 379–99.

Cressey, D. R. (1969) *Theft of the Nation*, New York: Harper and Row.

Cressey, P. G. (1932) *The Taxi-Dance Hall*, Chicago, IL: University of Chicago Press.

Creswell, J. W. (2003) *Research Design: Qualitative, Quantitative, and Mixed Methods*, 2nd edn, London: Sage.

Crewe, B. (2007) 'The Sociology of Imprisonment', in Y. Jewkes (ed.) *Handbook on Prisons*, Cullompton: Willan.

Crewe, B. (2009) *The Prisoner Society: Power, Adaptation, and Social Life in an English Prison*, Oxford: Oxford University Press.

Critcher, C. (2003) *Moral Panics and the Media*, Buckingham: Open University Press.

Critcher, C. (2011) 'For a Political Economy of Moral Panics', *Crime, Media, Culture*, 7 (3): 259–75.

Croall, H. (1992) *White Collar Crime*, Buckingham: Open University Press.

Croall, H. (1996) 'Crime: Understanding More and Condemning Less?', *Reviewing Sociology*, 10 (3).

Croall, H. (1998) *Crime and Society in Britain*, London: Longman.

Croall, H. (1998) 'Business, Crime and the Community', *International Journal of Risk, Security and Crime Prevention*, 3 (4): 281–92.

Croall, H. (2001) *Understanding White Collar Crime*, Buckingham: Open University Press.

Croall, H. (2007) 'Food Crime', in P. Beirne and N. South (eds) *Issues in Green Criminology*, Cullompton: Willan.

Croall, H. (2013) 'Food Crime: A Green Criminology Perspective', in N. South and A. Brisman (eds) *Routledge International Handbook of Green Criminology*, London: Routledge.

Cromwell, P. F. (ed.) (2003) *In Their Own Words: Criminals on Crime*, 3rd edn, Los Angeles, CA: Roxbury Park.

Crow, I. (2001) *The Treatment and Rehabilitation of Offenders*, London: Sage.

Crowther, C. (2000) *Policing Urban Poverty*, Basingstoke: Macmillan.

Cullen, F. T. and Agnew, R. (2003) *Criminological Theory: Past to Present (Essential Readings)*, 2nd edn, Los Angeles, CA: Roxbury Park.

Cumming, E., Cumming, I. and Edell, L. (1965) 'The Policeman as Philosopher, Guide and Friend', *Social Problems*, 12: 276–86.

Cunneen, C. (2008) 'State Crime, the Colonial Question and Indigenous Peoples', in A. Smeulers and R. Haverman (eds) *Supranational Criminology: Towards a Criminology of International Crimes*, Cambridge: Intersentia Press.

Cunneen, C. and White, R. (2006) 'Australia: Control, Containment or Empowerment?', in J. Muncie and B. Goldson (eds) *Comparative Youth Justice*, London: Sage.

Cunneen, C. and Hoyle, C. (2010) *Debating Restorative Justice*, Oxford: Hart.

Curran, J. and Seaton, J. (1994) *Power without Responsibility: The Press and Broadcasting in Britain*, London: Routledge.

Currie, E. (1996) *Is America Really Winning the War on Crime and Should Britain Follow Its Example?*, London: NACRO.

Currie, E. (2007) 'Against Marginality: Arguments for a Public Criminology', *Theoretical Criminology*, 11 (2): 175–90.

D'Cruze, S. (1998) *Crimes of Outrage: Sex, Violence and Victorian Working Women*, London: UCL Press.

D'Cruze, S. (ed.) (2000) *Everyday Violence in Britain, 1850–1950: Gender and Class*, Harlow: Longman.

D'Cruze, S., Walklate, S. and Pegg, S. (2006) *Murder: Social and Historical Approaches to Understanding Murder and Murderers*, Cullompton: Willan.

Daly, K. (1989) 'Criminal Justice Ideologies and Practices in Different Voices: Some Feminist Questions about Justice', *International Journal of the Sociology of Law*, 17: 1–18.

Daly, K. (1997) 'Different Ways of Conceptualizing Sex/Gender in Feminist Theory and Their Implications for Criminology', *Theoretical Criminology*, 1 (1): 25–51.

Daly, K. (2002) 'Restorative Justice: The Real Story', *Punishment and Society*, 4 (1): 55–79.

Daly, K. and Bordt, R. L. (1995) 'Sex Effects and Sentencing: An Analysis of the Statistical Literature', *Justice Quarterly*, 12 (1): 141–75.

Daly, K. and Chesney-Lind, M. (1988) 'Feminism and Criminology', *Justice Quarterly*, 5 (4): 498–543.

Daly, M. (2007) 'Plant Warfare', *Druglink*, March/April: 6–9.

Dandeker, C. (1990) *Surveillance, Power and Modernity: Bureaucracy and Discipline from 1700 to the Present Day*, Cambridge: Polity Press.

Darbyshire, P. (1991) 'The Lamp That Shows That Freedom Lives: Is It Worth the Candle?', *Criminal Law Review*, 740.

Davies, A. (1999) '"These Viragoes Are No Less Cruel Than the Lads": Young Women, Gangs and Violence in Late Victorian Manchester and Salford', *British Journal of Criminology*, 39: 72–89.

Davies, A. (2000) 'Youth Gangs, Gender and Violence, 1870–1900', in S. D'Cruze (ed.) *Everyday Violence in Britain, 1850–1950: Gender and Class*, Harlow: Longman.

Davies, M., Croall, H. and Tyrer, J. (2005) *Criminal Justice: An Introduction to the Criminal Justice System in England and Wales*, 3rd edn, Harlow: Longman.

Davies, P., Francis, P. and Jupp, V. (eds) (2003) *Victimisation: Theory, Research and Policy*, Basingstoke: Palgrave Macmillan.

Davis, J. (1989) 'From Rookeries to Communities: Race, Poverty and Policing in London, 1850–1985', *History Workshop*, 27: 66–85.

Davis, L. (1983) *Factual Fictions: The Origins of the English Novel*, New York: Columbia University Press.

Davis, M. (1992) *City of Quartz: Excavating the Future Los Angeles*, New York: Vintage; London: Verso, 1990.

Davis, M. (1993) 'Dead West: Ecocide in Marlboro Country', *New Left Review*, 200: 49–73.

Davis, M. (1994) *Beyond Blade Runner: Urban Control – The Ecology of Fear*, Open Magazine Pamphlet series, New York: New Press.

Davis, M. (1998) *Ecology of Fear: Los Angeles and the Imagination of Disaster*, New York: Metropolitan Books, Henry Holt (1999, Vintage Books).

Davis, P., Francis, P. and Jupp, V. (2000) *Victimization: Theory, Research and Policy*, London: Macmillan.

Day, D. (1991) *The Eco-wars*, London: Paladin.

De Giorgi, A. (2006) *Re-thinking the Political Economy of Punishment: Perspectives on Post-Fordism and Penal Politics*, Aldershot: Ashgate.

De Giorgi, A. (2010) 'Immigration Control, Post-Fordism, and Less Eligibility: A Materialist Critque of Immigration across Europe', *Punishment & Society*, 12 (2):147–67.

de Haan, W. (1990) *The Politics of Redress: Crime, Punishment and Penal Abolition*, London: Sage.

de Haan, W. and Loader, I. (2002) 'On the Emotions of Crime, Punishment and Social Control', *Theoretical Criminology*, 6 (3): 243–53.

Deehan, A. (1999) *Alcohol and Crime: Taking Stock, Policing and Crime Reduction Unit*, London: Home Office.

DeKeseredy, W. and Schwartz, M. (2010) 'Friedman Economic Policies, Social Exclusion and Crime: Toward a Gendered Left Realist Subcultural Theory', *Crime, Law and Social Change*, 54: 159–70.

DeKeseredy, W. and Dragiewicz, M. (eds) (2012) *Routledge Handbook of Critical Criminology*, London: Routledge.

DeKeseredy, W. and Schwartz, M. (2012) 'Left Realism', in W. DeKeseredy and M. Dragiewicz (eds) *Routledge Handbook of Critical Criminology*, London: Routledge.

Delgado, R. and Stefancic, J. (1997) *Must We Defend Nazis?*, New York: New York University Press.

Dell, S. (1971) 'Silence in Court', Occasional Papers on Social Administration 42, London: Bell.

della Porta, D. (1995) 'Left-wing Terrorism in Italy', in M. Crenshaw (ed.) *Terrorism in Context*, University Park, PA: Penn State Press.

Dench, G., Gavron, K. and Young, M. (2006) *The New East End: Kinship, Race and Conflict*, London: Profile Books.

Dennis, N. (1993) *Rising Crime and the Dismembered Family*, Choice in Welfare Series 13, London: IEA.

Dershowitz, A. (2002) *Why Terrorism Works: Understanding the Threat, Responding to the Challenge*, New Haven, CT: Yale University Press.

Desroches, F. (2007) 'Research on Upper Level Drug Trafficking: A Review', *Journal of Drug Issues*, 37: 827.

Di Filipo, J. (2000) 'Pornography on the Web', in D. Gauntlett (ed.) *Web.studies: Rewiring Media Studies for the Digital Age*, London: Arnold.

Dignan J, (2005) *Understanding Victims and Restorative Justice*, Maidenhead: Open University Press.

Dines, G. (2010) *Pornland: How Porn has Hijacked our Sexuality*, Boston, MA: Beacon Press.

Dingwall, G. (2005) *Alcohol and Crime*, Cullompton: Willan.

Ditton, J. (1977) *Part-Time Crime: An Ethnography of Fiddling and Pilferage*, Basingstoke: Macmillan.

Ditton, J., Bannister, J., Gilchrist, E. and Farrall, S. (1999) 'Afraid or Angry? Recalibrating the "Fear" of Crime', *International Review of Victimology*, 6: 83–99.

Dobash, R. E. and Dobash, R. P. (1992) *Women, Violence and Social Change*, London: Routledge.

Dobash, R. E., Dobash, R. P. and Noaks, L. (eds) (1995) *Gender and Crime*, Cardiff: University of Wales Press.

Dobash, R. P., Dobash, R. E. and Gutteridge, S. (1986) *The Imprisonment of Women*, Oxford: Blackwell.

Dobson, A. (1990) *Green Political Thought*, London: Unwin Hyman.

Doggett, M. (1992) *Marriage, Wife-Beating and the Law in Victorian England*, London: Weidenfeld and Nicolson.

Dorling, D. (2005) 'Prime Suspect: Murder in Britain', in P. Hillyard, C. Pantazis, S. Tombs, D. Gordon and D. Dorling (eds) *Criminal Obsessions: Why Harm Matters More than Crime*, London: Crime and Society Foundation.

Dorn, N. (2004) 'UK Policing of Drug Traffickers and Users: Policy Implementation in the Context of National Law, European Traditions, International Drug Conventions, and Security after 2001', *Journal of Drug Issues*, 34: 533–50.

Dorn, N. and South, N. (eds) (1987) *A Land Fit for Heroin?*, Basingstoke: Macmillan.

Dorn, N. and South, N. (1990) 'Drug Markets and Law Enforcement', *British Journal of Criminology*, 30 (2): 171–88.

Dorn, N., Murji, K. and South, N. (1992) *Traffickers: Drug Markets and Law Enforcement*, London: Routledge.

Dorn, N., Levi, M. and King, L. (2005) *Literature Review on Upper Level Drug Trafficking*, Online Report 22, London: Home Office.

Douglas, J. and Rasmussen, P. (1977) *The Nude Beach*, Beverly Hills, CA: Sage.

Douglas, M. (1966) *Purity and Danger*, Harmondsworth: Penguin.

Doward, J. (2008) 'UN Rejects British Denial on Rendition', *Observer*, 2 March: 3.

Dowie, M. (1979) 'The Corporate Crime of the Century', *Mother Jones*, November.

Downes, D. (1988) 'The Sociology of Crime and Social Control in Britain, 1960–1987', in P. Rock (ed.) special issue, *British Journal of Criminology*, 28 (2): 175–87.

Downes, D. and Rock, P. (1979) *Deviant Interpretations: Problems in Criminology*, Oxford: Clarendon Press.

Downes, D. and Rock, P. (1998) *Understanding Deviance: A Guide to the Sociology of Crime and Rule Breaking*, 3rd edn (4th edn, 2003), Oxford: Oxford University Press.

Downes, D., Rock, P., Chinkin, C. and Gearty, C. (eds) (2007) *Crime, Social Control and Human Rights: From Moral Panics to States of Denial, Essays in Honour of Stanley Cohen*, Cullompton: Willan.

Drake, C. (1998) *Terrorists' Target Selection*, London: Macmillan.

Drake, D. (2012) *Prisons, Punishment and the Pursuit of Security*, Basingstoke: Palgrave Macmillan.

Du Bois, W. E. B. (1901/2002) 'The Spawn of Slavery: The Convict–Lease System in the South',

reprinted in S. Gabbidon, H. T. Greene and V. D. Young (eds) (2001) *African American Classics in Criminology and Criminal Justice*, Thousand Oaks, CA: Sage.

Du Rees, H. (2001) 'Can Criminal Law Protect the Environment?', *Journal of Scandinavian Studies*, 2: 109–26.

Duff, P. and Hutton, N. (eds) (1999) *Criminal Justice in Scotland*, Aldershot: Ashgate.

Duff, R. (1996) 'Penal Communications: Recent Work in the Philosophy of Punishment', in M. Tonry (ed.) *Crime and Justice: A Review of Research*, 20: 1–97.

Duff, R. and Garland, D. (1994) 'Introduction: Thinking about Punishment', in R. Duff and D. Garland (eds) *A Reader on Punishment*, Oxford: Oxford University Press.

Dunbar, I. and Langdon, A. (1998) *Tough Justice: Sentencing and Penal Policies in the 1990s*, London: Blackstone.

Duneier, M. (1999) *Sidewalk*, New York: Farrar, Straus and Giroux.

Dunhill, C. (1989) 'Women, Racist Attacks and the Response from Anti-racist Groups', in C. Dunhill (ed.) *The Boys in Blue: Women's Challenge to the Police*, London: Virago.

Durkheim, É. (1893/1960) *The Division of Labor in Modern Society*, Glencoe, IL: Free Press.

Durkheim, É. (1895/1988) *The Rules of Sociological Method*, London: Routledge.

Durkheim, É. ([1897] 2002) *Suicide: A Study in Sociology*, London: Routledge Classics.

Durkheim, É. (1901/1984) 'Two Laws of Penal Evolution', in S. Lukes and A. Scull (eds) *Durkheim and the Law*, Oxford: Basil Blackwell.

Dworkin, A. (1981) *Pornography: Men Possessing Women*, London: Women's Press.

Dworkin, A. (1987) *Intercourse*, London: Arrow Books.

Dworkin, R. (1978) *Taking Rights Seriously*, London: Duckworth.

Eales, J. (1998) *Women in Early Modern England, 1500–1700*, London: UCL Press.

Eaton, M. (1986) *Justice for Women?*, Buckingham: Open University Press.

Eck, J. and Maguire, E. (2000) 'Have Changes in Policing Reduced Violent Crime? An Assessment of the Evidence', in A. Blumstein and J. Wallman (eds) *The Crime Drop in America*, Cambridge: Cambridge University Press.

Edelstein, D. (2006) 'Now Playing at your Local Multiplex: Torture Porn', *New York Movies*, http://nymag.com/movies/features/15622/ (accessed 2 April 2012).

Edgar, K., O'Donnell, I. and Martin, C. (2003) *Prison Violence: The Dynamics of Conflict, Fear and Power*, Cullompton: Willan.

Edmunds, M., Hough, M. and Urquia, M. (1996) 'Tackling Local Drug Markets, Crime Detection and Prevention', Series Paper 80, London: Home Office.

Edwards, A. and Gill, P. (eds) (2003) *Transnational Organised Crime: Perspectives on Global Security*, London: Routledge.

Edwards, S. (1984) *Women on Trial*, Manchester: Manchester University Press.

Edwards, S. (1989) *Policing Domestic Violence*, London: Sage.

Edwards, S. (1990) 'Violence against Women, Feminism and the Law', in L. Gelsthorpe and A. Morris (eds) *Feminist Perspectives in Criminology*, Milton Keynes: Open University Press.

Edwards, S., Edwards, T. and Fields, C. (eds) (1996) *Environmental Crime and Criminality: Theoretical and Practical Issues*, New York: Garland.

Eisenman, S. (2007) *The Abu Ghraib Effect*, Chicago, IL: University of Chicago Press.

Eisner, M. (2003) 'Long-term Historical Trends in Violent Crime', *Crime and Justice: A Review of Research*, 30: 83–142.

Elias, N. (1939/1978) *The Civilising Process*, trans E. Jephcott, Oxford: Blackwell.

Ellin, N. (ed.) (1997) *Architecture of Fear*, New York: Princeton Architectural Press.

Eman, K., Meško, G. and Fields, C. (2009) 'Crimes against the Environment: Green Criminology and Research Challenges in Slovenia', *Journal of Criminal Justice and Security*, 11 (4): 574–92.

Emsley, C. (1983) *Policing and Its Context, 1750–1870*, Basingstoke: Macmillan.

Emsley, C. (1996) *The English Police: A Political and Social History*, 2nd edn, Harlow: Longman.

Emsley, C. (2002) 'The History of Crime and Crime Control Institutions', in M. Maguire, R. Morgan and R. Reiner (eds) *Oxford Handbook of Criminology*, 3rd edn, Oxford: Oxford University Press.

Emsley, C. (2005) *Crime and Society in England 1750–1900*, 3rd edn, London: Longman.

Emsley, C. (2010) *The Great British Bobby: A History of British Policing from 1829 to the Present*, London: Quercus.

Emsley, C. and Knafla, L. A. (eds) (1996) *Crime and Histories of Crime: Studies in the Historiography of Crime and Criminal Justice in Modern History*, Westport, CT: Greenwood Press.

Engels, F. (1845/1958) *The Condition of the Working Class in England*, Oxford: Basil Blackwell.

Eribon, D. (1992) *Michel Foucault*, London: Faber and Faber.

Ericson, R. (1981) *Making Crime: A Study of Detective Work*, Toronto: Butterworths.

Ericson, R. (2007) *Crime in an Insecure World*, Cambridge: Polity.

Ericson, R. and Haggerty, K. (1997) *Policing the Risk Society*, Oxford: Clarendon Press.

Ericson, R., Baranek, P. and Chan, J. (1991) *Representing Order*, Milton Keynes: Open University Press.

Ettore, E. (1992) *Women and Substance Use*, Basingstoke: Macmillan.

European Committee for the Prevention of Torture (1991) *Report to the United Kingdom Government on the Visit to the United Kingdom Carried Out by the CPT from 29 July 1990 to 10 August 1990*, Strasbourg: Council of Europe.

Evans, D. J., Fyfe, N. R. and Herbert, D. T. (eds) (1992) *Crime, Policing and Place: Essays in Environmental Criminology*, London: Routledge.

Fanon, F. (1952) *Peau Noire, Masques Blanc*, Paris: Editions de Seuil. *Black Skin, White Masks*, London: Pluto, 1986.

Fanon, F. (1967) *The Wretched of the Earth*, Harmondsworth: Penguin.

Farnham, F. and James, D. (2001) '"Dangerousness" and Dangerous Law', *The Lancet*, 358: 1926.

Farrall, S. and Gadd, D. (2004) 'Research Note: The Frequency of the Fear of Crime', *British Journal of Criminology*, 44: 127–32.

Farrington, D. P. (1997) 'Human Developments and Criminal Careers', in M. Maguire, R. Morgan and R. Reiner (eds) *Oxford Handbook of Criminology*, 2nd edn, Oxford: Oxford University Press.

Farrington, D. P. (2002) 'Developmental Criminology and Risk-Focused Prevention', in M. Maguire, R. Morgan and R. Reiner (eds) *Oxford Handbook of Criminology*, 3rd edn, Oxford: Oxford University Press.

Farrington, D. P. and Morris, A. (1983) 'Sex, Sentencing and Reconviction', *British Journal of Criminology*, 23 (3): 229–48.

Fattah, E. A. (1986) 'On Some Visible and Hidden Dangers of Victim Movements', in E. A. Fattah (ed.) *From Crime Policy to Victim Policy*, Basingstoke: Macmillan.

Feeley, M. (1994) 'The Decline of Women in the Criminal Process: A Comparative History', *Criminal Justice History*, 15: 235–74.

Feeley, M. and Simon, J. (1992) 'The New Penology: Notes on the Emerging Strategy of Corrections and Its Implications', *Criminology*, 30 (4): 449–74.

Feeley, M. and Simon, J. (1994) 'Actuarial Justice: The Emerging New Criminal Law', in D. Nelken (ed.) *The Futures of Criminology*, London: Sage.

Feeley, M. and Simon, J. (2007) 'Folk Devils and Moral Panics: An Appreciation from North America', in D. Downes, P. Rock, C. Chinkin and C. Gearty (eds) *Crime, Social Control and Human Rights: From Moral Panics to States of Denial, Essays in Honour of Stanley Cohen*, Cullompton: Willan.

Felson, M. (1998) *Crime and Everyday Life*, Thousand Oaks, CA: Pine Forge.

Fenwick, M. and Hayward, K. J. (2000) 'Youth Crime Excitement and Consumer Culture: The Reconstruction of Aetiology in Contemporary Criminology', in J. Pickford (ed.) *Youth Justice: Theory and Practice*, London: Cavendish.

Ferrell, J. (1992) 'Making Sense of Crime: Review Essay on Jack Katz's Seductions of Crime', *Social Justice*, 19 (3): 111–23.

Ferrell, J. (1998) 'Criminological Verstehen: Inside the Immediacy of Crime', in J. Ferrell and M. Hamm (eds) *Ethnography at the Edge: Crime, Deviance and Field Research*, Boston, MA: Northeastern University Press.

Ferrell, J. (1999) 'Cultural Criminology', *Annual Review of Sociology*, 25: 395–418.

Ferrell, J. (2004) 'Boredom, Crime and Criminology', *Theoretical Criminology*, 8 (3): 287–302.

Ferrell, J. (2006) *Empire of Scrounge*, New York: New York University Press.

Ferrell, J. and Sanders, C. R. (eds) (1995) *Cultural Criminology*, Boston, MA: Northeastern University Press.

Ferrell, J. and Hamm, M. (eds) (1998) *Ethnography at the Edge: Crime, Deviance and Field Research*, Boston, MA: Northeastern University Press.

Ferrell, J. and Van De Voorde, C. (2010) 'The Decisive Moment: Documentary Photography and Cultural Criminology', in K. Hayward and M. Presdee (eds) *Framing Crime: Cultural Criminology and the Image*, London: Routledge.

Ferrell, J., Hayward, K., Morrison, W. and Presdee, M. (eds) (2004) *Cultural Criminology Unleashed*, London: Glasshouse Press.

Ferrell, J., Hayward, K. and Young, J. (2008) *Cultural Criminology: An Invitation*, London: Sage.

Fielder, L. (1982) *What was Literature?: Class Culture and Mass Society*, New York: Simon and Schuster.

Fijnaut, C. (1989) 'Researching Organized Crime', *Policing Organized Crime and Crime Prevention* (pp. 75–85), Bristol: Bristol and Bath Centre for Criminal Justice.

Findlay, M. (1999) *The Globalisation of Crime*, Cambridge: Cambridge University Press.

Findlay, M. and Duff, P. (eds) (1988) *The Jury under Attack*, London: Butterworths.

Fine, R. (1985) *Democracy and the Rule of Law*, London: Pluto.

Finn, J. (2009) *Capturing the Criminal Image: From Mug Shot to Surveillance Society*, Minneapolis: University of Minnesota Press.

Finney, A. (2006) *Domestic Violence, Sexual Assault and Stalking: Findings from the 2004/05 British Crime Survey*, Home Office Online Report 12/06. London: Home Office. http://www.home office.gov.uk/rds/pdfs06/rdsolr 1206.pdf

Fishbein, D. (2000) *Biological Perspectives on Criminology*, Belmont, CA: Wadsworth.

Fiske, J. (1992) 'Popularity and the Politics of Information', in P. Dahlgren and C. Sparks (eds) *Journalism and Popular Culture*, London: Sage.

Fiske, J. (1998) 'Surveilling the City: Whiteness, the Black Man and Democratic Totalitarianism', *Theory, Culture and Society*, 15 (2): 67–88.

Fitzgerald, M. (1993) *Ethnic Minorities and the Criminal Justice System*, Royal Commission on Criminal Justice, Research Study 20, London: HMSO.

Fitzgerald, M. and Sim, J. (1979) *British Prisons*, Oxford: Basil Blackwell.

Fitzgerald, M. and Hale, C. (1996) *Ethnic Minorities, Victimization and Racial Harassment: Findings from the 1988 and 1992 British Crime Surveys*, London: Home Office.

Fleming, N. (2010) 'Miaow-miaow on Trial: Truth or Trumped-up Charges?' 29 March, *New Scientist* (Health), http://www.newscientist.com/article/dn18712-miaowmiaow-on-trial-truth-or-trumpedup-charges.html?full=true#.UmZT_HA_s14

Flew, A. (1981) *The Politics of Procrustes*, London: Temple Smith.

Fogel, D. (1975) *We Are the Living Proof: The Justice Model for Corrections*, Cincinnati, OH: Anderson.

Foldy, M. S. (1997) *The Trials of Oscar Wilde: Deviance, Morality and Late Victorian Society*, New Haven, CT: Yale University Press.

Ford, T. (2008) 'Jails Full as Inmates Reach Record Number', *The Times*, 9 February: www.timesonline.co.uk/tol/news/politics/article3338037.ece?print=yes&randum=1208806844550 (accessed 21 April 2008).

Forrester, D., Chatterton, M. and Pease, K. (1988) 'The Kirkholt Burglary Prevention Project', Rochdale, Crime Prevention Unit Paper 13, London: Home Office.

Foster, J. (1989) 'Two Stations: An Ethnographic Study of Policing in the Inner City', in D. Downes (ed.) *Crime and the City*, Basingstoke: Macmillan.

Foster, J. (1990) *Villains: Crime and Community in the Inner City*, London: Routledge.

Foster, J. and Hope, T. (1993) *Housing, Community and Crime: The Impact of the Priority Estates Project*, Home Office Research Study 131, London: HMSO.

Foster, J., Newburn, T. and Souhami, A. (2005) *Assessing the Impact of the Stephen Lawrence Inquiry*, London: Home Office.

Foucault, M. (1975/1980) 'Prison Talk', in *Power/Knowledge: Selected Interviews and Other Writings*, Brighton: Harvester Press.

Foucault, M. (1977) *Discipline and Punish: The Birth of the Prison*, Harmondsworth: Penguin.

Foucault, M. (1978) *The History of Sexuality*, vol. 1, trans. R. Hurley, London: Allen Lane.

Foucault, M. (1991) 'Governmentality', in G. Burchell, C. Gordon and P. Miller (eds) *The Foucault Effect: Studies in Governmentality*, London: Harvester Wheatsheaf.

Foucault, M. (2004) *Society Must Be Defended: Lectures and the College de France 1975–76*, London: Penguin.

Fox, V. (1973) *Violence behind Bars: An Explosive Report on Prison Riots in the United States*, Westport, CT: Greenwood Press.

Fraser, F. (1994) *Mad Frank*, London: Little, Brown.

Frazier, E. F. (1949) *Crime and Delinquency: The Negro in the United States*, New York: Macmillan.

Freeman, N. (1996–7) 'That Was Business – This Is Personal: Professions of Violence in English Cinema from Brighton Rock to the Krays', *Close-Up: The Electronic Journal of British Cinema*, 1, Winter, www.shu.ac.uk/ services/lc/closeup

Freud, S. (1958) 'The Uncanny', in *On Creativity and the Unconscious: Papers on the Psychology of Art, Literature, Love, Religion*, New York: Harper and Row.

Frey, R. G. (1992) 'Torture', in L. C. Becker and C. B. Becker (eds) *Encyclopedia of Ethics*, Chicago, IL: St James Press.

Friedrichs, D. and Friedrichs, J. (2002) 'The World Bank and Crimes of Globalisation: A Case Study', *Social Justice*, 29: 1–12.

Friman, H. R. and Andreas, P. (1999) *The Illicit Global Economy and State Power*, Oxford: Rowman and Littlefield.

Furnell, S. (2010) 'Hackers, Viruses and Malicious Software', in Y. Jewkes and M. Yar (eds) *Handbook of Internet Crime*, Cullompton: Willan.

Fussey, P. (2007) 'Observing Potentiality in the Global City: Surveillance and Counterterrorism in London', *International Criminal Justice Review*, 17 (3): 171–92.

Fussey, P. (2011) 'An Economy of Choice? Terrorist Decision-making and Criminological Rational Choice Theories Reconsidered', *Security Journal*, 24 (1): 85–99.

Fussey, P. (2013) 'Contested Typologies of UK Counter-Terrorist Surveillance: The Rise and Fall of Project Champion', *Critical Studies on Terrorism*, 6 (3): 351–70.

Fussey, P. and Richards, A. (2008) 'Researching and Understanding Terrorism: A Role for

Criminology?' Special Issue: Terrorism Post 9/11, *Criminal Justice Matters*, 73 (1).

Fussey, P. and Coaffee, J. (2012) 'Urban Spaces of Surveillance', in D. Lyon, K. Haggerty and K. Ball (eds) *Routledge International Handbook of Surveillance Studies*, London: Routledge.

Fussey, P. and South, N. (2013) 'Heading toward a New Criminogenic Climate: Climate Change, Political Economy and Environmental Security', in R. White (ed.) *Climate Change from a Criminological Perspective*, New York: Springer.

Fussey, P., Coaffee, J., Armstrong, G. and Hobbs, D. (2011) *Securing and Sustaining the Olympic City: Reconfiguring London for 2012 and Beyond*, Aldershot: Ashgate.

Fussey, P., Coaffee, J., Armstrong, G. and Hobbs, D. (2012) 'The Regeneration Games: Purity and Security in the Olympic City', *British Journal of Sociology*, 63 (2): 260–84.

Fyfe, N. (ed.) (1998) *Images of the Street: Planning, Identity and Control in Public Space*, London: Routledge.

Fyfe, N. (2004) 'Zero Tolerance, Maximum Surveillance? Deviance, Difference and Crime Control in the Late Modern City' in L. Lees (ed.) *The Emancipatory City? Paradoxes and Possibilities*, London: Sage.

Fyfe, N. (2010) 'Crime and the "Re-moralization of City Spaces"', in S. Smith, R. Pain, S. Marston and J. Jones III (eds) *The Handbook of Social Geographies*, London: Sage.

Gabbidon, S., Greene, H. T. and Young, V. D. (eds) (2001) *African American Classics in Criminology and Criminal Justice*, Thousand Oaks, CA: Sage.

Gabor, T. (1994) *Everybody Does It*, Toronto: University of Toronto Press.

Gadd, D. and Jefferson, T. (2007) *Psychosocial Criminology: An Introduction*, London: Sage.

Gagnon, J. (1977) *Human Sexuality in Today's World*, New York: Foresman.

Gagnon, J. H. and Simon, W. (1973/2005) *Sexual Conduct: The Social Sources of Human Sexuality*, Piscataway, NJ: Transaction Publishers.

Galeotti, M. (ed.) (2003) *Russian and Post-Soviet Organised Crime*, Dartmouth: Ashgate.

Galliher, J. F. (1995) 'Chicago's Two Worlds of Deviance Research: Whose Side Are They On?', in G. A. Fine (ed.) *A Second Chicago School? The Development of a Postwar American Sociology*, Chicago, IL: University of Chicago Press.

Gallo, E. and Ruggiero, V. (1991) 'The "Immaterial" Prison: Custody as the Manufacture of Handicaps', *International Journal of the Sociology of Law*, 19 (3): 273–91.

Garafalo, J. (1979) 'Victimisation and the Fear of Crime', *Journal of Research in Crime and Delinquency*, 16: 80–97.

Garfinkel, H. (1956a) 'Conditions of Successful Degradation Ceremonies', *American Journal of Sociology*, 61: 420–4.

Garfinkel, H. (1956b) 'The Trial as a Degradation Ceremony', *American Journal of Sociology*, 66.

Garland, D. (1985) *Punishment and Welfare*, Aldershot: Gower.

Garland, D. (1990) *Punishment and Modern Society: A Study in Social Theory*, Oxford: Clarendon Press.

Garland, D. (1991) 'Sociological Perspectives on Punishment', in M. Tonry (ed.) *Crime and Justice: A Review of Research*, 14: 115–65.

Garland, D. (1996) 'The Limits of the Sovereign State: Strategies of Crime Control in Contemporary Society', *British Journal of Criminology*, 36 (4): 445–71.

Garland, D. (1997) '"Governmentality" and the Problem of Crime', *Theoretical Criminology*, 1 (2): 173–214.

Garland, D. (2000) 'The Culture of High Crime Societies: Some Preconditions of Recent "Law and Order" Policies', *British Journal of Criminology*, 40 (3): 445–71.

Garland, D. (2001a) 'Introduction: The Meaning of Mass Imprisonment', *Punishment and Society*, 3 (2): 5–7.

Garland, D. (2001b) *The Culture of Control: Crime and Social Order in Contemporary Society*, Oxford: Clarendon Press.

Garland, D. (2002) 'Of Crime and Criminals: The Development of Criminology in Britain', in M. Maguire, R. Morgan and R. Reiner (eds) *Oxford Handbook of Criminology*, 3rd edn, Oxford: Oxford University Press.

Garland, D. (2003) 'The Rise of Risk', in R. Ericson and A. Doyle (eds) *Risk and Morality*, Toronto: University of Toronto Press.

Garland, D. (2005) 'Capital Punishment and American Culture', *Punishment and Society*, 7 (4): 347–76.

Garland, D. (2007) 'Death, Denial, Discourse: On the Forms and Functions of American Capital Punishment', in D. Downes, P. Rock, C. Chinkin and C. Gearty (eds) *Crime, Social Control and Human Rights: From Moral Panics to States of Denial, Essays in Honour of Stanley Cohen*, Cullompton: Willan.

Garland, D. (2011) 'Criminology's Place in the Academic Field', in M. Bosworth and C. Hoyle (eds) *What is Criminology?*, Oxford: Oxford University Press.

Garland, D. and Sparks, R. (2000) 'Criminology, Social Theory and the Challenge of Our Times', *British Journal of Criminology*, 40 (2): 189–204.

Garner, R. (2001) *Environmental Politics*, 2nd edn, London: Prentice Hall.

Gatrell, V. A. C. (1990) 'Crime, Authority and the Policeman State', in F. M. L. Thompson (ed.) *Cambridge Social History of Britain, 1750–1950*, vol. 3, Cambridge: Cambridge University Press.

Gatrell, V. A. C. (1994) *The Hanging Tree: Execution and the English People, 1770–1868*, Oxford: Oxford University Press.

Gatrell, V. A. C. (2006) *City of Laughter: Sex and Satire in Eighteenth-Century London*, London: Atlantic.

Gatrell, V. A. C., Lenman, B. and Parker, G. (eds) (1980) *Crime and the Law: The Social History of Crime in Western Europe since 1500*, London: Europa.

Gauntlett, D. (2000) *Web.Studies: Rewiring Media Studies for the Digital Age*, London: Arnold.

Gay, P. (1973) *The Enlightenment: An Interpretation*, London: Wildwood House.

Geis, G. and Dimento, J. (1995) 'Should We Prosecute Corporations and/or Individuals?', in F. Pearce and L. Snider (eds) *Corporate Crime*, Toronto: University of Toronto Press.

Geis, G. and Dodge, M. (eds) (2002) *Lessons of Criminology*, Cincinnati, OH: Anderson.

Gelsthorpe, L. (1989) *Sexism and the Female Offender*, Aldershot: Gower.

Gelsthorpe, L. and Morris, A. (2002) 'Restorative Justice: The Last Vestiges of Welfare', in J. Muncie, G. Hughes and E. McLaughlin (eds) *Youth Justice: Critical Readings*, London: Sage.

Genders, E. and Player, E. (1987) 'Women in Prison: The Treatment, the Control and the Experience', in P. Carlen and A. Worrall (eds) *Gender, Crime and Justice*, Milton Keynes: Open University Press.

Genders, E. and Player, E. (1989) *Race Relations in Prison*, Oxford: Clarendon Press.

Gever, M. (2005) 'The Spectacle of Crime, Digitized: CSI: Crime Scene Investigation and Social Anatomy', *European Journal of Cultural Studies*, 8 (4): 445–63.

Gibbs, C., Gore, M., McGarrell, E., and Rivers, L. (2010) 'Introducing Conservation Criminology: Towards Interdisciplinary Scholarship on Environmental Crimes and Risks', *British Journal of Criminology*, 50 (1): 124–44.

Gibbs, P. and S. Hickson (2009) *Children: Innocent until Proven Guilty. A Report on the Overuse of Remand for Children in England and Wales and how it can be Addressed*, London: Prison Reform Trust.

Giddens, A. (1972) *Émile Durkheim: Selected Writings*, Cambridge: Cambridge University Press.

Giddens, A. (1990) *The Consequences of Modernity*, Cambridge: Polity.

Giddens, A. (1991) *Modernity and Self-Identity*, Cambridge: Polity.

Giddens, A. (1999) *Runaway World: How Globalisation Is Reshaping Our Lives*, London: Profile.

Giddens, A. (2005) 'Scaring People May Be the Only Way to Avoid the Risks of New Style Terrorism', *New Statesman*, 18 (840): 29–31.

Gilchrist, E., Bannister, J., Ditton, J. and Farrall, S. (1998) 'Women and the "Fear of Crime": Challenging the Accepted Stereotype', *British Journal of Criminology*, 38 (2): 283–98.

Gill, A. (2006) 'Patriarchal Violence in the Name of "Honour"', *International Journal of Criminal Justice Sciences*, 1 (1): 1–12.

Gill, P. and Phythian, M. (2006) *Intelligence in an Insecure World*, Cambridge: Polity.

Gill, R. (2007) *Gender and the Media*, Cambridge: Polity Press.

Gilligan, C. (1982) *In a Different Voice*, Cambridge, MA: Harvard University Press.

Gilmore, R. (2007) *Golden Gulag: Prisons, Surplus, and Opposition in Globalizing California*, Berkeley, CA: University of California Press.

Girling, E., Loader, I. and Sparks, R. (2000) *Crime and Social Change in Middle England: Questions of Order in an English Town*, London: Routledge.

Gladfelder, H. (2001) *Criminality and Narrative in Eighteenth-Century England: Beyond the Law*, Baltimore, MD: Johns Hopkins University Press.

Gleick, P. (2010) *Bottled and Sold: The Story Behind Our Obsession With Bottled Water*, Washington, DC: Island Press.

Glover, J. and Hibbert, P. (2009) *Locking Up or Giving Up? Why Custody Thresholds for Teenagers aged 12, 13 and 14 need to be Raised*, London: Barnados.

Gobert, J. and Punch, M. (2003) *Rethinking Corporate Crime*, London: Butterworths.

Godfrey, B.S., Emsley, C. and Dunstall, G. (eds) (2003a) *Comparative Histories of Crime*, Cullompton: Willan.

Godfrey, B.S., Emsley, C. and Dunstall, G. (2003b) 'Introduction: Do You Have Plane-Spotters in New Zealand? Issues in Comparative Crime History at the Turn of Modernity', in G. S. Godfrey, C. Emsley and G. Dunstall (eds) *Comparative Histories of Crime*, Cullompton: Willan.

Goffman, E. (1959) *The Presentation of Self in Everyday Life*, Garden City, NY: Doubleday.

Goffman, E. (1961) *Asylums: Essays on the Social Situation of Mental Patients and Other Inmates*, Harmondsworth: Penguin.

Goffman, E. (1963) *Stigma: Notes on the Management of Spoiled Identity*, Harmondsworth: Penguin.

Goldsmith, A. (2011) 'Policing's New Visibility', *British Journal of Criminology*, 50 (5): 914–34.

Goldson, B. (2000) *The New Youth Justice*, Lyme Regis: Russell House.

Goldson, B. (2006) 'Penal Custody: Intolerance, Irrationality and Indifference', in B. Goldson and J. Muncie (eds) *Youth Crime and Justice*, London: Sage.

Goldson, B. and Muncie, J. (eds) (2006) *Youth Crime and Justice*, London: Sage.

Goodey, J. (1997) 'Boys Don't Cry: Masculinities, Fear of Crime and Fearlessness', *British Journal of Criminology*, 47 (3): 401–18.

Goodey, J. (2000) 'Non-EU Citizens' Experiences of Offending and Victimization: The Case for Comparative European Research', *European Journal of Crime, Criminal Law and Criminal Justice*, 8 (1): 13–34.

Goodey, J. (2005) *Victims and Victimology: Research, Policy and Practice*, Harlow: Longman.

Goodman, E. and Moed, A. (2007) 'Community in Mashups: The Case of Personal Geodata', www.mashups.net (accessed 5 January 2008).

Goody, J. (2007) *The Theft of History*, Cambridge: Cambridge University Press.

Gordon, P. (1983) *White Law: Racism in the Police, Courts and Prisons*, London: Pluto.

Gordon, P. (1990) *Racial Violence and Harassment*, 2nd edn, London: Runnymede Trust.

Goring, C. (1913/1972) *The English Convict: A Statistical Study*, London: HMSO.

Gottfredson, M. (1984) *Victims of Crime: The Dimensions of Risk*, Home Office Research Study 81, London: HMSO.

Gottfredson, M. R. and Hirschi, T. (1990) *A General Theory of Crime*, Stanford, CA: Stanford University Press.

Gottschalk, M. (2006) *The Prison and the Gallows: The Politics of Mass Incarceration in America*, Cambridge: Cambridge University Press.

Gould, S. J. (1996) *The Mismeasure of Man*, 2nd edn, New York: W. W. Norton.

Gouldner, A. (1968/1973) 'The Sociologist as Partisan: Sociology and the Welfare State', in *For Sociology*, London: Allen Lane.

Gouldner, A. (1973) *For Sociology: Renewal and Critique in Sociology Today*, London: Allen Lane.

Gournelos, T. (2012) 'Breaking the News: Power and Secrecy in the Age of the Internet', in D. Gunkel and T. Gournelos (eds) *Transgression 2.0: Media, Culture, and the Politics of a Digital Age*, London: Continuum.

Grady, A. (2002) 'Female-on-Male Domestic Abuse: Uncommon or Ignored?', in C. Hoyle, R. Young and R. P. Young (eds) *New Visions of Crime Victims*, Portland, OR: Hart Publishing.

Graham, K. and Wells, S. (2003) '"Somebody's Gonna Get Their Head Kicked In Tonight!": Aggression among Young Males in Bars – a Question of Values?', *British Journal of Criminology*, 43 (3): 546–66.

Graham, S. (ed.) (2004) *Cities, War and Terrorism*, Oxford: Blackwell.

Graham, S. (2006) 'Surveillance, Urbanization and the US "Revolution" in Military Affairs', in D. Lyon (ed.) *Theorizing Surveillance: The Panopticon and Beyond*, Cullompton: Willan.

Graham, S. (2010) *Cities Under Siege: The New Military Urbanism*, London: Verso.

Gramsci, A. (1971) *Selections from Prison Notebooks*, London: Lawrence and Wishart.

Green, G., Smith, R. and South, N. (2005) 'Court-based Psychiatric Assessment: A Case for an Integrated and Diversionary Public Health Role', *Journal of Forensic Psychiatry and Psychology*, 16 (3): 577–91.

Greenberg, D. and Stender, F. (1972) 'The Prison as a Lawless Agency', *Buffalo Law Review*, 21: 799–839.

Greenberg, K. (ed.) (2006) *The Torture Debate in America*, Cambridge: Cambridge University Press.

Greene, H. T. and Gabbidon, S. L. (2000) *African American Criminological Thought*, Albany: State University of New York Press.

Greene, J. A. (1999) 'Zero Tolerance: A Case Study of Police Policies and Practices in New York', *Crime and Delinquency*, 45 (2): 171–87.

Greenwood, P., Chaiken, J. and Petersilia, J. (1977) *The Criminal Investigation Process*, Lexington, MA: D. C. Heath.

Greer, C. (2008) *Crime and Media: A Reader*, London: Routledge.

Greer, C. and McLaughlin, E. (2010) 'We Predict a Riot? Public Order Policing, New Media Environments and the Rise of the Citizen Journalist', *British Journal of Criminology*, 50 (6): 1041–59.

Greer, S. (1994) 'Miscarriages of Justice Reconsidered', *Modern Law Review*, 57: 58.

Gregory, D. and Urry, J. (eds) (1985) *Social Relations and Spatial Structures*, London: Macmillan.

Gregory, J. and Lees, S. (1999) *Policing Sexual Assault*, London: Routledge.

Griffin, S. (1971) 'Rape: The All American Crime', *Ramparts*, September: 26–35.

Griffiths, P. (1996) *Youth and Authority: Formative Experiences in England, 1560–1640*, Oxford: Clarendon Press.

Griffiths, P. (2002) 'Juvenile Delinquency in Time', in P. Cox and H. Shore (eds) *Becoming Delinquent: British and European Youth, 1650–1950*, Aldershot: Ashgate.

Gros, J.-G. (2003) 'Trouble in Paradise: Crime and Collapsed States in the Age of Globalisation', *British Journal of Criminology*, 43 (1): 63–80.

Guardian, The (2008) 'Just How Expert Are the Expert Witnesses?', 18 May, available: http://education.guardian.co.uk/egweekly/story/0,,2279458,00.html

Gusfield, J. (1981) *The Culture of Public Problems: Drinking–Driving and the Symbolic Order*, Chicago, IL: University of Chicago Press.

Guttenplan, D. D. (2000) 'The Holocaust on Trial', *Atlantic Monthly*, 285 (2): 45–66.

Habermas, J. (1987) *The Philosophical Discourse of Modernity*, Cambridge: Polity.

Hagan, J., Rymond-Richmond, W. and Parker, P. (2005) 'The Criminology of Genocide: The Death and Rape of Darfur', *Criminology*, 43 (3): 525–61.

Haggerty, K. and Ericson, R. (eds) (2006) *The New Politics of Surveillance and Visibility*, Toronto: University of Toronto Press.

Haines, K. and O'Mahony, D. (2006) 'Restorative Approaches, Young People and Youth Justice', in B. Goldson and J. Muncie (eds) *Youth Crime and Justice*, London: Sage.

Hale, C. (1992) *Fear of Crime: A Review of the Literature*, Canterbury: University of Kent.

Hale, C. (1996) 'Fear of Crime: A Review of the Literature', *International Review of Victimology*, 4: 79–150.

Halford, A. (1993) *No Way Up the Greasy Pole*, London: Constable.

Hall, M. (2012) 'State Responsibility for the Adverse Impacts of Climate Change on Individuals: Assessing the Potential for an Interdisciplinary Approach', in S. Farrall, D. French and T. Ahmed (eds) *Climate Change: Legal and Criminological Implications*, Oxford: Hart.

Hall, S. (2012) *Theorizing Crime and Deviance: A New Perspective*, London: Sage.

Hall, S. and Jefferson, T. (eds) (1976) *Resistance through Rituals: Youth Subcultures in Post-war Britain*, London: Routledge.

Hall, S. and Jefferson, T. (2006) 'Once More Around Resistance through Rituals', in S. Hall and T. Jefferson (eds) *Resistance through Rituals: Youth Subcultures in Post-war Britain*, 2nd edn, London: Routledge.

Hall, S., Critcher, C., Jefferson, T., Clarke, J. and Roberts, B. (1978) *Policing the Crisis: Mugging, the State and Law and Order*, London: Macmillan.

Hall, S., Winlow, S. and Ancrum, C. (2008) *Criminal Identities and Consumer Culture: Crime, Exclusion and the New Culture of Narcissism*, Cullompton: Willan.

Hamilton, P. (1996) 'The Enlightenment and the Birth of Social Science', in S. Hall, D. Held, D. Hubert and K. Thompson (eds) *Modernity: An Introduction to Modern Societies*, Oxford: Blackwell.

Hammersley, M. (2001) 'Which Side Was Becker On? Questioning Political and Epistemological Radicalism', *Qualitative Research*, 1 (1): 91–110.

Hammersley, R., Forsyth, A., Morrison, V. and Davis, J. (1989) 'The Relationship between Crime and Opioid Use', *British Journal of Criminology*, 84: 1029–44.

Hanmer, J. and Saunders, S. (1984) *Well Founded Fear*, London: Hutchinson.

Hanmer, J., Radford, J. and Stanko, E. (1989) *Women, Policing and Male Violence: International Perspectives*, London: Routledge.

Harcourt, B. (2001) *Illusion of Order*, London: Harvard University Press.

Harding, C., Hines, B., Ireland, B. and Rawlings, P. (1985) *Imprisonment in England and Wales: A Concise History*, London: Croom Helm.

Harland, D. (1985) 'Legal Aspects of the Export of Hazardous Products', *Journal of Consumer Policy*, 8 (3): 209–38.

Harman, C. (2009) *Zombie Capitalism*, London: Bookmark.

Harrison, P. and Pearce, F. (2000) *AAAS Atlas of Population and Environment*, Berkeley: University of California Press.

Hartless, J., Ditton, J., Nair, G. and Phillips, S. (1995) 'More Sinned against Than Sinning: A Study of Young Teenagers' Experience of Crime', *British Journal of Criminology*, 35 (1): 114–33.

Hassan, N. (2001) 'Letter from Gaza. An Arsenal of Believers: Talking to the "Human Bombs"', *New Yorker*, 19 November.

Hauck, M. (2007) 'Non-compliance in Small-scale Fisheries: A Threat to Security?', in P. Beirne and N. South (eds) *Issues in Green Criminology*, Cullompton: Willan.

Hay, D. (1975) 'Property, Authority, and the Criminal Law' in D. Hay, P. Linebaugh and E. P. Thompson (eds) *Albion's Fatal Tree: Crime and Society in Eighteenth-century England*, Harmondsworth: Penguin.

Hay, D., Linebaugh, P. and Thompson, E. P. (eds) (1975) *Albion's Fatal Tree: Crime and Society in Eighteenth-century England*, Harmondsworth: Penguin.

Hayes, P. (2001) 'Driving Up Treatment Standards: Interview', *Access*, 4 (Drugs Prevention Advisory Service newsletter).

Hayward, K. (2002) 'The Vilification and Pleasures of Youthful Transgression', in J. Muncie, G. Hughes and E. McLaughlin (eds) *Youth Justice: Critical Readings*, London: Sage.

Hayward, K. (2004) *City Limits: Crime, Consumer Culture and the Urban Experience*, London: Glasshouse Press.

Hayward, K. (2007) 'Situational Crime Prevention and its Discontents: Rational Choice Theory versus the "Culture of Now"', *Social Policy & Administration*, 41 (3): 232–50.

Hayward, K. (2010) 'Opening the Lens: Cultural Criminology and the Image', in K. Hayward and M. Presdee (eds) *Framing Crime: Cultural Criminology and the Image*, London: Routledge.

Hayward, K. (2012) 'Five Spaces of Cultural Criminology', *British Journal of Criminology*, 52 (3): 441–62.

Hayward, K. and Yar, M. (2006) 'The "Chav" Phenomenon: Consumption, Media and the Construction of a New Underclass', *Crime, Media, Culture*, 2 (1): 9–28.

Hebdige, D. (1988) *Hiding in the Light*, London: Comedia.

Hedderman, C. (2004), 'Why Are More Women Being Sentenced to Custody?', in G. McIvor (ed.) *Women Who Offend*, London: Jessica Kingsley.

Hedderman, C. and Moxon, D. (1992) *Magistrates' Court or Crown Court? Mode of Trial Decisions and Sentencing*, Home Office Research Study 125, London: HMSO.

Hedderman, C. and Hough, M. (1994) *Does the Criminal Justice System Treat Men and Women Differently?* Home Office Research Findings 10, London: Home Office.

Heidensohn, F. (1968) 'The Deviance of Women: A Critique and an Enquiry', *British Journal of Sociology*, 19: 160–75.

Heidensohn, F. (1987) 'Women and Crime: Questions of Criminology', in P. Carlen and A.

Worrall (eds) *Gender, Crime and Justice*, Buckingham: Open University Press.

Heidensohn, F. (1996) *Women and Crime*, 2nd edn, London: Macmillan.

Heidensohn, F. (ed.) (2006) *Gender and Justice – New Concepts and Approaches*, Cullompton: Willan.

Held, D., McGrew, A. G., Goldblatt, D. and Perraton, J. (1999) *Global Transformations: Politics, Economics and Culture*, Cambridge: Polity.

Hendrick, H. (1990) 'Constructions and Reconstructions of British Childhood: An Interpretative Survey 1800 to the Present', in A. James and A. Prout (eds) *Constructing and Reconstructing Childhood*, London: Falmer.

Henry, S. and Milovanovic, D. (1996) *Constitutive Criminology: Beyond Postmodernism*, London: Sage.

Her Majesty's Chief Inspectorate of Constabulary (2009) *Adapting to Protest: Nurturing the British Model of Policing*, London: HMIC

Her Majesty's Inspectorate of Constabulary (1999) *Police Integrity: Securing and Maintaining Public Confidence*, London: Home Office.

Herbert, S. (1997) *Territoriality and the Los Angeles Police Department*, Minneapolis: University of Minnesota Press.

Herbert, S. and Brown, E. (2006) 'Conceptions of Space and Crime in the Punitive Neoliberal City', *Antipode*, 38 (4): 755–77.

Herman, E. and Chomsky, N. (1988) *Manufacturing Consent: The Political Economy of the Mass Media*, New York: Pantheon.

Herman, M. (2003) 'Counter-Terrorism, Information Technology and Intelligence Change', *Intelligence and National Security*, 18 (4): 40–58.

Hermes, J. (2000) 'Of Irritation, Texts and Men: Feminist Audience Studies and Cultural Citizenship', *International Journal of Cultural Studies*, 3 (3): 351–67.

Herrnstein, R. and Murray, C. (1994) *The Bell Curve: Intelligence and Class Structure in American Life*, New York: Free Press.

Hershatter, G. (1997) *Dangerous Pleasures: Prostitution and Modernity in Twentieth-Century Shanghai*, Berkeley: University of California Press.

Hesketh, W. (2003) 'Medico-crime: Time for a Police–Health Professions Protocol?', *Police Journal*, 76: 121–31.

Hier, S. (2008) 'Thinking beyond Moral Panic: Risk, Responsibility, and the Politics of Moralization', *Theoretical Criminology*, 12 (2): 173–90.

Higgins, P. (1996) *Heterosexual Dictatorship: Male Homosexuality in Postwar Britain*, London: Fourth Estate.

Higgins, P., Short, D. and South, N. (2013) 'Protecting the Planet: A Proposal for a Law of Ecocide', *Crime, Law and Social Change*, 59 (3): 251–66.

Hill, A. (2002) '"No One Leaves This Place with Her Sanity Intact"', *Observer*, 1 December: 10–11.

Hill, P. (2003) *The Japanese Mafia: Yakuza, Law and the State*, Oxford: Oxford University Press.

Hillyard, P. (1993) *Suspect Community: People's Experience of the Prevention of Terrorism Acts in Britain*, London: Pluto.

Hillyard, P., Pantazis, C., Tombs, S. and Gordon, D. (2004) *Beyond Criminology: Taking Harm Seriously*, London: Pluto.

Hindelang, M. J., Gottfredson, M. R. and Garofalo, J. (1978) *Victims of Personal Crime: An Empirical Foundation for a Theory of Personal Victimization*, Cambridge, MA: Ballinger.

Hinsliff, G. (2003) 'Diet of Fish "Can Prevent" Teen Violence', *Observer*, 14 September.

Hinton, M. and Newburn, T. (eds) (2009) *Policing Developing Democracies*, London: Routledge.

Hirschfield, A., Brown, P. and Todd, P. (1995) 'GIS and the Analysis of Spatially Referenced Crime Data: Experiences in Merseyside UK', *International Journal of Geographical Information Systems*, 9 (2): 191–210.

Hirschi, T. (1969) *Causes of Delinquency*, Berkeley: University of California Press.

Hirst, P. (1975) 'Marx and Engels on Law, Crime and Morality', in I. Taylor, P. Walton and J. Young (eds) *Critical Criminology*, London: Routledge and Kegan Paul.

Hobbs, D. (1988) *Doing the Business: Entrepreneurship, the Working Class and Detectives in the East End of London*, Oxford: Clarendon Press.

Hobbs, D. (1991) 'Business as a Master Metaphor', in R. Burrows (ed.) *Deciphering the Enterprise Culture*, London: Routledge.

Hobbs, D. (1994) 'Professional and Organized Crime in Britain', in M. Maguire, R. Morgan and

R. Reiner (eds) *Oxford Handbook of Criminology*, Oxford: Oxford University Press.

Hobbs, D. (1995) *Bad Business: Professional Crime in Modern Britain*, Oxford: Oxford University Press.

Hobbs, D. (1997) 'Criminal Collaboration: Youth Gangs, Subcultures, Professional Criminals and Organized Crime', in M. Maguire, R. Morgan and R. Reiner (eds) *Oxford Handbook of Criminology*, 2nd edn, Oxford: Oxford University Press.

Hobbs, D. (1998) 'Going Down the Glocal: The Local Context of Organised Crime', *Howard Journal of Criminal Justice*, 37 (4): 407–22.

Hobbs, D. (2001) 'The Firm: Organizational Logic and Criminal Culture on a Shifting Terrain', *British Journal of Criminology*, 41 (4): 549–60.

Hobbs, D. (2013) *Lush Life: Constructing Organized Crime in the UK*, Oxford: Oxford University Press.

Hobbs, D., Lister, S., Hadfield, P., Winlow, S. and Hall, S. (2000) 'Receiving Shadows: Governance and Liminality in the Night-time Economy', *British Journal of Sociology*, 51 (4): 701–17.

Hobbs, D., Hadfield, P., Lister, S. and Winlow, S. (2002) '"Door Lore": The Art and Economics of Intimidation', *British Journal of Criminology*, 42: 352–70.

Hobbs, D., Hadfield, P., Lister, S. and Winlow, S. (2003) *Bouncers: Violence and Governance in the Night-time Economy*, Oxford: Oxford University Press.

Hobsbawm, E. (1972) *Bandits*, Harmondsworth: Penguin.

Hobsbawn, E. (1994) 'Barbarism: A User's Guide', *New Left Review*, July–August.

Hobsbawm, E. and Rudé, G. (1969) *Captain Swing*, London: Lawrence and Wishart.

Hochschild, A. (1983) *The Managed Heart: Commercialization of Human Feeling*, Berkeley: University of California Press.

Hodge, N. (2003) 'Manslaughter Business Placed on Hold', *Tribune*, 10 January, 67 (1): 3.

Hoffman, B. (2006) *Inside Terrorism*, New York: Columbia University Press.

Hoffman, B. (2008) 'The Myth of Grass-Roots Terrorism: Why Osama bin Laden Still Matters', *Foreign Affairs*, 87 (3): 133–8.

Hofrichter, R. (1993) *Toxic Struggles: The Theory and Practice of Environmental Justice*, Philadelphia, PA: New Society.

Holdaway, S. (1983) *Inside the British Police*, Oxford: Basil Blackwell.

Holdaway, S. (1996) *The Racialisation of British Policing*, Basingstoke: Macmillan.

Holdaway, S. and Barron, A. M. (1997) *Resigners: The Experience of Black and Asian Police Officers*, Basingstoke: Macmillan.

Holdaway, S. and Rock, P. (eds) (1998) *Thinking About Criminology*, London: UCL Press.

Hollin, C. (1999) 'Treatment Programmes for Offenders: Meta-analysis, "What Works", and Beyond', *International Journal of Psychiatry and Law*, 22: 361–72.

Hollway, W. and Jefferson, T. (1997) 'The Risk Society in an Age of Anxiety: Situating Fear of Crime', *British Journal of Sociology*, 48 (2): 255–66.

Hollway, W. and Jefferson, T. (2000) 'The Role of Anxiety in Fear of Crime', in T. Hope and R. Sparks (eds) *Crime, Risk and Insecurity*, London: Routledge.

Holmes, S. T. and Holmes, R. M. (2008) *Sex Crimes: Patterns and Behavior*, 3rd edn, Thousand Oaks, CA: Sage.

Home Office (1966) *Committee of an Enquiry into Prison Escapes and Security* (Mountbatten Report), Cmnd 3175, London: HMSO.

Home Office (1997) *Criminal Statistics for England and Wales 1996*, Cm 3764, London: Home Office.

Home Office (1998) *Crime and Disorder Act 1998. Racially Aggravated Offences*, http://www.home office. gov.uk/cdact/racagoff.htm

Home Office (1999) *Digest 4: Information on the Criminal Justice System*, Research, Development and Statistics Directorate, London: Home Office.

Home Office (2000a) *A Guide to the Criminal Justice System in England and Wales*, London: Home Office, www.homeoffice.gov.uk

Home Office (2000b) *Statistics on Race and the Criminal Justice System*, Research, Development and Statistics Directorate, London: Home Office.

Home Office (2001) *Prison Statistics England and Wales 2000*, Cmnd. 5250, London: HMSO.

Home Office (2002a) *Criminal Statistics England and Wales 2001*, Cm 5696, London: Home Office, www.archive.official-documents.co.uk

Home Office (2002b) *Prison Population Brief, England and Wales: June 2002*, London: HMSO.

Home Office (2002c) *Statistics on Race and the Criminal Justice System: A Home Office Publication under Section 95 of the Criminal Justice Act 1991*, London: Home Office.

Home Office (2004) *Statistics on Race and the Criminal Justice System – 2003*, London: HMSO.

Home Office (2005a) *Crime in England and Wales 2003/4, Supplementary Volume 1: Homicide and Gun Crime*, London: Home Office.

Home Office (2005b) *Crime against Retail and Manufacturing Premises: Findings from the 2002 Commercial Victimisation Survey* (http://www.crimereduction.homeoffice.gov.uk/business/business 42.htm).

Home Office (2005c) *Race and the Criminal Justice System: An Overview to the Complete Statistics, 2003–2004*, London: Home Office.

Home Office (2007a) *Home Office Statistical Bulletin: Crime in England and Wales, 2006–7*: http://www.homeoffice.gov.uk/rds/pdfs07/hosb1107.pdf

Home Office (2007b) *Organised Crime: Revenues, Economic and Social Costs, and Criminal Assets Available for Seizure*, Online Report 14/07, London: Home Office.

Home Office (2010) *Protecting our Border, Protecting the Public: The UK Border Agency's Five Year Strategy for Enforcing our Immigration Rules and Addressing Immigration and Cross Border Crime*, London: Home Office.

Home Office (2012) *Operation of Police Powers under the Terrorism Act 2000 and Subsequent Legislation: Arrests, Outcomes and Stops and Searches*, London: HMSO.

Home Office (2013) Crime Maps: https://www.gov.uk/government/news/crime-maps-made-to-measure-feature-adds-more-information

Honderich, T. (2002) *After the Terror*, Edinburgh: Edinburgh University Press.

Hood, R. (1992) *Race and Sentencing*, Oxford: Oxford University Press.

Hood, R. (2002) *The Death Penalty: A Worldwide Perspective*, 3rd edn, Oxford: Oxford University Press.

Hope, T. (1985) *Implementing Crime Prevention Measures*, Home Office Research Study 86, London: HMSO.

Hope, T. (2001) 'Crime Victimisation and Inequality in Risk Society', in R. Matthews and J. Pitts (eds) *Crime, Disorder and Community Safety*, London: Routledge.

Horgan, J. (2003) 'The Search for the Terrorist Personality', in A. Silke (ed.) *Terrorists, Victims and Society: Psychological Perspectives on Terrorism and its Consequences*, London: Wiley.

Horgan, J. (2005) *The Psychology of Terrorism*, London: Routledge.

Horgan, J. (2009) *Walking Away from Terrorism: Accounts of Disengagement from Radical and Extremist Movements*, London: Routledge.

Hough, M. (2012) 'Researching Trust in the Police and Trust in Justice: A UK Perspective', *Policing and Society* (on-line advanced access).

Hough, M. and Mayhew, P. (1983) *The British Crime Survey*, Home Office Research Study 76, London: HMSO.

Hovanissian, R. (ed.) (1986) *The Armenian Genocide in Perspective*, New Brunswick, NJ: Transaction.

Howe, A. (1994) *Punish and Critique: Towards a Feminist Analysis of Penality*, London: Routledge.

Howe, A. (2001) 'Deprivation and Violence in the Community: A Perspective from a UK Accident and Emergency Department', *Injury*, 32 (5): 349–51.

Hudson, B. (1987) *Justice through Punishment*, Basingstoke: Macmillan.

Hudson, B. (1989) 'Discrimination and Disparity: The Influence of Race on Sentencing', *New Community*, 16 (1): 23–34.

Hudson, B. (1993) *Penal Policy and Social Justice*, Basingstoke: Macmillan.

Hudson, B. (1996) *Understanding Justice*, London: Sage.

Hudson, B. (2003) *Understanding Justice*, 2nd edn, London: Sage.

Hudson, B. (2005) 'The Culture of Control: Choosing the Future', in M. Matravers (ed.) *Managing Modernity: Politics and the Culture of Control*, London: Routledge.

Hughes, G. (2002) 'Crime and Disorder Reduction Partnerships: The Future of Community Safety?', in G. Hughes, E. McLaughlin and J. Muncie (eds) *Crime Prevention and Community Safety: New Directions*, London: Sage.

Hughes, G. (2007) *The Politics of Crime and Community*, Basingstoke: Palgrave.

Hughes, G. and Follett, M. (2006) 'Community Safety, Youth and the "Anti-Social"', in B. Goldson and J. Muncie (eds) *Youth Crime and Justice*, London: Sage.

Human Rights Watch (2002) *Hopes Betrayed: Trafficking of Women and Girls to Post-Conflict Bosnia and Herzegovina for Forces Prostitution*, New York: Human Rights Watch.

Human Rights Watch (2010) *Without Suspicion: Stop and Search under the Terrorism Act 2000*, New York: Human Rights Watch.

Hunt, A. (1998) 'The Great Masturbation Panic and the Discourse of Moral Regulation in Nineteenth and Early Twentieth Century Britain', *Journal of the History of Sexuality*, 8 (4): 575–615.

Hunt, N. and Stevens, A. W. (2004) 'Whose Harm? Harm Reduction and the Shift to Coercion in UK Drug Policy', *Social Policy and Society*, 3 (4): 333–42.

Hutter, B. (1986) 'An Inspector Calls: The Importance of Proactive Enforcement in the Regulatory Context', *British Journal of Criminology*, 26 (2).

Hutton, W. (1995) *The State We're In*, London: Jonathan Cape.

Huxley, A. (1994) *Brave New World*, London: Flamingo.

Ianni, E. R. and Ianni, R. (1983) 'Street Cops and Management Cops: The Two Cultures of Policing', in M. Punch (ed.) *Control in the Police Organization*, Cambridge, MA: MIT Press.

Iganski, P. (2001) 'Hate Crimes Hurt More', *American Behavioral Scientist*, 45 (4): 626–38.

Iganski, P. (2006) 'Free to Speak, Free to Hate?', in L. Morris (ed.) *Rights: Sociological Perspectives*, London: Routledge.

Iganski, P. (2008) *'Hate Crime' and the City*, Bristol: Policy Press.

Ignatieff, M. (1978) *A Just Measure of Pain: The Penitentiary in the Industrial Revolution 1750–1850*, London: Macmillan.

Ignatieff, M. (1994) *Blood and Belonging: Journeys into the New Nationalism*, London: Vintage.

Inciardi, J. (1977) 'In Search of the Class Cannon: A Field Study of Professional Pickpockets', in R. S. Weppner (ed.) *Street Ethnography: Selected Studies of Crime and Drug Use in Natural Settings*, Beverly Hills, CA: Sage.

Inciardi, J. (1999) *The Drug Legalization Debate*, 2nd edn, Thousand Oaks, CA: Sage.

Innes, J. and Styles, J. (1993) 'The Crime Wave: Recent Writing on Crime and Justice in Eighteenth-Century England', in A. Wilson (ed.) *Rethinking Social History: English Society 1570–1920 and its Interpretation*, Manchester: Manchester University Press.

Institute for Jewish Policy Research (2000) *Combating Holocaust Denial through Law in the United Kingdom*, London: Institute for Jewish Policy Research.

Institute for Public Policy Research (2009) *Shared Responsibilities. A National Security Strategy for the UK*, London: Institute for Public Policy Research.

Institute of Race Relations (2009) *Spooked! How Not to Prevent Violent Extremism*, London: Institute of Race Relations.

International Centre for Prison Studies (2012) 'World Prison Brief', available at: http://www.prisonstudies.org/info/worldbrief/

International Federation of Red Cross and Red Crescent Societies (IFRC) (2003) *Disasters Report*, Geneva: IFRC.

Irwin, J. (1990) *The Jail: Managing the Underclass in American Society*, Berkeley: University of California Press.

Ishay, M. (ed.) (1997) *The Human Rights Reader*, London: Routledge.

Jackson, J., Tyler, T. R., Bradford, B., Taylor, D. and Shiner, M. (2010) 'Legitimacy and Procedural Justice in Prisons', *Prison Service Journal*, 191: 4–10.

Jackson, L. (2000) *Child Sexual Abuse in Victorian England*, London: Routledge.

Jackson, L. A. (2006) *Women Police: Gender, Welfare and Surveillance in the Twentieth Century*, Manchester: Manchester University Press.

Jackson, R., Breen Smyth, M. and Gunning, J. (2009) *Critical Terrorism Studies: A New Research Agenda*, London: Routledge.

Jackson, S. and Scott, S. (1996) *Feminism and Sexuality: A Reader*, Edinburgh: Edinburgh University Press.

Jacobs, J. (1961) *The Death and Life of Great American Cities*, New York: Random House.

Jacobson, J. (1999) *Policing Drug Hot-Spots*, Home Office Police Research Series 109, London: Home Office.

Jacobson, J., Bhardwa, B., Gyateng, T., Hunter, G. and Hough, M. (2010) *Punishing Disadvantage: A Profile of Children in Custody*, London: Prison Reform Trust.

Jacoby, J. (2002) 'Punish Crime, Not Thought Crime', in P. Iganski (ed.) *The Hate Debate*, London: Profile.

Jaggar, A. (1989) 'Love and Knowledge: Emotion in Feminist Epistemology', in S. Bordo and A. Jaggar (eds) *Gender/Body/Knowledge: Feminist Reconstructions of Being and Knowing*, New York: Rutgers University Press.

Jamieson, R. (1998) 'Towards a Criminology of War in Europe', in V. Ruggiero, N. South and I. Taylor (eds) *The New European Criminology: Crime and Social Order in Europe*, London: Routledge.

Jamieson, R., South, N. and Taylor, I. (1998) 'Economic Liberalization and Cross-border Crime: The North American Free Trade Area and Canada's Border with the USA', *International Journal of the Sociology of Law*, 26 (2): 245–72 and 26 (3): 285–319.

Janowitz, M. (ed.) (1996) *W. I. Thomas on Social Organization and Social Personality*, Chicago, IL: University of Chicago Press.

Jefferson, T. (1990) *The Case against Paramilitary Policing*, Milton Keynes: Open University Press.

Jefferson, T. (2002a) 'For a Psychosocial Criminology', in K. Carrington and R. Hogg (eds) *Critical Criminology: Issues, Debates, Challenges*, Cullompton: Willan.

Jefferson, T. (2002b) 'Masculinities and Crime', in M. Maguire, R. Morgan and R. Reiner (eds) *Oxford Handbook of Criminology*, 3rd edn, Oxford: Oxford University Press.

Jefferson, T. and Grimshaw, R. (1984) *Controlling the Constable: Police Accountability in England and Wales*, London: Muller/Cobden Trust.

Jefferson, T. and Walker, M. (1992) 'Ethnic Minorities in the Criminal Justice System', *Criminal Law Review*, 81: 83–95.

Jefferson, T. and Walker, M. (1993) 'Attitudes to the Police of Ethnic Minorities in a Provincial City', *British Journal of Criminology*, 33 (2): 251–66.

Jeffery-Poulter, S. (1991) *Peers, Queers, and Commons: The Struggle for Gay Law Reform from 1950 to the Present*, London: Routledge.

Jenkins, B. (2000) 'Terrorism', in E. Borgatta and R. Montgomery (eds) *Encyclopedia of Sociology*, New York: Macmillan.

Jenkins, P. (1998) *Moral Panic: Changing Concepts of the Child Molester in Modern America*, New Haven, CT: Yale University Press.

Jenkins, P. (2001) *Beyond Tolerance: Child Pornography on the Internet*, New York: New York University Press.

Jensen, Robert (2007) *Getting Off: Pornography and the End of Masculinity*, Cambridge, MA: South End Press.

Jesilow, P., Pontell, H. and Geis, G. (1985) 'Medical Criminals: Physicians and White-Collar Offences', *Justice Quarterly*, 2 (2): 149–65.

Jewkes, Y. (1999) *Moral Panics in a Risk Society: A Critical Evaluation, Crime, Order and Policing*, Occasional Paper Series 15, Scarman Centre, Leicester: University of Leicester.

Jewkes, Y. (ed.) (2003a) *Dot.cons: Crime, Deviance and Identity on the Internet*, Cullompton: Willan.

Jewkes, Y. (2003b) 'Policing the Net: Crime, Regulation and Surveillance in Cyberspace', in Y. Jewkes (ed.) *Dot.cons: Crime, Deviance and Identity on the Internet*, Cullompton: Willan.

Jewkes, Y. (2004) *Media and Crime*, London: Sage.

Jewkes, Y. (ed.) (2007a) *Crime Online*, Cullompton: Willan.

Jewkes, Y. (ed.) (2007b) *Handbook on Prisons*, Cullompton: Willan.

Jewkes, Y. and Andrews, C. (2005) 'Policing the Filth: The Problems of Investigating Online Child Pornography in England and Wales', *Policing and Society*, 15 (1): 42–62.

Johnston, L. (2000) *Policing Britain: Risk, Security and Governance*, Harlow: Longman.

Jones, S. and S. Mowlabocus (2009) 'Hard Times and Rough Rides: The Legal and Ethical Impossibilities of Researching "Shock" Pornographies', *Sexualities*, 12 (5): 613–28.

Jones, T. and Newburn, T. (1996) *Policing and Disaffected Communities: A Review of the Literature*, London: Policy Studies Institute.

Jones, T. and Newburn, T. (2002) 'The Transformation of Policing', *British Journal of Criminology*, 42 (1): 129–46.

Jones, T., Maclean, B. and Young, J. (1986) *The Islington Crime Survey*, Aldershot: Gower.

Jowit, J. (2007) 'Amazon Tribe Hits Back at Green "Colonialism"', *Observer*, 14 October: 43.

Jupp, V., Davies, P. and Francis, P. (1999) 'The Features of Invisible Crimes', in P. Davies, P. Francis and V. Jupp (eds) *Invisible Crimes: Their Victims and Their Regulation*, Basingstoke: Macmillan.

Jupp, V., Davies, P. and Francis, P. (eds) (2000) *Doing Criminological Research*, London: Sage.

Justice (1989) *Justice, Sentencing: A Way Ahead*, London: Justice.

Kalunta-Crumpton, A. (1999) *Race and Drug Trials: The Social Construction of Guilt and Innocence*, Aldershot: Ashgate.

Karmen, A. (1990) *Crime Victims: An Introduction to Victimology*, Pacific Grove, CA: Brooks Cole.

Karstedt, S. (2002) 'Emotions and Criminal Justice', *Theoretical Criminology*, 6 (3): 299–317.

Karstedt, S. and Farrall, S. (2007) 'Law-abiding Majority? The Everyday Crimes of the Middle Classes', Crime and Society Briefing 3, London: Centre for Crime and Justice Studies (http://www.crimeandjustice. org.uk/opus45/middle-class-crime-2007.pdf).

Karstedt, S., Levi, M. and Godfrey, B. (eds) (2006) 'Markets, Risk and "White Collar" Crimes: Moral Economies from Victorian Times to Enron', *British Journal of Criminology*, special issue, 46 (6).

Katz, J. (1988) *Seductions of Crime: Moral and Sensual Attractions of Doing Evil*, New York: Basic Books.

Keane, J. (1996) *Reflections on Violence*, London: Verso.

Kearon, A. and Leach, R. (2000) 'Invasion of the "Bodysnatchers": Burglary Reconsidered', *Theoretical Criminology*, 4 (4): 451–72.

Kearon, T. and Godfrey, B. (2007) 'Setting the Scene: A Question of History', in S. Walklate (ed.) *Handbook of Victims and Victimology*, Cullompton: Willan.

Keith, M. (1993) *Race, Riots and Policing: Law and Disorder in a Multi-racist Society*, London: UCL Press.

Kelly, D. (1990) 'Victim Participation in the Criminal Justice System', in A. J. Lurigio, W. G. Skoken and R. C. Davis (eds) *Victims of Crime: Problems, Policies and Programs*, Newbury Park, CA: Sage.

Kelly, L. (1988) *Surviving Sexual Violence*, Cambridge: Polity Press.

Kelly, L. (2005) *Fertile Fields: Trafficking in Persons in Central Asia*, Vienna: IOM.

Kelly, L., Lovett, J. and Regan, L. (2005) *A Gap or a Chasm? Attrition in Reported Rape Cases*, Home Office Research Study 293, London: Home Office.

Kelman, H. C. and Hamilton, V. L. (1989) *Crimes of Obedience*, New Haven, CT: Yale University Press.

Kempadoo, K. and Doezema, J. (1998) *Global Sex Workers: Rights, Resistance and Redefinition*, London: Routledge.

Kemper, T. (1978) *A Social Interactional Theory of Emotions*, New York: John Wiley.

Kemper, T. (1987) 'How Many Emotions Are There? Wedding the Social and Automatic Components', *American Journal of Sociology*, 93: 263–89.

Kennedy, H. (2004) *Just Law*, London: Chatto and Windus.

Kerr, P. (1992) *A Philosophical Investigation*, London: Arrow.

Kershaw, C., Budd, T., Kinshott, G., Mattinson, J., Mayhew, P. and Myhill, A. (2000) *The 2000 British Crime Survey*, London: Home Office.

Kersten, J. (1993) 'Street Youths, Bosozoku and Yakuza: Subculture Formation and Social Reactions in Japan', *Crime and Delinquency*, 39 (3): 277–95.

Kesteren, J. N. van, Mayhew, P. and Nieuwbeerta, P. (2000) *Criminal Victimisation in Seventeen Industrialised Countries: Key-findings from the 2000 International Crime Victims Survey*, The Hague: Ministry of Justice.

Kidd-Hewitt, D. (1995) 'Crime and the Media: A Criminological Perspective', in D. Kidd-Hewitt and R. Osborne (eds) *Crime and the Media: The Postmodern Spectacle*, London: Pluto.

Kiley, S. (2007) 'How Rare Shellfish Fuel Drug Mania', *Observer*, 23 September: 41.

King, C. (2003) 'A Case to Answer?', *Care and Health*, 42, 13–26 August: 10–11.

King, P. (1999) 'Locating Histories of Crime: A Bibliographical Study', *British Journal of Criminology*, 39 (1): 161–74.

King, R. (2007) 'Imprisonment: Some International Comparisons and the Need to Revisit Panopticisim', in Y. Jewkes (ed.) *Handbook on Prisons*, Cullompton: Willan.

King, R. D. and Wincup, E. (eds) (2007) *Doing Research on Crime and Justice*, 2nd edn, Oxford: Oxford University Press.

Kinsey, R. (1984) *Merseyside Crime Survey*, Edinburgh: Centre for Criminology, University of Edinburgh.

Kivisto, P. (1998) *Key Ideas in Sociology*, London: Sage/Pine Forge Press.

Klein, N. (2000) *No Logo*, London: Flamingo.

Klockars, C. (1975) *The Professional Fence*, London: Tavistock.

Knafla, L. A. (2003) 'Introduction', in L. A. Knafla (ed.) *Violent Crime in North America*, Westport, CT: Praeger.

Knepper, P. (2007) *Criminology and Social Policy*, London: Sage.

Kohn, M. (1992) *Dope Girls: The Birth of the British Drug Underground*, London: Lawrence and Wishart.

Kramer, R. (2010) 'From Guernica to Hiroshima to Baghdad: The Normalization of the Terror bombing of Civilians', in W. Chambliss, R. Michalowski and R. Kramer (eds) *State Crime in the Global Age*, Cullompton: Willan.

Kramer, R. and Michalowski, R. (1990) 'Toward an Integrated Theory of State–Corporate Crime'. Paper presented at the American Society of Criminology. Baltimore, MD.

Kramer, R. and Michalowski, R. (1993) 'State Corporate Crime: Case Studies in Organizational Deviance', unpublished manuscript.

Kramer, R. and Michalowski, R. (2005) 'War, Aggression and State Crime: A Criminological Analysis of the Invasion and Occupation of Iraq', *British Journal of Criminology*, 45: 446–9.

Kramer, R., Michalowshi, R. and Kauzlarich, D. (2002) 'The Origins and Development of the Concept and Theory of State–Corporate Crime', *Crime and Delinquency*, 48 (2): 263–82.

Kretsmer, D. (2007) 'The Torture Debate: Israel and Beyond', in D. Downes, P. Rock, C. Chinkin and C. Gearty (eds) *Crime, Social Control and Human Rights: From Moral Panics to States of Denial, Essays in Honour of Stanley Cohen*, Cullompton: Willan.

Kristof, N. (2008) Op-Ed column: 'Extended Forecast: Bloodshed', *New York Times*, April 13, NYTimes.com

Kuhn, T. S. (1962) *The Structure of Scientific Revolutions*, Chicago, IL: University of Chicago Press.

Lacey, N. (1988) *State Punishment: Political Principles and Community Values*, London: Routledge.

Lacey, N. (2000) *Narrative and Genre: Key Concepts in Media Studies*, Basingstoke: Macmillan.

Lacey, N. (2007) 'Legal Constructions of Crime', in M. Maguire, R. Morgan and R. Reiner (eds) *The Oxford Handbook of Criminology*, Oxford: Oxford University Press.

Lacey, N. (2008) *The Prisoners' Dilemma: Political Economy and Punishment in Contemporary Democracies* (The Hamlyn Lectures), Cambridge: Cambridge University Press.

Lancet, The (1999) 'Alcohol and Violence', *The Lancet*, 336, 17 November: 1223–4.

Landesco, J. (1929) *Organized Crime in Chicago*, Chicago: Illinois Association for Criminal Justice.

Langbein, J. (1983) 'Albion's Fatal Flaws', *Past and Present*, 98: 96–120.

Langfield, M. (2004) 'Voluntarism, Salvation, and Rescue: British Juvenile Migration to Australia and Canada, 1890–1939', *Journal of Imperial and Commonwealth History*, 32 (2): 86–114.

Lasch, C. (1979) *The Culture of Narcissism*, New York: Norton.

Latour, B. (2005) *Reassembling the Social: An Introduction to Actor-Network-Theory*, Oxford: Oxford University Press.

Lauer, J. (2005) 'Driven to Extremes: Fear of Crime and the Rise of the Sport Utility Vehicle in the United States', *Crime, Media, Culture*, 1 (2): 149–68.

Lawrence, F. M. (1999) *Punishing Hate: Bias Crimes under American Law*, Cambridge, MA: Harvard University Press.

Laycock, G. (2008) 'Special Edition on Crime Science Editorial: What is Crime Science?', *Policing: A Journal of Policy and Practice*, 2 (2): 149–53.

Lazarus, L. (2004) *Contrasting Prisoners' Rights: A Comparative Examination of Germany and England*, Oxford: Oxford University Press.

Lea, J. (1999) 'Social Crime Revisited', *Theoretical Criminology*, 3: 307–26.

Lea, J. (2000) 'The Macpherson Report and the Question of Institutional Racism', *Howard Journal of Criminal Justice*, 39 (2): 219–37.

Lea, J. (2002) *Crime and Modernity*, London: Sage.

Lea, J. and Young, J. (1984) *What Is To Be Done about Law and Order?*, London: Pluto.

Lee, J. A. (1981) 'Some Structural Aspects of Police Deviance in Relations with Minority Groups', in C. Shearing (ed.) *Organizational Police Deviance*, Toronto: Butterworths.

Lee, M. (1998) *Youth, Crime and Police Work*, Basingstoke: Macmillan.

Lee, M. (2001) 'The Genesis of "Fear of Crime"', *Theoretical Criminology*, 5 (4): 467–85.

Lee, M. (2007a) 'Women's Imprisonment as a Mechanism of Migration Control in Hong Kong', *British Journal of Criminology*, 47 (6): 847–60.

Lee, M. (ed.) (2007b) *Human Trafficking*, Cullompton: Willan.

Lee, M. (2011) *Trafficking and Global Crime Control*, London: Sage.

Lee, M. and South, N. (2003) 'Policing and Drugs', in T. Newburn (ed.) *Handbook of Policing*, Cullompton: Willan.

Lee, M. and South, N. (2008) 'Policing and Drugs', in T. Newburn (ed.) *Handbook of Policing*, 2nd edn, Cullompton: Willan.

Lees, S. (1996a) 'Unreasonable Doubt: The Outcomes of Rape Trials', in M. Hester, L. Kelly and J. Radford (eds) *Women, Violence and Male Power*, Buckingham: Open University Press.

Lees, S. (1996b) *Carnal Knowledge: Rape on Trial*, London: Penguin.

Legambiente, G. (2003) *The Illegal Trafficking in Hazardous Waste in Italy and Spain*, Rome: European Commission.

Leishman, F. and Mason, P. (2004) *Policing and the Media: Facts, Fictions and Factions*, Cullompton: Willan.

Lemert, E. (1967) *Human Deviance, Social Problems and Social Control*, Englewood Cliffs, NJ: Prentice Hall.

Lemert, E. (1951) *Social Pathology*, New York: McGraw-Hill.

Lemert, E. (1958) 'The Behavior of the Systematic Check Forger', *Social Problems*, 6: 141–9.

Leo, R. A. (1995) 'Trial and Tribulation: Courts, Ethnography, and the Need for Evidentiary Privilege for Academic Researchers', *American Sociologist*, 26: 113–34.

Leonard, E. B. (1982) *Women, Crime and Society*, New York: Longman.

Levi, M. (1981) *The Phantom Capitalists*, Aldershot: Gower.

Levi, M. (1993) *The Investigation, Prosecution and Trial of Serious Fraud*, Research Study No. 14, London: Royal Commission on Criminal Justice.

Levi, M. and Pithouse, A. (1992) 'The Victims of Fraud', in D. Downes (ed.) *Unravelling Criminal Justice*, Basingstoke: Macmillan.

Levi, M. and van Duyne, P. (2005) *Drugs and Money*, London: Routledge.

Levin, J. and McDevitt, J. (2002) *Hate Crimes Revisited: America's War on Those Who Are Different*, Boulder, CO: Westview Press.

Levy, A. (2005) *Female Chauvinist Pigs: Women and the Rise of Raunch Culture*, New York: Free Press.

Lewis, P., Newburn, T., Taylor, M. and Ball, J. (2011) 'Reading the Riots: Investigating England's Summer of Disorder', The Guardian.com http://www.theguardian.com/uk/2011/dec/05/anger-police-fuelled-riots-study

Lewis, R. (1989) 'European Markets in Cocaine', *Contemporary Crises*, 13: 35–52.

Liazos, A. (1972) 'The Poverty of the Sociology of Deviance: Nuts, Sluts and Preverts', *Social Problems*, 20: 103–20.

Liberty (2010) *Terrorism Pre-Charge Detention Comparative Law Study*, London: Liberty, available from http://www.liberty-human-rights.org.uk/policy/reports/comparative-law-study-2010-pre-charge-detention.pdf

Linebaugh, P. (1976) 'Karl Marx, the Theft of Wood and Working Class Composition', *Crime and Social Justice*, 6: 5–16.

Linebaugh, P. (1991) *The London Hanged: Crime and Civil Society in the Eighteenth Century*, London: Allen Lane/Penguin.

Lipstadt, D. (1994) *Denying the Holocaust: The Growing Assault on Truth and Memory*, New York: Plume.

Lister, R. et al. (eds) (1996) *Charles Murray and the Underclass: The Developing Debate*, London: IEA Health and Welfare Unit in association with the Sunday Times.

Livingstone, S. (1996) 'On the Continuing Problem of Media Effects', in J. Curran and M. Gurevitch (eds) *Mass Media and Society*, London: Arnold.

Loader, I. (1996) *Youth, Policing and Democracy*, Basingstoke: Macmillan.

Loader, I. (2000) 'Plural Policing and Democratic Governance', *Social and Legal Studies*, 9: 323–45.

Loader, I. (2002) 'Policing, Securitisation and Democratisation in Europe', *Criminal Justice*, 2 (2): 125–53.

Loader, I. and Sparks, R. (2007) 'Contemporary Landscapes of Crime, Order and Control', in M. Maguire, R. Morgan and R. Reiner (eds) *Oxford Handbook of Criminology*, 4th edn, Oxford: Oxford University Press.

Loader, I. and Walker, N. (2007) *Civilizing Security*, Cambridge: Cambridge University Press.

Loffreda, B. (2000) *Losing Matt Shepard: Life and Politics in the Aftermath of Anti-gay Murder*, New York: Columbia University Press.

Lofland, J. (1966) *Doomsday Cult*, Englewood Cliffs, NJ: Prentice Hall.

Lombroso, C. (1911/1968) *Crime: Its Causes and Remedies*, Montclair, NJ: Patterson Smith.

Lombroso, C. (1876) *L'uomo delinquente*, Turin: Fratelli Bocca.

Lombroso-Ferrero, G. (1911) *Criminal Man: According to the Classification of Cesare Lombroso*, New York: Putnam; repr. Montclair, NJ: Paterson Smith, 1972.

Loseke, D. (2003a) 'We Hold These Truths to Be Self Evident: Problems in Pondering the Pedophile Priest Problem: Symposium on Paedophile Priests', *Sexualities*, 6, February: 6–14.

Loseke, D. (2003b) *Thinking about Social Problems: An Introduction to Constructionist Perspectives*, 2nd edn, New York: Aldine de Gruyter.

Lovett, J. and Kelly, L. (2009) *Different Systems, Similar Outcomes? Tracking Attrition in Reported Rape Cases across Europe*, London: Child and Women Abuse Studies Unit, London Metropolitan University.

Low, D. (1982) *Thieves' Kitchen: The Regency Underworld*, London: Dent.

Lowman, J., Menzies, R. and Palys, T. (eds) (1987) *Transcarceration: Essays in the Sociology of Social Control*, Aldershot: Gower.

Lupton, D. and Tulloch, J. (1999) 'Theorizing Fear of Crime: Beyond the Rational/Irrational Opposition', *British Journal of Sociology*, 50 (3): 507–23.

Lupton, R., Wilson, A., May, T., Warburton, H. and Turnbull, P. (2002) *A Rock and a Hard Place: Drug Markets in Deprived Neighbourhoods*, Home Office Research Study 240, London: Home Office.

Lurigio, A. J., Skogan, W. G. and Davis, R. C. (eds) (1990) *Victims of Crime: Problems, Policies and Programs*, Newbury Park, CA: Sage.

Lury, K. (2005) *Interpreting Television*, London: Hodder Arnold.

Lustgarten, L. (1986) *The Governance of Police*, London: Sweet and Maxwell.

Lynch, M. (2012) 'Theorizing the Role of the "War on Drugs" in US Punishment', *Theoretical Criminology*, 16 (2):175–99.

Lynch, M. J. (1990) 'The Greening of Criminology: A Perspective on the 1990s', *Critical Criminologist*, 2 (3): 1–4, 11–12.

Lynch, M. and Stretesky, P. (2001) 'Toxic Crimes: Examining Corporate Victimization of the General Public Employing Medical and Epidemiological Evidence', *Critical Criminology*, 10: 153–72.

Lyng, S. (1990) 'Edgework: A Social Psychological Analysis of Voluntary Risk Taking', *American Journal of Sociology*, 95 (4): 851–86.

Lyng, S. (2004) 'Crime, Edgework and Corporeal Transaction', *Theoretical Criminology*, 8 (3): 359–75.

Lyng, S. and Snow, D. (1986) 'Vocabularies of Motive and High Risk Behavior: The Case of Skydiving', in E. J. Lawler (ed.) *Advances in Group Processes*, Greenwich, CT: JAI.

Lyon, D. (2001) *Surveillance Society: Monitoring Everyday Life*, Buckingham: Open University Press.

Lyon, D. (2003a) *Surveillance after September 11*, London: Blackwell

Lyon, D. (2003b) 'Surveillance as Social Sorting: Computer Codes and Mobile Bodies', in D. Lyon (ed.) *Surveillance as Social Sorting: Privacy, Risk and Digital Discrimination*, London: Routledge.

Lyon, D. (ed.) (2006) *Theorizing Surveillance: The Panopticon and Beyond*, Cullompton: Willan.

Lyons, H. A. and Harbinson, H. J. (1986) 'A Comparison of Political and Non-political Murderers in Northern Ireland, 1974–84', *Medicine, Science and the Law*, 26 (3): 193–8.

Mac an Ghaill, M. (1994) *The Making of Men*, Buckingham: Open University Press.

Mcalinden, A.-M. (2006) 'Managing Risk: From Regulation to the Reintegration of Sexual

Offenders', *Criminology and Criminal Justice*, 6 (2): 197–218.

Macalister, T. (2010) 'Cheap Prices and High Tax Revenues Underpin America's Love of Big Oil', *The Guardian*, 29 May.

McAllister, W. (2000) *Drug Diplomacy in the Twentieth Century*, London: Routledge.

McAra, L. (2005) 'Modelling Penal Transformation', *Punishment and Society*, 7 (3): 277–302.

McBarnet, D. (1981) *Conviction: Law, the State and the Construction of Justice*, London: Macmillan.

McCabe, A. and Raine, J. (1997) *Framing the Debate: The Impact of Crime on Public Health*, Birmingham: Public Health Alliance.

McConville, M. and Wilson, G. (2002) *Handbook of the Criminal Justice Process*, Oxford: Oxford University Press.

McConville, M., Sanders, A. and Leng, R. (1991) *The Case for the Prosecution*, London: Routledge.

McConville, S. (1998) 'The Victorian Prison: England, 1865–1965', in N. Morris and D. Rothman (eds) *Oxford History of the Prison: The Practice of Punishment in Western Society*, Oxford: Oxford University Press.

McCracken, S. (1998) *Pulp: Reading Popular Fiction*, Manchester: Manchester University Press.

McDermott, K. and King, R. (1988) 'Mind Games: Where the Action Is in Prisons', *British Journal of Criminology*, 28 (3): 357–77.

Macdonald, Lord (2011) *Review of Counter-Terrorism and Security Powers*, London: HMSO.

MacDonald, R. and Marsh, J. (2002) 'Crossing the Rubicon: Youth Transitions, Poverty, Drugs and Social Exclusion', *International Journal of Drug Policy*, 13: 27–38.

MacGlynn, C. (2010) 'Marginalizing Feminism? Debating Extreme Pornography Laws in Public and Policy Discourse', in K. Boyle (ed.) *Everyday Pornography*, London: Routledge.

McGoey, L. and Jackson, E. (2009) 'Seroxat and the Suppression of Trial Data: Regulatory Failure and the Uses of Legal Ambiguity', *Journal of Medical Ethics*, 36 (2): 107–12.

McGuire, J. (ed.) (1995) *What Works: Reducing Re-offending*, Chichester: Wiley.

McIntosh, M. (1975) *The Organisation of Crime*, London: Macmillan.

McIntosh, M. (1978) 'Who Needs Prostitutes?', in C. Smart (ed.) *Women, Sexuality and Social Control*, London: Routledge.

Mack, J. (1964) 'Full-Time Miscreants, Delinquent Neighbourhoods and Criminal Networks', *British Journal of Sociology*, 15: 38–53.

McKie, R. (2009) 'Britain Set to Become Most Populous Country in EU', *The Observer*, 22 March.

MacKinnon, C. A. (1987) *Feminism Unmodified: Discourses on Life and Law*, Cambridge, MA: Harvard University Press.

MacKinnon, C. A. (1998) 'Rape, Genocide, and Women's Human Rights', in S. G. French, W. Teays and L. M. Purdy (eds) *Violence Against Women: Philosophical Perspectives*, Ithaca, NY: Cornell University Press.

McLaren, A. (1997) *The Trials of Masculinity*, Chicago, IL: University of Chicago Press.

McLaughlin, E. (1994) *Community, Policing and Accountability*, Aldershot: Avebury.

McLaughlin, E. (2001) 'Political Violence, Terrorism and States of Fear', in J. Muncie and E. McLaughlin (eds) *The Problem of Crime*, 2nd edn, London: Sage/Open University.

McLaughlin, E. (2006) 'Terrorism', in E. McLaughlin and J. Muncie (eds) *Sage Dictionary of Criminology*, 2nd edn, London: Sage.

McLaughlin, E. (2007) *The New Policing*, London: Sage.

McLaughlin, E. and Murji, K. (1997) 'The Future Lasts a Long Time: Public Policework and the Managerialist Paradox', in P. Francis, P. Davies and V. Jupp (eds) *Policing Futures: The Police, Law Enforcement and the Twenty-First Century*, Basingstoke: Macmillan.

McLaughlin, E. and Muncie, J. (1999) 'Walled Cities: Surveillance, Regulation and Segregation', in S. Pile, C. Brook and G. Mooney (eds) *Unruly Cities*, London: Routledge.

McLaughlin, E. and Muncie, J. (2000) 'The Criminal Justice System: New Labour's New Partnerships', in J. Clarke, S. Gewirtz and E. McLaughlin (eds) *New Managerialism, New Welfare?*, London: Sage.

McLaughlin, E., Fergusson, R., Hughes, G. and Westmarland, L. (2003) *Restorative Justice: Critical Issues*, London: Sage.

McLeod, E. (1982) *Women Working: Prostitution Now*, London: Croom Helm.

McMurran, M. and Hollin, C. (1989) 'Drinking and Delinquency', *British Journal of Criminology*, 29 (4): 386–93.

McNair, B. (2002) *Striptease Culture: Sex, Media and the Democratisation of Desire*, London: Routledge.

McNair, B. (2010) 'From Porn Chic to Porn Fear: The Return of the Repressed', in F. Attwood (ed.) *Mainstreaming Sex*, London: I. B. Taurus.

McNaughton, J. (2003) 'Maddening Thing Is That Record Firms Could Have Done It', *Observer*, Business Section, 4 May: 6.

McNay, L. (1994) *Foucault: A Critical Introduction*, Cambridge: Polity.

Macpherson, Sir W. (1999) *The Stephen Lawrence Inquiry: Report of an Inquiry by Sir William Macpherson of Cluny*, Cm 4262, London: The Stationery Office.

McRobbie, A. (1994) *Postmodernism and Popular Culture*, London: Routledge.

McRobbie, A. (2005) *The Uses of Cultural Studies*, London: Sage.

McRobbie, A. (2006) 'Vulnerability, Violence and (Cosmopolitan) Ethics: Butler's Precarious Life', *British Journal of Sociology*, 57 (1): 69–86.

McRobbie, A. (2008) *The Aftermath of Feminism: Gender, Culture and Social Change*, London: Sage.

McRobbie, A. and Thornton, S. (1995) 'Rethinking Moral Panics for Multi-mediated Social Worlds', *British Journal of Sociology*, 46 (4): 559–74.

McVeigh, D. (2003) 'Rogue Advisors Profit from Asylum Misery', *Tribune*, 67 (3)2: 5.

Maguire, M. (1982) *Burglary in a Dwelling*, London: Heinemann.

Maguire, M. (1997) 'Crime Statistics, Patterns, and Trends: Changing Perceptions and their Implications', in M. Maguire, R. Morgan and R. Reiner (eds) *Oxford Handbook of Criminology*, 2nd edn, Oxford: Clarendon Press.

Maguire, M. (2012) 'Criminal Statistics and the Construction of Crime', in M. Maguire, R. Morgan, and R. Reiner (eds) *Oxford Handbook of Criminology*, 5th edn, Oxford: Oxford University Press

Maguire, M. and Corbett, C. (1987) *The Effects of Crime and the Work of Victim Support Schemes*, Aldershot: Gower.

Maguire, M. and Corbett, C. (1991) *A Study of the Police Complaints System*, London: Home Office.

Maguire, M. and John, T. (2006) 'Intelligence Led Policing, Managerialism and Community Engagement: Competing Priorities and the Role of the National Intelligence Model in the UK', *Policing and Society*, 16 (1): 67–85.

Maguire, M., Morgan, R. and Reiner, R. (2002) *Oxford Handbook of Criminology*, 3rd edn (4th edn, 2007; 5th edn, 2012), Oxford: Oxford University Press.

Maher, L. and Dixon, D. (1999) 'Policing and Public Health', *British Journal of Criminology*, 39 (4): 488–512.

Mahood, L. (1995) *Policing Gender: Class and Family in Britain, 1800–1945*, London: UCL Press.

Man, L.-H., Best, D., Marshall, J., Godfrey, C. and Budd, T. (2002) *Dealing with Alcohol-related Detainees in the Custody Suite*, Home Office Findings 178, London: Home Office.

Mandel, R. (1999) *Deadly Transfers and the Global Playground: Transnational Security Threats in a Disorderly World*, Westport, CT: Praeger.

Mann, N. (2012) *Doing Harder Time? The Experiences of an Aging Male Prison Population in England and Wales*, Aldershot: Ashgate.

Mannheim, H. (1965) *Comparative Criminology, Vol. 2*, London: Routledge and Kegan Paul.

Manning, P. (1979) 'The Social Control of Police Work', in S. Holdaway (ed.) *The British Police*, London: Edward Arnold.

Manning, P. K. (2000) 'Policing New Social Spaces', in J. Sheptycki (ed.) *Issues in Transnational Policing*, London: Routledge.

Manningham-Buller, E. (2011) *Terror*, BBC Reith Lectures 2011, available from: http://www.bbc.co.uk/programmes/b0145x77

Mars, G. (1982) *Cheats at Work: An Anthropology of Workplace Crime*, London: George Allen and Unwin.

Mars, G. (2006) 'Changes in Occupational Deviance: Scams, Fiddles and Sabotage in the 21st Century', *Crime, Law and Social Change*, 12: 285–96.

Martin, C. (1996) 'The Impact of Equal Opportunities Policies on the Day-to-Day Experiences of Women Police Constables', *British Journal of Criminology*, 36 (4): 510–28.

Martin, T. and Romero, A. (1992) *Multinational Crime*, London: Sage.

Martinson, R. (1974) 'What Works? Questions and Answers about Prison Reform', *The Public Interest*, 35: 22–54.

Marx, G. (2002) 'What's New about the New Surveillance? Classifying for Change and Continuity', *Surveillance and Society*, 1 (1): 9–29.

Marx, K. (1843/1971) *Critique of Hegel's 'Philosophy of Right'*, Cambridge: Cambridge University Press.

Marx, K. and Engels, F. (1845/1975) *Collected Works*, Vol. 4: 248–9, Moscow: Progress Publishers; London: Lawrence and Wishart.

Mason, P. (1970) *Patterns of Dominance*, Oxford: Oxford University Press.

Mason, P. (2006) 'Turn on, Tune in, Slop out', in P. Mason (ed.) *Captured by the Media: Prison Discourse in Popular Culture*, Cullompton: Willan.

Mason-Bish, H. (2012) 'Examining the Boundaries of Hate Crime Policy: Considering Age and Gender', *Criminal Justice Policy Review*, http://cjp. sagepub.com/content/early/2012/01/03/08 87403411431495

Mathiesen, T. (1965) *The Defences of the Weak*, London: Tavistock.

Mathiesen, T. (1974) *The Politics of Abolition*, London: Martin Robertson.

Matravers, M. (2000) *Justice and Punishment: The Rationale of Coercion*, Oxford: Oxford University Press.

Matravers, M. (ed.) (2005) *Managing Modernity: Politics and the Culture of Control*, London: Routledge.

Matrix Knowledge Group (2007) *The Illicit Drug Trade in the United Kingdom*, 2nd edn, London: Home Office Online Report 20/07.

Matthews, M. (2002) 'Crime Control in Late Modernity: A Review Essay', *Theoretical Criminology*, 6 (2): 217–27.

Matthews, R. (1989) *Privatizing Criminal Justice*, London: Sage.

Matthews, R. (1999) *Doing Time: An Introduction to the Sociology of Imprisonment*, Basingstoke: Macmillan.

Matthews, R. (2002) *Armed Robbery*, Cullompton: Willan.

Matza, D. (1964) *Delinquency and Drift*, New York: Wiley.

Matza, D. (1969) *Becoming Deviant*, Englewood Cliffs, NJ: Prentice Hall.

Mauer, M. (1997) *Intended and Unintended Consequences: State Racial Disparities in Imprisonment*, Washington, DC: The Sentencing Project.

Mauer, M. (2001) 'The Causes and Consequences of Prison Growth in the United States', *Punishment and Society*, 3 (2): 9–20.

Maung, N. A. (1995) *Young People, Victimisation and the Police*, Home Office Research Study 140, London: Home Office.

Mawby, R. (ed.) (1999) *Policing across the World: Issues for the Twenty-first Century*, London: UCL Press.

Mawby, R. (2001) *Burglary*, Cullompton: Willan.

Mawby, R. and Walklate, S. (1994) *Critical Victimology*, London: Sage.

Maxfield, M. G. and Babbie, E. (2007) *Research Methods for Criminal Justice and Criminology*, 5th edn, Belmont, CA: Wadsworth.

May, T. (1991) *Probation: Politics, Policy and Practice*, Milton Keynes: Open University Press.

Mayhew, P. and Van Dijk, J. J. M. (1997) *Criminal Victimisation in Eleven Industrialised Countries: Key Findings from the 1996 International Crime Victims Survey*, The Hague: Ministry of Justice, WODC.

Mead, G. H. (1918) 'The Psychology of Punitive Justice', *American Journal of Sociology*, 23: 577–602.

Mead, G. H. (1934) *Mind, Self and Society*, Chicago, IL: University of Chicago Press.

Measham, F. (2004) 'Play Space: Historical and Socio-cultural Reflections on Drugs, Licensed Leisure Locations, Commercialisation and Control', *International Journal of Drug Policy*, 15 (5): 337–45.

Measham, F. and Moore, K. (2008) 'The Criminalisation of Intoxication', in P. Squires (ed.) *ASBO Nation: The Criminalisation of Nuisance*, Bristol: Policy Press.

Measham, F. and South, N. (2012) 'Drugs, Alcohol and Crime', in M. Maguire, R. Morgan and R. Reiner (eds) *Oxford Handbook of Criminology*, 5th edn, Oxford: Oxford University Press.

Melossi, D. and Pavarini, M. (1978) *The Prison and the Factory: The Origins of the Penitentiary System*, Basingstoke: Macmillan.

Mena, F. and Hobbs, D. (2010) 'Narcophobia: Drugs Prohibition and the Generation of Human Rights Abuses', *Trends in Organized Crime*, 13 (1): 60–74.

Mendelsohn, B. (1956) 'Une nouvelle branche de la science bio-psycho-sociale: victimologie', *Revue Internationale de Criminologie et de Police Technique*: 10–31.

Mendelson, S. (2005) *Barracks and Brothels – Peacekeepers and Human Trafficking in the Balkans*, Washington, DC: Centre for Strategic and International Studies Press.

Merton, R. K. (1938) 'Social Structure and Anomie', *American Sociological Review*, 3: 672–82.

Messerschmidt, J. W. (1993) *Masculinities and Crime: Critique and Reconceptualization of Theory*, Lanham, MD: Rowman and Littlefield.

Messerschmidt, J.W. (1997) *Crime as Structured Action*, London: Sage.

Messerschmidt, J. W. (2000) *Nine Lives: Adolescence Masculinities, the Body and Violence*, Boulder, CO: Westview.

Messerschmidt, J. W. (2007) '"We Must Protect Our Southern Women": On Whiteness, Masculinities and Lynching', in M. Bosworth and J. Flavin (eds) *Race, Gender and Punishment: From Colonialism to the War on Terror*, New Brunswick, NJ: Rutgers University Press.

Meyers, M. (1997) *News Coverage of Violence against Women: Engendering Blame*, London: Sage.

Michalowski, R. (1985) *Order, Law and Crime*, New York: Random House.

Michalowski, R. and Kramer, R. (1987) 'The Space between Laws: The Problem of Corporate Crime in a Transnational Context', *Social Problems*, 34 (1): 34–53.

Miers, D. (1992) 'The Responsibilities and the Rights of Victims of Crime', *Modern Law Review*, 55: 482.

Miers, S. (2003) *Slavery in the Twentieth Century: The Evolution of a Global Problem*, Walnut Creek, CA: Alta Mira Press.

Miguel, E. (2005) 'Poverty and Witch Killing', *Review of Economic Studies*, 72 (4): 1153–72.

Milgram, S. (1963) 'Behavioural Study of Obedience', *Journal of Abnormal Social Psychology*, 67: 371–8.

Miller, A. (1962) 'The Bored and the Violent', *Harper's*, 25, November, reprinted in P. O'Malley and S. Mugford (1994) 'Crime, Excitement, and Modernity', in G. Barak (ed.) *Varieties of Criminology: Readings from a Dynamic Discipline*, Westport, CT: Praeger.

Miller, D. and Kitzinger, J. (1998) 'AIDS, the Policy Process and Moral Panics', in D. Miller, J. Kitzinger, K. Williams and P. Beharrell (eds) *The Circuit of Mass Communication*, London: Sage.

Miller, E. (1986) *Street Women*, Philadelphia, PA: Temple.

Miller, V. (2011) *Understanding Digital Culture*, London: Sage.

Millie, A., Jacobson, J. and Hough, M. (2005) 'Understanding the Growth in the Prison Population in England and Wales', in C. Elmsley (ed.) *The Persistent Prison: Problems, Images and Alternatives*, London: Francis Boutle.

Millington, G. (2005) 'Meaning, Materials and Melancholia: Understanding the Palace Hotel', *Social and Cultural Geography*, 6 (4): 531–49.

Mills, C.W. (1959) *The Sociological Imagination*, New York: Oxford University Press.

Milovanovic, D. (2012) 'Postmodern Criminology', in W. DeKeseredy and M. Dragiewicz (eds) *Routledge Handbook of Critical Criminology*, London: Routledge.

Ministry of Justice (2007) *Judicial and Court Statistics 2006*, London: Ministry of Justice.

Ministry of Justice (2008) *Statistics on Race and the Criminal Justice System, 2006/7*, London: HMSO.

Ministry of Justice (2010) *Statistics on Race and the Criminal Justice System, 2008/9*, London: Ministry of Justice.

Ministry of Justice (2011) *Statistics on Race and the Criminal Justice System, 2010*, London: HMSO.

Ministry of Justice (2012a) 'Offender Management Statistics Quarterly Bulletin: April to June 2012, England and Wales', London: Ministry of Justice.

Ministry of Justice (2012b) 'Prison Population Monthly Bulletin, September 2012'. London: Ministry of Justice.

Ministry of Justice (2012c) *Restorative Justice Action Plan for the Criminal Justice System*, London: Ministry of Justice.

Mirrlees-Black, C. (1999) *Domestic Violence: Findings from a New British Crime Survey Self-Completion Questionnaire*, Home Office Research Study 191, London: Home Office.

Mirrlees-Black, C. and Ross, A. (1995) *Crimes against Retail and Manufacturing Premises: Findings from the 1994 Commercial Victimization Survey*, Home Office Research Study 146, London: Home Office.

Mirrlees-Black, C., Budd, T., Partridge, S. and Mayhew, P. (1998) *The 1998 British Crime Survey*, Home Office Statistical Bulletin 19/96, London: Home Office.

Modood, T. and Berthoud, R. (1997) *Ethnic Minorities in Britain: Diversity and Disadvantage*, London: Policy Studies Institute.

Mollen Commission (1994) *Report of the Commission to Investigate Allegations of Police Corruption and the Anticorruption Procedures of the Police Department*, New York: Mollen Commission.

Monaghan, M. (2012) 'The Recent Evolution of UK Drug Strategies: from Maintenance to Behaviour Change?' *People, Place & Policy Online*, 6/1: 29–40.

Mooney, J. (1993) *The North London Domestic Violence Survey*, London: Middlesex University.

Mooney, J. (2012) 'Finding a Political Voice: The Emergence of Critical Criminology in Britain', in W. DeKeseredy and M. Dragiewicz (eds) *Routledge Handbook of Critical Criminology*, London: Routledge.

Moran, D. (2013) *Carceral Geography: Prisons, Power and Space*, Aldershot: Ashgate.

Moretti, F. (1990) 'Clues', in T. Bennett (ed.) *Popular Fiction: Technology, Ideology, Production, Reading*, London: Routledge.

Morgan, J. (2002) 'US Hate Crime Legislation: A Legal Model to Avoid in Australia', *Journal of Sociology*, 38 (1): 25–48.

Morgan, P. (1978) *Delinquent Fantasies*, London: Temple Smith.

Morgan, R. (2000) 'The Utilitarian Justification of Torture: Denial, Desert and Disinformation', *Punishment and Society*, 2 (2): 181–96.

Morgan, R. (2002) 'Imprisonment: A Brief History, the Contemporary Scene, and Likely Prospects', in M. Maguire, R. Morgan and R. Reiner (eds) *Oxford Handbook of Criminology*, 3rd edn, Oxford: Oxford University Press.

Morgan, R. (2007) 'Children and Young Persons', in Y. Jewkes (ed.) *Handbook on Prisons*, Cullompton: Willan.

Morgan, R. and Newburn, T. (1997) *The Future of Policing*, Oxford: Clarendon Press.

Morgan, R. and Sanders, A. (1999) *The Uses of Victim Statements*, Home Office RDS Occasional Paper, London: Home Office.

Morgan, R. and Russell, N. (2000) *The Judiciary in the Magistrates' Courts*, Home Office RDS Occasional Paper 66, London: Home Office.

Morgan, R. and Liebling, A. (2007) 'Imprisonment: An Expanding Scene', in M. Maguire, R. Morgan and R. Reiner (eds) *Oxford Handbook of Criminology*, 4th edn, Oxford: Oxford University Press.

Morris, J. (2006) 'The National Reassurance Policing Programme: A Ten-site Evaluation', Home Office Research Findings 273. Home Office: London.

Morris, L. (1994) *The Dangerous Classes: The Underclass and Citizenship*, London: Routledge.

Morris, L. (ed.) (2006) *Rights: Sociological Perspectives*, London: Routledge.

Mortimore, J. (2011) 'Policy Change and the Street Level Policing of Children and Young People in a Home Counties Police Force', Unpublished PhD Thesis, University of Bedfordshire.

Morton, J. (1992) *Gangland*, London: Little, Brown.

Moses, E. R. (1947) 'Differentials in Crime Rates between Negroes and Whites Based on Comparisons of Four Socio-economically Equated Areas', *American Sociological Review*, 12: 411–20.

Mullins, C. (2009) 'We are Going to Rape You and Taste Tutsi Women', *British Journal of Criminology*, 49: 719–35.

Muncie, J. (1999) *Youth and Crime: A Critical Introduction*, London: Sage.

Muncie, J. (2001) 'The Construction and Deconstruction of Crime', in J. Muncie and E. McLaughlin (eds) *The Problem of Crime*, 2nd edn, London: Sage/Open University.

Muncie, J. (2004) *Youth and Crime: A Critical Introduction*, 2nd edn, London: Sage.

Muncie, J (2009) *Youth and Crime*, London: Sage

Muncie, J., McLaughlin, E. and Langan, M. (eds) (1996) *Criminological Perspectives: A Reader* (2nd edn, 2003), London: Sage/Open University.

Murdock, G. (1997) 'Reservoirs of Dogma: An Archaeology of Popular Anxieties', in M. Barker and J. Petley (eds) *Ill Effects: The Media/Violence Debate*, London: Routledge.

Murphy, J. G. (1994) 'Marxism and Retribution', in R. Duff and D. Garland (eds) *A Reader on Punishment*, Oxford: Oxford University Press.

Murray, A. (1998) 'Debt-bondage and Trafficking: Don't Believe the Hype', in K. Kempadoo and J. Doezema (eds) *Global Sex Workers*, London: Routledge.

Murray, C. (1997) *Does Prison Work?*, London: Institute for Economic Affairs.

Murray, C. *et al.* (1990) *The Emerging British Underclass*, London: IEA Health and Welfare Unit.

Mythen, G. and Walklate, S. (2006) 'Criminology and Terrorism: Which Thesis? Risk Society or Governmentality?', *British Journal of Criminology*, 46 (3): 379–98.

NACRO (2001) 'Children, Health and Crime', *Impact: International Journal of Health Equality*, 1: 13–15.

NACRO (2001–2) 'Women Offenders', *Safer Society*, 11: 27–8.

NACRO (2002) 'Drug Misuse Is a Health Issue, Say Police Chiefs', *Safer Society*, 13: 14.

Nadelman, E. (1990) 'Global Prohibition Regimes: The Evolution of Norms in International Society', *International Organization*, 44 (4): 479–526.

Naffine, N. (1990) *Law and the Sexes*, London: Allen and Unwin.

Naffine, N. (1995) *Gender, Crime and Feminism*, Aldershot: Dartmouth.

Naffine, N. (1997) *Feminism and Criminology*, Cambridge: Polity.

Naím, M (2005) *Illicit: How Smugglers, Traffickers, and Copycats are Hijacking the Global Economy*, New York: Doubleday.

Namrouqa, H. (2007) 'Experts Focus on Water Management, Conflict Resolution', *The Jordan Times*, 23 October: 3.

National Board for Crime Prevention (1994) *Wise after the Event: Tackling Repeat Victimisation*, London: Home Office.

Naudé, C. M. B., Prinsloo, J. H. and Ladikos, A. (2006) *Experiences of Crime in Thirteen African Countries: Results from the International Crime Victim Survey*, Turin: UNICRI-UNODC.

Naughton, M. (2007) *Rethinking Miscarriages of Justice: Beyond the Tip of the Iceberg*, Basingstoke: Macmillan.

Neale, J. (2004) 'Measuring the Health of Scottish Drug Users', *Health and Social Care in the Community*, 12 (3): 202–11.

Nelken, D. (1989) 'Discipline and Punish: Some Notes on the Margin', *Howard Journal of Criminal Justice*, 28 (4): 245–54.

Nelken, D. (1994a) 'White Collar Crime', in M. Maguire, R. Morgan and R. Reiner (eds) *Oxford Handbook of Criminology*, Oxford: Oxford University Press.

Nelken, D. (ed.) (1994b) *The Futures of Criminology*, London: Sage.

Nellemann, C., Redmond, I. and Refisch, J. (eds) (2010) *The Last Stand of the Gorilla: Environmental Crime and Conflict in the Congo Basin*, A Rapid Response Assessment. United Nations Environment Programme, GRID-Arendal. Accessed at: http://www.grida.no/publications/rr/gorilla/

Nellis, M. (2003) 'News Media, Popular Culture and the Electronic Monitoring of Offenders in England and Wales', *Howard Journal of Criminal Justice*, 42 (1): 1–31.

New York Times, The (2013a) 'Poll Finds Strong Acceptance for Public Surveillance', 30 April, available: http://www.nytimes.com/2013/05/01/us/poll-finds-strong-acceptance-for-public-surveillance.html?pagewanted=all&_r=0

New York Times, The (2013b) 'Bombings Trip Up Reddit in Its Turn in Spotlight', 28 April, available: http://www.nytimes.com/2013/04/29/business/media/bombings-trip-up-reddit-in-its-turn-in-spotlight.html?pagewanted=all&_r=0

Newburn, T. (1999) *Understanding and Preventing Police Corruption: Lessons from the Literature*, Home Office Police Research Studies 110, London: Home Office.

Newburn, T. (2002a) 'Young People, Crime, and Youth Justice', in M. Maguire, R. Morgan and R. Reiner (eds) *Oxford Handbook of Criminology*, 3rd edn, Oxford: Oxford University Press.

Newburn, T. (2002b) 'Community Safety and Policing: Some Implications of the Crime and Disorder Act 1998', in G. Hughes, E. McLaughlin and J. Muncie (eds) *Crime Prevention and Community Safety: New Directions*, London: Sage.

Newburn, T. (ed.) (2003/2008) *Handbook of Policing*, Cullompton: Willan.

Newburn, T. (ed.) (2005) *Policing: Key Readings*, Cullompton: Willan.

Newburn, T. and Stanko, E. (eds) (1994) *Just Boys Doing Business?*, London: Routledge.

Newburn, T. and Sparks, R. (eds) (2004) *Criminal Justice and Political Cultures: National and International Dimensions of Crime Control*, Cullompton: Willan.

Newman, G. (ed.) (1999) *Global Report on Crime and Justice*, New York: Oxford University Press.

Newman, O. (1972) *Defensible Space*, New York: Macmillan.

Newman, O. (1996) *Creating Defensible Space*, New York: Rutgers and US Department of Housing and Urban Development.

Nicholas, S. and Walker, A. (2004) *Crime in England and Wales 2002/2003: Supplementary Volume 2: Crime, Disorder and the Criminal Justice System – Public Attitudes and Perceptions*, London: Home Office.

Nicholas, S., Povey, D., Walker, A. and Kershaw, C. (2005) *Crime in England and Wales 2004/2005*, Home Office Statistical Bulletin 11/05, London: Home Office.

Nicholas, S., Kershaw, C. and Walker, A. (2007) *Crime in England and Wales 2006/7*, 4th edn, London: Home Office.

Nietzsche, F. (1887/1996) *On the Genealogy of Morals*, Oxford: Oxford University Press.

Nightingale, C. (1993) *On the Edge*, New York: Basic Books.

Nikunen, K., Paasonen, S. and Saarenmaa, L. (eds) (2007) *Pornification: Sex and Sexuality in Media Culture*, Oxford: Berg.

Noaks, L. and Wincup, E. (2004) *Criminological Research: Understanding Qualitative Methods*, London: Sage.

Norris, C. and Armstrong, G. (1999) *The Maximum Surveillance Society*, Oxford: Berg.

Norris, C., Fielding, N., Kemp, C. and Fielding, J. (1992) 'Black and Blue: An Analysis of the Influence of Race on Being Stopped by the Police', *British Journal of Sociology*, 43: 207–24.

NSPCC (2013) 'Statistics on Children under One', http://www.nspcc.org.uk/Inform/resourcesforprofessionals/children_under_one_statistics_wda79305.html

O'Brien, M. (2008) 'Criminal Degradations of Consumer Culture', in R. Sollund (ed.) *Global Harms, Ecological Crime and Speciesism*, New York: Nova.

O'Byrne, D. J. (2003) *Human Rights: An Introduction*, Harlow: Longman.

O'Connell, R., Price, J. and Barrow, C. (2004) *Cyber Stalking, Abusive Cyber Sex and Online Grooming: A Programme for Teenagers*, Preston: Cyberspace Research Unit.

O'Donnell, I. and Milner, C. (2007) *Child Pornography: Crime, Computers and Society*, Cullompton: Willan.

O'Donovan, K. (1993) 'Law's Knowledge: The Judge, the Expert, the Battered Woman, and Her Syndrome', *Journal of Law and Society*, 20 (4): 427–37.

O'Duffy, B. (2007) 'The Liberation Tigers of Tamil Eelam (LTTE): Majoritarianism, Self-Determination and Military-to-Political Transitions in Sri Lanka', in M. Heiburg, B. O'Leary and J. Tirman (eds) *Terror, Insurgency and States*, Philadelphia, PA: University of Pennsylvania.

O'Hear, M. (2004) 'Sentencing the Green Collar Offender: Punishment, Culpability and Environmental Crime', *Journal of Criminal Law and Criminology*, 95 (1): 133–276.

O'Mahony, D. and Quinn, K. (1999) 'Fear of Crime and Locale: The Impact of Community Related Factors upon Fear of Crime', *International Review of Victimology*, 6: 231–51.

O'Malley, P. (1992) 'Risk, Power and Crime Prevention', *Economy and Society*, 21 (3): 242–75.

O'Malley, P. (1999) 'Volatile and Contradictory Punishment', *Theoretical Criminology*, 3 (2): 175–96.

O'Malley, P. and Mugford, S. (1994) 'Crime, Excitement and Modernity', in G. Barak (ed.) *Varieties of Criminology: Readings from a Dynamic Discipline*, Westport, CT: Praeger.

O'Toole, L. (1998) *Pornocopia: Porn, Sex, Technology and Desire*, London: Serpent's Tail.

Oberwittler, D. (2005) 'Social Exclusion and Youth Crime in Europe – The Spatial Dimension', Plenary Presentation at the Fifth Annual Conference of the European Society of Criminology, Krakow, Poland.

Office for National Statistics (2013) *Crime in England and Wales, year ending December 2012*, London: ONS.

Ogg, J. and Munn-Giddings, C. (1993) 'Researching Elder Abuse', *Ageing and Society*, 13: 389–413.

Ogletree, C. and Sarat, A. (eds) (2006) *From Lynch Mobs to the Killing State: Race and the Death Penalty in America*, New York: NYU Press.

Omand, D. (2010) *Securing the State*, London: Hurst.

Orwell, G. (1933) *Down and Out in Paris and London*, London: Victor Gollancz.

Osborne, R. (1995) 'Crime and the Media: From Media Studies to Post-modernism', in D. Kidd-Hewitt and R. Osborne (eds) *Crime and the Media: The Post-modern Spectacle*, London: Pluto.

Ost, S. (2004) 'Getting to Grips with Sexual Grooming? The New Offence under the Sexual Offences Act 2003', *Journal of Social Welfare and Family Law*, 26 (2): 147–59.

Owers, A. (2003) 'BIHR Human Rights Lecture: Prison Inspection and the Protection of Human Rights' www.homeoffice.gov.uk/docs2/bihr lecture.html (accessed 19 September 2004), reprinted in *European Human Rights Law Review*, 2004, No. 2.

Paasonen, S., Nikunen, K. and Saarenmaa, L. (eds) (2007) *Pornification: Sex and Sexuality in Media Culture*, Oxford: Berg.

Paehlke, R. (1995) 'Environmental Harm and Corporate Crime', in F. Pearce and L. Snyder (eds) *Corporate Crime: Contemporary Debates*, Toronto: University of Toronto Press.

Pain, R. (1991) 'Space, Sexual Violence and Social Control: Integrating Geographical and Feminist Analyses of Women's Fear of Crime', *Progress in Human Geography*, 15 (4): 415–31.

Pain, R. and Smith, S. J. (2008) *Fear: Critical Geopolitics and Everyday Life*, Aldershot: Ashgate.

Painter, K. and Farrington, D. (1998) 'Marital Violence in Great Britain and Its Relationship to Marital and Non-marital Rape', *International Review of Victimology*, 5: 257–76.

Pantazis, C. (1999) 'The Criminalization of Female Poverty', in S. Watson and L. Doyal (eds) *Engendering Social Policy*, Buckingham: Open University Press.

Pantazis, C. (2000) 'Tackling Inequalities in Crime and Social Harm', in C. Pantazis and D. Gordon (eds) *Tackling Inequalities: Where are We Now and What Can Be Done?*, Bristol: Policy Press.

Pantazis, C. and Pemberton, S. (2009) 'From the 'Old' to the 'New' Suspect Community: Examining the Impacts of Recent UK Counter-Terrorist Legislation' *British Journal of Criminology*, 49 (5): 646–66.

Paoli, L. (2003) *Mafia Brotherhoods: Organized Crime, Italian Style*, Oxford: Oxford University Press.

Paoli, L. and Fijnaut, C. (2006) 'Organised Crime and Its Control Policies', *European Journal of Crime, Criminal Law and Criminal Justice*, 13 (3): 307–27.

Pape, R. (2005) *Dying to Win: The Strategic Logic of Suicide Terrorism*, London: Random House.

Park, C. (2001) 'The Three Faces of Retail Theft', *New Zealand Security*, February/March (www.ecoliving.co.nz/nzsecurity/mag (accessed 20 December 2001)).

Park, E., Burgess, E. W. and McKenzie, R. D. (1925) *The City*, Chicago, IL: University of Chicago Press.

Parker, H. (1974) *View from the Boys: A Sociology of Down-Town Adolescents*, Newton Abbot: David and Charles.

Parker, H., Sumner, M. and Jarvis, G. (1989) *Unmasking the Magistrates: The 'Custody or Not' Decision in Sentencing Young Offenders*, Milton Keynes: Open University Press.

Parker, H., Aldridge, J. and Measham, F. (1998) *Illegal Leisure: The Normalization of Adolescent Recreational Drug Use*, London: Routledge.

Parmentier, R. (1999) 'Greenpeace and the Dumping of Waste at Sea: A Case of Non-State Actors' Intervention in International Affairs', *International Negotiation: A Journal of Theory and Practice*, 4 (3): 435–57.

Parsons, T. (1960) *Structure and Process in Modern Society*, New York: Free Press.

Parssinen, T. (1983) *Secret Passions, Secret Remedies: Narcotic Drugs in British Society, 1820–1930*, Manchester: Manchester University Press.

Pascoe, P. (1990) *Relations of Rescue: The Search for Female Moral Authority in the American West, 1874–1939*, New York: Oxford University Press.

Pashukanis, E. B. (1924/1978) *Law and Marxism: A General Theory*, London: Ink Links.

Passas, N. (1995) '"I Cheat, Therefore I Exist?" The BCCI Scandal in Context', in N. Passas (ed.) *Organized Crime*, Aldershot: Dartmouth.

Patel, R. (2010) 'Mozambique's Food Riots – the True Face of Global Warming', *The Observer*, 5 September, 31.

Patrick, J. (1973) *A Glasgow Gang Observed*, London: Eyre Methuen.

Pearce, F. (1976) *Crimes of the Powerful*, London: Pluto.

Pearce, F. and Tombs, S. (1998) *Toxic Capitalism: Corporate Crime and the Chemical Industry*, Aldershot: Ashgate.

Pearson, G. (1983) *Hooligan: A History of Respectable Fears*, London: Macmillan.

Pearson, G. (1987) 'Social Deprivation, Unemployment and Patterns of Heroin Use', in N. Dorn and N. South (eds) *A Land Fit for Heroin? Drug Policies, Prevention and Practice*, Basingstoke: Macmillan.

Pearson, G. (1992) 'The Role of Culture in the Drug Question', in G. Edwards, M. Lader and C. Drummond (eds) *The Nature of Alcohol and Drug Related Problems*, Oxford: Oxford University Press.

Pearson, J. (1973) *The Profession of Violence*, London: Panther.

Pease, K. (1998) *Repeat Victimisation: Taking Stock, Crime Detection and Prevention*, Paper 90, London: Home Office.

Peay, J. (2007) 'Detain – Restrain – Control: Sliding Scale or Slippery Slope?', in D. Downes, P. Rock, C. Chinkin and C. Gearty (eds) *Crime, Social Control and Human Rights: From Moral Panics to States of Denial, Essays in Honour of Stanley Cohen*, Cullompton: Willan.

Penfold-Mounce, R., Beer, D. and Burrows, R. (2011) 'The Wire as Social Science-fiction', *Sociology*, 45 (1): 152–67.

Percy, A. (1998) *Ethnicity and Victimization: Findings from the 1996 British Crime Survey*, Home Office Statistical Bulletin 6/98, London: Home Office.

Petchesky, R. P. (2000) 'Sexual Rights: Inventing a Concept, Mapping an International Practice', in R. Parker, R. M. Barbosa and P. Aggleton (eds) *Framing the Sexual Subject: The Politics of Gender, Sexuality and Power*, Berkeley: University of California Press.

Petley, J. (2012) 'Sick Stuff: Law, Criminality and Obscenity' in D. Gunkel and T. Gournelos (eds) *Transgression 2.0: Media, Culture, and the Politics of a Digital Age*, London: Continuum.

Petrow, S. (1994) *Policing Morals: The Metropolitan Police and the Home Office 1870–1994*, Oxford: Clarendon Press.

Philips, D. (1983) '"A Just Measure of Crime, Authority, Hunters and Blue Locusts": The "Revisionist" Social History of Crime and the Law in Britain, 1780–1850', in S. Cohen and A. Scull (eds) *Social Control and the State: Historical and Comparative Essays*, Oxford: Basil Blackwell.

Phillips, C. (2012) *The Multicultural Prison: Ethnicity, Masculinity and Social Relations among Prisoners*, Oxford: Oxford University Press.

Phillips, C. and Brown, D. (1998) *Entry into the Criminal Justice System: A Survey of Police Arrests and Their Outcomes*, Home Office Research Study 185, London: Home Office.

Phillips, C. and Bowling, B. (2007) 'Ethnicities, Racism, Crime, and Criminal Justice', in M. Maguire, R. Morgan and R. Reiner (eds) *Oxford Handbook of Criminology*, 4th edn, Oxford: Oxford University Press.

Phillips, C. and Bowling, B. (2012) 'Ethnicities, Racism, Crime, and Criminal Justice', in M. Maguire, R. Morgan and R. Reiner (eds) *Oxford Handbook of Criminology*, 5th edn, Oxford: Oxford University Press.

Phillips, M. (2001) *America's Social Revolution*, London: Civitas.

Phillips, M. (2002) 'Hate Crime: The Orwellian Response to Prejudice', in P. Iganski (ed.) *The Hate Debate: Should Hate be Punished as a Crime?*, London: Profile.

Phillips, T. (2005) *Knock-Off: The Deadly Trade in Counterfeit Goods*, London: Kogan Page.

Phillips, T. (2006) 'Counterfeiting Becomes a Really Big Business', *Manufacturing and Technology News*, at: http://www.manufacturingnews.com/news/editorials/phillips.html

Pick, D. (1989) *Faces of Degeneration: A European Disorder, c.1848–c.1918*, Cambridge: Cambridge University Press.

Pinder, D. (2003) 'Mapping Worlds: Cartography and the Politics of Representation', in A. Blunt, P. Gruffudd, J. May, M. Ogborn and D. Pinder (eds) *Cultural Geography in Practice*, London: Arnold.

Piquero, A. R., Farrington, D. P. and Blumstein, A. (2007) *Key Issues in Criminal Career Research: New*

Analyses of the Cambridge Study in Delinquent Development, Cambridge: Cambridge University Press.

Pitts, J. (2003) *The New Politics of Youth Crime: Discipline or Solidarity*, 2nd edn, Lyme Regis: Russell House.

Player, E. (1989) 'Women and Crime in the Inner City', in D. Downes (ed.) *Crime in the City*, Basingstoke: Macmillan.

Player, E. (2005) 'The Reduction of Women's Imprisonment in England and Wales: Will the Reform of Short Prison Sentences Help?', *Punishment and Society*, 7 (4): 419–39.

Plummer, K. (1979) 'Misunderstanding Labelling Perspectives', in D. Downes and P. Rock (eds) *Deviant Interpretations*, London: Martin Robertson.

Plummer, K. (1995) *Telling Sexual Stories*, London: Routledge.

Plummer, K. (ed.) (1997) *The Chicago School: Critical Assessments*, London: Routledge.

Plummer, K. (ed.) (2002) *Sexualities: Critical Concepts in Sociology*, London: Routledge.

Plummer, K. (2003) *Intimate Citizenship: Private Decisions and Public Dialogue*, Seattle: University of Washington Press.

Policy Studies Institute (1983) *Police and People in London*, 4 vols, London: Policy Studies Institute.

Polsky, N. (1967) *Hustlers, Beats and Others*, Chicago, IL: Aldine.

Powell, L. (2008) 'Cancer Drugs at Risk as Plant Species Die Off', *Observer*, 20 January: 12.

Pratt, J. (2007) *Penal Populism*, London: Routledge.

Presdee, M. (2000) *Cultural Criminology and the Carnival of Crime*, London: Routledge.

Presdee, M. (2004) 'The Story of Crime: Biography and the Excavation of Transgression', in J. Ferrell, K. Hayward, W. Morrison and M. Presdee (eds) *Cultural Criminology Unleashed*, London: Glasshouse Press.

Prime, J., White, S., Liriano, S. and Patel, K. (2001) *Criminal Careers of Those Born between 1953 and 1978, England and Wales*, Home Office Statistical Bulletin 4/01, London: Home Office.

Prison Reform Trust (2006) *Bromley Briefings: Prison Factfile November 2006*, London: Prison Reform Trust.

Prison Reform Trust (2011) *Reforming Women's Justice: Final Report of the Women's Justice Taskforce*, London: Prison Reform Trust.

Prison Reform Trust (2012) *Bromley Briefings Prison Factfile, November 2012*, London: Prison Reform Trust.

Prison Service (2001) *Prison Service: Annual Report and Accounts, April 2000 to March 2001*, HC 29, London: Prison Service.

Prison Service (2005) *Annual Report and Accounts, 2004–2005*, HC 193, London: Prison Service.

Prison Service (2008) 'Female Prisoners': www.hmprisonservice.gov.uk/adviceandsupport/prison_life/femaleprisoners/ (accessed 20 February 2008).

Prunier, G. (1995) *The Rwandan Crisis: History of a Genocide*, New York: Columbia University Press.

Pudney, S. (2002) *The Road to Ruin? Sequences of Initiation into Drug Use and Offending by Young People in Britain*, Home Office Research Studies 253, London: Home Office.

Pugh, R. (1968) *Imprisonment in Medieval England*, Cambridge: Cambridge University Press.

Punch, M. (1985) *Conduct Unbecoming*, London: Tavistock.

Punch, M. (1996) *Dirty Business: Exploring Corporate Misconduct*, London: Sage.

Punch, M. (1999) 'Tackling Business Crime Within Companies', *Security Journal*, 12 (2): 39–52.

Punch, M. (2000) 'Suite Violence: Why Managers Murder and Corporations Kill', *Crime, Law and Social Change*, 33: 243–80.

Punch, M. (2003) 'Rotten Orchards: "Pestilence", Police Misconduct and System Failure', *Policing and Society*, 13 (2): 171–96.

Punch, M. (2007) *Zero Tolerance Policing*, Bristol: Policy Press.

Punch, M. and Naylor, T. (1973) 'The Police: A Social Service', *New Society*, 24: 358–61.

Quayle, E. (2010) 'Child Pornography', in Y. Jewkes and M. Yar (eds) *Handbook of Internet Crime*, Cullompton: Willan.

Quinney, R. (1970) *The Social Reality of Crime*, Boston, MA: Little, Brown.

Quinton, P. and Morris, J. (2008) *Neighbourhood Policing: The Impact of Piloting and Early National Implementation*, London: Home Office.

Raco, M. (2003) 'Remaking Place and Securitising Space: Urban Regeneration and the Strategies, Tactics and Practices of Policing in the UK', *Urban Studies*, 40 (9): 1869–87.

Radford, J. (1987) 'Policing Male Violence – Policing Women', in J. Hanmer and M. Maynard (eds) *Women, Violence and Social Control*, Basingstoke: Macmillan.

Radzinowicz, L. and King, J. (1979) *The Growth of Crime: The International Experience*, Harmondsworth: Penguin.

Rafter, N. H. (1997) *Creating Born Criminals*, Chicago: University of Illinois Press.

Rafter, N. and Brown, M. (2011) *Criminology Goes to the Movies: Crime Theory and Popular Culture*, New York: New York University Press.

Raine, L. and Cilluffo, F. (eds) (1994) *Global Organized Crime: The New Empire of Evil*, Washington, DC: Center for Strategic and International Studies.

Raistrick, D., Hodgson, R. and Ritson, B. (eds) (1999) *Tackling Alcohol Together*, London: Free Association Books.

Ranstorp, M. (2007) *Mapping Terrorism Research: State of the Art, Gaps and Future Direction*, London: Routledge.

Rawlings, P. (1992) *Drunks, Whores and Idle Apprentices: Criminal Biographies of the Eighteenth Century*, London: Routledge.

Rawlings, P. (1995) 'The Idea of Policing: A History', *Policing and Society*, 5: 129–49.

Rawlings, P. (1999) *Crime and Power: A History of Criminal Justice, 1688–1998*, Harlow: Longman.

Rawlings, P. (2002) *Policing: A Short History*, Cullompton: Willan.

Rawlings, P. (2008) 'Policing before the Police', in T. Newburn (ed.) *Handbook of Policing*, 2nd edn, Cullompton: Willan.

Rawlinson, P. (1998) 'Russian Organised Crime: Moving Beyond Ideology', in V. Ruggiero, N. South and I. Taylor (eds) *The New European Criminology*, London: Routledge.

Rawls, J. (1972) *A Theory of Justice*, Oxford: Oxford University Press.

Ray, L., Smith, D. and Wastell, L. (2003) 'Understanding Racist Violence', in E. A. Stanko (ed.) *The Meanings of Violence*, London: Routledge.

Raynor, P. (2007) 'Community Penalties: Probation, "What Works", and Offender Management', in M. Maguire, R. Morgan and R. Reiner (eds) *Oxford Handbook of Criminology*, 4th edn, Oxford: Oxford University Press.

Raynor, P. and Vanstone, M. (2002) *Understanding Community Penalties*, Buckingham: Open University Press.

Reiman, J. (1979) *The Rich Get Richer and the Poor Get Prison: Ideology, Class and Criminal Justice*, New York: Wiley.

Reiman, J. (1988) 'The Justice of the Death Penalty in an Unjust World', in K. Haas and J. A. Inciardi (eds) *Challenging Capital Punishment: Legal and Social Science Approaches*, Newbury Park, CA: Sage.

Reiman, J. (2001) *The Rich Get Richer and the Poor Get Prison*, 6th edn (7th edn, 2005), Boston, MA: Allyn and Bacon.

Reiman, J. and Leighton, P. (2003) 'Getting Tough on Corporate Crime? Enron and a Year of Corporate Financial Scandals' (supplement to Reiman, 2001).

Reiner, R. (1992) 'Police Research in the United Kingdom: A Critical Review', in N. Morris and M. Tonry (eds) *Modern Policing*, Chicago, IL: University of Chicago Press.

Reiner, R. (1993) 'Race, Crime and Justice: Models of Interpretation', in L. Gelsthorpe (ed.) *Minority Ethnic Groups in the Criminal Justice System*, Cambridge: Institute of Criminology, University of Cambridge.

Reiner, R. (2000) *The Politics of the Police*, 3rd edn, Oxford: Oxford University Press.

Reiner, R. (2002) 'Media Made Criminality: The Representation of Crime in the Mass Media', in M. Maguire, R. Morgan and R. Reiner (eds) *Oxford Handbook of Criminology*, 3rd edn, Oxford: Oxford University Press.

Reiner, R. (2007a) 'Success or Statistics? New Labour and Crime Control', *Criminal Justice Matters*, 67: 4–5.

Reiner, R. (2007b) 'Political Economy, Crime, and Criminal Justice', in M. Maguire, R. Morgan and R. Reiner (eds) *Oxford Handbook of Criminology*, 4th edn, Oxford: Oxford University Press.

Reiner, R. (2007c) *Law and Order: An Honest Citizen's Guide to Crime and Control*, Cambridge: Polity.

Reiner, R. and Spencer, S. (eds) (1993) *Accountable Policing: Effectiveness, Empowerment and Equity*, London: Institute for Public Policy Research.

Reiner, R., Livingstone, S. and Allen, J. (2001) 'Casino Culture: Media and Crime in a Winner–Loser Society', in K. Stenson and R.

Sullivan (eds) *Crime, Risk and Justice: The Politics of Crime Control in Liberal Democracies*, Cullompton: Willan.

Renzetti, C. (2012) 'Feminist Perspectives in Criminology', in W. DeKeseredy and M. Dragiewicz (eds) *Routledge Handbook of Critical Criminology*, London: Routledge.

Retzinger, S. and Scheff, T. (1996) 'Strategy for Community Conferences: Emotions and Social Bonds', in B. Galaway and J. Hudson (eds) *Restorative Justice: International Perspectives*, Monsey, NY: Criminal Justice Press.

Reuter, P. (1984) *Disorganised Crime*, Cambridge, MA: MIT Press.

Reuter, P., MacCoun, R. J. and Murphy, P. (1990) *Money from Crime: A Study of the Economics of Drug Dealing in Washington, DC*, Santa Monica, CA: Rand.

Reynolds, L. (1974) 'Rape as Social Control', *Catalyst*, 8: 62–88.

Richards, A. (2010) 'The Problem with "Radicalization": The Remit of "Prevent" and the Need to Refocus on Terrorism in the UK', *International Affairs*, 87 (1): 143–52.

Ricolfi, L. (2005) 'Palestinians, 1981–2003', in D. Gambetta (ed.) *Making Sense of Suicide Missions*, Oxford: Oxford University Press.

Ridley, A. and Dunford, L. (1994) 'Corporate Liability for Manslaughter: Reform and the Art of the Possible', *International Journal of the Sociology of Law*, 22: 309–28.

Ringdal, N. J. (2003) *Love for Sale: A World History of Prostitution*, trans. R. Daly, New York: Grove/ Atlantic.

Ringius, L. (2001) *Radioactive Waste Disposal at Sea*, Cambridge, MA: MIT Press.

Ritzer, G. (2002) *The McDonaldization Reader*, London: Sage.

Robb, G. (1992) *White Collar Crime in Modern England: Financial Fraud and Business Morality 1845–1929*, Cambridge: Cambridge University Press.

Roberts, B. (2002) 'On Not Becoming Delinquent: Raising Adolescent Boys in the Dutch Republic, 1600–1750', in P. Cox. and H. Shore (eds) *Becoming Delinquent: British and European Youth, 1650–1950*, Aldershot: Ashgate.

Roberts, J. (1999) *Twentieth Century: The History of the World 1901 to 2000*, London: Allan Lane.

Roberts, M. (2003) *Drugs and Crime: From Warfare to Welfare*, Policy Report, London: NACRO.

Robertson, G. (1993) *Freedom, the Individual and the Law*, London: Penguin.

Robertson, G. (1999) *Crimes against Humanity*, London: Penguin.

Robertson, R. (1992) *Globalization*, London: Sage.

Robertson, R. (1995) 'Glocalization: Time-Space and Homogeneity-Heterogeneity', in M. Featherstone, S. Lash and R. Robertson (eds) *Global Modernities*, London: Sage.

Robinson, F., Keithley, J., Robinson, S. and Childs, S. (1998) *Exploring the Impacts of Crime on Health and Health Services: A Feasibility Study*, Durham: Sociology and Social Policy, University of Durham.

Rock, P. (1993) *The Social World of an English Crown Court*, Oxford: Clarendon Press.

Rock, P. (1996) *Reconstructing a Woman's Prison: The Holloway Redevelopment Project*, Oxford: Clarendon Press.

Rock, P. (1998) *After Homicide*, Oxford: Clarendon.

Rock, P. (2002) 'Sociological Theories of Crime', in M. Maguire, R. Morgan and R. Reiner (eds) *Oxford Handbook of Criminology*, 3rd edn, Oxford: Oxford University Press.

Rock, P. (2011) '"What Have We Done?" Trends in Criminological Theorising', *Acta Criminologica*, 24 (1):19–43.

Roebuck, J. and Windham, G. (1983) 'Professional Theft', in G. P. Waldo (ed.) *Criminal Careers*, Beverly Hills, CA: Sage.

Rojek, C. (2003) *Stuart Hall*, Cambridge: Polity.

Rolles, S. (2007) 'Field of Dreams', *Druglink*, March/April: 5.

Roper, L. (1994) *Oedipus and the Devil: Witchcraft, Sexuality and Religion in Early Modern Europe*, London: Routledge.

Roper, L. (2004) *Witch Craze: Terror and Fantasy in Baroque Germany*, New Haven, CT: Yale University Press.

Rose, N. (1996) 'The Death of the Social? Re-figuring the Territory of Government', *Economy and Society*, 25 (3): 327–56.

Rothe, D. (2009) *State Criminality: The Crime of all Crimes*, Lanham, MD: Lexington Books.

Rothe, D., Mullins, C. and Sandstrom, K. (2008) 'The Rwandan Genocide: International

Financial Policies and Human Rights', *Social Justice*, 35 (3).

Rothman, D. (1971) *The Discovery of the Asylum*, Boston, MA: Little, Brown.

Rothman, D. (1980) *Conscience and Convenience: The Asylum and Its Alternatives in Progressive America*, Boston, MA: Little, Brown.

Rothman, M., Entzel, P. and Dunlop, B. (eds) (2000) *Elders, Crime and the Criminal Justice System*, New York: Springer.

Rowell, A. (1996) *Green Backlash: Global Subversion of the Environment Movement*, London: Routledge.

Rowntree Foundation (1995) *Income and Wealth: Report of the Joseph Rowntree Foundation Inquiry Group*, York: Joseph Rowntree Foundation.

Royal College of Psychiatrists (1986) *Alcohol: Our Favourite Drug*, London: Tavistock.

Royal Commission on Criminal Justice (RCCJ) (1993) *Report*, Cm 2263, London: HMSO.

Royal Society of Arts Commission on Illegal Drugs, Communities and Public Policy (2007) *Drugs: Facing Facts*, London: Royal Society of Arts.

Rozenberg, J. (1993) 'Miscarriages of Justice', in E. Stockdale and S. Casale (eds) *Criminal Justice under Stress*, London: Blackstone.

Ruback, R. B. and Thompson, M. P. (2001) *Social and Psychological Consequences of Violent Victimisation*, Thousand Oaks, CA: Sage.

Rubin, G. (1984) 'Thinking Sex', in C. S. Vance (ed.) *Pleasure and Danger*, London: Routledge.

Rudé, G. (1964) *The Crowd in History*, New York: Wiley.

Ruff, J. R. (2001) *Violence in Early Modern Europe, 1500–1800*, Cambridge: Cambridge University Press.

Ruggiero, V. (1996) *Organized and Corporate Crime in Europe: Offers That Can't Be Refused*, Aldershot: Dartmouth.

Ruggiero, V. (2000) 'Transnational Crime: Official and Alternative Fears', *International Journal of the Sociology of Law*, 28: 187–99.

Ruggiero, V. (2010) 'War as Corporate Crime', in W. Chambliss, R. Michalowski and R. Kramer (eds) *State Crime in the Global Age*, Cullompton: Willan.

Ruggiero, V. and South, N. (1995) *Eurodrugs: Drug Use, Markets and Trafficking in Europe*, London: UCL Press.

Ruggiero, V. and Khan, K. (2006) 'British South Asian Communities and Drug Supply Networks in the UK: A Qualitative Study', *International Journal of Drug Policy*, 17: 473–83.

Ruggiero, V. and South, N. (2010) 'Green Criminology and Dirty-Collar Crime' *Critical Criminology*, 18 (4): 251–62.

Runciman Report (2000) *Report of the Independent Inquiry into the Misuse of Drugs Act 1971*, London: Police Foundation.

Rusche, G. and Kirchheimer, O. (1939/1968) *Punishment and Social Structure*, New York: Russell and Russell.

Russo, L. (2000) 'Date Rape: A Hidden Crime', *Australian Institute for Criminology, Trends in Crime and Criminal Justice*, 157: 1–6.

Ryan, M. and Ward, T. (1992) 'From Positivism to Postmodernism: Some Theoretical and Strategic Reflections on the Evolution of the Penal Lobby in Britain', *International Journal of the Sociology of Law*, 20 (4): 321–35.

Sageman, M. (2004) *Understanding Terror Networks*, Philadelphia: University of Pennsylvania Press.

Sageman, M. (2008) *Leaderless Jihad: Terror Networks in the Twenty-First Century*, Philadelphia: University of Pennsylvania Press.

Sampson, R. J. and Raudenbush, S. W. (2004) 'Seeing Disorder: Neighborhood Stigma and the Social Construction of "Broken Windows"', *Social Psychology Quarterly*, 67 (4): 319–42.

Samson, C. (2003) *A Way of Life that Does Not Exist: Canada and the Extinguishment of the Innu*, London: Verso.

Samuel, R. (1981) *East End Underworld: Chapters in the Life of Arthur Harding*, London: Routledge.

Sandberg, S. (2008) 'Street Capital: Ethnicity and Violence on the Streets of Oslo', *Theoretical Criminology*, 12 (2): 153–71.

Sanders, A. and Young, R. (2002) 'From Suspect to Trial', in M. Maguire, R. Morgan and R. Reiner (eds) *Oxford Handbook of Criminology*, 3rd edn, Oxford: Oxford University Press.

Sanders, A. and Young, R. (2007) *Criminal Justice*, 3rd edn, Oxford: Oxford University Press.

Sanders, A., Young, R. and Burton, M. (2010) *Criminal Justice*, 4th edn, Oxford: Oxford University Press.

Sanders, W. (1977) *Detective Work: A Study of Criminal Investigation*, New York: Free Press.

Sands, P. (2005) *Lawless World: America and Making and Breaking of Global Rules*, London: Allen Lane.

Santa-Olla, P. (2011) 'Women in Prison: It Really Doesn't Work', *POLIS*, 5, Summer: 1–42.

Sarraj, E. (1997) 'Why We have Turned into Suicide Bombers: Understanding Palestinian Terror', *Just Commentary*, no. 3, September: 1–2.

Sassen, S. (1998) *Globalization and its Discontents. Essays on the New Mobility of People and Money*, New York: New Press.

Savage, S., Charman, S. and Cope, S. (2000) *Policing and the Power of Persuasion: The Changing Role of the Association of Chief Police Officers*, London: Blackstone.

Savelsberg, J. and Sampson, R. (2002) 'Mutual Engagement: Criminology and Sociology?', *Crime, Law and Social Change*, 37 (2): 99–105.

Scarce, R. (1994) '(No) Trial (But) Tribulations: When Courts and Ethnography Conflict', *Journal of Contemporary Ethnography*, 23: 123–49.

Scarce, R. (1995) 'Scholarly Ethics and Courtroom Antics: Where Researchers Stand in the Eyes of the Law', *American Sociologist*, 26: 87–112.

Scarman, Lord (1981) *The Scarman Report: Report of an Inquiry*, London: HMSO.

Scarpitti, A. and Block, A. (1987) 'America's Toxic Waste Racket', in T. S. Bynum (ed.) *Organized Crime in America: Concepts and Controversies*, New York: Criminal Justice Publishers.

Scharf, T., Phillipson, C. and Smith, A. (2003) 'Older People's Perceptions of the Neighbourhood: Evidence from Socially Deprived Urban Areas', *Sociological Research Online*, 8 (4).

Schechter, H. (2005) *Savage Pastimes: A Cultural History of Violent Entertainment*, New York: St Martin's Press.

Scheff, T. J. (1966) *Being Mentally Ill*, London: Weidenfeld and Nicolson.

Scheff, T. J. (1979) *Catharsis in Healing, Ritual, and Drama*, Berkeley: University of California Press.

Scheff, T. J., Retzinger, S. M. and Ryan, M. T. (1989) 'Crime, Violence, and Self-Esteem: Review and Proposals', in A. Mecca, N. J. Smelser and J. Vasconcellos (eds) *The Social Importance of Self-Esteem*, Berkeley: University of California Press.

Scheper-Hughes, N. and Wacquant, L. (eds) (2002) *Commodifying Bodies*, London: Sage.

Schlesinger, P. and Tumber, H. (1994) *Reporting Crime: The Media Politics of Criminal Justice*, Oxford: Clarendon Press.

Schlesinger, P., Dobash, R., Dobash, R. and Weaver, K. (1992) *Women Watching Violence*, London: British Film Institute.

Schmid, A. and Jongman, A. (1988) *Political Terrorism*, London: Transaction Publishers.

Schone, J. (2001) 'The Short Life and Painful Death of Prisoners' Rights', *Howard Journal of Criminal Justice*, 40 (1): 70–82.

Schubart, R. (1995) 'From Desire to Deconstruction: Horror Films and Audience Reactions', in D. Kidd-Hewitt and R. Osborne (eds) *Crime and the Media: The Post-modern Spectacle*, London: Pluto.

Schulenberg, J. L. (2007) 'Analysing Police Decision-making: Assessing the Application of a Mixed-Method/Mixed-Model Research Design', *International Journal of Social Research Methodology*, 10 (2): 99–119.

Schulz, D. M. (1995) *From Social Worker to Crimefighter: Women in United States Municipal Policing*, London/ Westport, CT: Praeger.

Schur, E. (1965) *Crimes without Victims: Deviant Behavior and Public Policy*, Englewood Cliffs, NJ: Prentice Hall.

Schwendinger, H. J. and Schwendinger, J. (1970/1975) 'Guardians of Order or Defenders of Human Rights?', in I. Taylor, P. Walton and J. Young (eds) *Critical Criminology*, London: Routledge and Kegan Paul.

Scott, D. (2008) *Penology*, London: Sage.

Scott, J. (1996) *Stratification and Power: Structures of Class, Status and Command*, Cambridge: Polity.

Scott, J. (2005) 'Who Will Speak, and Who Will Listen? Comments on Burawoy and Public Sociology', *British Journal of Sociology*, 56 (3): 405–9.

Scott, M. (1968) *The Racing Game*, Chicago, IL: Aldine.

Scott, W. R. (2001) *Institutions and Organizations*, 2nd edn, London: Sage.

Scraton, P. (1990) 'Scientific Knowledge or Masculine Discourses? Challenging Patriarchy in Criminology', in L. Gelsthorpe and A. Morris (eds) *Feminist Perspectives in Criminology*, Milton Keynes: Open University Press.

Scraton, P. (1999) 'Policing with Contempt: The Degrading of Truth and Denial of Justice in the Aftermath of the Hillsborough Disaster', *Journal of Law and Society*, 26 (3): 273–97.

Scraton, P (2009) *Hillsborough: The Truth*, Edinburgh: Mainstream.

Scraton, P. and Moore, L. (2004) *The Hurt Inside: The Imprisonment of Women and Girls in Northern Ireland*, Belfast: Northern Ireland Human Rights Commission.

Scull, A. (1977) *Decarceration: Community Treatment and the Deviant – A Radical View*, Englewood Cliffs, NJ: Prentice Hall.

Seddon, T. (2002) 'Five Myths about Drugs and Crime', *Safer Society*, 14, Autumn.

Sekula, A. (1989) 'The Body and the Archive', in R. Bolton (ed.) *The Contest of Meaning*, Cambridge, MA: MIT Press.

Sennett, R. (1998) *The Corrosion of Character: The Personal Consequences of Work in the New Capitalism*, New York: W. W. Norton.

Serious Organized Crime Agency (SOCA) (2006/7) *The United Kingdom Threat Assessment of Serious Organised Crime*, London: SOCA. http://www.soca. gov.uk/assessPublications/downloads/threat_

Shapland, J. (1986) 'Victim Assistance and the Criminal Justice System', in E. A. Fattah (ed.) *From Crime Policy to Victim Policy*, Basingstoke: Macmillan.

Shapland, J. and Hobbs, D. (1989) 'Policing on the Ground', in R. Morgan and D. Smith (eds) *Coming to Terms with Policing*, London: Routledge.

Shapland, J., Willmore, J. and Duff, P. (1985) *Victims in the Criminal Justice System*, Aldershot: Gower.

Shapland, J., Robinson, G. and Sorsby, A. (2011) *Restorative Justice in Practice: Evaluating What Works for Victims and Offenders*, Cullompton: Willan.

Sharpe, J. A. (1999) *Crime in Early Modern England, 1550–1750*, 2nd edn, London: Longman.

Sharpe, J. A. (2001) *Witchcraft in Early Modern England*, Harlow: Longman.

Shaw, C. (1930) *The Jack Roller*, Chicago, IL: University of Chicago Press.

Shaw, C. R. and McKay, H. D. (1942) *Juvenile Delinquency and Urban Areas*, Chicago, IL: University of Chicago Press.

Shearing, C. and Stenning, P. (1987) '"Say Cheese!" The Disney Order That Is Not So Mickey Mouse', in C. Shearing and P. Stenning (eds) *Private Policing*, Newbury Park, CA: Sage.

Shelley, L. (1999) 'Transnational Organized Crime: The New Authoritarianism', in H. Friman and P. Andreas (eds) *Illicit Global Economy and State Power*, Lanham, MD: Rowman and Littlefield.

Shepherd, J. (1990) 'Violent Crime in Bristol: An Accident and Emergency Department Perspective', *British Journal of Criminology*, 30: 289–305.

Shepherd, J. and Farrington, D. (1993) 'Assault as a Public Health Problem', *Journal of the Royal Society of Medicine*, 86: 89–92.

Shepherd, J. and Lisles, C. (1998) 'Towards Multi-agency Violence Prevention and Victim Support', *British Journal of Criminology*, 3: 351–70.

Sheptycki, J. (1995) 'Transnational Policing and the Makings of a Postmodern State', *British Journal of Criminology*, 35 (4): 613–35.

Sheptycki, J. (1998) 'The Global Cops Cometh: Reflections on Transnationalization, Knowledge Work and Policing Subculture', *British Journal of Sociology*, 49 (1): 57–74.

Sherman, L. (1974) *Police Corruption*, New York: Anchor.

Sherman, L. W. (1995) 'Hot Spots of Crime and Criminal Careers of Places', in J. Eck and D. Weisburd (eds) *Crime and Place*, New York: Criminal Justice Press.

Sherman, L. W. (2005) 'The Use and Usefulness of Criminology, 1751–2005: Enlightened Justice and its Failures', *Annals of the American Academy of Political and Social Science*, 600: 115–35.

Shilling, C. (2002) 'The Two Traditions in the Sociology of Emotions', in J. Barbalet (ed.) *Emotions and Sociology*, Oxford: Blackwell.

Shiner, M. and Newburn, T. (1999) 'Taking Tea with Noel: The Place and Meaning of Drug Use in Everyday Life', in N. South (ed.) *Drugs, Cultures, Controls and Everyday Life*, London: Sage.

Shore, H. (1999) *Artful Dodgers: Youth and Crime in Early Nineteenth Century London*, Woodbridge: Boydell Press.

Shore, H. (2011) 'Criminality and Englishness in the Aftermath: The Racecourse Wars of the

1920s', *Twentieth Century British History*, 22 (4): 474–97.

Short, F. with L. Hughes (2007) 'Criminology, Criminologists, and the Sociological Enterprise', in C. Calhoun (ed.) *Sociology in America: A History*, Chicago, IL: University of Chicago Press.

Shover, N. (1991) 'Burglary', in M. Tonry (ed.) *Crime and Justice: A Review of Research*, 14, Chicago, IL: University of Chicago Press.

Shover, N. (1996) *Great Pretenders: Pursuits and Games of Persistent Thieves*, Boulder, CO: Westview Press.

Showalter, E. (1990) *Sexual Anarchy: Gender and Culture at the Fin de Siècle*, London: Bloomsbury.

Sibley, D. (1995) *Geographies of Exclusion: Society and Difference in the West*, London: Routledge.

Sikka, P. (2008) 'Heart of Darkness', 9 January, at: http://commentisfree.guardian.co.uk/prem_sikka_/2008/01/heart_of_darkness.html

Silke, A. (2001) 'The Devil You Know: Continuing Problems with Research on Terrorism', *Terrorism and Political Violence*, 13: 1–14.

Silke, A. (2003) 'Becoming a Terrorist', in A. Silke (ed.) *Terrorists, Victims and Society: Psychological Perspectives on Terrorism and its Consequences*, Chichester: Wiley.

Silke, A. (2008) 'Research on Terrorism: A Review of the Impact of 9/11 and the Global War on Terrorism', in H. Chen, E. Reid, J. Sinai, A. Silke and B. Ganor (eds) *Terrorism Informatics: Knowledge Management and Data Mining for Homeland Security*, New York: Springer.

Silke, A. (2009) 'Contemporary Terrorism Studies: Issues in Research', in R. Jackson, M. Breen Smith and J. Gunning (eds) *Critical Terrorism Studies: A New Research Agenda*, London: Routledge.

Silke, A. and Taylor, M. (2000) 'War Without End: IRA and Loyalist Vigilantism in Northern Ireland', *Howard Journal of Criminal Justice*, 39: 249–66.

Silverman, E. (1999) *NYPD Battles Crime: Innovative Strategies in Policing*, Boston, MA: Northeastern University Press.

Silverman, J. and Wilson, D. (2002) *Innocence Betrayed: Paedophilia, the Media and Society*, Cambridge: Polity.

Silverstone, D. and Savage, S. (2010) 'Farmers, Factories and Funds: Organised Crime and Illicit Drugs Cultivation within the British Vietnamese Community', *Global Crime*, 11 (1): 16–33.

Sim, J. (1990) *Medical Power in Prisons*, Buckingham: Open University Press.

Sim, J., Scraton, P. and Gordon, P. (1987) 'Introduction: Crime, the State and Critical Analysis', in P. Scraton (ed.) *Law, Order and the Authoritarian State*, Milton Keynes: Open University Press.

Simmons, J. et al. (2002) *Crime in England and Wales 2001/2*, Home Office Statistical Bulletin 7/02, London: Home Office.

Simmons, J. and Dodd, T. (2003) *Crime in England and Wales 2002/2003*, London: Home Office.

Simon, D. R. (2000) 'Corporate Environmental Crimes and Social Inequality', *American Behavioural Scientist*, 43: 633–45.

Simon, J. (2007) *Governing through Crime: How the War on Crime Transformed American Democracy and Created a Culture of Fear*, New York: Oxford University Press.

Simon, J. and Sparks, R. (2012) *The SAGE Handbook of Punishment and Society*, London: Sage.

Sims, L. and Myhill, A. (2001) *Policing and the Public: Findings from the 2000 British Crime Survey*, Home Office Research Findings 136, London: Home Office.

Singer, E. (2003) '"And Here Is the Local Crime Forecast . . ."', *New Scientist*, 16 August, 179 (2408): 13.

Skeggs, B. (2009) 'The Moral Economy of Person Production: The Class Relations of Self-performance on "Reality" Television', *Sociological Review*, 57 (4): 626–44.

Skogan, W. and Steiner, L. (2004) *Community Policing in Chicago, Year Ten: An Evaluation of Chicago's Alternative Policing Strategy*, Chicago: Illinois Criminal Justice Information Authority.

Skolnick, J. (1966) *Justice without Trial*, London: Wiley.

Skolnick, J. and Bayley, D. (1986) *The New Blue Line*, New York: Free Press.

Skrobankek, S., Boonpakdee, N. and Jatateero, C. (1997) *The Traffic in Women: Human Realities of the International Sex Trade*, London: Zed Books.

Slapper, G. and Tombs, S. (1999) *Corporate Crime*, Harlow: Longman.

Smandych, R. (ed.) (1999) *Governable Places: Readings on Governmentality and Crime Control*, Aldershot: Ashgate.

Smart, C. (1976) *Women, Crime and Criminology: A Feminist Critique*, London: Routledge and Kegan Paul.

Smart, C. (1979) 'The New Female Criminal: Reality or Myth?', British Journal of Criminology, 19: 50–9.

Smart, C. (1989) Feminism and the Power of the Law, London: Routledge.

Smart, C. (1990) 'Feminist Approaches to Criminology, or Postmodern Woman Meets Atavistic Man', in L. Gelsthorpe and A. Morris (eds) Feminist Perspectives in Criminology, Buckingham: Open University Press.

Smart, C. (1995) Law, Crime and Sexuality: Essays in Feminism, London: Sage.

Smelser, N. (1962) Theory of Collective Behavior, New York: Free Press.

Smeulers, A. and Hoex, L. (2010) 'Studying the Microdynamics of the Rwandan Genocide', British Journal of Criminology 50: 435–54.

Smith, D. (1994) The Sleep of Reason: The James Bulger Case, London: Century.

Smith, D. (2005) 'Probation and Social Work', British Journal of Social Work, 35: 621–37.

Smith, M. and Tilley, N. (2005) 'Introduction', in M. Smith and N. Tilley (eds) Crime Science: New Approaches to Preventing and Detecting Crime, Cullompton: Willan.

Smith, P. (2008) Punishment and Culture, Chicago, IL: University of Chicago Press.

Smith, R. (2010) 'Identity Theft and Fraud', in Y. Jewkes and M. Yar (eds) Handbook of Internet Crime, Cullompton: Willan.

Smithies, E. (1982) Crime in Wartime, London: Allen and Unwin.

Snider, L. (2000) 'The Sociology of Corporate Crime: An Obituary (or Whose Knowledge Claims Have Legs?)', Theoretical Criminology, 4 (2): 169–206.

Snodgrass, J. (1982) The Jack-Roller at Seventy, Lexington, MA: D. C. Heath.

Snyder, L. (1991) 'The Regulatory Dance: Understanding Reform Processes in Corporate Crime', International Journal of the Sociology of Law, 19: 209–36.

Sollund, R. (2008) Global Harms Ecological Crime and Speciesism, New York: Nova.

Sollund, R. (2013) 'The Victimisation of Women, Children and Non-human Species through Trafficking and Trade: Crimes Understood through an Ecofeminist Perspective', in N. South and A. Brisman (eds) The Routledge International Handbook of Green Criminology, London: Routedge.

Solomon-Godeau, A. (1991) Photography at the Dock, Minneapolis: University of Minnesota Press.

Soloway, I. and Walters, J. (1977) 'Workin' the Corner: The Ethics and Legality of Ethnographic Fieldwork among Active Heroin Addicts', in R. S. Weppner (ed.) Street Ethnography: Selected Studies of Crime and Drug Use in Natural Settings, Beverly Hills, CA: Sage.

Souness, H. (2007) Heist: The True Story of the World's Biggest Cash Robbery, London: Simon & Schuster.

South, N. (1988) Policing for Profit, London: Sage.

South, N. (ed.) (1995) Drugs, Crime and Criminal Justice, Aldershot: Dartmouth.

South, N. (1997) 'Late-Modern Criminology: "Late" as in "Dead" or "Modern" as in "New"?', in D. Owen (ed.) Sociology after Postmodernism, Thousand Oaks, CA: Sage.

South, N. (1998a) 'Corporate and State Crimes against the Environment: Foundations for a Green Perspective in European Criminology', in V. Ruggiero, N. South and I. Taylor (eds) The New European Criminology, London: Routledge.

South, N. (1998b) 'A Green Field for Criminology? A Proposal for a Perspective', Theoretical Criminology, 2 (2): 211–34.

South, N. (ed.) (1999a) Youth Crime, Deviance and Delinquency, 2 vols, Aldershot: Dartmouth.

South, N. (ed.) (1999b) Drugs: Cultures, Controls and Everyday Life, London: Sage.

South, N. (2002) 'Drugs, Alcohol and Crime', in M. Maguire, R. Morgan and R. Reiner (eds) Oxford Handbook of Criminology, 3rd edn, Oxford: Oxford University Press.

South, N. (2004) 'Managing Work, Hedonism and "the Borderline" between the Legal and Illegal Markets: Two Case Studies of Recreational Heavy Drug Users', Addiction Research and Theory, 12 (6): 525–38.

South, N. (2005) 'Inequalities, Crime and Citizenship', in M. Romero and E. Margolis (eds) The Blackwell Companion on Social Inequalities, Malden, MA: Blackwell.

South, N. (2007) 'The "Corporate Colonisation of Nature": Bio-Prospecting, Bio-Piracy and the Development of Green Criminology', in P. Beirne and N. South (eds) Toward a Green

Criminology: Confronting Harms Against Humanity, Animals and Nature, Cullompton: Willan.

South, N. (2010) 'The Ecocidal Tendencies of Late Modernity: Transnational Crime, Social Exclusion, Victims and Rights', in R. White (ed.) *Global Environmental Harm: Criminological Perspectives*, Cullompton: Willan.

South, N (2012) 'Climate Change, Environmental (In)security, Conflict and Crime', in S. Farrall, D. French and T. Ahmed (eds) *Climate Change: Legal and Criminological Implications*, Oxford: Hart.

South, N. and Beirne, P. (1998) in 'For a Green Criminology', special issue of *Theoretical Criminology*, 2 (2).

South, N. and Weiss, R. (eds) (1998) *Comparing Prison Systems: Toward a Comparative and International Penology*, Reading: Gordon and Breach.

South, N. and Beirne, P. (eds) (2006) *Green Criminology*, Aldershot: Dartmouth.

South, N. and Wyatt, T. (2011) 'Comparison of the Illicit Wildlife and Drug Trades: An Exploratory Study', *Deviant Behavior*, 32 (6): 538–61.

South, N. and Brisman, A. (eds) (2013) *Routledge International Handbook of Green Criminology*, London: Routledge.

Southwell, D. (2002) *Dirty Cash: Organised Crime in the 21st Century*, London: Virgin.

Spalek, B. (2001) 'Regulation, White Collar Crime and the Bank of Credit and Commerce International', *Howard Journal of Criminal Justice*, 40 (2): 166–79.

Spalek, B. (2007) 'Knowledgeable Consumers?: Corporate Fraud and Its Devastating Impacts', Briefing 4, London: Centre for Crime and Justice Studies. Available: http://www.crime andjustice.org.uk/opus309/KC_Final_version_ 200807.pdf

Sparks, R. (1992) *Television and the Drama of Crime: Moral Tales and the Place of Crime in Public Life*, Milton Keynes: Open University Press.

Sparks, R. (1993) 'Inspector Morse: "The Last Enemy"', in G. Brandt (ed.) *British Television Drama in the 1980s*, Cambridge: Cambridge University Press.

Sparks, R. (2000) 'Perspectives on Risk and Penal Politics', in T. Hope and R. Sparks (eds) *Crime, Risk and Insecurity*, London: Routledge.

Sparks, R. (2002) 'Prisons, Punishment and Penality', in E. McLaughlin and J. Muncie (eds) *Controlling Crime*, 2nd edn, London: Sage.

Sparks, R., Bottoms, A. and Hay, W. (1996) *Prisons and the Problem of Order*, Oxford: Clarendon Press.

Spelman, E. (1989) 'Anger and Insubordination', in A. Garry and M. Pearsall (eds) *Women, Knowledge, and Reality: Explorations in Feminist Philosophy*, Boston, MA: Unwin Hyman.

Spierenburg, P. (1984) *The Spectacle of Suffering: Executions and the Evolution of Repression*, Cambridge: Cambridge University Press.

Spierenburg, P. (ed.) (1998a) *Men and Violence: Gender, Honor, and Rituals in Modern Europe and America*, Columbus: Ohio State University Press.

Spierenburg, P. (1998b) 'The Body and the State: Early Modern Europe', in N. Morris and D. Rothman (eds) *The Oxford History of the Prison: The Practice of Punishment in Western Society*, Oxford: Oxford University Press.

Spierenburg, P. (2005) 'Origins of the Prison', in C. Emsley (ed.) *The Persistent Prison: Problems, Images and Alternatives*, London: Francis Boutle.

Spitzer, S. (1987) 'Security and Control in Capitalist Societies: The Fetishism of Security and the Secret Thereof', in J. Lowman, R. J. Menzies and T. S. Palys (eds) *Transcarceration: Essays in the Sociology of Social Control*, Aldershot: Gower.

Springhall, J. (1998) *Youth, Popular Culture and Moral Panics: Penny Gaffs to Gangsta-Rap, 1830–1996*, Basingstoke: Macmillan.

Squires, G. and Hartman, C. (2006) *There Is No Such Thing as a Natural Disaster: Race, Class and Katrina*, London: Routledge.

Stanko, B. (1987) 'Typical Violence, Normal Precaution: Men, Women, and Interpersonal Violence in England, Wales and the USA', in J. Hanmer and M. Maynard (eds) *Women, Violence and Social Control*, Basingstoke: Macmillan.

Stanko, B. (1988) 'Fear of Crime and the Myth of the Safe Home: A Feminist Critique of Criminology', in K. Yllo and M. Bograd (eds) *Feminist Perspectives on Wife Abuse*, London: Sage.

Stanko, B. (1997) 'Safety Talk: Conceptualising Women's Risk Assessment as a "Technology of the Soul"', *Theoretical Criminology*, 1 (4): 479–99.

Stanko, E. (1990) *Everyday Violence*, London: Pandora.

Stanko, E. (1994) *Perspectives on Violence*, London: Quartet.

Stanko, E., Marian, L., Crisp, D., Manning, R., Smith, J. and Cowan, S. (1998) *Taking Stock*, Uxbridge, Middlesex: Brunel University.

Stein, A. (2001) *Strangers in Our Midst*, Boston, MA: Beacon.

Stelfox, P. (1998) 'Policing Lower Levels of Organised Crime in England and Wales', *Howard Journal of Criminal Justice*, 37 (4): 393–406.

Sterling, C. (1990) *Octopus: The Long Reach of the International Sicilian Mafia*, New York: Norton.

Sterling, C. (1994) *Crime Without Frontiers*, London: Little, Brown.

Stern, V. (1993) *Bricks of Shame*, London: Penguin.

Stevens, A. (2011) *Drugs, Crime and Public Health: The Political Economy of Drug Policy*, London: Routledge.

Stevenson, D. (2003) *Cities and Urban Culture*, Buckingham: Open University Press.

Stevenson, N. (1999) *The Transformation of the Media: Globalisation, Morality and Ethics*, Harlow: Longman.

Steward, K. (2006) 'Gender Decisions in Remand Decision-Making', in F. Heidensohn (ed.) *Gender and Justice*, Cullompton: Willan.

Stimson, G. (1995) 'Aids and Injecting Drug Use in the United Kingdom, 1987–1993: The Policy Response and the Prevention of the Epidemic', *Social Science and Medicine*, 41 (5): 699–716.

Stoler, A. L. (2002) *Carnal Knowledge and Imperial Power: Race and the Intimate in Colonial Rule*, Berkeley: University of California Press.

Stones, R. (1996) *Sociological Reasoning*, Basingstoke: Macmillan.

Storch, R. (1975) 'The Plague of Blue Locusts: Police Reform and Popular Resistance in Northern England 1840–57', *International Review of Social History*, 20: 61–90.

Storch, R. (1976) 'The Policeman as Domestic Missionary', *Journal of Social History*, 9 (4): 481–509.

Strang, J. and Stimson, G. (eds) (1991) *AIDS and Drug Misuse*, London: Routledge.

Strang, J. and Gossop, M. (eds) (2004) *Heroin Addiction and the British System: Volume I, Origins and Evolution*, London: Routledge.

Strang, J. and Gossop, M. (2005) *Heroin Addiction and the British System: Volume II, Treatment and Other Responses*, London: Routledge.

Strang, J., Wilks, M., Wells, B. and Marshall, J. (1998) 'Missed Problems and Missed Opportunities for Addicted Doctors', Editorial, *British Medical Journal*, 7 (129): 316.

Straus, S. (2009) *The Order of Genocide: Race, Power, and War in Rwanda*, Ithaca, NY: Cornell University Press.

Streatfeild, D. (2002) *Cocaine: A Definitive History*, London: Virgin Books.

Strongman, K. (2003) *The Psychology of Emotion: From Everyday Life to Theory*, Chichester: Wiley.

Sumner, C. (1976) 'Marxism and Deviancy Theory', in P. Wiles (ed.) *Sociology of Crime and Delinquency in Britain*, vol. 2, London: Martin Robertson.

Sumner, C. (1994) *The Sociology of Deviance: An Obituary*, Milton Keynes: Open University Press.

Surette, R. (1998) *Media, Crime and Criminal Justice: Images and Realities*, Belmont, CA: Wadsworth.

Sutherland, E. (1924) *Criminology*, Philadelphia, PA: Lippincott.

Sutherland, E., with Locke, H. J. (1936) *Twenty Thousand Homeless Men*, Philadelphia, PA: J. B. Lippincott.

Sutherland, E. (1937) *The Professional Thief*, Chicago, IL: University of Chicago Press.

Sutherland, E. (1949) *White Collar Crime*, New York: Holt, Rinehart and Winston.

Sutherland, E. (1950) 'The Diffusion of Sexual Psychopath Laws', *American Journal of Sociology*, 56:

Sutherland, E. (1956) *The Sutherland Papers*, ed. A. K. Cohen, A. R. Lindesmith and K. Schlussler, Bloomington: Indiana University Press. Republished as Sutherland, E. (1973) *On Analyzing Crime*, ed. K. Schlussler, Chicago, IL: University of Chicago Press.

Sutton, M. (1998) *Handling Stolen Goods and Theft*, Home Office Research Study 178, London: Home Office.

Sutton, R. and Farrall, S. (2005) 'Gender, Socially Desirable Responding and the Fear of Crime: Are Women Really More Anxious about Crime?', *British Journal of Criminology*, 45 (2): 212–24.

Sykes, G. (1958) *The Society of Captives*, Princeton, NJ: Princeton University Press.

Sykes, G. M. and Matza, D. (1957) 'Techniques of Neutralization: A Theory of Delinquency', *American Sociological Review*, 22: 664–70.

Szasz, A. (1986) 'Corporations, Organised Crime and the Disposal of Hazardous Waste: An Examination of the Making of a Criminogenic Regulatory Structure', *Criminology*, 24 (1): 1–27.

Szasz, A. (1994) *EcoPopulism: Toxic Waste and the Movement for Environmental Justice*, Minneapolis: University of Minnesota Press.

Tagg, J. (1988) *The Burden of Representation: Essays on Photographies and Histories*, Basingstoke: Macmillan.

Talbot, J. (2010) *Seen and Heard: Supporting Vulnerable Children within the Youth Justice System*, London: Prison Reform Trust/Association of YOT Managers.

Tame, C. (1991) 'Freedom, Responsibility and Justice: The Criminology of the "New Right"', in K. Stenson and D. Cowell (eds) *The Politics of Crime Control*, London: Sage.

Tannenbaum, F. (1938) *Crime and the Community*, New York: McGraw-Hill.

Tappan, P. (1947) 'Who Is the Criminal?', *American Sociological Review*, 12: 96–102.

Tappan, P. (1954) 'The Legal Rights of Prisoners', *The Annals*, 293: 99–111.

Taverne, D. (2010) 'How to See Reality on Drugs', *New Scientist*, 30 November, 2788.

Taylor, I. (1996) 'Fear of Crime, Urban Fortunes and Suburban Social Movements: Some Reflections on Manchester', *Sociology*, 30 (2): 317–37.

Taylor, I. (1997) 'Crime, Anxiety, and Locality: Responding to the Condition of England at the End of the Century', *Theoretical Criminology*, 1 (1): 53–76.

Taylor, I. (1999) *Crime in Context: A Critical Criminology of Market Societies*, Cambridge: Polity.

Taylor, I. and Taylor, L. (eds) (1973) *Politics and Deviance*, Harmondsworth: Penguin.

Taylor, I. and Jamieson, R. (1997) '"Proper Little Mesters": Nostalgia and Protest in De-industrialised Sheffield', in S. Westwood and J. Williams (eds) *Imagining Cities: Scripts, Signs, Memory*, London: Routledge.

Taylor, I. and Jamieson, R. (1998) 'Fear of Crime and Fear of Falling: English Anxieties Approaching the Millennium', *Arch. European Journal of Sociology*, 39 (1): 149–75.

Taylor, I., Walton, P. and Young, J. (1973) *The New Criminology: For a Social Theory of Deviance*, London: Routledge and Kegan Paul.

Taylor, I., Walton, P. and Young, J. (eds) (1975) *Critical Criminology*, London: Routledge and Kegan Paul.

Taylor, J. (2004) *Crime against Retail and Manufacturing Premises: Findings from the 2002 Commercial Victimisation Survey*, Home Office Research Findings No. 259, London: Home Office.

Taylor, L. (1973) *Deviance and Society*, London: Joseph.

Taylor, M. and Horgan, J. (2006) 'A Conceptual Framework for Addressing Psychological Process in the Development of the Terrorist', *Terrorism and Political Violence*, 18: 585–601.

Taylor, P. (1999) *Hackers: Crime in the Digital Sublime*, London: Routledge.

Taylor, P. (2000) 'Hackers – Cyberpunks or Microserfs?', in D. Thomas, and B. D. Loader (eds) *Cybercrime: Law Enforcement, Security and Surveillance in the Information Age*, London: Routledge.

Taylor, P. (2003) 'Maestros or Misogynists? Gender and the Social Construction of Hacking', in Y. Jewkes (ed.) *Dot.cons: Crime, Deviance and Identity on the Internet*, Cullompton: Willan.

Taylor, P. and Chaplin, R. (eds) (2011) *Crimes Detected in England and Wales 2010/11*, Home Office Statistical Bulletin 11/11. London: Home Office.

Temkin, J. and Krahe, B. (2008) *Sexual Assault and the Justice Gap: A Question of Attitude*, Portland, OR: Hart Publishing.

Temko, N. (2006) 'Jail Racism Rife, Says Inquiry', *Observer*, 11 June: 5.

Thiel, D. (2009) *Policing Terrorism: A Review of the Evidence*, London: Police Foundation.

Thiel, D. (2013) *Double Injustice, Double Trauma: The Effects of Acquittal of Suspects upon the Families of Victims of Homicide*. Working paper, Social Science Research Network: http://ssrn.com/abstract+2364398/

Thomas, D. (2003) *An Underworld at War*, London: John Murray.

Thomas, D. and Loader, B. D. (eds) (2000) *Cybercrime: Law Enforcement, Security and Surveillance in the Information Age*, London: Routledge.

Thomas, H. (1997) *The Slave Trade, The Story of the Atlantic Slave Trade: 1440–1870*, New York: Simon & Schuster.

Thomas, T. (2000) *Sex Crime: Sex Offending and Society*, Cullompton: Willan.

Thomas, T. (2004) 'When Public Protection Becomes Punishment? The UK Use of Civil Measures to Contain the Sex Offender', *European Journal on Criminal Policy and Research*, 10 (4): 337–51.

Thomas, W. I. (1923) *The Unadjusted Girl*, Boston, MA: Little, Brown.

Thompson, E. P. (1963) *The Making of the English Working Class*, London: Victor Gollancz.

Thompson, E. P. (1975) *Whigs and Hunters: The Origin of the Black Act*, London: Allen Lane.

Thompson, E. P. (1991) *Customs in Common*, London: Merlin Press.

Thompson, J. (1995) *The Media and Modernity*, Cambridge: Polity.

Thompson, J. (2005) 'The New Visibility', *Theory, Culture and Society*, 22 (6): 31–51.

Thompson, K. (1998) *Moral Panics*, London: Routledge.

Thrasher, F. (1927) *The Gang*, Chicago, IL: University of Chicago Press.

Thurston, R. (2006) *The Witchhunts*, London: Longman.

Tikoff, V. (2002) 'Before the Reformatory: A Correctional Orphanage in Ancien Régime Seville', in P. Cox and H. Shore (eds) *Becoming Delinquent: British and European Youth, 1650–1950*, Aldershot: Ashgate.

Tilly, C. (1985) 'War Making and State Making as Organised Crime', in P. Evans *et al.* (eds) *Bringing the State Back In*, Cambridge: Cambridge University Press.

Tilly, N. (2008) 'Modern Approaches to Policing: Community, Problem-Oriented and Intelligence-led', in T. Newburn (ed.) *The Handbook of Policing*, 2nd edn, Cullompton: Willan.

Tithecott, R. (1997) *Of Men and Monsters: Jeffrey Dahmer and the Construction of the Serial Killer*, Madison: University of Wisconsin Press.

Tombs, S. (2000) 'Official Statistics and Hidden Crime: Researching Safety Crimes', in V. Jupp, P. Davies and P. Francis (eds) *Doing Criminological Research*, London: Sage.

Tombs, S. and Whyte, D. (eds) (2003) *Unmasking the Crimes of the Powerful: Scrutinizing States and Corporations*, New York: Peter Lang.

Tomsen, S. (1997) 'A Top Night: Social Protest, Masculinity and the Culture of Drinking Violence', *British Journal of Criminology*, 37 (1): 90–102.

Tonry, M. (2004) *Punishment and Politics: Evidence and Emulation in the Making of English Crime Control Policy*, Cullompton: Willan.

Tonry, M. (2011) *Punishing Race: A Continuing American Dilemma*, Oxford: Oxford University Press.

Travis, A. (2007) 'From Foreign Fields to UK Streets – The Anatomy of an £8bn Industry', *Guardian*, 21 November.

Treadwell, J. (2012) 'From the Car Boot to Booting It Up? eBay, Online Counterfeit Crime and the Transfromation of the Criminal Marketplace', *Criminology and Criminal Justice*, 12 (2): 175–91.

Treiber, K. (2012) 'Young People Are Mostly Crime-Averse': http://www.huffingtonpost.co.uk/kyle-treiber/crime-youth-young-people-are-mostly-c_b_1639536.html

Tremblay, M. (1986) 'Designing Crime: The Short Life Expectancy and the Workings of a Recent Wave of Credit Card Bank Frauds', *British Journal of Criminology*, 26: 234–53.

Trend, D. (2007) *The Myth of Media Violence: A Critical Introduction*, Oxford: Blackwell.

Tuan, Y. (1979) *Landscapes of Fear*, New York: Pantheon Books.

Turner, B. (1996) *The Body and Society*, 2nd edn, London: Sage.

Turner, J. and Stets, J. (2005) *The Sociology of Emotions*, Cambridge: Cambridge University Press.

Turner, J. and Kelly, L. (2009) 'Trade Secrets: Intersections of Diasporas and Crime Groups in the Constitution of the Human Trafficking Chain', *British Journal of Criminology*, 49 (2): 184–201.

Turton, J. (2008) *Child Abuse, Gender and Society*, London: Routledge.

Tyler, T. (1990) *Why People Obey the Law*, New Haven, CT: Yale University Press.

Uglow, S. (2002) *Criminal Justice*, London: Sweet and Maxwell.

UK Border Agency (2013) 'Immigration Removal Centres'. Available at: http://www.ukba.home

office.gov.uk/aboutus/organisation/immigrati onremovalcentres/

Ungar, S. (2001) 'Moral Panic versus the Risk Society: The Implications of the Changing Sites of Social Anxiety', British Journal of Sociology, 52 (2): 271–91.

United Nations (2002) Interim Report of the Panel of Experts on the Illegal Exploitation of Natural Resources and Other Forms of Wealth of the Democratic Republic of the Congo, United Nations Document S/2002/565/ 22 May: 1–19. Accessed at: http://www.unhcr. org/refworld/pdfid/3d0471ad4.pdf

United Nations Centre for International Crime Prevention (UNCICP) (2000) Assessing Transnational Organised Crime: Results of a Pilot Survey of 40 Selected Organised Criminal Groups in 16 Countries, Vienna: UNCICP.

United Nations Convention on Biological Diversity (2010) Global Biodiversity Outlook 3, Secretariat of the Convention on Biological Diversity, Montréal.

United Nations Educational, Scientific and Cultural Organization (UNESCO) (1997) Preventing the Illicit Traffic in Cultural Property. A Resource Handbook for the Implementation of the 1970 UNESCO Convention, Paris: UNESCO.

United Nations Office on Drugs and Crime (UNODC) (2007) Annual Report, Vienna: UNODC.

United Nations Office on Drugs and Crime (UNODC) (2010) The Globalization of Crime: A Transnational Organized Crime Threat Assessment, Vienna: UNODC.

United Nations Office on Drugs and Crime (UNODC) (2013) World Drugs Report 2013, Vienna: UNODC.

United Nations Security Council (2001) Resolution 1373, New York: UNSC.

United Nations Security Council (2004) Resolution 1566, New York: UNSC.

Urry, J. (2008) 'Climate Change, Travel and Complex Futures', British Journal of Sociology, 59 (2): 261–79.

US Federal Bureau of Investigation (1999) Hate Crime Data Collection Guidelines, Washington, DC: Federal Bureau of Investigation, US Department of Justice.

Useem, B. and Kimball, P. (1989) States of Siege: US Prison Riots, 1971–1986, Oxford: Oxford University Press.

Valier, C. (2002a) Theories of Crime and Punishment, Harlow: Pearson.

Valier, C. (2002b) 'Punishment, Border Crossings and the Powers of Horror', Theoretical Criminology, 6 (3): 319–37.

Valverde, M. (1996) 'Social Facticity and the Law: A Social Expert's Eyewitness Account of the Law', Social and Legal Studies, 5 (2): 201–18.

Valverde, M. (2006) Law and Order: Images, Meanings, Myths, New Brunswick, NJ: Rutgers University Press.

Valverde, M. (2012) 'Analyzing Punishment: Scope and Scale', Theoretical Criminology, 16 (2): 245–53.

van den Haag, E. (1975) Punishing Criminals: Concerning a Very Old and Painful Question, New York: Basic Books.

van den Haag, E. (1985) Deterring Potential Criminals, London: Social Affairs Unit.

Van Dijk, J. J. M. (1985) 'Regaining a Sense of Community and Order', in European Committee on Crime Problems, Research on Crime Victims, Strasbourg: Council of Europe, 145–64.

Van Duyne, P. (1993) 'Organised Crime and Business Crime Enterprises in the Netherlands', Crime, Law and Social Change, 19: 103–42.

van Zyl Smit, D. (2007) 'Prisoners' Rights', in Y. Jewkes (ed.) Handbook on Prisons, Cullompton: Willan.

Vann, I. B. and Garson, G. D. (2001) 'Crime Mapping and Its Extension to Social Science Analysis', Social Science Computer Review, 19 (4): 471–9.

Vanstone, M. (2007) Supervising Offenders in the Community: A History of Probation Theory and Practice, Aldershot: Ashgate.

Varese, F. (2011) Mafias on the Move: How Organized Crime Conquers New Territories, New York: Princeton University Press.

Vass, A. (1986) AIDS: A Plague in Us, Cambridge: Venus Academica.

Venkatesh, S. (2008) Gang Leader for a Day: A Rogue Sociologist Takes to the Streets, London: Penguin.

Vine, I. (1997) 'The Dangerous Psychologic of Media "Effects"', in M. Barker and J. Petley (eds) Ill Effects: The Media/Violence Debate, London: Routledge.

Virdee, S. (1997) 'Racial Harassment', in T. Modood and R. Berthoud (eds) Ethnic Minorities in Britain, London: Policy Studies Institute.

Vogel, D. (1986) *National Styles of Regulation: Environmental Policy in Great Britain and the United States*, Ithaca, NY: Cornell University Press.

Vold, G. B. (1958) *Theoretical Criminology*, Oxford: Oxford University Press.

von Hentig, H. (1948) *The Criminal and His Victim*, New Haven, CT: Yale University Press.

von Hirsch, A. (1976) *Doing Justice: The Choice of Punishments*, New York: Hill and Wang.

von Hirsch, A. (1985) *Past or Future Crimes: Deservedness and Dangerousness in the Sentencing of Criminals*, Manchester: Manchester University Press.

Von Lampe, K. (2001) 'Not a Process of Enlightenment: The Conceptual History of Organized Crime in Germany and the United States of America', *Forum on Crime and Society*, 1 (2): 99–116.

Wachholz, S. (2007) '"At Risk": Climate Change and its Bearing on Women's Vulnerability to Male Violence', in P. Beirne and N. South (eds) *Toward a Green Criminology: Confronting Harms Against Humanity, Animals and Nature*, Cullompton: Willan.

Wacquant, L. (2001) 'Deadly Symbiosis: When Prison and Ghetto Meet and Merge', *Punishment and Society*, 3 (1): 95–134.

Wacquant, L. (2009) *Punishing the Poor: The Neoliberal Government of Social Insecurity*, Durham, NC: Duke University Press.

Wacquant, L. (2010) 'Crafting the Neoliberal State: Workfare, Prisonfare, and Social Insecurity', *Sociological Forum*, 25 (2): 197–220.

Waddington, P. A. J. (1996) 'Public Order Policing: Citizenship and Moral Ambiguity', in F. Leishman, B. Loveday and S. Savage (eds) *Core Issues in Policing*, Harlow: Longman.

Waddington, P. A. J. (1999) 'Police (Canteen) Subculture: An Appreciation' *British Journal of Criminology*, 39 (2): 286–308.

Waddington, P. A. J. (2000) 'Public Order Policing: Citizenship and Moral Ambiguity', in F. Lieshman, B. Loveday and S. Savage (eds) *Core Issues on Policing*, 2nd edn, Harlow: Pearson.

Walker, A., Kershaw, C. and Nicholas, S. (2006) *Crime in England and Wales 2005/6*, Home Office Statistical Bulletin 12/06. London: Home Office.

Walker, C. and Starmer, K. (1999) *Miscarriages of Justice: A Review of Justice in Error*, London: Blackstone.

Walker, G. (2003) *Crime, Gender and Social Order in Early Modern England*, Cambridge: Cambridge University Press.

Walker, N. (1991) *Why Punish?*, Oxford: Oxford University Press.

Walker, N. (1999) 'Decoupling Police and State', in E. Bort and R. Keat (eds) *Boundaries of Understanding: Essays in Honour of Malcolm Anderson*, Edinburgh: University of Edinburgh International Social Sciences Institute.

Walklate, S. (1995) *Gender and Crime: An Introduction*, London: Prentice Hall.

Walklate, S. (1998) 'Excavating the Fear of Crime: Fear, Anxiety or Trust?', *Theoretical Criminology*, 2 (4): 403–18.

Walklate, S. (2001) *Gender, Crime and Criminal Justice* (2nd edn, 2004), Cullompton: Willan.

Walklate, S. (2007a) *Imagining the Victim of Crime*, Berkshire: Open University Press.

Walklate, S. (ed.) (2007b) *Handbook of Victims and Victimology*, Cullompton: Willan.

Walkowitz, J. (1984) 'Male Vice and Female Virtue: Feminism and the Politics of Prostitution in Nineteenth Century Britain', in A. Snitow, C. Stansell and S. Thompson (eds) *Power and Desire: The Politics of Sexuality*, London: Virago.

Walkowitz, J. R. (1992) *City of Dreadful Delight: Narratives of Sexual Danger in Late Victorian London*, London: Virago.

Wall, D. (2001) 'Cybercrimes on the Internet', in D. Wall (ed.) *Crime and the Internet*, London: Routledge.

Wall, D. (2007) *Cybercrime: The Transformation of Crime in the Information Age*, Cambridge: Polity.

Wall, D. and Yar, M. (2010) 'Intellectual Property Crime and the Internet: Cyber-piracy and "Stealing" Information Intangibles', in Y. Jewkes and M. Yar (eds) *Handbook of Internet Crime*, Cullompton: Willan.

Walmsley, R. (2003) *World Prison Population List*, 4th edn, London: The Stationery Office.

Walmsley, R. (2006) *World Prison Population List*, 7th edn, London: International Centre for Prison Studies.

Walmsley, R. (2011) *World Prison Population List*, 9th edn, London: International Centre for Prison Studies.

Walters, R. (2007) 'Crime, Regulation and Radioactive Waste', in P. Bierne and N. South (eds) *Toward a Green Criminology: Confronting Harms Against Humanity, Animals and Nature*, Cullompton: Willan.

Walters, R. (2010) 'Eco crime', in J. Muncie, D. Talbot and R. Walters (eds) *Crime: Local and Global*, Cullompton: Willan.

Walters, R. (2013) 'Air Crimes and Atmospheric Justice', in N. South and A. Brisman (eds) *The Routledge International Handbook of Green Criminology*, London: Routedge.

Walton, P. and Young, J. (1997) *The New Criminology Revisited*, Basingstoke: Macmillan.

Walzer, M. (1986) 'The Politics of Michel Foucault', in D. Couzens Hoy (ed.) *Foucault: A Critical Reader*, Oxford: Basil Blackwell.

Ward, T. (2005) 'State Crime in the Heart of Darkness' *British Journal of Criminology*, 45 (4): 434–45.

Wardlaw, G. (1982) *Political Terrorism: Theory, Tactics and Counter-Measures*, Cambridge: Cambridge University Press

Watney, S. (1997) *Policing Desire: Pornography, AIDS and the Media*, 3rd edn, London: Cassell.

Watt, P. (1998) 'Going Out of Town: Youth, Race and Place in the South East of England', *Environment & Planning D: Society and Space*, 16 (6): 687–703.

Weatherburn, D. and Lind, B. (2001) *Delinquent-Prone Communities*, Cambridge: Cambridge University Press.

Weber, M. (1958/1970) *From Max Weber: Essays in Sociology*, trans. and ed. H. J. H. Gerth and C. W. Mills, London: Routledge and Kegan Paul.

Webster, C. (1994) *The Keighley Crime Survey*, Bradford and Ilkley Community College.

Week, The (2007) 'The Cannabis Boom', *The Week*, 19 May: 13.

Weinberg, L. (2005) *Global Terrorism*, London: Oneworld Publications.

Weinberger, B. (1981) 'The Police and the Public in Mid-19th Century Warwickshire', in V. Bailey (ed.) *Policing and Punishment in 19th Century Britain*, London: Croom Helm.

Weisburd, D., Waring, E. and Chayel, E. (2001) *White Collar Crime and Criminal Careers*, Cambridge: Cambridge University Press.

Weiss, E. (1992) 'In Fairness to Future Generations and Sustainable Development', *American University International Law Review*, 8 (1): 19–26.

Weiss, R. P. (ed.) (1999) *Social History of Crime, Policing and Punishment*, Aldershot: Ashgate.

Weizman, E. (2007) *Hollow Land: Israel's Architecture of Occupation*, London: Verso.

Welch, M. (2007) 'The Re-emergence of Torture in Political Culture: Tracking Its Discourse and Genealogy', *Capítulo Criminológico*, 3 (4). http://www.serbi.luz.edu.ve/scielo.php?script=sci_arttext&pid=S0798–959820070120 (accessed 23 April 2008).

Welch, M. and Schuster, L. (2005) 'Detention of Asylum Seekers in the UK and USA: Deciphering Noisy and Quiet Constructions', *Punishment & Society*, 7 (4): 397–417.

Wells, C. (1993) *Corporations and Criminal Responsibility*, Oxford: Clarendon Press.

Wenar, L. (2008) 'Property Rights and the Resource Curse', *Philosophy and Public Affairs*, 36 (1): 2–32.

Western, B. (2006) *Punishment and Inequality in America*, New York: Russell Sage Foundation.

Westmarland, L. (2008) 'Police Cultures' in T. Newburn (ed.) *Handbook of Policing*, 2nd edn, Cullompton: Willan.

Westmarland, L. (2011) *Researching Crime and Justice: Tales from the Field*, London: Routledge.

Weston, B. (2012) 'The Theoretical Foundations of Intergenerational Ecological Justice: An Overview', *Human Rights Quarterly*, 34: 251–66.

White, K. (1993) *The First Sexual Revolution*, New York: New York Press.

White, R. (ed.) (2005) 'Green/Environmental Criminology', special issue, *Current Issues in Criminal Justice*, 16 (3).

White, R. (2008) *Crimes Against Nature: Environmental Criminology and Ecological Justice*, Cullompton: Willan.

White, R. (ed.) (2010) *Global Environmental Harm*, Cullompton: Willan.

White, R. and Sutton, A. (1995) 'Crime Prevention, Urban Space and Social Exclusion', *Journal of Sociology*, 31 (1): 82–99.

Whitehead, P. and Statham, R. (2006) *The History of Probation: Politics, Power and Cultural Change*, Crayford: Shaw and Sons.

Whitfield, J. (2004) *Unhappy Dialogue*, Cullompton: Willan.

Whyte, D. (2007) 'The Crimes of Neo-Liberal Rule in Occupied Iraq', *British Journal of Criminology*, 47 (2): 177–95.

Wiener, M. J. (1998) 'The Victorian Criminalization of Men', in P. Spierenburg (ed.) *Men and Violence: Gender, Honor, and Rituals in Modern Europe and America*, Columbus: Ohio State University Press.

Wiesner, M. E. (ed.) (2007) *Witchcraft in Early Modern Europe*, Boston, MA: Houghton Mifflin.

Wikström, P.-O. and Sampson, R. J. (2003) 'Social Mechanisms on Crime and Pathways into Criminality', in B. B. Lahey, T. E. Moffitt and A. Caspi (eds) *Causes of Conduct Disorder and Juvenile Delinquency*, New York: Conduct Press.

Wikström, P.-O., Oberwittler, D., Treiber, K. and Hardie, B. (2012) *Breaking Rules: The Social and Situational Dynamics of Young People's Urban Crime*, Oxford: Clarendon.

Wilkins, L. T. (1964) *Social Deviance: Social Policy, Action and Research*, London: Tavistock.

Wilkins, L. T. (1967) *Social Policy, Action and Research*, London: Tavistock.

Wilkinson, P. (2008) 'Al Qaeda Tactics and Strategies: Implications for London 2012', paper presented at the Terrorism & the Olympics: Critical Lessons and Key Issues conference, University of East London, May 9.

Williams, C. (1996) 'Environmental Victims: An Introduction', in C. Williams (ed.) 'Environmental Victims', special issue of *Social Justice*, 23 (4): 1–6.

Williams, S. (2001) *Emotion and Social Theory*, London: Sage.

Williams, L. (2004) 'Porn Studies: Proliferating Pornographies On/Scene: An Introduction', in Williams, L. (ed.) *Porn Studies*, Durham, NC: Duke University Press.

Willis, P. (1977) *Learning to Labour: How Working Class Kids Get Working Class Jobs*, London: Saxon House.

Wills, A. (2007) 'Historical Myth-making in Juvenile Justice Policy', *History and Policy* (website) http://www.historyandpolicy.org/papers/policy-paper-60.html

Wilson, D., Sharp, C. and Patterson, A. (2006) *Young People and Crime: Findings from the 2005 Offending, Crime and Justice Survey*, Home Office Statistical Bulletin 17/06, London: Home Office.

Wilson, J. Q. (1975) *Thinking about Crime*, New York: Basic Books.

Wilson, J. Q. and Kelling, G. (1982) 'Broken Windows: The Police and Neighbourhood Safety', *Atlantic Monthly*, 249: 29–38.

Winlow, S. (2001) *Badfellas: Crime, Tradition and New Masculinities*, Oxford: Berg.

Winlow, S. and Hall, S. (2006) *Violent Night: Urban Leisure and Contemporary Culture*, Oxford: Berg.

Wiseman, J. P. (1970) *Stations of the Lost*, Englewood Cliffs, NJ: Prentice Hall.

Witte, R. (1996) *Racist Violence and the State*, Harlow: Longman.

Wolch, J. and Dear, M. (eds) (1989) *The Power of Geography: How Territory Shapes Social Life*, Boston, MA: Unwin Hyman.

Wolfgang, M. (1958) *Patterns in Criminal Homicide*, Philadelphia: University of Pennsylvania Press.

Wolfgang, M. (1960) 'Cesare Lombroso', in M. Hermann (ed.) *Pioneers in Criminology*, London: Stevens.

Wollstein, J. (1967) *The Case Against Victimless Crimes*, Silver Springs, MD: Society for Individual Liberty.

Wood, D., Ball, K., Lyon, D., Norris, C. and Raab, C. (2006) *A Report on the Surveillance Society*, London: Information Commissioner's Office.

Woodiwiss, M. and Hobbs, D. (2009) 'Organized Evil and the Atlantic Alliance: Moral Panics and the Rhetoric of Organized Crime Policing in America and Britain', *British Journal of Criminology*, 49 (1): 106–28.

Woolf, H. and Tumim, S. (1991) *Prison Disturbances April 1990*, Cm 1456, London: HMSO.

Worrall, A. (1990) *Offending Women: Female Lawbreakers and the Criminal Justice System*, London: Routledge.

Worrall, A. (1997) *Punishment in the Community: The Future of Criminal Justice*, Harlow: Addison Wesley Longman.

Worrall, A. and Hoy, C. (2005) *Punishment in the Community: Managing Offenders, Making Choices*, 2nd edn, Cullompton: Willan.

Wright, A (2006) *Organised Crime*, Cullompton: Willan.

Wright, M. (1991) *Justice for Victims and Offenders*, Buckingham: Open University Press.

Webliography

2 Histories of Crime

National Archives
http://www.nationalarchives.gov.uk/
UK state document archive, including lots of material relating to crime and the criminal justice system.

Old Bailey
http://www.oldbaileyonline.org/proceedings/publishinghistory.html
Historical records from the Old Bailey (the Central Criminal Court in England).

The Times
http://historynews.chadwyck.com/noframes19/search
The Times newspaper online, 1790–1905 (Palmer's Index).

United Nations Asia and Far East Institute for the Prevention of Crime and the Treatment of Offenders
http://www.unafei.or.jp/english/index.htm

British Newspaper Archive
http://www.britishnewspaperarchive.co.uk/
Can be searched for national and local media coverage of specific criminal cases, national crime trends and popular and political debate about these.

3 Researching Crime

American Society of Criminology
http://www.asc41.com/

Australia and New Zealand Society of Criminology
http://www.anzsoc.org/

British Society for Criminology
http://www.britsoccrim.org/

European Society of Criminology
http://www.esc-eurocrim.org
Publishes the *European Journal of Criminology* http://www.esc-eurocrim.org/journal.shtml

Socio-Legal Studies Association
http://www.slsa.ac.uk/

British Journal of Criminology
http://bjc.oxfordjournals.org/

The Question Bank
http://qb.soc.surrey.ac.uk/
Questions from the British Crime Survey can be read online at the Question Bank, University of Surrey.

Dmoz Open Directory Project
http://www.dmoz.org/Society/Issues/Crime_and_Justice/Prisons/Organizations/
This section of this large web directory lists some of the many voluntary organizations working in the criminal justice field.

United Nations Office on Drugs and Crime
http://www.unodc.org/unodc/index.html

United Nations Interregional Crime and Justice Research Institute
http://www.unicri.it/

EC Europa – Justice and Home Affairs
http://ec.europa.eu/justice_home/fsj/crime/fsj_crime_intro_en.htm

Association of Southeast Asian Nations
http://www.aseansec.org/

UK Data Archive at the University of Essex
http://www.data-archive.ac.uk/
The UKDA provides resource discovery and support for secondary use of quantitative and qualitative data in research.

The Scottish Executive
http://www.scotland.gov.uk
The Scottish Executive is the devolved government for Scotland. It is responsible for most of the issues of day-to-day concern to the people of Scotland, including health, education, justice, rural affairs and transport.

http://www.culturalcriminology.org.
A website produced by criminologists based at the University of Kent, UK, that provides a resource for students interested in this growing area of criminology.

http://www.governing throughcrime.blogspot.com
Jonathan Simon's blog that interprets current events through his own distinctive criminological analysis.

http://www.deathpenaltyinfo.org
A useful website for data on the death penalty in America.

8 Crime, Place and Space

Home Office Statistical Bulletin: Crime in England and Wales, 2006–7
http://www.homeoffice.gov.uk/rds/pdfs07/hosb1107.pdf

Chicago Crime Map
http://www.chicagocrime.org/

ACORN
http://www.caci.co.uk/acorn/default.asp

UK Crime Statistics Maps
http://www.police.uk/

Liberty
http://www.liberty-human-rights.org.uk

Peterborough Adolescent and Young Adult Development Study
www.pads.ac.uk
An ongoing 10-year study investigating situational influences on young people, in particular the impact of their families, schools and communities on their social development.

Justice Mapping Center
http://www.justicemapping.org/
Provides visual data to argue that large numbers of US prisoners come from a small number of neighbourhoods in big cities.

Carceral Geography
http://carceralgeography.com/
A resource and networking site for those working on prisons, detention and space.

9 Victims and Victimization

Old Bailey online
http://www.oldbaileyonline.org/static/history.jsp
Examples of early discrepancies in justice for the victims of crime can be found in records of proceedings.

United Nations Declaration of Basic Principles of Justice for Victims of Crime and Abuse of Power
http://www2.ohchr.org/english/law/victims.htm
Declaration of basic principles of justice for victims of crime and abuse of power.

Victim Support
http://www.victimsupport.org.uk/
Charity giving free confidential advice and support to victims and their families.

Criminal Justice System Online: 'Victims Virtual Walkthrough'
http://webarchive.nationalarchives.gov.uk/20080107211250/http://www.cjsonline.gov.uk/witness/help_and_support/index.html
An interactive virtual tour that provides information about the British criminal justice process as it relates to victims of crime.

United Nations Interregional Crime and Justice Research Institute
http://www.unicri.it/documentation_centre/publications/icvs/
Provides information on various international crime victimization surveys.

Human Rights Watch
www.hrw.org
An international watchdog concerned with gathering information about breaches of human rights. The website provides details on their activities.

Hillsborough Independent Panel
http://hillsborough.independent.gov.uk/
Campaigns for justice for the families of the Hillsborough disaster.

Hillsborough Family Support Group
http://hfsg.co.uk/

10 Crime and Property

The Home Office: Research Development Statistics – Publications
http://www.homeoffice.gov.uk/rds/bcs.html

International Crime Victims Survey
http://www.unicri.it/services/library_documentation/publications/icvs/
Information, publications and statistics on international crime victim surveys are available at this site.

14 Drugs, Alcohol, Health and Crime

Drugscope
http://www.drugscope.org.uk/
An invaluable site with access to an online encyclopaedia about drugs and to Drugscope's library.

Alcohol Concern
http://www.alcoholconcern.org.uk/
This site provides links to many other useful sites and a good overview of key issues surrounding alcohol.

15 Thinking about Punishment

Restorative Justice online
www.restorativejustice.org
Excellent resource providing access to thousands of publications on restorative justice.

The Home Office: Publications: A Guide to the Criminal Justice System in England and Wales
http://www.homeoffice.gov.uk/rds/cjspub1.html
Publications available online, on the criminal justice process in England and Wales.

Criminal Justice System
http://www.cjsonline.org/home.html
This is another site that has useful information on the criminal justice process in England and Wales.

Crown Office and Procurator Fiscal Service
http://www.crownoffice.gov.uk/
This site has information on the Scottish criminal justice system plus a selection of other links for reference.

Criminal Justice System Northern Ireland
http://www.cjsni.gov.uk/
A site on the criminal justice process in Northern Ireland.

Proceedings of the Old Bailey
http://www.oldbaileyonline.org/
A fully searchable online edition of the largest body of texts detailing the lives of non-elite people ever published, containing accounts of over 100,000 criminal trials held at London's central criminal court.

16 The Criminal Justice Process

Home Office

http://www.homeoffice.gov.uk

The government ministerial office responsible for policing and related social control activities in England and Wales.

Ministry of Justice

http://www.justice.gov.uk

The government ministerial office responsible for key elements of the justice system including the courts and prisons in England and Wales.

Crown Prosecution Service

http://www.cps.gov.uk

Website of the organization that undertakes the prosecution of offenders on behalf of the government.

World Factbook of Criminal Systems

http://www.ojp.gov/bjs/abstract/wfcriminal justice.htm

This factbook provides narrative descriptions of the criminal justice systems of 45 countries around the world.

Criminal Justice System

http://www.criminaljusticeonline.org

This is another site that has useful information on the criminal justice process in England and Wales.

Crown Office and Procurator Fiscal Service

http://www.crownoffice.gov.uk/

This site has information on the Scottish criminal justice system plus a selection of other links for reference.

Criminal Justice System Northern Ireland

http://www.criminal justicesni.gov.uk/

A site on the criminal justice process in Northern Ireland.

Human Rights Watch

www.hrw.org

An international watchdog concerned with gathering information about breaches of human rights. The website provides detail on their activities.

Europe and Environmental Crime
http://europa.eu.int.comm/environment/crime/
The pages of the European online site that deals with the environment and crime.

Earthscan from Routledge
http://www.routledge.com/sustainability/
Provides resources and books giving information about the state of the environment.

Friends of the Earth
http://www.foe.org/

Greenpeace
http://www.greenpeace.org/international_en/
The two major activist websites.

20 Crime and the Media

Independent Media Centre
www.indymedia.org
Daily articles produced by a collective of independent media organizations and journalists.

Media Studies.Com
http://www.newmediastudies.com
A website for the study of new media, with articles, reviews, guides and other resources.

'Media Panics' podcast
http://britac.studyserve.com/home/lecture.asp?ContentContainerID=124
A discussion on 'Moral Panics: Then and Now' by Stan Cohen, Stuart Hall and David Garland at the British Academy in March 2007.

21 Political Violence, Terrorism and Counter-terrorism

Foreign Affairs: Security analysis
http://www.foreignaffairs.com/topics/Security
Analysis of US foreign policy and global affairs with detailed analysis of security issues and recent events.

MI5
https://www.mi5.gov.uk
Presentation of security issues from a UK government and security service perspective.

American Civil Liberties Union
http://www.aclu.org/keep-america-safe-and-free-0
A civil liberties NGO perspective on counter-terrorism in the US.

Liberty: Counter terrorism legislation

https://www.liberty-human-rights.org.uk/human-rights/terrorism/index.php

An overview of UK counter-terrorism law and its accompanying debates.

22 State Crime, War Crime and Human Rights

International State Crime Initiative

http://statecrime.og/

A cross-disciplinary community of scholars working to further the understanding of state crime, their website contains useful and up-to-date information about contemporary state crime and state crime research.

Universal Declaration of Human Rights

http://www.un.org/en/documents/udhr/index.shtml

Amnesty International

www.amnesty.org.uk

The worldwide movement campaigning for internationally recognized human rights.

Human Rights Watch

www.hrw.org

Produces regular reports into human rights abuses around the world.

Stanley Milgram's 'Behavioural study of obedience'

http://www.dailymotion.com/video/xlllu7_stranley-milgram-obedience_school

Arguably one of the most profound works of twentieth-century psychology, original film footage of Stanley Milgram's experiment into obedience to authority can be found at this site.

discourses 111–2

disorder, negotiations of 145–6

dispersal orders 102

dispersal policy 371

Dixon of Dock Green (TV programme) 343

DNA analysis 416

domestic violence 15, 37, 109, 164, 484

double deviance 108–9

double jeopardy 109

Douglas, Mary 68, 208

Drug Dependency Units 265

drugs and drug abuse 92–3, 94–5, 96, 235, 243, 482, 483; availability 270; control 262–4, 267, 278–80 *see also* corporate criminality and crime 261–2, 277–8; cross-cultural perspective 272; decriminalization/legalization 267–8; globalization 265, 269–72, **271**; harm reduction 267; and health 261–2, 282–3; heroin 269, **269**, 270, 277; legal highs 266; medicalization of 265; the mephedrone panic 266; the narco-economy 270; normalization 273; opium trade 269–70; and organized crime 267, 278; problem status 272–6, **275**; recreational 273; seizures **275**, 276; statistics 273–6, **275**, 277; stigmatization 272–3; trade 270–2, **271**; trafficking 124; treatment 266–7; UK legislation 279–80; UK politics and policy 264–8; upper level trafficking 270–2; user profiles 276

Du Bois, W.E.B 83–4, 84

due process 328

Duff, R. and Garland, D. 303, 306

Dugdale, Richard 23

Duggan, Mark, shooting of 344

Durkheim, Émile 50, 59, 67–8, 77, 115, 306–8, 462

Dworkin, Andrea 202, 204

Eaton, Mary 332

Echelon network, the 430–1

ecocide 397–8, 409

ecology of crime 135–7

ecology of fear 143, **143**, 144

economic divisions 6, 15

edgework 191, 234–5

Edwards, S. 108–9

effects studies 418–9

Eichmann, Adolf 470

Eisenman, Stephen 420

Eisner, Manuel 12, 16

elderly, the: fear of crime 225; victimization 163

electronic harassment 430

Elias, Norbert 12, 462

emotions 219–23; and crime 221–2, 234; fear 223–5, **224**; primary 222, 222; secondary 222, 222

empiricism 51

employment, insecurity of 116

Engels, Friedrich 69–70

England and Wales, spatial distribution of crime 137–42, **138**, **139**, **140**

Enlightenment, the 49, 51–2, 55

Enron 253–4, **254**

entertainment, crime as 414–5, 417, 424–5, 426–7, 428

Environment Agency 399

environmental crime 117, 155 *see also* green crimes and criminology

environmental criminology 135, 390

environmental damage 391

environmental degradation 394–5, 395

environmental justice 410

environmental legislation 408–10

environmental racism 405–6

environmental victimization 405–8

epistemology 4–5

Ericson, R. and Haggerty, K. 358

Ericson, Richard 129

Erikson, Kai 40

ethics 27, 39–40; codes of 40

ethnicity 6, 7–8, 23–4; and the criminal justice process 332–3; and organized crime 243–5; and prison 377–9; and property crime 184; residual discrimination 333; and victimization 166

ethnocentric assumptions 286

ethnographic research 28, 38–9; moral, ethical and legal issues 39–40

eugenics 58

European Convention on Human Rights 329

European Journal of Criminology 30

European Society of Criminology 30

Europol 358

evaluation research 28

evidence-based policy making 28

excitement, need for 234–5

exclusive society, the 117–8, 482–3

executions *see* capital punishment

experiential anarchy 234–5

experimental criminology 5, 28, 55

extinctions 400–1

extreme media 433–5

peer-group dynamics 445–6; sociological analysis 445–6; state 465; surveillance 452–5; suspect populations 454, 454–5, 467; target-hardening strategies 455–6, **456**, **457**; typologies 441; unstable terrorist thesis 444

Terrorism Act 2000 449, 450

Terrorism Act 2006 466

Terrorism and Allied Matters Fund 454

Thatcher, Margaret 101, 102, 104, 243

Thomas, Douglas, and Loader, Brian 429

Thomas, William I. 85, 92

Thompson, E. P. 310

Thrasher, Frederic M. 75, 239

thrill seeking 229–30, 234–5

Tiananmen Mothers, the 171

toleration 52

Tolstoy, Leo 294–5

Tomlinson, Ian, death of 345, 346, 423

torture 301, 302, 420, 464, **464**

torture porn 435

toxic waste *see* waste dumping

traditional understandings 50–1

transcarceration 313

transnational corporations [TNCs] 255–6

transnational policing 358

Treadwell, James 430

trust, abuse of 249

Turton, J. 202

twin studies 61

Uglow, S. 333

UN Conference on Sustainable Development 408–9

underclass, the 23, 57, 121, 192

underdog sociology 41–2

underground economy 116

unemployment 6

United Nations 109

United Nations Centre for International Crime Prevention 241

United Nations Conference on the Human Environment 408

United Nations Conference on Transnational Crime 123–4

United Nations Convention on Biological Diversity 400

United Nations Security Council (UNSC) 439–40, 462

United States of America: capital punishment 129–30, **130**; corporate criminality 253; counter-terrorism 447, 449, 451; crime rates 68; criminal justice process 326, 333–4; drugs and drug abuse 265, 267; ethnographic research 38–9; genocide 467; ghetto studies 233; and green crime 410; hate crimes 227, 228; Homeland Security model 447; legacy of slavery 468; lynching 228, 229; National Crime Victimization Survey 179; Native Americans 467; new penology 127–31, **130**; ordinary harms 398; organized crime 241, 243–4; PATRIOT Act 449, 466; plea bargaining 333–4; prison experiment 300–1; prison populations 117, 363, 468; prisons and the prison system 362, 383; Prohibition 241; property crime 179, 183, 185; prostitution 211; racist crime 34–5; spirals of denial 463, **464**; Sports Utility Vehicles 223–4, **224**; terrorism research 443; victim movements 171; waste dumping 407

universalism 52, 485

urban design, and crime 142–5, **143**

urban flight 146

urban fortress living 312

urban migration 21

urban sociology 135

urbanization 13, 15, 20, 67, 71–4, **73**

Urry, John 392

Useem, Bert, and Peter Kimball 383

utilitarianism 52, 54, 296, 301, 302, 303

Vallier, Claire 307

Valverde, Mariana 314

Venkatesh, Sudhir 72

vertigo 118

victim blaming 157–8

victim impact statement (VIS) 170

victim movements 171, 172

victim precipitation 157–8

victim statement (VS) 170

Victim Support 171

victim surveys 136

victimization 6, 154, 485; and age 162–3; crime victimization surveys 160–1; definition 155–7, **155**, **156**; distribution of risks 36–7; and ethnicity 166; and gender 163–4; hidden 159; hierarchy of 157–8; honour killings 165; indirect 169, **170**; primary 167; psychological impact 170; repeat 183–4; secondary 167, 169, 331; and social class 162; social variables in 162–6; waves of harm 169, **170**; women 164

victimization surveys 160–1; commercial 37; international 36; local 36–7; national 35–6

victimless crimes 94–5, 156–7